国家出版基金项目
NATIONAL PUBLICATION FOUNDATION

国际海事组织海员行为示范

MODEL COURSE 7.01

船长和大副

MASTER AND CHIEF MATE (2014)

中华人民共和国海事局 译

大连海事大学出版社
DALIAN MARITIME UNIVERSITY PRESS

国际海事组织 1991 年第一次出版

4 Albert Embankment, London SE1 7SR

图书在版编目(CIP)数据

船长和大副：汉英对照 / 国际海事组织著；中华人民共和国海事局译. — 大连：大连海事大学出版社，2016.2

(国际海事组织海员行为示范)

书名原文: MASTER AND CHIEF MATE

ISBN 978-7-5632-3298-7

Ⅰ. ①船… Ⅱ. ①国… ②中… Ⅲ. ①船长—技术培训—教材—汉、英②船员—技术培训—教材—汉、英
Ⅳ. ①U661.32 ②U676.2

中国版本图书馆 CIP 数据核字(2016)第 029135 号

大连海事大学出版社出版

地址：大连市凌海路 1 号　邮编：116026　电话：0411-84728394　传真：0411-84727996

http://www.dmupress.com E-mail:cbs@dmupress.com

大连住友彩色印刷有限公司印装　　大连海事大学出版社发行

2016 年 2 月第 1 版　　2016 年 2 月第 1 次印刷

幅面尺寸：210 mm×297 mm　　印数：1~3000 册

印张：44.25　　字数：1373 千

出 版 人：徐华东　　策　　划：徐华东

责任编辑：刘长影　　责任校对：宋彩霞　刘若实

封面设计：解瑶瑶　　版式设计：孟　冀　解瑶瑶

ISBN 978-7-5632-3298-7　　定价：111.00 元

国际海事组织海员行为示范
编审委员会

《船长和大副》

翻　译：郭党华　王当利　郑绍华

审　校：胡甚平　付耀芳

CONTENTS

Page

Foreword ..... **viii**

Introduction **2**
- Purpose of the model courses 2
- Use of the model course 2
- Lesson plans 4
- Presentation 4
- Implementation 4
- Course objective 6
- Entry standards 6
- Course intake limitations 6
- Textbooks, videos and bibliography 8
- Computer applications 8
- Conventions, regulations and legislation 10

Part A: Course Framework for all functions **12**
- Aims 12
- Objective 12
  - Function 1 12
  - Function 2 12
  - Function 3 14
- Entry standards 14
- Course certificate 16
- Staff requirements 16
- Teaching facilities and equipment 16
- Teaching aids (A) 18
- Videos (DVDs), CD-ROMs, CBTs (V) 20
- IMO references (R) 28
- Textbooks (T) 38
- Bibliography (B) 42

目　录

页码

前言 ································ **ix**

介绍 ································ **3**

示范课程的目的 ································ 3
示范课程的使用 ································ 3
教案 ································ 5
学员展示 ································ 5
实施 ································ 5
课程目标 ································ 7
入学标准 ································ 7
课程人数限制 ································ 7
教科书、录像和参考文献 ································ 9
计算机应用 ································ 9
公约、规则和立法 ································ 11

A 部分:所有功能的课程框架 ································ **13**

目的 ································ 13
目标 ································ 13
功能 1 ································ 13
功能 2 ································ 13
功能 3 ································ 15
入学标准 ································ 15
课程证书 ································ 17
教员要求 ································ 17
教学设施和设备 ································ 17
教具(A) ································ 19
录像 (DVDs),光盘,基于计算机的训练(V) ································ 21
IMO 参考书目(R) ································ 29
教科书(T) ································ 39
参考文献(B) ································ 43

Function 1: Navigation at the Management Level ······ **66**

Part B1: Course Outline ······ **70**
Timetable ······ 70
Lectures ······ 70
Course outline ······ 70

Part C1: Detailed Teaching Syllabus ······ **82**
Introduction ······ 82
Explanation of information contained in the syllabus tables ······ 82

Part D1: Instructor Manual ······ **202**
1.1 PLAN A VOYAGE AND CONDUCT NAVIGATION ······ 204
1.2 DETERMINE POSITION AND THE ACCURACY OF RESULTANT POSITION FIX BY ANY MEANS ······ 210
1.3 DETERMINE AND ALLOW FOR COMPASS ERRORS ······ 216
1.4 COORDINATE SEARCH AND RESCUE OPERATIONS ······ 218
1.5 ESTABLISH WATCHKEEPING ARRANGEMENTS AND PROCEDURES ······ 218
1.6 MAINTAIN SAFE NAVIGATION THROUGH THE USE OF INFORMATION FROM NAVIGATION EQUIPMENT AND SYSTEMS TO ASSIST IN COMMAND DECISION MAKING ······ 222
1.7 MAINTAIN SAFE NAVIGATION THROUGH THE USE OF ECDIS AND ASSOCIATED NAVIGATION SYSTEMS TO ASSIST COMMAND DECISION MAKING ······ 222
1.8 FORECAST WEATHER AND OCEANOGRAPHIC CONDITIONS ······ 222
1.9 RESPOND TO NAVIGATIONAL EMERGENCIES ······ 226
1.10 MANOEUVRE AND HANDLE A SHIP IN ALL CONDITIONS ······ 230
1.11 OPERATE REMOTE CONTROLS OF PROPULSION PLANT AND ENGINEERING SYSTEMS AND SERVICES ······ 236

Function 2: Cargo Handling and Stowage at the Management Level ······ **248**

Part B2: Course Outline ······ **252**
Timetable ······ 252
Lectures ······ 252
Course outline ······ 252

Part C2: Detailed Teaching Syllabus ······ **260**

Part D2: Instructor Manual ······ **360**
2.1 PLAN AND ENSURE SAFE LOADING, STOWAGE, SECURING, CARE DURING THE VOYAGE AND UNLOADING OF CARGOES ······ 360
2.2 ASSESS REPORTED DEFECTS AND DAMAGE TO CARGO SPACES, HATCH COVERS AND BALLAST TANKS AND TAKE APPROPRIATE ACTION ······ 378
2.3 CARRIAGE OF DANGEROUS GOODS ······ 378

功能 1:管理级航行 …… **67**

B1 部分:课程概要 …… **71**
时间表 …… 71
教学 …… 71
课程概要 …… 71

C1 部分:教学大纲细则 …… **83**
介绍 …… 83
教学大纲细则里的信息说明 …… 83

D1 部分:教员手册 …… **203**
1.1 制订航次计划并引导航行 …… 205
1.2 定位和确定通过任一定位方法获取的最终船位的精度 …… 211
1.3 测定并修正罗经差 …… 217
1.4 协调搜寻与救助行动 …… 219
1.5 确定值班安排和程序 …… 219
1.6 通过辅助决策的导航设备和系统的信息保持安全航行 …… 223
1.7 通过辅助决策的 ECDIS 及相关的航行系统保持安全航行 …… 223
1.8 预报天气和海洋水文状况 …… 223
1.9 航行中的应急反应 …… 227
1.10 在各种状况下操纵和操作船舶 …… 231
1.11 推进装置和轮机系统的遥控操作与维护 …… 237

功能 2:管理级货物装卸与积载 …… **249**

B2 部分:课程概要 …… **253**
时间表 …… 253
教学 …… 253
课程概要 …… 253

C2 部分:教学大纲细则 …… **261**

D2 部分:教员手册 …… **361**
2.1 计划并确保在航行期间货物的安全装载、积载、系固、照管以及货物的卸载 …… 361
2.2 评估报告中的货舱、舱盖和压载舱的缺陷和损坏以及采取适当的行动 …… 379
2.3 危险货物运输 …… 379

Function 3: Controlling the Operation of the Ship and Care for Persons on Board at the Management Level **382**

Part B3: Course Outline **386**
- Timetable 386
- Lectures 386
- Course outline 386

Part C3: Detailed Teaching Syllabus **394**

Part D3: Instructor Manual **568**
- 3.1 CONTROL TRIM, STABILITY AND STRESS 570
- 3.2 MONITOR AND CONTROL COMPLIANCE WITH LEGISLATIVE REQUIREMENTS AND MEASURES TO ENSURE SAFETY OF LIFE AT SEA AND THE PROTECTION OF THE MARINE ENVIRONMENT 594
- 3.3 MAINTAIN SAFETY AND SECURITY OF CREW AND PASSENGERS AND THE OPERATIONAL CONDITION OF SAFETY SYSTEMS 614
- 3.4 DEVELOP EMERGENCY AND DAMAGE CONTROL PLANS AND HANDLE EMERGENCY SITUATIONS 620
- 3.5 USE OF LEADERSHIP AND MANAGERIAL SKILLS 620
- 3.6 ORGANIZE AND MANAGE THE PROVISION OF MEDICAL CARE ON BOARD 628

Appendix 1 .... **630**
- Stability Data 630
- Loading Scale 632
- KN Curves 634

Appendix 2 .... **636**
- Trim Table 636

Part E: Evaluation **638**
- Initial/Diagnostic assessment 638
- Formative assessment 638
- Summative assessment 638
- Evaluation for quality assurance 640
- Assessment planning 640
- Validity 640
- Reliability 640
- STCW Code 642
- Calculations 644
- Compiling tests 646
- Quality of test items 646
- Advantages and disadvantages of oral and practical tests 654

Attachment: Guidance on the implementation of IMO model courses **656**

功能 3:管理级船舶作业管理和人员管理 ······ **383**

B3 部分:课程概要 ······ **387**
时间表 ······ 387
教学 ······ 387
课程概要 ······ 387

C3 部分:教学大纲细则 ······ **395**

D3 部分:教员手册 ······ **569**
3.1 控制吃水差、稳性和应力 ······ 571
3.2 根据立法要求的监督与控制以及确保海上人命安全和海洋环境保护的措施 ······ 595
3.3 维护船员和乘客的安全和治安与安全系统的操作条件 ······ 615
3.4 制定破损控制图并处理紧急状况 ······ 621
3.5 领导力和管理技能的运用 ······ 621
3.6 船上医护的组织与管理 ······ 629

附录 1 ······ **631**
稳性数据 ······ 631
载重表尺 ······ 633
KN 曲线 ······ 635

附录 2 ······ **637**
吃水差表 ······ 637

E 部分:评估 ······ **639**
初始性 / 诊断性评估 ······ 639
形成性评估 ······ 639
终结性评估 ······ 639
质量保证评价 ······ 641
评估计划 ······ 641
有效性 ······ 641
可靠性 ······ 641
STCW 规则 ······ 643
计算 ······ 645
测试命题 ······ 647
试题质量 ······ 647
口试和实操考试的优缺点 ······ 655

附件:IMO 示范课程实施指南 ······ **657**

Foreword

Since its inception the International Maritime Organization (IMO) has recognized the importance of human resources to the development of the maritime industry and has given the highest priority to assisting developing countries in enhancing their maritime training capabilities through the provision or improvement of maritime training facilities at national and regional levels. IMO has also responded to the needs of developing countries for postgraduate training for senior personnel in administrations, ports, shipping companies and maritime training institutes by establishing the World Maritime University in Malmö, Sweden, in 1983.

Following the adoption of the International Convention on Standards of Training, Certification and Watchkeeping for Seafarers, 1978 (STCW), a number of IMO Member Governments had suggested that IMO should develop model training courses to assist in the implementation of the Convention and in achieving a more rapid transfer of information and skills regarding new developments in maritime technology. IMO training advisers and consultants also subsequently determined from their visits to training establishments in developing countries that the provision of model courses could help instructors improve the quality of their existing courses and enhance their implementation of the associated Conference and IMO Assembly resolutions.

In addition, it was appreciated that a comprehensive set of short model courses in various fields of maritime training would supplement the instruction provided by maritime academies and allow administrators and technical specialists already employed in maritime administrations, ports and shipping companies to improve their knowledge and skills in certain specialized fields. With the generous assistance of the Government of Norway, IMO developed model courses in response to these generally identified needs and now keeps them updated through a regular revision process taking into account any amendments to the requirements prescribed in IMO instruments and any technological developments in the field.

These model courses may be used by any training institution and, when the requisite financing is available, the Organization is prepared to assist developing countries in implementing any course.

Koji Sekimizu

Secretary-General

前 言

国际海事组织(IMO)自成立伊始就认识到人力资源在海运业发展中的重要性,并最优先考虑通过在国家和地区层面上提供或改善培训设备来帮助发展中国家增强其海事培训能力。为应对发展中国家主管机关、港口、航运公司及海事培训机构高层人员对研究生培训的需求,IMO 于 1983 年在瑞典的马尔默成立了世界海事大学。

在《1978 年海员培训、发证和值班标准国际公约》(STCW)通过的初期,一些 IMO 成员国政府就建议 IMO 应制定示范课程,以帮助对该公约的实施以及对航海技术新发展方面信息和技能的迅速转化。IMO 培训顾问和咨询专家在对发展中国家的培训机构进行访问后确定,提供示范课程有助于教员改进现有课程的质量,也有助于提升对相关会议和 IMO 大会决议的实施。

此外,令人欣慰的是,海事培训领域中一套综合性简短课程将对海事院校提供的授课加以补充,并使得已在海事行政机关、港口和航运公司工作的行政管理人员和技术专家能够提高其在某些专业领域中的知识和技能。为此,在挪威政府的慷慨帮助下,IMO 编写了示范课程以应对那些普遍发现的需求, 同时考虑到对 IMO 文件中规定要求的任何修正及该领域内的任何技术发展,通过定期修订程序对示范课程进行更新。

任何培训机构可以使用这些示范课程, 在筹措到必需的资金时本组织也准备帮助发展中国家实施任何课程。

关水康司

秘书长

7.01 MODEL COURSE

Introduction

■ Purpose of the model courses

The purpose of the IMO model courses is to assist maritime training institutes and their teaching staff to introduce and organize new training courses and enhance existing training material, whereby the quality and effectiveness of the training may be improved.

It is not the intention of the model course programme to present instructors with a rigid "teaching package" which they are expected to "follow blindly". Nor is it the intention to substitute audio-visual or "programmed" material for the instructor's presence. As in all training endeavours, the knowledge, skills and dedication of the instructors are the key components in the transfer of knowledge and skills to those being trained through IMO model course material.

Rather, this document should be used as a guide with the course duration given as indicative of the expected time required to cover the required outcomes. The parties may modify this course to suit their respective training schemes.

For those following planned training schemes approved by the Administration, it is intended that this training may form an integral part of the overall training plan and be complementary to other studies. The training may be undertaken in progressive stages; for such candidates, it is not appropriate to specify the duration of the learning, provided achievement of the specified learning outcomes is properly assessed and recorded.

The educational systems and the cultural backgrounds of trainees in maritime subjects vary considerably from country to country. For this reason, the model course material has been designed to identify the basic entry requirements and trainee target group for each course in universally applicable terms, and to specify clearly the technical content and levels of knowledge and skill necessary to meet the technical intent of IMO conventions and related recommendations.

This is the next major revision to this model course. In order to keep the training programme up to date in future, it is essential that users provide feedback. New information will provide better training in safety at sea and protection of the marine environment. Information, comments and suggestions should be sent to the Head of the STCW and Human Element Section at IMO, London.

■ Use of the model course

To use the model course the instructor should review the course plan and detailed syllabus, taking into account the information provided under the entry standards specified in the course framework. The actual level of knowledge and skills and the prior technical education of the trainees should be kept in mind during this review, and any areas within the detailed syllabus which may cause difficulties because of differences between the actual trainee entry level and that assumed by the course designer should be identified. To compensate for such differences, the instructor is expected to delete from the course, or reduce the emphasis on, items dealing with knowledge or skills already attained by the trainees. They should also

介 绍

■ 示范课程的目的

IMO示范课程的目的是协助海事培训机构及其教学人员组织和引入新的培训课程，提高、更新或补充现有的培训材料，以此改进培训课程的质量和培训效果。

本示范课程计划的意图并不是向教员呈交一个他们期望“盲目遵循”的“教学包”，其意图也不是用视听或“编排的”材料来代替教员的存在。在所有的培训努力中，知识、技能和教员的奉献是向IMO示范课程材料的受训者传授知识和技能的关键构成要素。

此外，本示范课程是作为培训过程的指导性文件，表明为达到公约要求培训结果所需预计时间，各缔约国可酌情对本示范课程进行修改以满足培训要求。

对于那些已由主管机关批准的培训计划，本示范课程可以作为其整体培训计划的组成部分，也可作为其他相应学科培训的补充。培训须分阶段实施，对于那些已进行正确评估和记录特定学习成果的学员，不宜再规定其持续学习时间。

鉴于各缔约国海上科目的培训学员所属教育体制和所具文化基础差异较大，IMO示范课程采用通俗易懂的文字明确了基本入学条件及课程培训目标群体，并明确阐明学员应掌握的技术内容、须达到的知识和技能水平，以符合相关IMO公约及议定书技术要求。

本示范课程为第二修订版。为保持培训课程不断更新，由用户提供相关反馈信息十分关键。新的信息能够促使完善有关海上安全和海洋环境保护的知识培训。欢迎用户将新的信息、评论和建议提交给伦敦IMO人力资源及STCW总部。

■ 示范课程的使用

为使用示范课程，教员应当审视课程计划和教学大纲细则，考虑课程框架中规定的入学标准所提供的信息。在审视过程中，应当牢记学员知识和技能的实际水准以及从前的技术教育水平，并应当识别出在教学大纲细则范围内由于学员实际入门水准与课程设计者假定的水准之间的差异，可能引起困难的任何部分。为弥补这些差异，希望教员将涉及学员已经掌握的知识和技能的项目从课程中删去或不做重视。此外，教员应当识别出学员可能还没有掌握的任何学术知识、技能或技术训练。

identify any academic knowledge, skills or technical training which they may not have acquired.

By analysing the detailed syllabus and the academic knowledge required to allow training in the technical area to proceed, the instructor can design an appropriate pre-entry course or, alternatively, insert the elements of academic knowledge required to support the technical training elements concerned at appropriate points within the technical course.

Adjustment of the course objective, scope and content may also be necessary if in your maritime industry the trainees completing the course are to undertake duties which differ from the course objectives specified in the model course.

Within the course plan, the course designers have indicated their assessment of the time that should be allotted to each area of learning. However, it must be appreciated that these allocations are arbitrary and assume that the trainees have fully met all entry requirements of the course. The instructor should therefore review these assessments and may need to re-allocate the time required to achieve each specific learning objective or training outcome.

■ Lesson plans

Having adjusted the course content to suit the trainee intake and any revision of the course objectives, the instructor should draw up lesson plans based on the detailed syllabus. Where no adjustment has been found necessary in the learning objectives of the detailed syllabus, the lesson plans may simply consist of the detailed syllabus with keywords or other reminders added to assist the instructor in making his presentation of the material.

■ Presentation

The presentation of concepts and methodologies must be repeated in various ways until the instructor is satisfied, by testing and evaluating the trainee's performance and achievements, that the trainee has attained each specific learning objective or training outcome. The syllabus is laid out in learning objective format and each objective specifies a required performance or what the trainee must be able to do as the learning or training outcome. Taken as a whole, these objectives aim to meet the knowledge, understanding and proficiency specified in the appropriate tables of the STCW Code.

■ Implementation

For the course to run smoothly and to be effective, considerable attention must be paid to the availability and use of:

- properly qualified instructors
- support staff
- rooms and other spaces
- workshops and equipment
- suggested references, textbooks, technical papers, bibliography
- other reference material.

通过分析教学大纲细则以及技术领域培训所需的学术知识，教员可以设计出适当的预科课程,或者在技术课程中的适当处加入技术课程需要的学术知识。

如果完成该课程的学员在其所处的航海事业中要从事有别于本示范课程规定的课程目标的职责,则可能有必要调整课程的目标、范围和内容。

在课程计划中,课程设计者已经表明了其估计的、应分配给每一个学习部分的时间。但是,必须清楚的是,这些分配是主观的,并假设了学员完全符合本课程的入门要求。因此,教员应当对这些估计进行重新审视而且可能需要重新分配时间以符合每一个特定培训目标的需要。

■ 教案

在为适应招收的学员以及课程目标的修正而调整课程内容之后，教员应当基于大纲细则拟定教案。教案可以包括添加了关键词或提示语的大纲细则,以帮助教员授课,在这种情况下就没有必要调整大纲细则的培训目标。

■ 学员展示

必须以不同的方式反复讲授概念和方法，直到通过试验和评估学员的表现和成绩使教员感到满意:学员已经达到了每一个具体的培训目标或培训效果。教学大纲以培训目标的格式排列编排,而且每个目标规定了技能要求,或者学员必须能做的事情作为学习或培训的效果。从整体上看,这些目标的目的在于满足STCW规则相应表格规定的知识、理解和熟练。

■ 实施

为使课程顺利进行和卓有成效,必须充分注意下列资源的获得和使用:

- 完全合格的教员
- 辅助人员
- 教室或其他场所
- 车间和设备
- 建议性的参考书目、教科书、技术论文、参考文献
- 其他参考资料

Thorough preparation is the key to successful implementation of the course. IMO has produced a booklet entitled 'Guidance on the implementation of IMO model courses', which deals with this aspect in greater detail.

In certain cases, the requirements for some or all of the training in a subject are covered by another IMO model course. In these cases, the specific part of the STCW Code, which applies, is given and the user is referred to the other model course.

■ Course objective

This model course comprises three functions at the management level. On successful completion of the course and the requisite watchkeeping experience, officers will be prepared for taking full responsibility for the safety of the ship, its passengers, crew and cargo. They will be aware of their obligations under international agreements and conventions concerning safety and the protection of the marine environment and will be prepared for taking the practical measures necessary to meet those obligations.

In this model course, one combined course has been written for both Masters and chief officers. The material is set out assuming that trainees have previously completed the operational level training content required for watchkeeping officer and they have some watchkeeping experience. This does not preclude some of the content for both levels being run within the same training course but it is very important that trainees are familiar with the operational level content before attempting to develop the management level competence outlined in this model course.

The teaching schemes should be carefully scrutinized to ensure that all of the tabulated training outcomes are covered, that repetition is avoided and that essential underpinning knowledge at any stage has already been covered. A certain amount of duplication under different subjects will probably occur, provided it is not excessive, the different approaches can provide useful reinforcement of work already learned. Care should be taken to see that items not included in the syllabus or treatment beyond the depth indicated by the objectives have not been introduced except where necessary to meet additional requirements of the Administration. The teaching scheme should be adjusted to take account of those matters and the timing of any modular courses (such as training in firefighting), that are to be included.

■ Entry standards

Entrants should have successfully completed a course covering the minimum standards required for certification as officer in charge of a navigation watch with content similar to IMO model course 7.03, Officer in charge of a navigational watch.

■ Course intake limitations

Class sizes should generally be limited to not more than 24 in order to allow the instructor to give adequate attention to individual trainees. Larger numbers may be admitted if extra staff and tutorial periods are provided to deal with trainees on an individual basis. In addition, for scheduling access to learning facilities and equipment, attention to strict time management is necessary. In large classes trainees should have their own reference books, unless sufficient

充分备课是成功实施本示范课程的关键。IMO已出版“IMO示范课程实施指南”更加详细说明其实施方法。

某些情况下,其他IMO示范课程会覆盖或包含某一科目的部分或所有培训要求。STCW公约相应于此种情况给出了特定要求,建议使用者参考和使用其他示范课程。

■ 课程目标

本示范课程由管理级的三部分职能组成。成功地完成本课程并具备必要的值班经验,高级船员将能够承担与船舶、乘客、船员和货物安全有关的所有职责。他们将知晓有关安全和防止海洋污染的国际协议和公约所要求的义务,并为履行这些义务采取必要的措施。

本示范课程是一门为船长和大副编写的综合课程。列出本课程的资料是设想学员以前已经结束了值班船员的操作级培训内容,已经具备了值班的经验。这并不排除在同样培训课程中两个级别都包括的一些内容, 但学员在发展本示范课程管理级适任能力之前熟悉操作级的内容非常重要。

应仔细审核教学机制以确保涵盖表中所列出的所有培训效果和每一阶段必要的基础知识,避免重复。不同的课程中可能会发生内容重复现象。如果这些重复的内容不是很多,可以应用不同的教学方法以巩固已学的内容。应特别注意教学大纲中没有要求的或超出教学目标难度的,但应满足主管机关额外要求的内容。教学机制应考虑到这些因素以及任何示范课程(如消防培训)所包含的学时选择并加以调整。

■ 入学标准

学员应顺利通过500总吨或以上船舶负责航行值班的高级船员认证所要求的最低标准的课程(参见IMO示范课程7.03“负责航行值班的高级船员”)。

■ 课程人数限制

为了使教员能够充分关照到每一个学员,班级人数不应超过24人。若对个别受训人员能够提供额外的教员和指导时间,班级人数可以增加。此外,为了能够进行定期的关于设施和设备的学习,有必要对时间进行严格的分配。除非图书馆能够提供足够的复印教材,否则大型班的学生应拥有自己的参考书。教室应能够容纳所有的学生。

copies can be provided in a central library. Classrooms should be big enough to seat all trainees so they can see and hear the instructor.

During practical sessions and group activities, there will be additional restraints on class size. Where applicable, a recommendation on class size is contained in the framework for each of the individual functions.

■ Textbooks, videos and bibliography

References to books, videos and bibliography are made in the Instructor's Manual of the individual subjects to aid both instructors and trainees in finding relevant information and to help in defining the scope and depth of treatment intended.

The mention of a particular textbook does not imply that it is essential to use that book only that it appeared to be best suited to the course at the time of its design. In many instances there are a number of suitable books, and instructors are free to use whatever texts they consider to be most suited to their circumstances and trainees.

Every effort has been made to quote the latest editions of the publications mentioned but new editions are constantly being produced. Instructors should always use the latest edition for preparing and running their courses.

Full use should be made of technical papers and other publications available from maritime and other professional organizations. Such papers contain new developments in techniques, equipment, design, management and opinion, and are an invaluable asset to a maritime training establishment.

■ Computer applications

In view of the rapid growth of information technology (IT) and widespread use of computers aboard ship, it is recommended that at the discretion of the Administration, computer applications at an advanced level should be included in the training for Masters and chief engineers. If this topic has not been covered during training as officer in charge of a navigational watch, some basic training may also be required.

Particulars of the training will depend upon the computer facilities available and the needs of the trainees. The following outline provides guidance on topics that could be included:

- The care and storage of magnetic media; use of simple utility programs for identifying disk problems and fixes; LAN maintenance; back-up management; virus protection.
- IT and the use of applications, for communications (email, data, etc.), the internet, intranets and the worldwide web (www).
- The installation and set-up of multi-media applications.
- Accessing and evaluating information through the internet.

在进行实践练习和分组活动时,应对班级人数另行限制。如可行,建议班级人数应限定在对应职能课程结构中所要求的人数内。

■ 教科书、录像和参考文献

每一课程的教员手册中所列出的参考性的图书、录像和参考文献旨在帮助教员和学员查找相关的信息以及确定教学的范围和深度。

提及某一专门的教科书并不意味着必须使用该教科书,仅表示这本教科书是在编写本课程时最适合本课程的教科书。在多数情况下,适合的教科书有很多,教员可以根据具体情况自由选择最适合教学情境和学员的教科书。

虽然所提及的出版物都是引用最新的版本,但新的版本仍然不断地出版。教员应使用最新版本进行备课和教学。

应充分利用航海和其他专业机构的技术论文和出版物。这些论文包含了技术、设备、设计、管理和信息的最新发展,对航海培训的建立十分有价值。

■ 计算机应用

鉴于目前信息技术(IT)的迅速发展以及计算机在船舶上的广泛应用,建议主管机关决定在船长和轮机长的培训中包含计算机的应用。若负责航行值班的高级船员的培训中没有涉及这些内容,应进行一些计算机应用基础的培训。

培训的具体细节应视可以使用的计算机设备和受训人员的需求而定。以下是一些计算机培训内容的建议:

- 磁介质的保管和储存;识别硬盘问题和修复的简单应用程序的使用、局域网的维护、备份管理、防病毒。
- 通信(电子邮件、数据等)、国际互联网、内部互联网以及万维网等中信息技术的使用。
- 多媒体应用程序的安装与启动。
- 通过国际互联网查找和评价信息。

The use of multi-media applications can enhance learning in topics in many areas of knowledge and prove of value to Masters and chief officers. Many of the IMO rules and Assembly resolutions are available on CD-ROM. Up-to-date details may be found on the IMO website at http://www.imo.org.

■ Conventions, regulations and legislation

These are constantly being revised and updated. It is essential that the up-to-date version of these are being used and that all references to particular versions in this model course should be taken to include all future amendments and revisions.

多媒体应用程序的使用在许多知识领域能增强学习的效果，并已表明对一般的船长和高级船员具有很好的促进作用。IMO的许多规则和大会决议都配有光盘。IMO网站http://www.imo.org有最新的更新信息。

■ 公约、规则和立法

本示范课程须不断地进行修订和更新。至关重要的是须使用最新版本的示范课程,以及将来对本示范课程修改和修订时须包含特定版本的所有参考资料。

Part A: Course Framework for all functions

■ Aims

This model course aims to meet the mandatory minimum requirements for knowledge, understanding and proficiency in table A-II/2 of STCW Code for the function Navigation at the Management Level, for the function Cargo Handling and Stowage at the Management Level and the background knowledge to support Controlling the Operation of the Ship and Care for Persons on Board at the Management Level.

■ Objective

Function 1

The syllabus covers the requirements of the STCW Code, chapter II, section A-II/2. This functional element provides the detailed knowledge to support the training outcomes related to Navigation at the Management Level.

This section provides the background knowledge to support the tasks, duties and responsibilities in:

- planning a voyage and conducting navigation
- determining position and the accuracy of resultant position fix by any means
- determining and allowing for compass errors
- coordinating search and rescue operations
- establishing watchkeeping arrangements and procedures
- maintaining safe navigation through information from navigation equipment and systems to assist command decision making
- maintaining safe navigation through the use of ECDIS and associated navigation systems to assist command decision making
- forecasting weather and oceanographic conditions
- response to navigational emergencies
- manoeuvring and handling a ship in all conditions
- operation of remote controls of propulsion plant and engineering systems and services

Function 2

The syllabus covers the requirements of the STCW Code, chapter II, section AII/2. This functional element provides the detailed knowledge to support the training outcomes related to Cargo Handling and Stowage at the Management Level.

A部分：所有功能的课程框架

■ 目的

本课程旨在符合STCW公约表A-Ⅱ/2管理级航行功能、货物装卸与积载功能和船舶作业管理和人员管理背景知识的知识、理解和熟练的强制性最低要求。

■ 目标

功能1

本课程大纲涵盖了STCW公约第二章A-II/2节的要求。本功能部分为保证有关管理级航行的培训效果提供了详细的内容。

本部分为支持以下情况中的任务、职能和责任提供了背景知识：

- 制订航次计划并引导航行
- 定位和确定通过任一定位方法获取的最终船位的精度
- 测定并修正罗经差
- 协调搜寻与救助行动
- 确定值班安排和程序
- 通过辅助决策的导航设备和系统的信息保持安全航行
- 通过辅助决策的ECDIS及相关的航行系统保持安全航行
- 预报天气和海洋水文状况
- 航行中的应急反应
- 在各种状况下操纵和操作船舶
- 推进装置和轮机系统的遥控操作与维护

功能2

本课程大纲涵盖了STCW公约第二章A-II/2节的要求。本功能部分为保证有关管理级货物装卸与积载的培训效果提供了详细的内容。

This section provides the background knowledge to support the tasks, duties and responsibilities in:

- planning safe loading, stowage, securing and care during the voyage and unloading of cargoes
- the carriage of dangerous goods.

This includes topics such as ship trim, stability, ballasting, cargo securing, tankers and tanker operations and carriage of dangerous, hazardous and harmful cargoes.

Function 3

The syllabus covers the requirements of the STCW Code, chapter II, section A-II/2. This functional element provides the detailed knowledge to support the training outcomes related to Controlling the Operation of the Ship and Care for Persons on Board at the Management Level.

This section provides the background knowledge to support the tasks, duties and responsibilities in:

- controlling trim, stability and stress
- monitoring and controlling compliance with legislation to ensure
  - safety of life at sea
  - protection of the marine environment
- maintaining safety and security of crew and passengers
- developing emergency and damage control plans
- organizing and managing the crew
- organizing and providing medical care on board

This includes topics such as ship construction and stability, dry-docking, search and rescue, personnel management and contingency planning.

■ Entry standards

This course is principally intended for officers for certification as Master and Chief Mate on ships of 500 gross tonnage or more. Entrants should have successfully completed a course covering the minimum standards required for certification as officer in charge of a navigational watch on ships of 500 gross tonnage or more (see IMO model course 7.03, Officer in charge of a navigational watch). In addition they should have completed approved seagoing service as officer in charge of a navigational watch in accordance with STCW Convention, 1978, as amended, regulation II/2, paragraph 2 prior to certification.

本部分为支持以下情况中的任务、职能和责任提供了背景知识：

- 在航行和货物卸载过程中安全装载、积载、系固和照管
- 危险货物运输

本部分包括了例如船舶吃水差、稳性、压载、货物系固、油船和油船操作、危险和有害货物运输的内容。

功能3

本课程大纲涵盖了STCW公约第二章A-II/2节的要求。本功能部分为保证有关管理级船舶作业管理和人员管理的培训效果提供了详细的内容。

本部分为支持以下情况中的任务、职能和责任提供了背景知识：

- 控制吃水差、稳性和应力
- 根据立法监督和控制以确保
  - 海上人命的安全
  - 海洋环境保护
- 维护船员和乘客的安全和治安
- 制定紧急和破损控制图
- 组织和管理船员
- 组织和提供船上医护

本部分包括诸如船舶结构和稳性、进入干船坞、搜救、人员管理和应急计划的内容。

■ 入学标准

本课程主要面向500总吨及以上考船长和大副证书的学员开设。学员应顺利通过负责航行值班的500总吨及以上驾驶员考证所要求的最低标准的课程(参见IMO示范课程7.03“负责航行值班的高级船员”)。此外，他们还应具有经认可符合经修订的STCW1978公约第二章A-II/2节认证之前第二段要求的航行值班驾驶员海上服务的资历。

Course certificate

On successful completion of the course and assessments, a document may be issued certifying that the holder has successfully completed a course of training which meets or exceeds the level of knowledge and competence specified in table A-II/2 of STCW Code, for the function.

A certificate may be issued only by centres approved by the Administration.

Staff requirements

Instructors shall be qualified in the task for which training is being conducted and have appropriate training in instructional techniques and training methods (STCW Code, section AI/6). Depending on the complexity of the exercises set, an assistant instructor with similar experience is desirable for certain practical exercises.

Teaching facilities and equipment

A classroom equipped with an overhead projector and a blackboard, whiteboard or interactive board or flipchart should be provided for teaching the theory of the course and holding group discussions.

The following items are necessary for use in group work:

For Function 1:

COLREGS 1972 — a set of table-top models displaying proper signals or lights, a magnetic board or a navigation light simulator.

Manoeuvring — a set of models to represent ships, jetties, piers and other dock configurations, which can be used on a table top to illustrate ship, handling techniques STCW provides for trainees to have practical competence in ship manoeuvring. The practical components of this may be developed and assessed on vessels in service; however, those training centres completing the practical element of this competence within a training course will need to provide an approved ship simulator, manned ship models or a training ship for this purpose.

For Functions 2 and Function 3:

- a collec tion of photographs, drawings and plans, illustrating various types of ship and constructional details, should be provided; cutaway models also can be used to reinforce this knowledge
- a floating ship stability demonstration model and a flotation tank are recommended
- the model should be capable of demonstrating the effects of adding or removing masses, of shifting masses, of suspending masses and of free surface liquid working models of heavy-lift derricks
- a ship's loading instrument or manufacturers' descriptions of examples, capacity plans and hydrostatic data for one or more ships' electronic calculators.

■ 课程证书

学员顺利完成本课程及其评估之后，将会获得培训合格证，表明其能力达到或超过STCW公约表A-II/2所列知识水平及适任能力。

该证书仅由主管机关批准的机构签发。

■ 教员要求

教员应能胜任所承担的培训任务，并经过相应的教学技能和培训方法训练（参见STCW 规则AI/6节）。根据实操课程的复杂性，可以安排一位具有相应资历的助教承担某些实操项目的教学。

■ 教学设施和设备

应提供一个配有高射投影仪和黑板（白板、互动板）或活动挂图的教室供课程的理论教学和进行分组讨论使用。

在分组作业中有必要应用以下内容：

对于功能1：

COLREGS 1972——一套正确显示号型或号灯的桌面模型，一块磁力板或一台航行灯模拟器。

操纵——一套显示船舶、防波堤、码头及码头其他结构的模型，该模型用在桌面上以展示STCW公约所要求学员适任能力的船舶操纵技艺。虽然本部分的实操内容可以在学员所在船上进行和评估，但是，完成培训课程中实操适任能力培训，必须提供船舶模拟器或有人驾驶船舶模型或实习船来进行此项培训。

对于功能2和功能3：

- 应有一批照片、图纸、平面图说明各种船舶及其结构细节，采用剖面模型也能够强化此类知识
- 推荐一个浮动的船舶稳性展示模型和一个浮动的液舱
- 该模型应能展示增减重量、移动重量、悬挂重量和重吊工作模式下的自由液面的影响效果
- 一台船舶装载仪或制造商提供的由一个或多个电子计算器使用的舱容表和静水力参数表的示例说明

■ Teaching aids (A)

The list of teaching aids and references are recommendations only and are intended to support the learning outcomes of the course.

A1 Instructor Manual (Part D of this course)
A2 Catalogue of British Admiralty charts and other hydrographic publications
A3 British Admiralty Notices to Mariners
A4 Nautical Almanac
A5 Nautical tables (Norie's, Burton's or others)
A6 Pre-computed altitude and azimuth tables (e.g. H0229)
A7 Pocket calculator
A8 Working chart
A9 Ocean plotting sheet
A10 Passage planning charts
A11 Routeing charts
A12 *Ocean Passages for the World* (NP 136), Taunton, Hydrographer of the Navy, 1987
A13 Distance tables
A14 British Admiralty List of Lights
A15 National list of lights and buoyage system
A16 British Admiralty tide table of the area concerned
A17 Local tide table
A18 Tidal stream atlas
A19 British Admiralty "Pilot" book for the area concerned
A20 National sailing directions
A21 Port information books
A22 IALA Maritime Buoyage System, Admiralty NP 735
A23 British Admiralty List of Radio Signals, Vol. 2: Radio Aids to Navigation, Satellite Navigation Systems, Legal Time, Radio Time Signals and Electronic Position Fixing System
A24 British Admiralty List of Radio Signals, Vol. 5: Global Maritime Distress and Safety System (GMDSS)
A25 British Admiralty List of Radio Signals, Vol. 6: Pilot Services, Vol. 7: Vessel Traffic Services and Port Operations
A26 British Admiralty List of Radio Signals, Vol. 3: Maritime Safety Information Services
A27 Ship's logbook
A28 Loran-C Receiver
A29 Magnetic compass in a binnacle with necessary correcting devices for identification of various parts only
A30 Pelorus and azimuth mirror
A31 Gyrocompass
A32 GPS Receivers
A33 Differential GPS (DGPS) Receiver
A34 Enhanced Loran (eLoran) Receiver
A35 Global Navigation Satellite System (GLONASS) Receiver
A36 Galileo Receiver
A37 Automatic Identification System (AIS) Receiver
A38 Long Range Identification and Tracking (LRIT) Receiver
A39 Voyage Data Recorder (VDR) and Simplified Voyage Data Recorder (S-VDR)

■ 教具(A)

教辅材料及参考资料清单只是建议性的,其目的是支持课程的培训效果。

A1 教员手册(本课程的D部分)
A2 英版海图及其他水道出版物总目录
A3 英版航海通告
A4 航海天文历
A5 航海表(Norie's,Burton's 或其他)
A6 天体高度方位表(如H0229)
A7 袖珍计算器
A8 航用海图
A9 空白定位图
A10 航路设计图
A11 航线设计图
A12 世界大洋航路(NP 136)(Taunton, 海军水道测量家,1987)
A13 里程表
A14 英版灯标表
A15 英国灯标表及浮标系统
A16 相关地区的英版潮汐表
A17 当地潮汐表
A18 潮流图册
A19 相关地区的英版航路指南
A20 英国航路指南
A21 港口信息手册
A22 IALA海上浮标系统,英版NP 735
A23 英版无线电信号表,第2卷:无线电航标、卫星导航系统、法定时间、无线电授时信号和电子定位系统
A24 英版无线电信号表,第5卷:全球海上遇险和安全系统(GMDSS)
A25 英版无线电信号表,第6卷:引航服务,第7卷:船舶交管服务及港口运营
A26 英版无线电信号表,第3卷:海上安全信息服务
A27 船舶航海日志
A28 劳兰-C接收机
A29 置于罗盘内并配有必要的供识别不同部件用校正设备的磁罗经
A30 罗经刻度盘和方位镜
A31 陀螺罗经
A32 GPS接收机
A33 差分GPS接收机
A34 增强型劳兰(eLoran)接收机
A35 全球导航卫星系统(GLONASS)接收机
A36 伽利略定位系统接收机
A37 自动识别系统(AIS)接收机
A38 远距离识别和跟踪(LRIT)接收机
A39 航行数据记录仪(VDR)和简式航行数据记录仪(S-VDR)

A40 Bridge Navigational watch alarm system (BNWAS)
A41 Ship's Drawings/Plan (GA, Mid section)
A42 Simulators (wherever applicable to enhance understanding of topics, especially, COLREGS and Ship handling)

■ Videos (DVDs), CD-ROMs, CBTs (V)

V1 Ships' Routeing on CD, Version 4 (2008) (IMO Code No. DC927E, ISBN 978-92-801-70207)
V2 IMO – Safe, Secure and Efficient Shipping on Clean Oceans on DVD (2006 Edition) (IMO Code No. V010M, ISBN 978-92-801-70023)
V3 Ship handling – Part 1 (Code No. 95)
V4 Ship handling – Part 2 (Code No. 129)
V5 Ship handling – Part 3 (Code No. 321)
V6 Anchoring safely (Code No. 928)
V7 Interaction (Code No. 13)
V8 Ship handling in following seas (Code No. 636)
V9 Ship handling in head seas (Code No. 661)
V10 Ship handling in restricted waters – ship squat and shallow (Code No. 697)
V11 Ship handling in restricted waters – bank effect & interaction (Code No. 748)
V12 Manoeuvring characteristics of special car carriers (Code No. 696)
V13 Manoeuvring and control characteristics of special type ships: Part 1 Focusing on the wind pressure effect on a PCC (Code No. 9985)
V14 Manoeuvring and control characteristics of special type ships: Part 2 Anchoring and mooring of a PCC (Code No. 9986)
V15 Working with tugs (Code No. 972)
V16 Tractor tugs (Code No. 165)
V17 Ship handling with Tractor Tugs (Code No. 359)
V18 Navigating in ICE (Code No. 927)
V19 Helicopter operations at sea (edition 2) (Code No. 704)
V20 Margins of safety (Code No. 73)
V21 Voyage planning (Code No. 758)
V22 Bridge watchkeeping (Code No. 497)
V23 Master/pilot relationship (Code No. 498)
V24 Accident prevention – the human factor (Code No. 637)
V25 Emergency procedures (Code No. 638)
V26 Navigational charts & associated publications (Code No. 639)
V27 Working with VTS (Code No. 640)
V28 Five case studies (Code No. 781)
V29 Shipping Casualty Emergency response (Code No. 467)
V30 Safer mooring (Code No. 997)
V31 Theory of mooring – edition 4 (Code No. 1104)
V32 Safe mooring practice – edition 4 (Code No. 1105)
V33 Maintenance of mooring systems – edition 4 (Code No. 1106)

A40 驾驶台航行值班报警系统(BNWAS)
A41 船舶图纸/平面图(GA图,舯剖面图)
A42 模拟器(用于能提高对主题的理解特别是避碰规则和船舶操纵的情况下)

■ 录像(DVDS),光盘,基于计算机的训练(V)

V1 航线设计的CD,2008年第4版(IMO 规则编号DC927E,ISBN 978-92-801-70207)
V2 IMO—有关清洁海洋的安全、保安和有效航运的DVD (2006版)(IMO规则编号V010M, ISBN 978-92-801-70023)
V3 船舶操纵—第1部分(规则编号第95号)
V4 船舶操纵—第2部分(规则编号第129号)
V5 船舶操纵—第3部分(规则编号第321号)
V6 安全锚泊(规则编号第928号)
V7 相互作用(规则编号第13号)
V8 在下列海域的船舶操纵(规则编号第636号)
V9 船舶顶浪操纵(规则编号第661号)
V10 受限水域船舶操纵—浅水区船舶下沉(规则编号第697号)
V11 受限水域船舶操纵—岸壁效应和相互作用(规则编号第748号)
V12 汽车专用运输船舶的操纵特性(规则编号第696号)
V13 特种船舶的操控特性:第1部分关注汽车专用运输船的风压效应(规则编号第9985号)
V14 特种船舶的操控特性:第2部分汽车专用运输船的锚泊和系泊(规则编号第9986号)
V15 拖船作业(规则编号第972号)
V16 牵引船(规则编号第165号)
V17 在牵引船作业时的船舶操纵(规则编号第359号)
V18 冰区航行(规则编号第927号)
V19 海上直升机作业(第2版)(规则编号第704号)
V20 安全余地(规则编号第73号)
V21 航次计划(规则编号第758号)
V22 驾驶台值班(规则编号第497号)
V23 船长/引航员关系(规则编号第498号)
V24 事故预防—人为因素(规则编号第637号)
V25 应急程序(规则编号第638号)
V26 航用海图与相关出版物(规则编号第639号)
V27 VTS作业(规则编号第640号)
V28 5个案例研究(规则编号第781号)
V29 船舶遇险应急响应(规则编号第467号)
V30 安全系泊(规则编号第997号)
V31 系泊理论(第4版)(规则编号第1104号)
V32 安全系泊实践(第4版)(规则编号第1105号)
V33 系泊系统的维护(第4版)(规则编号第1106号)

V34 Pilot on board, working together (Code No. 945)
V35 Basic instincts (passenger mustering & crowd control) (Code No. 603)
V36 The cold and heavy weather file (Code No. 626)
V37 Meteorology for safe navigation in cyclones (Code No. 695)
V38 Wind, waves and storms Part 1 – understanding weather system (Code No. 738)
V39 Wind, waves and storms Part 2 – coping with hazardous weather (Code No. 743)
V40 AIS – automatic identification systems (Code No. 926)
V41 The safe use of electronic charts (Code No. 705)
V42 Target tracking devices (Code No. 948)
V43 Gyrocompass – Part 1 (Code No. 9897)
V44 Gyrocompass – Part 2 (Code No. 9898)
V45 Gyrocompass – Part 3 (Code No. 9899)
V46 Watchkeeping in port (Code No. 659)
V47 Dangerous goods at sea series (edition 5) (Code No. 713)
V48 Dangerous goods at sea series part 2 (edition 5) (Code No. 719)
V49 Centrifugal pumps – theory & operation (Code No. 9)
V50 Crude oil washing operations (edition 3) (Code No. 707)
V51 Operation & maintenance of inert gas systems (edition 3) (Code No. 708)
V52 The ship-shore interface (petroleum tankers) (Code No. 709)
V53 Safe cargo stowage & securing (Code No. 747)
V54 Ship to ship transfer – petroleum and liquid cargoes (Code No. 751)
V55 Tank purging and line cleaning onboard chemical tankers (Code No. 752)
V56 Introduction to liquefied gas carriers (edition 2) (Code No. 753)
V57 Safe log carrier operations (Code No. 760)
V58 Successful reefer container operations (Code No. 788)
V59 Bulk carriers – handle with care (Code No. 691)
V60 Hatch covers – a practical guide (Code No. 938)
V61 Chemical tank cleaning & inspection (edition 2) (Code No. 950)
V62 Chemical tanker operations: safety and pollution prevention part 1 (Code No. 951)
V63 Chemical tanker operations: safety and pollution prevention part 2 (Code No. 952)
V64 Tank cleaning practice (Code No. 982)
V65 Over and under pressurization of tanks (edition 2) (Code No. 984)
V66 Handling vegetable oils (Code No. 988)
V67 Dangerous & difficult bulk cargoes (Code No. 1101)
V68 Vapour emission control (Code No. 1118)
V69 Ro-ro safety and cargo operations (Code No. 162)
V70 Portable tanks and tank containers (Code No. 314)
V71 Reefer container operations (Code No. 481)
V72 Fire fighting & safe cargo operations on car carriers (Code No. 540)
V73 Don't gamble with safety on chemical tankers (Code No. 595)
V74 Cargo loss prevention on board bulk carriers (Code No. 598)
V75 Cargo lashing operations (ro-ro) (Code No. 631)
V76 Safe use of rigging equipment (Code No. 700)
V77 Manual handling techniques (Code No. 703)
V78 Tanker practices series
Pumping cargo part 1 (Code No. 501)
Pumping cargo part 2 (Code No. 502)
Tank cleaning – part 3 (Code No. 503)
Heating cargo – part 4 (Code No. 504)
Measuring cargo – part 5 (Code No. 505)

V34 引航员上船,共同工作(规则编号第945号)
V35 基本技能(召集乘客和聚集人群控制)(规则编号第603号)
V36 寒冷和恶劣天气读本(规则编号第626号)
V37 气旋天气安全航行的气象学(规则编号第695号)
V38 风、浪、风暴第1部分—了解天气系统(规则编号第738号)
V39 风、浪、风暴第2部分—应对灾害天气(规则编号第743号)
V40 AIS—自动识别系统(规则编号第926号)
V41 电子海图的安全使用(规则编号第705号)
V42 目标跟踪装置(规则编号第948号)
V43 陀螺罗经—第1部分(规则编号第9897号)
V44 陀螺罗经—第2部分(规则编号第9898号)
V45 陀螺罗经—第3部分(规则编号第9899号)
V46 在港值班(规则编号第659号)
V47 海运危险货物系列(第5版)(规则编号第713号)
V48 海运危险货物系列(第5版)第2部分(规则编号第719号)
V49 离心泵—理论与操作(规则编号第9号)
V50 原油洗舱作业(第3版)(规则编号第707号)
V51 惰性气体系统作业与维护(第3版)(规则编号第708号)
V52 船岸连接(油船)(规则编号第709号)
V53 货物安全积载与系固(规则编号第747号)
V54 船对船转驳—石油和液体货物(规则编号第751号)
V55 化学品船的洗舱和管线清洁(规则编号第752号)
V56 液化气船简介(第2版)(规则编号第753号)
V57 原木船安全作业(规则编号第760号)
V58 成功的冷藏集装箱作业(规则编号第788号)
V59 散货船—小心轻放(规则编号第691号)
V60 舱盖—实操指南(规则编号第938号)
V61 化学品舱清洁及检查(第2版)(规则编号第950号)
V62 化学品船:安全与防污染第1部分(规则编号第951号)
V63 化学品船:安全与防污染第2部分(规则编号第952号)
V64 液货舱清洁实操(规则编号第982号)
V65 液货舱的压力控制(第2版)(规则编号第984号)
V66 装卸菜油(规则编号第988号)
V67 危险散货和特殊散货(规则编号第1101号)
V68 蒸汽排放控制(规则编号第1188号)
V69 滚装船的安全与货物作业(规则编号第162号)
V70 可移式液货舱与液货集装箱维护(规则编号第314号)
V71 冷藏集装箱作业(规则编号第481号)
V72 汽车运输船上的消防与货物安全作业(规则编号第540号)
V73 别拿化学品船的安全赌博(规则编号第595号)
V74 防止散货船货物损耗(规则编号第598号)
V75 货物绑扎作业(滚装船)(规则编号第631号)
V76 索具设备的安全使用(规则编号第700号)
V77 人工装卸技艺(规则编号第703号)
V78 液货船实操系列
泵送货物—第1部分(规则编号第501号)
泵送货物—第2部分(规则编号第502号)
液舱清洁—第3部分(规则编号第503号)
加热货物—第4部分(规则编号第504号)
货物测量—第5部分(规则编号第505号)

V79 Fighting pollution – preventing pollution at sea (edition 3) (Code No. 755)
V80 Good bunkering practice (edition 2) (Code No. 962)
V81 Permit to work (Code No. 621)
V82 Safe gangway and ladder operations (Code No. 946)
V83 Personal safety on tankers (edition 2) (Code No. 970)
V84 Personal safety on chemical tankers (Code No. 980)
V85 Seven steps to ship stability part 1 (Code No. 622)
Seven steps to ship stability part 2 (Code No. 623)
V86 Entering into enclosed spaces (edition 2) (Code No. 682)
V87 Death in minutes – rescue techniques from confined spaces (Code No. 750)
V88 Permit to work (Code No. 621)
V89 Safe hot work procedures (Code No. 701)
V90 Waste and garbage management (Code No. 627)
V91 Medical first aid (edition 2) (Code No. 990)
V92 Hull stress monitoring (Code No. 550)
V93 Mistaken identity (Code No. 14)
V94 Survival (Code No. 681)
V95 Basic fire fighting (edition 3) (Code No. 674)
V96 Enclosed lifeboats, freefall lifeboats rescue boats (Code No. 679)
V97 STCW and flag state implementation (Code No. 629)
V98 Search techniques (Code No. 935)
V99 Security at sea (Code No. 484)
V100 Immersion suits – the difference between life and death (Code No. 947)
V101 Muster lists, drills & helicopter operations (Code No. 678)
V102 MLC 2006 (Code No. 986)
V103 Shipshape. A guide to good housekeeping part 1: on deck (Code No. 974)
V104 The shipboard management role (edition 2) (Code No. 969)
V105 Port state control – tightening the net (edition 2) (Code No. 977)
V106 Health & welfare advice for seafarers (Code No. 510)
V107 Personal hygiene (Code No. 993)
V108 Load line surveys – part 1 (Code No. 544)
V109 Safety construction survey – part 2 (Code No. 545)
V110 Safety equipment survey – part 3 (Code No. 546)
V111 Management for seafarer series (Code No. 607 – 612)
V112 Ballast water management
V113 Emergency Response – the vital first minutes
V114 Interpreting weather at sea
V115 MARPOL. The new rules
V116 Oily water separators

V79 防污染—海上防污染 (第3版) (规则编号第755号)
V80 好的加油做法 (第2版)(规则编号第962号)
V81 作业许可 (规则编号第621号)
V82 舷梯和绳梯安全作业(规则编号第946号)
V83 液货船个人安全 (第2版)(规则编号第970号)
V84 化学品船个人安全(规则编号第980号)
V85 船舶稳性的7个步骤第1部分(规则编号第622号)
船舶稳性的7个步骤第2部分(规则编号第623号)
V86 进入封闭场所(第2版)(规则编号第682号)
V87 和死神争分夺秒—受限空间救援技巧(规则编号第750号)
V88 作业许可(规则编号第621号)
V89 热工作业安全程序(规则编号第701号)
V90 废物和垃圾管理 (规则编号第627号)
V91 医疗急救(第2版) (规则编号第990号)
V92 船体应力监测(规则编号第550号)
V93 错误识别(规则编号第14号)
V94 求生(规则编号第681号)
V95 基本消防 (第3版) (规则编号第674号)
V96 封闭式救生艇、自由降落式救生艇、救助艇 (规则编号第679号)
V97 STCW 和船旗国履约(规则编号第629号)
V98 搜索技巧(规则编号第935号)
V99 海上保安 (规则编号第484号)
V100 浸水保温服—生死之别 (规则编号第947号)
V101 应变部署表、演习和直升机作业(规则编号第678号)
V102 MLC(国际海事劳工公约)2006(规则编号第986号)
V103 井然有序—良好的内务管理指南第1部分：甲板上(规则编号第974号)
V104 船舶管理的作用(第2版) (规则编号第969号)
V105 港口国监督—收紧网 (第2版)(规则编号第977号)
V106 海员健康和福利建议(规则编号第510号)
V107 个人健康 (规则编号第993号)
V108 载重线检查—第1部分(规则编号第544号)
V109 安全结构检查—第2部分 (规则编号第545号)
V110 安全设备检查—第3部分 (规则编号第546号)
V111 海员管理系列 (规则编号第607—612号)
V112 压载水管理
V113 应急响应—至关重要的前几分钟
V114 海上天气释疑
V115 MARPOL—新规则
V116 油水分离器

V117 Stowaways! A new view on prevention
V118 SOPEP (CBT # 0004)
V119 ISM Code (CBT # 0005)
V120 Vessel Structural Conditions (CBT # 0014)
V121 Corrosion Protection I (CBT # 0015)
V122 Corrosion Protection II (CBT # 0016)
V123 Steering Gear (CBT # 0017)
V124 Auxiliary Engine (CBT # 0024)
V125 Voyage Planning (CBT # 0026)
V126 Ballast Water Management (CBT # 0027)
V127 Protection and Indemnity (CBT # 0028)
V128 Emergency Towing system (CBT # 0031)
V129 Liquid Cargo Properties (CBT # 0032)
V130 Medical First Aid (CBT # 0036)
V131 Operation of Generators (CBT # 0041)
V132 Bilge Water Separator (CBT # 0043)
V133 Auxiliary Boiler Plant (CBT # 0046)
V134 Radar Observation and Plotting (CBT # 0049)
V135 ARPA Theory (CBT # 0050)
V136 HAZMAT – IMDG Code (CBT # 0053)
V137 COW (CBT # 0054)
V138 ODME (CBT # 0055)
V139 Satellite Navigation GPS (CBT # 0059)
V140 Navigation in Ice (CBT # 0060)
V141 Stability II, Damage Stability (CBT # 0061)
V142 Basic Ship Handling (CBT # 0066)
V143 Sulzer Medium Speed Diesel Engine (CBT # 0074)
V144 Pumps and Pumping Operations (CBT # 0078)
V145 Human Relations (CBT # 0088)
V146 Medical Care (CBT # 0089)
V147 Incinerators (CBT # 0091)
V148 Introduction to MARPOL (CBT # 0092)
V149 Fresh Water Generator (CBT # 0098)
V150 INS – Integrated Navigation System (CBT # 0103)
V151 AIS – Automatic Identification System (CBT # 0109)
V152 Heavy Weather Damage (Container Vessels) (CBT # 0111)
V153 Risk Assessment and Management (CBT # 0123)
V154 HAZMAT – IMDG Code, Advanced (CBT # 0151)
V155 Hatch Cover Maintenance and Operation (CBT # 0152)
V156 Stowaways, migrants and refugees (CBT # 0155)
V157 Introduction to the Maritime Labour Convention (MLC 2006) (CBT # 0191)

V117 预防偷渡的新视角!
V118 SOPEP (CBT编号第0004号)
V119 ISM 规则 (CBT编号第0005号)
V120 船舶结构状况 (CBT编号第0014号)
V121 防腐蚀1 (CBT 编号第0015号)
V122 防腐蚀2 (CBT编号第0016号)
V123 舵机 (CBT 编号第0017号)
V124 辅机 (CBT编号第0024号)
V125 航行计划 (CBT 编号第0026号)
V126 压载水管理 (CBT编号第0027号)
V127 保赔 (CBT 编号第0028号)
V128 应急拖带系统 (CBT编号第0031号)
V129 液体货物性质 (CBT 编号第0032号)
V130 医疗急救 (CBT编号第0036号)
V131 发电机的操作 (CBT 编号第0041号)
V132 舱底水分离器 (CBT编号第0043号)
V133 辅助锅炉装置 (CBT 编号第0046号)
V134 雷达观测与标绘(CBT编号第0049号)
V135 ARPA 理论 (CBT 编号第0050号)
V136 危险品—IMDG 规则 (CBT编号第0053号)
V137 COW (CBT编号第0054号)
V138 ODME (CBT 编号第0055号)
V139 卫星导航 GPS (CBT编号第0059号)
V140 冰区航行 (CBT 编号第0060号)
V141 稳性2,破损稳性 (CBT编号第0061号)
V142 船舶操纵基础 (CBT 编号第0066号)
V143 苏尔寿中速柴油机(CBT编号第0074号)
V144 泵及泵的操作 (CBT 编号第0078号)
V145 人际关系 (CBT编号第0088号)
V146 医疗保健 (CBT 编号第0089号)
V147 焚烧炉 (CBT编号第0091号)
V148 MARPOL公约简介 (CBT 编号第0092号)
V149 淡水造水机 (CBT编号第0098号)
V150 INS—组合导航系统 (CBT编号第0103号)
V151 AIS—自动识别系统 (CBT编号第0109号)
V152 恶劣天气的危害性 (集装箱船) (CBT编号第0111号)
V153 风险评估与管理 (CBT 编号第0123号)
V154 危险品— IMDG 规则(高级) (CBT编号第0151号)
V155 舱盖维护与操作 (CBT编号第0152号)
V156 偷渡、移民和难民 (CBT编号第0155号)
V157 海事劳工公约 (MLC 2006) 简介(CBT编号第0191号)

V158 MLC 2006 – Onboard Responsibilities (CBT # 0192)
V159 Culture Management (CBT # 0251)
V160 Active Listening (CBT # 0252)
V161 Corrective Feedback (CBT # 0253)
V162 Meeting Management (CBT # 0254)
V163 Question Techniques (CBT # 0255)
V164 Team Leadership (CBT # 0256)
V165 Stress Management (CBT # 0257)
V166 Personal Safety (DVD # 2001)
V167 SOPEP (DVD # 2004)
V168 Mooring and Anchoring (DVD # 2063)
V169 Counting the cost
V170 Any fool can stuff a container
V171 No Room for Error
V172 Bulk Matters
V173 Container Matters
V174 Gas Matters
V175 Tanker Matters

■ IMO references (R)

CHECKS SHOULD BE MADE THAT THESE ARE THE LATEST EDITIONS AVAILABLE

R1 International Convention on Standards of Training, Certification and Watchkeeping for Seafarers (STCW), 2011 edition (IMO Sales No. 938, ISBN 978-92-801-52884)
R2 International Convention for the Safety of Life at Sea (SOLAS), as amended (IMO Sales No. IE110E) SOLAS – Consolidated Edition, 2009 (ISBN 978-92-801-15055)
R3 Ships' Routeing (2010, 10th ed.) (IMO Sales No. ID927E)
R4 Assembly resolution A.665(16): Performance standards for radio direction-finding systems
R5 Assembly resolution A.574(14): Recommendation on general requirements for electronic navigational aids
R6 Assembly resolution A.382(X): Magnetic compasses: carriage and performance standards
R7 Assembly resolution A.424(XI): Performance standards for gyrocompasses

V158 MLC 2006—船上责任(CBT 编号第0192号)
V159 文化管理(CBT编号第0251号)
V160 主动倾听(CBT 编号第0252号)
V161 反馈与纠正(CBT编号第0253号)
V162 会议管理(CBT 编号第0254号)
V163 提问技巧(CBT编号第0255号)
V164 团队领导(CBT 编号第0256号)
V165 压力管理(CBT编号第0257号)
V166 个人安全(DVD 编号第2001号)
V167 SOPEP(DVD编号第2004号)
V168 系泊与锚泊(DVD编号第2063号)
V169 成本计算
V170 任何一个傻瓜都能装满集装箱
V171 无处容错
V172 散货业务
V173 集装箱业务
V174 气体业务
V175 油船业务

■ IMO 参考书目(R)

应对这些参考文献进行检查,以确保它们都是最新版本

R1 国际海员训练、发证与值班标准公约(STCW)2011 版(IMO销售号第938号,ISBN 978-92-801-52884)
R2 经修订的国际海上人命安全公约(SOLAS)(IMO销售号IE110E)(综合版,2009)(ISBN 978-92-801-15055)
R3 船舶航线(2010,第10版.)(IMO销售号ID927E)
R4 A.665(16)号大会决议:无线电测向系统的性能标准
R5 A.574(14)号大会决议:关于电子导航设备一般要求的建议
R6 A.382(X)号大会决议:磁罗经安装和性能标准
R7 A.424(XI)号大会决议:陀螺罗经性能标准

R8 Convention on the International Regulations for Preventing Collisions at Sea, 1972 (COLREGS 1972), as amended (IMO Sales No. IB904E) Consolidated Edition, 2003 (ISBN 978-92-801-41672)

R9 International Convention for the Prevention of Pollution from Ships, 1973 (MARPOL 1973) (IMO Sales No. IC520E) Consolidated Edition, 2006 (ISBN 978-92-801-42167)

R10 Regulations for the Prevention of Pollution by Oil – Annex 1, MARPOL 73/78 (IMO Sales No. 520)

R11 Regulations for the Control of Pollution by Noxious Substances in Bulk – Annex II, MARPOL 73/78 (IMO Sales No. 520)

R12 Guidelines for the implementation of Annex V of MARPOL 73/78 (IMO Sales No. 520)

R13 Manual on Oil Pollution, Section 1 – Prevention (IMO Sales No. 557)

R14 Assembly resolution A.648 (16) – General Principles for Ship Reporting Systems and Ship Reporting Requirements, including Guidelines for Reporting Incidents Involving Dangerous Goods, Harmful Substances and/or Marine Pollutants

R15 Assembly resolution A.626(15) – Amendments to the International Regulations for Preventing Collisions at Sea, 1972

R16 Assembly resolution A.678(16) – Amendments to the International Regulations for Preventing Collisions at Sea, 1972

R17 Assembly resolution A.601(15) – Provision and display of manoeuvring information on board ships Assembly resolution A.751(18) – Interim standards for ship manoeuvrability

R18 Assembly resolution A.160(ES.IV) – Recommendation on data concerning manoeuvring capabilities and stopping distances of ships

R19 Assembly resolution A.269(VIII) – Recommendation for skippers of fishing vessels on ensuring a vessel's endurance in conditions of ice formation

R20 Assembly resolution A.889(21) – Pilot transfer arrangements

R21 International Convention on Salvage, 1989. The London Salvage Convention

R22 Assembly resolution A.528(13) – Recommendation on weather routeing

R23 Comitee Maritime International, International Conventions on Maritime Law (Antwerp, CMI Secretariat (Firma Henry Voet-Genicot, Borzestraat 17, B-2000 Antwerp), 1987)

R24 Assembly resolution A.439(XI) – IMCO Search and Rescue Manual

R25 Assembly resolution A.530 (13) – Use of radar transponders for search and rescue purposes

R26 MEPC.14(20) Amendments to Annex I of MARPOL 73/78

R27 MEPC.16(22) Amendments to Annex II of MARPOL 73/78

R28 MEPC.21 (22) Amendments to Protocol I of MARPOL 73/78 and the text of the Protocol, as amended, annexed thereto

R29 MSC.35(63) – Guidelines for emergency towing arrangements on tankers

R30 INTERNATIONAL CONVENTION ON THE CONTROL OF HARMFUL ANTI-FOULING SYSTEMS (AFS) ON SHIPS, 2001 (2005 Edition) IMO Sales No. IA680E, ISBN 978-92-801-41955

R31 International Aeronautical and Maritime Search and Rescue Manual (IAMSAR Manual) Volume I – Organization and Management, Volume II – Mission Coordination, Volume III – Mobile Facilities (2008 Edition, IMO Sales No. IF960E, IC961E, IF962E, ISBN 978-92-801-14881, ISBN 978-92-801-14898, ISBN 978-92-801-14904)

R32 International Code of Signals (2005 edition) (IMO Sales No. IA994E, ISBN 978-92-801-41986)

R8　经修订的1972年国际海上避碰规则（COLREGS 1972）(IMO销售号IB904E)（综合版，2003）(ISBN 978-92-801-41672)

R9　1973年国际防止船舶造成污染公约(MARPOL 1973)(IMO销售号IC520E)(综合版,2006)(ISBN 978-92-801-42167)

R10　防止油类污染规则—MARPOL 73/78,附则Ⅰ(IMO销售号第520号)

R11　控制散装有毒液体物质污染规则—MARPOL 73/78,附件Ⅱ(IMO销售号第520号)

R12　MARPOL 73/78附件Ⅴ的操作指南(IMO销售号第520号)

R13　油污手册,第1节—预防(IMO销售号第557号)

R14　A.648(16)号大会决议—船舶报告系统与船舶报告要求总则,包括涉及危险货物、有害物质和/或海上污染物事故的报告指南

R15　A.626(15)号大会决议—1972年国际海上避碰规则修正案

R16　A.626(16)号大会决议—1972年国际海上避碰规则修正案

R17　A.601(15)号大会决议—船舶操纵信息的规定和显示,A.751(18)号大会决议—船舶操纵性能的暂行标准

R18　A.160(ES.Ⅳ)号大会决议—关于船舶操纵性和冲程有关数据的建议

R19　A.269(Ⅷ)号大会决议—关于渔船船长在结冰情况下保证船舶续航力的建议

R20　A.889(21)号大会决议—引航员登离船装置

R21　1989国际救助公约(伦敦救助公约)

R22　A.528(13)号大会决议—关于气象航线的建议

R23　国际海事委员会,关于海事法的国际公约,1987[安特卫普,国际海事委员会秘书处（Firma Henry Voet-Genicot,Borzestraat 17,B-2000 Antwerp)]

R24　A.439(Ⅺ)号大会决议—IMCO搜寻与救助手册

R25　A.530(13)号大会决议—搜救中雷达应答器的使用

R26　MEPC.14(20) MARPOL 73/78附件Ⅰ修正案

R27　MEPC.16(22) MARPOL 73/78附件Ⅱ修正案

R28　MEPC.21(22) MARPOL 73/78议定书Ⅰ修正案和经修订的议定书文本及其附录

R29　MSC.35(63)—油船应急拖带装置指南

R30　2001年关于船舶有害防污染系统控制的国际公约(2005 版)（IMO销售号IA680E)(ISBN 978-92-801-41955)

R31　国际航空与航海收寻与救助手册(IAMSAR Manual),第1卷—组织及管理,第2卷—任务协调，第3卷—移动设备（2008版）（IMO销售号IF960E,IC961E,IF962E,ISBN 978-92-801-14881,ISBN 978-92-801-14898,ISBN 978-92-801-14904)

R32　国际信号规则(2005版)（IMO销售号IA994E,ISBN 978-92-801-41986)

R33 IMO Standard Marine Communication Phrases (IMO SMCP) (2002 Edition) (IMO Sales No. IA987E, ISBN 978-92-801-51374)
R34 Assembly resolution A.954(23) – Proper use of VHF channels at sea
R35 Assembly resolution A.953(23) – World–wide radio navigation system
R36 Assembly resolution A.577 (14) – Operational Status of Electronic Position-Fixing Systems
R37 Assembly resolution A.615(15) – Radar Beacons and Transponders
R38 Assembly resolution A.280 (VIII) – Recommendations on Performance Standards for Gyrocompasses
R39 Assembly resolution A.382(X) – Magnetic Compasses: Carriage and Performance Standards
R40 Assembly resolution A.384(X) – Performance Standards for Radar Reflectors
R41 Assembly resolution A.823(19) – Performance standards for automatic radar plotting aids (ARPAs)
R42 Assembly resolution A.424(XI) – Performance Standards for Gyrocompasses
R43 Assembly resolution A.479(XII) – Performance Standards for Shipborne Receivers for Use with Differential Omega
R44 Assembly resolution A.281(VIII) – Recommendation on general requirements for electronic navigational aids
R45 Assembly resolution A.694 (17)* – General Requirements for Shipborne Radio Equipment Forming Part of the Global Maritime Distress and Safety System (GMDSS) and for Electronic Navigational Aids
R46 Assembly resolution A.918(22) – IMO standard marine communication phrases
R47 Assembly resolution A.488(XII) – Use of the Standard Marine Navigational Vocabulary
R48 Assembly resolution A.429(XI) – Routeing Systems
R49 MSC.71(69) – Amendments to the General Provisions on Ships' routeing
R50 Assembly resolution A.528(13) – Recommendation on Weather Routeing
R51 Assembly resolution A.113(V) – Revised International Code of Signals
R52 MSC.165(78) – Adoption of amendments to the general provisions on ships' routeing
R53 International Convention on Load Lines, 1966 (2005 Edition) IMO Sales No. IB701E, ISBN 978-92-801-41948
R54 International Maritime Dangerous Goods Code (IMDG Code), 2008 Edition (incorporating amendment 34-08) IMO Sales No. IG200E, ISBN 978-92-801-42419
R55 International Maritime Dangerous Goods Code (IMDG Code) Supplement, 2008 Edition, IMO Sales No. IG210E, ISBN 978-92-801-42426
R56 International Maritime Solid Bulk Cargoes Code (IMSBC Code) and Supplement (2009 Edition) IMO Sales No. IE260E, ISBN 978-92-801-42396
R57 Code of Safe Practice for Ships Carrying Timber Deck Cargoes, 1991 (1992 Edition) IMO Sales No. I275E, ISBN 978-92-801-12856
R58 Assembly resolution A.489 (XII) – Safe Stowage and Securing of Cargo Units and Other Entities in Ships Other Than Cellular Container Ships
R59 Assembly resolution A.533(13) – Elements to Be Taken Into Account When Considering the Safe Stowage and Securing of Cargo Units and Vehicles in Ships
R60 Assembly resolution A.581(14) – Guidelines for Securing Arrangements for the Transport of Road Vehicles on Ro-Ro Ships
R61 Code of Safe Practice for Cargo Stowage and Securing (CSS Code) (2003 Edition) IMO Sales No. IA292E, ISBN 978-92-801-51459
R62 International Code for the Safe Carriage of Grain in Bulk (International Grain Code) (1991 Edition) IMO Sales No. I240E, ISBN 978-92-801-12757

R33 IMO标准海事用语（IMO SMCP）（2002版）（IMO销售号IA987E，ISBN 978-92-801-51374）
R34 A.954(23)号大会决议—海上VHF的正确使用
R35 A.953(23)号大会决议—全球无线电导航系统
R36 A.577（14）号大会决议—电子定位系统的运行状态
R37 A.615（15）号大会决议—雷达信标和应答器
R38 A.280（Ⅷ）号大会决议—关于标准陀螺罗经性能的建议
R39 A.382（Ⅹ）号大会决议—磁罗经:安装和性能标准
R40 A.384（Ⅹ）号大会决议—雷达反射器的性能标准
R41 A.823(19)号大会决议—自动雷达标绘仪(ARPAs)性能标准
R42 A.424（Ⅺ）号大会决议—陀螺罗经的性能标准
R43 A.479（Ⅻ）号大会决议—船用差分欧米伽接收机的性能标准
R44 A.281(Ⅷ)号大会决议—关于电子助航仪器一般要求的建议
R45 A.694（17）* 号大会决议—对船用全球海上遇险和安全系统(GMDSS)与电子助航设备的无线电组成部分的一般要求
R46 A.918(22)号大会决议— IMO 标准航海用语
R47 A.488（Ⅻ）号大会决议—标准航海用语的使用
R48 A.429（Ⅺ）号大会决议—航路设计系统
R49 MSC.71(69)号决议—对船舶航路定线总则的修正案
R50 A.528（13）号大会决议—对气象航线的修正案
R51 A.113（Ⅴ）号大会决议—经修订的国际信号规则
R52 MSC.165(78)号决议—采纳船舶定线总则的修正案
R53 1966年国际载重线公约(2005 版)（IMO销售号IB701E，ISBN 978-92-801-41948）
R54 国际海上危险货物运输规则（IMDG 规则），2008 版（34-08修正案）（IMO销售号IG200E，ISBN 978-92-801-42419）
R55 国际海上危险货物运输规则（IMDG Code）补篇，2008 版（IMO销售号IG210E，ISBN 978-92-801-42426）
R56 国际海上散装固体货物运输规则（IMSBC 规则）及其补篇(2009 版)(IMO销售号IE260E，ISBN 978-92-801-42396）
R57 1991年船载甲板原木安全操作规则(1992版)(IMO销售号I275E，ISBN 978-92-801-12856）
R58 A.489（Ⅻ）号大会决议—非集装箱船的船载货物单元和其他物体的安全积载与系固
R59 A.533（13）号大会决议— 船载货物单元和车辆的安全积载与系固所应注意的因素
R60 A.581（14）号大会决议—滚装船车辆运输系固设施指南
R61 货物积载与系固安全操作规则（CSS 规则）(2003 版)（IMO 销售号 IA292E，ISBN 978-92-801-51459）
R62 国际散装谷物安全运输规则（国际谷物规则）(1991 版)（IMO销售号 I240E，ISBN 978-92-801-12757）

R63 Guidelines on the Enhanced Programme of inspections during survey of Bulk Carriers and Oil Tankers (2008 Edition) IMO Sales No. IA265E, ISBN 978-92-801-14966

R64 Code of Practice for the Safe Loading and Unloading of Bulk Carriers (BLU Code) (1998 Edition) IMO Sales No. I266E, ISBN 978-92-801-14584

R65 Manual on loading and unloading of Solid Bulk cargoes for Terminal representative (BLU Manual) (2008 Edition) IMO Sales No. I267E, ISBN 978-92-801-14928

R66 International Convention for Safe Containers (CSC), 1972 (1996 Edition) IMO Sales No. IA282E, ISBN 978-92-801-14119

R67 Guidelines for the Transport and Handling of Limited Amounts of Hazardous and Noxious Liquid Substances in Bulk on Offshore Support Vessels (LHNS) (2007 Edition) IMO Sales No. I289E, ISBN 978-92-801-14874

R68 REVISED RECOMMENDATIONS ON THE SAFE TRANSPORT OF DANGEROUS CARGOES AND RELATED ACTIVITIES IN PORT AREAS (2007 Edition) IMO Sales No. IB290E, ISBN 978-92-801-14720

R69 Guidelines for the Preparation of the Cargo Securing Manual (1997 Edition) IMO Sales No. I298E, ISBN 978-92-801-14416

R70 CRUDE OIL WASHING SYSTEMS (2000 Edition) IMO Sales No. IA617E, ISBN 978-92-801-50940

R71 BALLAST WATER MANAGEMENT CONVENTION AND THE GUIDELINES FOR ITS IMPLEMENTATION (2009 Edition) IMO Sales No. I621E, ISBN 978-92-801-15031

R72 MARPOL – How to do it, 2002 Edition. IMO Sales No. IA636E, ISBN 978-92-801-41528

R73 Pollution prevention equipment under MARPOL, 2006 Edition. IMO Sales No. IA646E, ISBN 978-92-801-14706

R74 Manual on Oil Pollution – Section II – Contingency Planning, 1995 Edition. IMO Sales No. IA560E, ISBN 978-92-801-13303

Manual on Oil Pollution – Section III – Salvage, 1997 Edition. IMO Sales No. IA566E, ISBN 978-92-801-14423

Manual on Oil Pollution – Section IV – Combating Oil spills, 2005 Edition. IMO Sales No. IA569E, ISBN 978-92-801-41771

Manual on Oil Pollution – Section V – Administrative Aspects of Oil Pollution Response, 2009 Edition. IMO Sales No. IA572E, ISBN 978-92-801-15000

Manual on Oil Pollution – Section VI – IMO Guidelines for Sampling and Identification of Oil Spills, 1998 Edition. IMO Sales No. I578E, ISBN 978-92-801-14515

MANUAL ON CHEMICAL POLLUTION – Section 1 – Problem Assessment and Response Arrangements (1999 Edition) IMO Sales No. IA630E, ISBN 978-92-801-60963

MANUAL ON CHEMICAL POLLUTION – Section 2 – Search and Recovery of Packaged Goods Lost at Sea (2007 Edition) IMO Sales No. IA633E, ISBN 978-92-801-42228

R75 United Nations Conference on the Law of the Sea, Official Records Volume II Plenary Meetings. Geneva, 1958 (United Nations Publication Sales No. 58.VA, Vol II) containing:

Geneva Convention of the Territorial Sea and the Contiguous Zone, 1958

Geneva Convention on the High Seas, 1958

Geneva Convention on the Continental Shelf, 1958

R76 United Nations Convention on the Law of the Sea. New York, 1983 (United Nations Publication Sales No. E.83.V.5)

R77 IMO Assembly resolution A.671 (16) – Safety Zones and Safety of Navigation Around Offshore Installations and Structures

R78 Supplement relating to the International Convention on Load Lines, 1966 (IMO Sales No. 705)

R63 散货船和油轮加强检查程序指南(2008版)(IMO销售号IA265E,ISBN 978-92-801-14966)

R64 固体散货船安全装卸操作规则 (BLU规则)(1998版)(IMO销售号I266E,ISBN 978-92-801-14584)

R65 码头代表用固体散货装卸规则 (BLU手册)(2008版)(IMO销售号I267E,ISBN 978-92-801-14928)

R66 1972年国际集装箱安全公约(CSC),(1996版)(IMO销售号IA282E,ISBN 978-92-801-14119)

R67 近海补给船限量散装有害和有毒液体物质运输与装卸指南(LHNS)(2007版)(IMO销售号I289E,ISBN 978-92-801-14874)

R68 经修订的有关港内危险货物运输及其相关活动安全的议定书 (2007版)(IMO销售号IB290E,ISBN 978-92-801-14720)

R69 货物系固手册编制指南(1997版)(IMO销售号I298E, ISBN 978-92-801-14416)

R70 原油洗舱系统(2000版)(IMO销售号 IA617E, ISBN 978-92-801-50940)

R71 压载水管理公约及其实施指南(2009版)(IMO销售号 I621E,ISBN 978-92-801-15031)

R72 MARPOL公约—如何执行(2002版)(IMO销售号 IA636E,ISBN 978-92-801-41528)

R73 MARPOL所要求的防污染设备(2006版)(IMO销售号 IA646E,ISBN 978-92-801-14706)

R74 油污手册—第2部分应急计划(1995版)(IMO销售号IA560E,ISBN 978-92-801-13303)
油污手册—第3部分救助(1997版)(IMO销售号 IA566E,ISBN 978-92-801-14423)
油污手册—第4部分溢油处理(2005版)(IMO销售号 IA569E,ISBN 978-92-801-41771)
油污手册—第5部分油污应急管理方面 (2009版)(IMO销售号IA572E,ISBN 978-92-801-15000)
油污手册—第6部分IMO溢油取样与识别指南 (1998版)(IMO销售号I578E,ISBN 978-92-801-14515)
化学品污染手册—第1部分问题评估与应急处理 (1999版) (IMO销售号 IA630E,ISBN 978-92-801-60963)
化学品污染手册—第2部分海上遗失包装货物的搜索与回收 (2007版)(IMO销售号IA633E,ISBN 978-92-801-42228)

R75 关于海洋法的联合国会议,1958年日内瓦全体会议官方记录第2卷 (联合国出版物销售编号58.VA,Vol II)包括:
1958年日内瓦领海及其毗连区公约
1958年日内瓦公海公约
1958年日内瓦大陆架公约

R76 联合国海洋法公约(1983,纽约)(联合国出版物销售编号E.83.V.5)

R77 IMO大会A.671 (16)号决议—近岸设施与结构附近的安全水域与安全航行

R78 1966年国际载重线公约补篇(IMO销售编号第705号)

R79 IMO Assembly resolution A.760 (18) 1993. Symbols related to life-saving appliances and arrangements

R80 PROCEDURES FOR PORT STATE CONTROL (2000 Edition) IMO Sales No. IA650E, ISBN 978-92-801-50995

R81 GUIDELINES FOR THE DEVELOPMENT OF SHIPBOARD MARINE POLLUTION EMERGENCY PLANS (2010 Edition) IMO Sales No. IB586E, ISBN 978-92-801-15185

R82 International Code for the Construction and Equipment of Ships Carrying Dangerous Chemicals in Bulk (IBC Code) (2007 Edition) IMO Sales No. IC100E, ISBN 978-92-801-42266

R83 INTERNATIONAL CODE FOR THE CONSTRUCTION AND EQUIPMENT OF SHIPS CARRYING LIQUEFIED GASES IN BULK (IGC Code) (1993 Edition) IMO Sales No. I104E, ISBN 978-92-801-12771

R84 INTERNATIONAL CONFERENCE ON SPECIAL TRADE PASSENGER SHIPS,1971 (1972 Edition) IMO Sales No. I727B, ISBN 978-92-801-00136

R85 WHO International Health Regulations (1969), 3rd annotated ed. (Geneva, World Health Organization, 1983, ISBN 92-4-158007-0)

R86 INTERNATIONAL CONFERENCE ON SPACE REQUIREMENTS FOR SPECIAL TRADE PASSENGER SHIPS, 1973 (1973 Edition) IMO Sales No. I734B, ISBN 978–92-801-00228

R87 IMO Assembly resolution A.494(XII) – Revised Interim Scheme for Tonnage Measurement for Certain Ships

R88 IMO Assembly resolution A.540 (13) – Tonnage Measurement for Certain Ships Relevant to the International Convention on Standards of Training, Certification and Watchkeeping for Seafarers, 1978

R89 IMO Assembly resolution A.541(13) – Interim Scheme for Tonnage Measurement for Certain Ships for the Purpose of the International Convention for the Prevention of Pollution From Ships, 1973, As Modified by the Protocol of 1978 Relating Thereto

R90 IMO Assembly resolution A.769(18) – Procedures and Arrangements for Issuing GMDSS Certificates to Holders of Non-GMDSS Certificates

R91 INTERNATIONAL SAFETY MANAGEMENT CODE (ISM Code) AND GUIDELINES ON IMPLEMENTATION OF THE ISM CODE (2010 Edition) IMO Sales No. IB117E, ISBN 978-92-801-51510

R92 International Life Saving Appliance Code (LSA Code) (2010 edition) IMO Sales No. ID982E, ISBN 978-92-801-15079

R93 International Code for Fire Safety Systems (FSS Code) IMO Sales No. IA155E, ISBN 978-92-801-14812

R94 INTERNATIONAL CODE FOR APPLICATION OF FIRE TEST PROCEDURES (FTP Code) (1998 Edition) IMO Sales No. IB844E, ISBN 978–92–801–14522

R95 GRAPHICAL SYMBOLS FOR FIRE CONTROL PLANS (2006 Edition) IMO Sales No. IA847E, ISBN 978-92-801-42259

R96 INTERNATIONAL CODE ON INTACT STABILITY, 2008 (2009 Edition)IMO Sales No. IB874E, ISBN 978-92-801-15062

R97 PREVENTION OF CORROSION ON BOARD SHIPS (2010 Edition)IMO Sales No. I877M, ISBN 978-92-801-00358

R98 IMO Assembly resolution A.1001 (25) 2007. Criteria for the provision of mobile satellite communication systems in the global maritime distress and safety system (GMDSS)

R99 IMO Assembly resolution A.705 (17) 2008. Amendments to resolution A.705 (17) – Promulgation of Maritime Safety Information

R100 IMO Assembly resolution A.706 (17) 2008. Amendments to resolution A.706 (17) – World-Wide Navigational Warning Service

R79　1993年IMOA.760(18号)大会决议—关于救生设备和装置的表示符号
R80　港口国监督程序 (2000 版)(IMO销售号 IA650E,ISBN 978-92-801-50995)
R81　船舶油污应急计划编制指南 (2010 版)(IMO销售号 IB586E,ISBN 978-92-801-15185)
R82　国际散装运输危险化学品船舶构造和设备规则(IGC公约)(IBC Code) (2007 版) (IMO销售号 IC100E, ISBN 978-92-801-42266)
R83　国际散装运输液化气体船舶构造和设备规则 (1993 版)(IMO销售号 I104E,ISBN 978-92-801-12771)
R84　1971年有关乘客专运船舶的国际会议 (IGC公约)(1972 版) (IMO销售号 I727B,ISBN 978-92-801-00136)
R85　WHO国际卫生条例 (1969)(第3注解版)(日内瓦，世界卫生组织,1983)(ISBN 92-4-158007-0)
R86　1973年有关乘客专运船舶空间要求的国际会议 (1973 版)(IMO销售号 I734B,ISBN 978-92-801-00228)
R87　IMOA.494(Ⅻ)号大会决议 —经修订的某些船舶吨位丈量过渡方案
R88　IMOA.540 (13)号大会决议—1978年海员培训、发证和值班标准国际公约之有关某些船舶吨位丈量
R89　IMOA.541 (13)号大会决议—经1978年议定书修正的1973年国际防止船舶造成污染公约之某些船舶吨位丈量过渡方案
R90　IMO A.769(18)号大会决议—向无GMDSS证书人员签发GMDSS证书程序及安排
R91　关于国际安全管理规则 (ISM规则) 及其履行指南 (2010 版)(IMO销售号 IB117E,ISBN 978-92-801-51510)
R92　国际救生设备规则(LSA规则) (2010 版) (IMO销售号 ID982E,ISBN 978-92-801-15079)
R93　火灾安全系统国际规则(FSS规则) (IMO销售号 IA155E,ISBN 978-92-801-14812)
R94　火灾试验程序应用国际规则 (FTP 规则)(1998 版)(IMO 销售号 IB844E,ISBN 978-92-801-14522)
R95　防火控制图图例 (2006 版) (IMO销售号 IA847E,ISBN 978-92-801-42259)
R96　2008年完整稳性国际规则(2009 版)(IMO销售号 IB874E,ISBN 978-92-801-15062)
R97　船舶防腐蚀(2010 版)(IMO销售号 I877M, ISBN 978-92-801-00358)
R98　2007年IMOA.1001(25)号大会决议—全球海上遇险和安全系统(GMDSS)中有关移动卫星通信系统的规定标准
R99　2008年IMOA.705(17)号大会决议—对A.705(17)号决议—海上安全信息播发的修正案
R100　2008年IMOA.706(17)号大会决议—对A.706(17)号决议—全球航行警告业务的修正案

R101 MSC.306 (87) 2010. Revised performance standards for enhanced group call (EGC) equipment

R102 IMO/UNEP GUIDELINES ON OIL SPILL DISPERSANT APPLICATION INCLUDING ENVIRONMENTAL CONSIDERATIONS (1995 Edition) IMO Sales No. IA575E, ISBN 978-92-801-13327

R103 MANUAL ON OIL SPILL RISK EVALUATION AND ASSESSMENT OF RESPONSE PREPAREDNESS (2010 Edition) IMO Sales No. I579E, ISBN 978-92-801-15123

R104 ILO, Maritime Labour Convention 2006

R105 Convention on limitation of liability for maritime claims, 1976 (LLMC 1976) (IMO Sales No. 444)

R106 Inter-Governmental Conference on the Dumping of wastes at Sea (LDC 1972) (IMO Sales No. 532)

R107 International Convention relating to Intervention on High Seas in cases of Oil Pollution Casualties, 1979 (Intervention) (IMO Sales No. 402)

R108 International Convention on Civil Liability for Oil Pollution Damage,1969 (CLC 1969)

R109 Intact Stability Criteria for Passenger & Cargo Ships (1987 edition) (IMO Sales No. 832)

R110 FAL.2/Circ.123/MEPC.1/Circ.769/MSC.1/Circ.1409, List of Certificates and Documents Required to be Carried on Board

■ Textbooks (T)

T1 Admiralty Manual of Navigation. Vol 1. London, The Stationary Office 1999 4th impression (ISBN 0-11-772880-2)

T2 Bole, A.G. and Dineley, W.O. and Nicholls, C.E. The Navigation Control Manual. 2nd ed. Oxford, Heinemann Professional, 1992 (ISBN 0-7506-0542-1)

T3 House, D.J. Seamanship techniques. 3rd ed. Oxford, Elsevier Butterworth – Heinemann, 2005 (ISBN 0-7506-6315-4)

T4 Derrett, D.R. Ship Stability for Masters and Mates, 6th ed. Butterworth-Heinemann, 2006 (ISBN 0-7506-6784-2)

T5 Eyres, D.J. Ship Construction, 5th ed. London, Butterworth-Heinemann, 2001 (ISBN 0-7506-4887-2)

T6 Frost, A. Practical Navigation for Second Mates. 6th ed. Glasgow, Brown, Son & Ferguson, 1985 (ISBN 0-8517-4397-8)

T7 Frost, A. The Principles and Practice of Navigation. 3rd ed. Glasgow, Brown, Son & Ferguson, 1988 (ISBN 0-8517-4443-3)

T8 Gylden, S.G. & Petterson, B. Plotting and parallel index. Constant radius turns: Navigation in fog. 2nd ed. Ytterby (Sweden), Micronav Consultants, 1991

T9 Hensen, Capt. H. Tug Use In Port, A practical guide, 2nd ed. The Nautical Institute (ISBN 1-8700-7739-3)

T10 Hill, C. Maritime Law, 4th ed. London, Lloyd's of London Press, 1995 (ISBN 1-850-44-888-4)

T11 Hooyer, H.H. The Behaviour and Handling of Ships. Cornell Maritime Press (ISBN 0-7870-33306-2)

T12 International Chamber of Shipping, Bridge Procedures Guide, 3rd ed. 1998 London. Marisec Publications

T13 International Medical Guide for Ships. World Health Organization, 1989

R101 2010年MSC.306(87)号决议—经修订的增强群呼(EGC)设备性能标准
R102 IMO/UNEP关于考虑环境影响的消油剂使用指南 (1995 版)(IMO销售号 IA575E, ISBN 978-92-801-13327)
R103 溢油风险评估和应急预案评价手册(2010 版)(IMO销售号 I579E, ISBN 978-92-801-15123)
R104 ILO2006年国际劳工公约
R105 1976年海事赔偿责任限制国际公约(LLMC 1976) (IMO销售号第444号)
R106 海洋倾倒废弃物国际会议(LDC 1972) (IMO销售号第532号)
R107 1979年公海油污事件干预国际公约 (干预) (IMO销售号第402号)
R108 1969年国际油污损害民事责任公约(CLC 1969)
R109 客船及货船完整稳性标准(1987 版) (IMO销售号第832号)
R110 便利委员会FAL.2/Circ.123号通函 / 环境保护委员会.1/Circ.769号通函 / 海上安全委员会 MSC.1/Circ.1409号通函, 要求船上携带的证书和文件清单

■ 教科书(T)

T1 英版航海手册. 第1卷. 伦敦, The Stationary Office出版, 1999年第4次印刷 (ISBN 0-11-772880-2)
T2 Bole, A.G. 和 Dineley, W.O. 以及Nicholls, C.E. 航海操纵手册. 第2版. 牛津, Heinemann Professional出版, 1992年 (ISBN 0-1506-0542-1)
T3 House, D.J. 航海技术. 第3版. 牛津, Elsevier Butterworth-Heinemann出版, 2005年 (ISBN 0-7506-6315-4)
T4 Derrett, D.R . 面向船长与驾驶员的船舶稳性知识, 第6版. Butteworth-Heinemann出版, 2006年 (ISBN 0-7506-6784-2)
T5 Eyres, D.J. 船舶结构. 第5版. 伦敦, Butterworth-Heinemann出版, 2001年 (ISBN 0-7506-4887-2)
T6 Frost, A. 面向二副的航行实践. 第6版. 格拉斯哥, Brown, Son & Ferguson出版, 1985年 (ISBN 0-8517-4397-8)
T7 Frost, A. 航海原理与实践. 第3版. 格拉斯哥, Brown, Son & Ferguson出版, 1985年 (ISBN 0-8517-4443-3)
T8 Gylden, S.G. & Petterson, B. 雾中航行之定常旋回时的标绘与平行标线. 第2版. 于特比(瑞典), Micronav Consultants出版, 1991年
T9 H. Hensen船长. 港内拖船使用的实操指南. 第2版, The Nautical Institute出版 (ISBN 1-8700-7739-3)
T10 Hill, C. 海商法. 第4版. 伦敦, 劳氏伦敦出版社, 1995年 (ISBN 1-850-44-888-4)
T11 Hooyer, H.H. 船舶行为与操纵. Cornell Maritime出版社 (ISBN 0-7870-33306-2)
T12 国际航运公会.驾驶台程序指南. 第3版. 1998年, 伦敦. Marisec 出版物
T13 国际船用医疗指南. 世界卫生组织, 1989年

T14 International Safety Guide for Oil Tankers and Terminals. 5th ed. ICS/OCIMF. London, Witherby & Co. Ltd, 2006 (ISBN 978-1856-092-913)

T15 Immer, J.R. Cargo Handling. Marine Education Textbooks, 1984 (ISBN 1-877977-806-8)

T16 Kemp, J.F. and Young, P. Notes on Compass Work. 2nd ed. London, Stanford Maritime, 1972; reprinted 1987 (ISBN 0-5400-0362-X)

T17 La Dage, J. and Van Gemert, L. (Eds). Stability and Trim for the Ship's Officer. 3rd ed. Centreville, Maryland, US, Cornell Maritime Press, 1983 (ISBN 0-8703-3-297-X)

T18 MacElvrey, D.H. Shiphandling for the Mariner. 3rd ed. Centreville, Maryland, US, Cornell Maritime Press, 1995 (ISBN 0-8703-3464-6)

T19 Morton, G.S. Tanker Operations. A Handbook for the Ship's Officer 3rd ed., 1992 (ISBN 0-8703-3-432-8)

T20 Maritime Meteorology, 2nd ed., 1997. Thomas Reed Publications (ISBN 0-9012-8167-0)

T21 McGuire and White. Liquefied Gas Handling Principles on Ships and Terminals. 2nd ed. London, Witherby, 1996 (ISBN 1-8560-9087-6)

T22 Merrifield, F.G. Ship Magnetism and The Magnetic Compass, Pergamon Press

T23 Meteorological Office, Marine Observer's Handbook. 11th ed. (Met.0.887). London, HMSO, 1995 (ISBN 0-1140-0367-X)

T24 Meteorological Office, Meteorology for Mariners, 3rd ed. 8th impression. London, HMSO, 1978 (ISBN 0-1140-0311-4)

T25 Rowe, R.W. The Shiphandler's Guide. The Nautical Institute. 1996 (ISBN 1-8700-77 35-0)

T26 Ship Captain's Medical Guide. 1985. Department of Transport HMSO published by HMSO

T27 Swift, Capt. A.J. Bridge Team Management – A Practical Guide. The Nautical Institute, 1993 (ISBN 1-8700-7714-8)

T28 Taylor, D.A. Merchant Ship Construction. 3rd ed. London, Institute of Marine Engineers,1992 (ISBN 0-9072-0646-8)

T29 Tetley, L. and Calcutt, D. Electronic Aids to Navigation: Position Fixing. 2nd ed. 1986 London, Edward Arnold, 1991 (ISBN 0-3405-4380-9)

T30 The Mariner's Handbook (NP 100). 6th ed. Taunton (UK), Hydrographer of the Navy,1989

T31 Thomas, O.O., Agnew, J. and Cole, K.L. Thomas' Stowage: The Properties and Stowage of Cargoes, 3rd ed. Glasgow, Brown, Son & Ferguson, 1996

T32 Taylor, D.A. Introduction to Marine Engineering. 2nd ed. London, Butterworth, 1990 (ISBN 0-4080-5706-8)

T33 Medical First Aid Guide for use in Accidents involving Dangerous Goods (MFAG). 5th ed. 1994 (ISBN 92-801-1322-4)

T34 Guidelines for the Inspection and Maintenance of Double Hull Tanker Structures. OCIMF. London, Witherby, 1995 (ISBN 1-8560-9090-9)

T35 Bulk Carriers: Guidance and information on bulk cargo loading and discharging to reduce the likelihood of overstressing the hull structures. IACS. London 1997

T36 Code of Safe Working Practices for Merchant Seamen, London. The Stationery Office Publications Centre, 1998 (ISBN 01 1551 8363)

T37 Holder, L.A. Training and Assessment on Board. 3rd ed. London, Witherby & Co Ltd, 2002 (ISBN 1-8560-9228-3)

T38 Anwar, Capt. N. – Navigation Advanced – Mates/Masters, Witherby Seamanship International Ltd, 2006 (ISBN 1-905331-15-0)

T14　油船与油码头国际安全指南. 第5版. ICS/OCIMF. 伦敦, Witherby & Co. Ltd出版,2006年(ISBN 978-1856-092-913)

T15　Immer, J.R. 货物装卸,航海教育教材, 1984年 (ISBN 1-877977-806-8)

T16　Kemp, J.F. and Young, P. 罗经使用注意事项. 第2版. 伦敦, Stanford Maritime出版,1972年; 1987再版 (ISBN 0-5400-0362-X)

T17　La Dage, J. and Van Gemert, L. (Eds). 面向驾驶员的稳性与吃水差. 第3版. 森特维尔(马里兰,美国)Cornell Maritime 出版社, 1983年 (ISBN 0-87033-297-X)

T18　MacElvrey, D.H. 航海者的船舶操纵. 第3版. 森特维尔(马里兰,美国) Cornell Maritime出版社,1995年(ISBN 0-8703-3464-6)

T19　Morton, G.S. 船舶驾驶员手册之油轮作业. 第3版. 1992 (ISBN 0-87033-432-8)

T20　海洋气象学.第2版. 1997年. Thomas Reed 出版物 (ISBN 0-9012-8167-0)

T21　McGuire and White. 液化气船舶与码头装卸原理. 第2版. 伦敦,Witherby出版,1996年(ISBN 1-8560-9087-6)

T22　Merrifield, F.G.船磁与磁罗经, Pergamon 出版社

T23　气象局, 海上观测员手册. 第11版.(Met.0.887). 伦敦,HMSO出版,1995年 (ISBN 0-1140-0367-X)

T24　气象局,航海气象.第3版. 第8次印刷. 伦敦,HMSO出版,1978年 (ISBN 0-1140-0311-4)

T25　Rowe, R.W. 船舶操纵指南. The Nautical Institute出版,1996年 (ISBN 1-8700-7735-0)

T26　船长医疗指南. 1985年. Department of Transport HMSO, HMSO出版

T27　Swift, A.J船长. 驾驶台团队管理—实操指南. The Nautical Institute出版,1993年(ISBN 1-8700-7714-8)

T28　Taylor, D.A. 商船建造. 第3版. 伦敦,Institute of Marine Engineers出版,1992年 (ISBN 0-9072-0646-8)

T29　Tetley, L.和Calcutt,D. 电子导航设备:定位. 第2版. 1986年,伦敦,爱德华·阿诺德,1991年(ISBN 0-3405-4380-9)

T30　航海员手册.(NP 100). 第6版. Taunton(英国),海军水道部出版,1989年

T31　Thomas, O.O., Agnew, J. and Cole, K.L. Thomas' 积载:货物性能与积载, 第3版. 格拉斯哥, Brown, Son & Ferguson出版, 1996年

T32　Taylor, D.A. 船舶轮机介绍. 第2版. 伦敦,Butterworth出版,1990年(ISBN 0-4080-5706-8)

T34　双壳油船结构检查与维护指南. OCIMF. 伦敦,Witherby出版,1995年 (ISBN 1-8560-9090-9)

T35　散货船: 减少船体结构超负荷可能的散货装卸指南与信息. 伦敦, IACS出版. 1997年

T36　商船船员安全工作实践规则, 伦敦. The Stationery Office Publications Centre出版,1998年(ISBN 01 1551 8363)

T37　Holder, L.A. 船上培训与评估. 第3版. 伦敦,Witherby & Co Ltd出版,2002年(ISBN 1-8560-9228-3)

T38　Anwar, N船长. 高级航海—驾驶员/船长,Witherby Seamanship International Ltd出版,2006年(ISBN 1-905331-15-0)

T39 Anwar, Capt. N. & Khalique, A. – Passage Planning – Practice, Witherby Seamanship International Ltd, 2006 (ISBN 1-8560-9323-9)

T40 Cockcroft, A.N. – A guide to the collision avoidance rules. 6th ed. Oxford: Elsevier Butterworth-Heinemann, 2004 (ISBN 0-7506-6179-8)

T41 JACKSON, L. – Reed's instrumentation and control systems. 4th ed. London: Thomas Reed Publications Ltd, 1992 (Reed's Marine Engineering Series Vol. 10). (ISBN 0-947637-86-9)

T42 Maclachlan, Malcolm – The Shipmaster's Business Companion (Book and CD), 4th ed., 2004 (ISBN 978 1 870077 45 3)

T43 Maclachlan, Malcolm – Shipmaster's Business Self-Examiner, 7th ed., 2009 (ISBN 978 1 906915 00 1)

T44 Rhodes, M. – Ship Stability Mates Masters, 1st ed., Witherby Seamanship International Ltd, 2012 (ISBN 978-0-9534379-3-1)

■ Bibliography (B)

B1 ANDERSON, P. – ISM Code: A guide to the legal and insurance implications. London, Lloyd's of London Press (ISBN 1-859-786-21-9)

B2 ARROYO, D.W. – International maritime conventions. Deventer (Netherlands), Kluwer Law and Taxation Publishers, 1991 (ISBN 90-6544-4408)

B3 BARRASS, C.B. – Ship stability: Notes and examples. 3rd ed. Oxford, Butterworth-Heinemann, 2001 (ISBN 0-7506-4850-3)

B4 BAUGHEN, S. – Shipping law. London: Cavendish Publishing Ltd, 1998 (ISBN 1–85941–313–7)

B5 BENNET, H. – Law of marine insurance. 2nd ed. Oxford, Oxford University Press, 2006 (ISBN 0-19-927359-6)

B6 BIRNIE, P. & BOYLE, A.E. – International law and the environment. 2nd ed. Oxford, Oxford University Press, 2002 (ISBN 0-19-8766553-3)

B7 Bowditch, N. – American practical navigator (Combined edition Vol. 1 & 2). Riverdale, (MD) (USA), National Ocean Servicing, 1995

B8 Brown & Perring Ltd – Admiralty charts. London, Brown & Perrings Ltd (Various regions, published individually)

B9 BROWN, E.D. – The International law of the sea. 2 Vols. Aldershot, Dartmouth Publishing Co. Ltd, 1994 (ISBN 1-85521-306-0)

B10 BROWN, R.H. – Marine insurance. Vol. 1 – Principles and basic practice. 6th ed. London, Witherby & Co. Ltd, 1999 (ISBN 1-85609-150-3)

B11 BROWN, R.H. – Marine insurance. Vol. 2 – Cargo practice. 5th ed. 1997 (ISBN 1-85609-132-5); Vol. 3 – Hull practice. 2nd ed. 1992 (ISBN 0-948691-45-X).

B12 Brown, Son & Ferguson – Brown's nautical almanac daily tide and tables. Glasgow: Brown, Son & Ferguson Ltd (Annual)

B13 Brown, Son & Ferguson – Regulations for preventing collisions at sea. Revised. Glasgow (UK), Brown, Son & Ferguson Ltd, 1995 (ISBN 0-85174-645-4)

B14 BRUBAKER, D. – Marine pollution and international law: principles and practices. London, Belhaven Press, 1993 (ISBN 1-85293-273-2)

B15 BUNDOCK, M. – Shipping law handbook. 3rd ed. London, Lloyd's of London Press, 2003 (ISBN 1-84311-209-4)

B16 Buyese, Capt. J. – Handling Ships in Ice. A practical guide to handling class 1A and 1AS ships. The Nautical Institute, 2007 (ISBN 1-8700-7784-2)

T39 Anwar, N船长.& Khalique, A. 航线设计 —实践, Witherby Seamanship International Ltd出版, 2006年 (ISBN 1-8560-9323-9)

T40 Cockcroft, A.N. 避碰规则指南. 第6版.牛津:Elsevier Butterworth-Heinemann出版, 2004年 (ISBN 0-7506-6179-8)

T41 JACKSON, L. 里德仪表与控制系统. 第4版. 伦敦 : Thomas Reed Publications Ltd出版, 1992 年(里德船用轮机系列第10卷). (ISBN 0-947637-86-9)

T42 Maclachlan, Malcolm. 船长业务伴侣 (书和CD), 第4版, 2004年 (ISBN 978 1 870077 45 3)

T43 Maclachlan, Malcolm. 船长业务自我考核,第7版, 2009年 (ISBN 978 1 906915 00 1)

T44 Rhodes, M. 船舶稳性—驾驶员/船长, 第1版, Witherby Seamanship International Ltd出版, 2012年 (ISBN 978-0-9534379-3-1)

■ 参考文献 (B)

B1 ANDERSON, P. —ISM 规则: 法律与保险关联性指导. 伦敦, 伦敦劳氏出版社. (ISBN 1-859-786-21-9)

B2 ARROYO, D.W. —国际海事公约. Deventer (荷兰), Kluwer Law and Taxation Publishers 出版, 1991年(ISBN 90-6544-4408)

B3 BARRASS, C.B. —船舶稳性: 注释与范例.第3版.牛津, Butterwoth-Heinemann出版, 2001年(ISBN 0-7506-4850-3)

B4 BAUGHEN, S. —航运法. 伦敦: Cavendish Publishing Ltd 出版, 1998 年 (ISBN 1-85941-313-7)

B5 BENNET, H. —海上保险法. 第2版. 牛津, 牛津大学出版社, 2006年 (ISBN 0-19-927359-6)

B6 BIRNIE, P. & BOYLE, A.E. —国际法与环境. 第2版. 牛津, 牛津大学出版社, 2002年 (ISBN 0-19-8766553-3)

B7 Bowditch, N. —美国实用航海. (1卷与2卷合订本). 里弗代尔, (MD) (美国), National Ocean Servicing出版, 1995年

B8 Brown & Perring Ltd. —英版海图. 伦敦, Brown & Perrings Ltd出版. (不同地区各自出版)

B9 BROWN, E.D. —国际海洋法. 第2卷. 奥尔德肖特, Dartmouth Publishing Co. Ltd. 出版, 1994年 (ISBN 1-85521-306-0)

B10 BROWN, R. H. —海上保险.第1卷—原理与基本实践. 第6版. 伦敦, Witherby & Co. Ltd出版, 1999年(ISBN 1-85609-150-3)

B11 BROWN, R. H. —海上保险.第2卷—货物实操. 第5版. 1997年(ISBN 1-85609-132-5);第3卷—船体实操. 第2版. 1992(ISBN 0-948691-45-X)

B12 Brown, Son & Ferguson. —布朗航海天文历每日潮汐表. 格拉斯哥 :Brown, Son & Ferguson Ltd出版(年刊)

B13 Brown, Son & Ferguson. —海上避碰规则. Revised. 格拉斯哥 (英国), Brown, Son & Ferguson Ltd出版, 1995年(ISBN 0-85174-645-4)

B14 BRUBAKER, D. —海洋污染与国际法: 原理与实践. 伦敦, Belhaven 出版社, 1993年 (ISBN 1-85293-273-2)

B15 BUNDOCK, M. —航运法手册. 第3版. 伦敦, 伦敦劳氏出版社, 2003 年 (ISBN 1-84311-209-4)

B16 Buyese, J船长. —冰区船舶操纵. 1A级 和 1AS级船舶操纵指南. The Nautical Institute出版, 2007年 (ISBN 1-8700-7784-2)

B17 Cahill, R.A. – Collisions and their causes. 2nd ed. London, The Nautical Institute, 2002 (ISBN 1-870077-60-6; Ref: 0268)

B18 Cahill, R.A. – Disaster at sea: From the Titanic to the Exxon Valdez. London, Century Publishing, 1990

B19 Cahill, R.A. – Strandings and their causes. 2nd ed. London, The Nautical Institute, 2002 (ISBN 1-870077-61-3 Ref: 0269)

B20 CAMINOS, H. (Ed.) – Law of the sea. Aldershot: Dartmouth Publishing Co., 2001 (ISBN 1-84014-090-9)

B21 CHEMICAL INDUSTRIES ASSOCIATION – Guidelines for shipping packaged dangerous goods by sea. London: Chemical Industries Association, 1997 (ISBN 1-85897-062-8)

B22 CHEN, X. – Limitation of liability for maritime claims. The Hague, Kluwer Law International, 2001 (ISBN 90-411-1598-6)

B23 CHURCHILL, R. & LOWE, A. – Law of the sea. 3rd ed. Manchester University Press, 1989 (ISBN 0-7190-4381-6)

B24 Clark, I.C. – Mooring and Anchoring Ships Vol. 1 – Principles and Practice. London, The Nautical Institute, 2009 (ISBN 1-870077-93-4)

B25 Clark, I.C. – Ship dynamics for mariners. London, The Nautical Institute, 2005 (ISBN 1-870077-68-7)

B26 Cockroft, A.N. – Nicholl's Seamanship and Nautical Knowledge. 26th ed. Glasgow (UK), Brown, Son & Ferguson Ltd, 1993 (ISBN 0-85174-407-1)

B27 Collins, L. – Global Positioning System (GPS): Theory and practice. 5th ed. New York: Springer-Verlag, 2001 (ISBN 3-211-83534-2)

B28 Cornish, M. & Ives, E. – Reed's maritime meteorology. 3rd ed. Hampton Court (UK), Reed (Thomas) Publications, 2009 (ISBN 0-901281-67-0)

B29 CURTIS, S. – The law of shipbuilding contracts. 3rd ed. London, Lloyd's of London Press, 2002

B30 DAVIES, D. – Commencement of laytime, 3rd. ed. London, Lloyd's of London Press, (ISBN 1-85978-196-9)

B31 DAVIES, M. & DICKEY, A. – Shipping law. 3rd ed. Sydney, Lawbook Co. 2004 (ISBN 0-455-22081-6)

B32 DAVISON, R. & SNELSON, A. – The law of towage. London, Lloyd's of London Press, 1990 (ISBN 1-85044-347-5)

B33 DURNFORD, J.R. Technical sketching for deck and engineer officers. London, Nautical Institute, 1996 (ISBN 1-870077-34-2)

B34 EMBLETON, W. – Engineering knowledge: Instruments and control systems for deck officers. 5th ed. Hampton Court (UK), Reed (Thomas) Publications Ltd, 1995 (ISBN 0-90128-115-8)

B35 FAIRPLAY PUBLICATIONS – Tonnage measurement of ships. 2nd ed. Coulsdon (UK), Fairplay Publications Ltd, 1980 (ISBN 0-905045-03-3)

B36 Fifield, L.W.J. – Navigation for watchkeepers. Oxford, Heinemann Professional Publishing, 1980 (ISBN 0-434-90564-X)

B37 FISHER, A., ECON, D. – Principles of marine insurance. London, Chartered Insurance Institute, 1999 (ISBN 1-85369-267-0)

B38 FISHER, W. – Engineering for nautical students. Glasgow (UK), Brown, Son & Ferguson (ISBN 0-851740-40)

B39 FOGARTY – Merchant shipping legislation. 2nd ed. London, Lloyd's of London Press, 2004 (ISBN 1-84311-329-5)

B40 Forsberg, G. – Salvage from the sea. Glasgow, Brown, Son & Ferguson Ltd, 1977 (ISBN 0-71008698-9)

B17 Cahill, R.A. —碰撞及其原因. 第2版. 伦敦, The Nautical Institute出版, 2002年 (ISBN 1-870077-60-6; Ref: 0268)

B18 Cahill, R.A. —海难: 从泰坦尼克到埃克森·瓦尔迪兹. 伦敦, Century Publishing出版, 1990年

B19 Cahill, R.A. —搁浅及其原因. 第2版. 伦敦, The Nautical Institute出版, 2002年(ISBN 1-870077-61-3 Ref: 0269)

B20 CAMINOS, H. (Ed.) —海洋法. Aldershot:Dartmouth Publishing Co.出版, 2001年 (ISBN 1-84014-090-9)

B21 化学工业协会—海运包装危险品指南. 伦敦: 化学工业协会出版, 1997年(ISBN 1-85897-062-8)

B22 CHEN, X. —海事赔偿责任限制. 海牙, Kluwer Law International出版, 2001年(ISBN 90-411-1598-6)

B23 CHURCHILL, R. & LOWE, A. —海洋法. 第3版. 曼彻斯特大学出版社出版, 1989年 (ISBN 0-7190-4381-6)

B24 Clark, I.C. —船舶系泊与锚泊第1卷—原理与实践. 伦敦, The Nautical Institute出版, 2009年(ISBN 1-870077-93-4)

B25 Clark, I.C. —航海者的船舶动力学. 伦敦, The Nautical Institute出版, 2005年 (ISBN 1-870077-68-7)

B26 Cockroft, A.N.—Nicholl's 船艺和航海知识. 第26版. 格拉斯哥 (英国), Brown, Son & Ferguson Ltd出版 1993年 (ISBN 0-85174-407-1)

B27 Collins, L. —全球定位系统(GPS):理论与实践. 第5版. 纽约:Springer-Verlag出版, 2001年 (ISBN 3-211-83534-2)

B28 Cornish, M. & Ives, E. —里德海洋气象学. 第3版. 汉普顿法院(英国), Reed (Thomas) 出版物, 2009年 (ISBN 0-901281-67-0)

B29 CURTIS, S. —船舶建造合同法. 第3版. 伦敦, 伦敦劳氏出版社, 2002年

B30 DAVIES, D. —装卸货开始时间. 第3版. 伦敦, 伦敦劳氏出版社, (ISBN 1-85978-196-9)

B31 DAVIES, M. & DICKEY, A. —航运法. 第3版. 悉尼, Lawbook Co出版, 2004年 (ISBN 0-455-22081-6)

B32 DAVISON, R. & SNELSON, A. —拖带法. 伦敦, 伦敦劳氏出版社, 1990年 (ISBN 1-85044-347-5)

B33 DURNFORD, J.R.驾驶员和轮机员技术概述. 伦敦, Nautical Institute出版社出版, 1996年 (ISBN 1-870077-34-2)

B34 EMBLETON, W, —轮机知识: 面向驾驶员的仪器与控制系统. 第5版. 汉普顿法院 (英国), Reed (Thomas) Publications Ltd出版, 1995年 (ISBN 0-90128-115-8)

B35 FAIRPLAY出版物—船舶吨位丈量. 第2版. 库尔斯东 (英国), Fairplay Publications Ltd出版, 1980年(ISBN 0-905045-03-3)

B36 Fifield, L.W.J. —航行值班. 牛津, Heinemann Professional Publishing出版, 1980年(ISBN 0-434-90564-X)

B37 FISHER, A. / ECON, D. —海上保险原理. 伦敦, Chartered Insurance Institute出版, 1999年(ISBN 1-85369-267-0)

B38 FISHER, W. —面向航海学生的工程学. 格拉斯哥 (英国), Brown, Son & Ferguson出版 (ISBN 0-851740-40)

B39 FOGARTY, —商船航运立法. 第2版. 伦敦, 伦敦劳氏出版社 ,2004年(ISBN 1-84311-329-5)

B40 Forsberg, G. —海上救助. 格拉斯哥, Brown, Son & Ferguson Ltd出版 ,1977年(ISBN 0-71008698-9)

B41 Frampton, R. & Uttridge, P. – Meteorology for seafarers. 3rd ed. Glasgow, Brown, Son & Ferguson Ltd, 2008 (ISBN 978-0-85174-799-6)

B42 Gale, Capt. H – From Paper Charts to ECDIS – A practical voyage plan. The Nautical Institute, 2009 (ISBN 1-8700-7798-9)

B43 GASKELL, N. et al – Bills of lading: Law and contracts. London, Lloyd's of London Press, 2000 (ISBN 1-85978-480-1)

B44 GAUCI, G. – Oil pollution at sea: Civil liability and compensation for damage. Chichester (West Sussex): John Wiley & Sons, 1997 (ISBN 0-471-97066-2)

B45 Gibilisco, S – Meteorology Demystified, McGraw-Hill. 2006 (ISBN 0-071-48790-0)

B46 GOLD, E. – Gard handbook on marine pollution. 2nd ed. Arendal (Norway), Assurance for engine Gard, 1997 (ISBN 82-90344-11-2)

B47 GORTON, L., HILLENIUS, P., IHRE, R., SANDERVARN, A. – Ship broking and chartering practice. 6th ed. London, Lloyd's of London Press, 2004 (ISBN 1-8431-322-8)

B48 GUERRERO Jr, J. – Maritime cargo insurance. London, Witherby & Co. Ltd, 2003 (ISBN 1-85609-263-1)

B49 HAZELWOOD, S.J. – P & I Clubs: Law and practice. 3rd ed. London, Lloyd's of London Press, 2000 (ISBN 1-85978-531-X)

B50 Hensen, Capt, H. – Ship bridge simulators: A project handbook. London, Nautical Institute, 1999

B51 Hobbs, R.R. – Marine navigation. Piloting, celestial and electronic navigation. 3rd ed. Annapolis (MD) (USA), Naval Institute Press, 1994 (ISBN 0-87021-294-X)

B52 HODGES, S. & HILL, C. – Principles of maritime law. London, Lloyd's of London Press, 2001 (ISBN 1-85978-998-6)

B53 HODGES, S. – Law of marine insurance. London, Cavendish Publishing Ltd, 1996 (ISBN 1-85941-227-0)

B54 HOPKINS, F.N. – Business and law for the shipmaster. 7th ed. Glasgow (UK), Brown, Son & Ferguson Ltd, 1989 (ISBN 0-85174537-7)

B55 House, D.J. – Anchor Practice: A Guide for Industry, London, Witherby & Co. Ltd, 2006 (ISBN 1-8560-9212-7)

B56 House, D.J. – Marine survival and rescue systems. 2nd ed. London, Witherby & Co. Ltd, 1997 (ISBN 1-85609-127-9)

B57 House, D.J. – Navigation for masters. 3rd ed. London, Witherby & Co. Ltd, 2006 (ISBN 1-85609-271-2)

B58 House, D.J. – Seamanship techniques. 3rd. ed. Oxford, Elsevier Butterworth-Heinemann, 2005 (ISBN 0-7506-6315-4)

B59 House, D.J. – Seamanship techniques: for shipboard & maritime operations. 3rd ed. Butterworth-Heinemann, 2004 (ISBN 0-7506-6315-1)

B60 House, D.J. – Ship Handling – Theory and practice. Butterworth-Heinemann, 2007 (ISBN 0–7506–8530–6)

B61 House, D.J. – The Command companion of seamanship techniques. Vol. 3. Oxford, Butterworth-Heinemann, 2000 (ISBN 0-7506-4443-5)

B62 House, D.J. & Saeed, F. – The Seamanship Examiner: For STCW Certification Examinations. Butterworth-Heinemann, 2005 (ISBN 0-7506-6701-2)

B63 House, Lloyd, Toomey & Dickin – The Ice Navigation Manual, Witherby Seamanship International Ltd, 2009 (ISBN 1-9053-3159-8)

B64 HUDSON, N. and ALLEN, J. – Marine claims handbook. 5th ed. London, Lloyd's of London Press, 1996 (ISBN 1-85978-048-2)

B65 Hydrographer of the Navy – Admiralty list of radio signals. 6 Vols. Taunton (UK), Hydrographer of the Navy, 2001

B41 Frampton, R. & Uttridge, P. —海洋气象学. 第3版. 格拉斯哥, Brown, Son & Ferguson Ltd 出版,2008年 (ISBN 978-0-85174-799-6)

B42 Gale, H船长—从纸质海图到ECDIS —航行计划实操. The Nautical Institute出版,2009年 (ISBN 1-8700-7798-9)

B43 GASKELL, N. et al —提单: 法律与合同. 伦敦, 伦敦劳氏出版社,2000年(ISBN 1-85978-480-1)

B44 GAUCI, G. —海上油污染: 损害民事责任与赔偿. 奇切斯特 (西苏塞克斯郡):John Wiley & Sons出版,1997年(ISBN 0-471-97066-2)

B45 Gibilisco, S. —气象揭秘, McGraw-Hill出版. 2006年(ISBN 0-071-48790-0)

B46 GOLD, E. —海洋污染加德手册.第2版. 阿伦达尔(挪威),Assurance for engine Gard出版, 1997年(ISBN 82-90344-11-2)

B47 GORTON, L. HILLENIUS, P., IHRE, R., SANDERVARN, A. —船舶经纪与租船实践. 第6版. 伦敦,伦敦劳氏出版社,2004年 (ISBN 1-8431-322-8)

B48 GUERRERO Jr, J. —海上货物保险. 伦敦,Witherby & Co. Ltd出版,2003年(ISBN 1-85609-263-1)

B49 HAZELWOOD, S.J. —船东互保协会:法律与实践. 第3版. 伦敦, 伦敦劳氏出版社,2000年 (ISBN 1-85978-531-X)

B50 Hensen, H船长. —船舶驾驶模拟器:工程手册. 伦敦,Nautical Institute出版,1999年

B51 Hobbs, R.R. —海上航行. 引航、天文和电子航海.第3版. 安纳波利斯(马里兰,美国),海军学院出版社,1994年(ISBN 0-87021-294-X)

B52 HODGES, S & HILL, C. —海商法原理, 伦敦, 伦敦劳氏出版社,2001年(ISBN 1-85978-998-6)

B53 HODGES, S. —海上保险法. 伦敦,Cavendish Publishing Ltd出版,1996年 (ISBN 1-85941-227-0)

B54 HOPKINS, F.N. —船长业务与法律. 第7版. 格拉斯哥 (英国), Brown, Son & Ferguson Ltd 出版, 1989年(ISBN 0-85174537-7)

B55 House, D.J. —锚的运用: 行业指导, 伦敦,Witherby & Co. Ltd出版,2006年 (ISBN 1-8560-9212-7)

B56 House, D.J. —海上求生与救援系统. 第2版. 伦敦,Witherby & Co. Ltd出版,1997年(ISBN 1-85609-127-9)

B57 House, D.J. —面向船长的航海学. 第3版. 伦敦, Witherby & Co. Ltd出版,2006年(ISBN 1-85609-271-2)

B58 House, D.J. —航海技术. 第3版. 牛津, Elsevier Butterworth-Heinemann出版,2005年(ISBN 0-7506-6315-4)

B59 House, D.J. —航海技术: 船舶和海上作业. 第3版. Butterworth-Heinemann出版,2004年 (ISBN 0-7506-6315-1)

B60 House, D.J. —船舶操纵—理论与实践. Butterworth-Heinemann出版,2007年(ISBN 0-7506-8530-6)

B61 House, D.J. —共同指挥航海技术. 第3卷. 牛津,Butterworth-Heinemann出版,2000年 (ISBN 0-7506-4443-5)

B62 House, D.J. & Saeed, F —航海考官: STCW 发证考试. Butterworth-Heinemann出版,2005年 (ISBN 0-7506-6701-2)

B63 House, Lloyd, Toomey & Dickin —冰区航行手册,Witherby Seamanship International Ltd出版, 2009年 (ISBN 1-9053-3159-8)

B64 HUDSON, N and ALLEN, J. —海事索赔手册. 第5版. 伦敦, 伦敦劳氏出版社,1996年 (ISBN 1-85978-048-2)

B65 海军水道部—英版无线电信号表.第6卷. 汤顿(英国),海军水道部出版,2001年

B66 Hydrographer of the Navy (UK) – Admiralty manual of hydrographic surveying. Vol. 1, 1965. Taunton (UK), Hydrographer of the Navy

B67 Hydrographer of the Navy (UK) – Admiralty manual of hydrographic surveying. Vol. II, Taunton (UK), Hydrographer of the Navy

B68 Hydrographer of the Navy (UK) – Catalogue of admiralty charts and publications 2000. Taunton (UK), Hydrographer of the Navy, 2000

B69 Hydrographer of the Navy (UK) – Symbols and abbreviations used on admiralty charts (Chart 5011), 2nd ed. Taunton (UK), Hydrographer of the Navy, 1998

B70 Hydrographer of the Navy (UK) – The mariner's handbook. 7th ed. Taunton (UK), Hydrographer of the Navy, 1999 (ISBN 0-707-71123-1)

B71 INTERNATIONAL ASSOCIATION OF CLASSIFICATION SOCIETIES (IACS) – Bulk carriers: Guidance and information to shipowners and operators. London: IACS, 1992

B72 INTERNATIONAL ASSOCIATION OF CLASSIFICATION SOCIETIES (IACS) – Bulk carriers: Guidelines for surveys, assessment and repair of hull structure. 3rd ed. London: Witherby and Co. Ltd, 1995 (ISBN 1-85609-135-X)

B73 INTERNATIONAL ASSOCIATION OF CLASSIFICATION SOCIETIES (IACS) – Bulk carriers: Handle with care. London, IACS, 1998

B74 INTERNATIONAL ASSOCIATION OF CLASSIFICATION SOCIETIES (IACS) – Bulk carriers: Guidelines for surveys, assessment and repair of hull structure. 3rd ed. London, Witherby & Co. Ltd, 1995 (ISBN 1-85609-135-X)

B75 INTERNATIONAL ASSOCIATION OF CLASSIFICATION SOCIETIES (IACS) – Container ships: Guidelines for surveys, assessment and repair of hull structures. London, Witherby & Co. Ltd, 2005 (ISBN 1-85609-296-8)

B76 INTERNATIONAL ASSOCIATION OF CLASSIFICATION SOCIETIES (IACS) – General cargo ships: Guidelines for surveys, assessment and repair of hull structure. London, Witherby & Co. Ltd, 1999 (ISBN 1-85609-189-9)

B77 INTERNATIONAL ASSOCIATION OF CLASSIFICATION SOCIETIES (IACS) – Guidelines for coatings maintenance and repairs. London, Witherby & Co. Ltd, 2005 (ISBN 1-85609-308-5)

B78 INTERNATIONAL ASSOCIATION OF DRY CARGO SHIPOWNERS (INTERCARGO) – Bulk carrier casualty report 2005, the previous ten years (1996-2005) and the trends. London, Intercargo, 2006

B79 INTERNATIONAL ASSOCIATION OF DRY CARGO SHIPOWNERS (INTERCARGO) – Port state control: A guide for ships involved in the dry bulk trades. London, Intercargo, 2000

B80 INTERNATIONAL ASSOCIATION OF DRY CARGO SHIPOWNERS (INTERCARGO) – Bulk carriers: Guidelines for surveys, assessment and repair of hull structures. 2nd ed. London, Witherby & Co. Ltd, 2002 (ISBN 1-85609-223-2)

B81 INTERNATIONAL ASSOCIATION OF INDEPENDENT TANKER OWNERS (INTERTANKO) – A guide to crude oil washing and cargo heating criteria. Oslo, Intertanko, 2004

B82 INTERNATIONAL ASSOCIATION OF INDEPENDENT TANKER OWNERS (INTERTANKO) – A guide for correct entries in the Oil Record Book (Part I – Machinery space operations). Revised edition. Oslo, Intertanko, 2006

B83 INTERNATIONAL ASSOCIATION OF INDEPENDENT TANKER OWNERS (INTERTANKO) – A guide for vetting inspections. 3rd ed. Oslo: Intertanko, 1997

B84 INTERNATIONAL ASSOCIATION OF INDEPENDENT TANKER OWNERS (INTERTANKO) – A Guide to International Environmental Management Systems (EMS). Oslo: Intertanko, 2002

B66　海军水道部(英国)—英版水道测量手册. 第1卷.汤顿 (英国),海军水道部出版,1965年

B67　海军水道部(英国)—英版水道测量手册. 第2卷,汤顿 (英国),海军水道部出版

B68　海军水道部(英国)—英版航海图书总目录. 汤顿(英国),海军水道部出版,2000年

B69　海军水道部(英国)—英版海图符号与缩写(5011号海图),第2版.汤顿(英国),海军水道部出版, 1998年

B70　海军水道部 (英国)—海员手册. 第7版. 汤顿 (英国), 海军水道部出版,1999年(ISBN 0-707-71123-1)

B71　国际船级社协会(IACS)—散装船:船东和经营人指南与资讯. 伦敦 :IACS出版,1992年

B72　国际船级社协会 (IACS)—散装船：船体结构的检验、评估与修理指南. 第3版. 伦敦：Witherby and Co. Ltd出版,1995年(ISBN 1-85609-135-X)

B73　国际船级社协会(IACS)—散装船:谨慎装卸. 伦敦,IACS出版, 1998年

B74　国际船级社协会 (IACS)—散装船：船体结构的检验、评估与修理指南. 第3版. 伦敦,Witherby & Co. Ltd出版,1995年(ISBN 1-85609-135-X)

B75　国际船级社协会(IACS)—化学品船:船体结构的检验、评估与修理指南. 伦敦, Witherby & Co. Ltd出版,2005年(ISBN 1-85609-296-8)

B76　国际船级社协会(IACS)—杂货船:船体结构的检验、评估与修理指南. 伦敦, Witherby & Co. Ltd出版, 1999年(ISBN 1-85609-189-9)

B77　国际船级社协会 (IACS)—涂层维护和修理指南. 伦敦, Withcrby & Co. Ltd出版, 2005年(ISBN 1-85609-308-5)

B78　国际干散货船东协会(INTERCARGO)—2005散货船事故报告, 前10年 (1996—2005) 及其趋势. 伦敦, Intercargo出版, 2006年

B79　国际干散货船东协会 (INTERCARGO)—港口国监督：干散货船舶贸易指南. 伦敦, Intercargo出版, 2000年

B80　国际干散货船东协会(INTERCARGO)—散货船:船体结构的检验、评估与修理指南.第2版. 伦敦,Witherby & Co. Ltd出版, 2002年 (ISBN 1-85609-223-2)

B81　国际独立油船船东协会 (INTERTANKO)—原油洗舱及货油加热标准指南. 奥斯陆, Intertanko出版,2004年

B82　国际独立油船船东协会(INTERTANKO)—正确填写油类记录簿指南 (第1部分机械场所作业). 修订版. 奥斯陆, Intertanko出版,2006年

B83　国际独立油船船东协会 (INTERTANKO)—审核检查指南. 第3版. 奥斯陆:Intertanko出版, 1997年

B84　国际独立油轮船东协会 (INTERTANKO)—国际环境管理系统 (EMS) 指南. 奥斯陆：Intertanko出版,2002年

B85 INTERNATIONAL ASSOCIATION OF INDEPENDENT TANKER OWNERS (INTERTANKO) – A guide to bunkering of ships for the purposes of Annex VI to MARPOL. Oslo, Intertanko, 2004

B86 International Association of Lighthouses Authorities (IALA) – IALA aids to navigation guide (NAVGUIDE). Edition 4. Paris: IALA, 2001

B87 International Association of Lighthouses Authorities (IALA) – IALA Vessel Traffic Services manual. Paris, IALA, 1993 (ISBN 2-910312-01-1)

B88 INTERNATIONAL CARGO HANDLING COORDINATION ASSOCIATION (ICHCA) – The loading and unloading of solid bulk cargoes. London: ICHCA, 1998 (ISBN 1-85330-096-9)

B89 INTERNATIONAL CARGO HANDLING COORDINATION ASSOCIATION (ICHCA) – The loading and unloading of solid bulk cargoes. London, ICHCA, 1998 (ISBN 1-85330-096-9)

B90 INTERNATIONAL CHAMBER OF SHIPPING (ICS) – Condition evaluation and maintenance of tanker structure. London, Witherby & Co. Ltd, 1992 (ISBN 1-85609-039-6)

B91 INTERNATIONAL CHAMBER OF SHIPPING (ICS) – International Safety Guide for Oil Tankers and Terminals (ISGOTT). 5th ed. London, Witherby & Co. Ltd, 2006 (ISBN 1-85609-291-7)

B92 INTERNATIONAL CHAMBER OF SHIPPING (ICS) – Safety in chemical tankers. London, Witherby & Co. Ltd, 1977

B93 INTERNATIONAL CHAMBER OF SHIPPING (ICS) – Safety in liquefied gas tankers. London, Witherby & Co. Ltd, 1980

B94 INTERNATIONAL CHAMBER OF SHIPPING (ICS) – Safety in oil tankers. London, Witherby & Co. Ltd, 1978

B95 INTERNATIONAL CHAMBER OF SHIPPING (ICS) – Ship shore safety checklist for bulk carriers. London, ICS, 2000

B96 INTERNATIONAL CHAMBER OF SHIPPING (ICS) – Shipping and the environment: A code of practice. 3rd ed., London, ICS, 1999

B97 INTERNATIONAL CHAMBER OF SHIPPING (ICS) – Tanker safety guide: Chemicals. 3rd ed. London, ICS, 2002 (ISBN 0-906270-04-9)

B98 INTERNATIONAL CHAMBER OF SHIPPING (ICS) – Tanker safety guide: Liquefied gas. 2nd ed. London, ICS, 1995 (ISBN 0-906270-03-0)

B99 International Chamber of Shipping (ICS)/Oil Companies International Marine Forum (OCIMF) – Peril at sea and salvage: A guide for masters. 5th ed. London, Witherby & Co. Ltd, 1998 (ISBN 1-5609-095-7)

B100 INTERNATIONAL CHAMBER OF SHIPPING (ICS)/OIL COMPANIES INTERNATIONAL MARINE FORUM (OCIMF) – Clean seas guide for oil tankers. 4th ed. London Witherby & Co. Ltd, 1994 (ISBN 1-85609-058-2)

B101 INTERNATIONAL CHAMBER OF SHIPPING (ICS)/OIL COMPANIES INTERNATIONAL MARINE FORUM (OCIMF) – Guidance manual for the inspection and condition assessment of tanker structures. London, Witherby & Co. Ltd, 1986 (ISBN 0-948691-11-5)

B102 INTERNATIONAL CHAMBER OF SHIPPING (ICS)/OIL COMPANIES INTERNATIONAL MARINE FORUM (OCIMF) – Ship to ship transfer guide: Liquefied gases. 2nd ed. London, Witherby & Co. Ltd, 1995 (ISBN 1-85609-082-5)

B103 INTERNATIONAL CHAMBER OF SHIPPING (ICS)/OIL COMPANIES INTERNATIONAL MARINE FORUM (OCIMF) – Ship to ship transfer guide: (Petroleum). 4th ed. London, Witherby & Co. Ltd, 2005 (ISBN 1-85609-258-5)

B85 国际独立油轮船东协会 (INTERTANKO) —对实施MARPOL附件Ⅵ的船舶加油指南. 奥斯陆, Intertanko出版, 2004年.

B86 国际灯塔协会 (IALA)—IALA 助航标志指南 (NAVGUIDE). 第4版. 巴黎 : IALA出版, 2001年

B87 国际灯塔协会(IALA) —IALA 船舶交管手册. 巴黎, IALA, 1993年 (ISBN 2-910312-01-1)

B88 国际货物装卸协调联合会 (ICHCA)—固体散货装卸. 伦敦:ICHCA出版, 1998年 (ISBN 1-85330-096-9)

B89 国际货物装卸协调联合会 (ICHCA)—固体散货装卸. 伦敦: ICHCA出版, 1998年 (ISBN 1-85330-096-9)

B90 国际航运公会 (ICS)—液货船结构状况评估及维护. 伦敦, Witherby & Co. Ltd出版, 1992年 (ISBN 1-85609-039-6)

B91 国际航运公会 (ICS)—国际油船和油码头安全指南 (ISGOTT). 第5版. 伦敦, Witherby & Co. Ltd出版, 2006(ISBN 1-85609-291-7)

B92 国际航运公会(ICS)—化学品船安全. 伦敦, Witherby & Co. Ltd出版, 1977年

B93 国际航运公会(ICS)—液化气船安全. 伦敦, Witherby & Co. Ltd出版, 1980年

B94 国际航运公会(ICS)—油船安全. 伦敦 , Witherby & Co. Ltd出版, 1978年

B95 国际航运公会(ICS)—散货船船岸安全检查表. 伦敦, ICS出版, 2000年

B96 国际航运公会(ICS)—航运与环境:实践规则.第3版. 伦敦, ICS出版, 1999年

B97 国际航运公会 (ICS) —液货船安全指南: 化学品. 第3版. 伦敦, ICS出版, 2002年(ISBN 0-906270-04-9)

B98 国际航运公会 (ICS) —液货船安全指南: 液化气. 第2版. 伦敦, ICS出版, 1995年(ISBN 0-906270-03-0)

B99 国际航运公会 (ICS) /石油公司国际海上论坛 (OCIMF)—海上危险与救助: 船长指南. 第5版. 伦敦, Witherby & Co. Ltd出版, 1998年(ISBN 1-5609-095-7)

B100 国际航运公会 (ICS) /石油公司国际海上论坛(OCIMF) —油船防污染指南. 第4版.伦敦 Witherby & Co. Ltd出版, 1994年 (ISBN 1-85609-058-2)

B101 国际航运公会 (ICS) /石油公司国际海上论坛(OCIMF)—液货船结构检查和状况评估指南手册. 伦敦, Witherby & Co. Ltd出版, 1986年(ISBN 0-948691-11-5)

B102 国际航运公会 (ICS) / 石油公司国际海上论坛(OCIMF)—船对船转驳指南:液化气. 第2版. 伦敦, Witherby & Co. Ltd出版, 1995年(ISBN 1-85609-082-5)

B103 国际航运公会 (ICS) / 石油公司国际海上论坛(OCIMF)—船对船转驳指南:石油. 第4版. 伦敦, Witherby & Co. Ltd出版, 2005年(ISBN 1-85609-258-5)

B104 INTERNATIONAL CHAMBER OF SHIPPING et al – Bulk carrier checklists. London, ICS, 1996

B105 International Hydrography Organization (IHO) – IHO/IMO world-wide navigational warning service. Guidance document. Monaco, IHO, 1995 (Special Publication No. 53. Language(s): E, F

B106 INTERNATIONAL INSTITUTE OF MARINE SURVEYING – Code of practice for draught surveys. London, Witherby & Co. Ltd, 1998 (ISBN 1-85609-152-X)

B107 INTERNATIONAL LABOUR ORGANIZATION (ILO) – Maritime labour convention 2006. CD-ROM. Geneva, ILO, 2006 (ISBN 92-2-018784-1)

B108 International Maritime Pilot's Association (IMPA) – Required boarding arrangements for pilots. London, Witherby & Co. Ltd, 1995

B109 INTERNATIONAL ORGANIZATION FOR STANDARDIZATION (ISO) – Ships and marine technology: Bulk carriers: Construction quality of hull structure. Geneva, ISO, 2000 (ISO 15401)

B110 INTERNATIONAL ORGANIZATION FOR STANDARDIZATION (ISO) – Ships and marine technology: Bulk carriers: Repair quality of hull structure. Geneva, ISO, 2000 (ISO 15402)

B111 INTERNATIONAL SHIPPING FEDERATION (ISF) – ILO Maritime Labour Convention: A guide for the shipping, London, ISF, 2006

B112 Irving, M. – Marine pilot safety. London, Nautical Institute, 1996 (ISBN 1-870077-31-8)

B113 ISBESTER, J. – Bulk carrier practice. London: The Nautical Institute, 1993 (ISBN 1-870077-16-4)

B114 JACKSON, D. – Enforcement of maritime claims. 4th ed. London, Lloyd's of London Press, 2005 (ISBN 1-84311-424-0)

B115 JERVIS, B. – Reeds marine insurance. London, Adlard Coles Nautical, 2005 (ISBN 0-7136-7396-6) (http://www.adlardcoles.com)

B116 Jones, T.G. – Seamanship notes. 5th ed. Oxford, Butterworth-Heinemann, 1992 (ISBN 0-7506-0281-3)

B117 KEMP, J.F. & YOUNG, P. – Kandy: Cargo work. 5th ed. Oxford, Butterworth-Heinemann, 1982 (ISBN 0-7506-0524-3)

B118 KEMP, J.F. & YOUNG, P. – Ship construction: Sketches and notes. Oxford, Butterworth-Heinemann, 1991 (ISBN 0-7506-0381-X)

B119 Khalique, A. – Nav Basics. Witherby Seamanship International Ltd, 2009 (ISBN 9781905331581)

B120 Lee, Capt., G.W.U. and Parker, C.J. – Managing Collision Avoidance at Sea. The Nautical Institute, 2007 (ISBN 1-8700-7786-6)

B121 Lloyd, Capt., M. – Captains Legal. Witherby Seamanship International Ltd, 2009 (ISBN 9781905331406)

B122 Lloyd, Capt., M. – In Command. Witherby Seamanship International Ltd, 2007 (ISBN 978 1 85609 353)

B123 Lloyd, Capt., M. – The Complete Chief Officer. Witherby Seamanship International Ltd, 2006 (ISBN 1-8560-9359-0)

B124 Lloyd, Capt., M. – The Masters Pocketbook Series – Checklists. Witherby Seamanship International Ltd, 2009 (ISBN 9781905331444)

B125 Lloyd, Capt., M. – The Pocket Book of Anchoring. Witherby Seamanship International Ltd, 2006 (ISBN 9781905331451)

B126 LLOYD'S OF LONDON PRESS (LLP) – Marine claims: A guide for the handling and prevention of marine claims. Lloyd's list practical guide. 2nd ed. London, LLP, 1996 (ISBN 1-85978-047-4)

B104 国际航运公会等 —散货船检查表. 伦敦, ICS出版, 1996 年

B105 国际水道组织 (IHO) —IHO/IMO 全球航行警告服务指导性文件. 摩纳哥, IHO出版, 1995年(专门出版物编号第53号.语言: 英语、法语)

B106 国际海洋测绘研究所—吃水测量实践规则. 伦敦, Witherby & Co. Ltd出版, 1998年 (ISBN 1-85609-152-X)

B107 国际劳工组织 (ILO) — 2006年国际劳工公约. CD-ROM.日内瓦, ILO出版, 2006年(ISBN 92-2-018784-1)

B108 国际海上引航员协会 (IMPA) —引航员登船安排的要求. 伦敦, Witherby & Co. Ltd出版, 1995年

B109 国际标准组织(ISO) —船舶和海上技术: 散货船: 船体建造质量. 日内瓦, ISO出版, 2000年 (ISO 15401)

B110 国际标准组织 (ISO) —船舶和海上技术: 散货船:船体修理质量. 日内瓦, ISO出版, 2000年(ISO 15402)

B111 国际航运联合会(ISF) —ILO海事劳工公约: 航运指南. 伦敦, ISF出版, 2006 年

B112 Irving, M. —海上引航安全. 伦敦,Nautical Institute出版, 1996年(ISBN 1-870077-31-8)

B113 ISBESTER, J. —散货船实践. 伦敦 ;The Nautical Institute 出版 ,1993 年 (ISBN 1-870077-16-4)

B114 JACKSON, D. —海事索赔之实施. 第4版. 伦敦, 伦敦劳氏出版社 ,2005年(ISBN 1-84311-424-0)

B115 JERVIS, B. —里德海上保险. 伦敦 ,Adlard Coles Nautical 出版 ,2005 年 (ISBN 0-7136-7396-6) (http://www.adlardcoles.com)

B116 Jones, T.G. —航海笔记. 第5版. 牛津 ,Butterworth-Heinemann 出版 ,1992 年 (ISBN 0-7506-0281-3)

B117 KEMP, J. F. & YOUNG, P, — Kandy:货物作业. 第5版. 牛津, Butterworth-Heinemann出版, 1982年(ISBN 0-7506-0524-3)

B118 KEMP, J.F. & YOUNG, P. —造船:草图与注释. 牛津, Butterworth-Heinemann出版,1991年 (ISBN 0-7506-0381-X)

B119 Khalique, A —航海基础. Witherby Seamanship International Ltd 出版 ,2009 年 (ISBN 9781905331581)

B120 Lee, 船长 ,G.W.U and Parker,C.J. —海上避碰管理. The NAUTICAL INSTITUTE出版 , 2007年(ISBN 1-8700-7786-6)

B121 Lloyd, M. 船长. —船长法律. Witherby Seamanship International Ltd出版 ,2009年(ISBN 9781905331406)

B122 Lloyd, M. 船长. —指挥. Witherby Seamanship International Ltd出版 ,2007年 (ISBN 978 1 85609 353)

B123 Lloyd, M. 船长. —完美大副. Witherby Seamanship International Ltd出版 ,2006年(ISBN 1-8560-9359-0)

B124 Lloyd, M. 船长. —船长袖珍字典系列—检查表. Witherby Seamanship International Ltd出版, 2009年 (ISBN 9781905331444)

B125 Lloyd, M. 船长. —锚泊袖珍书. Witherby Seamanship International Ltd出版 ,2006年 ,(ISBN 9781905331451)

B126 伦敦劳氏出版社 (LLP) — 海事索赔: 海事索赔处理与预防指南. 劳氏系列实操指南. 第2版. 伦敦 ,LLP出版 ,1996年(ISBN 1-85978-047-4)

B127 Lloyd's of London Press – Lloyd's Nautical Yearbook, 2000. LLP Professional Publishing, 1999 (ISBN 1–85978–540–9)
B128 LLOYD'S REGISTER OF SHIPPING – Bulk carriers – The safety issues. London: Lloyd's Register of Shipping, 1991
B129 LLOYD'S REGISTER OF SHIPPING – Bulk carriers: An update (January 1996). London: Lloyd's Register of Shipping, 1996
B130 LLOYD'S REGISTER OF SHIPPING – Bulk carriers: Guidance to operators on the inspection of cargo holds. London: Lloyd's Register of Shipping, 1991
B131 LLOYD'S REGISTER OF SHIPPING – Lloyd's register and the Standard. A master's guide to hatch cover maintenance. London, Witherby & Co. Ltd, 2002 (ISBN 1-85609-232-1)
B132 LUDDEKE, C. & JOHNSON, A. – The Hamburg Rules. 2nd ed. London, Lloyd's of London Press, 1995 (ISBN 1-85044-84-1)
B133 LUX, J. (Ed). – Classification societies. London, Lloyd's of London Press, 1993 (ISBN 1-85044-491-9)
B134 M Notices – Consolidated list to August 1996. 3 Vols. (ISBN 0-11-551853-3)
B135 MANDARAKA –SHEPPARD, A. – Modern admiralty law. London, Cavendish Publishing Ltd, 2001 (ISBN 1-85941-531-8)
B136 Maritime And Coastal Agency – Code of safe working practice for merchant seamen. London, HMSO, 1998 (ISBN 0-11-551836-3)
B137 MEESON, N. – Admiralty jurisdiction and practice. 3rd ed. London, LLP Professional Publishing, 2003 (ISBN 1-84311-271-X)
B138 Meteorological Office, The marine Observer's Handbook. 11th ed. (Met.0.,887). London, HMSO, 1996 (ISBN 0-1140-0367-X)
B139 Ministry Of Defence (UK) – Admiralty manual of navigation. Vol. 1 – General navigation, 1986. London, HMSO
B140 Ministry Of Defence (UK) – Admiralty manual of navigation. Vol. 2 – Ocean navigation, 1973. London, HMSO
B141 Ministry Of Defence (UK) – Admiralty manual of navigation. Vol. 3 – Radio aids, etc. 1987. London, HMSO
B142 Moore, D.A. – International light, shape and sound signals. 2nd ed. Oxford, Butterworth-Heinemann, 1982 (ISBN 0-434-913-103)
B143 Morgans Technical Books – Seaman's guide to the rule of the road. 6th ed. Morgans Technical Books Ltd, 1995 (ISBN 0-948254-00-9)
B144 NAUTICAL INSTITUTE – Improving ship operational design. London, The Nautical Institute, 1998
B145 NAUTICAL INSTITUTE – Master's role in collecting evidence. London, Nautical Institute, 1989 (ISBN 1-870077-05-9)
B146 NAUTICAL INSTITUTE – Safe operation of bulk carriers. London, Nautical Institute, 1991
B147 NAUTICAL INSTITUTE – Seaworthiness: The Marine and the Maritime Law Series No. 3. London, Nautical Institute, 1992
B148 NAUTICAL INSTITUTE – Signing bills of lading. London, Nautical Institute, 1992
B149 NAUTICAL INSTITUTE – Unsafe berths and ports. London, Nautical Institute, 1992
B150 Norris, Dr. A. – Radar and AIS-Vol. 1 Integrated Bridge Systems. The Nautical Institute, 2008 (ISBN 1-8700-7795-8)
B151 Norris, Dr. A. – Integrated Bridge Systems, Vol. 2 ECDIS and Positioning. The Nautical Institute, 2010 (ISBN 1-9069-1511-3)

B127 伦敦劳氏出版社—2000年劳氏航海年鉴. LLP Professional Publishing出版, 1999年(ISBN 1-85978-540-9)

B128 劳氏船级社— 散货船:安全问题. 伦敦:Lloyd's Register of Shipping出版, 1991年

B129 劳氏船级社—散货船: 一个更新 (1996年1月). 伦敦:Lloyd's Register of Shipping出版, 1996年

B130 劳氏船级社—散货船: 货舱检查指南. 伦敦:Lloyd's Register of Shipping出版, 1991 年

B131 劳氏船级社—劳氏登记和标准. 船长舱盖维护指南. 伦敦, Witherby & Co. Ltd出版, 2002年(ISBN 1-85609-232-1)

B132 LUDDEKE, C. & JOHNSON, A. —汉堡规则. 第2版. 伦敦, 伦敦劳氏出版社, 1995年(ISBN 1-85044-84-1)

B133 LUX, J. (Ed). —船级社. 伦敦, 伦敦劳氏出版社, 1993年 (ISBN 1-85044-491-9)

B134 汇总至1996年8月的航运通知.第3卷. (ISBN 0-11-551853-3)

B135 MANDARAKA-SHEPPARD, A. —现代海事法, 伦敦, Cavendish Publishing Ltd出版, 2001年(ISBN 1-85941-531-8)

B136 海上和沿海代理—商船海员安全工作守则. 伦敦, HMSO出版, 1998年 (ISBN 0-11-551836-3)

B137 MEESON, N. —海事审判与实践. 第3版, 伦敦, LLP Professional出版, 2003年(ISBN 1-84311-271-X)

B138 气象局, 海洋观察员手册. 第11版 (Met.0.,887). 伦敦, HMSO出版, 1996年 (ISBN 0-1140-0367-X)

B139 国防部 (英国) —海上航行手册. 第1卷— 一般情况下航行. 伦敦, HMSO, 1986年

B140 国防部 (英国) —海上航行手册. 第1卷—大洋航行. 伦敦, HMSO出版, 1973年

B141 国防部 (英国) —海上航行手册. 第3卷—无线电助航等. 伦敦, HMSO出版,1987年

B142 Moore, D.A. —国际号灯、号型和声响信号. 第2版. 牛津, Butterworth-Heinemann出版, 1982年(ISBN 0-434-913-103)

B143 Morgans Technical Books —航行规则海员指南.第6版. Morgans Technical Books Ltd出版, 1995年(ISBN 0-948254-00-9)

B144 航海学院—改善船舶操作设计. 伦敦, The Nautical Institute出版, 1998年

B145 航海学院—船长在收集证据中的作用. 伦敦, The Nautical Institute出版, 1989年(ISBN 1-870077-05-9)

B146 航海学院—散货船安全操作. 伦敦, Nautical Institute出版, 1991年

B147 航海学院—适航性: 海洋和海事法律.第3卷. 伦敦, Nautical Institute出版, 1992年

B148 航海学院—签发提单. 伦敦, Nautical Institute出版, 1992年

B149 航海学院—不安全的泊位和港口. 伦敦, Nautical Institute出版, 1992年

B150 Norris, Dr. A. —雷达和AIS—第1卷 组合驾驶台系统. The Nautical Institute出版, 2008年(ISBN 1-8700-7795-8)

B151 Norris, Dr.A. —组合驾驶台系统,第2卷 ECDIS和定位. The Nautical Institute出版, 2010年(ISBN 1-9069-1511-3)

B152 OIL COMPANIES INTERNATIONAL MARINE FORUM (OCIMF) – Guide on marine terminal fire protection and emergency evacuation. London, Witherby & Co. Ltd, 1987 (ISBN 0-948691-30-1)

B153 OIL COMPANIES INTERNATIONAL MARINE FORUM (OCIMF) – Marine and terminal operations survey guidelines. London, Witherby & Co. Ltd, 1994 (ISBN 1-85609-62-0)

B154 OIL COMPANIES INTERNATIONAL MARINE FORUM (OCIMF) – Oil spill contingency planning: A brief guide. London, Witherby & Co. Ltd, 1990 (ISBN 0-900886-40-4)

B155 OIL COMPANIES INTERNATIONAL MARINE FORUM (OCIMF) – Oil spill fate and impact on the marine environment. London, Witherby & Co. Ltd, 1980 (ISBN 0-900-80086-49-8)

B156 OIL COMPANIES INTERNATIONAL MARINE FORUM (OCIMF) – Recommendations for oil tanker manifolds and associated equipment. 4th ed. London, Witherby & Co. Ltd, 1991 (ISBN 1-85609-017-5)

B157 OIL COMPANIES INTERNATIONAL MARINE FORUM (OCIMF) – Recommendations on equipment for towing of disabled tankers. London, Witherby & Co. Ltd, 1981 (ISBN 0-900886-65-X)

B158 OIL COMPANIES INTERNATIONAL MARINE FORUM (OCIMF) – Safety guide for terminals handling ships carrying liquefied gases in bulk. 2nd ed. London, Witherby & Co. Ltd, 1993 (ISBN 1-85609-057-4)

B159 OIL COMPANIES INTERNATIONAL MARINE FORUM (OCIMF) – Vessel inspection questionnaire for bulk oil/chemical carriers and gas carriers – V.I.Q. 2nd ed. London, Witherby & Co. Ltd, 2000 (ISBN 1-85609-200-3)

B160 OIL COMPANIES INTERNATIONAL MARINE FORUM (OCIMF)/INTERNATIONAL TANKER OWNERS POLLUTION FEDERATION (ITOPF) – Guidelines for the preparation of shipboard oil spill contingency plans. London, Witherby & Co. Ltd, 1990 (ISBN 1-85609-016-7)

B161 OIL COMPANIES INTERNATIONAL MARINE FORUM (OCIMF)/SOCIETY OF INTERNATIONAL GAS TANKERS AND TERMINAL OPERATORS (SIGTTO) – Inspection guidelines for ships carrying liquefied gases in bulk. 2nd ed. London: Witherby & Co. Ltd, 1998 (ISBN 1-85609-139-2)

B162 OIL COMPANIES INTERNATIONAL MARINE FORUM (OCIMF)/SOCIETY OF INTERNATIONAL GAS TANKERS AND TERMINAL OPERATORS (SIGTTO) – Ship information questionnaire for gas carriers. 2nd ed. London, Witherby & Co. Ltd, 1998 (ISBN 1-85609-138-4)

B163 Oil Companies International Marine Forum (OCIMF) – Anchoring Systems and Procedures, 2nd edition. Witherby Seamanship International Ltd, 2010 (ISBN 1-8560-9404-9)

B164 Oil Companies International Marine Forum (OCIMF) – Effective mooring. London, Witherby & Co. Ltd, 1989 (ISBN 0-948691-88-3)

B165 Oil Companies International Marine Forum (OCIMF) – Guidelines and recommendations for the safe mooring of large ships at piers and sea islands. 2nd ed. London, Witherby & Co. Ltd, 1992 (ISBN 1-85609-041-8)

B166 Oil Companies International Marine Forum (OCIMF) – The Use of Large Tankers in Seasonal First-Year Ice and Severe Sub-Zero Conditions. Witherby Seamanship International Ltd, 2010 (ISBN 1-8560-9429-4)

B167 OIL INTERNATIONAL COMPANIES MARINE FORUM (OCIMF) – Vessel inspection questionnaire for bulk oil/chemical carriers and gas carriers – V.I.Q. 2nd ed. London, Witherby & Co. Ltd, 2000 (ISBN 1-85609-200-3)

B152 石油公司国际海上论坛 (OCIMF) —海上码头防火和应急疏散指南. 伦敦, Witherby & Co. Ltd出版, 1987年(ISBN 0-948691-30-1)

B153 石油公司国际海上论坛 (OCIMF) —海上和码头作业检测指南. 伦敦, Witherby & Co. Ltd出版, 1994年(ISBN 1-85609-62-0)

B154 石油公司国际海上论坛 (OCIMF) —溢油应急计划:简明指南. 伦敦, Witherby & Co. Ltd出版, 1990年(ISBN 0-900886-40-4)

B155 石油公司国际海上论坛 (OCIMF) —溢油事故及其对海洋环境的影响. 伦敦, Witherby & Co. Ltd出版, 1980年(ISBN 0-900-80086-49-8)

B156 石油公司国际海上论坛 (OCIMF) —油船歧管和相关设备建议. 第4版. 伦敦, Witherby & Co. Ltd出版, 1991年(ISBN 1-85609-017-5)

B157 石油公司国际海上论坛 (OCIMF)—失控油轮拖带设备建议. Witherby & Co. Ltd出版, 1981年(ISBN 0-900886-65-X)

B158 石油公司国际海上论坛 (OCIMF) —载运液化气船舶码头装卸安全指南. 第2版. 伦敦, Witherby & Co. Ltd出版. 1993年(ISBN 1-85609-057-4)

B159 石油公司国际海上论坛 (OCIMF) —对散装油类、化学品和气体船舶检查问卷—V.I.Q. 第2版. 伦敦, Witherby & Co. Ltd出版, 2000年 (ISBN 1-85609-200-3)

B160 石油公司国际海上论坛 (OCIMF) / 国际油船船东油污联合会(ITOPF) —船舶油污应急计划编制指南. 伦敦, Witherby & Co. Ltd出版, 1990年(ISBN 1-85609-016-7)

B161 石油公司国际海上论坛 (OCIMF) / 国际气体船东及码头经营者协会 (SIGTTO)—散装液化气体运输船舶检查指南. 第2版. 伦敦: Witherby & Co. Ltd出版, 1998年(ISBN 1-85609-139-2)

B162 石油公司国际海上论坛 (OCIMF) /国际气体船东及码头经营者协会(SIGTTO) —气体运输船舶的船舶信息问卷. 第2版. 伦敦, Witherby & Co. Ltd出版, 1998年 (ISBN 1-85609-138-4)

B163 石油公司国际海上论坛 (OCIMF). —锚泊系统与程序, 第2版. Witherby Seamanship International Ltd出版, 2010年 (ISBN 1-8560-9404-9)

B164 石油公司国际海上论坛 (OCIMF). —有效系泊. 伦敦, Witherby & Co. Ltd出版, 1989年 (ISBN 0-948691-88-3)

B165 石油公司国际海上论坛 (OCIMF). —大型船舶安全系泊码头和海岛指南与建议. 第2版. 伦敦, Witherby & Co. Ltd出版, 1992年(ISBN 1-85609-041-8)

B166 石油公司国际海上论坛 (OCIMF). —在季节性首年冰和严重零下天气条件下大型液体船舶操作. Witherby Seamanship International Ltd出版, 2010年(ISBN 1-8560-9429-4)

B167 石油公司国际海上论坛(OCIMF) —对散装油类、化学品和气体船舶检查问卷—V.I.Q. 第2版. 伦敦,Witherby & Co. Ltd出版, 2000年 (ISBN 1-85609-200-3)

B168 Owen, P. – High speed craft: A practical guide for deck officers. London, The Nautical Institute, 1995 (ISBN 1-870077-22-9)

B169 OZCAYIR, Z.O. – Liability for oil pollution and collisions. London, Lloyd's of London Press (ISBN 1-85978-179-9)

B170 PAMBORIDES, G.P. – International shipping law: Legislation and enforcement. The Hague: Kluwer Law International, 1999 (ISBN 90-411-1193-X)

B171 PAYNE & IVAMY – Marine insurance. 4th ed. Sevenoaks (UK), Butterworth & Co. Ltd, 1985 (ISBN 0-406-25313-7)

B172 Peacock, Lt Cmdr A. – Astro Navigation – Admiralty Manual of Navigation Vol. 2, 2004 (ISBN 1-8700-7765-1)

B173 Peacock, Lt Cmdr A. – The Principles of Navigation – The Admiralty Manual of Navigation Vol. 1, 10th ed. 2008 (ISBN 1-8700-7790-3)

B174 PHILIPS, N., CRAIG, N. – Merchant shipping act 1995 – Annotated guide. 2nd ed. London, Lloyd's of London Press, 2001 (IBSN 1-8597-8563-8)

B175 POLAND, S., ROOTH, T. – Gard handbook on P & I insurance. 4th ed. Arendal (Norway), Assuranceforeningen Gard, 1996 (ISBN 82-90344-16-3)

B176 RAINEY, S. – The Law of tug and tow. 2nd ed. London, Lloyd's of London Press, 2002 (ISBN 1–84311.169.1)

B177 Reed (Thomas) Publication Ltd – Reed marine distance tables. 7th ed. Hampton Court (UK). Reed (Thomas) Publication Ltd, 1992 (ISBN 0-947637-27-3)

B178 REYNOLDS, M. – Arbitration. London, Lloyd's of London Press, 1995 (ISBN 1-85044-550-8)

B179 RHIDIAN THOMAS, D. (Ed.) – Modern law of marine insurance. Vol. 1. London, Lloyd's of London Press, 1996 (ISBN 1-85978-033-4)

B180 RHIDIAN THOMAS, D. (Ed.) – Modern law of marine insurance. Vol. 2. London Lloyd's of London Press, 2002 (ISBN 1-84311-120-9)

B181 RICHARDSON, J. – The Hague and Hague-Visby rules. 4th ed. London: Lloyd's of London Press, 1999 (Lloyd's Practical Shipping Guides) (ISBN 1-85978-180-2)

B182 ROGERS, P., et al – Coal: Carriage by sea. 2nd ed. London, Lloyd's of London Press, 1997 (ISBN 1-85978-108-X)

B183 Rose, F. – Marine Insurance: law and practice. Informa, 2004 (ISBN 1-8431-1247-7)

B184 ROSES, F. – General average: Law and practice. London, Lloyd's of London Press, 1997 (ISBN 1-85978-158-6)

B185 SANDS, P. – Principles of international environmental law. 2nd ed. Cambridge, Cambridge University Press, 2003 (ISBN 0-521-81794-3)

B186 SCHOENBAUM, T.J. – Admiralty and maritime law. 3rd ed. St. Paul (Minn.) (USA), West Publishing Co., 2001 (ISBN 0-314-02711-4)

B187 SCHOFIELD, J. – Laytime and demurrage. 5th ed. London, Lloyd's of London Press, 2005 (ISBN 1-84311-419-4)

B188 Society Of International Gas Tanker And Terminal Operators (SIGTTO) – A guide for passage planning for the transit of the Straits of Malacca and Singapore for vessels of draughts of less than 12 metres London, Witherby & Co. Ltd, 2000 (ISBN 1-85609-195-3)

B189 SOCIETY OF INTERNATIONAL GAS TANKER AND TERMINAL OPERATORS (SIGTTO) – Crew safety standards and training for LNG carriers: Essential best practices for the industry. London, Witherby & Co. Ltd, 2003 (ISBN 1-85609-257-7)

B190 SOCIETY OF INTERNATIONAL GAS TANKER AND TERMINAL OPERATORS (SIGTTO) – Liquefied gas fire hazard management. London, Witherby & Co. Ltd, 2004 (ISBN 1-85609-265-8)

B168 Owen, P. —高速船: 驾驶员实操指南. 伦敦, The Nautical Institute出版, 1995年 (ISBN 1-870077-22-9)

B169 Ozcayir, Z.O. —油污与碰撞责任. 伦敦,伦敦劳氏出版社 (ISBN 1-85978-179-9)

B170 Pamborides, G.P. —国际航运法: 立法与实施. 海牙 ,Kluwer 国际法, 1999 年 (ISBN 90-411-1193-X)

B171 Payne & Ivamy—海上保险. 第4版. 七橡树 (英国), Butterworth & Co. Ltd出版, 1985年 (ISBN 0-406-25313-7)

B172 Peacock, Lt Cmdr A. —天文航海—英国海军航行手册第2卷, 2004年(ISBN 1-8700-7765-1)

B173 Peacock, Lt Cmdr A. —航海原理—英国海军航行手册第1卷, 第10版. 2008年(ISBN 1-8700-7790-3)

B174 Philips, N. / CRAIG, N. —1995年商船航运法注释指南. 第2版. 伦敦, 伦敦劳氏出版社, 2001年(IBSN 1-8597-8563-8)

B175 Poland, S. Rooth, T. —保赔保险加德手册. 第4卷. 阿伦达尔 (挪威), Assuranceforeningen Gard 出版, 1996年(ISBN 82-90344-16-3)

B176 Rainey, S. —拖船与拖带法. 第2版. 伦敦, 伦敦劳氏出版社, 2002年(ISBN 1-84311-169-1)

B177 Reed (Thomas) Publication Ltd —里德航海里程表. 第7版. 汉普顿法院 (英国). Reed (Thomas) Publication Ltd出版, 1992年(ISBN 0-947637-27-3)

B178 Reynolds, M. - 仲裁. 伦敦, 伦敦劳氏出版社, 1995年(ISBN 1-85044-550-8)

B179 Rhidian Thomas, D. (Ed) —现代海上保险法.第1卷. 伦敦,伦敦劳氏出版社, 1996年 (ISBN 1-85978-033-4)

B180 Rhidian Thomas, D. (Ed) —现代海上保险法.第2卷. 伦敦,伦敦劳氏出版社, 2002年 (ISBN 1-84311-120-9)

B181 Richardson, J. — 海牙规则和海牙—维斯比规则.第4版. 伦敦,伦敦劳氏出版社, 1999年, (劳氏实用航运指南) (ISBN 1-85978-180-2)

B182 Rogers, P, et al —煤: 海运. 第2版. 伦敦, 伦敦劳氏出版社, 1997年(ISBN 1-85978-108-X)

B183 Rose, F. —海上保险: 法律与实践. Informa出版, 2004年(ISBN 1-8431-1247-7)

B184 Roses, F. —共同海损: 法律与实践. 伦敦, 伦敦劳氏出版社, 1997年(ISBN 1-85978-158-6)

B185 Sands, P. —国际环境法原理.第2版. 剑桥, 剑桥大学出版社, 2003 年(ISBN 0-521-81794-3)

B186 Schoenbaum, T.J. —海事海商法. 第3版.圣保罗 (明尼苏达州,美国), West Publishing Co.出版, 2001年(ISBN 0-314-02711-4)

B187 Schofield, J. —装卸货时间与滞期.第5版. 伦敦, 伦敦劳氏出版社, 2005年(ISBN 1-84311-419-4)

B188 国际气体船东及码头经营者协会 (SIGTTO) — 吃水小于12米的船舶通过马六甲和新加坡海峡航线设计指南.伦敦, Witherby & Co. Ltd出版, 2000年(ISBN 1-85609-195-3)

B189 国际气体船东及码头经营者协会 (SIGTTO) — LNG船舶船员安全与培训标准: 行业最佳实践必备. 伦敦, Witherby & Co.Ltd出版, 2003年 (ISBN 1-85609-257-7)

B190 国际气体船东及码头经营者协会 (SIGTTO) — 液化气船火灾管理. 伦敦, Witherby & Co. Ltd出版, 2004年 (ISBN 1-85609-265-8)

B191 SOCIETY OF INTERNATIONAL GAS TANKER AND TERMINAL OPERATORS (SIGTTO) – Liquefied gas carriers: Your personal safety guide. London, Witherby & Co. Ltd, 2002 (ISBN 1-85609-217-8)

B192 SOCIETY OF INTERNATIONAL GAS TANKER AND TERMINAL OPERATORS (SIGTTO) – LNG Operations in port areas: Essential best practices for the industry. London, Witherby & Co. Ltd, 2004 (ISBN 1-85609-256-9)

B193 SPARKS, A. – Steel: Carriage by Sea. 4th ed. London, Lloyd's of London Press, 2003.

B194 Squairy W.H. – Modern chart work. 6th ed. Glasgow (UK), Brown, Son & Ferguson Ltd, 1992 (ISBN 0-85174-548-2)

B195 Subramaniam, Capt. – Practical Navigation. 4th Edition. Nutshell Series Book 1. Vijaya Publications

B196 TANKER STRUCTURE COOPERATIVE FORUM – Guidance manual for tanker structures. London, Witherby & Co, Ltd, 1997 (ISBN 1-85609-093-0)

B197 TANKER STRUCTURE COOPERATIVE FORUM/INTERNATIONAL ASSOCIATION OF CLASSIFICATION SOCIETIES (IACS) – Guidelines for the inspection and maintenance of double hull tanker structures. London, Witherby & Co. Ltd, 1995 (ISBN 1-85609-080-9)

B198 TAYLOR, L.G. – Cargo work. 12th ed. Glasgow, Brown, Son & Ferguson Ltd, 1992 (ISBN 0–85174–605–5)

B199 TETLEY, W. – Maritime liens and claims. 2nd ed. Montreal, International Shipping Publications, 1998 (ISBN 2-89451-227-9)

B200 The Standard – A Master's Guide to Berthing. Witherby Seamanship International Ltd (ISBN 9781856092906)

B201 The Stationery Office – Admiralty manual of seamanship. London HMSO, 1995 (ISBN 0-11-772695-8) Loose-leaf

B202 The Stationery Office – The Nautical Almanac. London, HMSO (Annual)

B203 THE TANKER STRUCTURE COOPERATIVE FORUM – Guidelines for ballast tank coating systems and surface preparation. London, Witherby & Co. Ltd, 2002 (ISBN 1-85609-214-3)

B204 THOMAS, D.R. – Maritime liens. Andover (Hants, UK), Stevens, 1998 (ISBN 0-4216-0920-6)

B205 TODD, P. – Bills of lading and bankers' documentary credits. 3rd ed. London, Lloyd's of London Press, 1998 (ISBN 1-85978-113-6)

B206 TUPPER, E.C. – Introduction to naval architecture. Butterworth-Heinemann, 1996 (ISBN 0–75062–529–5)

B207 UNITED NATIONS (UN) – United Nations Convention on the carriage of goods by sea, 1978 (Hamburg Rules). New York, 1994 (ISBN 92-1-133494-2)

B208 Van Kluijven, P.C. et al – IMO standard marine communication phrases (Dutch-English). Alkmaar (The Netherlands): De Alk & Heijnen bv, 2003 (ISBN 90-5961-008-3)

B209 Various authors. Bridge Watchkeeping. 2nd ed. The Nautical Institute, 2003 (ISBN 1-8700-7717-0)

B210 Vervloesem, W. – Mooring and Anchoring Ships Vol. 2 – Inspection and Maintenance. The Nautical Institute, 2009 (ISBN 1-8700-7794-1)

B211 VIDEOTEL MARINE INTERNATIONAL – Fighting pollution (Book, video and posters), London, Videotel Marine International, 1991

B212 Waugh, I. – The mariner's guide to marine communications. 2nd ed. London: The Nautical Institute, 2006 (ISBN 1-870077-78-4) (http://www.nautinst.org)

B213 WILFORD, M. et al – Time charters. 5th ed. London, LLP Professional Publishing, 2003 (ISBN 1-84311-210-8)

B191 国际气体船东及码头经营者协会 (SIGTTO) — 液化气体船: 个人安全指南. 伦敦, Witherby & Co. Ltd出版, 2002年(ISBN 1-85609-217-8)

B192 国际气体船东及码头经营者协会 (SIGTTO) —港内LNG作业: 行业最佳实践必备. 伦敦, Witherby & Co. Ltd出版, 2004年(ISBN 1-85609-256-9)

B193 Sparks, A. —钢铁:海运.第4版. 伦敦, 伦敦劳氏出版社, 2003年

B194 Squairy W.H. —现代海图作业. 第6版. 格拉斯哥 (英国), Brown, Son & Ferguson Ltd出版, 1992年(ISBN 0-85174-548-2)

B195 Subramaniam船长—航海实践. 第4版. Nutshell 系列丛书第1册. Vijaya Publications出版

B196 液货船结构合作论坛—液货船结构指南手册. 伦敦, Witherby & Co, Ltd出版, 1997年(ISBN 1-85609-093-0)

B197 液货船结构合作论坛/国际船级社联合会 (IACS) —双壳液货船结构检查与维护指南. 伦敦, Witherby & Co. Ltd出版, 1995年(ISBN 1-85609-080-9)

B198 Taylor, L. G. —货物作业. 第12版, 格拉斯哥, Brown, Son & Ferguson Ltd出版. 1992年(ISBN 0-85174-605-5)

B199 Tetley, W. —船舶优先权与索赔. 第2版. 蒙特利尔, International Shipping Publications出版, 1998年(ISBN 2-89451-227-9)

B200 The Standard. —船长靠泊指南. Witherby Seamanship International Ltd 出版 (ISBN 9781856092906)

B201 英国文书局. —英版航海技术手册. 伦敦,HMSO出版, 1995年 (ISBN 0-11-772695-8) 活页装

B202 英国文书局. —航海天文历. 伦敦, HMSO出版(年刊)

B203 液货船结构合作论坛—压载舱涂层系统和表面处理指南. 伦敦,Witherby & Co. Ltd出版, 2002年(ISBN 1-85609-214-3)

B204 Thomas, D.R. —船舶优先权. 安多 (汉普郡, 英国), Stevens出版, 1998年(ISBN 0-4216-0920-6)

B205 Todd, P. —提单与银行信用证. 第3版. 伦敦, 伦敦劳氏出版社, 1998年(ISBN 1-85978-113-6)

B206 Tupper, E.C. —造船概论. Butterworth-Heinemann出版, 1996年(ISBN 0-75062-529-5)

B207 联合国 (UN) —1978年联合国海上货物运输公约 (汉堡规则). 纽约, 1994年(ISBN 92-1-133494-2)

B208 Van Kluijven, P.C. et al—IMO 标准航海用语 (荷兰语—英语). 阿尔克马尔(荷兰) De Alk & Heijnen bv出版, 2003年(ISBN 90-5961-008-3)

B209 多位作者. 驾驶台值班.第2版. The Nautical Institute出版, 2003年(ISBN 1-8700-7717-0)

B210 Vervloesem, W. —船舶系泊与锚泊第2卷—检查和维护. The Nautical Institute出版, 2009年 (ISBN 1-8700-7794-1)

B211 Videotel Marine International—防治污染 (书、录像带、海报). 伦敦, Videotel Marine International出版, 1991年

B212 Waugh, I. —海上通信航海者指南. 第2版. 伦敦,The Nautical Institute出版, 2006年(ISBN 1-870077-78-4) (http://www.nautinst.org)

B213 Wilford, M. et al —期租. 第5版. 伦敦, LLP Professional Publishing出版, 2003年(ISBN 1-84311-210-8)

B214 Williamson, P.R. – Ship manoeuvring principles and pilotage. London, Witherby & Co. Ltd, 2001 (ISBN 1-85609-210-0)
B215 WITHERBY & CO. LTD – Condition evaluation and maintenance of tanker structures. London, Witherby & Co. Ltd, 1992 (ISBN 1-85609-039-6)
B216 WITHERBY SEAMANSHIP INTERNATIONAL – Chemical tankers: A pocket safety guide. London, Witherbys Publishing Ltd, 2006 (ISBN 1-85609-324-7)
B217 WITHERBY SEAMANSHIP INTERNATIONAL – LNG: Operational practice. London, Witherbys Publishing Ltd, 2006 (ISBN 1-85609-321-7)
B218 Witherby Seamanship International Ltd – Macneil's Seamanship Examiner MATES/ MASTERS Pocket Book, 2010 (ISBN 9781856094146)
B219 Witherby Seamanship International Ltd – Macneil's Seamanship Examiner COLREGS Pocket Book, 2010 (ISBN 9781 856094122)
B220 Witherby Seamanship International Ltd – Passage Planning Guide – English Channel and Dover Strait, 2010 (ISBN 1-9053-3194-0)
B221 Witherby Seamanship International Ltd – Passage Planning Guide – Malacca & Singapore Straits 2nd ed., 2010 (ISBN 1905331940)
B222 Witherby Seamanship International Ltd – Regulatory Primer for Mates & Masters Covering Current and New Regulations, 2010 (ISBN 9781856094207)
B223 World Meteorological Organization (WMO) – Handbook on marine meteorological services. Geneva, WMO, 1991
B224 World Meteorological Organization (WMO) – Manual on marine meteorological services. 2 Vols. Geneva, WMO, 1990
B225 Jeffery, R. (2007) *Leadership Throughout*. London: The Nautical Institute
B226 Bass, B.M. (1990) *Bass and Stodgill's Handbook of Leadership*. Third Edition. London: The Free Press
B227 Carnegie, Dale (1936 rev 1981) *How to Win Friends and Influence People*. Random House
B228 Drucker, P.F. (1968) *The Practice of Management. London*. William Heinemann
B229 Drucker, P.F. (2003) *The New Realities. New Brunswick,* NJ. Transaction Publishers
B230 Drucker, P.F. (2004) *The Daily Drucker: 365 Day of Insight and Motivation for Getting the Right Things Done*. Harper
B231 Goleman, D. (1996) *Emotional Intelligence: Why It Can Matter More Than IQ*. London, Bloomsbury
B232 Grint, K. (2005) *Leadership: Limits and Possibilities*. Basingstoke, Palgrave Macmillan
B233 Handy, C.B. (1993) *Understanding Organisations*. London, Penguin
B234 Hart, D. (1994) *Authentic Assessment: A Handbook for Educators*, Menlo Park, CA; Addison Wesley. Excerpted from *Classroom Teacher's Survival Guide*
B235 Jones, S. & Glosling, J. *Nelson's Way: Leadership Lessons from the Great Commander*. London; Nicholas Brealey
B236 Kotter, J. (1990) *A Force for Change: How Leadership Differs from Management*. New York, The Free Press
B237 Moon, J.A. (2002) *Reflection in Learning and Development*. London, Kogan Page
B238 Maritime & Coastguard Agency (MCA) UK (2010) *The Human Element: A Guide to the Human Behaviour in the Shipping Industry*. London, The Stationery Office
B239 Reason, J. (1990) *Human Error*. New York, Cambridge University Press
B240 Reason, J. (1997) *Managing the risks of organizational accidents*. Aldershot, Ashgate
B241 Senge, P.M. (1994) *The Fifth Discipline*. New York, Doubleday Business
B242 B18 Western, S. (2008) *Leadership: A Critical Test*. London, Sage
B243 Sidney Dekker (2007) *Just Culture: Balancing Safety and Accountability*. Aldershot, Ashgate

B214 Williamson, P.R. —船舶操纵原理与引航. 伦敦，Witherby & Co. Ltd. 出版, 2001年(ISBN 1-85609-210-0)

B215 Witherby & CO. LTD.出版—液货船结构状况评估与维护. 伦敦, Witherby & Co. Ltd.出版, 1992年(ISBN 1-85609-039-6)

B216 Witherby Seamanship International—化学品船：袖珍安全指南. 伦敦, Witherbys Publishing Ltd.出版, 2006年(ISBN 1-85609-324-7)

B217 Witherby Seamanship International—LNG: 操作实践. 伦敦, Witherbys Publishing Ltd. 出版, 2006年(ISBN 1-85609-321-7)

B218 Witherby Seamanship International Ltd —Macneil's航海技术考试船舶驾驶员/船长袖珍书, 2010年(ISBN 9781856094146)

B219 Witherby Seamanship International Ltd—Macneil's 航海技术考试避碰规则袖珍书, 2010年(ISBN 9781 856094122)

B220 Witherby Seamanship International Ltd—航线设计指南—英吉利海峡和多佛尔海峡, 2010年(ISBN 1-9053-3194-0)

B221 Witherby Seamanship International Ltd—航线设计指南—马六甲和新加坡海峡. 第2版, 2010年 (ISBN 1905331940)

B222 Witherby Seamanship International Ltd—驾驶员和船长现行新规则管理入门, 2010年(ISBN 9781856094207)

B223 世界气象组织 (WMO)—海洋气象服务手册. 日内瓦, WMO, 1991年

B224 世界气象组织 (WMO)—海洋气象服务手册第2卷. 日内瓦, WMO, 1990年

B225 Jeffery, R (2007). 无处不在的领导力. 伦敦, The Nautical Institute出版

B226 Bass, B.M. (1990). Bass and Stodgill's 领导力手册. 第3版. 伦敦: 自由出版社

B227 Carnegie, Dale (1936—1981). 如何赢得朋友和影响他人. 兰登书屋出版

B228 Drucker, P.F. (1968). 管理实践. 伦敦. William Heinemann出版

B229 Drucker, P.F. (2003). 新现实. New Brunswick, NJ. Transaction Publishers出版

B230 Drucker, P.F. (2004). Daily Drucker日报: 成功做事的领悟与动机之365天. Harper出版

B231 Goleman, D. (1996). 情商：它为什么比智商更重要. 伦敦, Bloomsbury出版

B232 Grint, K. (2005). 领导力：局限与可能. Basingstoke, Palgrave Macmillan出版

B233 Handy, C.B. (1993). 了解组织. 伦敦, Penguin出版

B234 Hart, D. (1994). 真实性评价：教师手册. Menlo Park, CA; Addison Wesley. 摘自课堂教师生存指南

B235 Jones, S. & Glosling, J. Nelson之路：来自伟大统帅的领导经验. London; Nicholas Brealey出版

B236 Kotter, J. (1990). 改变的力量：领导如何不同于管理. 纽约，自由出版社

B237 Moon, J. A. (2002). 在学习与进步中思考. London, Kogan Page出版

B238 英国海事和海岸警备局(MCA)英国(2010). 人为因素：航运业人类的行为指南.伦敦, The Stationery Office出版

B239 Reason, J. (1990). 人类错误.纽约，剑桥出版社

B240 Reason, J. (1997). 组织事故的风险管理.奥尔德肖特，Ashgate出版

B241 Senge, P. M. (1994). 第5大纪律.纽约，Doubleday Business出版

B242 B18 Western, S. (2008). 领导力：关键的考验.伦敦，Sage出版

B243 Sidney Dekker (2007). 只是文化：安全与责任的平衡. 奥尔德肖特, Ashgate出版

B244 Gunnar Fahlgren (2011) *Human Factors*. Bloomington, Author House
B245 Grech, Horberry, Koester (2008) *Human Factors in the Maritime Domain*. London, CRC Press
B246 Beaty, David (1995) *The Naked Pilot*. Shrewsbury, Airlife Publishing

B244　Gunnar Fahlgren (2011). 人为因素. 布卢明顿, Author House出版
B245　Grech, Horberry, Koester (2008). 海事领域的人为因素. London, CRC出版社
B246　Beaty, David (1995). 缺乏保护的引航员. 什鲁斯伯里, Airlife Publishing出版

Master and Chief Mate

Function 1: Navigation at the Management Level

船长和大副

功能1:
管理级航行

Master and Chief Mate

Function 1: Navigation at the Management Level

INDEX

Page

Part B1: **Course Outline** **70**
Timetable
Lectures
Course outline

Part C1: **Detailed Teaching Syllabus** **82**
Introduction
Explanation of information contained in the syllabus tables
1.1 Plan a voyage and conduct navigation
1.2 Determine position and the accuracy of resultant position fix by any means
1.3 Determine and allow for compass errors
1.4 Coordinate search and rescue
1.5 Establish watchkeeping arrangements and procedures
1.6 Maintain safe navigation through the use of information from navigation equipment and systems to assist command decision making
1.7 Maintain safe navigation through the use of ECDIS and associated navigation systems to assist command decision making
1.8 Forecast weather and oceanographic conditions
1.9 Respond to navigational emergencies
1.10 Manoeuvre and handle a ship in all conditions
1.11 General knowledge of remote controls of propulsion plant and engineering systems and services

Part D1: **Instructor Manual** **202**

船长和大副

功能1:管理级航行

索引

页码

B1部分: **课程概要** **71**
时间表
教学
课程概要

C1部分: **教学大纲细则** **83**
介绍
教学大纲细则里的信息说明
1.1 制订航次计划并引导航行
1.2 定位和确定通过任一定位方法获取的最终船位的精度
1.3 测定并修正罗经差
1.4 协调搜寻与救助行动
1.5 确定值班安排和程序
1.6 通过辅助决策的导航设备和系统的信息保持安全航行
1.7 通过辅助决策的ECDIS及相关的航行系统保持安全航行
1.8 预报天气和海洋水文状况
1.9 航行中的应急反应
1.10 在各种状况下操纵和操作船舶
1.11 推进装置和轮机系统的遥控操作与维护常识

D1部分: **教员手册** **203**

Part B1: Course Outline

■ Timetable

No formal example of a timetable is included in this model course.

Development of a detailed timetable depends on the level of skills of the officers entering the course and the amount of revision work of basic principles that may be required.

Lecturers must develop their own timetable depending on:

- the level of skills of trainees
- the numbers to be trained
- the number of instructors

and normal practices at the training establishment.

Preparation and planning constitute an important factor which makes a major contribution to the effective presentation of any course of instruction.

■ Lectures

As far as possible, lectures should be presented within a familiar context and should make use of practical examples. They should be well illustrated with diagrams, photographs and charts where appropriate, and be related to matter learned during seagoing time.

An effective manner of presentation is to develop a technique of giving information and then reinforcing it. For example, first tell the trainees briefly what you are going to present to them; then cover the topic in detail; and, finally, summarize what you have told them. The use of an overhead projector and the distribution of copies of the transparencies as trainees handouts contribute to the learning process.

■ Course outline

The tables that follow list the competencies and areas of knowledge, understanding and proficiency, together with the estimated total hours required for lectures and practical exercises. Teaching staff should note that timings are suggestions only and should be adapted to suit individual groups of trainees depending on their experience, ability, equipment and staff available for training.

B1部分:课程概要

■ 时间表

本示范课程中没有包含正式的示例课时表。

详细的时间表要根据学员技术等级和对基本原理的复习量来制定。

教员必须根据下面情况制定自己的课程表:

- 学员的技术水平
- 需培训的项目
- 教员数量

以及在培训地的常规实践操作。

教学前的准备及计划是任何课程教学中取得良好教学效果的重要因素。

■ 教学

教员应尽可能在熟悉的背景范围内讲解并结合实际例子。讲课中也应在适当的时候运用示意图、照片、图表等进行图示说明,并联系航海实践中遇到的一些实际问题进行讲解。

一个有效实施方式就是先进行授课,再加强提高。例如:先向学员概述授课内容;然后进行详解;最后进行总结。利用投影仪及向学员分发教学资料幻灯片拷贝等方式有助于其学习进程。

■ 课程概要

以下课程表中列出了对知识、理解与熟练程度及对适任能力的要求,列出了授课、实习的总时数。教员须注意此处的总时数为建议性的,要根据学员的经验、能力、设备及师资力量等不同情况进行调整。

Course outline

Knowledge, understanding and proficiency	Total hours for each topic	Total hours for each subject area of required performance
Competence:		
1.1 PLAN A VOYAGE AND CONDUCT NAVIGATION		
1.1.1 VOYAGE PLANNING AND NAVIGATION FOR ALL CONDITIONS	24	
.1 Voyage planning for all conditions by acceptable methods of plotting ocean tracks		
.2 Navigation and monitoring of the voyage	12	
.3 Logbooks and voyage records	2	38
1.1.2 ROUTEING IN ACCORDANCE WITH THE GENERAL PROVISIONS ON SHIP'S ROUTEING		
.1 Routeing	12	12
1.1.3 REPORTING IN ACCORDANCE WITH THE GENERAL PRINCIPLES FOR SHIP REPORTING SYSTEMS AND WITH VTS PROCEDURES		
.1 Ship reporting systems	1	1
1.2 DETERMINE POSITION AND THE ACCURACY OF RESULTANT POSITION FIX BY ANY MEANS		
1.2.1 POSITION DETERMINATION IN ALL CONDITIONS		
.1 Celestial navigation	10	
.2 Terrestrial observations, including the ability to use appropriate charts, notices to mariners and other publications to assess the accuracy of the resulting fix	16	
.3 Modern electronic navigational aids with specific knowledge of their operating principles, limitations, sources of error, detection of misrepresentation of information and methods of correction to obtain accurate position fixing	20	46
1.3 DETERMINE AND ALLOW FOR COMPASS ERRORS		
1.3.1 PRINCIPLES OF THE MAGNETIC COMPASS		
.1 Parts of the magnetic compass and their function	3	
.2 Errors of the magnetic compass and their correction	27	30
1.3.2 PRINCIPLES AND ERRORS OF GYROCOMPASSES		
.1 Principles of gyrocompasses	3	
.2 Gyrocompass errors and corrections	7	10
1.3.3 SYSTEMS UNDER THE CONTROL OF THE MASTER GYRO AND THE OPERATION AND CARE OF THE MAIN TYPES OF GYROCOMPASS		
.1 Systems under the control of the master gyro and the operation and care of the main types of gyrocompass	2	2

课程概要

知识、理解和熟练	每一标题的总学时	技能要求中每一科目的总学时
适任:		
1.1 制订航次计划并引导航行		
1.1.1 各种状况下的航次计划和航行		
.1 各种状况下利用可接受的标绘航迹方法进行航次计划和航行	24	
.2 航行及其监控	12	
.3 航海日志和航次记录	2	38
1.1.2 根据船舶定线制总则制定航线		
.1 制定航线	12	12
1.1.3 根据船舶报告系统总则和 VTS 程序报告		
.1 船舶报告系统	1	1
1.2 定位和确定通过任一定位方法获取的最终船位的精度		
1.2.1 确定各种状况下的定位		
.1 天文航海	10	
.2 陆标定位,包括使用适当的海图、航海通告和其他航海出版物评估定位精度的能力	16	
.3 现代电子导航设备的工作原理、局限性 、误差源、探测虚假信息和更正后得到准确定位的方法等专门知识	20	46
1.3 测定并修正罗经差		
1.3.1 磁罗经的原理		
.1 磁罗经各个部分及其功能	3	
.2 磁罗经的误差与修正	27	30
1.3.2 陀螺罗经的原理及其误差		
.1 陀螺罗经的原理	3	
.2 陀螺罗经的误差与修正	7	10
1.3.3 主陀螺罗经控制下的系统与主要类型的陀螺罗经的操作与维护		
.1 主陀螺罗经控制下的系统与主要类型的陀螺罗经的操作与维护	2	2

Knowledge, understanding and proficiency	Total hours for each topic	Total hours for each subject area of required performance
1.4 COORDINATE SEARCH AND RESCUE OPERATIONS		
See IMO model course 1.08 and STCW reg. I/12		
1.5 ESTABLISH WATCHKEEPING ARRANGEMENTS AND PROCEDURES		
1.5.1 INTERNATIONAL REGULATIONS FOR PREVENTING COLLISIONS AT SEA		
.1 Thorough knowledge of content, application and intent of the International Regulations for Preventing Collisions at Sea, 1972, as amended	30	30
1.5.2 PRINCIPLES TO BE OBSERVED IN KEEPING A NAVIGATIONAL WATCH		
.1 Thorough knowledge of the content, application and intent of the principles to be observed in keeping a navigational watch at a management level	12	12
1.5.3 BRIDGE WATCHKEEPING EQUIPMENT AND SYSTEMS		
.1 Knowledge of voyage data recorders (VDR) and bridge navigational watchkeeping alarm systems (BNWAS)	6	6
1.6 MAINTAIN SAFE NAVIGATION THROUGH THE USE OF INFORMATION FROM NAVIGATION EQUIPMENT AND SYSTEMS TO ASSIST COMMAND DECISION MAKING		
See IMO model courses 1.08, 1.22, 1.27, 1.34 and STCW reg. I/12		60
1.7 MAINTAIN SAFE NAVIGATION THROUGH THE USE OF ECDIS AND ASSOCIATED NAVIGATION SYSTEMS TO ASSIST COMMAND DECISION MAKING		
See IMO model courses 1.27 in association with 1.08 and 1.22		40
1.8 FORECAST WEATHER AND OCEANOGRAPHIC CONDITIONS		
1.8.1 SYNOPTIC CHARTS AND WEATHER FORECASTING		
.1 Synoptic and prognostic charts and forecasts from any source	6	
.2 Range of information available through fax transmission, internet and email	3	
.3 Weather forecasting	15	24
1.8.2 CHARACTERISTICS OF VARIOUS WEATHER SYSTEMS		
.1 Tropical revolving storms (TRS)	8	
.2 Main types of floating ice, their origins and movements	2	
.3 Guiding principles relating to the safety of navigation in the vicinity of ice	2	
.4 Conditions leading to ice accretion on ship's superstructures, dangers and remedies available	2	14

知识、理解和熟练	每一标题的总学时	技能要求中每一科目的总学时
1.4　协调搜寻与救助行动		
参见 IMO 示范课程 1.08 以及 STCW 公约 I/12 条。		
1.5　确定值班安排和程序		
1.5.1　国际海上避碰规则		
.1　理解 1972 年国际海上避碰规则及其修正案的内容、应用及意图	30	30
1.5.2　保持航行值班应遵循的原则		
.1　全面了解管理级航行值班应遵循原则的内容、运用和目的	12	12
1.5.3　驾驶台值班设备与系统		
.1　船舶数据记录仪(VDR)和驾驶台航行值班报警系统(BNWAS)的常识	6	6
1.6　通过辅助决策的导航设备和系统的信息保持安全航行		
参见 IMO 示范课程 1.08、1.27、1.34 以及 STCW 公约 I/12 条。		60
1.7　通过辅助决策的 ECDIS 及相关的航行系统保持安全航行		
参见 IMO 示范课程 1.27 及 1.08、1.22 相关部分。		
1.8　预报天气和海洋水文状况		40
1.8.1　气象图与天气预报		
.1　气象图与预报图以及任何来源的预报	6	
.2　通过传真、互联网和电子邮件发送的可用信息的范围	3	
.3　天气预报	15	24
1.8.2　各种天气系统的特点		
.1　热带气旋风暴(TRS)	8	
.2　浮冰的主要类型、来源及其运动	2	
.3　在冰区附近航行安全的指导性原则	2	
.4　导致船舶上层建筑积冰的条件、危险性和可用的补救措施	2	14

Knowledge, understanding and proficiency	Total hours for each topic	Total hours for each subject area of required performance
1.8.3 OCEAN CURRENT SYSTEMS		
.1 Surface water circulation of the ocean and principal adjoining seas	3	
.2 Principle of voyage planning with respect to weather conditions and wave height	2	
.3 Formation of sea waves and swell waves	2	7
1.8.4 CALCULATION OF TIDAL CONDITIONS		
.1 Ability to calculate tidal conditions	6	6
1.8.5 APPROPRIATE NAUTICAL PUBLICATIONS ON TIDES AND CURRENTS		
.1 Nautical publications on tides and currents and information which can be obtained via internet and email	3	3
1.9 RESPOND TO NAVIGATIONAL EMERGENCIES		
1.9.1 PRECAUTIONS WHEN BEACHING A SHIP		
.1 Precautions when beaching a ship	2	2
1.9.2 ACTION TO BE TAKEN IF GROUNDING IS IMMINENT AND AFTER GROUNDING		
.1 Action to be taken if grounding is imminent and after grounding	2	2
1.9.3 REFLOATING A GROUNDED SHIP WITH AND WITHOUT ASSISTANCE		
.1 Refloating a grounded ship with and without assistance	1	1
1.9.4 ACTION TO BE TAKEN IF COLLISION IS IMMINENT AND FOLLOWING A COLLISION OR IMPAIRMENT OF THE WATERTIGHT INTEGRITY OF THE HULL BY ANY CAUSE		
.1 Action to be taken if collision is imminent and following a collision or impairment of the watertight integrity of the hull by any cause	2	2
1.9.5 ASSESSMENT OF DAMAGE CONTROL		
.1 Assessment of damage control	1	1
1.9.6 EMERGENCY STEERING		
.1 Emergency steering	2	2
1.9.7 EMERGENCY TOWING ARRANGEMENTS AND TOWING PROCEDURES		
.1 Emergency towing arrangements and towing procedures	2	2

知识、理解和熟练	每一标题的总学时	技能要求中每一科目的总学时
1.8.3 洋流系统		
.1 海洋表面的水循环以及主要的邻接水域	3	
.2 与天气条件和浪高相关的航次计划原理	2	
.3 海浪与涌浪的形成	2	7
1.8.4 潮汐计算		
.1 计算潮汐状况的能力	6	6
1.8.5 有关潮汐和潮流的航海出版物		
.1 有关潮汐和潮流的航海出版物以及通过互联网和电子邮件获取的信息	3	3
1.9 航行中的应急反应		
1.9.1 船舶抢滩的预防措施		
.1 船舶抢滩的预防措施	2	2
1.9.2 即将搁浅与搁浅后所采取的行动		
.1 即将搁浅与搁浅后所采取的行动	2	2
1.9.3 在有援助和无援助下搁浅船舶的脱浅		
.1 在有援助和无援助下搁浅船舶的脱浅	1	1
1.9.4 即将碰撞、碰撞后或任何原因造成船体水密性的破坏所要采取的行动		
.1 即将碰撞、碰撞后或任何原因造成船体水密性的破坏所要采取的行动	2	2
1.9.5 破损控制的评估		
.1 破损控制的评估	1	1
1.9.6 应急操舵		
.1 应急操舵	2	2
1.9.7 应急拖带部署与拖带程序		
.1 应急拖带部署与拖带程序	2	2

Knowledge, understanding and proficiency	Total hours for each topic	Total hours for each subject area of required performance
1.10 MANOEUVRE AND HANDLE A SHIP IN ALL CONDITIONS (Also refer to IMO model course 1.22, Ship simulator and bridge teamwork and STCW reg. I/12)		
1.10.1 MANOEUVRING AND HANDLING A SHIP IN ALL CONDITIONS		
.1 Approaching pilot stations and embarking or disembarking pilots, with due regard to weather, tide, head reach and stopping distances	4	
.2 Handling ship in rivers, estuaries and restricted waters, having regard to the effects of current, wind and restricted water on helm response	10	
.3 Application of constant rate of turn techniques	3	
.4 Manoeuvring in shallow water including the reduction in under-keel clearance caused by squat, rolling and pitching	2	
.5 Interaction between passing ships and between own ship and nearby banks (canal effect)	2	
.6 Berthing and unberthing under various conditions of wind, tide and current with and without tugs	20	
.7 Ship and tug interaction	3	
.8 Use of propulsion and manoeuvring systems including different types of rudder	4	
.9 Types of anchor; choice of anchorage; anchoring with one or two anchors in limited anchorages and factors involved in determining the length of anchor cable to be used	6	
.10 Procedures for anchoring in deep water and in shallow water	1	
.11 Dragging anchor; clearing fouled anchors	1	
.12 Dry-docking, both with and without damage	4	
.13 Management and handling ships in heavy weather including assisting a ship or aircraft in distress; towing operations; means of keeping an unmanageable ship out of a sea trough, lessening lee drift and use of oil	6	
.14 Precautions in manoeuvring to launch rescue boats and survival craft in bad weather	2	
.15 Methods of taking on board survivors from rescue boats and survival craft	1	
.16 Ability to determine the manoeuvring and propulsion characteristics of common types of ships, with special reference to stopping distances and turning circles at various draughts and speeds	3	
.17 Importance of navigating at reduced speed to avoid damage caused due to own ship's bow and stern waves	1	
.18 Practical measures to be taken when navigating in or near ice or in conditions of ice accumulation on board	4	
.19 Use of, and manoeuvring in and near traffic separation schemes and in vessel traffic service (VTS) areas	4	81

知识、理解和熟练	**每一标题的总学时**	**技能要求中每一科目的总学时**
1.10　在各种状况下操纵和操作船舶		
(还应参见IMO示范课程1.22船舶模拟器和驾驶台团队及STCW公约I/12条)		
1.10.1 在各种状况下操纵和操作船舶		
.1 考虑天气、潮汐、冲程、停船距离后接近引航船、上下引航员	4	
.2 考虑流、风、受限水域对舵效的影响下，在河流、河口和受限水域里的船舶操纵	10	
.3 恒定旋转率的应用技巧	3	
.4 船体下沉、横倾和纵倾引起富余水深减少时的浅水操纵	2	
.5 船舶间、船岸间的相互作用(运河效应)	2	
.6 在各种风、潮汐和海流时有拖船和无拖船情况下的靠泊与离泊	20	
.7 船舶与拖船的相互作用	3	
.8 推进系统和包括各种类型舵的操纵系统的使用	4	
.9 锚的种类;锚地的选择;在受限锚地单锚泊或双锚泊以及决定出链长度时所考虑的因素	6	
.10 深水区锚泊和浅水区锚泊程序	1	
.11 走锚与锚绞缠时的清理	1	
.12 有损伤、无损伤入干船坞	4	
.13 在恶劣天气下管理与操纵船舶,包括救援遇险船舶、飞机,拖带作业,使失控船舶脱离海上低压槽的方法,减少下风漂移和油的使用	6	
.14 恶劣天气下施放救生艇筏应采取的预防措施	2	
.15 将遇险者从救生艇筏救上船舶的方法	1	
.16 确定常见船舶操纵和推进的特性的能力,特别应考虑不同吃水和速度下的冲程和旋回圈	3	
.17 为避免本船首尾船行波造成浪损而减速航行的重要性	1	
.18 在冰区内或附近以及积冰情况下的实用应对措施	4	
.19 在分道通航制与船舶交管服务(VTS)中或其附近的操纵	4	81

Knowledge, understanding and proficiency	Total hours for each topic	Total hours for each subject area of required performance
1.11 GENERAL KNOWLEDGE OF REMOTE CONTROLS OF PROPULSION PLANT AND ENGINEERING SYSTEMS AND SERVICES		
1.11.1 OPERATING PRINCIPLES OF MARINE POWER PLANTS	25	25
1.11.2 SHIPS' AUXILIARY MACHINERY	25	25
1.11.3 GENERAL KNOWLEDGE OF MARINE ENGINEERING SYSTEMS		
.1 Marine engineering terms and fuel consumption	4	
.2 Arrangements necessary for appropriate and effective engineering watches to be maintained for the purpose of safety under normal circumstances and UMS operations	2	
.3 Arrangements necessary to ensure a safe engineering watch is maintained when carrying dangerous cargo	2	8
Total for Function 1: Navigation at the Management Level		**451 hours**

Teaching staff and Administrations should note that the hours for lectures and exercises are suggestions only as regards sequence and length of time allocated to each objective. These factors may be adapted by lecturers to suit individual groups of trainees depending on their experience, ability, equipment and staff available for teaching.

知识、理解和熟练	每一标题的总学时	技能要求中每一科目的总学时
1.11　推进装置和轮机系统的遥控操作与维护常识		
1.11.1　船舶动力装置的操作原理	25	25
1.11.2　船舶辅机	25	25
1.11.3　船舶轮机系统常识		
.1　船舶轮机术语与燃油消耗	4	
.2　为保证正常情况和机舱无人值班情况下的安全,适当而有效的轮机值班所必需的安排	2	
.3　当运载危险货物时为保证机舱值班安全所必需的安排	2	8
功能 1 总计学时:管理级航行		**451 学时**

教员和主管机关应注意到课程概要中各学习任务的先后次序和时间安排仅仅是建议,可根据各班组学员的经验、能力、设备和师资配备等实际情况进行适当的调整。

Part C1: Detailed Teaching Syllabus

■ Introduction

The detailed teaching syllabus is presented as a series of learning objectives. The objective, therefore, describes what the trainee must do to demonstrate that the specified knowledge or skill has been transferred.

Thus each training outcome is supported by a number of related performance elements in which the trainee is required to be proficient. The teaching syllabus shows the Required performance expected of the trainee in the tables that follow.

In order to assist the instructor, references are shown to indicate IMO references and publications, textbooks and teaching aids that instructors may wish to use in preparing and presenting their lessons.

The material listed in the course framework has been used to structure the detailed teaching syllabus; in particular,

- Teaching aids (indicated by A)
- IMO references (indicated by R)
- Textbooks (indicated by T) and
- Bibliography (indicated by B)

will provide valuable information to instructors.

■ Explanation of information contained in the syllabus tables

The information on each table is systematically organized in the following way. The line at the head of the table describes the FUNCTION with which the training is concerned. A function means a group of tasks, duties and responsibilities as specified in the STCW Code. It describes related activities which make up a professional discipline or traditional departmental responsibility on board.*

In this model course there are three functions:

- Navigation at the Management Level
- Cargo Handling and Stowage at the Management Level
- C ontrolling the Operation of the Ship and Care for Persons on Board at the Management Level

The header of the first column denotes the **COMPETENCE** concerned. Each function comprises a number of competences. For example, Function 1, Navigation at the Management Level, comprises a total of eleven COMPETENCES. Each competence is uniquely and consistently numbered in this model course.

* Morrison, W.S.G. Competent crews = safer ships. Malmo, WMU Press, 1997 (ISBN 91-973372-0-X)

C1部分:教学大纲细则

■ 介绍

教学大纲细则是以一系列的学习目标的形式呈现的。因此,目标描述的是学员必须做什么以表明专业知识或技能已经得到传授。

因此每一个培训效果都包括学员需要熟练的诸多任务要求。教学大纲在下表中列出期待学员达到的程度的内容。

为了有助于教员,列出教员希望在备课和讲课中使用的IMO参考书目、出版物、教科书和辅助教学设备。

课程框架里列出的材料用于构成教学大纲细则,特别是,

- 教具(以A开头)
- IMO参考书目(以R开头)
- 教科书(以T开头)
- 参考文献(以B开头)

将为教员提供有价值的信息。

■ 教学大纲细则里的信息说明

每一个课程表的信息用以下的方法系统地进行组织。表头的一行描述了与培训有关的功能。“功能”指的是STCW公约里规定的一组的任务、职责以及责任,描述了一些与构成船上的专业准则或传统的部门责任相关的活动*。

本示范课程中有3个功能:

- 管理级航行
- 管理级货物装卸与积载
- 管理级船舶作业管理和人员管理

第一列的标题表示相关的适任能力。每个功能含有许多个适任能力。例如,功能1管理级航行,含有11个适任能力。每个适任能力在本示范课程中是唯一的并有永久的编号。

* 莫里森, W.S.G. 适任海员 = 安全船舶. 马尔默, 世界海事大学出版社, 1997(ISBN 91-973372-0-X)

The first is **Plan a Voyage and Conduct Navigation**. It is numbered 1.1, that is the first competence in Function 1. The term competence should be understood as the application of knowledge, understanding, proficiency, skills, experience for an individual to perform a task, duty or responsibility on board in a safe, efficient and timely manner.

Shown next is the required TRAINING OUTCOME. The training outcomes are the areas of knowledge, understanding and proficiency in which the trainee must be able to demonstrate knowledge and understanding. Each COMPETENCE comprises a number of training outcomes. For example, the competence **Plan a Voyage and Conduct Navigation** comprises a total of seven training outcomes. The first is in VOYAGE PLANNING AND NAVIGATION FOR ALL CONDITIONS. Each training outcome is uniquely and consistently numbered in this model course. That concerned with Voyage Planning and Navigation for all Conditions is uniquely numbered 1.1.1. For clarity, training outcomes are printed in black on grey, for example TRAINING OUTCOME.

Finally, each training outcome embodies a variable number of required performances – as evidence of competence. The instruction, training and learning should lead to the trainee meeting the specified required performance. For the training outcome Voyage Planning and Navigation for all Conditions, there are two areas of performance. These are:

1.1.1.1 Logbooks

1.1.1.2 Navigation Planning for all Conditions

Following each numbered area of required performance there is a list of activities that the trainee should complete and which collectively specify the standard of competence that the trainee must meet. These are for the guidance of teachers and instructors in designing lessons, lectures, tests and exercises for use in the teaching process. For example, under the topic 1.1.1.2 Navigation Planning for all Conditions, to meet the Required performance, the trainee should be able to:

- plan navigation in restricted waters by day, using terrestrial observations...
- plan navigation in restricted waters by night...
- plan navigation in restricted visibility...

and so on.

IMO references (Rx) are listed in the column to the right hand side. Teaching aids (Ax), videos and CBTs (Vx), textbooks (Tx) and bibliography (Bx) relevant to the training outcome and required performances are placed immediately following the TRAINING OUTCOME title.

It is not intended that lessons are organized to follow the sequence of required performances listed in the Tables. The Syllabus Tables are organized to match with the competence in the STCW Code, table A-II/2. Lessons and teaching should follow college practices. It is not necessary, for example, for celestial navigation to be studied before tides. What is necessary is that all the material is covered and that teaching is effective to allow trainees to meet the standard of the required performance.

首先是“制订航次计划并引导航行”。编号为1.1,是功能1的第一个适任能力。术语“适任能力”应被理解为船上个人以安全、有效和及时的方式为完成任务、职责或责任而对知识、理解、熟练、技能、经验的应用。

紧接着是所要求的“培训效果”。培训效果是学员必须能够表现其对所学知识的熟悉、理解和熟练程度。每个适任能力含有多个培训效果。例如,“制订航次计划并引导航行”的适任能力含有7个培训效果。首先是各种状况下的航次计划和航行。每个培训效果在本示范课程中是唯一的并有永久的编号。有关的“各种状况下的航次计划和航行”的编号为1.1.1。为清楚起见,培训效果用灰底黑字印刷,例如,**培训效果**。

最后,每个培训效果表现为多个不一样的所要求的内容——作为适任能力的证明。教学、训练和学习应使学员完成具体规定的内容。“各种状况下的航次计划和航行”的培训结果含有两方面的标准。它们为:

1.1.1.1　航海日志

1.1.1.2　各种状况下的航行计划

不同的技能要求后有一个学员必须完成的活动清单,它集中详细列明学员必须满足的适任能力标准。这是教师和教员在教学过程中设计课程内容、讲稿、测试及练习所依据的指南。例如,在“1.1.1.2各种状况下的航行计划”主题中,为满足所要求的内容,学员应能够:

- 白天利用陆标定位,在受限水域内计划航行……
- 夜晚在受限水域内计划航行……
- 在能见度受限时计划航行……

等等。

IMO参考书目(Rx)排在列的右边。与培训效果及所要求的内容相关的教具(Ax)、录像(Vx)、教科书(Tx)及参考文献(Bx)紧接在培训效果标题之后。

在表中把课程安排在所要求的内容之后不是故意的。大纲课程表的安排是与STCW公约里的表A-II/2的适任能力相匹配的。教与学应遵循院校的做法。例如,没有必要在学习潮汐前学习天文航海。有必要的是拥有所有的资料和有效的教学以使学员满足技能要求的标准。

<table>
<tr><td>COMPETENCE 1.1</td><td>Plan a Voyage and Conduct Navigation</td><td>IMO Reference</td></tr>
<tr><td colspan="2">TRAINING OUTCOMES:

Demonstrate a knowledge and understanding of:
1.1.1 VOYAGE PLANNING AND NAVIGATION FOR ALL CONDITIONS
1.1.2 ROUTEING IN ACCORDANCE WITH THE GENERAL PROVISIONS ON SHIP'S ROUTEING
1.1.3 REPORTING IN ACCORDANCE WITH THE GENERAL PRINCIPLES FOR SHIP REPORTING SYSTEMS</td><td>STCW Code table A-II/2</td></tr>
</table>

<table>
<tr><td>适任 1.1</td><td>制订航次计划并引导航行</td><td>IMO
参考书目</td></tr>
<tr><td colspan="2">培训效果:

讲授下列内容知识与理解:
1.1.1　各种状况下的航次计划和航行
1.1.2　根据船舶定线制总则制定航线
1.1.3　根据船舶报告系统总则报告</td><td>STCW 公约
表 A-II/2</td></tr>
</table>

COMPETENCE 1.1	Plan a Voyage and Conduct Navigation	IMO Reference
1.1.1 VOYAGE PLANNING AND NAVIGATION FOR ALL CONDITIONS **Textbooks/Bibliography:** T2, T12, T38, T39, B7, B8, B12, B26, B36, B51, B57, B58, B60, B68, B69, B70, B86, B87, B105, B108, B119, B127, B134, B136, B138, B139, B140, B141, B142, B172, B173, B177, B194, B202, B209, B212, B220, B221 **Teaching aids:** A1, A2, A3, A8, A10, A13, A14, A15, A16, A17, A18, A19, A20, A21, A22, A23, A24, A25, A26, A27, V20, V21, V22, V23, V34, V40, V41, V125 Required performance:		
1.1 Voyage planning for all conditions (24 hours) *Note that trainees must be familiar with the passage planning, position monitoring, chartwork, sailings using plane, Mercator and great circle sailing methods, tidal, meteorology and oceanography content of IMO model course 7.03 before completing these performance requirements. This knowledge is considered so fundamental for much of the management level content within this course that there is merit in reviewing the operational level content quickly before covering the additional elements required at management level. The learning time has been reduced for many elements on the basis that trainees will be reviewing rather than learning much of this content at this level. It may be necessary for some trainees to refresh their knowledge of such techniques before undertaking this management level content* – determines key parameters for the voyage to be planned and briefs officers appropriately – fully appraises all information that may be relevant to the voyage, including information from: – Routeing and pilot charts – Ocean Passages for the World – Sailing Directions – Charts – IMO Routeing Guide – Lists of Lights – Lists of Radio Signals – Tidal and Tidal Stream Information – Load line, insurance and charter party parameters – Port Information – Notices to Mariners – Navigation Warnings – Meteorological information – Vessel condition, draught, trim and handling characteristics – plans voyages from berth to berth using appropriate strategies and contingency plans in order to deal with various factors, such as: – encountering restricted visibility – expected meteorological conditions – navigational hazards and no go areas – making landfall – accuracy of position fixing required in critical areas – encountering or navigating in ice		R1, R3, R32, R33, R34, R48, R49

<table>
<tr><td>适任 1.1</td><td>制订航次计划并引导航行</td><td>IMO
参考书目</td></tr>
<tr><td colspan="2">
1.1.1 各种状况下的航次计划和航行
教科书/参考文献:T2, T12, T38, T39, B7, B8, B12, B26, B36, B51, B57, B58, B60, B68, B69, B70, B86, B87, B105, B108, B119, B127, B134, B136, B138, B139, B140, B141, B142, B172, B173, B177, B194, B202, B209, B212, B220, B221
教具:A1, A2, A3, A8, A10, A13, A14, A15, A16, A17, A18, A19, A20, A21, A22, A23, A24, A25, A26, A27, V20, V21, V22, V23, V34, V40, V41, V125
技能要求:
1.1 各种状况下的航行计划(24 学时)
注意:在完成这些要求的内容之前,学员必须熟悉 IMO 示范课程 7.03 中的航线设计,船位监控,海图作业,航用海图、墨卡托和大圆航法,潮汐,气象和海洋学的内容。本课程中的知识对多数管理级内容非常重要, 以至于在涉及管理级额外要求的知识点之前,在迅速复习操作级内容方面颇具价值。基于学员将复习而不是学习该级别内容,已经减少了许多知识点的学时。对某些学员而言,在学习管理级内容之前,可能有必要更新这些技能的知识
– 决定航次计划中的重要参数并向船员简要介绍
– 充分评估包括信息表在内的所有可能相关的航次信息:
  – 航线设计和导航图
  – 世界大洋航路
  – 航路指南
  – 海图
  – IMO 航路指南
  – 灯标表
  – 无线电信号表
  – 潮汐和潮流信息
  – 载重线、保险和租船参数
  – 港口信息
  – 航海通告
  – 航行警告
  – 气象信息
  – 船舶状况、吃水、纵倾和操纵性能
– 使用适当的策略制订从泊位到泊位的航次计划和应急计划,以应对以下各种因素:
  – 遭遇能见度受限
  – 预期的气象条件
  – 航行中的危险和禁航区
  – 登陆
  – 在关键区域要求的定位精度
  – 遭遇海冰或冰区航行
</td><td>R1, R3, R32, R33, R34, R48, R49</td></tr>
</table>

COMPETENCE 1.1	Plan a Voyage and Conduct Navigation	IMO Reference

- areas of restricted/confined/pilotage waters
- traffic separation schemes en route
- expected traffic density
- operational requirements in terms of passage time and fuel consumption
- areas of extensive tidal effects
- ensuring adequate fuel, water and provisions
- ensuring the safety of the personnel, property and the environment
- ship reporting requirements in vessel traffic service (VTS) and other reporting areas
- vessel condition, draught, trim and handling characteristics

- ensures that charts, course cards and other voyage planning documentation, i.e. navigation notebooks etc. accurately detail the plan and are prepared in accordance with industry practice including ECDIS where appropriate
- ensures that positions, distances and ETAs or average speed required calculations completed using mercator sailing, great circle sailing, composite great circle sailing and limited latitude sailing are accurate
- ensures that there is adequate fuel, water and provisions on board for the voyage
- ensures that all watchkeeping officers are fully briefed and familiar with the voyage plan
- ensures that watchkeeping officers understand the circumstances in which they may deviate from the initial plan and the requirement to update the plan where this occurs

1.2 Navigation and monitoring of the voyage (12 hours)

- plans and establishes parameters and guidance to watchkeeping officers to ensure that the navigation and monitoring of the voyage is appropriate for the area being navigated, with particular regard to navigation in areas of:
  - restricted waters
  - meteorological conditions
  - ice
  - restricted visibility
  - traffic separation schemes
  - vessel traffic service (VTS) areas
  - areas of extensive tidal effects
- ensures that the vessel's position is monitored using two or more independent position determination systems appropriate to the area
- ensures that the vessel's position is determined at appropriate intervals and monitored continuously
- ensures that the execution of the voyage plan is monitored and that any required alterations are appraised, evaluated and approved where these are outside the authority of the watchkeeping officer

1.3 Logbooks and voyage records (2 hours) R1

- ensures that proper log and voyage records are maintained in accordance with maritime shipping acts and other laws and regulations

适任 1.1	制订航次计划并引导航行	IMO 参考书目
– 限制/受限/引航水域 – 定线制航路 – 预期的船舶交通流密度 – 航行时间和燃料消耗方面的操作要求 – 受潮汐影响的大片水域 – 确保足够的燃料、淡水和食品 – 确保人员、财产和环境安全 – 在船舶交管服务(VTS)和其他报告水域的船舶报告要求 – 船舶状况、吃水、纵倾和操纵性能 – 确保海图、航向表和其他航次计划文件,如航行记录簿等,准确详述该计划并按行业惯例予以备妥,包括 ECDIS 如果适用的话 – 确保利用墨卡托航法、大圆航法、混合航法和限制纬度航法按要求完成的位置、距离和 ETA 或平均速度的计算准确无误 – 确保在开航前船上有足够的燃料、淡水和食品 – 确保向所有值班驾驶员简要介绍并使之熟悉航次计划 – 确保值班驾驶员知晓可能偏离初始航线的情况以及在此情况下更新航次计划的要求		
1.2 航行及其监控(12 学时) – 给值班驾驶员计划并设置限制因素和指南,以确保在当前水域航行及其监控,特别在下列相关水域: – 限制水域 – 气象条件恶劣 – 冰区 – 能见度受限 – 分道通航制 – 船舶交管服务(VTS)水域 – 潮汐影响较大的水域 – 确保船位是由两个或多个适合于该水域的相互独立的定位系统所监控 – 确保以合适的间隔连续定位与监控 – 确保航次计划的执行处在监控之下,超出值班驾驶员职权之外的所要求的任何改变都应得到评价、评估和经过批准		
1.3 航海日志和航次记录(2 学时) – 确保根据航运法及其他的法律和规则妥善保管航海日志与航次记录		R1

<table>
<tr><th>COMPETENCE 1.1</th><th>Plan a Voyage and Conduct Navigation</th><th>IMO Reference</th></tr>
<tr><td colspan="2">1.1.2 ROUTEING IN ACCORDANCE WITH GENERAL PROVISIONS ON SHIP'S ROUTEING
Textbooks/Bibliography: T2, T3, B8, B57, B68, B177
Teaching aids: A1, A3, A11, A12, A13, A23, A24, V1
Required performance:
2.1 Routeing (12 hours)
– selects ocean and coastal routes that appropriately consider:
– mandatory or recommended requirements including the IMO Routeing Guide
– distance
– average passage speed and fuel consumption
– availability of position monitoring
– safety of life, property and the environment
– selects appropriate routes using:
– weather routeing information received from shore-based providers
– weather routeing techniques using synoptic and prognosis information observed and received from ashore
1.1.3 REPORTING IN ACCORDANCE WITH THE GENERAL PRINCIPLES FOR SHIP REPORTING SYSTEMS AND WITH VTS PROCEDURES
Textbooks/Bibliography: T2
Teaching aids: A1, A3, A25, V27
Required performance:
3.1 Ship reporting systems (1 hour)
– explains the general principles for various ship reporting systems
– explains the general principles for reporting as per VTS procedures
– determines the reporting requirements for particular reporting and VTS systems
– explains the use of AIS within reporting systems
– makes reports in accordance with published procedures and criteria</td><td>R2, R3, R48, R49, R50

R1
R2 reg. V/8-1
R3, R14</td></tr>
</table>

适任 1.1	制订航次计划并引导航行	IMO 参考书目
1.1.2　根据船舶定线制总则制定航线 **教科书/参考文献:**T2, T3, B8, B57, B68, B177 **教具:**A1, A3, A11, A12, A13, A23, A24, V1 技能要求: **2.1　制定航线(12 学时)** – 选择大洋航路和沿海航路应适当考虑: – 包括 IMO 定线规则在内的强制性或建议的要求 – 距离 – 平均通过速度和燃料消耗 – 定位监控的可靠性 – 人命、财产、环境的安全 – 选择适当的航路可使用: – 从岸上的信息提供者处获得的气象定线信息 – 根据观察到的或从岸上收到的气象信息、预报信息进行定线的技能		R2, R3, R48, R49, R50
1.1.3　根据船舶报告系统总则和 VTS 程序报告 **教科书/参考文献:**T2 **教具:**A1, A3, A25, V27 技能要求: **3.1　船舶报告系统(1 学时)** – 解释各种船舶报告系统总则 – 按照 VTS 程序解释船舶报告系统的总则 – 确定特别报告和 VTS 系统的报告要求 – 解释在报告系统中 AIS 的使用 – 根据出版的指南和标准制定报告		R1 R2 规则 V/8-1 R13,R14

<table>
<tr><td>COMPETENCE 1.2</td><td>Determine Position and the Accuracy of Resultant Position Fix by any Means</td><td>IMO Reference</td></tr>
<tr><td colspan="2">TRAINING OUTCOME:

Demonstrates a knowledge and understanding of:
1.2.1 POSITION DETERMINATION IN ALL CONDITIONS</td><td>STCW Code table A-II/2</td></tr>
</table>

适任 1.2	定位和确定通过任一定位方法获取的最终船位的精度	IMO 参考书目
培训效果: 讲授下列内容知识与理解: 1.2.1　确定各种状况下的船位		STCW 公约表 A-II/2

<table>
<tr><th>COMPETENCE 1.2</th><th>Determine Position and the Accuracy of Resultant Position Fix by any Means</th><th>IMO Reference</th></tr>
<tr><td colspan="2">1.2.1 POSITION DETERMINATION IN ALL CONDITIONS
Textbooks/Bibliography: T1, T2, T6, T7, T29, T38, T39, B7, B8, B12, B26, B27, B42, B50, B51, B57, B58, B119, B139, B140, B141, B150, B151, B172, B173, B195, B202
Teaching aids: A1, A2, A4, A5, A6, A7, A8, A9, A10, A16, A17, A18, A26, A28, A30, A32, A33, A34, A35, A36, A37, A38, A39, A40, V26, V40, V41, V42, V139, V150, V151
Required performance:</td><td></td></tr>
<tr><td colspan="2">1.1 Celestial navigation (10 hours)
Note that trainees must be familiar with the celestial techniques covered in IMO model course 7.03 before completing these performance requirements. This knowledge is considered so fundamental for much of the management level content within this course that there is merit in reviewing the operational level content quickly before covering the additional elements required at management level. The learning time has been reduced for many elements on the basis that trainees will be reviewing rather than learning much of this content at this level. It may be necessary for some trainees to refresh their knowledge of such techniques before undertaking this management level content
– determines parameters for position monitoring on ocean passages using celestial observations of the sun and stars uses appropriate techniques, frequency and is completed accurately
– verifies that celestial techniques are correctly applied by watchkeeping officers
– provides guidance and support to cadets and watchkeeping officers in the correct application of celestial techniques
– assesses the accuracy of position monitoring using celestial techniques</td><td>R1</td></tr>
<tr><td colspan="2">1.2 Terrestrial observations, including the ability to use appropriate charts, notices to mariners and other publications to assess the accuracy of the resulting fix (16 hours)
Note that trainees must be familiar with the terrestrial position determination techniques covered in IMO model course 7.03 before completing these performance requirements. This knowledge is considered so fundamental for much of the management level content within this course that there is merit in reviewing the operational level content quickly before covering the additional elements required at management level. The learning time has been reduced for many elements on the basis that trainees will be reviewing rather than learning much of this content at this level. It may be necessary for some trainees to refresh their knowledge of such techniques before undertaking this management level content
– selects and applies the most appropriate techniques for position monitoring using terrestrial observations in any area being navigated
– verifies that the position is determined at appropriate frequencies and monitored continuously using terrestrial observations and techniques where these are possible
– provides guidance and support to cadets and watchkeeping officers in the correct application of terrestrial position fixing techniques
– assesses the accuracy of position monitoring using terrestrial techniques, particularly considering:
  – the limitations and errors of the technique used
  – information from charts, notices to mariners and other publications
– ensures charts and publications are up to date</td><td>R1</td></tr>
</table>

适任 1.2	定位和确定通过任一定位方法获取的最终船位的精度	IMO 参考书目
1.2.1 确定各种状况下的定位 **教科书/参考文献**:T1, T2, T6, T7, T29, T38, T39, B7, B8, B12, B26, B27, B42, B50, B51, B57, B58, B119, B139, B140, B141, B150, B151, B172, B173, B195, B202 **教具**:A1, A2, A4, A5, A6, A7, A8, A9, A10, A16, A17, A18, A26, A28, A30, A32, A33, A34, A35, A36, A37, A38, A39, A40, V26, V40, V41, V42, V139, V150, V151 技能要求:		
1.1 天文航海(10 学时) 注意:在完成这些要求的内容之前,学员必须熟悉 IMO 示范课程 7.03 中的天文学的技能。本课程中的知识对多数管理级内容非常重要,以至于在涉及管理级额外要求的知识点之前,在迅速复习操作级内容方面颇具价值。基于学员将复习而不是学习该级别内容,已经减少了许多知识点的学时。对某些学员而言,在学习管理级内容之前,可能有必要更新这些技能的知识 – 通过适当的技术、频率准确地对太阳和星星进行天文测量以确定大洋航行时的船位监控参数 – 核查值班驾驶员正确运用天文技能 – 在正确运用天文技能方面给实习生和值班驾驶员提供指导和支持 – 评估利用天文技能监控船位的精度		R1

1.2 陆标定位,包括使用适当的海图、航海通告和其他航海出版物评估定位精度的能力(16 学时)
注意:在完成这些要求的内容之前,学员必须熟悉 IMO 示范课程 7.03 中的陆标定位技能。本课程中的知识对多数管理级内容非常重要,以至于在涉及管理级额外要求的知识点之前,在迅速复习操作级内容方面颇具价值。基于学员将复习而不是学习该级别内容,已经减少了许多知识点的学时。对某些学员而言,在学习管理级内容之前,可能有必要更新这些技能的知识
– 在任何航行水域利用陆标定位选择并运用最适合的技巧来监控船位
– 可能时,利用陆标定位技术以适当频率核实定位和连续监控船位
– 在正确运用陆标定位技能方面给实习生和值班驾驶员提供指导和支持
– 评估利用地文技巧监控船位的精度,特别考虑:
  – 所用技巧的局限性和误差
  – 海图、航海通告和其他出版物信息
– 确保图表和出版物都是最新的
		R1

COMPETENCE 1.2	Determine Position and the Accuracy of Resultant Position Fix by any Means	IMO Reference
1.3 Modern electronic navigational aids with specific knowledge of their operating principles, limitations, sources of error, detection of misrepresentation of information and methods of correction to obtain accurate position fixing (20 hours) *Note that trainees must be familiar with the principles, operation, limitations and errors of the electronic navigation aids covered in IMO model course 7.03 before completing these performance requirements. These aids include Loran C, eLoran, GNSS including GPS and augmented satellite systems, Echo Sounders and Speed Measurement systems. This knowledge is considered so fundamental for much of the management level content within this course that there is merit in reviewing the operational level content quickly before covering the additional elements required at management level. The learning time has been reduced for many elements on the basis that trainees will be reviewing rather than learning much of this content at this level. It may be necessary for some trainees to refresh their knowledge of such techniques before undertaking this management level content* – ensures that the most appropriate electronic systems and electronic navigation aids are used for position monitoring in any area given the information the system may provide and the limitations, errors and accuracy of the available system – verifies that each electronic navigation aid used is set up and operated effectively – provides guidance and support to cadets and watchkeeping officers in the correct set-up and use of electronic navigation aids – assesses the accuracy of position monitoring using electronic navigation aids – ensures that the vessel position is determined at appropriate frequencies and monitored continuously using the most appropriate electronic navigation aids available and this is cross checked with terrestrial or celestial observations where these are possible		R1, R5, R36, R44, R45

1.4 Integrated Navigation system (INS) and Integrated Bridge system (IBS)
– briefly describe that Integrated Navigation system (INS) "supports safety of navigation by evaluating inputs from several independent and different sensors, combining them to provide information giving timely warnings of potential dangers and degradation of integrity of this information"
– evaluate the three categories of INS as defined by IMO, namely:
  – INS(A), which as a minimum provides the information of position, speed, heading and time, each clearly marked with an indication of integrity
  – INS(B), which automatically, continually and graphically indicates the ship's position, speed and heading and, where available, depth in relation to the planned route as well as to known and detected hazards
  – INS(C), which provides means to automatically control heading, track or speed and monitor the performance and status of these controls
– states that Integrity monitoring is an intrinsic function of the INS and that in the INS the integrity of information is verified by comparison of the data derived from two or more sources if available
– states that in Integrity monitoring by the INS, the integrity is verified before essential information is displayed or used and information with doubtful integrity should be clearly marked by the INS and not used for automatic control systems		

适任 1.2	定位和确定通过任一定位方法获取的最终船位的精度	IMO 参考书目
1.3 现代电子导航设备的工作原理、局限性、误差源、探测虚假信息和更正后得到准确定位的方法等专门知识 (20 学时) 注意:在完成这些要求的内容之前,学员必须熟悉 IMO 示范课程 7.03 中的电子导航设备的原理、操作、局限性和误差。这些设备包括劳兰 C、eLoran, 包含 GPS, DGPS, Glonass, Galileo 在内的 GNSS、测深仪和测速系统。本课程中的知识对多数管理级内容非常重要，以至于在涉及管理级额外要求的知识点之前，在迅速复习操作级内容方面颇具价值。基于学员将复习而不是学习该级别内容,已经减少了许多知识点的学时。对某些学员而言,在学习管理级内容之前,可能有必要更新这些技能的知识。 – 在任何水域确保使用最合适的电子系统和电子导航设备以监控船位以及可用系统的局限性、误差和精度 – 核实每个电子航行导航设备已启动和有效运行 – 在正确启动和使用电子导航设备方面给实习生和值班驾驶员提供指导和支持 – 评估使用电子导航设备进行船位监控的精度 – 确保利用最合适的电子导航设备以适当的频率定位并连续监控船位,可能时与陆标定位、天文定位交叉检查		R1, R5, R36, R44, R45

1.4 组合导航系统(INS)和综合船桥系统(IBS)
– 简述组合导航系统（INS）通过评估几个彼此独立的传感器的输入信息支持航行安全,结合传感器的信息对于潜在的危险和信息完整性的降低及时发出警告
– 简要说明 IMO 定义的 3 种 INS,即：
  – INS(A), 至少提供位置、速度、航向和时间等信息,各信息清楚标示完整性
  – INS(B), 自动、连续、以图形方式显示船位、速度和航向,并且如可行,显示与计划航线相关的深度、已知和探得的危险信息
  – INS(C),能提供自动控制航向、轨迹或速度并监控这些控制的性能与状态
– 阐述完整性监控是 INS 的一种固有的功能,在 INS 中,信息的完整性可由来自两个或更多数据来源比较验证
– 阐述由 INS 监控完整性时,在显示或使用基本信息之前进行完整性检查,完整性存在疑问的信息应清楚标示并不被用于自动控制系统		

COMPETENCE 1.2	Determine Position and the Accuracy of Resultant Position Fix by any Means	IMO Reference
– explains that the Integrated Bridge systems (IBS) is "a combination of systems which are interconnected in order to allow centralized access to sensor information or command/control workstations, with the aim of increasing safe and efficient ship's management by suitably qualified personnel" – states that IBS recommendation apply to a system performing two or more operations, namely: passage execution; communication; machinery control; loading, discharging and cargo control; and safety and security – describes the limitations of the systems		

适任 1.2	定位和确定通过任一定位方法获取的最终船位的精度	IMO 参考书目
– 阐述综合船桥系统(IBS)是一个为了集中访问传感器信息或命令 / 控制工作站而相互关联的系统组合,其目的是提升适任人员的安全、有效管理 – 阐述 IBS 推荐应用于一个执行两个或多个操作的系统,这些操作为:航行、通信、机械控制、装卸和控制货物、安全和保安 – 描述系统的局限性		

COMPETENCE 1.3	Determine and Allow for Compass Errors	IMO Reference
TRAINING OUTCOMES: Demonstrates a knowledge and understanding of: 1.3.1 PRINCIPLES OF THE MAGNETIC COMPASS AND THEIR CORRECTION 1.3.2 PRINCIPLES AND ERRORS OF GYROCOMPASSES 1.3.3 SYSTEMS UNDER THE CONTROL OF THE MASTER GYRO AND THE OPERATION AND CARE OF THE MAIN TYPES OF GYROCOMPASS		STCW Code table A-II/2

适任 1.3	测定并修正罗经差	IMO 参考书目
培训效果: 讲授下列内容知识与理解： 1.3.1　磁罗经的原理及其误差修正 1.3.2　陀螺罗经的原理及其误差 1.3.3　主陀螺罗经控制下的系统与主要类型的陀螺罗经的操作与维护		STCW 公约 表 A-II/2

COMPETENCE 1.3	Determine and Allow for Compass Errors	IMO Reference
1.3.1 PRINCIPLES OF THE MAGNETIC COMPASS AND THEIR CORRECTION **Textbooks/Bibliography:** T16, T22 **Teaching aids:** A1, A27, A29, A30 Required performance: *Note that trainees must be familiar with the principles of magnetism and the magnetic compass covered in IMO model course 7.03 before completing these performance requirements. This knowledge is considered so fundamental for much of the management level content within this course that there is merit in reviewing the operational level content quickly before covering the additional elements required at management level. The learning time has been reduced for many elements on the basis that trainees will be reviewing rather than learning much of this content at this level. It may be necessary for some trainees to refresh their knowledge of such techniques before undertaking this management level content*		
1.1 Parts of the magnetic compass and their function (3 hours) – explains the requirements of SOLAS chapter V, regulation 19, in regard to the requirements for the carriage of magnetic compasses – explains that ships must also be fitted with a pelorus, or other means, to take bearings over an arc of 360° of the horizon and a means for correcting heading and bearings to true at all times – describes the parts of the magnetic compass and explains their function – briefly explains the operating principle of Transmitting Magnetic Compass (TMC) – outlines the performance standards for magnetic compasses		R2, ch. V reg. 19, R6, R39
1.2 Errors of the magnetic compass and their correction (27 hours) – explains the importance of keeping a record of observed deviations – determines deviations and prepares a table or graph of deviations – defines the approximate coefficients *A*, *B*, *C*, *D* and *E* – states the equation for the deviation on a given heading in terms of the coefficients – describes the conditions which give rise to each of the coefficients – explains the use of the approximate coefficients *A*, *B*, *C*, *D* and *E* – describes why coefficients *A* and *E* may exist at a badly sited compass – explains the non-magnetic causes of an apparent coefficient *A* – explains that coefficient *B* results partly from the ship's permanent magnetism and partly from induced magnetism – explains that induced magnetism may also contribute to coefficient *C* in a badly sited compass – describes how the deviation associated with the coefficient permanent *B* varies with magnetic latitude		R2, ch. V reg. 19, R6, R39

适任 1.3	测定并修正罗经差	IMO 参考书目
1.3.1　磁罗经的原理及其误差修正 **教科书/参考文献:**T16, T22 **教具:**A1, A27, A29, A30 技能要求: 注意:在完成这些要求的内容之前,学员必须熟悉 IMO 示范课程 7.03 中的磁力学和磁罗经原理。本课程中的知识对多数管理级内容非常重要，以至于在涉及管理级额外要求的知识点之前,在迅速复习操作级内容方面颇具价值。基于学员将复习而不是学习该级别内容,已经减少了许多知识点的学时。对某些学员而言,在学习管理级内容之前,可能有必要更新这些技能的知识		
1.1　磁罗经各个部分及其功能(3 学时) – 解释 SOLAS 公约第 5 章 19 条磁罗经的安装要求 – 解释船舶还必须配备哑罗经或其他设施来测量 360° 的水平方位和任何时候可以将航向和方位修正为真航向和真方位的设施 – 描述磁罗经的组成及其功能 – 简要解释传送磁罗经(TMC)的工作原理 – 概述磁罗经的性能标准		R2,ch. V 第 19 条 R6,R39
1.2　磁罗经的误差与修正(27 学时) – 解释保存所观测的自差记录的重要性 – 测定自差并制作自差表或自差曲线 – 定义修正系数 A、B、C、D、E – 阐述根据系数在给定船首向的自差方程 – 描述每个系数产生的条件 – 解释修正系数 A、B、C、D、E 的使用 – 描述罗经放置不当会存在系数 A、E 的原因 – 解释修正系数 A 的非磁性原因 – 解释部分源于永久磁性和部分源于感应磁性的系数 B – 解释罗经放置不当感应磁性也能产生系数 C – 描述与修正系数 B 相关的自差如何随磁纬度的不同而变化		R2,ch. V 第 19 条 R6,R39

COMPETENCE 1.3	Determine and Allow for Compass Errors	IMO Reference
– explains why the deviation due to permanent magnetism should be compensated by permanent magnets and deviation due to induced magnetism by spherical soft iron correctors, where possible – describes the causes of heeling error and how it varies with heel, course and magnetic latitude – describes the correction of heeling error and why the correction does not remain effective with change of magnetic latitude – defines the constants lambda 1 and lambda 2 – defines the constant mu – explains how the soft iron spheres increase the mean directive force towards magnetic north and that the value of lambda with the spheres in place is called the ship's multiplier – describes the vertical force instrument and its use in correcting heeling error – describes methods of obtaining a table of deviations – analyses a table of deviations to obtain approximate coefficients – states that anything which could affect the deviation of the compass should be stowed in its seagoing position before correcting it – explains the adjustment of the compass by the analysis and/or tentative methods and obtains a table of residual deviations *(Administrations shall determine whether trainees should be capable of adjusting the compass themselves or whether they require only the competence to supervise the adjustment of the compass by a licensed compass adjuster)* – states the order in which corrections should be made and explains why they are made in that order – describes how heeling error may produce an unsteady compass on certain headings after a large change of magnetic latitude and how to deal with it – explains why a large coefficient *B* may appear after a large change of magnetic latitude and how to correct it – describes how subpermanent magnetism gives rise to retentive error – states that deviations may be affected by cargo of a magnetic nature, the use of electromagnets for cargo handling, or repairs involving hammering or welding of steelwork in the vicinity of the compass – defines the magnetic moment of a bar magnet as the product of the pole strength and the length of the magnet – states that, for a suspended magnet vibrating in a magnetic field, T^2 is proportional to $1/H$, where T is the period of vibration and H is the field strength – explains how the relative strengths of two fields may be found		

适任 1.3	测定并修正罗经差	IMO 参考书目
	– 解释为何由永久磁性引起的自差应当用永久磁铁加以抵消以及由感应磁性引起的自差有可能用软铁校正器加以校正 – 描述倾斜误差产生的原因以及它是如何随倾斜角、航向和磁纬度的不同而变化的 – 描述倾斜误差的校正以及为何在磁纬度发生变化时校正不能有效地保持 – 定义常数 λ_1 和 λ_2 – 定义常数 μ – 解释软铁球如何增大平均指向磁北的力以及放置适当的软铁球的 λ 值称为船舶的放大器 – 描述垂直力校正设备以及它在校正倾斜误差中的应用 – 描述获得自差表的方法 – 分析自差表以获得修正系数 – 阐述在校正罗经自差前，可能影响罗经自差的任何物品都应按其在航行时的位置存放 – 解释以分析和/或试验的方式校正罗经并获得剩余自差表 （主管机关应决定学员是否应具备亲自校正罗经的能力或是否只要求他们能适任监督由持证罗经师进行的罗经校正） – 阐述进行校正的顺序,并解释为何要按此顺序进行校正 – 描述在磁纬度发生较大变化后倾斜误差如何使罗经某些航向上不稳定,以及如何处理 – 解释在磁纬度发生较大的变化后为何会出现大的系数 B,以及如何校正 – 描述亚永久磁性如何产生固有误差 – 阐述磁性货物、装卸货物时电磁铁的使用、对罗经附近的钢结构的敲打或电焊的修理可能会影响自差 – 定义一个条形磁铁的磁力矩为该磁极强度和磁铁长度的乘积 – 阐述一个在磁场中振动的悬浮磁铁,T^2 与 $1/H$ 成正比，其中 T 为振动周期,H 为磁场强度 – 解释如何可发现两个磁场的相对强度	

COMPETENCE 1.3	Determine and Allow for Compass Errors	IMO Reference
1.3.2 PRINCIPLES AND ERRORS OF GYROCOMPASSES **Textbooks/Bibliography:** T16, T29 **Teaching aids:** A1, A29, A31, V43, V44, V45 Required performance: *Note that trainees must be familiar with the principles of the gyrocompass covered in IMO model course 7.03 before completing these performance requirements. This knowledge is considered so fundamental for much of the management level content within this course that there is merit in reviewing the operational level content quickly before covering the additional elements required at management level. The learning time has been reduced for many elements on the basis that trainees will be reviewing rather than learning much of this content at this level. It may be necessary for some trainees to refresh their knowledge of such techniques before undertaking this management level content*		
2.1 Principles of gyrocompass (3 hours) – reviews the operating principles of the mechanical/ballistic gyrocompass – explains the operating principle of other types of gyrocompass such as fibre optic gyrocompass and ring laser gyrocompass and their advantages over the mechanical/ballistic gyrocompass		R1, R7, R38, R42
2.2 Gyrocompass errors and corrections (7 hours) – explains why a gyrocompass that is damped in tilt will settle with its spin axis at a small angle to the meridian, except when at the equator – states that the resulting error is known as latitude error or damping error and varies directly as the tangent of the latitude – states that latitude error can be removed by a manual setting that mechanically moves the lubber line and the follow-up system to show the correct heading – states that course and speed error is caused by the tilting of the spin axis, resulting from the ship's motion over the surface of the earth – states that the rate of tilting, in minutes of arc per hour, is equal to the north south component of the ship's velocity – explains how the tilt causes precession in azimuth to the west on northerly headings and to the east on southerly headings in compasses with liquid ballistic control – states that the velocity error is removed by manual settings of latitude and speed to offset the lubber line and the follow-up system in liquid-controlled compasses – explains how the correction is made in compasses that employ other methods of detecting tilt – states that ballistic deflection results from changes in the ship's north-south component of velocity – explains the behaviour of a liquid ballast during a change of speed or an alteration of course – explains that the precession resulting from ballistic deflection may be arranged to move the compass to the correct settling position, after allowance for the change in course and speed error, by choosing a suitable period for the compass – explains that the pendulum of a tilt detector will be thrown out of the vertical during a change of course or speed, producing an error in its output		

<table>
<tr><td>适任 1.3</td><td>测定并修正罗经差</td><td>IMO
参考书目</td></tr>
<tr><td colspan="2">1.3.2　陀螺罗经的原理及其误差
教科书/参考文献:T16, T29
教具:A1, A29, A31, V43, V44, V45
技能要求:
注意:在完成这些要求的内容之前,学员必须熟悉 IMO 示范课程 7.03 中的陀螺罗经原理。本课程中的知识对多数管理级内容非常重要,以至于在涉及管理级额外要求的知识点之前,在迅速复习操作级内容方面颇具价值。基于学员将复习而不是学习该级别内容,已经减少了许多知识点的学时。对某些学员而言,在学习管理级内容之前,可能有必要更新这些技能的知识
2.1　陀螺罗经的原理(3 学时)
– 复习机械 / 弹道陀螺罗经的工作原理
– 解释其他种类的陀螺罗经,如光纤罗经和环形激光陀螺罗经的工作原理,以及相对于机械 / 弹道陀螺罗经的优点
2.2　陀螺罗经的误差与修正(7 学时)
– 解释为何除在赤道外,倾斜时被阻尼的陀螺罗经的主轴将与子午面保持一个小夹角
– 阐述由此产生的误差称为纬度误差、阻尼误差以及直接随纬度的正切而变化
– 阐述纬度误差可以通过机械地调整罗盘准线和跟踪系统以显示正确船首向来进行人工修正
– 阐述船舶在地球表面的运动而使旋转轴倾斜从而产生了航向和速度误差
– 阐述倾斜率以每小时弧度分为单位,等于船舶速度的南北分量
– 解释在液体连通控制的罗经里,倾斜如何造成在船首向偏北时方位向西进动,船首向偏南时向东进动
– 阐述在液体控制的罗经里,速度误差可通过人工调整纬度和速度、重设罗盘基线和跟踪系统
– 解释如何在采用其他检测倾斜方法的罗经中进行误差校正
– 阐述由于船舶速度南北分量的变化而产生冲击误差
– 解释在速度或航向发生变化期间液体连通器的动作
– 解释通过选择合适的罗经周期,在虑及航向和速度误差之后,可以把罗经移动到正确的稳定位置来解决由冲击误差产生的进动
– 解释在航向或航速发生变化期间,倾斜探测器的单摆失去垂直分量,在输出结果中会产生误差</td><td>

R1, R7, R38, R42</td></tr>
</table>

COMPETENCE 1.3	Determine and Allow for Compass Errors	IMO Reference
– explains that the method used in the above objective is not applicable for compasses without liquid ballistic control since course and speed error is fully corrected for all headings – explains that errors are limited by damping the pendulum and limiting the applied torque for large deflections of the pendulum – states that the sensitive element of a gyrocompass is made such that its moment of inertia about any axis is the same, thus preventing any tendency to turn when swinging pendulously as a result of rolling or pitching – describes the effect of rolling on a liquid ballistic for various ship's headings – explains why the movement of the liquid causes an error except on the cardinal headings – explains how intercardinal rolling error is reduced to negligible proportions – states that intercardinal rolling error does not occur in compasses having no gravitational control attachments to the gyroscope – states that errors caused by acceleration of the compass during rolling and pitching can be reduced by sitting the master compass low down, near the rotational centre of the ship – outlines the performance standards for gyrocompasses 1.3.3 SYSTEMS UNDER THE CONTROL OF THE MASTER GYRO AND THE OPERATION AND CARE OF THE MAIN TYPES OF GYROCOMPASS **Textbooks/Bibliography:** T34, T59 **Teaching aids:** A1, A29, A31 Required performance:		
3.1 Systems under the control of the master gyro and the operation and care of the main types of gyrocompass in use at sea (2 hours) – defines the main systems under the control of the master gyro – defines the main types of gyrocompass in use at sea – refers to manufacturers' manuals to determine necessary maintenance tasks		R1

<table>
<tr><td>适任 1.3</td><td>测定并修正罗经差</td><td>IMO
参考书目</td></tr>
<tr><td colspan="2">
– 解释因为航向和速度的误差完全被所有船首向更正,以上所用的方法并不适用无液体连通器的罗经
– 解释误差受减幅单摆的约束,并在大幅单摆方面制约着施加的扭矩
– 阐述陀螺罗经的灵敏元件是如此构成的,任何轴的惯性矩都相同,以防止船舶横摇或纵摇产生悬垂摇摆时的转动趋势
– 描述各种船首向横摇对液体连通器的影响
– 解释为什么液体的运动会产生误差,除了在基点船首向外
– 解释隅点方向的横摇误差如何减小到可忽略的程度
– 阐述隅点方向的横摇误差不会在没有陀螺仪重力控制附件的罗经里产生
– 阐述在船舶横摇和纵摇期间罗经加速产生的误差可以通过在船舶转心的附近降低主罗经的位置来加以减小
– 概述陀螺罗经的性能标准

1.3.3 主陀螺罗经控制下的系统与主要类型的陀螺罗经的操作和维护
教科书/参考文献:T34,T59
教具:A1, A29, A31
技能要求:
3.1 主陀螺罗经控制下的系统与海上使用的主要类型的陀螺罗经的操作与维护(2 学时)
– 定义主陀螺罗经控制下的主要系统
– 定义海上使用的陀螺罗经主要类型
– 参照制造商的说明书确定必要的保养任务
</td><td>

R1</td></tr>
</table>

COMPETENCE 1.4	Coordinate Search and Rescue	IMO Reference
TRAINING OUTCOME: 1.4.1 PROCEDURES CONTAINED IN INTERNATIONAL AERONAUTICAL AND MARITIME SEARCH AND RESCUE MANUAL (IAMSAR) VOL III See IMO model course 1.08, Radar navigation – management level		STCW Code table A-II/2 R24, R25, R31, R37

适任 1.4	协调搜寻与救助行动	IMO 参考书目
培训效果: 1.4.1 国际航空和海上搜救手册(IAMSAR)Ⅷ卷里所包含的程序 参见 IMO 示范课程 1.08“雷达航行——管理级”		STCW 公约 表 A-II/2 R24, R25, R31, R37

<table>
<tr><td>COMPETENCE 1.5</td><td>Establish Watchkeeping Arrangements and Procedures</td><td>IMO Reference</td></tr>
<tr><td colspan="2">TRAINING OUTCOME:

Demonstrates a knowledge and understanding of:
1.5.1 INTERNATIONAL REGULATIONS FOR PREVENTING COLLISIONS AT SEA
1.5.2 PRINCIPLES TO BE OBSERVED IN KEEPING A NAVIGATIONAL WATCH
1.5.3 BRIDGE WATCHKEEPING EQUIPMENT AND SYSTEMS</td><td>STCW Code table A-II/2</td></tr>
</table>

适任 1.5	确定值班安排和程序	IMO 参考书目
培训效果: 讲授下列内容知识与理解: 1.5.1　国际海上避碰规则 1.5.2　保持航行值班应遵循的原则 1.5.3　驾驶台值班设备与系统		STCW 公约 表 A-II/2

COMPETENCE 1.5	Establish Watchkeeping Arrangements and Procedures	IMO Reference
1.5.1 INTERNATIONAL REGULATIONS FOR PREVENTING COLLISIONS AT SEA **Textbooks/Bibliography:** T40, B17, B18, B142 **Teaching aids:** A1, V134, V135 Required performance: *Note that trainees must be familiar with the content and application of the International Regulations for Preventing Collisions at Sea covered in IMO model course 7.03 before completing these performance requirements. This knowledge is considered so fundamental for much of the management level content within this course that there is merit in reviewing the operational level content quickly before covering the additional elements required at management level. The learning time has been reduced for many elements on the basis that trainees will be reviewing rather than learning much of this content at this level. It may be necessary for some trainees to refresh their knowledge of such techniques before undertaking this management level content*		
1.1 International Regulations for Preventing Collisions at Sea, 1972, as amended (30 hours) – demonstrates a thorough knowledge of the content, application and intent of the International Regulations for Preventing Collisions at Sea, 1972, as amended – describes the lights, shapes and sound signals that should be shown or made by own ship in any situation – demonstrates the ability to determine risk of collision and to take appropriate action when encountering all types of vessel when in sight of one another by day or night – demonstrates the ability to determine the risk of collision and the proper action to take to avoid collision in restricted visibility – determines a safe speed for any situation – demonstrates the ability to take appropriate actions when manoeuvring in narrow channels and traffic separation schemes including encounters with other vessels – demonstrates the ability to maintain situational awareness, determine risk of collision and to take appropriate action in situations of high traffic density both when vessels are in sight and when in restricted visibility – demonstrates the ability to take appropriate action when another vessel is believed not to be taking the action required under the Regulations or where a collision cannot be avoided by the action of this vessel alone		R1, R8, R15, R16, R41
1.5.2 PRINCIPLES TO BE OBSERVED IN KEEPING A NAVIGATIONAL WATCH **Textbooks/Bibliography:** T12, T27, B7, B8, B12, B13, B16, B17, B18, B19, B24, B25, B26, B27, B36, B42, B50, B51, B55, B57, B62, B63, B65, B69, B70, B86, B87, B105, B108, B112, B119, B134, B136, B138, B139, B140, B141, B142, B143, B150, B151, B172, B173, B177, B195, B202, B208, B209, B212 **Teaching aids:** A1, V21, V22, V23, V26, V27, V28, V46		STCW Code section A-VIII/2 part 3-1, R32, R33, R34

<table>
<tr><td>适任 1.5</td><td>确定值班安排和程序</td><td>IMO
参考书目</td></tr>
<tr><td colspan="2">1.5.1 国际海上避碰规则
教科书/参考文献:T40, B17, B18, B142
教具:A1, V134, V135
技能要求:
注意:在完成这些要求的内容之前,学员必须熟悉 IMO 示范课程 7.03 中的国际海上避碰规则的内容及其适用。本课程中的知识对多数管理级内容非常重要,以至于在涉及管理级额外要求的知识点之前，在迅速复习操作级内容方面颇具价值。基于学员将复习而不是学习该级别内容,已经减少了许多知识点的学时。对某些学员而言,在学习管理级内容之前,可能有必要更新这些技能的知识
1.1 1972 年 COLREGS 及其修正案(30 学时)
– 全面演示 1972 年国际海上避碰规则及其修正案的知识、适用和目的
– 描述本船在任何情况下都要显示或发出的号灯、号型和声响信号
– 演示在白天或夜间,与所有种类的船舶会遇、互见时判定碰撞危险和采取适当行动的能力
– 演示判定碰撞危险以及如何在能见度受限时采取正确避碰行动的能力
– 任何情况下确定安全航速
– 演示在狭水道和分道通航制航行采取正确行动的能力,包括与他船相遇时
– 演示在互见中和能见度受限时,保持态势感知、碰撞危险的判断和船舶交通密度很大时采取适当行动的能力
– 演示按照避碰规则单凭来船的行动无法避免碰撞,而该船被认为没有采取避碰行动时采取适当行动的能力</td><td>R1, R8, R15, R16, R41</td></tr>
<tr><td colspan="2">1.5.2 保持航行值班应遵循的原则

教科书/参考文献:T12, T27, B7, B8, B12, B13, B16, B17, B18, B19, B24, B25, B26, B27, B36, B42, B50, B51, B55, B57, B62, B63, B65, B69, B70, B86, B87, B105, B108, B112, B119, B134, B136, B138, B139, B140, B141, B142, B143, B150, B151, B172, B173, B177, B195, B202, B208, B209, B212
教具:A1, V21, V22, V23, V26, V27, V28, V46</td><td>STCW 公约表 A-Ⅷ/2 节 3-1 部分, R32, R33, R34</td></tr>
</table>

COMPETENCE 1.5	Establish Watchkeeping Arrangements and Procedures	IMO Reference

Required performance:

Note that trainees must be familiar with the content and application of the Principles of Keeping a Safe Navigational Watch from IMO model course 7.03. This knowledge is considered so fundamental for much of the management level content within this course that there is merit in reviewing the operational level content quickly before covering the additional elements required at management level. The learning time has been reduced for many elements on the basis that trainees will be reviewing rather than learning much of this content at this level. It may be necessary for some trainees to refresh their knowledge of such techniques before undertaking this management level content

2.1 Thorough knowledge of the content, application and intent of the principles to be observed in keeping a navigational watch (12 hours)

- determines appropriate watchkeeping arrangements that are adequate for maintaining safe watchkeeping, taking into account the prevailing circumstances and conditions
- determines the appropriate composition of the watch for differing situations
- determines and posts watch schedules that ensure that rest periods are observed and that watchkeepers are fit for duty for operational conditions
- ensures that the responsibilities and expected actions of the Master when in charge of the navigational watch and the officer of the watch at other times are consistent with the Principles outlined in the STCW Code and that these are clearly understood by these officers, including:
  - calling the Master
  - expectation of action until the Master formally takes control of the watch
  - physical presence on the bridge
  - maintaining an effective lookout
  - not undertaking any duties that interfere with watchkeeping
  - determining if there is risk of collision and the correct application of Colreg
  - monitoring and adjusting the vessel position in a accordance with the voyage plan
  - knowing the handling characteristics of their ship, including its stopping distances
  - using the helm, engines and sound signalling apparatus
  - familiarization and operational use of all bridge equipment, charts, and publications
  - checks and tests
  - actions expected when encountering restricted visibility or distress situations
  - actions when pilots are embarked
  - actions when there is any doubt
- prepares standing orders for watchkeeping at anchor or under way
- ensures that an appropriate lookout is maintained at all times
- states that watch schedules must be posted and accessible
- states the contents of the STCW Code, section A-VIII/2, part 4-1 Principles to be observed in keeping a navigational watch
- states that watch duties should be so arranged to comply with rest periods prescribed in the STCW Code, chapter VIII Standards regarding watchkeeping, section A-VIII/1 Fitness for duty

适任 1.5	确定值班安排和程序	IMO 参考书目

技能要求:
注意:在完成这些要求的内容之前,学员必须熟悉 IMO 示范课程 7.03 中的保持安全航行值班原则的内容及其适用。本课程中的知识对多数管理级内容特别重要,以至于在涉及管理级额外要求的知识点之前,在简要复习操作级内容方面颇具价值。基于学员将复习而不是学习该级别内容,已经减少了许多知识点的学时。对某些学员而言,在学习管理级内容之前,可能有必要更新这些技能的知识
2.1 全面了解航行值班应遵循原则的内容、适用和目的(12 学时)
– 结合当时环境和情况,做出适当的安排以保持安全值班
– 根据不同情形确定值班人员配备
– 确定并设置值班安排表,保证休息时间并确保值班人员胜任其各自工作条件下的职责
– 确保负责航行值班的船长和该班的驾驶员在其他时候的职责和期望的行为与 STCW 公约中概述的原则相一致,对此他们明白无误,包括:
  – 呼叫船长
  – 在船长正式接过值班控制前预期的行动
  – 值守在驾驶台
  – 保持有效瞭望
  – 不从事影响值班的活动
  – 确定是否存在碰撞危险和正确运用避碰规则
  – 按照航次计划监控和调整船位
  – 知道船舶操纵性能,包括停车距离
  – 使用舵、主机和声响设备
  – 熟悉和使用所有驾驶台仪器、海图和出版物
  – 检测
  – 能见度不良或遇险时预期的行动
  – 引航员在船时的行动
  – 有任何疑问时的行动
– 准备锚泊或航行值班的常规命令
– 确保任何时候保持正规瞭望
– 阐述值班安排表必须张贴并在手边
– 阐述航行值班应遵守的 STCW 公约 A-Ⅷ/2,4-1 部分的原则
– 阐述应按照 STCW 公约第Ⅷ章 A-Ⅷ/1 关于合适的值班职责规定的休息周期来安排值班职责		

COMPETENCE 1.5	Establish Watchkeeping Arrangements and Procedures	IMO Reference

- states that the officer in charge of the navigational watch is the Master's representative and is primarily responsible at all times for the safe navigation of the ship and for complying with the International Regulations for Preventing Collisions at Sea, 1972, as amended
- states that officers in charge of the navigational watch under the Master's general direction are responsible for navigating the ship safely during their periods of duty, when they should be physically present on the navigating bridge or in a directly associated location such as the chartroom or bridge control room at all times
- states that the Master, chief engineer officer and officer in charge of watch duties should maintain a proper watch, making the most effective use of the resources available, such as information, installations/equipment and other personnel
- states that the lookout must be able to give full attention to the keeping of a proper lookout and that no other duties should be undertaken or assigned which could interfere with that task
- states that the duties of the lookout and helmsperson are separate and that the helmsperson should not be considered to be the lookout while steering, except in small ships where an unobstructed all-round view is provided at the steering position and there is no impairment of night vision or other impediment to the keeping of a proper lookout
- lists all factors to be considered to decide if the officer in charge of the navigational watch can be the sole lookout in daylight
- lists all relevant factors to be taken into account by the Master in determining that the composition of the navigational watch is adequate to ensure that a proper lookout can continuously be maintained, including those described in the STCW Code
- outlines all factors to be taken into account when deciding the composition of the watch on the bridge, which may include appropriately qualified ratings
- states that the officer in charge of the navigational watch should:
  1. keep the watch on the bridge;
  2. in no circumstances leave the bridge until properly relieved; and
  3. continue to be responsible for the safe navigation of the ship, despite the presence of the Master on the bridge, until informed specifically that the Master has assumed that responsibility and this is mutually understood
- states that the officer in charge of the navigational watch should not be assigned or undertake any duties which will interfere with the safe navigation of the ship
- states that in cases of need, the officer in charge of the navigational watch should not hesitate to use the helm, engines and sound signalling apparatus. However, timely notice of intended variations of engine speed should be given where possible or effective use should be made of UMS engine controls provided on the bridge in accordance with the applicable procedures
- states that the officers of the navigational watch should know the handling characteristics of their ship, including its stopping distances, and should appreciate that other ships may have different handling characteristics
- states that the officer in charge of the navigational watch should make sure that a proper lookout is maintained at all times

适任 1.5	确定值班安排和程序	IMO 参考书目
– 阐述值班驾驶员是船长的代表，任何时候对船舶安全航行和遵守 1972 国际海上避碰规则及其修正案负主要责任 – 阐述航行值班驾驶员在值班期间在船长指导下对船舶安全航行负责,且应任何时候都在驾驶台或海图室或海图控制室等直接相关位置值守 – 阐述船长、轮机长和值班驾驶员应保持适当的值守,最有效地利用可用资源,如信息、装置 / 设备和其他人员 – 阐述瞭望人员必须能全神贯注地保持瞭望,不应进行可能干扰瞭望的其他职责 – 阐述瞭望人员和舵工的职责是分离的,舵工在操舵时不应被认为是瞭望人员,除非在小船上提供一个不受阻碍的 360°视野的操舵位置，且无不利于夜视或妨碍保持正规瞭望的设置 – 列出决定夜间负责值班的驾驶员作为唯一瞭望人员时应考虑的因素 – 列出应被考虑的相关因素,包括 STCW 公约中的相关规定,为确保正规瞭望得以保持,船长决定适当的驾驶台值班人员的时候 – 概述应被考虑的所有因素,当决定驾驶台值班人员时可能包括留足胜任的普通船员 – 阐述值班驾驶员应： 1. 在驾驶台保持值班； 2. 无论如何不离开驾驶台直到被正常接班;且 3. 继续对船舶安全负责,尽管船长在驾驶台,除非船长明确通知其对船舶安全负责且为双方理解 – 阐述值班驾驶员不应被安排或从事任何妨碍船舶航行安全的职责 – 阐述一旦有需要,值班驾驶员应毫不犹豫地使用舵、主机和声响信号装置。但可能时，应不时地注意主机的不同速度或按照驾驶台的操作程序有效使用 UMS 主机控制 – 阐述值班驾驶员应知道其所操纵船舶的性能,包括停车距离,并应了解他船具有不同的操纵性能 – 阐述值班驾驶员应确保任何时候都保持正规瞭望		

COMPETENCE 1.5	Establish Watchkeeping Arrangements and Procedures	IMO Reference

- states that in a ship with a separate chartroom, the officer in charge of the navigational watch may visit the chartroom, when essential, for a short period for the necessary performance of navigational duties, but should first ensure that it is safe to do so and that proper lookout is maintained
- lists all the checks that should be carried out during the navigational watch by the officer in charge of the navigational watch
- states that the officers of the navigational watch should be thoroughly familiar with the use of all electronic navigational aids carried, including their capabilities and limitations, and should use each of these aids when appropriate and should bear in mind that the echo-sounder is a valuable navigational aid
- states that whenever restricted visibility is encountered or expected, the officer in charge of the navigational watch should use the radar, and at all times in congested waters, having due regard to its limitations
- lists all the circumstances when the officer in charge of the navigational watch should notify the Master immediately, which are:
  1. if restricted visibility is encountered or expected;
  2. if the traffic conditions or the movements of other ships are causing concern;
  3. if difficulty is experienced in maintaining course;
  4. on failure to sight land, or a navigation mark or to obtain soundings by the expected time;
  5. if, unexpectedly, land or a navigation mark is sighted or a change in soundings occurs;
  6. on breakdown of the engines, propulsion machinery remote control, steering gear or any essential navigational equipment, alarm or indicator;
  7. if the radio equipment malfunctions;
  8. in heavy weather, if in any doubt about the possibility of weather damage;
  9. if the ship meets any hazard to navigation, such as ice or a derelict; and
  10. in any other emergency or if in any doubt
- states that the officer in charge of the navigational watch should not hesitate to take immediate action for the safety of the ship, where circumstances so require, despite notifying the Master immediately in the circumstances considered important for his presence on the bridge
- states that the officer in charge of the navigational watch should give watchkeeping personnel all appropriate instructions and information which will ensure the keeping of a safe watch, including a proper lookout
- states that in clear weather the officer in charge of the navigational watch should take frequent and accurate compass bearings of approaching ships as a means of early detection of risk of collision and should bear in mind that such risk may sometimes exist even when an appreciable bearing change is evident, particularly when approaching a very large ship or a tow or when approaching a ship at close range
- states that the officer in charge of the navigational watch should also take early and positive action in compliance with the applicable International Regulations for Preventing Collisions at Sea, 1972, as amended and subsequently check that such action is having the desired effect

适任 1.5	确定值班安排和程序	IMO 参考书目
– 阐述具有独立海图室的船舶的负责航行值班的驾驶员,虽然必要时为履行航行职责可以到海图室去,但首先应确保这样做是安全的,且正规瞭望得以保持 – 列出值班驾驶员在航行值班期间应进行的所有检查 – 阐述值班驾驶员应完全熟悉所有的船载电子导航设备,包括其能力与局限性,适当的时候使用每一个导航设备,牢记测深仪是一个宝贵的航行设备 – 阐述当遭遇或预期能见度受限时,负责航行值班的驾驶员应使用雷达,且任何时候在拥挤水域都应注意其局限性 – 列出值班驾驶员应立即通知船长的所有情况,它们是: 1. 遭遇或预期能见度不良; 2. 船舶交通情况或他船的运动引起了关注; 3. 保持航向遇到困难; 4. 在预定的时间未见陆地或航标,或得到水深数据; 5. 假如,意外地看到陆地或航标,或水深异常变化; 6. 主机或推进机械遥控或舵机或任何其他主要设备、警报或指示器发生故障; 7. 无线电设备发生故障; 8. 恶劣天气时如对气象灾害的可能性存在怀疑时; 9. 如船舶遭遇任何航行危险,比如冰或废弃物;和 10. 其他紧急情况或对此有任何怀疑 – 阐述当情形非常需要时,值班驾驶员应为了船舶安全毫不犹豫地采取紧急行动,尽管在此情况下船长在驾驶台时立刻通知船长是重要的 – 阐述值班驾驶员应向所有值班人员发出确保值班安全的适当指令和信息,包括正规瞭望 – 阐述天气晴朗时,值班驾驶员应经常而准确地测量来船的罗经方位,以此作为一种早期探测碰撞危险的手段,并应记住有时这种危险是存在的,即使是有明显的方位变化,特别是接近一艘非常大的船舶或拖带时或近距离接近一艘船舶时 – 阐述值班驾驶员还应按照适用的 1972 年国际避碰规则及其修正案及早采取积极行动,并随后检查这种行动正在取得预期的效果		

COMPETENCE 1.5	Establish Watchkeeping Arrangements and Procedures	IMO Reference
– states that when restricted visibility is encountered or expected, the first responsibility of the officer in charge of the navigational watch is to comply with the relevant rules of the International Regulations for Preventing Collisions at Sea, 1972, as amended with particular regard to the sounding of fog signals, proceeding at a safe speed and having the engines ready for immediate manoeuvre – states that in addition to the above, the officer in charge of the navigational watch shall: 1. inform the Master; 2. post a proper lookout; 3. exhibit navigation lights; and 4. operate and use the radar – states that when arranging lookout duty, in hours of darkness, the Master and the officer in charge of the navigational watch should have due regard to the bridge equipment and navigational aids available for use, their limitations, procedures and safeguards implemented – states that in coastal and congested waters the largest scale chart on board, suitable for the area and corrected with the latest available information, should be used – states that fixes in coastal and congested waters should be taken at frequent intervals, and should be carried out by more than one method whenever circumstances allow – states that when using ECDIS, in coastal and congested waters, appropriate scale of electronic navigational charts should be used and the ship's position should be checked by an independent means of position fixing at appropriate intervals – states that in coastal and congested waters the officer in charge of the navigational watch should positively identify all relevant navigation marks – states that when navigating with pilot on board, despite the duties and obligations of pilots, their presence on board does not relieve the Master or the officer in charge of the navigational watch from their duties and obligations for the safety of the ship – states that when navigating with pilot on board, the Master and the pilot should exchange information regarding navigation procedures, local conditions and the ship's characteristics – states that when navigating with pilot on board, the Master and/or the officer in charge of the navigational watch should cooperate closely with the pilot and maintain an accurate check on the ship's position and movement – states that when navigating with pilot on board, if in any doubt as to the pilot's actions or intentions, the officer in charge of the navigational watch should seek clarification from the pilot and, if doubt still exists, should notify the Master immediately and take whatever action is necessary before the Master arrives		

适任 1.5	确定值班安排和程序	IMO 参考书目
– 阐述当遭遇或预期能见度不良时,负责航行值班的驾驶员的首要责任是应遵守1972年国际避碰规则及其修正案的相关规定,特别注意鸣放雾号、以安全航速航行和备妥主机以备紧急操作 – 阐述除上述诸点以外,值班驾驶员应: 1. 通知船长; 2. 设置瞭望人员; 3. 显示航行灯;和 4. 操作和使用雷达 – 阐述在安排夜间的瞭望职责时,船长和值班驾驶员适当注意可用的驾驶台设备和导航设备及其局限性、执行的程序和安全措施 – 阐述在沿海和拥挤水域应使用适于该水域并更新至拥有最新信息的最大比例尺海图 – 阐述在沿海和拥挤水域应采取适当时间间隔定位,且当环境许可时采取多种方法进行 – 阐述在沿海和拥挤水域使用ECDIS时,应采用适当比例尺的电子航行图,并以适当间隔用独立的方式检查船位 – 阐述值班驾驶员在沿海和拥挤水域应积极辨别所有相关航标 – 阐述引航员在船航行时,不管引航员在船的职责如何,都不应减轻船长或值班驾驶员在船舶安全方面承担的职责和义务 – 阐述引航员在船航行时,船长和引航员应交换关于航行程序、当地情况和船舶性能的信息 – 阐述引航员在船航行时,船长和/或值班驾驶员应与引航员密切合作,对船舶位置及其移动保持准确检查 – 阐述引航员在船航行时,如对引航员的行动或意图存有任何疑问,值班驾驶员应向引航员寻求澄清,且如仍有疑问,应立刻通知船长并在船长到来前采取必要的行动		

COMPETENCE 1.5	Establish Watchkeeping Arrangements and Procedures	IMO Reference

1.5.3 BRIDGE WATCHKEEPING EQUIPMENT AND SYSTEMS

3.1 Knowledge of voyage data recorders (VDR) and bridge navigational watchkeeping alarm systems (BNWAS) (6 hours)

Voyage data recorder (VDR) and simplified voyage data recorder (S-VDR)

- explains that voyage data recorder (VDR) and simplified voyage data recorder (S-VDR) means a complete system, including any items required to interface with the sources of input data, for processing and encoding the data, the final recording medium in its capsule, the power supply and dedicated reserve power source
- explains that the purpose of a voyage data recorder (VDR) and simplified voyage data recorder (S-VDR) is to maintain a store, in a secure and retrievable form, of information concerning the position, movement, physical status, command and control of a vessel over the period leading up to and following an incident having an impact thereon
- explains that the information contained in a VDR and S-VDR is made available to both the Administration and the shipowner and this information is for use during any subsequent investigation to identify the cause(s) of the incident
- describes the operation of a VDR and S-VDR, that is it:
  - continuously maintains sequential records of preselected data items relating to the status and output of the ship's equipment, and command and control of the ship
  - permits subsequent analysis of factors surrounding an incident, the method of recording ensures that the various data items are co-related in date and time during playback on suitable equipment. The final recording medium is installed in a protective capsule and in case of S-VDR of either a fixed or float-free type that meets all of the following requirements:
    - is capable of being accessed following an incident but secure against tampering;
    - for VDR – it maximizes the probability of survival and recovery of the final recorded data after any incident;
    - for S-VDR – it maintains the recorded data for a period of at least two years following termination of recording;
    - is of a highly visible colour and marked with retro-reflective materials; and
    - is fitted with an appropriate device to aid location
- explains the requirements set out in MSC resolution A.861(20) on the fixed type protective capsule for S-VDR
- explains that the equipment is so designed that, as far as is practical, it is not possible to tamper with the selection of data being input to the equipment, the data itself nor that which has already been recorded, and any attempt to interfere with the integrity of the data or the recording is recorded
- explains that the recording method is such that each item of the recorded data is checked for integrity and an alarm is given if a non-correctable error is detected
- describes the continuity of operation of VDR and S-VDR

适任 1.5	确定值班安排和程序	IMO 参考书目

1.5.3 驾驶台值班设备与系统

3.1 航行数据记录仪(VDR)和驾驶台航行值班报警系统(BNWAS)的常识(6 学时)

航行数据记录仪(VDR)和简易航行数据记录仪(S-VDR)

- 解释航行数据记录仪(VDR)和简易航行数据记录仪(S-VDR)是一整套系统,包括要求连接输入数据源、数据处理与数据编码、其容器中的最终记录介质、电源和专用的储备电源
- 解释航行数据记录仪(VDR)和简易航行数据记录仪(S-VDR)的目的是以一种安全和可回收的形式保持存储事故发生前后有关船舶位置、运动、物理状态、命令等信息
- 解释主管机关和船东都可得到 VDR 和 S-VDR 所包含的信息,该信息可为以后调查事故原因时所使用
- 描述 VDR 和 S-VDR 的操作,即
  - 连续保持有关船舶设备状态和输出以及船舶命令与控制的预选数据项的顺序记录
  - 允许随后围绕事故因素进行分析,记录方法确保在适合的设备里回放各种数据项是与日期和时间相关联的。最终记录媒介被安装在保护容器内,固定类或自由上浮类 S-VDR,均应满足下列所有要求:
    - 事故之后能被访问但防止篡改;
    - 对于 VDR,它使事故之后最终记录数据的保存和回收的可能性最大化;
    - 对于 S-VDR,它至少能在记录终止后的两年内保留记录的数据;
    - 采用高度可见的色彩并用反光材料标记;且
    - 安装有辅助定位装置
- 解释 MSC A.861(20)决议中有关固定种类的 S-VDR 保护容器的要求
- 解释只要可能,如此设计设备以使得无法篡改所选输入到其中的数据,也不能对已记录数据本身加以篡改,并记录任何干涉数据或记录完整性的企图
- 解释记录方法是每一项被记录的数据都进行完整性检查,如探测到不可纠正的错误则发出警报
- 介绍 VDR 和 S-VDR 运行的连续性

COMPETENCE 1.5	Establish Watchkeeping Arrangements and Procedures	IMO Reference

- lists and states the data items recorded in the VDR and S-VDR, which are:
- date and time
- ship's position
- ship's speed
- bridge audio
- communications audio
- radar data, post-display selection (or, for S-VDR only, AIS data if radar data is not available) in addition to the above data sets, a VDR should also record:
  - depth under the keel
  - status of all mandatory bridge alarms
  - rudder order and rudder position
  - engine orders and engine response (rev/min or pitch), including any transverse-thrusters
  - status of hull openings
  - status of watertight doors and fire doors
  - wind speed and direction
- explains the data output interface of VDR and S-VDR, that they provide an interface for downloading the stored data and playback the information to an external computer. This interface is compatible with an internationally recognized format, such as Ethernet, USB, FireWire, or equivalent
- describes the software for data downloading and playback
- states that the shipowner, in all circumstances and at all times, owns the VDR and its information
- explains that in the event of an accident the owner of the ship makes all decoding instructions available as necessary to recover the recorded information and maintains the same
- explains the recovery and relevant information of VDR and S-VDR
- explains the custody, read-out and access to the VDR and S-VDR information
- describes the limitations of the receivers
Bridge navigational watch alarm system (BNWAS)
- explains that the carriage requirement of bridge navigational watch alarm system (BNWAS) is set out by SOLAS, chapter V/19 and the requirements will be mandatory for new ships and phased in for existing ships
- states when BNWAS must be fitted to existing ships
- explains that the purpose of BNWAS is to monitor bridge activity and detect operator disability, which could lead to marine accidents
- explains that this purpose is achieved by a series of indications and alarms to alert first the OOW and, if he/she is not responding, then to alert the Master or another qualified OOW
- explains that the system monitors the awareness of the officer-on-watch (OOW) and automatically alerts the Master or other qualified OOW if for any reason the OOW becomes incapable of performing watch duties
- explains that additionally, the BNWAS may provide the OOW with a means of calling for immediate assistance if required		

适任 1.5	确定值班安排和程序	IMO 参考书目

– 列出并阐述 VDR 和 S-VDR 记录的数据项,它们是:
  – 日期和时间
  – 船位
  – 船速
  – 驾驶台通话
  – 联系通话
  – 雷达数据,后显示选择(或如得不到雷达数据仅对 S-VDR 的 AIS 数据),除上述数据集外,一台 VDR 还应记录:
    – 龙骨下水深
    – 驾驶台所有强制性报警的状态
    – 舵角命令和舵的位置
    – 主机命令和主机响应(转 / 分钟或螺距),包括任何横移—侧推器
    – 船体开口状态
    – 水密门和防火门状态
    – 风速和风向
– 解释 VDR 和 S-VDR 的数据输出接口,这些接口提供下载所存储数据和对外部计算机的回放信息。该接口与诸如 Ethernet、USB、FireWire 或等效的国际认可格式兼容
– 介绍数据下载和回放的软件
– 阐述船东在任何情况下的任何时候都拥有 VDR 及其信息
– 解释一旦发生事故,船东应使所有解码指令可用,以有必要恢复所记录的信息和保持信息不变
– 解释 VDR 和 S-VDR 的回收与相关信息
– 解释 VDR 和 S-VDR 信息的保管、解读与获取
– 描述接收机的局限性
驾驶台航行值班报警系统(BNWAS)
– 解释 SOLAS 公约第五章Ⅴ/19 规定的驾驶台航行值班报警系统(BNWAS)安装要求,该要求对新船是强制实施,对现有船舶分阶段实施
– 详述什么时候现有船舶必须配备 BNWAS
– 解释 BNWAS 的目的是要监控驾驶台的活动和探测可能导致海上事故操作者的失误
– 解释 BNWAS 的目的是首先通过一系列的指示和报警提醒值班驾驶员, 如果他 / 她没有响应,然后通知船长或另一名合格的值班驾驶员
– 解释该系统监控值驾驶员的警觉度,当出于任何原因值班驾驶员无法履行其职责时自动地通知船长或其他的值班驾驶员
– 解释 BNWAS 可另外提供给值班驾驶员一种当需要时呼叫紧急救援的工具		

COMPETENCE 1.5	Establish Watchkeeping Arrangements and Procedures	IMO Reference

	– explains that the BNWAS should be operational whenever the ship's heading or track control system is engaged, unless inhibited by the Master
	– explains that the system has the following operational modes: Automatic, Manual On and Manual Off
	– lists and explains the operational sequence of indications and alarms:
	  – once operational, the alarm system remains dormant for a period of between 3 and 12 min (Td – selected dormant period)
	  – at the end of this dormant period, the alarm system initiates a visual indication on the bridge
	  – if not reset, the BNWAS additionally sounds a first stage audible alarm on the bridge 15 sec after the visual indication is initiated
	  – if not reset, the BNWAS additionally sounds a second stage remote audible alarm in the back-up officer's and /or Master's location 15 sec after the first stage audible alarm is initiated
	  – if not reset, the BNWAS additionally sounds a third stage remote alarm at locations of further crew members capable of taking corrective actions 90 seconds after the second stage remote audible alarm is initiated
	  – in vessels other than passenger vessels, the second or third stage remote audible alarms may sound in all the above locations at the same time. If the second stage audible alarm is sounded in this way, the third stage alarm may be omitted
	– states that in larger vessels, the delay between the second stage and third stage may be set to a longer value on installation, up to a maximum of 3 min, to allow sufficient time for back-up officer and /or Master to reach the bridge
	– lists and explains the resetting function of the BNWAS, which are as follows:
	  – it is not possible to initiate the reset or cancel any audible alarm from any device, equipment or system not physically located in areas of the bridge providing proper lookout
	  – the reset function does, by a single operator action, cancel the visual indication and all audible alarms and initiate a further dormant period. If the reset function is activated before the end of the dormant period, the period is re-initiated to run for its full duration from the time of reset
	  – to initiate the reset function, an input representing a single operator action by the OOW is required. This input may be generated by reset devices forming an integral part of the BNWAS or by external inputs from other equipment capable of registering physical activity and mental alertness of the OOW
	  – a continuous activation of any reset device does not prolong the dormant period or cause a suppression of the sequence of indications and alarms
	– explains that the emergency call facility may be provided on the bridge to immediately activate the second, and subsequently third stage, remote audible alarms by means of an "Emergency Call" push button or similar
	– explains that the means of selecting the operational mode and the duration of the dormant period (Td) is security protected so that access to these controls should be restricted to the master only
	– describes the limitation of the system	

适任 1.5	确定值班安排和程序	IMO 参考书目

– 解释每当船舶航向或轨迹控制系统运行时,BNWAS 就响应工作,除非其被船长关停
– 解释该系统具有如下工作模式:自动、手动开启和手动关闭
– 列出并解释指示和报警的操作顺序:
  – 一旦投入使用,该报警系统保持一个 3~12 分钟的休眠期(Td—选择休眠期)
  – 休眠期结束时,该报警系统在驾驶台发出一个视觉标识
  – 如没有被复位,在视觉标识启动后 15 秒,BNWAS 在驾驶台另外发出一级听觉报警
  – 如没有被复位,在一级听觉报警启动后 15 秒,BNWAS 在驾驶台另外发出二级遥控听觉报警至后备驾驶员和 / 或船长所在位置
  – 如没有被复位,在二级听觉报警启动后 90 秒,BNWAS 在驾驶台另外发出三级遥控听觉报警至更多能采取纠正行动的船员所在位置
  – 在除了客船以外的船舶,二、三级遥控听觉报警可以同时在上述所有位置发出。如二级听觉报警以此方式发出,则三级报警可以省略
– 阐述在大船上,二、三级报警之间的延时在安装时可以设置较大的值,最长达 3 分钟,以允许后备驾驶员和 / 船长有足够时间到达驾驶台
– 列出并解释 BNWAS 的复位功能如下:
  – 从非驾驶台实际提供正规瞭望位置的任何装置、仪器或系统不能启动复位或删除任何听觉报警
  – 复位功能由一个操作者采取行动,取消了视觉指示和所有听觉警报,并启动休眠期。如果复位功能在休眠期结束前被激活,则该休眠期从复位时开始重新启动其运行周期
  – 需要一个代表值班驾驶员单一操作者行动的输入来启动复位功能。该输入可由组成 BNWAS 的装置或其他能记录值班驾驶员身体活动和心理警觉性的外部设备产生
  – 连续激活任何复位装置并不延长休眠期或对标识和警报顺序造成抑制
– 解释在驾驶台可提供紧急呼叫的设施,通过“紧急呼叫”按钮或类似物立刻启动二级和随后的三级遥控听觉报警
– 解释选择操作模式和休眠期(Td)周期具有安全防护,以便这些控制仅应限于船长操作
– 介绍该系统的局限性		

COMPETENCE 1.6	Maintain Safe Navigation through the Use of Information from Navigation Equipment and Systems to Assist Command Decision Making	IMO Reference
TRAINING OUTCOMES: Demonstrates a knowledge and understanding of: 1.6.1 SYSTEM ERRORS AND OPERATIONAL ASPECTS OF MODERN NAVIGATION SYSTEMS INCLUDING RADAR AND ARPA 1.6.2 BLIND PILOTAGE TECHNIQUES 1.6.3 EVALUATION OF NAVIGATIONAL INFORMATION TO AID IN COMMAND DECISIONS FOR AVOIDING COLLISION AND SAFE NAVIGATION OF THE SHIP 1.6.4 INTERRELATIONSHIP AND OPTIMUM USE OF ALL NAVIGATIONAL DATA Required performance: *Note that trainees must be familiar with the content and application of modern navigation systems, navigation techniques, collision avoidance and bridge resource management from IMO model course 7.03. This knowledge is considered so fundamental for much of the management level content within this course that there is merit in reviewing the operational level content quickly before covering the additional elements required at management level. The learning time has been reduced for many elements on the basis that trainees will be reviewing rather than learning much of this content at this level. It may be necessary for some trainees to refresh their knowledge of such techniques before undertaking this management level content* See IMO model courses 1.08 Radar navigation – management level, 1.22 Ship simulator and bridge teamwork and 1.27 Operational use of electronic chart display and information systems (ECDIS) and 1.34 AIS Operator course	STCW Code table A-II/2

适任 1.6	通过辅助决策的导航设备和系统的信息保持安全航行	IMO 参考书目
培训效果: 讲授下列内容知识与理解: 1.6.1　现代导航系统(包括雷达与 ARPA)的操作事项与系统误差 1.6.2　盲航导航术 1.6.3　对有助于避免碰撞和船舶安全航行的指挥决策信息评估 1.6.4　所有导航数据的内在关系和最优应用 技能要求: 注意:在完成这些要求的内容之前,学员必须熟悉 IMO 示范课程 7.03 中的现代航行系统、航行技术、避碰及驾驶台资源管理的内容及其适用。本课程中的知识对多数管理级内容非常重要,以至于在涉及管理级额外要求的知识点之前,在迅速复习操作级内容方面颇具价值。基于学员将复习而不是学习该级别内容,已经减少了许多知识点的学时。对某些学员而言,在学习管理级内容之前,可能有必要更新这些技能的知识 参见 IMO 示范课程 1.08"雷达航行——管理级"、1.22"船舶模拟器和驾驶台团队工作"、1.27"电子海图显示与信息系统(ECDIS)的操作使用"、1.34 "AIS 操作员课程"		STCW 公约 表 A-II/2

COMPETENCE 1.7	Maintain Safe Navigation through the Use of ECDIS and Associated Navigation Systems to Assist Command Decision Making	IMO Reference
TRAINING OUTCOMES: Demonstrates a knowledge and understanding of: 1.7.1 COMMAND DECISION MAKING USING THE INFORMATION PROVIDED BY ECDIS AND ASSOCIATED NAVIGATION SYSTEMS (40 hours) Required performance: *Note that trainees must be familiar with the content and operational use of ECDIS from IMO model course 1.27. This knowledge is considered so fundamental for much of the management level content within this course that there is merit in reviewing the operational level content quickly before covering the additional elements required at management level. The learning time has been reduced for many elements on the basis that trainees will be reviewing rather than learning much of this content at this level. It may be necessary for some trainees to refresh their knowledge of operational level content before undertaking this management level content* See IMO model courses 1.27, Operational use of electronic chart display and information systems (ECDIS), 1.34, AIS Operator course and STCW reg. I/12 from the perspective of command decision making, 1.08 Radar navigation – management level and 1.22, Ship simulator and bridge teamwork		STCW Code table A-II/2 STCW Code table A-II/2

适任 1.7	通过辅助决策的 ECDIS 及相关的航行系统保持安全航行	IMO 参考书目
培训效果: 讲授下列内容知识与理解: 1.7.1　使用 ECDIS 和相关航行系统信息进行指挥决策(40 学时) 技能要求: 注意:在完成这些要求的内容之前,学员必须熟悉 IMO 示范课程 1.27 中使用 ECDIS 的内容及其操作。本课程中的知识对多数管理级内容非常重要,以至于在涉及管理级额外要求的知识点之前,在迅速复习操作级内容方面颇具价值。基于学员将复习而不是学习该级别内容,已经减少了许多知识点的学时。对某些学员而言,在学习管理级内容之前,可能有必要更新这些技能的知识 参见 IMO 示范课程 1.27“电子海图显示与信息系统(ECDIS)的操作使用”、IMO 示范课程 1.34“AIS 操作员课程”和 STCW(Ⅰ/12)有关指挥决策规定、1.08“雷达航行——管理级”及 1.22“船舶模拟器和驾驶台团队工作”		STCW 公约 表 A-II/2 STCW 公约 表 A-II/2

COMPETENCE 1.8	Forecast Weather and Oceanographic Conditions	IMO Reference
TRAINING OUTCOMES: Demonstrates a knowledge and understanding of: 1.8.1 SYNOPTIC CHARTS AND WEATHER FORECASTING 1.8.2 CHARACTERISTICS OF VARIOUS WEATHER SYSTEMS 1.8.3 OCEAN CURRENT SYSTEMS 1.8.4 CALCULATION OF TIDAL CONDITIONS 1.8.5 APPROPRIATE NAUTICAL PUBLICATIONS ON TIDES AND CURRENTS		STCW Code table A-II/2

适任 1.8	预报天气和海洋水文状况	IMO 参考书目
培训效果: 讲授下列内容知识与理解: 1.8.1　气象图与天气预报 1.8.2　各种天气系统的特点 1.8.3　洋流系统 1.8.4　潮汐计算 1.8.5　有关潮汐和潮流的航海出版物		STCW 公约 表 A-II/2

COMPETENCE 1.8	Forecast Weather and Oceanographic Conditions	IMO Reference

1.8.1 SYNOPTIC CHARTS AND WEATHER FORECASTING — STCW Code section A-VIII/2

Textbooks/Bibliography: T23, T24, B28, B41, B63, B138, B223, B224
Teaching aids: A1, V36, V37, V38, V39, V114
Required performance:
Note that trainees must be familiar with the content and application of the Meteorology content from IMO model course 7.03. This knowledge is considered so fundamental for much of the management level content within this course that there is merit in reviewing the operational level content quickly before covering the additional elements required at management level. The learning time has been reduced for many elements on the basis that trainees will be reviewing rather than learning much of this content at this level. It may be necessary for some trainees to refresh their knowledge of such techniques before undertaking this management level content

1.1 Synoptic and prognostic charts and forecasts from any source (6 hours) — R1
- interprets the isobaric patterns of a synoptic weather chart with interpolation and extrapolation as necessary
- determines the geostrophic and approximate surface wind speeds from the chart by use of the geostrophic wind scale
- determines the weather associated with specific places within the plots
- determines the likely movement of pressure systems
- evaluates the use of prognostic charts
- evaluates the information given in shipping forecasts
- evaluates the information received from internet and email

1.2 Range of information available (3 hours) — R1, R2 ch. V, R100
- lists the information available to the mariner in fax transmissions
- discusses the source of information relating to radio stations, and their transmissions
- evaluates the information given in surface synoptic and prognostic fax charts
- interprets the information given in wave charts
- evaluates the information given in ice charts
- evaluates the use of 500 hPa charts in forecasting the progress of depressions
- evaluates the value of personal observations of weather signs, in evaluating weather trends
- lists the information available to the mariner via internet and email
- evaluates the information received from internet and email

1.3 Weather Forecasting (15 hours) — R1, R2 ch. V, R100
- forecasts anticipated local weather from synopsis and prognosis information received, the movement of meteorological systems, knowledge of local influences, observation of local conditions and movement of own ship

适任 1.8	预报天气和海洋水文状况	IMO 参考书目
1.8.1　气象图与天气预报 **教科书/参考文献**:T23, T24, B28, B41, B63, B138, B223, B224 **教具**:A1, V36, V37, V38, V39, V114 技能要求: 注意:在完成这些要求的内容之前,学员必须熟悉 IMO 示范课程 7.03 中的气象学内容及其适用。本课程中的知识对多数管理级内容非常重要，以至于在涉及管理级额外要求的知识点之前,在迅速复习操作级内容方面颇具价值。基于学员将复习而不是学习该级别内容,已经减少了许多知识点的学时。对某些学员而言,在学习管理级内容之前,可能有必要更新这些技能的知识		STCW 公约 A-Ⅷ/2 节
1.1　天气图与预报图以及任何来源的预报(6 学时) – 解释必要时用内推和外推的方法分析天气图的等压模式 – 利用地转风比例尺在图上确定地转风近地面风速 – 确定在所标绘的区域内,特定地域有关的天气 – 确定气压系统可能的运动 – 评估预报图的使用 – 评估船舶预报所给出的信息 – 评估从互联网和电子邮件所接收到的信息		R1
1.2　可用信息的范围(3 学时) – 列出传真发送的对海员可用的信息 – 讨论与无线以及它们的发送电台有关的信息源 – 评估地面传真天气图和地面传真预报图中的信息 – 解释波浪图中的信息 – 评估冰况图中的信息 – 评估在预测低气压运动过程中 500 百帕图的使用 – 评估在评估天气趋势中,个人观测天气的价值 – 列出海员可用的互联网和电子邮件发送的信息 – 评估从互联网和电子邮件所接收到的信息		R1, R2 ch. V, R100
1.3　天气预报(15 学时) – 根据收到的天气和预报信息、气象系统的移动、当地影响的知识、当地状况的观测和本船的移动,对可能影响地区的天气进行预报		R1, R2 ch. V, R100

COMPETENCE 1.8	Forecast Weather and Oceanographic Conditions	IMO Reference
1.8.2 CHARACTERISTICS OF VARIOUS WEATHER SYSTEMS **Textbooks/Bibliography:** T23, T24, B28, B41, B63, B138, B223, B224 **Teaching aids:** A1, V36, V37, V38, V39 Required performance: **2.1 Tropical revolving storms (TRS) (8 hours)** – states the definitions adopted by the WMO with respect to tropical storms – states local nomenclature of TRS – states regions and seasons of greatest frequency of TRS – states the conditions associated with the formation of tropical revolving storms – states the factors that affect the future movement of a TRS – describes with the aid of diagrams typical and possible tracks of TRS – explains the factors associated with the decay of TRS – draws a plan of a TRS showing isobars, wind circulation, path, track, vortex or eye, trough line, dangerous semicircle, dangerous quadrant and navigable semicircle (for north and south hemispheres) – explains the reasons for the naming of the dangerous semicircle – draws a cross-section through a TRS showing areas of cloud and precipitation – describes the characteristics of a TRS, i.e. size, wind, pressure, eye, cloud and precipitation sequence – describes the signs which give warning of the approach for the TRS – explains the methods of determining the approximate bearing of an approaching TRS – explains the method of determining in which sector of a TRS the ship is situated – states the correct avoidance procedure when in the vicinity of a TRS – given the position and direction of travel of a TRS and ship's voyage information, describes appropriate measures to avoid the danger sector of a TRS – describes the messages required to be sent in accordance with the requirements of SOLAS, when a TRS is encountered, or suspected to be in the vicinity – describes the message required to be sent in accordance with the requirement of SOLAS when a wind of or above storm force 10 is encountered which has not previously been reported		 R1, R2

适任 1.8	预报天气和海洋水文状况	IMO 参考书目
1.8.2　各种天气系统的特点 **教科书/参考文献**:T23, T24, B28, B41, B63, B138, B223, B224 **教具**:A1, V36, V37, V38, V39 技能要求: **2.1　热带气旋风暴(TRS)(8 学时)** – 阐述 WMO 所采纳的有关热带风暴的定义 – 阐述 TRS 的地方命名 – 阐述 TRS 出现频率最大的区域和季节 – 阐述热带风暴形成的有关条件 – 阐述影响 TRS 未来运动的因素 – 利用图表描述 TRS 典型和可能的轨迹 – 解释与 TRS 减弱有关的因素 – 画出有等压线、风循环、路径、轨迹、旋涡或眼区、槽线、危险半圆、危险象限及可航半圆的 TRS 平面图(南、北半球) – 解释命名“危险半圆”的原因 – 画出显示 TRS 云区和降水区的横剖面图 – 描述 TRS 的特点,即尺度、风、气压、眼区、云和降水的顺序 – 描述显示 TRS 接近的警报符号 – 解释确定 TRS 接近的大概方位的方法 – 解释确定船舶位于 TRS 哪个区域的方法 – 阐述在 TRS 附近正确规避的程序 – 在已知 TRS 位置和运动方向以及船舶航行信息的情况下，描述避开 TRS 危险区的适当措施 – 描述当遭遇 TRS 或怀疑在其附近,根据 SOLAS 的要求应发送的信息 – 描述当遭遇先前没有报告的 10 级以上的风暴,根据 SOLAS 要求应发送的信息	 R1, R2

COMPETENCE 1.8	Forecast Weather and Oceanographic Conditions	IMO Reference
2.2	**Main types of floating ice, their origins and movements (2 hours)** – explains the formation of icebergs from floating glacier tongues and from ice shelves, and the characteristics of each – discusses the formation of sea ice – defines ice tongue, ice shelf – defines pack ice and fast ice – discusses the normal seasons and probable tracks of North Atlantic bergs from origin to decay – defines the outer limits of the area in which icebergs may be encountered in the North Atlantic – discusses the normal and extreme limits of iceberg travel in the southern oceans during summer and winter – explains the reasons for the decay of icebergs – describes the areas affected by sea ice in regions frequented by shipping – discusses the seasonal development and recession of sea ice on the coastlines of the northern oceans, and in the latitude of the normal trade routes	R1
2.3	**Guiding principles relating to the safety of navigation in ice (2 hours)** – states the signs which may indicate the proximity of ice on clear days and nights – defines the ranges at which observers may expect to detect ice visually in varying conditions of visibility, see T61 – discusses the limitations of radar as a means of detecting ice – states the precautions to be taken when navigating near ice, and when ice is suspected in the vicinity	R1, R2 ch. V
2.4	**Conditions leading to ice accretion on ship's superstructures, dangers and the remedies available (2 hours)** – describes the factors which may give rise to ice accretion – describes the use of data in the Mariner's Handbook, for estimating the rate of ice accretion – evaluates the methods of avoiding or reducing ice accretion – explains the reports to be made under international conventions when ice is encountered – lists the information to be given in radio messages reporting dangerous ice – states the iceberg nomenclature in use by the International Ice Patrol – lists the information to be given in radio messages reporting conditions leading to severe ice accretion on ship's superstructures	R1

适任 1.8	预报天气和海洋水文状况	IMO 参考书目
2.2　浮冰的主要类型、来源及其运动(2 学时) – 解释来自漂浮的冰河舌和冰架形成的冰山,以及它们各自的特性 – 讨论海冰的形成 – 定义冰河舌、冰架 – 定义密集冰和固定冰 – 讨论北大西洋冰山从源地到融化的正常季节和行程 – 定义在北大西洋可能遇上冰山的地区外边界 – 讨论夏季和冬季期间在南部海洋冰山移动的正常和最大的界线 – 解释冰山融化的原因 – 描述在船舶频繁航行的水域受海冰影响的区域 – 讨论在北部海洋海岸线和正常的贸易航线的纬度上,海冰的季节性发展和消退		R1
2.3　在冰区附近航行安全的指导性原则(2 学时) – 阐述晴朗的白天和夜间指向附近存在冰的迹象 – 定义各种能见度情况下,观察者可以视觉看见冰的距离,参见 T61 – 讨论雷达用作探冰工具的局限性 – 阐述当航行在冰区附近,以及怀疑附近有冰的时候,应采取的预防措施		R1, R2 ch. V
2.4　导致船舶上层建筑积冰的条件、危险性以及可用的补救措施(2 学时) – 描述产生积冰的因素 – 描述为估计积冰率,《海员手册》里的数据的使用 – 评估避免或减少积冰的方法 – 解释当遭遇浮冰,按照国际规则所做的报告 – 列出报告危险浮冰无线电报所给出的信息 – 阐述国际冰区巡逻所使用的冰山的命名 – 列出报告导致船舶上层建筑积冰情况的无线电报所给出的信息		R1

COMPETENCE 1.8	Forecast Weather and Oceanographic Conditions	IMO Reference
1.8.3 OCEAN CURRENT SYSTEMS **Textbooks/Bibliography:** T23, T24, T30, B28, B41, B63, B223, B224 **Teaching aids:** A1, A12, A19, V36, V37, V38, V39 Required performance: **3.1 Surface water circulation of the ocean and principal adjoining seas (3 hours)** – defines qualitatively the effect of geostrophic force on surface currents – discusses the generation of drift currents by prevailing winds – discusses the generation of gradient currents from differences in water temperature and salinity – discusses the generation of gradient currents resulting from the indirect effect of wind causing a piling up of water on windward coasts, as in the case of the Equatorial Counter Currents – analyses the nature of currents formed by a combination of the above as experienced by western shores of large land masses – relates the general pattern of surface water circulation to the atmospheric pressure distribution – constructs a chart showing global surface water circulation applicable to the above – describes the seasonal changes in the above in areas under the influence of the Asian monsoons – identifies the principal individual currents by name – analyses the causes of individual currents where explicitly stated in Meteorology for Mariners – explains the classification of individual currents as warm or cold where appropriate – describes the form in which surface current data is presented in current atlases and on routeing charts – evaluates qualitatively the use of this data in passage planning – explains the derivation of the current rose – explains the derivation of the predominant current – shows the meaning of the term constancy when applied to predominant currents – explains the derivation of the vector mean current – compares qualitatively the values of the information given by the current rose, the predominant current and the vector mean current as aids to passage planning		R1
3.2 Voyage planning principles with respect to weather conditions and wave height (2 hours) – selects and uses data from *Ocean Passages for the World* – describes climatological routeing – defines significant wave height – discusses the factors affecting wave height and direction – describes the methods employed in forecasting wave heights – describes optimum (least time) routeing – evaluates the forms of routeing in the above objectives		R1, R2

适任 1.8	预报天气和海洋水文状况	IMO 参考书目
1.8.3 洋流系统 **教科书/参考文献:**T23, T24, T30, B28, B41, B63, B223, B224 **教具:**A1, A12, A19, V36, V37, V38, V39 技能要求:		
3.1 海洋表面的水循环以及主要的邻接水域(3 学时) – 定性定义地转力对表层流的影响 – 讨论风生流的产生 – 讨论温度和盐度不同导致梯度流的产生 – 讨论在赤道逆流的情况下,由于风造成上风岸海水堆积,间接影响梯度流的产生 – 分析大陆西岸上述因素共同作用所形成的流的性质 – 表层水循环的一般模式与大气压力分布的联系 – 画图表示适合上述内容的地球表面水循环 – 描述上述内容中亚洲季风影响区域的季节变化 – 按名称逐个辨认主要的洋流 – 逐个分析《航海气象学》中明确阐述的洋流产生的原因 – 逐个按照暖流和寒流的区别对洋流进行说明 – 描述在洋流图集和航路图里给出的表层流数据的形式 – 定性评估这些数据在航线设计中的应用 – 解释海流玫瑰图的来源 – 解释主要洋流的来源 – 说明应用在主要洋流中的术语定常性的意思 – 解释矢量平均洋流的来源 – 定性比较有助于航线设计的海流玫瑰图、主要洋流和矢量平均洋流所给出信息的价值		R1
3.2 与天气条件和浪高有关的航次计划原理(2 学时) – 从《世界大洋航路》里选择和使用数据 – 描述气候航线 – 定义显著浪高 – 讨论影响浪高和方向的因素 – 描述预测浪高所采用的方法 – 描述最优(时间最短)航线 – 评估上述目的航线的形式		R1, R2

COMPETENCE 1.8	Forecast Weather and Oceanographic Conditions	IMO Reference
– describes the methods of constructing a least time track – appraises the relative merits of ship and shore-based routeing, and their limitations – describes the construction of ships' performance curves – demonstrates the use of monthly Routeing Charts – explains the construction and use of a Baillie wind rose – demonstrates familiarity with the forms of climatological, meteorological and current data presented in the Sailing Directions (Pilot Books) and in the Mariner's Handbook		
3.3 Formation of sea waves and swell waves (2 hours)		R1
– selects and uses data from *Ocean Passages for the World* – explains the role of wind in wave formation – explains the importance of wind force in wave formation – explains the importance of duration of wind causing waves – explains the importance of fetch in the growth of waves – uses Dorrenstein's nomogram for forecasting significant wave heights – states the relationship between sea waves and swell waves – explains the decay of swell waves as they travel from the area of origin		
1.8.4 CALCULATION OF TIDAL CONDITIONS **Textbooks/Bibliography:** T1, B28, B41, B63, B138, B223, B224 **Teaching aids:** A1, V36, V37, V38, V39 Required performance: *Note that trainees must be familiar with the content and application of the tidal calculation content from IMO model course 7.03. This knowledge is considered so fundamental for much of the management level content within this course that there is merit in reviewing the operational level content quickly before covering the additional elements required at management level. The learning time has been reduced for many elements on the basis that trainees will be reviewing rather than learning much of this content at this level. It may be necessary for some trainees to refresh their knowledge of such techniques before undertaking this management level content*		
4.1 Ability to calculate tidal conditions (6 hours)		R1
– explains the non-astronomical component of sea level – explains other irregularities of the tide – states that the predicted tide level is not an accurate value – demonstrates the use of tide tables – determines height and time for high and low water in secondary ports – determines the predicted height of water at a given time in a tabulated port – determines the predicted time for a given tide level – demonstrates the use of tidal stream charts – defines the zero level of the charts – evaluates qualitatively the effect of high or low atmospheric pressure on tide levels		

适任 1.8	预报天气和海洋水文状况	IMO 参考书目
– 描述设计时间最短航迹的方法 – 评价海上航路设计和陆地航路设计的相对优点及其局限性 – 描述船舶性能曲线的组成 – 按月演示航路设计图的使用 – 解释 Baillie 风玫瑰图的组成和使用 – 演示对《航路指南》(引航手册)和《海员手册》里给出的气候、气象和洋流数据形式的熟练程度		
3.3 波浪与涌浪的形成(2 学时) – 从《世界大洋航路》中选择和使用数据 – 解释风玫瑰图在海浪形成中的作用 – 解释风力在海浪形成中的重要性 – 解释产生波浪的风周期的重要性 – 解释在波浪发展的过程中风区的重要性 – 使用 Dorrenstein's 诺模图预测显著浪高 – 阐述波浪和涌浪之间的关系 – 解释涌浪从发源地传来后的衰减		R1
1.8.4 潮汐计算 **教科书/参考文献**:T1, B28, B41, B63, B138, B223, B224 **教具**:A1, V36, V37, V38, V39 技能要求: 注意:在完成这些要求的内容之前,学员必须熟悉 IMO 示范课程 7.03 中的潮汐计算内容及其适用。本课程中的知识对多数管理级内容非常重要,以至于在涉及管理级额外要求的知识点之前,在迅速复习操作级内容方面颇具价值。基于学员将复习而不是学习该级别内容,已经减少了许多知识点的学时。对某些学员而言,在学习管理级内容之前,可能有必要更新这些技能的知识		
4.1 计算潮汐状况的能力(6 学时) – 解释海平面的非天体学成分 – 解释潮汐的其他不规则性 – 阐述预测的潮高水面不是一个精确的值 – 演示潮汐表的使用 – 确定副港涨潮和落潮的潮高和潮时 – 确定表列港口在给定时间的预测潮高 – 确定给定潮高的预计潮时 – 演示潮流图的使用 – 定义潮流图的零水位 – 定性评估高压或低压对潮位的影响		R1

COMPETENCE 1.8	Forecast Weather and Oceanographic Conditions	IMO Reference
– evaluates qualitatively the effect of persistent winds on tide levels and tidal times – evaluates qualitatively the effect of abrupt changes of weather conditions on tidal levels – describes seismic waves, their origin and areas of prevalence – demonstrates use of computer program to obtain tidal information – explains briefly the use of harmonic constant method of tidal prediction – explains the reliability of tidal predictions (awareness of the factors influencing the accuracy and reliability of predictions, e.g. local weather conditions, flooding, local area knowledge, etc.) 1.8.5 APPROPRIATE NAUTICAL PUBLICATIONS ON TIDES AND CURRENTS **Textbooks/Bibliography:** T1, B28, B41, B63, B138, B223, B224 **Teaching aids:** A1, A16, A17 Required performance: **5.1 Nautical publications and information which can be obtained via internet and email on tides and currents (3 hours)** – uses tidal height calculations in passage planning, with regard to limiting draughts and times of available depth of water – uses tidal stream information in passage planning, with regard to effect on course made good, and effect on speed and timing of events – uses current information in passage planning, with regard to effect on course made good, and effect on speed and timing of events – uses information which can be obtained via internet and email on tides and currents in passage/voyage planning		 R1

适任 1.8	预报天气和海洋水文状况	IMO 参考书目
– 定性评价持续的风对潮位和潮时的影响 – 定性评估天气的突然变化对潮位的影响 – 描述地震波及其来源以及盛行的区域 – 演示使用计算机程序获得潮汐信息 – 简述潮汐预报的调和常数法的使用 – 解释潮汐预报的可靠性(影响预测的精度和可靠性因素的认识,如当地天气情况、洪水、当地情况,等等) 1.8.5 有关潮汐和潮流的航海出版物 **教科书/参考文献:**T1, B28, B41, B63, B138, B223, B224 **教具:**A1, A16, A17 技能要求: **5.1 有关潮汐和潮流的航海出版物以及通过互联网和电子邮件获取的信息(3学时)** – 在航线设计中使用潮高计算时考虑受限吃水和可用水深的时间的利用 – 在航次计划中使用潮流信息时考虑对地航向、航速以及航次时间计算的影响 – 在航次计划中使用海流信息时考虑对地航向、航速以及航次时间计算的影响 – 在航线设计/航次计划中对通过互联网和电子邮件获得的潮汐和海流信息的利用		R1

<table>
<tr><td>COMPETENCE 1.9</td><td>Respond to Navigational Emergencies</td><td>IMO Reference</td></tr>
<tr><td colspan="2">TRAINING OUTCOMES:

Demonstrates a knowledge and understanding of:
1.9.1 PRECAUTIONS WHEN BEACHING A SHIP
1.9.2 ACTIONS TO BE TAKEN IF GROUNDING IS IMMINENT AND AFTER GROUNDING
1.9.3 REFLOATING A GROUNDED SHIP WITH AND WITHOUT ASSISTANCE
1.9.4 ACTIONS FOR IMMINENT COLLISION, AFTER COLLISION AND IMPAIRMENT OF THE WATERTIGHT INTEGRITY OF THE HULL BY ANY CAUSE
1.9.5 ASSESSMENT OF DAMAGE CONTROL
1.9.6 EMERGENCY STEERING
1.9.7 EMERGENCY TOWING ARRANGEMENTS AND TOWING PROCEDURES</td><td>STCW Code table A-II/2</td></tr>
</table>

适任 1.9	航行中的应急反应	IMO 参考书目
培训效果: 讲授下列内容知识与理解: 1.9.1 船舶抢滩的预防措施 1.9.2 即将搁浅与搁浅后所采取的行动 1.9.3 在有援助和无援助下搁浅船舶的脱浅 1.9.4 即将碰撞、碰撞后和任何原因破坏船体水密性时所采取的行动 1.9.5 破损控制的评估 1.9.6 应急操舵 1.9.7 应急拖带部署与拖带程序		STCW 公约 表 A-II/2

COMPETENCE 1.9	Respond to Navigational Emergencies	IMO Reference
1.9.1 PRECAUTIONS WHEN BEACHING A SHIP **Textbooks/Bibliography:** T3, B58, B59, B62 **Teaching aids:** A1, V24, V25, V28, V29 Required performance: **1.1 Precautions when beaching a ship (2 hours)** – describes the circumstances in which a vessel may be beached – states that a gently shelving beach of mud, sand or gravel should be chosen if possible – states that beaching should be at slow speed – states that, when trimmed heavily by the head, beaching stern first may be advantageous – compares the relative advantages of beaching broadside-on and at rightangles to the beach – states that wind or tide along the shore will quickly swing the ship broadsideon to the beach – describes measures which can be taken to prevent the ship driving further ashore and to assist with subsequent refloating – states that ballast should be added or transferred to counteract a tendency to bump on the bottom – states that all tanks and compartments should be sounded and an assessment made of damage to the ship – states that soundings should be taken to establish the depth of water round the ship and the nature of the bottom		R1
1.9.2 ACTIONS TO BE TAKEN IF GROUNDING IS IMMINENT AND AFTER GROUNDING **Textbooks/Bibliography:** T10, T3, B58, B59, B62 **Teaching aids:** A1, V24, V25, V28, V29, V113 Required performance: **2.1 Grounding (2 hours)** – states that, on stranding, the engines should be stopped, watertight doors closed, the general alarm sounded and, if on a falling tide, the engines should be put full astern to see if the ship will immediately refloat – states that the engineers should be warned to change to high-level water intakes – states that a distress or urgency signal should be transmitted and survival craft prepared if necessary – states that all tanks and compartments should be sounded and the ship should be inspected for damage – states that any discharge or probable discharge of harmful substances should be reported to the nearest coast radio station – states that soundings should be taken to establish the depth of water round the ship and the nature of the bottom		R1, R2

适任 1.9	航行中的应急反应	IMO 参考书目
1.9.1 船舶抢滩的预防措施 **教科书/参考文献**:T3, B58, B59, B62 **教具**:A1, V24, V25, V28, V29 技能要求:		
1.1 船舶抢滩的预防措施(2 学时) – 描述船舶可以抢摊的环境 – 阐述如果可能的话,应选择海底坡度小的泥质、沙质或砾石质的海滩 – 阐述应以低速抢摊 – 阐述当船舶艄倾严重时,船尾首先抢摊可能有利 – 比较侧对滩和与滩有个合适角度的相对优点 – 阐述沿岸的风或潮汐将很快使船舶偏转为侧对滩 – 描述防止船舶进一步向岸移动以及有助于以后的脱浅应采取的措施 – 阐述应增加或调驳压载水以抵消触底趋势 – 阐述所有液舱应测深并应进行船舶破损的评估 – 阐述应进行测深以确定船舶附近的水深和海底的性质		R1
1.9.2 即将搁浅与搁浅后所采取的行动 **教科书/参考文献**:T10, T3, B58, B59, B62 **教具**:A1, V24, V25, V28, V29, V113 技能要求:		
2.1 搁浅(2 学时) – 阐述在搁浅时,主机应停转,水密门应关闭,全船警报应启动,以及如果正在落潮,主机应全速后退应查明是否船舶能立即脱浅 – 阐述应警告轮机员更换高水位进水口 – 阐述应发射遇险或紧急信号,如有必要应准备救生筏 – 阐述所有的液舱应测深并检查船舶的破损 – 阐述任何有害物质的排放或可能的排放应向最近的海岸无线电台报告 – 阐述应进行测深以确定船舶附近的水深和海底的性质		R1, R2

COMPETENCE 1.9	Respond to Navigational Emergencies	IMO Reference
1.9.3 REFLOATING A GROUNDED SHIP WITH AND WITHOUT ASSISTANCE **Textbooks/Bibliography:** T10, T3, B58, B59, B62 **Teaching aids:** A1, V24, V25, V28, V29 Required performance: **3.1 Refloating (1 hour)** – describes measures which can be taken to prevent further damage to the ship and to assist with subsequent refloating – explains how ballast or other weights may be moved, taken on or discharged to assist refloating – describes the use of ground tackle for hauling off – describes ways in which tugs may be used to assist in refloating – describes the use of the main engine in attempting to refloat and the danger of building up silt from its use		R1
1.9.4 ACTION TO BE TAKEN IF COLLISION IS IMMINENT, AND FOLLOWING A COLLISION OR IMPAIRMENT OF THE WATERTIGHT INTEGRITY OF THE HULL BY ANY CAUSE **Textbooks/Bibliography:** T10, T3, B58, B59, B62 **Teaching aids:** A1, V24, V25, V28, V29 Required performance: **4.1 Action to be taken if collision is imminent and following a collision or impairment of the watertight integrity of the hull by any cause (2 hours)** – lists the duties of the Master following a collision – states that after impact the engines should be stopped, all watertight doors closed, the general alarm sounded and the crew informed of the situation – states that in calm weather the colliding ship should generally remain embedded to allow the other ship time to assess the damage or prepare to abandon ship – states that survival craft should be made ready for abandoning ship or assisting the crew of the other ship – states that a distress or urgency signal should be made, as appropriate – states that requests for information may be received from coastal States – states that, if not in danger, own ship should stand by to render assistance to the other for as long as necessary – states that any discharge or portable discharge of harmful substances should be reported to the nearest coast radio station – states that the owners should be informed and all details of the collision and subsequent actions entered in the logbook		R1 R2

适任 1.9	航行中的应急反应	IMO 参考书目

1.9.3 在有援助和无援助下搁浅船舶的脱浅

教科书/参考文献:T10, T3, B58, B59, B62

教具:A1, V24, V25, V28, V29

技能要求:

3.1 脱浅(1学时) R1

- 描述防止船舶进一步破损以及有助于以后的脱浅所应采取的措施
- 解释为了有助于脱浅,如何移动、加载或卸载压载水或其他重物
- 描述使用锚泊索具脱离
- 描述使用拖船帮助脱浅的方法
- 描述为帮助脱浅主机的使用以及淤泥的累积对使用主机的危险性

1.9.4 即将碰撞、碰撞后或任何原因破坏船体水密完整性时所采取的行动

教科书/参考文献:T10, T3, B58, B59, B62

教具:A1, V24, V25, V28, V29

技能要求:

4.1 即将碰撞、碰撞后或任何原因造成船体水密性的破坏所要采取的行动(2学时)

- 列出碰撞后船长的职责 R1
- 阐述碰撞后主机应停转,全部水密门应关闭,全船警报应启动,以及应通知船员当前情形 R2
- 阐述在平静的天气里,碰撞船一般应保持碰撞状态,以允许他船有时间评估损坏或准备弃船
- 阐述为了弃船或帮助他船船员,应准备好救生艇
- 阐述在合适的时候应发出遇险或紧急信号
- 阐述信息需求可从海岸国家获得
- 阐述如果没有危险,只要有必要,本船应做好准备为他船提供帮助
- 阐述任何有害物质的排放或可能的排放都应向最近的海岸无线电台报告
- 阐述应通知船东,所有碰撞细节及其随后的行动应写入航海日志

COMPETENCE 1.9	Respond to Navigational Emergencies	IMO Reference
1.9.5 ASSESSMENT OF DAMAGE CONTROL **Textbooks/Bibliography:** T10, T3, B58, B59, B62 **Teaching aids:** A1, V24, V25, V28, V29 Required performance: **5.1 Assessment of damage control (1 hour)** – states that damage to own ship should be determined – describes measures to attempt to limit damage and salve own ship		R1
1.9.6 EMERGENCY STEERING **Textbooks/Bibliography:** T10, T3, B58, B59, B62 **Teaching aids:** A1, V24, V25, V28, V29 Required performance: **6.1 Emergency steering (1 hour)** – describes typical arrangements of auxiliary steering gear – describes how the auxiliary steering gear is brought into action – describes how to change from bridge control to local control in the steering gear compartment – states that, when appropriate, a disabled ship should report to a coastal State that it is a potential hazard to other ships or to the environment – lists possible course of action which may be taken by a disabled ship – states the navigational safety message to broadcast and signals to be displayed by a disabled vessel		R1 R14
1.9.7 EMERGENCY TOWING ARRANGEMENTS AND TOWING PROCEDURES **Textbooks/Bibliography:** T10, T3, B58, B59, B62 **Teaching aids:** A1, V128 Required performance: **7.1 Emergency towing arrangements (2 hours)** – states that permission from the owners or charterers is usually required before towing, except for the purpose of saving life – states that a coastal State may intervene when a disabled ship presents a potential risk to the environment – states that early communication should be established between the vessels to agree on the method of connecting the tow – states that both vessels should have everything prepared and have agreed on communication before the arrival of the towing ship – describes how to approach a disabled vessel and pass the first connection by line-throwing apparatus or other methods – states that the tow normally passes a messenger followed by a wire messenger to the towing vessel to haul across the towing line – describes how to pay out the towing wire under control – describes methods of securing the towing wire at the towing ship		R1

适任 1.9	航行中的应急反应	IMO 参考书目
1.9.5 破损控制的评估 **教科书/参考文献**:T10, T3, B58, B59, B62 **教具**:A1, V24, V25, V28, V29 技能要求: **5.1 破损控制的评估(1 学时)** – 阐述应确定本船的损坏 – 描述试图控制破损和救助本船的措施		R1
1.9.6 应急操舵 **教科书/参考文献**:T10, T3, B58, B59, B62 **教具**:A1, V24, V25, V28, V29 技能要求: **6.1 应急操舵(1 学时)** – 描述典型的辅助操舵装置的设置 – 描述如何使辅助操舵装置投入运行 – 描述如何在舵机间里将驾驶台控制切换到本机控制 – 描述在合适的时候,失控船应向海岸当局报告其对他船或环境存在潜在的危险 – 列出失控船可能采取行动的方案 – 阐述失控船应广播的航海安全信息以及应发出的信号		R1 R14
1.9.7 应急拖带部署与拖带程序 **教科书/参考文献**:T10, T3, B58, B59, B62 **教具**:A1, V128 技能要求: **7.1 应急拖带部署(2 学时)** – 描述除了救助人命外,在拖带之前通常需要得到船东或承租人的许可 – 阐述当失控船对环境存在潜在危险时,海岸当局可以进行干预 – 阐述船舶间应建立早期通信,以在连接到拖船的方法上达成一致 – 阐述在拖带船到达之前,两船应准备就绪并在通信中达成一致 – 描述如何接近失控船以及如何利用抛绳器或其他手段进行初次连接 – 阐述拖船通常将一根带有钢丝引缆的传递到拖带船以拉过拖绳 – 描述如何控制拖带钢丝缆的送出 – 描述在拖带船上系固拖带钢丝缆的方法		R1

COMPETENCE 1.9	Respond to Navigational Emergencies	IMO Reference
– explains why the wire is usually shackled to the anchor cable of the tow – describes the preparations made by the disabled ship – states that the towing wire should be protected from chafing at fairleads – states that wires and cables should be inspected frequently and the nip freshened if any sign of wear or chafe is found – describes how to take the weight of the tow – explains how the towing speed should be decided – describes how to disconnect the tow on arrival at the destination – describes the emergency towing arrangements for all tankers of not less than 20,000 dwt		

适任 1.9	航行中的应急反应	IMO 参考书目
– 解释为什么这根钢丝绳通常用卸扣固定在被拖船的锚链上 – 描述失控船应进行的准备 – 描述拖带钢丝绳应在导缆孔处加以保护以防止磨损 – 阐述应经常检查钢丝绳和锚链,如果发现任何的磨损或破损的迹象,应更换损伤处 – 描述如何承受被拖船的重量 – 描述如何决定拖带速度 – 描述在到达目的地后如何解拖 – 描述不低于 20 000 dwt 油船的应急拖带部署		

COMPETENCE 1.10	Manoeuvre and Handle a Ship in all Conditions	IMO Reference
TRAINING OUTCOME: Demonstrates a knowledge and understanding of: 1.10.1 MANOEUVRING AND HANDLING A SHIP IN ALL CONDITIONS		STCW Code table A-II/2

适任 1.10	在各种状况下操纵和操作船舶	IMO 参考书目
培训效果: 讲授下列内容知识与理解: 1.10.1　在各种状况下操纵和操作船舶		STCW 公约 表 A-II/2

COMPETENCE 1.10	Manoeuvre and Handle a Ship in all Conditions	IMO Reference
1.10.1 MANOEUVRING AND HANDLING A SHIP IN ALL CONDITIONS **Textbooks/Bibliography:** T3, T8, T11, T18, T25, T10, B16, B24, B25, B58, B59, B60, B61,B62, B63, B99, B125, B163, B164, B165, B200, B214 **Teaching aids:** A1, V3, V4, V5, V6, V7, V8, V9, V10, V11, V12, V13, V14, V15, V16, V17, V18, V19, V30, V31, V32, V33, V98, V140, V142, V152, V168 Required performance: * The STCW Convention requires trainees to be able to demonstrate practical competence in performing the manoeuvres stated under this competence. This competence may be developed and demonstrated in service, in which case the practical elements of actual ship handling may not be included in the training course. The required performances indicated with an asterix are therefore applicable only where the competence is to be developed and assessed as part of a training course using simulators, manned ship models or training ships.		
1.1 Approaching pilot stations and embarking or disembarking pilots, with due regard to weather, tide, headreach and stopping distances (4 hours)		R1
– explains the importance and the procedure of making a passage plan from sea to berth		R2, R20
– describes the preparations for picking up a pilot		R2
– states that a second steering-gear power unit should be in operation where possible		R1
– states that steering should be changed to manual in ample time and tested – states that anchors should be cleared and ready for letting go – explains how to reduce speed when approaching the pilot station, taking account of wind and tidal set – explains why the ship's speed should be reduced to a suitable speed for the pilot boat to come alongside – describes how to make a lee for the pilot boat – states that extra care should be taken after dropping the pilot until clear of inward ships manoeuvring to embark pilots – plans manoueuvres for the embarking and disembarking of pilots under varying environmental conditions – performs manoeuvres to embark and disembark pilots in varying environmental conditions*		
1.2 Handling ship in rivers, estuaries and restricted waters having regard to the effects of current, wind and restricted water on helm response (10 hours)		R1
– defines shallow water as a depth of less than 2 times the ship's draught – explains that shallow-water effects become more marked as the under-keel clearance decreases		

适任 1.10	**在各种状况下操纵和操作船舶**	**IMO 参考书目**

1.10.1　在各种状况下操纵和操作船舶

教科书/参考文献:T3, T8, T11, T18, T25, T3, B16, B24,B25, B58, B59, B60, B61, B62, B63, B99, B125, B163, B164, B165, B200, B214

教具:A1, V3, V4, V5, V6, V7, V8, V9, V10,V11, V12, V13, V14, V15, V16, V17, V18, V19, V30, V31, V32, V33, V98,V140, V142, V152, V168

技能要求:

*STCW 公约要求学员能够展示在完成本适任能力中阐述的操纵方面的实际能力。这种能力可加以培养和在服务中体现,在这种情况下,培训课程可能不包括实船操纵的实用因素。因此,用 * 标出的技能要求的内容仅在利用模拟器、有人船模或实习船培养和评估该能力作为部分培训课程的情况下适用。

1.1　考虑天气、潮汐、冲程和停车距离后接近引航站、上下引航员(4 学时) R1

- 解释从海上到靠泊的航线设计的重要性和程序 R2, R20

R2

- 描述迎接引航员的准备工作
- 阐述可能情况下应运行舵机的备用电源 R1
- 阐述在时间充裕时切换到人工操舵并进行测试
- 阐述锚应清爽并准备抛锚
- 解释考虑风和潮流流向情况下接近引航站时如何降低船速
- 解释为什么船速应降低到一个适当值以使引航艇靠拢
- 描述如何为引航艇制作下风
- 阐述在引航员离船后应格外小心直到让清正在进行接引航员操作的进口船
- 在各种情况下上下引航员的操纵计划
- 在各种情况下上下引航员的操纵 *

1.2　考虑流、风、受限水域对舵效的影响下,在河流、河口和受限水域里的船舶操纵(10 学时) R1

- 把小于 2 倍船舶吃水的水深定义为浅水
- 解释当船舶富余水深减小时,浅水效应变得更加明显

COMPETENCE 1.10	Manoeuvre and Handle a Ship in all Conditions	IMO Reference

– lists shallow-water effects as:
  – increased directional stability and sluggish response to helm
  – the speed falls less during turns
  – a large increase in turning radius
  – a more pronounced effect from transverse propeller thrust
  – a possibility that transverse thrust may act opposite to that expected
  – the ship carries her way longer and responds slowly to changes in engine speed
  – the trim changes, usually by the head for a full hull form
  – an increase in squat
– defines squat as the reduction of under-keel clearance resulting from bodily sinkage and change of trim which occurs when a ship moves through the water
– calculates the approximate sinkage due to squat in deep water
– states that the squat in shallow water (ratio of water depth/draught = 2) may be double that in deep water
– states that squat in canals and restricted channels in proximity to other vessels may be significantly greater
– uses a squat estimation diagram
– explains the meaning of "blockage factor" in restricted channels
– explains how squat and trim effects increase with blockage factor
– describes the reduction in keel clearance resulting from rolling and pitching and heel or list
– states that speed should be moderate in rivers, estuaries, etc. to reduce shallow-water effects and to provide reserve power for correcting a sheer
– describes how to round bends in a channel with a current in either direction, taking account of the effect of wind
– describes the use of an anchor to assist in rounding a bend
– describes how to turn short round in a narrow channel, with or without a wind
– describes the use of an anchor to assist turning in a channel
– explains the importance of navigating at reduced speed to avoid damage caused by own ship's bow wave or stern wave
– describes how a passing ship affects a moored ship
– plans manoeuvres in rivers, estuaries and restricted waters in varying environmental conditions
– performs manoeuvres in rivers, estuaries and restricted waters in varying environmental conditions*		

1.3 Application of constant rate of turn techniques (3 hours) – describes the circumstances in which a constant rate turn is appropriate – describes how to plan a constant rate turn – describes how to judge the correct execution of a constant rate turn by visual means – describes how radar can be used to assist in monitoring a constant rate turn – describes how to determine the wheel over position bearing for a constant rate turn		R1

适任 1.10	在各种状况下操纵和操作船舶	IMO 参考书目
	– 列出浅水效应 – 航向稳定性变好,舵变得不灵敏 – 旋转时船速下降幅度小 – 旋转半径增大 – 螺旋桨横向推力效应变得更加明显 – 有可能横向推力作用到预计的反方向 – 船舶保持航向的时间更长,对主机变速反应缓慢 – 吃水差发生变化,通常整体艏倾 – 船体下沉量增大 – 把由于船舶整体下沉以及当船舶对水航行时吃水差的变化而产生的富余水深的减小定义为船体下沉量 – 计算在深水区由于船体下沉而产生的大约下沉量 – 阐述浅水区的船体下沉量(水深与吃水的比为2)可以是深水区的2倍 – 解释在运河和受限航道与其他船舶邻近时船体下沉会明显加大 – 使用船体下沉量估计图表 – 解释在受限航道“堵塞系数”的意思 – 解释下沉量和纵倾效如何随堵塞系数的增加而增加 – 描述由于横摇和纵摇以及倾斜或横倾造成富余水深的减少 – 阐述为减少浅水效应和提供修正偏航的储备动力,船速在河里或河口应保持中等 – 描述在考虑风的影响下,如何顶流或顺流过弯道 – 描述锚在协助过弯道时的运用 – 描述在有风或无风的情况下,如何在狭水道里进行小半径的旋转 – 描述锚在协助航道里旋转时的运用 – 解释为避免由本船首航行波或尾航行波造成的浪损而减速航行的重要性 – 描述路过的船舶对系泊船的影响 – 在各种情况下,在河流、河口和受限水域里的操纵计划 – 在各种情况下,在河流、河口和受限水域里的操纵 *	
1.3	**恒定旋转率的应用技巧(3学时)** – 描述适合恒定旋转率的环境 – 描述如何计划恒定旋转 – 描述如何用视觉判断恒定旋转的正确执行 – 描述如何使用雷达协助监控恒定旋转 – 描述如何确定舵轮转动的位置以达到恒定旋转	R1

COMPETENCE 1.10	Manoeuvre and Handle a Ship in all Conditions	IMO Reference
	– describes how a constant rate turn is effective in helping a vessel maintain its planned trail – plans turns using constant rate of turn techniques – performs turns using constant rate of turn techniques*	
1.4	**Manoeuvring in shallow water including the reduction in under-keel clearance caused by squat, rolling and pitching (2 hours)** – describes the effect of squat on under-keel clearance, trim and vessel manoeuvring characteristics – describes the changes in dynamic under-keel clearance when manoeuvres are conducted in shallow water in conjunction with turning or the effects of sea and swell – describes the use of the kick-ahead to control the speed and direction of the vessel – explains how a ship will respond to helm before increasing speed when using a kick-ahead – identifies the danger of taking a sheer in shallow water and what corrective action can be taken – describes how tugs can be used to assist in maintaining slow speed control – describes how anchors can be used to assist in manoeuvring a vessel in shallow water – plans manoeuvres to be conducted in shallow water with and without the effects of sea and swell – performs manoeuvres in shallow water*	R1
1.5	**Interaction between passing ships and between own ship and nearby banks (canal effect) (2 hours)** – explains and describes the interaction between ship and shore – explains and describes the interaction between ships when meeting end-on – explains and describes the interaction between ships in an overtaking situation – explains the particular dangers of interaction when working close by other craft such as tugs – describes the pattern of pressure changes round the hull of a moving ship – explains the interaction between a ship and nearby banks (bank cushion and bank suction) – describes the interaction between passing ships – describes how to pass or overtake another ship safely in a narrow channel – explains that shoal patches may give rise to bank cushion or suction, resulting in an unexpected sheer – explains the possible effects on squat, trim and vessel manoeuvring characteristics with different blockage factors and speeds – plans manoeuvres where ship to ship and ship to topography interaction are anticipated – performs manoeuvres where ship to ship and ship to topography interaction are experienced*	R1

适任 1.10	在各种状况下操纵和操作船舶	IMO 参考书目
– 描述在帮助船舶保持计划航迹时恒定旋转如何起作用 – 运用恒定旋转率技术的转向计划 – 运用恒定旋转率技术的转向 *		
1.4 船体下沉、横倾和纵倾引起富余水深减少时的浅水操纵(2 学时)		R1
– 描述船体下沉对富余水深、吃水差和船舶操纵性能的影响 – 描述在浅水区转向操纵或海浪和涌的共同影响下,富余水深的动态变化 – 描述运用前冲来控制航向和船速 – 解释当运用前冲时,在船舶提速前,船舶如何响应舵 – 识别在浅水区域船舶偏转的危险以及应采取纠正措施 – 描述拖船保持船舶低速控制的应用 – 描述如何用锚协助在浅水区操纵船舶 – 有海浪和涌以及无海浪和涌时,浅水区的操纵计划 – 进行浅水区的操纵 *		
1.5 船舶间、船岸间的相互作用(运河效应)(2 学时)		R1
– 解释并描述船与岸之间的相互作用 – 解释并描述后船首接近前船尾的两船之间的相互作用 – 解释并描述追越局面船舶之间的相互作用 – 解释当如拖船这类小船在船舶附近作业而相互作用的特殊危险性 – 描述运动船体周围压力变化的模型 – 描述船舶与附近岸壁之间的相互作用(岸推和岸吸) – 描述相互驶过两船间的相互作用 – 描述如何在狭水道内安全驶过或追越他船 – 解释点滩可能产生岸推或岸吸,导致意外的偏航 – 解释不同堵塞系数和速度情况下对船体下沉、吃水差和船舶操纵性能的可能影响 – 在预计中的船对船和船对岸相互作用情况下的操纵计划 – 在船对船和船对岸相互作用情况下的操纵 *		

COMPETENCE 1.10	Manoeuvre and Handle a Ship in all Conditions	IMO Reference

1.6 Berthing and unberthing under various conditions of wind, tide and current with and without tugs (20* hours)
– describes the effects of right-and left-handed propellers on manoeuvring
– describes the use of twin screws for manoeuvring
– explains the advantages and disadvantages of controllable-pitch propellers with regard to ship handling
– describes the use of lateral thrusters
– states that lateral thrusters cease to be effective above a certain speed, which has to be determined by trial
– describes, with reference to ship type and trim, the likely effect of wind on a ship when moving ahead or astern and when stopped
– explains how an anchor or anchors may be used to assist in manoeuvring
– describes the use of anchors for stopping in an emergency
– describes the different ways in which tugs may be made fast and used
– explains fully how to use engine, helm, tugs, anchors and mooring lines to berth and unberth under various conditions of wind and tide at:
  – river berths
  – piers
  – locks
  – enclosed docks
  – a single buoy
  – two buoys
  – multibuoy berths
  – Mediterranean moorings
– describes the mooring lines to be used, their leads and methods of securing at the berths listed above
– explains that when wind blows against a ship, a force acts almost in the opposite direction to the relative wind direction and the magnitude is proportional to the square of the relative velocity of the wind
– states that knowing the magnitude of the wind force and how it affects the ship is of great importance during berthing/unberthing
– explains that the knowledge of above mentioned magnitude, will assist the Master to:
  – decide whether the available tugs have sufficient power to hold the ship against a crosswind or to move the ship against a crosswind
  – decide whether the thrusters have the necessary power to manoeuvre the ship safely under the prevailing wind conditions
  – determine the effect of a longitudinal wind in respect of its effect on the ship's stopping distance
		R1

适任 1.10	在各种情况下操纵和操作船舶	IMO 参考文献

1.6 在各种风、潮汐和海流时有拖船和无拖船情况下的靠泊与离泊(20* 学时) R1

- 描述右旋式和左旋式螺旋桨的操纵效应
- 描述使用双螺旋桨的操纵
- 解释可变螺距螺旋桨在船舶操纵方面的优点和缺点
- 描述侧推器的使用
- 阐述须经试验确定,侧推器在超过某一速度时将失去作用
- 根据船舶的类型和吃水差,在船舶时,描述风在船舶前进或后退和静止时可能的影响
- 解释如何利用单锚或多锚进行操纵
- 描述锚在紧急情况下停止船舶的应用
- 描述可以挽牢拖船及使用的不同方法
- 详细解释如何应用主机、舵、锚以及系船缆,在各种风和潮汐条件下,在下列位置靠泊和离泊:
  - 河流泊位
  - 码头
  - 船闸
  - 封闭式船坞
  - 单浮筒
  - 双浮筒
  - 多浮筒泊位
  - 地中海系泊泊位
- 描述在以上泊位中所用缆绳、导缆孔以及挽牢的方法
- 解释当风吹向船舶,产生一个几乎与相对风向相反方向的作用力,其大小和相对风速的平方成正比
- 说明在靠/离泊期间,了解风力大小及其如何影响船舶是极其重要的
- 解释了解上述风力的大小将有助于船长:
  - 决定现有拖船是否具有足够动力在横风中驻留船舶或使船受横风时向上风移动
  - 决定侧推器是否具有足够动力在当前风的情况下安全操纵船舶
  - 确定首尾方向来风对停船距离的影响

COMPETENCE 1.10	Manoeuvre and Handle a Ship in all Conditions	IMO Reference

- explains that the wind force in tonnes may, with a certain approximation, be expressed by the formula:
  K (wind) = $k \times A \times V^2$
  where K = wind force in tonnes
  k = constant depending on the ship and direction of the wind (as an average figure for k, the following constants can be used: $k = 0.52 \times 10^{-4}$ (for a beam wind) and $k = 0.39 \times 10^{-4}$ (for a longitudinal wind)
  A = windage area in square metres
  V = relative velocity of the wind in m/sec
- explains that normally tugs cannot hold a ship against a cross current, as the power, which is necessary for such an operation, is enormous
- explains that the force (K) required to oppose a cross current in deep waters might be determined approximately by the formula:
  $K = k_{deep} \times L \times d \times V^2$ (where K = current force in tonnes, k = constant, 0.033 for deep water, L = vessel length in metres, d = vessel draft in metres and V = current speed in m/sec)
- explains that the force (K) required to oppose a cross current in shallow waters might be determined approximately by the formula:
  $K = 0.033 \times f \times L \times d \times V^2$ (where K = current force in tonnes, 0.033 is the constant, f = the shallow water constant modifier derived from a graph, L = vessel length in metres, d = vessel draft in metres and V = current speed in m/sec)
- plans manoeuvres to berth and unberth in varying environmental conditions and with and without tugs
- performs manoeuvres to berth and unberth in varying environmental conditions and with and without tugs*

1.7 Ship and Tug interaction (3 hours) R1

- describes the type of tug, i.e. conventional single or twin-screw tugs fitted or not fitted with nozzles, tractor type tugs and the ASD (azimuth stern drive) tugs
- describes the main difference resulting from the location of tug's propulsion and towing point
- explains the dangers related to ship-tug interaction
- explains the dangers for relatively small tugs when compared with the size of assisted ships in relation to interaction phenomenon
- states the special attention to be paid by the Master on the condition of own vessel, i.e. ships in ballast condition or for ships having particular overhanging stern, found generally on large container vessels, the danger of interaction which is created and the danger of damages that can be caused to the tug's hull and superstructure, during the ship-tug cooperation
- explains the tug bow-cushion effect
- explains the risk during the ship-tug cooperation of the tug getting sucked under the bow of the ship with risk of capsizing, and the importance of immediate action required by the tug master, by the application of rudder and the use of available power to go full astern, to avoid above
- explains why tractor type tugs are generally found to be less vulnerable in the above mentioned situation
- explains "girting" and the dangers associated with it
- explains the dangers of ships high speed during ship-tug cooperation

适任 1.10	在各种状况下操纵和操作船舶	IMO 参考书目
– 解释以吨为单位的风力可以用近似公式计算： $K(\text{wind}) = k \times A \times V^2$ 式中：K—风力（吨）； k—由船和风的方向决定的常数。k 取平均值时，可用下列常数： $k = 0.52 \times 10^{-4}$（横风）和 $k = 0.39 \times 10^{-4}$（首尾来风）； A—每平方米受风面积； V—风速（米 / 秒） – 解释通常拖船不能使船在横流中驻留，因为此种作业所需动力巨大 – 解释在深水需要对抗所受横流的力（K）可用近似公式计算： $K = k_{\text{deep}} \times L \times d \times V^2$ 式中：K—水流力（吨）；k—常数，深水中取 0.033；L—船长（米）；d—吃水（米）； V—流速（米 / 秒） – 解释在浅水需要对抗所受横流的力（K）可用近似公式计算： $K = 0.033 \times f \times L \times d \times V^2$ 式中：K—水流力（吨）；0.033 是常数；f 为来自于图表的常数修正量，L—船长（米），d—吃水（米）；V—流速（米 / 秒） – 在各种情况下有拖船和无拖船靠离泊的操纵计划 – 在各种情况下有拖船和无拖船靠离泊的操纵 *		
1.7 船舶和拖船的相互作用（3 学时） – 描述拖船种类，即传统的配备或没有配备喷管的单桨或双桨拖船、牵引式拖船和 ASD（方位尾驱动）拖船 – 描述由于拖船不同驱动位置和拖带点所产生的主要差别 – 解释有关船—拖相互作用的危险 – 解释当拖船与被拖船舶尺度相比相对较小而出现有关相互作用现象的危险 – 阐述船长应特别注意本船情况，即船舶压载情况，具有特殊悬伸船尾通常是大型集装箱船尾部，这在船—拖协作期间会出现船—拖相互作用的危险和损坏拖船船体及其上层建筑的危险 – 解释拖船首推效应 – 解释在船—拖协作期间，大船存在倾覆危险时，拖船有被吸入大船船首之下的危险，以及拖船船长要求采取立即行动的重要性，通过用舵和全力后拉来避免上述情况的发生 – 解释牵引式拖船在上述情况下不太容易受损的原因 – 解释“束缚”及与其相关的危险 – 解释在船—拖协作期间高船速的危险		R1

COMPETENCE 1.10	Manoeuvre and Handle a Ship in all Conditions	IMO Reference

	– describes the meaning of "gob rope", and how its use on conventional tugs can improve the situation of "girting"
	– explains how the use of such "gob rope" limits the manoeuvrability of the towing tug
	– explains the precaution needed to be exercised for the tug's safety, while using the tugs, in respect to:
	  – the visibility of ship's bulbous bow
	  – short towlines
	  – excessive forward speed of the ship or sudden changes in a ship's heading and speed
	  – experience and the ability of the crew in releasing tug's towline, when needed
	  – underestimating wind and current forces
	  – information exchange pilot-shipmaster-tug captain
	  – operating bow-to-bow
	– explains the importance of keeping the ship's speed and heading constant when passing or taking a towline
	– explains the knowledge necessary for a Master when ordering the number and total bollard pull of tugs
	– explains the important criteria of ships' loading conditions when planning for the number of tugs and the tug position along the hull
	– describes the effectiveness of tug(s), during ship-tug cooperation, in relation to pivot point, leverage, and tendency of the ship to swing in a particular direction, in the following conditions:
	  – when the ship is stopped and making no way through the water (dead in the water)
	  – when the ship is making headway
	  – when the ship is making sternway
	– plans manoeuvres involving tugs to minimize adverse interaction effects and optimize tug efficiency
	– performs manoeuvres involving tugs to minimize adverse interaction effects and optimize tug efficiency*	

1.8	**Use of propulsion and manoeuvring systems including various types of rudder (4* hours)**
	– describes various types of rudders, including:
	  – Flap rudder (commonly known as the "Becker rudder")
	  – Rotor rudder (commonly known as the "Jastram rudder")
	  – T-shaped rudder (commonly known as the "Single Schilling rudder")
	  – Twin Schilling rudders and explains their advantages with regard to ship handling
	– describes how the use of bow-thrust can be used to assist in manoeuvring
	– describes how the use of stern-thrust can be used to assist in manoeuvring
	– describes the use of high-lift rudder systems to improve ship manoeuvrability
	– describes the use of dynamically positioned vessels and their control systems
	– describes the use of rudder cycling to reduce head reach in an emergency
		R1

适任 1.10	在各种状况下操纵和操作船舶	IMO 参考书目

– 解释“水兵绳”的含义以及常规的拖船如何用它来改善“束缚”情形
– 解释如何用“水兵绳”来限制拖带中的拖船的操纵能力
– 解释在以下方面采取必要的预防措施来保证拖船安全工作:
  – 船舶球鼻艏的能见度
  – 短拖缆
  – 过大的前进速度或航向和速度的突然改变
  – 必要时,船员解拖的经验和能力
  – 低估风、流的作用力
  – 引航员—船长—拖船船长间的信息交换
  – 艏对艏作业
– 解释在传递和接受拖缆时保持速度和航向不变的重要性
– 解释船长在预订拖船数量和总拖力方面的必要的知识
– 解释在计划拖船数量和船体拖带位置时船舶装载情况的重要标准
– 描述在下列情况下,船—拖协作期间,拖船在转心、杠杆力、向某一特定方向旋回船舶趋势方面的有效性:
  – 当船舶停车且不对水移动(静止于水中)
  – 当船舶前进时
  – 当船舶后退时
– 计划减少拖船不利相互作用的操纵及优化拖船效率
– 进行减少拖船不利相互作用的操纵及优化拖船效率 *		

1.8 推进系统和包括各种类型舵的操纵系统的使用(4* 学时)
– 描述各种舵,包括:
  – 襟翼舵(通常称为“Becker 舵”)
  – 转子舵(通常称为“Jastram 舵”)
  – T 形舵(通常称为“单 Schilling 舵”)
  – 双 Schilling 舵及其船舶操纵方面的优点
– 描述如何使用艏侧推器协助操纵
– 描述如何使用艉侧推器协助操纵
– 描述使用高升力舵提高船舶操纵性
– 描述动态定位船舶的应用及其控制系统
– 描述舵循环系统在紧急情况下减小冲程的应用
		R1

COMPETENCE 1.10	Manoeuvre and Handle a Ship in all Conditions	IMO Reference
	– compares the effectiveness of rudder cycling with a crash stop – plans manoeuvres using bow and stern thrusters – performs manoeuvres using rudder cycling to control speed and bow and stern thrusters*	

1.9	**Choice of anchorage; anchoring with one or two anchors in limited anchorages and factors involved in determining the length of anchor cable to be used (6 hours)**
	– explains how to choose an anchorage and lists the factors which influence the choice
	– states that an anchoring plan should be prepared in advance, showing the direction and speed of approach and the dropping position(s), with check bearings
	– explains how to judge that a ship is stopped ready for letting go
	– explains that positions should be obtained on letting go and again when brought up
	– describes the use of anchor buoys
	– lists the factors to consider in determining the length of anchor cable to be used as:
	  – the nature of the bottom
	  – the strength of current or wind
	  – the strength and direction of the tidal stream
	  – the exposure of the anchorage to bad weather
	  – the amount of room to swing
	  – the expected length of stay at anchor
	– plans anchorage positions and manoeuvres to anchor the vessel using one and two anchors
	– performs manoeuvres to anchor the vessel using one and two anchors*
		R1

1.10	**Procedures for anchoring in deep water and in shallow water (1 hour)** – describes holding powers of different anchors – describes the preparation of anchors, including walking the anchor back for anchoring in deep water – explains that when lowering anchor under power, excessive load on the anchor cable could cause damage or wear of the windlass engine and gearing	
1.11	**Dragging anchor; clearing fouled anchors (1 hour)** – defines dragging and explains how to detect it – describes the actions to be taken when the anchor starts to drag – explains how excessive yawing may break the anchor out of its holding and describes measures to control yaw – describes how to bring a ship to an open moor – explains what is meant by 'foul hawse' and how it occurs – describes how to clear a foul hawse – describes how to clear a fouled anchor – describes how to buoy and slip an anchor	R1

适任 1.10	在各种状况下操纵和操作船舶	IMO 参考书目
– 紧急停车情状下舵循环系统的有效性的比较 – 计划艏侧推器和艉侧推器的操纵 – 进行舵循环系统在控制船速中的运用、艏侧推器和艉侧推器的操纵 *		

1.9 锚地的选择;在受限锚地单锚泊或双锚泊以及决定出链长度时所考虑的因素(6 学时)
– 解释如何选择锚地并列出影响锚地选择的因素
– 阐述应事先准备锚泊计划,表明抵达锚地的方向和船速,抛锚的位置以及核实的方位
– 解释如何判断船舶已停妥可以抛锚
– 解释在抛锚时以及抓牢时应获得的船位
– 描述锚位浮标的应用
– 列出在确定应使用链长时需考虑的因素:
  – 底质
  – 流或风的强度
  – 潮流的方向和强度
  – 锚地受恶劣天气影响情况
  – 回旋余地大小
  – 在锚地预计停留时间
– 计划锚地位置和使用单锚、双锚进行锚泊操纵
– 使用单锚和双锚进行锚泊操纵 *
		R1

1.10 深水区锚泊和浅水区锚泊程序(1 学时) – 描述不同锚的抓力 – 描述抛锚准备工作,包括收回走锚以备在深水区锚泊 – 解释用锚机松锚时,锚链过大负荷可能造成锚机和传动装置损坏或磨损		
1.11 走锚与锚绞缠时的清理(1 学时) – 定义走锚以及如何检测走锚 – 描述开始走锚时应采取的行动 – 解释过大的偏荡会破坏锚抓底,并描述控制偏荡的措施 – 描述如何将船舶带到开阔的锚地 – 解释何谓“锚链绞缠”以及它是如何发生的 – 描述如何清解锚链绞缠 – 描述如何清解被链缠住的锚 – 描述如何使用浮标定位锚以及如何弃锚		R1

COMPETENCE 1.10	Manoeuvre and Handle a Ship in all Conditions	IMO Reference

1.12 Dry-docking (4 hours)
– lists the information required by the dry-dock authorities as:
  – length, beam and rise of floor, if any
  – draughts and trim
  – position of bilge keels and appendages such as a bulbous bow
  – whether single or twin screw
  – the weight and disposition of any cargo on board
  – position of any hull damage for inspection or repair
– states that a plan showing the position of bulkheads, main structural members and drain plugs is required for the preparation of beds and shores when dry-docking in the loaded condition
– explains why a slight trim by the stern is the ideal condition for dry-docking
– explains the need for adequate statical stability and states when the most critical condition occurs
– determines that the vessel has adequate statical stability for docking by calculation
– plans the distribution of deadweight items to ensure adequate statical stability during docking
– describes the use of bilge blocks, breast shores and bilge shores and their placement during pumping out
– states that all tanks should be sounded and the readings recorded when the ship takes the keel blocks
– explains why, as far as possible, tanks should be full or empty
– explains that tanks and movable weights should be restored to their original condition before flooding the dock to ensure the same trim and zero list on refloating
– explains why a ship may be left partially waterborne if damage is accessible
– explains how an adequate supply of water for firefighting and a telephone for calling emergency services should be arranged
– lists the precautions to be taken and the preparations to be made before flooding the dock
		R1

1.13 Management and handling ships in heavy weather, including assisting a ship or aircraft in distress; towing operations; means of keeping an unmanageable ship out of a sea trough; lessening drift and use of oil (6 hours) – states that the use of weather routeing can reduce the number of occasions on which heavy weather is encountered – explains that the most common reason for heavy weather damage is lack of proper route planning taking into consideration the 96 hrs, 72 hrs and 48 hrs forecasts during planning – describes the precautions to be taken before the onset of heavy weather – explains the importance of understanding the enormous stresses encountered by the ship in heavy weather conditions – defines wavelength, period, and period of encounter of waves and swell – explains that high wave heights are one of the most common reasons for heavy weather damage		R1

适任 1.10	在各种状况下操纵和操作船舶	IMO 参考文献
1.12 入干船坞(4 学时) – 列出干船坞管理部门要求的信息: – 船长、船宽及船底的倾斜度 – 吃水和吃水差 – 舭龙骨和船体附件(如球鼻艏)的位置 – 单螺旋桨还是双螺旋桨 – 船上任何货物的重量和分布 – 需要检查或修理的任何船体破损的位置 – 阐述应要求一份具有舱壁、主要结构部分及泄水孔塞位置的平面图,以利船舶在装载情况下入干船坞时,准备支船架和支船柱 – 解释为何轻微艉倾入干船坞是理想的情况 – 解释适当静稳性的必要性以及何时出现最关键的情况 – 通过计算确定船舶入干船坞的适度静稳性 – 制作载重量各项分布计划以确保入干船坞时适度静稳性 – 描述在抽水时,舭龙骨墩、横撑木和舭撑柱的使用以及它们的布置 – 阐述在船舶安放龙骨墩时,所有液舱应进行测深并进行记录 – 解释为什么应尽可能把舱注满或排空 – 解释在向船坞注水之前,液舱和可移动的重物应恢复原状,以确保船舶重新浮起时,具有同样的吃水差和无横倾 – 解释如果船舶易受损,为何船舶应部分留在水中 – 解释如何提供足够的消防水以及如何安排紧急报警电话呼叫服务 – 列出在向船坞注水之前,应采取的预防措施和准备工作		R1
1.13 在恶劣天气下管理与操纵船舶,包括救援遇险船舶、飞机,拖带作业,使失控船舶脱离海上低压槽的方法,减少下风漂移和油的使用(6 学时) – 阐述气象航线的使用能减少遭遇恶劣天气的次数 – 解释最常见的恶劣天气损坏是由于在航线设计时没有适当考虑 96 小时、72 小时和 48 小时天气预报 – 描述在受恶劣天气影响前应采取的预防措施 – 解释理解船在恶劣天气里承受巨大应力的重要性 – 定义海浪和涌浪的波长、周期和遭遇周期 – 解释大的浪高是恶劣天气损坏的最常见原因之一		R1

COMPETENCE 1.10	Manoeuvre and Handle a Ship in all Conditions	IMO Reference

	– describes the methods of observing the frequency of wave beating and the formula with which it can be calculated (for ships less than 250 m in length and for ships whose length exceeds 250 m)
	– defines rolling period and synchronous rolling
	– explains how synchronous rolling can be avoided by an alteration of speed or course to change the period of encounter
	– describes synchronous pitching and how to prevent it
	– explains that parametric rolling is caused due to changes in parameters of stability which are: Displacement *W* (constant), Righting lever *GZ* (variable), $W \times GZ$ = righting moment
	– explains that parametric roll motions with large and dangerous roll amplitudes in waves are due to the variation of stability between the position on the wave crest and the position in the wave trough
	– explains that among the measures which the vessel can take to avoid parametric rolling and synchronous rolling are ensuring that the vessel has adequate intact stability and that the course and speed of the ship should be selected in a way to avoid conditions for which the encounter period is
	  – close to the ship roll period or
	  – the encounter period is close to one half of the ship roll period
	– describes how excessive speed into head seas can cause severe panting and slamming stresses
	– states that excessive slamming may be almost unnoticed on the bridge of a very large ship
	– explains that heavy pitching also gives rise to high longitudinal stresses, racing of the propeller and the shipping of water
	– defines "pooping" and describes the conditions in which it may occur
	– defines "broaching-to" and describes the conditions in which it may occur
	– explains that a reduction in speed combined with an alteration of course can reduce the danger of broaching-to and of being pooped
	– describes how to turn a ship in heavy seas
	– states that a ship may be hove-to with the wind on the bow or on the quarter or stopped
	– describes the circumstances in which each of the methods above may be used
	– describes methods of turning a disabled ship's head to keep it out of a sea trough and of lessening lee drift
	– explains that a ship may drift at an angle to the downwind direction and that its direction of drift will depend upon which side it has the wind
	– describes how to use oil to reduce breaking seas when hove-to and when manoeuvring in heavy seas
	– describes actions to prevent a ship being driven on to a lee shore
	– describes how to assist a ship or aircraft in distress
	– describes towing operations		

适任 1.10	在各种状况下操纵和操作船舶	IMO 参考书目

	– 描述观测波浪拍击频率及其用来计算的公式(用于船长小于250米和船长大于250米船舶)
	– 定义横摇周期和谐摇
	– 解释如何通过改变航速或航向来改变遭遇周期以避免横向谐摇
	– 描述纵向谐摇以及应如何避免
	– 解释参数横摇是由于稳性参数变化所引起:排水量W(常数量)、复原力臂GZ(变量),$W\times GZ$=复原力矩
	– 解释波浪中大而危险的参数横摇运动是由于在波峰与波谷之间位置的稳性变化所致
	– 解释船舶能采取避免参数横摇和横向谐摇的措施是,确保船舶具有足够的完整稳性和选择航向和速度以避免如下情形
	  – 遭遇周期接近船舶横摇周期或
	  – 遭遇周期接近船舶横摇周期的一半
	– 描述以过大的速度进入艏向浪如何会产生严重的拍底和冲击应力
	– 阐述超大型船舶的驾驶台可能注意不到过大的冲击
	– 解释严重的纵摇会产生纵向应力、螺旋桨空转以及船舶上浪
	– 定义“艉淹”以及可能产生的条件
	– 定义“正横受浪”以及可能产生的条件
	– 解释减速加变向能减少“正横受浪”和“艉淹”的危险
	– 描述船舶如何在大浪中掉头
	– 阐述船舶可能会顶风或顺风停船或停止不前
	– 描述以上所使用的每种方法的情形
	– 描述使失控船远离浪槽和减少下风漂移的转向方法
	– 解释船舶可以以一定的漂移角度向下风漂移以及船舶漂移的方向取决于它哪边受风
	– 描述当顶风停船和在大风浪中航行时如何洒油镇浪
	– 描述防止船舶被迫驶向下风岸的行动
	– 描述如何帮助遇险船舶或飞机
	– 描述拖带作业	

COMPETENCE 1.10	Manoeuvre and Handle a Ship in all Conditions	IMO Reference
1.14	**Precautions in manoeuvring to launch rescue boats and survival craft in bad weather (2 hours)** – explains how to make a lee for launching/recovering rescue and survival craft – describes the effect of speed and the effect of flowlines around the vessel – plans manoeuvres to enable launching and recovery of rescue and survival craft – performs manoeuvres to enable launching and recovery of rescue and survival craft*	R1, section A-VI/2
1.15	**Methods of taking on board survivors from rescue boats and survival craft (1 hour)** – describes the methods of manoeuvring the ship and the precautions needed to take on board survivors from rescue boats and survival craft	R1
1.16	**Ability to determine the manoeuvring and propulsion characteristics of common types of ships, with special reference to stopping distances and turning circles at various draughts and speeds (3 hours)** – explains the IMO recommendations for ship manoeuvrability, which are: 1. Standards for Ship Manoeuvrability, adopted by resolution MSC.137(76) on 4 December 2002 2. explanatory Notes to the Standards for Ship Manoeuvrability, adopted by MSC/Circ.1053 on 16 December 2002 3. provision and Display of Manoeuvring Information on Board Ships, adopted by resolution A.601(15) on 19 November 1987	R1, R2 ch. V reg. 23, R17, R18

	– states in particular to IMO's recommendation, with respect to the turning ability of the ship, that the advance should not exceed 4.5 ship lengths and the tactical diameter should not exceed 5 ship lengths in the turning circle manoeuvre
	– states in particular to IMO's recommendation, with respect to the stopping ability of the ship, that the track reach in the full astern stopping test should not exceed 15 ship lengths and also keeping in mind, as guided by the recommendation, that this value may be modified by the Administration where ships of large displacement make this criterion impracticable but in no case exceed 20 ship lengths
	– states that opportunity should be taken to check and supplement the information in the ship's manoeuvring booklet for intermediate draughts and for various weather conditions
	– states that turning circles in shallow water at various manoeuvring speeds should be recorded when possible
	– states that details of an accelerated turn in shallow water should be obtained
	– explains how trials of stopping ability under various conditions should be recorded
	– states that the effect of wind on the behaviour of the ship should be recorded, in particular:
	  – the drifting behaviour when stopped
	  – the speed at which steerage is lost in various conditions of loading and wind
	  – the behaviour of the ship when making sternway
		R1 section B-V/a

适任 1.10	在各种状况下操纵和操作船舶	IMO 参考书目
1.14	**恶劣天气下施放救生艇筏应采取的预防措施(2 学时)** – 解释如何为施放 / 回收救援和救生艇筏创造下风 – 描述速度的影响和船舶附近流水线的影响 – 能够施放 / 回收救援和救生艇筏的操纵计划 – 进行能够施放 / 回收救援和救生艇筏的操纵 *	R1, A-VI/2 节
1.15	**将遇险者从救生艇筏救上船舶的方法(1 学时)** – 描述将救援和救生艇筏上的幸存者救上船的操船方法和需要采取的预防措施	R1
1.16	**确定常见船舶操纵和推进的特性的能力,特别应考虑不同吃水和速度下的冲程和旋回圈(3 学时)** – 解释 IMO 有关船舶操纵性的下列建议: 1. 海安会 2002 年 12 月 4 日 MSC.137 (76) 号决议通过的有关船舶操纵性标准 2. 2002 年 12 月 16 日海安会 MSC/Circ.1053 号通函通过的船舶操纵性标准解释性说明 3. 1987 年 11 月 19 日 A.601 (15) 号决议通过的船舶操纵信息的提供与展示	R1, R2 ch. V 23 条, R17, R18
	– 特别阐述有关船舶旋回能力的 IMO 建议,在旋回操纵中,进距不超过 4.5 倍船长,旋回初径不超过 5 倍船长 – 特别阐述有关船舶停车能力的 IMO 建议,全速倒车停船试验的倒车冲程应不超过 15 倍船长,并记住,如建议中指出的,大排水量船舶无法达到此值时,主管机关可以调整,但无论如何不应超过 20 倍船长 – 阐述应利用机会核实和补充《操纵手册》里船中吃水和不同天气条件下的信息 – 阐述可能时应记录浅水中各种操纵速度下的旋回圈 – 阐述应获得浅水区里加速旋回的详细情况 – 解释如何记录在各种情况下船舶停航性能的试验 – 解释应记录风对船舶行为的影响,特别是: – 当船舶停航时的飘航行为 – 在各种装载和风的情况下,失去舵效的速度 – 当船舶后退时的行为	R1 B-V/a 节

COMPETENCE 1.10	Manoeuvre and Handle a Ship in all Conditions	IMO Reference
	– states why the minimum operating revolutions of the engine and the resulting speed should be checked – states that any details of manoeuvring behaviour which would be useful to a pilot or future Master should be recorded – states that STCW Code section B-V/a recommends additional training for Masters and Chief Mates of large ships and ships with unusual manoeuvring characteristics	
1.17	**Importance of navigating at reduced speed to avoid damage caused by own ship's bow and stern waves (1 hour)** – explains damage to shore due to excessive bow waves and stern waves – explains the effects of passing ships on ships moored alongside – states the precautions that should be taken by ships alongside to minimize the effect of passing traffic	R1

1.18	**Navigating in or near ice; practical measures to be taken when navigating in or near ice or in conditions of ice accumulation on board (4 hours)**
	– states that all possible information about ice located on or in the vicinity of the intended track should be obtained
	– states that information is available from:
	  – daily bulletins of the International Ice Patrol in the North Atlantic
	  – ice warnings from countries where ice is a regular problem
	  – Hydrographic Office ice charts
	  – pilot books
	  – facsimile ice charts
	  – warnings from other ships in the vicinity
		R1, R9, R19

	– defines the following terms used in ice warnings:
	  – solid ice
	  – soft ice
	  – drift ice
	  – pack ice
	  – growler
	  – iceberg
	– states the Master's obligation to report dangerous ice or sub-freezing air temperatures associated with gale-force winds causing severe ice accretion on superstructures
	– states that, when ice is reported on or near the course, the Master of every ship is bound to proceed at a moderate speed or to alter course so as to go well clear of the danger zone
	– explains that radar may not detect small icebergs and growlers
	– states that navigation marks may be removed without warning in coastal areas threatened by ice
	– states that no attempt should be made to enter a region of thick ice in a ship not specially strengthened for navigation in ice
		R2

适任 1.10	在各种状况下操纵和操作船舶	IMO 参考书目
	– 阐述为什么要检测最小的主机转速及其速度 – 阐述应记录对引航员或未来船长有用的船舶操纵行为的详细情况 – 阐述 STCW 公约 B-V/a 节建议大型船舶和具有特殊操纵性能船舶的船长和大副的附加培训	
1.17	**为避免本船首尾船行波造成浪损而减速航行的重要性(1 学时)**	R1
	– 解释过大的船首波和船尾波对岸的损坏 – 解释驶过的船舶对锚泊船舶的影响 – 阐述为减小驶过的船舶对靠泊船舶的影响应采取的预防措施	
1.18	**在冰区内或附近航行;在冰区内或附近航行或船上积冰情况下采取的实用措施(4 学时)**	R1, R2, R19

	– 阐述应获得计划航线上或附近所有可能的冰况信息
	– 阐述可从以下来源获取信息:
	  – 北大西洋的国际冰情巡逻的每日公告
	  – 常为冰情所困扰国家的冰况警告
	  – 气象局的冰况图
	  – 航路指南
	  – 传真冰况图
	  – 来自附近其他船舶的警告	

	– 定义冰况警告里所使用的以下术语:
	  – 固态冰
	  – 软冰
	  – 浮冰
	  – 密集冰
	  – 碎冰山
	  – 冰山
	– 阐述船长有义务报告危险冰况与造成船舶上层建筑严重积冰的大风有关的冰点以下气温
	– 阐述当据报航向上或其附近有冰时，每一船舶的船长应采用中速航行或改向以完全让清危险区域
	– 解释雷达可能不能探测到小冰山和碎冰山
	– 阐述在受冰威胁的沿岸的航行标志可能在没有警告的情况下被移除
	– 阐述不要在船舶没有特别加强的情况下试图进入厚冰区航行
		R2

COMPETENCE 1.10	Manoeuvre and Handle a Ship in all Conditions	IMO Reference
– lists precautions to take when entering ice as: – estimating the thickness and concentration of ice and assessing whether the ship can safely pass through it – avoiding entry to pressure areas (shown by hummocks and rafting) – following leads used by previous ships, where possible – entering on the lee side of the ice, if practicable – entering at right angles to the ice edge, to avoid damage to hull, propeller and rudder – approaching at as slow a speed as possible, and increasing the power to maintain headway when the bow contacts the ice – explains that leads through the ice show well on radar when set to short range – explains precautions to be taken to avoid damaging the propeller and rudder when manoeuvring in ice – explains how to obtain assistance from an ice-breaker – states that it is important to follow the ice-breaker's instructions regarding speed and manoeuvring – states that fenders should be ready for use when negotiating sharp turns in leads – describes the precautions which should be taken to prevent freezing up of tailend shafts, deck machinery and services – describes how to heave-to in an ice field – describes the need to keep a lookout, when hove-to at night, for large ice drifting through the pack – states that soft ice may block seawater intakes – describes the conditions in which ice accumulates on decks and superstructures – explains the dangers resulting from heavy accumulation of ice – states that a change of course or speed should be made to reduce the shipping of freezing spray – states that accumulated ice and snow should be cleared away as quickly as possible – describes methods of clearing decks, rigging and superstructure of ice		
1.19 Use of, and manoeuvring in and near, traffic separation schemes (TSS) and in vessel traffic service (VTS) (4 hours) – explains the requirements of the International Regulations for preventing Collisions at Sea with respect to traffic separation schemes and narrow channels – discusses the actions that can be taken to manoeuvre the vessel in case of emergency – describes the information that may be required by VTS officers before entering, leaving or manoeuvring within a VTS controlled area – plans manoeuvres in and near traffic separation schemes – performs manoeuvres in and near traffic separation schemes*		R1, R2 ch. V, R14

适任 1.10	在各种状况下操纵和操作船舶	IMO 参考书目
	– 列出在进入冰区时应采取的预防措施: – 估计冰的厚度和密集程度,并评估船舶是否能安全通过 – 避免进入高压区(由冰丘和浮冰区域所显示) – 如果可行的话,跟随前船的航迹 – 如果可行的话,从冰的下风侧进入 – 以与冰的边缘成直角进入,避免损坏船体、螺旋桨和舵 – 尽可能地以低速接近,当船首碰到冰时,加大马力以保持前进 – 解释当雷达设置为小量程时,通过冰区的航道完全显示在雷达上 – 解释在冰区操纵船舶时防止螺旋桨和舵受损应采取的预防措施 – 解释如何从破冰船处获得帮助 – 阐述重要的是在航速和操纵方面遵照破冰船的指导 – 阐述当通过急转弯处时应准备好碰垫 – 描述为防止螺旋桨尾轴、甲板机械和设备冰冻应采取的预防措施 – 描述如何在冰区里顶风停船 – 描述当夜间顶风停船时,对漂过积冰的大块浮冰保持瞭望的必要性 – 阐述软冰可能会堵塞海水进入口 – 描述冰积累在甲板和上层建筑的条件 – 解释严重积冰产生的危险 – 阐述应改变航向或航速以减少甲板上浪、结冰 – 阐述应尽快地清除积冰和积雪 – 描述清扫甲板、索具和上层建筑的冰的方法	
1.19	**在分道通航制(TSS)与船舶交管服务(VTS)中或其附近的操纵(4 学时)** – 解释国际海上避碰规则关于分道通航制和狭水道方面的要求 – 讨论在紧急情况下操纵船舶应采取的行动 – 描述在进入或离开或在 VTS 控制区域内操纵船舶之前,VTS 官员可能会要求的信息 – 在分道通航制中或其附近的操纵计划 – 在分道通航制中或其附近进行操纵 *	R1, R2 ch. V, R14

COMPETENCE 1.11	General Knowledge of Remote Controls of Propulsion Plant and Engineering Systems and Services	IMO Reference
TRAINING OUTCOMES: Demonstrates a knowledge and understanding of: 1.11.1 OPERATING PRINCIPLES OF MARINE POWER PLANTS 1.11.2 SHIPS' AUXILIARY MACHINERY 1.11.3 GENERAL KNOWLEDGE OF MARINE ENGINEERING TERMS		STCW Code table A-II/2

适任 1.11	推进装置和轮机系统的遥控操作与维护常识	IMO 参考书目
培训效果: 讲授下列内容知识与理解: 1.11.1　船舶动力装置的操作原理 1.11.2　船舶辅机 1.11.3　船舶轮机术语的常识		STCW 公约 表 A-II/2

COMPETENCE 1.11	General Knowledge of Remote Controls of Propulsion Plant and Engineering Systems and Services	IMO Reference
1.11.1 OPERATING PRINCIPLES OF MARINE POWER PLANTS **Textbooks/Bibliography:** T28, T41, B33, B34, B38 **Teaching aids:** A1, V143 Required performance: **1.1 Operating principles of marine power plants (25 hours)** – Diesel engines – uses generally accepted engineering terms – describes the 2-stroke diesel cycle – describes the 4-stroke diesel cycle – describes the operating principles of marine diesel engine propulsion plant – describes the advantages and disadvantages of a slow-speed diesel engine – explains the cause of scavenge fires and how they are dealt with – describes methods of supercharging – describes the fuel oil system from bunker tank to injection – describes the lubrication system – describes engine cooling-water systems – describes the advantages and disadvantages of a medium-speed diesel – explains the need for gearing with medium-speed diesels – describes the arrangement of clutch and turning gears – describes how a diesel engine is prepared for stand-by – describes the method of starting, stopping and reversing of a direct propulsion diesel engine – states that the number of starts is limited by the capacity of the starting air reservoir – describes the waste heat recovery system of the 2-stroke main propulsion engine – Steam turbine systems – describes the turbine, the feed system and the boiler as a system – explains the working of an impulse turbine and a reaction turbine – describes a steam turbine installation and its gearing – distinguishes between and describes open and closed feed systems – states that a steam turbine needs a large water-tube boiler – describes the main features of a water-tube boiler – describes in outline the procedure for raising steam – describes the procedure for warming through a steam turbine ready for manoeuvring – describes the procedures for manoeuvring when using a steam turbine – Gas turbine system – describes the gas turbine system – describes the compressor part of the gas turbine – describes the combustion chamber or combustor part of the gas turbine – describes the turbine part of the gas turbine – describes the two main types of compressors		R1

适任 1.11	推进装置和轮机系统的遥控操作与维护常识	IMO 参考书目
1.11.1 船舶动力装置的操作原理 **教科书/参考文献**:T28, T41, B33, B34, B38 **教具**:A1, V143 技能要求: **1.1　船舶动力装置的操作原理(25学时)** – 柴油机 　– 使用普遍认可的轮机术语 　– 描述二冲程柴油机循环 　– 描述四冲程柴油机循环 　– 描述船用柴油机推进装置的操作原理 　– 描述低速柴油机的优点和缺点 　– 解释扫气箱起火的原因以及如何处理 　– 描述增压的方法 　– 描述从燃油舱到喷油的燃油系统 　– 描述润滑系统 　– 描述主机冷却水系统 　– 描述中速柴油机的优点和缺点 　– 解释中速柴油机传动装置的必要性 　– 描述离合器装置和转动齿轮装置 　– 描述柴油机如何备车 　– 描述直接推进柴油机的启动、停止和倒车的方法 　– 阐述启动的次数受到启动空气瓶容量的限制 　– 描述二冲程主推进器的废热回收系统 – 蒸汽涡轮系统 　– 描述涡轮机、给水系统和作为一个系统的锅炉 　– 解释冲击式涡轮机和反向式涡轮机的工作原理 　– 描述蒸汽涡轮机装置及其传动装置 　– 描述开放式系统和封闭式系统及其之间的区别 　– 阐述蒸汽涡轮机需要大型水管锅炉 　– 描述水管锅炉的主要特点 　– 概述制备蒸汽的详细过程 　– 描述蒸汽涡轮机的暖机程序以备操纵 　– 描述使用蒸汽涡轮机的操纵程序 – 燃气轮机系统 　– 描述燃气轮机系统 　– 描述燃气轮机的增压部分 　– 描述燃气轮机的燃烧室 　– 描述燃气轮机的涡轮部分 　– 描述两种主要的增压器		R1

COMPETENCE 1.11	General Knowledge of Remote Controls of Propulsion Plant and Engineering Systems and Services	IMO Reference

– Propeller and propeller shaft
  – describes the arrangement of thrust shaft, intermediate shafts and tailshaft
  – explains how propeller thrust is transmitted to the hull
  – describes how the propeller shaft is supported between the thrust block and the stern tube
  – sketches and describes an oil-lubricated stern-tube bearing
  – describes how the propeller is secured to the tailshaft
  – defines pitch, slip and efficiency of a propeller
  – calculates the percentage apparent slip from given data
  – calculates the ship's speed, given the engine revolutions per minute, mean pitch and percentage slip
  – describes the arrangement and operation of a controllable-pitch propeller (CPP)
  – states the precautions to take with a CPP before:
    – starting the main engines
    – going to sea
    – entering harbour or confined waters
– states that changing control positions and the use of emergency hand control pitch and engine revolutions should be exercised
– Bridge control[1]
  – describes a control system for the main engine, including control from bridge, machinery control room, engine control local and changeover controls
  – describes bridge control of controllable-pitch propellers
  – describes bridge control of slow speed diesel engines
  – describes bridge control of steam turbines with associated boilers
  – describes bridge control for gas turbines with associated gas generators
  – lists the indicators and alarms provided with bridge control
  – describes the arrangement and operations of lateral thrusters
  – describes the bridge control and indicators for lateral thrusters
  – describes the concept of control systems
  – describes the terminology used in control systems
  – explains when is the control system "fail-safe"
  – explains when is the control system "fail-run"
  – explains the meaning of safety interlocks in a control system
  – describes the types of controls (open and closed loop)		

1 Administrations may wish to provide specialized training in bridge control systems for personnel who are to serve on higher technology ships fitted with complex bridge control systems.

适任 1.11	推进装置和轮机系统的遥控操作与维护常识	IMO 参考书目
– 螺旋桨和螺旋桨轴 – 描述推力轴装置、中间轴装置和艉轴装置 – 解释螺旋桨推力是如何作用于船体的 – 描述推力轴承和艉轴管是如何支撑螺旋桨轴的 – 简要概述加了润滑油的艉轴管轴承 – 描述螺旋桨是如何被固定在艉轴上的 – 定义螺旋桨的螺距、滑失率和效率 – 由已知数据计算视滑距百分比 – 已知主机转数、平均螺距和滑失百分比,计算船速 – 描述可控螺距螺旋桨(CPP)设备和操作 – 阐述在使用CPP之前应采取的预防措施: – 启动主机 – 航行出海 – 进港或进入受限水域 – 阐述应练习转换控制位置、螺距和主机转数的手动应急控制 – 驾驶台控制[1] – 描述主机控制系统,包括驾驶台控制、集控室控制、机旁控制和转换控制 – 描述可变螺距螺旋桨的驾驶台控制 – 描述低速柴油机的驾驶台控制 – 描述蒸汽轮机及其锅炉的驾驶台控制 – 描述燃气轮机及其燃气发动机的驾驶台控制 – 列出驾驶台控制的指示器和报警器 – 描述侧推器设备和操作 – 描述驾驶台控制和侧推器指示器 – 描述控制系统的概念 – 描述控制系统中使用的术语 – 解释什么时候是“绝对安全”控制系统 – 解释什么时候是“可靠运行”控制系统 – 解释控制系统中安全联锁装置的意义 – 描述控制系统的种类(开环和闭环)		

1 主管当局希望能够为在配有复杂的驾驶台控制系统的更高技术船舶上服务的人员提供驾驶台控制系统的专业培训。

<table>
<tr><th>COMPETENCE 1.11</th><th>General Knowledge of Remote Controls of Propulsion Plant and Engineering Systems and Services</th><th>IMO Reference</th></tr>
<tr><td colspan="2">1.11.2 SHIPS' AUXILIARY MACHINERY
Textbooks/Bibliography: T28, B33, B34, B38
Teaching aids: A1, V49, V116, V123, V124, V131, V132, V133, V144, V147, V149
Required performance:
2.1 Ships' auxiliary machinery (25 hours)
– distinguishes between water-tube and fire-tube boilers
– describes auxiliary boilers
– describes a waste-heat boiler
– describes exhaust-gas heat exchangers
– describes steam-to-steam generators and explains where and why they are used
– describes a boiler fuel oil supply system
– describes the effect of dissolved salts in the feedwater and how it is treated
– explains what is meant by "priming"
– states that carry-over of water may cause serious damage to turbine blading and to steam cylinders
Distillation and fresh-water systems
– describes a distillation system
– explains the operation of a flash evaporator
– describes the treatment of fresh water intended for drinking
– describes a domestic water system
Pumps and pumping systems
– classifies pumps as displacement, axial-flow or centrifugal
– describes the operation of a reciprocating pump
– describes rotary displacement pumps and states typical applications
– describes a screw pump and states possible uses
– describes an axial-flow pump and states possible applications
– describes a centrifugal pump and states typical applications
– explains the need to prime a centrifugal pump
– describes the head losses in a pumping system and how they are expressed
– explains net positive suction head and its significance in pump operation
– describes a typical bilge system and ballast system for a dry cargo vessel
– states that the engine-room emergency bilge suction is connected to the main circulating pump in the engine-room
Steering gear
– describes ram-type hydraulic steering gear
– describes rotary-vane steering gear
– explains how hydraulic power is provided by variable-delivery pumps
– describes the IMO requirements for auxiliary steering gear and how they are met by ram-type and rotary-vane steering gear</td><td>R1</td></tr>
</table>

适任 1.11	推进装置和轮机系统的遥控操作与维护常识	IMO 参考书目
1.11.2 船舶辅机 **教科书/参考文献**:T28, B33, B34, B38 **教具**:A1, V49, V116, V123, V124, V131, V132, V133, V144, V147, V149 技能要求: **2.1 船舶辅机(25学时)** – 区分水管锅炉和火管锅炉 – 描述辅助锅炉 – 描述废热锅炉 – 描述废气热交换器 – 描述蒸汽—蒸汽发生器并解释为何要用以及何处用蒸汽—蒸汽发生器 – 描述锅炉燃油供应系统 – 描述供给水管路中未融化盐的影响以及应如何解决 – 解释“引灌” – 阐述残留水会对涡轮机叶片和蒸汽机汽缸造成严重损坏 蒸馏和淡水系统 – 描述蒸馏系统 – 解释闪发式造水机的操作 – 描述处理饮用淡水 – 描述生活用水系统 泵和泵水系统 – 将泵分为容积泵、轴流泵或离心泵 – 描述往复泵的操作 – 描述旋转容积泵并阐述其典型的应用 – 描述螺杆泵并阐述其可能的应用 – 描述轴流泵并阐述其可能的应用 – 描述离心泵并阐述其典型的应用 – 解释注满离心泵的必要性 – 描述泵系统的压头损失以及如何表达之 – 解释吸口净正压头以及其在泵操作中的重要性 – 描述干货船典型的舱底水系统和压载水系统 – 阐述机舱应急污水系统吸口连至机舱里的主循环泵 舵机 – 描述柱塞式液压舵机 – 描述转叶式舵机 – 解释变量泵如何提供液压力 – 描述IMO关于辅助舵机的要求以及柱塞式和转叶式舵机如何满足要求		R1

COMPETENCE 1.11	General Knowledge of Remote Controls of Propulsion Plant and Engineering Systems and Services	IMO Reference
– describes a telemotor control system – describes electric steering control – explains how the change from remote to local control in the steering-gear compartment is made – describes the requirement for power supplies to electric and electrohydraulic steering gear – describes the requirements for emergency control of the steering gear – states the IMO requirements for testing steering gear and for drills Generators, alternators and electrical distribution – describes the operation of a D.C. generator – explains the functioning of shunt- and compound-wound D.C. motors – describes the operation of an alternator – explains the functioning of induction motors – explains the relative advantages and disadvantages of generation and distribution of D.C. and A.C. – describes D.C. and A.C. distribution systems – describes the use of circuit-breakers and fuses – describes and draws a navigation light circuit with indicators and alarm, showing an alternative power supply – describes the use of rectifiers – describes the characteristics of lead-acid batteries and of alkaline batteries – describes the maintenance of batteries – describes the safety precautions to be observed for battery compartments – outlines the starting requirements for emergency generating sets – lists the services to be supplied from the emergency generator – describes the supplementary emergency lighting for ro-ro passenger ships Refrigeration, air-conditioning and ventilation – describes a vapour-compression-cycle refrigeration plant – states desirable properties of a refrigerant – states the properties of commonly used refrigerants – describes the use of secondary refrigerants for cooling compartments – explains the co-efficient of performance of a refrigeration plant – describes an air-conditioning plant – describes a ventilation system for accommodation – describes a mechanical ventilation system for ships' holds Stabilizers – describes the construction and operation of fin stabilizers – describes the arrangement and operation of a flume stabilizer Sewage treatment plants – describes the operation of a chemical sewage treatment plant – describes the operation of a biological sewage treatment plant		

适任 1.11	推进装置和轮机系统的遥控操作与维护常识	IMO 参考书目
– 描述液压传动控制系统 – 描述电力操舵控制 – 解释如何在舵机间里进行遥控和机旁控制的切换 – 描述电力舵机和电力液压舵机的电源供应的要求 – 描述舵机的应急控制要求 – 阐述IMO关于舵机试验和演习的要求 发电机、交流发电机及电力分配 – 描述直流发电机的操作 – 描述并激直流电动机和复励直流电动机的功能 – 描述交流发电机的操作 – 解释感应电动机的功能 – 解释直流电和交流电的产生和分配的相对优点和缺点 – 描述直流电和交流电的分配系统 – 描述电路开关和保险丝的使用 – 描述并绘出带有指示器和报警器的航行灯的电路图,标明备用电源 – 描述整流器的使用 – 描述铅酸蓄电池和碱性蓄电池的特点 – 描述电池的保养 – 描述蓄电池间应遵循的安全预防措施 – 概述应急发电设备的启动要求 – 列出应急发电机可提供的服务 – 描述滚装船的辅助应急照明设备 制冷、空调及通风 – 描述蒸汽—压缩—循环制冷设备 – 阐述冷冻剂理想的性能 – 阐述常用冷冻剂的性能 – 描述冷却舱室中备用冷冻剂的使用 – 解释制冷设备的性能系数 – 描述空调设备 – 描述生活区的通风系统 – 描述船舶货舱的机械通风系统 减摇装置 – 描述减摇鳍的结构和操作 – 描述水槽式减摇装置的布置和操作 污水处理设备 – 描述化学污水处理设备的操作 – 描述生物污水处理设备的操作		

COMPETENCE 1.11	General Knowledge of Remote Controls of Propulsion Plant and Engineering Systems and Services	IMO Reference
	Oily water separators and oil filtering equipment – describes the operation of an oily water separator (producing effluent that contains less than 100 ppm of oil) – describes the operation of oil filtering equipment (producing effluent that contains not more than 15 ppm of oil) – explains why oily water separators, even if well maintained and correctly operated, may not function properly – describes how an oil-content meter functions – describes an oil discharge monitoring and control system Incinerators – describes the functioning of a waste incinerator Deck machinery – states that the design and performance of anchor windlasses is subject to approval by a classification society – sketches and describes a windlass driving two de-clutchable cable lifters and warping drums – explains the gearing necessary between the prime mover and cable lifters – states that both winches may be coupled mechanically to provide either a stand-by drive, in case one prime mover should fail, or the power of both prime movers on one windlass, if required – describes the arrangement of vertical anchor capstans with driving machinery below deck – describes a spooling device to distribute the wire evenly on the drum of a mooring winch – explains the working of self-tensioning winches – briefly explains the advantages and disadvantages of steam, electric and hydraulic drive for mooring winches and capstans – describes a cargo winch – sketches and describes a slewing deck crane, its motors and its controls – describes the lubrication of deck machinery Hydraulic systems – states that a hydraulic system consists of an oil tank, pumps, control valves, hydraulic motors and pipework – distinguishes between open- and closed-loop systems – describes a live-line circuit supplied by a centralized hydraulic power system – describes radial-piston and axial-piston variable-stroke pumps – explains how the variable-stroke pump can act as controller and power supply – sketches and describes a simple spool valve with shutoff and control of flow direction – describes ram and rotary-vane actuators – states that hydraulic systems can provide stepless control of speed for winches, cranes and other lifting devices	

适任 1.11	推进装置和轮机系统的遥控操作与维护常识	IMO 参考书目
油水分离器及滤油设备 – 描述油水分离器(产生油含量低于100 ppm的排放物)的操作 – 描述滤油设备(产生油含量低于15 ppm的排放物)的操作 – 解释为何油水分离器即使保养得当且正确操作,也可能不正常工作 – 描述油量计如何工作 – 描述排油监控系统 焚烧炉 – 描述垃圾焚烧炉的功能 甲板机械 – 阐述锚机的设计和性能应经船级社批准 – 简要概述锚机驱动两个可离合的链轮和卷缆滚筒 – 解释在原动机和持轮之间必要的传动装置 – 阐述两台绞车可以机械地耦合,为一台原动机不能工作时提供备用驱动,或者在需要时将两台原动机的动力用于一台锚机 – 描述驱动机械在甲板下的垂直锚机设备 – 描述将钢丝绳均匀分布在系泊绞车滚筒的排缆设备 – 解释自动绞车的工作原理 – 简要解释用蒸汽、电力和液压驱动绞缆机和绞盘的优点和缺点 – 描述货物起重机 – 简要概述回旋式甲板克林吊、其发电机及控制 – 描述甲板机械的润滑 液压系统 – 阐述液压系统包括油舱、泵、控制阀、液压马达以及管道系统 – 区分开系统环和闭环系统 – 描述中央液压动力系统供应的带电线路 – 描述径向活塞和轴向活塞变量泵 – 描述变量泵如何能作为控制器和提供电源 – 概述带遮断和流向控制的简易滑阀 – 描述柱塞式和转叶式传动装置 – 阐述液压系统能够为起重机、克令吊和其他起重设备提供无级速度控制		

COMPETENCE 1.11	General Knowledge of Remote Controls of Propulsion Plant and Engineering Systems and Services	IMO Reference

- describes a hydraulic accumulator and explains its purpose
- states that cooling of the hydraulic oil is necessary during operation to maintain the correct viscosity of the oil
- states that the oil may need to be heated before starting from cold
- states that cleanliness of the oil is essential for satisfactory operation and that all systems contain filters
- states that air in a system leads to erratic functioning

1.11.3 GENERAL KNOWLEDGE OF MARINE ENGINEERING SYSTEMS

Textbooks/Bibliography: T28, T41, B33, B34, B38

Teaching aids: A1

Required performance:

3.1 Marine engineering terms and fuel consumption (4 hours) R1

- uses the correct engineering terms when describing and explaining the operation of the machinery and equipment mentioned above
- defines mass, force, work, power, energy, pressure, stress, strain and heat and states the units in which each is measured
- explains what is meant by the efficiency of machine
- describes an indicator diagram and the information obtainable from it
- defines indicated power, shaft power, propeller power and thrust
- defines the Admiralty coefficient (AC) as:

$$AC = \frac{(\text{displacement})^{2/3} \times (\text{speed})^3}{\text{engine power}}$$

- defines the fuel coefficient (FC) as:

$$FC = \frac{(\text{displacement})^{2/3} \times (\text{speed})^3}{\text{daily fuel consumption}}$$

- explains that for a given period of time:

$$\frac{\text{fuel consumption}^1}{\text{fuel consumption}^2} = \left[\frac{\text{displacement}^1}{\text{displacement}^2}\right]^{2/3} \times \left[\frac{\text{speed}^1}{\text{speed}^2}\right]^3$$

- explains that for a given distance:

$$\frac{\text{fuel consumption}^1}{\text{fuel consumption}^2} = \left[\frac{\text{displacement}^1}{\text{displacement}^2}\right]^{2/3} \times \left[\frac{\text{speed}^1}{\text{speed}^2}\right]^2$$

- explains that:

$$\frac{\text{Voyage consumption}^1}{\text{Voyage consumption}^2} = \left[\frac{\text{displacement}^1}{\text{displacement}^2}\right]^{2/3} \times \left[\frac{\text{speed}^1}{\text{speed}^2}\right]^2 \times \frac{\text{Voyage distance}^1}{\text{Voyage distance}^2}$$

- given data from the previous performance, calculates:
  - the daily consumption at service speed
  - the bunker fuel required for a voyage
  - the speed for a given daily consumption
  - the reduced speed required to complete a voyage with a given consumption

适任 1.11	推进装置和轮机系统的遥控操作与维护常识	IMO 参考书目

- 描述液压蓄能器并解释其用途
- 阐述为保持油的适当黏度,在运行期间冷却液压油是必要的
- 阐述在冬天启动之前,可能需要对油进行加热
- 阐述对满意的操作而言,油的清洁度至关重要,所有的系统都有过滤器
- 阐述系统中的空气会导致不稳定的运行

1.11.3　船舶轮机系统常识

教科书/参考文献:T28, T41, B33, B34, B38

教具:A1

技能要求:

3.1　船舶轮机术语和燃油消耗(4学时)　　R1

- 当描述和解释上文提及的机械和设备的操作时,使用正确的轮机术语
- 定义质量、力、功、功率、能量、压力、应力、拉力和热并阐述它们各自的衡量单位
- 解释机械效率的含义
- 描述示功图以及可以从中获得的信息
- 定义指示功率、轴功率、螺旋桨功率和推力
- 定义海军系数:

$$AC = \frac{(\text{排水量})^{2/3} \times (\text{船速})^3}{\text{主机功率}}$$

- 定义燃油系数:

$$FC = \frac{(\text{排水量})^{2/3} \times (\text{船速})^3}{\text{日燃油消耗量}}$$

- 解释在一个给定的时段:

$$\frac{\text{燃油消耗量}^1}{\text{燃油消耗量}^2} = \left[\frac{\text{排水量}^1}{\text{排水量}^2}\right]^{2/3} \times \left[\frac{\text{船速}^1}{\text{船速}^2}\right]^3$$

- 解释在个给定的距离:

$$\frac{\text{燃油消耗量}^1}{\text{燃油消耗量}^2} = \left[\frac{\text{排水量}^1}{\text{排水量}^2}\right]^{2/3} \times \left[\frac{\text{船速}^1}{\text{船速}^2}\right]^2$$

- 解释:

$$\frac{\text{燃油消耗量}^1}{\text{燃油消耗量}^2} = \left[\frac{\text{排水量}^1}{\text{排水量}^2}\right]^{2/3} \times \left[\frac{\text{船速}^1}{\text{船速}^2}\right]^2 \times \frac{\text{航次航程}^1}{\text{航次航程}^2}$$

- 由上述性能的数据计算:
  - 以服务速度航行的日消耗量
  - 航次需要的燃油
  - 给定日消耗量的船速
  - 在给定日消耗量下为完成航次要求降低的船速

COMPETENCE 1.11	General Knowledge of Remote Controls of Propulsion Plant and Engineering Systems and Services	IMO Reference
– explains that, for fuel economy, the actual speed at any stage of a voyage should be as near as practicable to the required average speed – explains how the condition of the hull affects the fuel coefficient and the fuel consumption – explains that keeping the leading edges and tips of propeller blades dressed and polished improves propeller efficiency and reduces fuel consumption **3.2 Arrangements necessary for appropriate and effective engineering watches to be maintained for the purpose of safety under normal circumstances and UMS operations (2 hours)** – explains briefly the general engine room safety that should be observed at all given times – describes the main dangers and sources of risk in an engine room – explains the importance and implementation of risk assessment and risk management in an engine room – describes the safe systems of work and permits to work that should be observed in an engine room – explains the types and importance of wearing personal protective equipment (PPE) while working in an engine room – describes the arrangements necessary for appropriate and effective engineering watches to be maintained for the purpose of safety under normal circumstances and UMS operations **3.3 Arrangements necessary to ensure a safe engineering watch is maintained when carrying dangerous cargo (2 hours)** – describes the arrangements necessary to ensure a safe engineering watch is maintained when carrying dangerous cargo		

适任 1.11	推进装置和轮机系统的遥控操作与维护常识	IMO 参考书目
– 解释为了节省燃油,在航次的任意阶段应尽可能地接近所要求的平均船速 – 解释船体的状况如何影响燃油消耗系数和燃油消耗 – 解释保持螺旋桨桨叶的导边和叶梢的刨光和磨光以提高螺旋桨效率和降低燃油消耗量 **3.2 为保证正常情况和机舱无人值班情况下的安全，适当而有效的轮机值班所必需的安排（2学时）** – 简要解释在任何给定时刻都应遵守的机舱一般安全守则 – 描述机舱的主要危险和风险源 – 解释机舱里风险评估和风险管理的重要性及其实施 – 阐述机舱里的安全工作系统和应遵守的安全许可制度 – 解释在机舱工作个人防护设备的种类及穿戴它们重要性 – 描述为保证正常情况和机舱无人值班情况下的安全,适当而有效的轮机值班所必需的安排 **3.3 当运载危险货物时为保证机舱值班安全所必需的安排(2学时)** – 描述当运载危险货物时为保证机舱值班安全所必需的安排		

Part D1: Instructor Manual

The following notes are intended to highlight the main objectives or training outcomes of each part of the function. The notes also contain some material on topics which are not adequately covered in the quoted references.

This function covers the theoretical knowledge, understanding and proficiency for the safe navigation of a ship in coastal waters and in the open ocean.

Function 1: Navigation at the Management Level

On completion of training for this function, the officer should possess a thorough understanding and capability in navigation. This together with knowledge gained in other areas, will enable the officer to carry out passages independently in a proper and safe manner and to be able to solve those problems that may arise during a voyage.

The officer will be able to fix positions and analyse in a practical way the quality of the fix, make great circle calculations, read tide tables and predict times and heights of tides at different ports worldwide.

In voyage planning the officer will be able to:

- use appropriate means of navigation in coastal waters
- make use of publications and other information sources for safe voyage planning in coastal waters
- use pilot charts, *Ocean Passages for the World* and other publications to select a safe and economic 'best' route
- organize and manage the bridge team

Officers will be thoroughly conversant with the content, application and intent of the International Regulations for Preventing Collisions at Sea (COLREG 1972), as amended.

The interpretations arising from court decisions should be used when teaching these rules. They will be able to apply them correctly in all situations as Master of a ship.

Officers will be able to arrange and monitor the keeping of a safe navigational watch at sea and an effective deck watch in port taking account of the standards regarding watchkeeping in the STCW code, chapter VIII. They will have a knowledge of all modern navigational aids, enabling them to navigate safely in all parts of the world. They will have specific knowledge of operating principles, limitations, sources of error, detection of misrepresentation of information and methods of correction to obtain accurate position fixing. Officers will appreciate the danger of exclusive reliance on information gained from instruments and the necessity for calibration and frequent checking of the instruments.

On completion of the function, officers will be able to identify the various parts of the magnetic compass and explain their functions. They will understand the reasons for the change of compass deviation with time and position and the need for routine checking of the ship's deviation. They will also be able to produce and analyse a deviation table. Officers will have

D1部分:教员手册

以下注意事项旨在突出主要的教学目标或本功能每部分的培训效果。注意事项也包含了一些所引用的参考文献中没有充分涵盖的主题的资料。

本功能涵盖船舶在沿海水域和公海安全航行的理论知识、理解和熟练的内容。

功能1:管理级航行

完成本功能培训后,驾驶员应在航行方面具备充分的理解和能力。结合其他领域所学到的知识,将使他能以一个适当和安全的方式独立地进行航行,并能够解决航行中可能出现的问题。

驾驶员将能定位,以实用的方式分析定位的质量,进行大圆计算,阅读潮汐表以及预测世界上不同港口的潮时和潮高。

在航次计划方面,驾驶员将能:

- 在沿海水域采用适当的航行方式
- 在沿海水域利用出版物和其他信息源制订安全的航次计划
- 利用引航图、《世界大洋航路》和其他出版物选择安全而经济的最佳航线
- 组织和管理驾驶台团队

驾驶员将精通经修订的国际海上避碰规则(COLREG 1972)的内容、适用范围及意图。

在讲授这些规则时,应使用法院判决所产生的解释。他们应能像船舶的船长那样在所有情况下正确应用这些规则。

驾驶员将能够安排和监控在海上保持安全航行值班与港内有效的甲板值班, 并考虑到STCW公约第八章有关值班标准。他们将具有所有现代导航设备知识,能使用它们在世界各地安全航行,具有工作原理、局限性、误差源、探测虚假信息和得到准确定位的更正方法的专门知识。他们将领会完全依赖来自于仪器的信息的危险性与矫正和经常检查仪器的必要性。

完成本职能培训后,驾驶员们将能够识别磁罗经的各个部分并解释其功能,将懂得自差随时间和地点变化和需要常规检查船舶自差的原因。他们还将能制作并分析自差表,具有陀螺罗经误

a knowledge and understanding of gyrocompass errors and will be able to evaluate possible errors and appreciate the limitations of the instrument.

On completion of the function, officers will:

- possess a general understanding of the elements and processes which determine the weather;
- be able to draw conclusions on the basis of observations made on board and from information available;
- be able to utilize information from weather and wave charts; and
- have a basic knowledge of the elements of oceanography.

This knowledge will, as part of the training programme as a whole, enable the trainee to take into account climatic conditions, the weather prognosis, ocean currents and information on the presence of ice, for the safe operation of the ship.

The officer will understand and interpret a synoptic chart, predict area weather, have a knowledge of the characteristics of various weather systems and ocean current systems and be able to use all appropriate navigational publications.

Officers will also be aware of all of the factors affecting the manoeuvring and handling of ships. They will be able to plan berthing or anchoring procedures, taking account of prevailing conditions of wind and tide and their own ship's characteristics, and to make use of assisting tugs when necessary. They will, after having gained seagoing experience or training on a ship-handling simulator, also be able to handle a ship so as to minimize the risk of damage or stranding resulting from heavy weather. Officers will be aware of the dangers to be encountered when navigating in ice or conditions of ice accumulation on board and the precautions to take for the safety of the ship and crew.

Officers will know the procedures to use in VHF communications and be able to use radiotelephones, particularly with respect to distress, urgency, safety and navigational messages. They will also know the procedures for emergency distress signals by radiotelegraphy, as prescribed in the Radio Regulations, and will be able to send a distress call by using an automatic keying device and the emergency transmitter.

1.1 PLAN A VOYAGE AND CONDUCT NAVIGATION

First of all, the officers should be well acquainted with publications which supply appropriate information for voyage planning. The officers should plan navigation after analysing and evaluating current legislations (if applicable) with regard to Passage and Voyage Planning and as per the requirements of International Maritime Organization resolution A.893. Intelligent use of the information, together with professional ability and watchfulness, leads to a successful voyage. Proper safe working procedures are very important and should be stressed. Instructors will find T12 a valuable source of reference.

差的知识与理解,将能评估可能的误差和辨析该仪器的局限性。

完成本功能后,驾驶员将:

- 具有对决定天气的要素和过程的常识;
- 能根据船上的观测和得到的资料做出结论;
- 能利用天气图和波浪图;并
- 具有海洋学要素的基本知识。

作为整个培训计划的一部分,该知识将使学员为了船舶安全营运,能考虑相关的气候条件、天气预报、洋流和有关存在冰况的信息。

驾驶员将理解和解读天气图、预报地区天气,具有不同天气系统和洋流系统特征的知识,还能利用所有相关航海出版物。

驾驶员还将意识到所有影响船舶操纵和控制的因素,能考虑当时风和潮汐的情况及其船舶特性,计划靠泊或锚泊程序,必要时利用拖船协助。在获得远洋经验或在船舶操纵模拟器训练之后,他们还将能操控船舶使恶劣天气所致的破损或搁浅风险减至最小。他们将意识到在冰区航行或船上积冰时遭遇的危险,并采取保证船舶和船员安全的预防措施。

驾驶员将了解使用VHF通信的程序,能使用无线电话,特别是有关遇险、紧急、安全和航行信息的通信程序。他们还将了解无线电规则中规定的无线电报紧急遇险信号的程序,并能用自动发报设备和应急发射机发送遇险呼叫。

1.1 制订航次计划并引导航行

首先,驾驶员们应熟悉为航次计划提供适当的信息的出版物。他们应按照国际海事组织A.893决议要求,在分析和评价关于航线和航次计划的现行法规(如适用)后设定航行计划。结合专业能力和警觉性,合理使用信息促成一个成功的航次。正确的安全工作程序是非常重要的,应加以强调。教师将发现T12是一份有用的参考书目。

1.1.1 VOYAGE PLANNING AND NAVIGATION FOR ALL CONDITIONS

Voyage planning and navigation for all conditions by acceptable methods of plotting ocean tracks **(24 hours)**

This content builds on the passage planning elements of IMO model course 7.03 and is intended to ensure that management level officers can effectively plan voyages from berth to berth in accordance with guidance on passage planning and that they can manage passage planning tasks performed by operational level officers. Additional learning time may be required for trainees who have not retained competence in the operational level tasks.

The importance of preparing oneself and the vessel before setting off on a sea passage is irrefutable, especially on a coastal passage where the sheer number and proximity of hazards can quickly spell disaster for the unprepared. Navigation planning should be carried out after utilizing the principles of passage planning to make a complete appraisal of a proposed passage also taking into account restricted waters, while en route, in conjunction and utilizing Navigational charts, Admiralty Routeing charts, *Ocean Passages for the World*, Admiralty Sailing Directions, Tide tables to appraise a proposed ocean passage and a coastal or pilotage passage. Appropriate strategies and contingency plans should also be used in order to deal with various factors, as mentioned in the detailed teaching syllabus.

Navigation Safety recommends that:

1) all of the ship's navigation is planned in adequate detail
2) there is a systematic bridge organization that provides for:
    (a) comprehensive briefing of personnel;
    (b) close monitoring of position;
    (c) cross-checking.

Logbooks and voyage records **(3 hours)**

On board ship, various conditions need to be watched and taken care of. In a nautical context this means navigation, including watchkeeping, weather, ship handling, handling of cargo, condition of ship as to stability, trim, stress, etc., personnel management and communications, which are the most important subjects. Proper and effective keeping of logbooks is important as a record of the various circumstances. Special emphasis should be placed on conditions involving maritime shipping legislation and other regulations and on keeping logbooks in normal circumstances.

1.1.2 ROUTEING IN ACCORDANCE WITH THE GENERAL PROVISIONS ON SHIP'S ROUTEING

Routeing **(12 hours)**

This content builds on the routeing and passage planning elements of IMO model course 7.03 and is intended to ensure that management level officers can effectively plan voyages from berth to berth in accordance with guidance on passage planning and that they can manage passage planning tasks performed by operational level officers. This knowledge is

1.1.1 各种状况下的航次计划和航行

各种状况下利用可接受的标绘航迹方法进行航次计划和航行 **(24学时)**

此内容建立在IMO示范课程7.03航线设计要素的基础上,旨在确保管理级人员按照航线设计指南,能有效地计划从泊位到泊位的航行,应对由操作级船员完成的航线设计任务。对不适任操作级任务的学员,可要求增加额外的学习时间。

起航前的自我准备和船舶做好准备的重要性无可争辩,特别是在沿海航行,数量众多的临近的危险物会迅速给未经准备者带来灾难。应在利用航线设计原理,考虑航行途中的限制水域,结合并使用航用海图、英版航路图、《世界大洋航路》、航路指南、潮汐表评估拟定的大洋航线和沿海航线或引航航线之后,做出航行计划。在教学大纲细则中,也应该使用适当的策略和应急计划来针对各种因素。

航行安全建议:

1) 船舶航行的各个方面都应详细确切地制订计划

2) 具有一个系统的驾驶台团队提供:

(a) 人员的全面介绍;

(b) 密切的位置监控;

(c) 交叉检查。

航海日志和航次记录 **(3 学时)**

船上需要监视和关注所有状况。在海上环境下,这意味着航行活动,包括值班、天气、船舶操纵、货物装卸、船舶状况(如稳性、吃水差、应力等)、人员管理和通信,这些最重要的方面。作为各种情况下的记录,准备和有效保管航海日志是重要的。应特别强调的是涉及海上运输法规和其他规定的情况,以及正常状况下航海日志的保管。

1.1.2 根据船舶定线制总则制定航线

制定航线 **(12 学时)**

此内容建立IMO示范课程7.03航线设计要素基础上，旨在确保管理级人员按照航线设计指南,能有效地计划从泊位到泊位的航行,完成由操作级船员完成的航线设计任务。本课程中的知识对多数管理级内容非常重要,以至于在涉及管理级额外要求的知识点之前,在迅速复习操作级

considered so fundamental for much of the management level content within this course that there is merit in reviewing the operational level content quickly before covering the additional elements required at management level. The learning time has been reduced for many elements on the basis that trainees will be reviewing rather than learning much of this content at this level. Additional learning time may be required for trainees who have not retained competence in the operational level tasks.

The procedures for weather routeing by a shore–based service should be covered in this topic.

On-board routeing can be carried out by the Master if the ship is equipped with a facsimile receiver and is in a region for which the necessary prognostic charts are available. The internet and email facility can also be used in order to obtain charts from various sources providing these facilities. This topic should be taught in conjunction with the voyage planning.

Ocean voyage

Because traffic concentrations are low and navigational hazards are relatively few on an ocean crossing, the main data to be appraised are environmental, such as seasonal prevailing weather, local and actual weather, ocean currents, tides, ice, etc. In addition, data of the ship's characteristics, cargo and navigational/operational data need to be taken into account.

The main reason for selection of alternative routes is one of safety and economics. Route selection is to some extent regulated by insurance restrictions, load line zones, IMO routeings and similar regulations.

A thorough analysis of all of the conditions relevant to passage planning should be covered in this subject area. Such an analysis may start with calculating distances of possible tracks and then evaluating weather conditions, current, characteristics of the ship and of its cargo, regulations, etc. Very often the "best" route is not the shortest.

1.1.3 REPORTING IN ACCORDANCE WITH THE GENERAL PRINCIPLES FOR SHIP REPORTING SYSTEMS AND WITH VTS PROCEDURES

Ship reporting systems **(1 hour)**

Instructors should note that reference R3 contains full information on ship's routeing and reporting.

Planning of navigation should be carried in accordance to the ship's routeing as these systems contribute to safety of life at sea, safety and efficiency of navigation and/or protection of the marine environment. The instructor should also refer to MSC/Circ.1060 Guidance Note on the Preparation of Proposals on Ships' Routeing Systems and Ship Reporting Systems, especially while appraising and preparing a coastal Navigation plan while teaching this topic.

They should also note that the measures mentioned on the ship's routeing, that are described or defined in parts A and H of this publication are individually described in parts B (traffic separation schemes), C (deep-water routes), D (areas to be avoided), E (other routeing measures, such as recommended tracks, two-way routes and recommended direc ions of traffic flow), F (the rules and recommendations on navigation that are associated with

内容方面颇具价值。基于学员将复习而不是学习该级别内容,已经减少了许多知识点的学时。对不适任操作级任务的学员,可要求增加额外的学习时间。

本主题应涵盖通过岸基服务进行气象导航的程序。

如船舶配备传真接收机,处于可接收必要的预报图区域,则船长可进行在船航线设计。互联网和电子邮件设施也可用来从各种资源获得它们提供的图表。本主题应结合航次计划讲授。

大洋航行

由于跨洋航行交通流密度低,航海危险相对较少,要评估的主要数据为环境,如季节性盛行天气、局部的实际天气、洋流、潮汐、冰等。此外,必须考虑船舶特性、货物和航行/运行的数据。

选择替代航线的主要原因是安全性和经济性。航线选择在某种程度上受保险约束条件、载重线区、IMO定线制和类似规则控制。

在本课程内容内,应包括有关航线设计所有条件的透彻分析。这样的分析可从计算可能路径的距离开始,然后评估大气条件、海流、船舶和货物特性、法规等。"最佳"航线常常不是最短航线。

1.1.3 根据船舶报告系统总则和VTS程序报告

船舶报告系统 **(1学时)**

教员们应注意,参考文献R3包括有关船舶定线和船舶报告的全部信息。

应根据船舶定线进行航线设计,因为这些系统有助于海上人命安全、航行安全及效率和/或保护海洋环境。讲授本主题时,教员还应参考关于船舶定线制和船舶报告系统的准备建议的MSC/Circ.1060指导性说明,特别是在评估和准备沿海航行计划时。

教员还应注意该出版物A部分和H部分中描述或定义的有关船舶定线的措施,在B(分道通航制)、C(深水航路)、D(避航区)、E(诸如推荐航路、双向航路和推荐交通流向这些其他定线措施)、F(关于特殊通航区域和海峡航行的规则和建议)、G(强制性的船舶报告系统、定线制和禁止抛锚

particular traffic areas and straits), G (mandatory ship reporting systems, mandatory routeing systems and mandatory no anchoring areas) and H (archipelagic sea lanes).

Routeing measures were adopted on May 2010.

1.2 DETERMINE POSITION AND THE ACCURACY OF RESULTANT POSITION FIX BY ANY MEANS

This content builds on the position determination elements of IMO model course 7.03 and is intended to ensure that management level officers ensure that effective position monitoring occurs during the voyage, watchkeeping officers are encouraged to use the most appropri ate position fixing systems available and that the accuracy of the position monitoring is evaluated. The content assumes that trainees have retained their competence in the techniques required for operational level certification. This knowledge is considered so fundamental for much of the management level content within this course that there is merit in reviewing the operational level content quickly before covering the additional elements required at management level. The learning time has been reduced for many elements on the basis that trainees will be reviewing rather than learning much of this content at this level. Additional learning time may be required for trainees who have not retained competence in the operational level tasks.

1.2.1 POSITION DETERMINATION IN ALL CONDITIONS

The main objective of this subject area is that management level officers retain the ability to use celestial and terrestrial based techniques and to ensure that watchkeeping officers monitor the position effectively at all times.

Celestial navigation **(10 hours)**

The main objective of this subject area is that the trainee shall retain the knowledge and ability in position fixing by using all celestial bodies.

To compute the altitude of the celestial body, three methods are available:

- the cosine formula and a pocket calculator;
- the haversine formula;
- pre-computed altitude and azimuth tables.

Which of these should be chosen is optional. After having introduced these methods, it is recommended to select one of them and specialize on that particular method. These days with universal access to inexpensive pocket calculators, the first method may be preferable.

The Longitude by chronometer method to obtain the longitude (a position line) should be carried out before the body is on the observer's meridian.

The Marcq St. Hilaire method (also known as Intercept method) for obtaining a position line is universal and can be utilized for any celestial body in any direction, the body in the meridian included.

区)和H(群岛海区航路)部分中都独自加以描述。

2010年5月采纳了定线制措施。

1.2 定位和确定通过任一定位方法获取的最终船位的精度

此内容建立IMO示范课程7.03定位要素的基础上,旨在确管理保级人员保证在航行期间有效监控船位,鼓励值班驾驶员使用最恰当的定位系统,并评估定位精度。本内容假设学员在操作级证书要求的技巧方面已经适任。本课程中的知识对多数管理级内容非常重要,以至于在涉及管理级额外要求的知识点之前,在迅速复习操作级内容方面颇具价值。基于学员将复习而不是学习该级别内容,已经减少了许多知识点的学时。对不胜任操作级任务的学员,可要求增加额外的学习时间。

1.2.1 确定各种状况下的定位

本课程内容的主要目的在于管理级驾驶员具备使用天文和地文基础技巧及确保值班驾驶员始终有效监控船位的能力。

天文航海 **(10学时)**

本课程内容的主要目的在于使学员具备利用天体定位的知识和能力。

有3种方法计算天体高度:

- 余弦公式和袖珍计算器;
- 半正矢公式;
- 预先计算的地平纬度和方位表。

应选择其一。在介绍了这些方法之后,建议选择其中之一,并专注于该方法。当今随着便宜的袖珍计算器的普遍使用,第一种方法最可取。

应在天体到达测者子午线之前通过计时方法获得经度(一条位置线)。

Marcq St. Hailar's 法(也被称为拦截方法)可用于求位置线,其应用也是很广泛的,并能应用于在任何方向的任何天体,包括天顶的天体。

The Latitude by Meridian Altitude method should be used when the body is on the observer's meridian after applying the true zenith distance to the declination of the celestial body in order to obtain the observer's latitude.

The officers should also be able to obtain the corrections from pole star tables in the nautical almanac and apply them to the altitude of Polaris to find the latitude of the observer.

Finally the officers should be able to find the position of the observer at the time of the final observation, given two or more position lines with the courses and distances run between the observations.

Fixing positions might be carried out as geometrical problems, using simultaneous or staggered observations of celestial bodies, preferably on an ocean plotting sheet which can then be transferred onto the navigational chart (if scale permits).

The examination of trainees in celestial navigation should be mainly limited to their demonstrating the ability to explain the most common definitions and, in a written examination, to the ability to carry out the calculations related to the various observations and obtain a fix from celestial bodies.

Terrestrial navigation including the ability to use appropriate charts, notices to mariners and other publications to assess the accuracy of the resulting fix (16 hours)

This subject area is intended to ensure that the trainee retains appropriate sufficient knowledge and ability in:

1) sailing calculations, using the Mercator formula
2) great circle and composite great circle calculation
3) simple analysis of errors that may occur in position fixing
4) correct usage of appropriate charts, notices to mariners and other publications to assess the accuracy of the resulting fix
5) correct usage of chart catalogue and correcting of charts using information from notices to mariners

The analysis of errors is a very important task. As far as mathematical knowledge permits, statistical methods may be used. A more practical approach to the problem may be more fruitful. The trainees' ability to make critical judgements and to adopt a critical attitude should be encouraged. In particular, the understanding of possible errors, limitations of accuracy and the need for repeated observations must be stressed.

Calculation of the course, distance and intermediate positions should be practised by working a sufficient number of exercises. The choice of formulae and the method of calculation are optional. In the case of a pocket calculator being chosen, which these days is a natural choice, use of the cosine formula for the distance and of the cotangent formula for the course is convenient. The cotangent formula cannot be used close to the equator, where the great circle method is of little or no benefit. Except for this restriction, the formulae can be used in any position.

当将真顶距用于天体赤纬后,天体位于测者子午线时,应用天顶高度求纬度方法来求测者纬度。

驾驶员还应能从航海天文历中的北极星表获得修正值,并将其用于北极星高度,以求得测者纬度。

在两次观测间的航向和航程时,已知两个或多个位置线,最终驾驶员应能得到最后观测时刻的测者位置。

同时或交错使用天体观测,定位可以看作是几何问题来进行,最好在能转换为航用海图(如果比例尺允许)的大洋标绘图上。

学员的天文航海考试应主要限于其展示解释最普通定义的能力上,在书面考试中,限于进行各种观测计算和测天定位的能力上。

包括使用适当海图、航海通告和其他出版物评估所得船位精度能力的地文航海 (16 学时)

本课程内容旨在确保学员具备下列适当和足够的知识:

1) 利用墨卡托公式进行航行计算
2) 大圆和混合大圆计算
3) 定位中可能出现误差的简单分析
4) 正确使用适当海图、航海通告和其他出版物评估所得船位精度
5) 海图目录的正确使用和利用航海通告信息改正海图

误差分析是非常重要的任务。只要数学知识允许,可使用统计方法。解决问题的方法越实用,成果可能越丰硕。应鼓励学员做出批判的判断和具备采取批判态度的能力。必须特别强调理解可能的误差、精度的局限性和重复观测的必要。

应通过足够数量的练习进行航向、距离和中间船位的计算。计算公式和方法可以选择。目前通常选择袖珍计算器,在此情况下,用余弦公式计算距离、用余切公式计算航向较为方便。靠近赤道处不能使用余切公式,在此情况下大圆方法很少使用或无意义。除此限制之外,该公式可用于其他任何位置。

Despite great circle sailing having the advantage over Mercator sailing, for a shorter distance, the method has certain disadvantages. In some cases, use of the method may lead to a latitude which is too high, and composite sailing has to be used. The latitude of vertex is important and if there are restrictions pertaining to weather or commercial aspects, composite sailing has to be used. Composite exercises, including various observation methods, dead reckoning and great circle sailing, should be a part of the learning process.

Discussion of routes and the analysis of the optimum track may start in this subject area and continue in the subject area of voyage planning.

Modern electronic navigational aids (20 hours)

At the level of the training for Chief Mate and Master there are two main areas of emphasis in this subject. First, there should be a review of principles, more thorough consideration of the limitations of the systems, of the instruments and of the presentation of information than for the watchkeeping officer. Secondly, emphasis should be put on procedures for setting up the instruments, on sources of errors, detection of wrong information and on the use of corrections and estimation of accuracy.

In particular, methods of checking and calibration should be thoroughly covered.

New modern electronic aids have been added since the previous edition of the book, as many more are in operational use and the officers should be familiar with these electronic navigational aids.

Loran C is covered in IMO model course 7.03, Officer in charge of a navigational watch – Operational level. Now overtaken by enhanced Loran(eLoran), little background knowledge is required to reinforce the knowledge gained previously, especially as it will benefit in understanding eLoran as Integrated GPS/DGPS/eLoran systems are already in use.

Enhanced Loran (eLoran): The officers should know that eLoran is an independent, dissimilar, complement to Global Navigation Satellite Systems (GNSS). Its operation limitation should also be covered.

Differential GPS (DGPS): The trainees should be able to explain the principle of the DGPS and its use, including the two working methods.

Global Navigation Satellite System (GLONASS): The instructors should explain the principle on which GLONASS works and the advantage of the receiver capable of operating both GLONASS and GPS. Combined GPS/GLONASS receiver equipment utilizes a global datum based on the Soviet Geocentric Coordinate System 1990 (SGS 90).

Galileo: The instructor should explain that Galileo is the European satellite navigation system, designed as a wholly civil system, operated under public control and is a 2nd generation Global Navigation Satellite System (GNSS).

Integrated Navigation system (INS) and Integrated Bridge system (IBS): Integrated Navigation system (INS) "supports safety of navigation by evaluating inputs from several independent and different sensors, combining them to provide information giving timely

尽管大圆航行比墨卡托航行具有航程更短的优势，但大圆航行也有一些缺点。在某些情况下,大圆航法会导致纬度太高,不得不使用混合航行。顶点纬度很重要,如果存在有关天气或商业方面的限制,必须使用混合航行。综合练习,包括各种观测方法、推算和大圆航行,应是本部分内容学习过程的一部分。

在本课程内容,可以开始进行航线的讨论和最优航迹的分析,并且在航次计划课程内容中继续学习。

现代电子导航设备 **(20 学时)**

在大副和船长级的培训水平上,本课程强调两点主要内容。首先,应有原理的回顾,比值班驾驶员更全面地考虑系统、仪器和信息表述的局限性。其次,应强调设定仪器程序、误差源、错误信息探测及进行精度的修正和估计。

特别指出,应彻底涵盖检查和校正方法。

本书的现行版本中已增加了新的现代电子助航设备的内容，由于还有更多的在实际操作使用,驾驶员应熟悉这些电子导航设备。

劳兰C包括在IMO 7.03示范课程负责值班的驾驶员——操作级中。现已被增强型劳兰(eLoran)超越,无须什么背景知识来加强以前获得的知识,特别是因为它将有益于将eLoran理解为已在使用中的GPS/DGPS/eLoran组合系统。

增强型劳兰 (eLoran):驾驶员应了解eLoran是一个独立的、与全球导航卫星系统(GNSS)不同的仪器,对全球导航卫星系统是一个补充。也应包括了解其操作局限性。

差分 GPS (DGPS):学员应能解释DGPS的原理及其使用,包括两种工作方法。

全球导航卫星系统 (GLONASS):教员应解释其工作原理和其接收机可作为GLONASS和GPS兼用的优点。组合GPS / GLONASS接收机设备利用基于苏联的地心坐标系统1990 (SGS 90)的全球基准面。

伽利略:教员应解释是欧洲卫星导航系统,被设计为一个完全的民用系统,在公共控制下操作,是第二代全球导航卫星系统(GNSS)。

组合导航系统(INS)和综合船桥系统(IBS):组合导航系统(INS)通过评估几个独立的和不同的传感器输入，结合它们提供的信息给予及时警告潜在的危险和完整解读该信息来支持航行胜

warnings of potential dangers and degradation of integrity of this information". The three categories of INS namely (A), (B) and (C) should be explained to the officers.

The Integrated Bridge systems (IBS) is "a combination of systems which are interconnected in order to allow centralized access to sensor information or command/control workstations, with the aim of increasing safe and efficient ship's management by suitably qualified personnel". IBS recommendations apply to a system performing two or more operations, namely: passage execution; communication; machinery control; loading, discharging and cargo control; and safety and security. The instructors should explain the limitations of these systems clearly to the officers.

Exercises in the use and calibration of instruments are suitable for group activities.

1.3 DETERMINE AND ALLOW FOR COMPASS ERRORS

1.3.1 PRINCIPLES OF THE MAGNETIC COMPASS

Parts of the magnetic compass and their function **(30 hours)**

The officers should be able to identify the various parts of the magnetic compass and explain their functions and to explain the principles of the magnetic compass including a knowledge of the cause and correction of errors. Resolution A.382(X) details the performance standards for magnetic compasses and resolution MSC.86 (70), annex 2 for Transmitting magnetic heading devices.

The practical correction of the compass should be undertaken during training where Administrations continue to permit Masters to undertake compass adjustment but an understanding only of the process is sufficient where compass correction must only be performed by a licensed compass adjuster.

Although the magnetic compass is mainly used only as a stand-by for the gyrocompass, its errors should be regularly checked and recorded.

1.3.2 PRINCIPLES AND ERRORS OF GYROCOMPASSES

Gyrocompass errors and corrections **(10 hours)**

The instructor should remind trainees that the meridian-seeking property and damping both depend upon detection and measurement of the tilt of the spin axis of the gyroscope resulting from the earth's rotation. That applies equally to compasses controlled by liquidballistic attachments and those controlled by electrical signals to torque motors. Any tilt, other than that resulting from the earth's rotation, and any apparent tilt resulting from horizontal acceleration of the compass is a source of error.

The errors and the methods of correcting or limiting them should be treated non-mathematically.

The various errors may be referred to the performance standards for gyrocompasses to give trainees an indication of the limits of the accuracy that can be expected.

任人员安全。应向驾驶员解释A、B、C三种INS。

综合船桥系统(IBS)是一个相互关联的结合系统,以允许集中访问传感器信息或指挥/控制工作站,目的在于增加具有适任资格人员管理船舶的安全性和效率。IBS建议适用于一个完成两项或多项作业的系统,即:航行、通信、机械控制、装卸货和货物控制、安全和保安。教员应向驾驶员解释清楚这些系统的局限性。

仪器的使用和校正练习适合于小组作业。

1.3 测定并修正罗经差

1.3.1 磁罗经的原理

磁罗经的部件与功能 **(30学时)**

驾驶员应能识别磁罗经各种部件,解释其功能和磁罗经原理,包括造成误差和改正误差知识。决议A.382(X)决议详细说明了磁罗经性能标准,MSC.86(70)决议附件2详述了发送磁航向装置的标准。

培训期间应进行罗经校正实操,虽然主管机关依然允许船长进行罗经校正,但在罗经校正必须只能由持证罗经校正师进行的情况下,学员仅理解该过程就够了。

尽管磁罗经仅主要用作于陀螺罗经的备用,但应定期检查和记录其误差。

1.3.2 陀螺罗经的原理及其误差

陀螺罗经的误差与修正 **(10学时)**

教员应提醒学员指向特性和阻尼都取决于由地球自转导致的陀螺仪主轴倾斜的探测与测量。那同样适合于液体连通器控制的罗经和力矩马达产生电信号控制的罗经。除了由地球自转产生的倾斜以外的任何倾斜和由罗经水平加速所产生的任何视倾斜都是误差来源。

误差及其校正或限制的方法应以非数学的方式加以处理。

各种误差可以参照陀螺罗经性能标准以给学员一个期望达到的精度范围的指示。

1.4 COORDINATE SEARCH AND RESCUE OPERATIONS

See IMO model course 1.08 Radar navigation – management level and STCW reg. I/12

Instructors should note that the International Aeronautical and Maritime Search and Rescue Manual, R31 published jointly by IMO and the International Civil Aviation Organization (ICAO) in three volumes provides guidelines for a common approach to organizing and providing SAR services.

Volume III, Mobile Facilities, is intended to be carried aboard rescue units, aircraft and vessels to help with performance of a search, rescue or on-scene coordination function, and with aspects of SAR that pertain to their own emergencies.

1.5 ESTABLISH WATCHKEEPING ARRANGEMENTS AND PROCEDURES

1.5.1 INTERNATIONAL REGULATIONS FOR PREVENTING COLLISIONS AT SEA

Thorough knowledge of content, application and intent of the International Regulations for Preventing Collisions at Sea, 1972, as amended (30 hours)

This section will be dealt with mainly by question-and-answer sessions, using models, magnetic boards and computer or simulator based real-time situations. Trainees should already be thoroughly familiar with COLREGS and their application, so these sessions will be for the purposes of revision and consolidation. The response "call the Master" will, of course, no longer be available to them.

The attention of trainees should be drawn to collision cases and court judgements when discussing their answers and the actions they propose.

When dealing with the use of and manoeuvring in traffic separation schemes, particular attention should be drawn to the proper use of inshore traffic zones where they exist.

Exercises should involve planning passages during which it would be necessary to join or to leave lanes, including cases which involve crossing the other lane.

The use of radar for collision avoidance in restricted visibility is covered in IMO model course 1.08, Radar navigation, but some attention should be paid to the posting of lookouts, the proper use of sound signals, and the actions to take on hearing the fog signal of another ship and other matters which do not lend themselves to simulation.

1.5.2 PRINCIPLES TO BE OBSERVED IN KEEPING A NAVIGATIONAL WATCH

Thorough knowledge of the content, application and intent of the principles to be observed in keeping a navigational watch (12 hours)

This is based on ensuring that the requirements of STCW regulations and recommendations are complied with. The regulations are contained in the STCW Code, section A-VIII/2. The emphasis should be on the officer demonstrating that they have the ability to establish and monitor watchkeeping practice that is consistent with the principles in practice rather than a simple recall of the principles.

1.4　协调搜寻与救助行动

参见IMO示范课程1.08雷达航行——管理级以及STCW规则I/12。

教员应注意由IMO和国际民航组织(ICAO)联合出版的R31,国际航空航海搜寻与救助手册的三卷中有关于组织和进行搜寻与救助服务的通行方法指南。

第Ⅲ卷—移动设备,指计划在船携带的救助装置、飞机和船舶,以帮助执行搜寻、救助或现场协调功能和SAR自身紧急情况。

1.5　确定值班安排和程序

1.5.1　国际海上避碰规则

完全理解经修订的1972国际海上避碰规则的内容、适用范围和目的　(30学时)

本节主要以问答的形式进行,使用模型或磁力板和计算机或基于实时情境的模拟器。学员应已完全熟悉COLREGS及其适用范围,因此本节授课以复习和巩固为目的。当然,"呼叫船长"的反应将不再适合他们。

当学员在讨论他们的回答及他们建议的行动时,应注意到碰撞案例和法庭判决。

当在考虑分道通航制的应用及在其中的操纵时,应特别注意在有沿岸通航带时的正确使用。

练习应包括有必要进入或离开通航分道时的航线设计,包括横穿其他通航分道的情况。

IMO示范课程1.08——雷达航行,涵盖了能见度受限时避碰雷达的使用,但应注意设置瞭望人员、声响信号的正确使用和听到他船雾号所采取的行动以及不适于模拟的其他事件。

1.5.2　保持航行值班应遵循的原则

完全理解保持航行值班应遵循的原则的内容、适用范围和目的　(12学时)

这是基于确保STCW公约的要求和建议的执行。STCW公约A-Ⅷ/2节含有此规则。强调驾驶员展示其具有建立和保持与实操原理相一致的值班实操的能力,而不是简单地回忆这些原理。

The references provide examples of stranding which became the subject of official investigations. In most cases, a failure to keep an adequate navigational watch caused or contributed to the accident. A criticism made in a number of cases was the absence of Master's standing or special orders and the lack of any routine regarding effective navigational and watchkeeping procedures, such as the planning of passages in confined waters and the checking of courses and positions on the chart. In other cases there was uncertainty about calling the Master and confusion about who was conning the ship after the Master had come to the bridge.

1.5.3 BRIDGE EQUIPMENT AND SYSTEMS (6 hours)

In recent years, bridge equipment that has become a mandatory requirement and which is not strictly an electronic navigation aid has been introduced. It is important that this equipment is considered within the management of the watchkeeping practice on board ship.

Automatic Identification System (AIS): The international requirement for the carriage AIS as ship-borne navigational equipment on vessels is detailed within chapter V (Safety of Navigation) regulation 19, of the revised SOLAS Convention. The information received from the AIS is displayed on an electronic chart, computer display or compatible radar and the information received can help situational awareness as well as assist in collision avoidance.

The reasons why AIS should not be used as an aid for collision avoidance should be emphasized to the officers.

Long Range Identification and Tracking (LRIT): The purpose of LRIT is to improve maritime safety, security and assist in search and rescue (SAR) operation. The officers should have the knowledge that the data transmitted from the LRIT, which ships are required to transmit LRIT messages. There is no interface between LRIT and AIS. AIS is a broadcast system and data derived through LRIT will be available only to the parties entitled to receive such information; regulatory provisions will include safeguards concerning the confidentiality of data.

SOLAS contracting Governments will be entitled to receive information about ships navigating within a distance not exceeding 1,000 nautical miles off their coast.

Voyage Data Recorder (VDR) and Simplified Voyage Data Recorder (S-VDR): The purpose of a voyage data recorder (VDR) and Simplified Voyage Data Recorder (S-VDR) is to maintain and store, in a secure and retrievable form, information concerning the position, movement, physical status, command and control of a vessel over the period leading up to and following an incident having an impact thereon. The officers should know that the information contained in a VDR and S-VDR is made available to both the Administration and the shipowner and this information is for use during any subsequent investigation to identify the cause(s) of the incident. The equipment is so designed that, as far as is practical, it is not possible to tamper with the selection of data being input to the equipment, the data itself nor that which has already been recorded and any attempt to interfere with the integrity of the data or the recording is recorded. The various data items recorded in the VDR and S-VDR should be explained to the officers. The officers should know that the shipowner, in all circumstances and at all times, owns the VDR and its information and in the event of an accident the owner of the ship makes all decoding instructions available as necessary to recover the recorded information and maintains the same.

参考文献提供了已成为官方调查主题的搁浅例子。在大多数情况下,没有保持适当的航行值班会导致或产生事故。对一些案例提出批评的是因为缺乏船长常规或特殊命令簿和对有效的航行和值班的程序缺乏日常的关注，像在受限水域的航线设计以及在海图上检查航向和船位这些方面。在其他情况下,存在对呼叫船长的不定性以及在船长上驾驶台后由谁来操纵船舶感到模棱两可的情况。

1.5.3 驾驶台值班设备与系统 (6 学时)

近年来,驾驶台设备已成为一种强制性的要求,已不再是严格意义上的电子助航设备。重要的是该设备在船舶值班实践管理考虑之内。

自动识别系统(AIS):AIS作为船载导航设备的国际要求,在经修订的SOLAS公约第五章(航行安全)第19条中有详细规定。来自AIS的信息在电子海图、计算机屏幕或兼容的雷达上显示,收到的信息可有助于情境认识和避碰。

应对驾驶员强调AIS为何不能用作避碰设施的理由。

远距离识别和跟踪(LRIT):LRIT 旨在提高海上安全、保安和协助搜救(SAR)作业。驾驶员应了解LRIT发送的数据，要求船舶发送LRIT信息。LRIT 和 AIS间没有接口。 AIS 是一个广播系统,通过LRIT所获数据将只提供给有权获得此类信息的各有关方;监管规定将包括有关数据保密性的保卫措施。

SOLAS公约缔约国政府将有权接收在距海岸不超过1 000海里的航行船舶的信息。

船载航行数据记录仪(VDR)和简易船载航行数据记录仪(S-VDR):船载航行数据记录仪(VDR)和简易船载航行数据记录仪(S-VDR)旨在在导致事故发生和随后产生的事故影响期间,以安全和可回收的形式保持和存储有关船舶位置、运动、物理状态、指挥和控制的信息。驾驶员应知晓,主管机关和船东二者都可得到包含在VDR和S-VDR中的信息,该信息用于随后的辨明事故原因的调查。只要可行,如此设计该设备,既不可能篡改所选输入该设备的数据,也不可能篡改已被记录的数据,并记录任何干涉数据或记录完整性的企图。应向驾驶员解释VDR和S-VDR中记录的各种数据项。驾驶员应知道,在任何情况下,任何时候船东都拥有VDR及其信息,一旦发生事故,当有必要恢复记录的信息并保持不变的时候,船东使所有解码指令可用。

Bridge Navigational Watch Alarm System (BNWAS): The carriage requirement of Bridge Navigational Watch Alarm System (BNWAS) is set out by SOLAS chapter V/19 and the requirements will be mandatory for new ships and phased-in for existing ships. The instructors should explain the purpose of BNWAS is to monitor bridge activity and detect operator disability, which could lead to marine accidents and this purpose is achieved by a series of indications and alarms to alert first the OOW and, if he/she is not responding, then to alert the Master or another qualified OOW. The system monitors the awareness of the officer-onwatch(OOW) and automatically alerts the Master or other qualified OOW if for any reason the OOW becomes incapable of performing watch duties. The officers should be able to list and explain the operational sequence of indications and alarms of the system.

Officers should be fully conversant with the limitations of all the equipment.

1.6 MAINTAIN SAFE NAVIGATION THROUGH THE USE OF INFORMATION FROM NAVIGATION EQUIPMENT AND SYSTEMS TO ASSIST IN COMMAND DECISION MAKING

See IMO model courses 1.08, Radar navigation – management level, 1.22, Ship simulator and bridge teamwork, 1.27, Operational use of electronic chart display and information systems (ECDIS) and STCW reg. I/12

This competence requires the trainee to develop the practical ability to use the information from a range of navigation equipment and systems and to make sound command level decisions using this information. Trainees should undertake a range of activities from relatively simple to complex that involve both navigation and anti-collision situations in real time. Appropriate simulators and/or training ships allow realistic situations to be created and the competence of the trainee to be assessed with some validity.

1.7 MAINTAIN SAFE NAVIGATION THROUGH THE USE OF ECDIS AND ASSOCIATED NAVIGATION SYSTEMS TO ASSIST COMMAND DECISION MAKING

See IMO model course 1.27, Operational use of electronic chart display and information systems (ECDIS) and STCW reg. I/12

The emphasis at management level should be on the trainee utilizing ECDIS and AIS effectively within watchkeeping practice in the typically complex situations where the Master is required to take charge of the bridge watchkeeping. There should also be an emphasis on ensuring that watchkeeping officers set up, maintain and utilize this equipment appropriately and understand the limitations of the systems.

1.8 FORECAST WEATHER AND OCEANOGRAPHIC CONDITIONS

1.8.1 SYNOPTIC CHARTS AND WEATHER FORECASTING (24 hours)

Weather forecasting

The emphasis should be on identifying sources of and obtaining synoptic information and then utilizing this information and the meteorological knowledge gained at operational level to

驾驶台航行值班报警系统 (BNWAS):SOLAS 公约第5章19条规定了驾驶台航行值班报警系统(BNWAS)的配备要求,该要求对新船是强制性的,对现有船舶是分阶段性的。驾驶员应解释BNWAS旨在监控驾驶台活动和探测操作者可导致海上事故的操作失误,通过先用一系列的指示和警报传感器警示值班驾驶员,如他/她没有反应,然后向船长或另一合格的值班驾驶员发出警报来达到此目的。该系统监控值班驾驶员的意识,如由于任何原因导致值班驾驶员不能履行其职责,将自动向船长或其他值班驾驶员报警。驾驶员应能列出并解释该系统的指示和警报的操作顺序。

驾驶员应完全熟悉所有设备的局限性。

1.6 通过辅助决策的导航设备和系统的信息保持安全航行

参见IMO 示范课程1.08——雷达航行管理级、示范课程1.22——船舶模拟器和驾驶台团队、示范课程1.27——电子海图显示与信息系统(ECDIS)的操作使用以及STCW 规则Ⅰ/12。

本适任能力内容要求学员形成使用一系列导航仪器和系统信息的实操能力和利用该信息做出合理命令级别决定的能力。在实时的航行和避碰情境下,学员应从相对简单到复杂地进行一系列活动。适当的模拟器和/或实习船可以创造真实情境,在评估学员的适任能力方面具有一定的效果。

1.7 通过辅助决策的ECDIS及相关的航行系统保持安全航行

参见IMO 示范课程1.27——电子海图显示与信息系统(ECDIS)的操作使用以及STCW 规则Ⅰ/12。

管理级应注重在要求船长负责驾驶台值班的典型复杂情境下,学员在进行值班期间有效地利用ECDIS和AIS。还应注重确保值班驾驶员适当正确建立、维护和使用该设备,懂得该系统的局限性。

1.8 预报天气和海洋水文状况

1.8.1 气象图与天气预报 (24学时)

天气预报

应注重识别天气信息来源和获取天气信息,然后利用这些信息和操作级所获得的气象知识,能预测船舶预期将经历的天气状况。

be able to forecast the weather conditions that the vessel is anticipated to experience in the future.

If a facsimile receiver, internet and email facility is available, receiving and interpreting the weather chart of the day should be part of the training process.

Climatology

Trainees should have a general idea of the climate of the oceans and the seasonal changes to be expected. The Mariner's Handbook (T30) contains world climatic charts.

1.8.2 CHARACTERISTICS OF VARIOUS WEATHER SYSTEMS (14 hours)

Tropical revolving storms

The instructor should make use of drawings of the structure of a tropical storm, graphical representations of temperature, pressure and wind speed, satellite pictures and charts showing actual storm tracks.

Trainees should be fully conversant with the means of avoiding tropical storms, where to find details of radio storm warnings and the information which should be transmitted if the Master has good reason to believe that a tropical storm is developing or exists in the neighbourhood.

Ice

There is little coverage of ice in the operational level model course. Trainees therefore need to understand the formation and characteristics of different types of ice and to learn appropriate strategies for navigating the vessel in or near ice. The use of visual aids such as videos and photographs will enhance the ability of trainees to differentiate ice and to relate the learning content to real situations.

Trainees should know where information on ice reports can be found and understand the terms and descriptions used in them. The Marine Observer's Handbook (T23) and The Mariner's Handbook (T30) contain the Ice Nomenclature drawn up by the World Meteorological Organization.

Trainees should also recognize the conditions which may give rise to severe accumulation of ice on the ship.

1.8.3 OCEAN CURRENT SYSTEMS (7 hours)

Ocean currents

Trainees should possess sufficient knowledge of ocean currents and sources of information on currents to enable them to select an optimal route for a sea passage and season. As an aid to the instructors, there are: sample Lesson plan for Ocean Current Systems, sample participants handout, sample power point presentation and activities, included in this model course. The instructors may find them useful when preparing for lectures. These samples are given as guidance only to demonstrate the use of extensive research and pedagogy.

如传真接收机、互联网和电子邮件设施可用,则接收当天的天气图并加以解读应作为该培训过程的一部分。

气候学

学员应具有海洋气候的和预期的季节变化的一般概念。海员手册(T30)含有世界气候图。

1.8.2 各种天气系统的特点 (14 学时)

热带气旋风暴

教员应利用热带风暴的结构图,气温、压力和风速的示意图,卫星图片以及显示实际风暴轨迹的图。

学员应完全熟悉避让热带风暴的方法，获知无线电风暴警告的详细内容以及如果船长有充分的理由相信热带风暴正在发展或存在于附近,应发送的信息。

海冰

在操作级示范课程中很少涵盖有关冰的内容。因此,学员需要了解不同类型的冰的形成和特性,并学习在冰区或接近冰区船舶航行的适当策略。使用视觉辅助工具,如视频和照片,将提高学员区分冰的能力和将学习内容与实际情况相联系的能力。

学员应知道在哪里可以找到冰况报告的信息,理解其中所用的术语和描述。《航海观察员手册》(T23)和《海员手册》(T30)里含有世界气象组织制定的冰况术语。

学员也应知道可在船上产生严重的积冰的条件。

1.8.3 洋流系统 (7学时)

洋流

学员应对洋流及其信息源具有足够的了解,以便能为大洋航行和季节选择最优的航线。作为教员的辅助工具,本示范课程含有:洋流系统的教案范本、学员讲义范本、幻灯片放映和活动范本。教员在备课时可发现它们是有用的。给出这些范本仅作为示教学科研使用的指南。

Waves

The dangers of crossing areas of shallow water in heavy weather should be stressed.

If facsimile wave charts of the area are available, trainees should make use of them in weather forecasting.

1.8.4 TIDAL CALCULATIONS (6 hours)

Trainees should review their knowledge of tidal theory and basic calculations from their operational level training and practice. The emphasis at management level should be on more complex secondary port calculations that, where possible, can be integrated into voyage planning tasks.

It is very important that trainees appreciate the meteorological and local conditions that can significantly influence the actual tide level.

1.9 RESPOND TO NAVIGATIONAL EMERGENCIES

1.9.1 PRECAUTIONS WHEN BEACHING A SHIP

Precautions to be taken when beaching a vessel **(2 hours)**

Although a gently shelving beach of sand or gravel is ideal, in many cases the urgency of the operation will dictate that the nearest beach is used regardless of the nature of the bottom. Similarly, the state of the tide can seldom be chosen.

A loss of stability similar to that experienced on taking the blocks in dry-dock will occur. If the ship has a large trim or the slope of the bottom is large, a heavy list may develop as the tide falls. The ship will list similarly when one end lifts again on the rising tide. Transfer of ballast or flooding a compartment may be necessary to prevent the list becoming excessive.

Beaching with the ship parallel to the beach may avoid that problem; the ship will settle with a list equal to the slope of the beach. If boats are to be used to transfer passengers or nonessential crew members ashore, the broadside-on position will provide a lee from onshore waves and surf for the boat work.

On the other hand, a ship end-on to the beach with ground tackle laid out to keep, the stern in place would be better able to withstand heavy onshore weather and would be easier to haul off eventually.

1.9.2 ACTIONS TO BE TAKEN IF GROUNDING IS IMMINENT AND AFTER GROUNDING

Grounding **(2 hours)**

Many of the actions to take after beaching a ship apply also to stranding.

When planning an attempt at refloating, consideration should be given to the extent of damage, the height of the tide, the assistance available and whether the ship can be

波浪

在恶劣天气里穿越浅水域的危险性应加以强调。

如果水域的波浪传真图可供使用,学员应在天气预报中加以应用。

1.8.4 潮汐计算 (6学时)

学员应复习其在操作级培训和实操中获得的潮汐理论和基本计算知识。管理级应注重更复杂的副港计算,可能情况下,可合并到航次计划任务中。

学员了解可显著影响实际潮高的气象和当地状况是十分重要的。

1.9 航行中的应急反应

1.9.1 船舶抢滩的预防措施

船舶抢摊时应采取的预防措施 **(2学时)**

尽管逐渐倾斜的沙滩或砂砾滩是理想的,但在许多情况下操纵的紧迫性将指示使用最近的滩,而不管其海底的性质。同样,很少选择潮汐的状况。

同在干船坞里放上墩木相类似,稳性的损失将会发生。如果船舶有大的吃水差或有大的船底倾斜,当潮水退潮时,会产生严重的横倾。同样地,当船舶的一端又被涨潮抬起时,船舶将会横倾。为了防止形成过多的横倾,可能有必要进行调驳压载水或在一舱室中注水。

与滩平行的船舶抢摊可以避免上述问题;船舶将以一个与滩坡度相等的横倾坐滩。如果可以利用小艇向岸上转运乘客或非重要船员,为了防止向岸浪和拍岸浪,船舶向海一舷的位置应为小艇作业提供一个下风。

另一方面,船舶远离滩的一端布置锚具以保持船尾的位置,将能更好地抵御海岸的恶劣天气以及将更易于最后的脱离。

1.9.2 即将搁浅与搁浅后所采取的行动

搁浅 **(2学时)**

在船舶抢摊后需采取的许多措施也适用于搁浅。

当要进行脱浅计划时,应考虑将产生的损坏程度、潮高、可供使用的帮助以及是否船舶能通过排出载水或卸下货物来减轻船舶的重量。从小艇上测得的水深将为船舶在脱浅期间尽量向最

lightenedby discharging ballast or cargo. Soundings, taken from a boat, will give an indication of the most favorable direction in which to try to move the ship during refloating.

The release or probable release of oil or other harmful substances should be reported at once to the nearest coast radio station. Where a serious threat of pollution exists, the coastal State involved may intervene in the salvage operations.

1.9.4 ACTION TO BE TAKEN IF COLLISION IS IMMINENT, AFTER A COLLISION OR IMPAIRMENT OF THE WATERTIGHT INTEGRITY OF THE HULL

Collision **(2 hours)**

The duties of the Master following a collision are set out in the appropriate regulations and annexes.

There may also be national requirements regarding the recording and notification of collision accidents. In any case, full details of the collision, engine and helm orders prior to impact, estimates of the heading and speed at the time of impact and the angle of contact with the other ship should be entered in the logbook for future reference. The trace from the course recorder should be appended to the logbook.

1.9.5 ASSESSMENT OF DAMAGE CONTROL (1 hour)

Even a small hole in the shell plating below the waterline will admit water faster than the capacity of bilge pumps to deal with it. A rapid assessment is needed of the tonnage of water in the space, the lost buoyancy and change of trim and the effect of these factors on stability. Cross-flooding may be needed to reduce the list in certain ships, if only to aid abandonment.

The release or probable release of oil or other harmful substances should be reported to the nearest coast radio station at the first opportunity.

1.9.6 EMERGENCY STEERING (1 hour)

When a ship in a coastal region or area of high traffic density has become disabled as a result of engine or steering failure which cannot readily be repaired, she should report her situation to the coastal State concerned.

It is unlikely that jury steering can be arranged for a large deeply loaded ship, such as a VLCC or a bulk carrier, which would be effective in conditions of strong wind. Recognizing that, the most prudent course of action would be to call for tug assistance at an early stage, before a dangerous situation has developed.

1.9.7 EMERGENCY TOWING ARRANGEMENTS AND TOWING PROCEDURES (2 hours)

Before undertaking a tow, the Master should check that he is permitted to do so by the terms of the charter party or bills of lading. In any case, he should contact the owners for their agreement. They will have to arrange additional insurance.

合适的方向移动提供一个标识。

应立即向最近的海岸无线电电台报告油或其他有害物质的释放或可能的释放。在有严重污染威胁的地方,相关沿岸国可以干涉救助作业。

1.9.4 即将碰撞和碰撞后或船体的水密完整性损坏后所采取的行动

碰撞 **(2学时)**

碰撞后船长的职责列在相应的规则和附录里。

可能还有关于碰撞事故的记录和告示的国内要求。在任何情况下,碰撞的全部细节、碰撞前的车钟和舵令、碰撞时的船首向和速度的估计以及与他船的触碰角度均应记入航海日志供将来参考。航向记录仪上的航迹应附在航海日志上。

1.9.5 破损控制的评估 (1学时)

即使是水线下船壳板的一个小漏洞,其漏水的能力比用于应对它的污水泵的排水能力还要快。需要快速评估舱室里水的吨数、损失的浮力和吃水差的变化以及这些因素对稳性的影响。如果仅为了有助于弃船,在某些船上为了减少横倾,可以进行交错注水。

应立即在第一时间向最近的海岸无线电电台报告油或其他有害物质的释放或可能的释放。

1.9.6 应急操舵 (1学时)

当船舶处在沿岸或高密度交通流的水域,由于不能立即修复的主机故障或操舵失灵使船舶失控,她应向相关沿岸国报告她的状况。

在强风情况下,不可能对像VLCC或散货船这样的大型重载船舶安排应急操纵,这将不会奏效。应认识到,最审慎的行动为在危险态势发展之前的早期阶段请求拖船协助。

1.9.7 应急拖带部署与拖带程序 (2学时)

在进行拖带之前,船长应核实租船合同或提单条款允许这样做。在任何情况下,他应与船东联系以得到他们的同意。他们将不得不安排额外的保险。

Towing for the purpose of saving life is always permitted. For example, towing a disabled vessel away from a lee shore may be the safest way of saving the crew in some circumstances.

The Master should also be satisfied that the towing operation has a reasonable chance of successful completion. He should consider the relative sizes of the ships, the power of the engines, fuel reserves, equipment available and distance to a safe port.

The towing wires used by salvage tugs are much longer than the towing wires carried by merchant ships, which do not have sufficient weight on their own to provide a catenary to absorb shock loadings. To provide the extra weight it is usual to shackle the towing wire to the anchor cable of the towed ship and to walk back the cable sufficiently to keep the towing wire submerged throughout the towing operation.

When starting to tow, the weight should be taken up gradually, the speed being slowly increased until towing speed is reached. Care should be taken to avoid jerking the tow wire on first taking the weight. The towing speed is adjusted so that the tow wire remains submerged. If the tow wire shows signs of clearing the water and straightening, the engine revolutions should be reduced until a catenary has been restored.

A method of slipping the tow in an emergency (such as the foundering of the towed vessel, for example) should be decided and known to all of the watchkeepers.

Disconnecting the tow, particularly in confined waters at a port approach, can be a critical operation and should be planned and agreed between the two vessels. Speed will have to be reduced gradually over a long distance. As the depth of water decreases, the towed ship should shorten the tow by heaving in cable, to prevent the tow line fouling on the bottom. Harbor tugs should be arranged to assist with manoeuvring during disconnection and to take the tow into a berth. Alternatively, both ships may be brought to anchor before disconnecting.

1.10 MANOEUVRE AND HANDLE A SHIP IN ALL CONDITIONS

The STCW Convention requires trainees to be able to demonstrate practical competence in performing the manoeuvres stated under this competence in addition to any examination of their knowledge and understanding of principles. This practical competence may be developed and demonstrated in service, in which case the practical elements of actual ship handling may not be included in the training course.

Administrations and training centres need to evaluate whether is is likely that their trainees will get sufficient opportunity to develop their practical ability and to demonstrate competence on board ships in service.

Where this is unlikely, the use of appropriate simulators, manned ship models or training ships will be required. The content below assumes that practical demonstrations will be part of the training course. Under each manoeuvre, trainees should undertake a number of practical exercises ranging from relatively simple to more complex.

以救助人命为目的的拖带总是允许的。例如,拖带一条失控船舶远离下风岸在某些环境下可能是最安全的救助船员的方法。

船长也应对拖带作业有一个成功完成的合理机会感到满意。他应考虑船舶的相对尺度、主机功率、燃油储备、可供使用的设备以及到达安全港口的距离。

救助拖船使用的拖带钢丝绳应比商船上的拖带绳索长得多,商船的拖带钢丝绳自身没有足够的强度以提供能吸收冲击负荷的悬链线。为了能提供额外的强度,通常是将拖带钢丝绳用卸扣连接在被拖船的锚链上并放出足够的锚链以使整个拖带作业过程中拖带钢丝绳都浸在水中。

开始拖带时,强度逐渐增大,速度慢慢增加直至达到拖带速度。注意在首次拖动拖缆时应避免急拉。应调节拖带速度使拖缆保持浸入水中。如果拖缆有出水或绷直的迹象,应减小主机转数直至恢复悬链线。

应决定并让所有值班人员都知道在紧急情况下(例如被拖船沉没)解拖的方法。

解拖,特别是在港口进口处的受限水域内,可能是关键操作,应在两船之间协商并达成一致。经过长距离的航行船速将逐渐减小。当水深减小时,被拖船应绞进锚链缩短拖带长度,避免拖缆缠绕海底。在解拖期间,应安排港口拖船协助操纵以及拖带拖轮靠泊。可供选择的是两船在解拖前都抛锚。

1.10 在各种状况下操纵和操作船舶

STCW公约要求学员在除了检查他们对原理的知识与理解的任何考试之外,在执行本适任能力规定的操纵方面能够展示实操能力。这种实操能力,在船上服务期间可以培养和展示,在这种情况下,船舶实际操纵的实操要素可不包括本培训课程中。

主管机关和培训中心必须评估其学员在船上服务期间,是否将获得足够机会发展其实操能力和展示其适任能力。

在船上实操不可能获得的情况下,将需要使用适当的模拟器、有人船模或实习船。在每一操纵情况下,学员应进行相对地从简单到复杂的实操练习。

1.10.1 MANOEUVRING AND HANDLING A SHIP IN ALL CONDITIONS

(V3, V4, V5, V6, V7, V8, V9, V10, V11, V12, V13, V14, V15, V16, V17, V18, V19, V30, V31, V32, V33, V98, V140, V142, V152, V168)

Approaching pilot stations and embarking or disembarking pilots, with due regard to weather, tide, head reach and stopping distances (4 hours)

This section can be introduced with discussion led by the instructor prior to the trainee undertaking practical exercises. Trainees should be encouraged to contribute, from their own experiences, cases of difficult approaches, problems with embarking a pilot in heavy weather or ice and the slowing of very large ships.

The instructor should impress on trainees that the passage plan should extend to the berth and not finish at the pilot station. The officer in charge of the navigational watch will need the plan to monitor the ship's progress to the berth (T25).

Handling ship in rivers, estuaries and restricted waters having regard to the effects of current, wind and restricted water on helm response (10 hours)

The approximate mean squat can be calculated by using formulae. Trainees should be reminded that values obtained from the formula or from squat diagrams are theoretical and that the actual squat and trim of their vessels may differ somewhat (T18, T25, V4, V7).

The variable effect of current, under-keel clearance and bottom topography in restricted waters and the typical effects on vessel handling should be covered in depth before practical exercises are undertaken.

Application of constant rate of turn techniques (3 hours)

Such techniques may be demonstrated and practised using a radar simulator, ship simulator or training ship. Radar navigation – management level is covered in IMO model course 1.08.

Manoeuvring in shallow water including the reduction in under-keel clearance caused by squat, rolling and pitching (2 hours)

Theories on the cause and estimation of squat effects and the impact this may have on ship manoeuvring should be covered. The effect of reduced under-keel clearance on turning ability and on increasing/reducing speed should be introduced.

There continues to be a number of casualties where the dynamic effects of rolling, pitching and changing water levels in high sea and swell lead to grounding. Trainees should be introduced to theories that estimate the static water level that would be required in order to safely transit a shallow where these dynamic effects are anticipated.

Interaction between passing ships and own ship nearby banks (2 hours)

Trainees should be able to describe in detail the anticipated effect of interaction with other ships and with the bottom and sides of restricted channels or canals including encounters

1.10.1 在各种状况下操纵和操作船舶

(V3, V4, V5, V6, V7, V8, V9, V10, V11, V12, V13, V14, V15, V16, V17, V18, V19, V30, V31, V32, V33, V98, V140, V142, V152, V168)

考虑天气、潮汐、冲程和停车距离后接近引航站、上下引航员 **(4 学时)**

在进行实操练习前,在教员的带领下讨论本节。应鼓励学员从他们自身的经验提供难以接近的案例、在恶劣天气或冰区引航员难以登船和超大型船舶难以减速的难题。

教员应向学员强调航行计划应延伸至靠泊而并非终止于引航站。负责航行值班的高级船员将需要监视船舶靠泊进程的计划(T25)。

考虑流、风、受限水域对舵效的影响下,在河流、河口和受限水域里的船舶操纵 **(10 学时)**

利用公式能计算近似的平均下沉量。应提醒学员从公式或下沉量图表获得的数值只是理论上的,与实际的下沉量及船舶的吃水差可能有些差异(T18, T25, V4, V7)。

在进行实操练习前,在受限水域多变的流、富余水深和海底地形的影响和对船操纵的典型影响应都包含在水深之中。

恒定旋转率的应用技巧 **(3 学时)**

该技巧可使用雷达模拟器、船舶操纵模拟器或实习船进行演示和练习。IMO 示范课程1.08里涵盖了雷达航行——管理级。

船体下沉、横倾和纵倾引起富余水深减少时的浅水操纵 **(2 学时)**

应涵盖有关下沉作用及其可能对船舶操作的影响的原因和估计理论。应介绍富余水深减少对旋回能力和船速增减的影响。

在横倾、纵倾和大幅度水位变化及涌的动力作用造成搁浅的情况下,仍会造成一定的损失伤亡。应向学员介绍在预期存在这些动力作用的情况下需要估计静态水位,以安全通过浅水区的理论知识。

船舶间、船岸间的相互作用 **(2 学时)**

学员应能详细描述预计与他船的相互影响和限制航道或运河的底部及两侧的相互影响,包括限制航道两船相遇的相互影响。他们还应能解释这些影响的原因。

between ships in restricted channels. They should also be able to explain the causes of these effects.

Berthing and unberthing under various conditions of wind, tide and current with and without tugs **(20 hours)**

Trainees should demonstrate, with the use of models on a large table, how to berth and unberth at given port facilities, under various conditions of wind and current, detailing the helm and engine orders, anchors, mooring lines and instructions to tugs that they would use prior to undertaking practical exercises.

Instructors should also emphasize theory on the magnitude of wind and current force and how it affects the ship during berthing or unberthing. This knowledge will assist a Master, to decide whether the available tugs have to hold the ship against a crosswind or to move the ship against a crosswind. Normally tugs cannot hold a ship against a cross current, as the power, which is necessary for such an operation, is enormous. The class should be asked to evaluate and criticize the actions taken and suggest alternative methods where applicable (V5).

Ship and tug interaction **(3 hours)**

Different types of tugs and the main difference resulting from the location of tug's propulsion and towing point should be pointed out. The dangers related to ship-tug interaction and the precautions that the trainee, when acting as Master, should take is of importance.

Use of propulsion and manoeuvring systems including various types of rudder **(4 hours)**

Various types of rudder and their advantages with regard to ship handling should be pointed out to the trainees. Knowledge on the appropriate use of bow and stern thrusters is also important. Trainees should also have adequate knowledge on the use of rudder cycling and its effectiveness.

Anchoring **(6 hours)**

Exercises in anchoring are particularly suitable for practice with a training vessel where one is available. Trainees should be required to produce a plan for anchoring in a given position and then carry out the plan, acting as a bridge team. Their roles in the bridge team would be rotated in subsequent exercises. Mention should be made of the importance of checking lateral as well as fore-and-aft movement when anchoring very large ships.

Procedures for anchoring in deep water and in shallow water **(1 hour)**

Many ships reportedly have experienced large damage to ships and its ancillary equipment, as the required knowledge on anchoring ships in deep or shallow waters were found inadequate. The procedures and precautions when anchoring in these waters should be explained to the trainees.

在各种风、潮汐和海流时有拖船和无拖船情况下的靠泊与离泊 **(20 学时)**

利用大桌子上的船模,学员应在实操练习前给定码头设施,各种风、流情况,详细的舵和车钟令,锚,系船缆和将对拖船使用指令的情况下,演示如何靠泊和离泊。

教员还应强调有关风流等级以及它如何影响船舶靠离泊的理论。该知识将有助于船长决定是否必须使用现有的拖船在横风中顶推或移动船舶。拖船通常不能在横流中顶住船舶,因为这种作用需要的功率巨大。要求该课程评估和评判所采取的行动,并建议提供合适的替代方法(V5)。

船舶与拖船的相互作用 **(3 学时)**

应该指出,不同类型的拖船和由于拖船推进和拖带点位置产生的主要差别。有关船舶—拖船相互作用的危险和学员作为船长所采取的预防措施是重要的。

推进系统和包括各种类型舵的操纵系统的使用 **(4 学时)**

应对学员指出各种舵及其与船舶操纵有关的优点。关于适当使用首尾侧推器的知识也很重要。学员还应具有有关舵的回转使用及其效果的知识。

锚泊 **(6 学时)**

锚泊练习特别适合于有实习船可供使用的练习。应要求学员制订一份在指定位置锚泊的计划,并以驾驶台团队的形式执行该计划。驾驶台团队中的角色应在随后的练习中轮流担任。当锚泊超大型船舶时,应提到检查横向和前后移动的重要性。

深水区锚泊和浅水区锚泊程序 **(1学时)**

据许多船舶报告,因发现在深水或浅水锚泊所需要知识不足,其船舶和附属设备都遭受了巨大的损坏。应向学员解释这些水域中锚泊的程序和预防措施。

Procedures for dry-docking **(4 hours)**

Managing the stability implications during dry-docking and the practical aspects of both preparing a ship for dry-docking and managing the vessel throughout the dry-dock should be pointed out to trainees.

Management and handling the ship in heavy weather **(6 hours)**

Full use should be made of trainees' personal experiences when covering this section. When dealing with methods of keeping a disabled vessel out of a sea trough and lessening lee drift, trainees should be restricted to using materials which are available aboard their ships. The importance of understanding the enormous stresses encountered by the ship in heavy weather conditions is vital. Dangers and precautions to be exercised when the ships experience synchronous rolling/pitching, parametric rolling to be pointed out to the trainees (V5, V8, V9).

Ability to determine the manoeuvring and propulsion characteristics of common types of ships, with special reference to stopping distances and turning circles at various draughts and speeds **(3 hours)**

Draw attention to the warning in the manoeuvring booklet and the wheelhouse poster that the performance of the ship may differ from that shown, due to environmental, hull and loading conditions. Also point out that much of the information is estimated; for example, the manoeuvring characteristics in wind. Records of actual behaviour, together with the conditions in which they were observed, form a valuable addition to the manoeuvring booklet. IMO's recommendation, with respect to the turning ability of the ship, that the advance should not exceed 4.5 ship lengths and the tactical diameter should not exceed 5 ship lengths in the turning circle manoeuvre should be pointed out to the trainees. Opportunities for determining characteristics arise, for example, when approaching pilot stations or anchoring to await a tide or berth (R17).

Practical measures to be taken when navigating in or near ice, or in conditions of ice accumulation on board **(4 hours)**

The Mariner's Handbook (T30) contains a full treatment of ice conditions, well illustrated with photographs.

1.11 OPERATE REMOTE CONTROLS OF PROPULSION PLANT AND ENGINEERING SYSTEMS AND SERVICES

1.11.1 OPERATING PRINCIPLES OF MARINE POWER PLANTS (25 hours)

Marine power plants

Diesel engines

The principles of the working of 2-stroke and 4-stroke diesels should be covered, together with their essential services such as fuel, lubricating and cooling systems. Details of particular makes of engines are not required. Trainees should be aware of the procedures for

入干船坞程序 **(4学时)**

应向学员指出进坞期间管理稳性的含义、船舶进坞准备和在坞中管理船舶两方面。

在恶劣天气下管理和操纵船舶 **(6 学时)**

当在讲授本节时,应完全利用学员的个人经验。当运用使失控船驶离波谷并减少向下风漂移的方法时,学员应局限于使用他们船上可供使用的材料。理解恶劣天气条件下船舶遭遇的巨大压力至关重要。应向学员指出当船舶经历横向谐摇/纵向谐摇、参数横摇的危险和采取的预防措施(V5, V8, V9)。

特别注意各种吃水和速度时停车距离和旋回圈情况下,确定普通船舶操纵和推进性能的能力 **(3 学时)**

应注意《操纵手册》和驾驶台张贴的公告里列出的由于环境、船体及载重情况不同船舶的性能可能不同的警告,也应指出许多信息是估计的;例如,风中的操纵特性。实际行为的记录,应结合他们所遵守的条件形成一份有价值的《操纵手册》的补充。应向学员指出,IMO关于旋回能力的建议,在旋回操纵中,进距不超过4.5倍船长,旋回初径不超过5倍船长。例如,当接近引航站或抛锚等待潮汐或泊位时,是确定特性的机会(R17)。

在冰区内或其附近航行,或船上积冰情况下采取的实用措施 **(4 学时)**

航海者手册 (T30) 包含了全部冰况处理措施,配照片加以清楚说明。

1.11 推进装置和轮机系统的遥控操作与维护

1.11.1 船舶动力装置的操作原理 (25 学时)

船舶动力装置

柴油机

应讲授两冲程和四冲程柴油机的工作原理,并结合它们必要的辅助系统,如燃油、润滑油及冷却系统,主机特别构造的细节不做要求。学员应意识到准备使用主机以及从海上全速到操纵速

preparing the engine for use and the change-over from full sea speed to manoeuvring, with the likely times involved. They should also know what is involved in starting and controlling the engine.

The rules regarding the capacity of the starting air reservoir are laid down by the classification societies.

Steam turbine systems

The boiler, feed system and turbine should be treated as a single main propulsion system. Trainees should be able to produce schematic drawings of the complete system and explain the purpose of the various parts. Details of particular makes of equipment are not required. Trainees should be aware of those faults which lead to automatic shut-down. The procedures and time taken to raise steam and prepare the engine for manoeuvring and the procedures for controlling a steam turbine engine should be known.

Propeller and propeller shaft

The bridge control for controllable-pitch propellers is usually arranged to give about 60 to 70 per cent of engine full speed when set for zero pitch. Movement of the lever forward or aft initially affects the pitch only. Full pitch is usually reached by moving the control lever through half of its travel, further movement increasing the engine revolutions. There may also be a means of adjusting the maximum pitch available. The engine and CPP can be controlled from the machinery control room and facilities may be provided for overriding all remote controls. Standing orders should lay down the procedure for informing the bridge if this has to be done.

Before starting the main engine, the propeller pumps should be running and a check made that control is possible from all control positions. During starting, control will be from the machinery control room. The propeller should be set for zero thrust and a check made that it is all clear to start the propeller turning. After starting, control is transferred to the bridge.

Before letting go or weighing anchor, the officer of the watch should check which position has control, and that it is effective, by making a small movement of the pitch control and observing the result. Before entering harbour or restricted waters, a check should be made on the control of engine speed and propeller pitch while sea room is still available.

Throughout this section instructors should keep in mind that officers should be able to explain the principles of operating and maintaining marine power plants. Officers should be familiar with the correct and commonly used engineering terminology in this context. The officer must have sufficient knowledge to be able to understand and manage the issues – he therefore does not need to have a detailed engineering knowledge. It is important that he understands the consequences of any malfunctioning and the actions to be taken to restore proper operations, or avoid problems if the machinery cannot be restored.

Bridge control

Technical details are not required. Trainees should be able to draw block diagrams of the systems, showing the information paths between the various components. The requirements for bridge indicators and alarms and the emergency stop are set out in SOLAS Regulations.

度的转换可能花费的时间,他们也应知道启动和控制主机所涉及的内容。

关于启动空气瓶的容量的规则由船级社制定。

蒸汽涡轮机系统

锅炉、燃料供油系统和涡轮机应被看成一个单一的主推进系统。学员应能画出整个系统的示意图并能解释各个部分的作用,设备特别构造的细节不做要求。学员应意识到导致停车的那些故障。应知道获得蒸汽和准备操纵主机所需的程序和时间以及控制蒸汽涡轮机的程序。

螺旋桨和螺旋桨轴

为了给出60%~70%的主机全速,驾驶台通常控制可变螺距螺旋桨的螺距为零。操纵杆最初的向前或向后的移动仅影响螺距。移动操纵杆至中间位置,通常可获得全部的螺距,进一步移动操纵杆可增加主机转速。也有可以调节最大可用螺距的方法,主机和可变螺距螺旋桨可以通过机舱集控室加以控制并可提供压制所有遥控设备的设施。如果不得不通知驾驶台,常规命令应制定通知驾驶台的程序。

在启动主机前,应运行螺旋桨的泵,并应进行所有控制位置的控制检查。启动期间,应从集控室控制。螺旋桨应设置成零推力并且应进行检查,待一切就绪开始运行螺旋桨。启动后,控制转移给驾驶台。

在开始抛锚或起锚前,值班驾驶员应通过小范围地移动螺距控制杆并观察其结果来检测控制杆在哪个位置是有效的。在进港或进入受限水域之前,在海上水域仍可用的情况下,应进行主机速度和螺旋桨螺距的检查。

贯穿本节的整个过程,教员应实记驾驶员应能够解释操作和维护航海动力装置的原理。在本课程内容中,驾驶员应熟悉正确以及通常使用的轮机术语。驾驶员必须具有足够的知识以便能理解和处理这些问题——他不必具有详细的轮机工程知识。驾驶员理解任何故障的后果,以及如果机器不能恢复,为恢复正确操作所采取的行动或避免问题是重要的。

驾驶台控制

技术细节不做要求。学员应能够画出系统的方框图,标出各个部件之间的信息路径。SOLAS规则中列出了驾驶台指示器和警报器以及紧急停船的要求。

1.11.2 SHIPS' AUXILIARY MACHINERY (25 hours)

This section deals with machinery and equipment other than the main propulsion, although some of the equipment would be necessary to keep the main engine running; for example, pumps.

Trainees should be able to draw simple line drawings of boilers and heat exchangers. Today, when most ships are equipped with diesel main engines, their use is restricted to providing ship's services. In tankers, the use of steam is important for heating cargo and for the driving of cargo pumps.

Instructors should keep in mind that officers should be able to explain the principles of operating and maintaining auxiliary machinery. Officers should be familiar with the correct and commonly used engineering terminology in this context. The officer must have sufficient knowledge to be able to understand and manage the issues – he therefore does not need a detailed engineering knowledge. It is important that he understands the consequences of any malfunctioning and the actions to be taken to restore proper operations, or avoid problems if the machinery cannot be restored.

Distillation and fresh-water systems

The production of fresh water from seawater in sufficient quantities enables a ship to carry a larger deadweight of cargo and ensures a supply of water free from dissolved salts for the boiler feed. The temperature at which flash evaporators work is not high enough to sterilize water for drinking purposes. Evaporators should not be run for the production of drinking water in coastal areas because of the risk of biological contamination. In any case, water from distillers or evaporators must be treated before it is safe to drink.

As an alternative to traditional distillation methods, reverse osmosis process may be used for generating fresh water at sea and should be mentioned.

Pumps and pumping systems

Trainees should have a qualitative knowledge of the losses in a pumping system and the characteristic curve for centrifugal pumps. They should also understand net positive suction head and realize that, when it approaches zero, gassing will occur at the pump, leading to cavitation which may cause damage to the impellers of centrifugal pumps.

Steering gears

The operation of ram and rotary-vane hydraulic steering gears and how the power required is supplied by variable-delivery pumps should be known. Trainees should also be able to explain how the SOLAS requirements for auxiliary steering and emergency control of steering gear are met. They should also be aware of the requirements for testing the steering gear and having drills in the change-over to auxiliary steering gear. Records of the tests and drills should be entered in the logbook.

1.11.2　船舶辅机 (25 学时)

虽然一些设备对于保持主机运行是必需的,例如泵,但本节涉及的是除主推进设备外的机械和设备。

学员应能画出简单的锅炉和热交换器的曲线图。当今, 在大多数船舶配备柴油主机的情况下,它们的作用仅限于提供船舶辅助服务。在油船上,因加热货物以及驱动货泵而使蒸汽的使用变得重要的。

教员应记住,驾驶员应能够解释操作和维护辅机的原理。在本课程内容中,驾驶员应熟悉正确的及常用的轮机术语。驾驶员必须具有足够的知识以便能够理解和处理问题——他不必具有详细的轮机工程知识。驾驶员理解任何故障的后果,以及如果机器不能恢复,为恢复正确操作所采取的行动或避免问题是重要的。

蒸馏和淡水系统

从海水转化而来的大量淡水会使货物载重量增大,并能确保为锅炉供应不含溶解盐的水。闪发式造水机的工作温度不够高,不能为饮用水消毒。在沿岸地区,由于生物污染的危险,蒸发器不能运行以生产饮用水。在任何情况下,蒸馏器或蒸发器生产的水必须加以处理方可安全饮用。

应当提到的是,反渗透工艺取代传统的蒸馏方法,可用于在海上生产淡水。

泵和泵水系统

学员应具有泵水系统的排吸损失以及离心泵特性曲线的定性知识。他们也应理解净压头并应认识到,当净压头为零时,在泵里将产生气化,导致会对离心泵的叶片造成损坏的气穴现象。

航机

应知道液压千斤顶和转叶式液压舵机的操作以及变量泵如何供电。学员也应能解释如何符合SOLAS关于辅助舵机和应急舵机的要求。他们也应意识到测试舵机和进行辅助舵机转换的演习的要求。测试和演习记录应记入航海日志中。

Generators, alternators and electrical distribution

Trainees should have a qualitative understanding of electrical generation and distribution, including the connection between the main and emergency switchboard during normal operation. The treatment of A.C. motors is confined to the induction motor, which is the only type found aboard most ships.

The considerations in loading generators and parallel operations may be covered.

During charging, lead-acid batteries evolve hydrogen, which is easily ignited over a wide range of concentration. The electrolytes of both acid and alkaline batteries are highly corrosive to many materials and to the person. In addition, there is a risk of electric shock from large installations such as the traditional sources of electrical power.

Refrigeration, air-conditioning and ventilation

Trainees should be able to sketch a vapour-compression-cycle refrigeration system and explain what happens at the various components. The coefficient of performance is defined as the rate of heat extraction at the evaporator divided by the power used to circulate the refrigerant. It is a measure of the plant efficiency but, since its value is greater than one, the term "coefficient of performance" is used instead of "efficiency". Trainees should deal with refrigerated cargo systems. The arrangements can be considered in three parts: the central primary refrigeration plant, the brine circulating system and the air circulating system for cooling the holds.

Mechanical ventilation systems for ships' holds often incorporate remote-reading dewpoint sensors and drying units for the circulated air to maintain the dewpoint in the hold below the temperature of the cargo and of its steelwork, so as to prevent condensation damage.

Stabilizers

The quantity of water and the setting of the control valves of flume stabilizers need to be adjusted to the ship's condition of loading, which determines its natural rolling period.

Adjustment may be necessary after an alteration of course which produces a large change in wave encounter period.

Sewage treatment plants

The discharge of untreated sewage into coastal waters is prohibited by some countries and most port authorities. Ships will then either have to retain sewage aboard for subsequent discharge to shore facilities or more than 12 miles from the nearest land, or be equipped with an approved sewage plant producing an effluent which can be discharged anywhere. The latter would require a biological treatment plant. Discharges from an approved chemical treatment plant would be permitted when more than four miles from the nearest land.

Oily water separators and oil filtering equipment

The term "separator", as used in the regulations for preventing pollution by oil, means equipment which reduces the oil content below 100 ppm even if it uses filters to achieve that

发电机、交流发电机及电力分配

学员应对电力的产生和分配有定性的了解,包括在通常操作中,主配电板与应急配电板之间的连接。交流电动机的处置限于感应电动机,这是大多数船上能找到的唯一类型的电动机。

可以考虑装载发电机和并行操作。

在发电期间,铅酸蓄电池产生氢气,氢气在较大范围的浓度内容易被点燃。酸性电池和碱性电池的电解液对大多数物质和人具有高腐蚀性。此外,像传统的大型发电设备存在电击的危险。

制冷、空调及通风

学员应能绘判蒸汽—压缩—循环制冷系统草图,并解释各部分的作用。性能系数被作为用于循环制冷剂的电源分开的蒸发器热除去率加以定义。它是设备效率的衡量标准,但由于它的值比较大,因此以“效率”来代替术语“性能系数”。学员应能处理冷藏货物系统。考虑三个部分的设施:中央主制冷设备、盐水循环系统以及冷却货舱的空气循环系统。

船舶货舱机械通风系统常包含遥测露点传感器和循环空气干燥装置, 以保持货舱露点低于货舱货物和钢结构的温度,防止冷凝损坏。

减摇装置

根据船舶的装载情况,需要调节水的数量以及自由液面减摇装置控制阀的设置,这决定了船舶的自身横摇周期。

在产生大的波浪遭遇周期变化的改向之后有必要进行调节。

污水处理设备

一些国家和大多数港口当局禁止在沿岸水域排放未经处理的污水。船舶要么在船上积累污水直到排入岸上的设备,要么在离最近海岸大于12海里处排放,要么配备经批准的能产生随处都能排放的合格排放物的污水设备,后者要求一台生物处理设备。在离最近海岸大于4海里处允许排放经批准的化学处理设备处理过的排放物。

油水分离器及滤油设备

术语“分离器”,用在防止油污染规则中,指的是即使使用过滤器,能达到把油的含量减少到低于100 ppm 的设备。“滤油设备”指的是把油的含量减少15 ppm或以下的设备。

level. “Oil filtering equipment” refers to equipment which reduces the oil content to 15 ppm or less.

The approval for an oily water separator includes the pump supplying it. No other pump should be used with it. Even when used correctly, a separator may fail to reduce the oilcontent to the required limits if the oil is emulsified or the water contains a lot of particulate matter to which the oil adheres.

Incinerators

An incinerator can be used to burn residual oil and sludge collected from oil purifiers and the oily water separator. It can also be used for the disposal of sewage sludge and rubbish. Ships fitted with an incinerator may not be dependent on the availability of shore reception facilities.

Deck machinery

The requirements for windlasses vary between the classifications societies, but, basically, require that:

- the windlass brakes are able to control the running anchor and cable when letting go;
- the windlass can heave a specified weight of cable and anchor at a specified speed, typically between 4 and 6 times the weight of one anchor at a speed of between 0.12 and 0.2 m/s.

Hydraulic systems

The majority of marine hydraulic systems are medium-pressure systems and may be either open-or closed-circuit.

Accumulators damp out fluctuations in pressure which may occur in the pressure line. They may also be used to provide a small store of pressurized fluid which can be used in an emergency. One example is for the closing of watertight doors after power to the hydraulic pump has been lost.

Hydraulic systems also contain non-return valves, to prevent reverse flow, and pressure-control valves, including pressure-relief valves.

Hydraulic steering gear provides an example of a variable-stroke pump acting as controller and power supply.

Dirt or sediment in a system causes abrasion of moving parts and blockage of control valves, leading to a failure of the machinery. Filters are fitted at pump suctions and upstream of control valves. When any part of the system is disconnected for repair or replacement, it is important to cover and seal openings through which dust or water could enter. Hydraulic systems should not be opened up or reassembled when other work in the vicinity is creating dirty conditions.

认可的油水分离器应包括专用泵的辅助,其他的泵不适合与其一起使用。甚至在正确使用的情况下,如果油是乳化的或水中含有很多能吸附油的物质,分离器可能无法把油的含量减少到所要求的标准。

焚烧炉

焚烧炉用于焚烧从净油器和油水分离器处搜集来的残油和淤泥。它也能用于污水和垃圾的处理。船舶配有焚烧炉即可以不依赖岸上备用设备。

甲板机械

不同的船级社对锚机的要求是不同的,但基本的要求为:

- 抛锚时,锚机刹车时能控制下降的锚和锚链;
- 锚机能以一定的速度拉起一定重量的锚链和锚,有代表性的是以0.12~0.2米/秒的速度拉起一个锚重量的4~6倍的重量。

液压系统

大多数航海液压系统是中压系统,并且可以是开环或是闭环的。

蓄能器抑制压力管路中可能会产生的压力波动。它们也可被用于在紧急的时候提供小型的加压液体的存储。一个例子是水压泵失电后水密门的关闭。

液压系统也包括阻止倒转水流的止回阀,以及压力控制阀,包括压力释放阀。

液压操舵装置就是一个可变冲程泵作为控制器和电源的例子。

系统里的灰尘或碎片磨损运动部件并阻塞控制阀,导致机械故障。在泵的吸头和控制阀的上游处配备过滤器。当系统的任何部分被拆开进行修理或更新时,盖上和密封灰尘或水能进入的开口都是重要的。液压系统不能在附近有其他产生灰尘的操作正在进行的情况下进行拆开或重装。

1.11.3 GENERAL KNOWLEDGE OF MARINE ENGINEERING SYSTEMS (8 hours)

Some of the terms listed in the syllabus may already have been covered in the teaching of Physical Science.

Marine engineering terms and fuel consumption

When using the fuel coefficient to estimate fuel requirements for a passage, it should be remembered that the value of the constant depends to some extent on the roughness of the hull.

A ship lying in water of high temperature for some time may attract considerable fouling of the hull and propeller, resulting in increased fuel consumption during the subsequent passages. Generally, performance falls off with time since the previous dry-docking. Clearly, the state of maintenance of the engine also affects fuel consumption.

When it is known that the ship cannot be berthed or is not required before a certain time at the next port, fuel may be saved by reducing speed, to arrive shortly before the required time, rather than proceeding at full speed and waiting at anchor.

Arrangements necessary for appropriate and effective engineering watches to be maintained for the purpose of safety under normal circumstances and UMS operations.

Main dangers and sources of risk in an engine room should be pointed out. The importance of and implementation of risk assessment and risk management in an engine room should be highlighted to the trainees.

1.11.3 船舶轮机系统常识 (8学时)

教学大纲里所列的一些术语可能在物理学教学中已经涉及了。

船舶轮机术语和燃油消耗

当使用燃油系数估计航次所需的燃油需求时,应记住常数值在某些程度上依赖于船体的粗糙程度。

船舶停泊在高温水里一段时间可能会引起船体和螺旋桨积累相当多的污垢,导致在随后的航次中增加燃油的消耗量。一般地,自从上一次入干船坞后,随着时间的推移,性能会有所下降。很明显,主机的保养状况将影响燃油的消耗。

当得知船舶无法靠泊或不要求在某一时间前到达下一港口, 可以通过减速来节省燃油,以便在要求的时间稍提前前到达,而不是全速航行并抛锚等候。

在正常情况下和UMS作业情况下,有必要安排适当而有效的轮机值班,以策安全。

应指出机舱的主要危险和风险源, 并应向学员强调在机舱进行风险评估和风险管理的重要性。

Master and Chief Mate

Function 2:
Cargo Handling and Stowage at the Management Level

船长和大副

功能2:
管理级货物装卸与积载

Master and Chief Mate

Function 2: Cargo Handling and Stowage at the Management Level

INDEX

Page

Part B2: **Course Outline** **252**
Timetable
Lectures
Course outline

Part C2: **Detailed Teaching Syllabus** **260**
Introduction
Explanation of information contained in the syllabus tables
2.1 Plan and ensure safe loading, stowage, securing, care during the voyage and unloading of cargoes
2.2 Assess reported defects and damage to cargo spaces, hatch covers and ballast tanks and take appropriate action
2.3 Carriage of dangerous goods

Part D2: **Instructor Manual** **360**

船长和大副

功能2:管理级货物装卸与积载

索引

页码

B2部分: **课程概要** 253
时间表
教学
课程概要

C2部分: **教学大纲细则** 261
介绍
教学大纲细则里的信息说明
2.1 计划并确保在航行期间货物的安全装载、积载、系固、照管以及货物的卸载
2.2 评估报告中的货舱、舱盖和压载舱的缺陷和损坏以及采取适当的行动
2.3 危险货物运输

D2部分: **教员手册** 361

Part B2: Course Outline

Cargo Handling and Stowage at the Management Level

■ Timetable

No formal example of a timetable is included in this model course.

Development of a detailed timetable depends on the level of skills of the officers entering the course and the amount of revision work of basic principles that may be required.

Lecturers must develop their own timetable depending on:

- the level of skills of trainees
- the numbers to be trained
- the number of instructors

and normal practices at the training establishment.

Preparation and planning constitute an important factor which makes a major contribution to the effective presentation of any course of instruction.

■ Lectures

As far as possible, lectures should be presented within a familiar context and should make use of practical examples. They should be well illustrated with diagrams, photographs and charts where appropriate, and be related to matter learned during seagoing time.

An effective manner of presentation is to develop a technique of giving information and then reinforcing it. For example, first tell the trainees briefly what you are going to present to them; then cover the topic in detail; and, finally, summarize what you have told them. The use of an overhead projector and the distribution of copies of the transparencies as trainees handouts contribute to the learning process.

■ Course outline

The tables that follow list the competencies and areas of knowledge, understanding and proficiency, together with the estimated total hours required for lectures and practical exercises. Teaching staff should note that timings are suggestions only and should be adapted to suit individual groups of trainees depending on their experience, ability, equipment and staff available for training.

B2部分:课程概要

管理级货物装卸与积载

■ 时间表

本示范课程中没有包含正式的示例课时表。

详细的时间表要根据学员技术等级和对基本原理的复习量来制定。

教员必须根据下面情况制定自己的课程表:

- 学员的技术水平
- 需培训的项目
- 教员数量

以及在培训地的常规实践操作。

教学前的准备及计划是任何课程教学中取得良好教学效果的重要因素。

■ 教学

教员应尽可能在熟悉的背景范围内讲解并结合实际例子。讲课中也应在适当的时候运用示意图、照片、图表等进行图示说明,并联系航海实践中遇到的一些实际问题进行讲解。

一个有效实施方式就是先进行授课,再加强提高。例如:先向学员概述授课内容;然后进行详解;最后进行总结。利用投影仪及向学员分发教学资料幻灯片拷贝等方式有助于其学习进程。

■ 课程概要

以下课程表中列出了对知识、理解与熟练程度及对适任能力的要求,列出了授课、实习的总时数。教员须注意此处的总时数为建议性的,要根据学员的经验、能力、设备及师资力量等不同情况进行调整。

Course outline

Knowledge, understanding and proficiency	Total hours for each topic	Total hours for each subject area of required performance
Competence:		
2.1 PLAN AND ENSURE SAFE LOADING, STOWAGE, SECURING, CARE DURING VOYAGE AND UNLOADING OF CARGOES		
2.1.1 APPLICATION OF INTERNATIONAL REGULATIONS, CODES AND STANDARDS CONCERNING THE SAFE HANDLING, STOWAGE, SECURING AND TRANSPORT OF CARGOES		
.1 Plans and actions conform with international regulations	6	6
2.1.2 EFFECT ON TRIM AND STABILITY OF CARGOES AND CARGO OPERATIONS		
.1 Draft, trim and stability	20	20
2.1.3 STABILITY AND TRIM DIAGRAMS AND STRESS-CALCULATING EQUIPMENT		
.1 Shear forces, bending moments and torsional moments	8	
.2 Compliance with minimum freeboard requirements of the load line regulations	6	
.3 Use of automatic data-based (ADB) equipment	2	
.4 Knowledge of loading cargoes and ballasting in order to keep hull stress within acceptable limits	6	22
2.1.4 STOWAGE AND SECURING OF CARGOES ON-BOARD SHIP, CARGO HANDLING GEAR AND SECURING AND LASHING EQUIPMENT		
.1 Timber deck cargoes	3	
.2 Procedures for receiving and delivering cargo	3	
.3 Care of cargo during carriage	4	
.4 Requirements applicable to cargo handling gear	4	
.5 Maintenance of cargo gear	3	
.6 Maintenance of hatch covers	2	19
2.1.5 LOADING AND UNLOADING OPERATIONS, WITH SPECIAL REGARD TO THE TRANSPORT OF CARGOES IDENTIFIED IN THE CODE OF SAFE PRACTICE FOR CARGO STOWAGE AND SECURING		
.1 Loading, stowage and discharge of heavy weights	3	
.2 Care of cargo during carriage	1	
.3 Methods and safeguards when fumigating holds	2	6

课程概要

知识、理解和熟练		每一标题的总学时	技能要求中每一科目的总学时
适任:			
2.1	**计划并确保在航行期间货物的安全装载、积载、系固、照管以及货物的卸载**		
2.1.1	有关货物安全装卸、积载、系固和运输的国际规则、公约和标准的应用		
	.1 符合国际规则的计划和措施	6	6
2.1.2	货物和货物操作对吃水差和稳性的影响		
	.1 吃水、吃水差和稳性	20	20
2.1.3	稳性和吃水差曲线图以及应力计算设备		
	.1 剪力、弯矩和扭矩	8	
	.2 遵循载重线规则中最小干舷的要求	6	
	.3 自动数据(ADB)设备的使用	2	
	.4 为保持船体应力在可接受极限内的装载和压载知识	6	22
2.1.4	船上货物积载与系固、货物装卸设备及系固和绑扎设备		
	.1 木材甲板货	3	
	.2 接货和交货程序	3	
	.3 运载期间货物的照管	4	
	.4 货物装卸设备的要求	4	
	.5 货物设备的维护	3	
	.6 舱盖的维护	2	19
2.1.5	装卸作业,特别注意货物积载与系固安全操作公约中确认的货物运输内容		
	.1 重型货物的装载、积载和卸载	3	
	.2 运载期间货物的照管	1	
	.3 熏舱的方法和防护措施	2	6

Knowledge, understanding and proficiency	Total hours for each topic	Total hours for each subject area of required performance
2.1.6 GENERAL KNOWLEDGE OF TANKERS AND TANKER OPERATIONS		
.1 Terms and definitions	1	
.2 Contents and application of ISGOTT	2	
.3 Oil tanker operations and related pollution prevention regulations	3	
.4 Chemical tankers	3	
.5 Tank cleaning and control of pollution in chemical tankers	2	
.6 Gas tankers	3	
.7 Cargo operations in gas tankers	2	16
2.1.7 KNOWLEDGE OF THE OPERATIONAL AND DESIGN LIMITATIONS OF BULK CARRIERS		
.1 Operational and design limitations of bulk carriers	3	
.2 SOLAS chapter XII Additional safety measures for bulk carriers	1	
.3 CSR Bulk	1	5
2.1.8 LOADING, CARE AND UNLOADING OF BULK CARGOES		
.1 Application of all available shipboard data related to loading, care and unloading of bulk cargoes	5	
.2 Code of practice for the safe loading and unloading of bulk carriers (BLU Code)	1	6
2.1.9 SAFE CARGO HANDLING IN ACCORDANCE WITH THE PROVISIONS OF THE RELEVANT INSTRUMENTS		
.1 Establish procedures for safe cargo handling in accordance with the provisions of the relevant instruments such as: – IMDG Code – IMSBC Code – MARPOL 73/78, Annexes III and V	3	3
2.1.10 EFFECTIVE COMMUNICATIONS AND IMPROVING WORKING RELATIONSHIPS		
.1 Basic principles for establishing effective communications and improving working relationships between ship and terminal personnel	1	1
2.2 ASSESS REPORTED DEFECTS AND DAMAGE TO CARGO SPACES, HATCH COVERS AND BALLAST TANKS AND TAKE APPROPRIATE ACTION		
2.2.1 LIMITATIONS ON STRENGTH OF THE VITAL CONSTRUCTIONAL PARTS OF A STANDARD BULK CARRIER AND INTERPRET GIVEN FIGURES FOR BENDING MOMENTS AND SHEAR FORCES	3	3
2.2.2 METHODS TO AVOID THE DETRIMENTAL EFFECTS ON BULK CARRIERS OF CORROSION, FATIGUE AND INADEQUATE CARGO HANDLING	3	3

知识、理解和熟练	**每一标题的总学时**	**技能要求中每一科目的总学时**
2.1.6 油船和油船作业的常识		
.1 术语和定义	1	
.2 ISGOTT 的内容和应用	2	
.3 油船操作和有关的防污染规则	3	
.4 化学品船	3	
.5 化学品船的洗舱和污染控制	2	
.6 液化气船	3	
.7 液化气船的货物操作	2	16
2.1.7 散货船作业与设计限制的知识		
.1 散货船作业与设计限制	3	
.2 SOLAS 公约第 12 章有关散货船的附加安全措施	1	
.3 CSR 散货船	1	5
2.1.8 散货的装载、照管与卸载		
.1 与散货的装载、照管和卸载有关的所有船舶数据的运用	5	
.2 散货船安全装卸操作规则(BLU 规则)	1	6
2.1.9 按照相关文件规定安全装卸货物		
.1 按照下列文件规定建立安全装卸货物程序: – IMDG 规则 – IMSBC 规则 – MARPOL 73/78,附件Ⅲ、附件Ⅴ	3	3
2.1.10 有效的沟通与改善工作关系		
.1 船舶和码头人员间建立有效沟通和改善工作关系的基本原则	1	1
2.2 评估报告中的货舱、舱盖和压载舱的缺陷和损坏以及采取适当的行动		
2.2.1 对标准散货船重要结构的强度限制和解释给出的弯矩与剪力数据	3	3
2.2.2 避免腐蚀、疲劳和不当装卸对散货船造成不利影响的方法	3	3

Knowledge, understanding and proficiency	Total hours for each topic	Total hours for each subject area of required performance
2.3 CARRIAGE OF DANGEROUS GOODS 2.3.1 INTERNATIONAL REGULATIONS, STANDARDS, CODES AND RECOMMENDATIONS ON CARRIAGE OF DANGEROUS CARGOES .1 International regulations and codes including the International Maritime Dangerous Goods (IMDG) Code and the International Maritime Solid Bulk Cargoes (IMSBC) Code	3	3
2.3.2 CARRIAGE OF DANGEROUS, HAZARDOUS AND HARMFUL CARGOES; PRECAUTIONS DURING LOADING AND UNLOADING AND CARE DURING THE VOYAGE OF DANGEROUS, HAZARDOUS AND HARMFUL CARGOES		
.1 Dangerous goods in packages	10	
.2 Solid bulk cargoes	9	
.3 International Code for the Safe Carriage of Grain in Bulk (International Grain Code)	7	26
Total for Function 2: Cargo Handling and Stowage at the Management Level		**139 hours**

Teaching staff and Administrations should note that the hours for lectures and exercises are suggestions only as regards sequence and length of time allocated to each objective. These factors may be adapted by lecturers to suit individual groups of trainees depending on their experience, ability, equipment and staff available for teaching.

知识、理解和熟练	每一标题的总学时	技能要求中每一科目的总学时
2.3 危险货物运输		
2.3.1 关于危险货物运输的国际规定、标准、规则和建议的内容		
.1 国际规定、规则包括《国际海运危险货物规则》(IMDG)和《国际海运固体散装货物规则》(IMSBC 规则)在内的国际规则和规范	3	3
2.3.2 危险货物、有毒货物和有害货物的运载；装卸期间的预防措施及危险货物、有毒货物和有害货物航行期间的照管		
.1 包装类危险货物	10	
.2 固体散货	9	
.3 《国际散装谷物安全运输规则》(国际谷物规则)	7	26
功能 2 总计学时:管理级货物装卸与积载		**139 学时**

教员和主管机关应注意到课程概要中各学习任务的先后次序和时间安排仅仅是建议，可根据各班组学员的经验、能力、设备和师资配备等实际情况进行适当的调整。

Part C2: Detailed Teaching Syllabus

<table>
<tr><th>COMPETENCE 2.1</th><th>Plan and Ensure Safe Loading, Stowage, Securing, Care During the Voyage and Unloading of Cargoes</th><th>IMO Reference</th></tr>
<tr><td colspan="2">TRAINING OUTCOMES:

Demonstrates a knowledge and understanding of:
2.1.1 APPLICATION OF INTERNATIONAL REGULATIONS, CODES AND STANDARDS CONCERNING SAFE HANDLING, STOWAGE, SECURING AND TRANSPORT OF CARGOES
2.1.2 EFFECT ON TRIM AND STABILITY OF CARGOES AND CARGO OPERATIONS
2.1.3 USE OF STABILITY AND TRIM DIAGRAMS AND STRESS-CALCULATING EQUIPMENT INCLUDING AUTOMATIC DATA-BASED EQUIPMENT AND KNOWLEDGE OF LOADING CARGOES AND BALLASTING IN ORDER TO KEEP HULL STRESS WITHIN ACCEPTABLE LIMITS
2.1.4 STOWAGE AND SECURING OF CARGOES ON BOARD SHIP, CARGO HANDLING GEAR AND SECURING AND LASHING EQUIPMENT
2.1.5 LOADING AND UNLOADING OPERATIONS, WITH SPECIAL REGARD TO THE TRANSPORT OF CARGOES IDENTIFIED IN THE CODE OF SAFE PRACTICE FOR CARGO STOWAGE AND SECURING
2.1.6 GENERAL KNOWLEDGE OF TANKERS AND TANKER OPERATIONS
2.1.7 KNOWLEDGE OF THE OPERATIONAL AND DESIGN LIMITATIONS OF BULK CARRIER
2.1.8 LOADING, CARE AND UNLOADING OF BULK CARGOES
2.1.9 SAFE CARGO HANDLING IN ACCORDANCE WITH THE PROVISIONS OF THE RELEVANT INSTRUMENTS
2.1.10 EFFECTIVE COMMUNICATIONS AND IMPROVING WORKING RELATIONSHIPS</td><td>STCW Code table A-II/2</td></tr>
</table>

C2部分:教学大纲细则

适任 2.1	**计划并确保在航行期间货物的安全装载、积载、系固、照管以及货物的卸载**	**IMO 参考书目**
培训效果: 讲授下列内容知识与理解: 2.1.1 有关货物安全装卸、积载、系固和运输的国际规则、公约和标准的应用 2.1.2 货物和货物操作对吃水差和稳性的影响 2.1.3 稳性和吃水差曲线图以及应力计算设备(包括自动数据设备)以及将船体应力保持在可接受范围的货物装载和压载的常识 2.1.4 船上货物积载与系固、货物装卸设备及系固和绑扎设备 2.1.5 装卸作业,特别注意货物积载与系固安全操作公约中确认的货物运输内容 2.1.6 油船和油船作业的常识 2.1.7 散货船作业与设计限制的知识 2.1.8 散货的装载、照管与卸载 2.1.9 按照相关文件规定安全装卸货物 2.1.10 有效的沟通与改善工作关系		STCW 公约 表 A-Ⅱ/2

COMPETENCE 2.1	Plan and Ensure Safe Loading, Stowage, Securing, Care During the Voyage and Unloading of Cargoes	IMO Reference

2.1.1 APPLICATION OF INTERNATIONAL REGULATIONS, CODES AND STANDARDS CONCERNING SAFE HANDLING, STOWAGE, SECURING AND TRANSPORT OF CARGOES — R2, R55, R56, R57, R58, R59, R60, R61, R62, R64, R66, R67, R68, R69, R82, R83

Textbooks/Bibliography: T15

Teaching aids: A1

Required performance:

1.1 Plans and actions conform with international regulations (6 hours) — R1

- plans loading to comply with the Load Line Convention in terms of:
  - freeboard
  - seasonal restrictions
  - zones
  - statical and dynamic stability requirements
  - bunker requirements, and considers
  - expected weather patterns
- plans loading to comply with the IMO Intact Stability Code
- plans cargo stowage and carriage in compliance with the Code of Safe Practice for Cargo Stowage and Securing — R2, Res. A.714(17)
- states that an approved cargo securing manual is required to be carried on board all ships except those engaged solely in the carriage of bulk cargoes
- lists the information provided in the cargo securing manual
- uses data from the cargo securing manual to plan securing a range of cargo types
- lists the certificates required for inspection by port state control officers
- plans loading and securing to comply with the Code of Practice for the Carriage of Timber Deck Cargoes

2.1.2 EFFECT ON TRIM AND STABILITY OF CARGOES AND CARGO OPERATIONS

Textbooks/Bibliography: T4, T14, T15, T21, T34, B3, B198

Teaching aids: A1

Required performance:

Note that trainees must be familiar with the content and application of the stability and trim calculations from IMO model course 7.03. This knowledge is considered so fundamental for much of the management level content within this course that there is merit in reviewing the operational level content quickly before covering the additional elements required at management level. The learning time has been reduced for many elements on the basis that trainees will be reviewing rather than learning much of this content at this level. It may be necessary for some trainees to refresh their knowledge of such techniques before undertaking this management level content

2.1 Draught, trim and stability (20 hours)

- given the draughts forward, aft and amidships, calculates the draught to use with the deadweight scale, making allowance for trim, deflection and density of the water

适任 2.1	计划并确保在航行期间货物的安全装载、积载、系固、照管以及货物的卸载	IMO 参考书目
2.1.1　有关货物安全装卸、积载、系固和运输的国际规则、公约和标准的应用 **教科书/参考文献:**T15 **教具:**A1 技能要求: **1.1　符合国际规则的计划和措施(6 学时)** – 装载计划的以下内容符合《载重线公约》: 　– 干舷 　– 季节限制 　– 载重线区 　– 静稳性和动稳性要求 　– 燃料要求和计划 　– 预期的天气模式 – 装载计划符合 IMO 完整稳性规则 – 根据《货物积载和系固安全操作规则》计划货物积载和运输 – 阐述除了专门从事散货运输的船舶外,所有船舶都要求配有经批准的货物系固手册 – 列出《货物操作手册》中提供的信息 – 使用《货物系固手册》中的数据,计划系固某一范围的货物类型 – 列出港口国监督检查官检查的证书 – 根据《甲板运输木材货物安全操作规则》计划货物积载和运输 2.1.2　货物和货物操作对吃水差和稳性的影响 **教科书/参考文献:**T4, T14, T15, T21, T34, B3, B198 **教具:**A1 技能要求: 注意:在完成这些要求的内容之前,学员必须熟悉 IMO 示范课程 7.03 中的稳性和吃水差计算内容及其适用。本课程中的知识对多数管理级内容非常重要,以至于在涉及管理级额外要求的知识点之前,在迅速复习操作级内容方面颇具价值。基于学员将复习而不是学习该级别内容,已经减少了许多知识点的学时。对某些学员而言,在学习管理级内容之前,可能有必要更新这些技能的知识 **2.1　吃水、吃水差和稳性(20 学时)** – 在已知艏吃水、艉吃水和船中吃水的情况下,考虑吃水差、修正量和水的密度,应用载重表尺计算吃水		R2, R55, R56, R57, R58, R59, R60, R61, R62, R64, R66, R67, R68, R69, R82, R83 R1 R2 Res. A.714(17)

COMPETENCE 2.1	Plan and Ensure Safe Loading, Stowage, Securing, Care During the Voyage and Unloading of Cargoes	IMO Reference

- given a ship's hydrostatic data, the weight and the intended disposition of cargo, stores, fuel and water, calculates the draughts, allowing for trim, deflection and water density
- calculates changes of draught resulting from change in distribution of masses
- calculates changes of draught resulting from change in water density
- calculates the quantity of cargo to move between given locations to produce a required trim or maximum draught
- calculates how to divide a given mass between two given locations to produce a required trim or maximum draught after loading
- calculates the locations at which to load a given mass so as to leave the after draught unchanged
- given a ship's hydrostatic data and the disposition of cargo, fuel and water, calculates the metacentric height (*GM*)
- calculates the arrival *GM* from the conditions at departure and the consumption of fuel and water
- identifies when the ship will have the worst stability conditions during the passage
- calculates the maximum weight which can be loaded at a given height above the keel to ensure a given minimum *GM*
- constructs a *GZ* curve for a given displacement and *KG* and checks that the ship meets the minimum intact stability requirements
- determines the list resulting from a change in distribution of masses
- determines the expected maximum heel during the loading or discharging of a heavy lift with the ship's gear
- calculates the increased draught resulting from the heel
- plans the loading and movement of cargo and other deadweight items to achieve specified draughts and/or stability conditions in terms of required statical and dynamic stability

2.1.3 USE OF STABILITY AND TRIM DIAGRAMS AND STRESS-CALCULATING EQUIPMENT INCLUDING AUTOMATIC DATA-BASED EQUIPMENT AND KNOWLEDGE OF LOADING CARGOES AND BALLASTING IN ORDER TO KEEP HULL STRESS WITHIN ACCEPTABLE LIMITS

Textbooks/Bibliography: T4, T14, T15, T21, T34, B3, B198

Teaching aids: A1

Required performance:

3.1 Shear forces, bending moments and torsional moments (8 hours) — R1

- states that the carriage of loading calculators in large ships carrying dry or liquid cargo in bulk is a requirement of the classification societies
- states that the maximum permissible values of shear force and bending moment in harbour and at sea are laid down by the classification societies
- states that maximum torsional moments are also laid down for some container ships

适任 2.1	计划并确保在航行期间货物的安全装载、积载、系固、照管以及货物的卸载	IMO 参考书目
– 在已知船舶静水力参数、载重量,货物、备用品、燃油和水的预计配置情况下,考虑吃水差、修正量和水的密度,计算吃水 – 计算由于货物分布的变化而产生的吃水变化 – 计算由于水密度的变化而产生的吃水变化 – 计算为达到所要求的吃水差或最大吃水,在给定的位置之间应移动的货物数量 – 计算在装载以后为达到所要求的吃水差或最大吃水,如何在给定的位置之间分配所给定的货物 – 计算装载所给定的货物重量使艉吃水没有变化的位置 – 在已知船舶静水力参数,货物、燃油和水的配置情况下,计算稳性高度(*GM*) – 由离港和燃油与水的消耗情况,计算到达的 *GM* – 识别船舶在航行期间何时稳性最差 – 计算在给定距龙骨基线高度,为保证所要求的最小 *GM* 能装载的最大载重量 – 构建一个由所给定的排水量和 *KG* 组成的 *GZ* 曲线图,并核实船舶满足最低完整稳性的要求 – 确定由丁重量分布的改变而产生的横倾 – 确定在用船舶设备进行重件货的装卸过程中预计的最大倾斜 – 计算由于倾斜而增加的吃水 – 根据要求的静稳性和动稳性,计划货物和其他重物的装载、移动以达到特定的吃水和/或稳性状况 2.1.3 稳性和吃水差曲线图以及应力计算设备(包括自动数据设备)以及将船体应力保持在可接受范围的货物装载和压载的常识 **教科书/参考文献**:T4, T14, T15, T21, T34, B3, B198 **教具**:A1 技能要求: **3.1 剪力、弯矩和扭矩(8 学时)** – 阐述在大型运载干散货或液体散货的船舶上,配备装载计算器是船级社的要求 – 阐述船级社制定的船舶在港内和海上所允许的最大剪力值和弯矩值 – 解释集装箱船也有最大扭转力矩		R1

COMPETENCE 2.1	Plan and Ensure Safe Loading, Stowage, Securing, Care During the Voyage and Unloading of Cargoes	IMO Reference
	– describes the use of typical cargo loading instruments and lists the information obtainable from them – interprets the information regarding stress limits provided to the ship – explains that harbour stress limits should not be exceeded during loading, discharging or ballasting operations and that it is not sufficient just to finish within the limits – explains that sufficient information to arrange for the loading and ballasting of the ship in such a way as to avoid the creation of unacceptable stresses should be on board, unless the Administration considers it unnecessary for that ship – plans the loading and discharge of a ship to ensure that maximum allowable stress limits are not exceeded	
3.2	**Compliance with the minimum freeboard requirements of the Load Line Regulations (6 hours)** – uses the chart of zones and seasonal areas to determine the load lines which apply for all stages of a particular passage – plans the loading, discharge and consumption of deadweight items to determine the minimum departure freeboards and maximum quantities to load in one or more loading ports to ensure that the vessel is not overloaded at any stage of a voyage through multiple load line zones and seasonal zones	R1, R4, R5
3.3	**Use of automatic data-based (ADB) equipment (2 hours)** – provides an understanding of information obtained from ship stress indicators and loading programmes – uses stress indicators and loading programmes in planning for the safe carriage of dry and liquid cargoes – advantages and limitations of analogue and digital stability and loading programmes	

3.4	**Knowledge of loading cargoes and ballasting in order to keep hull stress within acceptable limits (6 hours)**
	– explains the importance of devising a cargo stowage plan and loading/ unloading plan
	– states that the officer in charge should always refer to the loading manual to ascertain an appropriate cargo load distribution, satisfying the imposed limits on structural loading
	– explains the stages of development of a safe cargo loading or unloading plan
	– explains that in any event if the cargo needs to be distributed differently from that described in the loading manual, calculations must always be made to determine, for any part of the voyage, that still water shear force (SWSF), still water bending moments (SWBM) and local loading limits are not exceeded
	– explains the reason to keep the hull stress levels below the permissible limits by the greatest possible margin
	– explains that when making a plan for cargo operations, the officer in charge must consider the ballasting operation, to ensure:
	  – correct synchronization is maintained with the cargo operations
	  – that the de-ballasting/ballasting rate is specially considered against the loading rate and the imposed structural and operational limits
	  – that ballasting and de-ballasting of each pair of symmetrical port and starboard tanks is carried out simultaneously
		R64, R65

适任 2.1	计划并确保在航行期间货物的安全装载、积载、系固、照管以及货物的卸载	IMO 参考书目
	– 描述典型装载仪器的使用并列出可从装载仪器获得的信息 – 说明有关提供给船舶的极限应力信息 – 解释在装载、卸载或压载作业期间不能超过港内应力极限,且仅在极限内完成是不够的 – 解释船上应具有使船舶在进行装载和压载时能避免产生不可接受应力的足够信息,除非主管当局认为该船没必要如此 – 计划船舶装卸以确保不超过最大许可应力极限	
3.2	**遵循载重线规则中最小干舷的要求(6 学时)** – 应用区带和季节区域图以确定适合某一航次各阶段的载重线 – 计划装卸和载重量的消耗，决定在一个或多个装载港口的最小干舷和最大装载量,以确保船舶在穿过多个载重线区带和季节区的各个阶段不超载	R1, R4, R5
3.3	**自动数据(ADB)设备的使用(2 学时)** – 给出从船舶应力指示器和装载程序中获得的信息的理解 – 在计划干散货和液体货物的安全运输中应力指示器和装载程序的使用 – 模拟稳性与装载程序和数字稳性与装载程序的优点和局限性	

3.4	**为保持船体应力在可接受极限内的装载和压载知识(6 学时)**
	– 解释制订货物积载计划和装 / 卸计划的重要性
	– 阐述负责的驾驶员应参考装载手册来确定合适的货物分配,满足规定的结构负荷限制
	– 解释制订一个安全的装卸计划的各个阶段
	– 解释在任何情况下,如果需要不按照装载手册中的规定分配货物,则在该航次的各个阶段都必须计算确定静水剪力(SWSF)、静水弯矩(SWBN)和局部载荷极限未超标
	– 解释尽最大可能保持船体应力水平低于许可极限的原因
	– 解释当制订货物作业计划时,负责的驾驶员必须考虑压载作业,以确保：
	  – 保持与货物作业的适当同步
	  – 尤其要考虑排压载水 / 打入压载水的速度与装载速度、规定的结构和操作限制相对应
	  – 每一对左右舷舱同时打入压载水和排压载水
		R64, R65

COMPETENCE 2.1	Plan and Ensure Safe Loading, Stowage, Securing, Care During the Voyage and Unloading of Cargoes	IMO Reference

- explains the importance to know the exact pumping rates achieved on board their ship to ascertain and ensure the plans are devised and modified accordingly
- plans loading/de-ballasting operations within acceptable stress parameters
- plans discharging/ballasting operations within acceptable stress parameters

2.1.4 STOWAGE AND SECURING OF CARGOES ON BOARD SHIP, CARGO HANDLING GEAR AND SECURING AND LASHING EQUIPMENT

Textbooks/Bibliography: T36, B21, B71, B72, B73, B74, B75, B76, B77, B78, B80, B81, B82, B83, B88, B89, B90, B91, B92, B93, B94, B95, B97, B98, B101, B102, B104, B106, B109, B110, B113, B117, B128, B129, B130, B146, B152, B153, B156, B158, B159, B161, B162, B167, B182, B189, B190, B191, B192, B193, B196, B197, B198, B215, B216, B217

Teaching aids: A1, V60, V86, V170, V172, V173, V174, V175

Required performances:

4.1 Timber deck cargoes (3 hours) — R57

- outlines the contents of the Code of Safe Practice for Ships Carrying Timber Deck Cargoes with respect to:
  - stowage of sawn timber, logs, cants and wood pulp
  - fitting of uprights
  - lashings and the arrangements for tightening them, including the use of a wiggle wire
- states that vibration and movement of the ship in a seaway compacts the stow and slackens the lashings
- states that lashings should be inspected regularly and tightened as necessary
- states that inspections of lashings should be entered in the log book
- explains the dangers of heavy seas breaking aboard and how to minimize that risk
- states the action to take if cargo is lost overboard or jettisoned
- states the maximum height of cargo permitted on deck in a seasonal winter zone in winter
- describes the controlling factors for height of cargo at other times
- describes the requirements for fencing, for provision of walk-ways and for access to the top of the cargo
- describes the requirements when loading to timber load lines
- lists the stability information that should be available to the Master
- explains when the worst stability conditions during a voyage are likely to occur
- describes the rolling period test for the approximate determination of a ship's stability and the limitations of the method
- explains the actions to take in the event of the ship developing an angle of loll
- plans the loading and securing of a timber deck cargo

4.2 Procedures for receiving, and delivering cargo (3 hours) — R1

- states the period for which the ship is deemed responsible for the cargo under conventions for the carriage of goods and under typical carriage contracts evidenced by bills of lading or charter parties

适任 2.1	计划并确保在航行期间货物的安全装载、积载、系固、照管以及货物的卸载	IMO 参考书目
– 解释获知本船泵水速率以弄清和确认安排已适当设计和修正 – 在可接受的应力范围内安排装载/排出压载水的操作 – 在可接受的应力范围内安排卸货/打入压载水的操作 2.1.4 船上货物积载与系固、货物装卸设备及系固和绑扎设备 **教科书/参考文献**:T36, B21,B71, B72, B73, B74, B75, B76, B77, B78, B80, B81, B82, B83, B88, B89, B90, B91, B92, B93, B94, B95, B97, B98, B101, B102, B104, B106, B109, B110, B113, B117, B128, B129, B130, B146, B152, B153, B156, B158, B159, B161, B162, B167, B182, B189, B190, B191, B192, B193, B196, B197, B198, B215, B216, B217 **教具**:A1, V60, V86, V170, V172, V173, V174, V175 技能要求:		
4.1 木材甲板货(3 学时) – 概括《运载木材甲板货船舶安全操作规则》有关方面内容: – 锯材、原木、木方和木纸浆的积载 – 扶正设备 – 绑扎绳索及其拧紧设施,包括扭转钢丝的使用 – 阐述船舶在海上的振动和运动使积载变紧凑、绑扎变松弛 – 阐述应定时地检查绑扎,如有必要应拉紧 – 阐述绑扎的检查应记入航海日志 – 解释大浪打在船上的危险以及如何最大限度地减少危险 – 阐述货物落水或抛弃货物后的行动 – 阐述在冬季里冬季区带所允许的甲板货的最大高度 – 描述在其他季节货物高度的控制因素 – 描述对围栏、过道和货物顶层通道的要求 – 描述装载到木材载重线的要求 – 列出应为船长所用的稳性信息 – 解释在航行期间何时可能会发生稳性最差的情况 – 描述用横摇周期试验近似确定船舶稳性及该方法的局限性 – 解释船舶产生静止角时应采取的措施 – 计划木材甲板货的装载和系固		R57
4.2 接货和交货程序(3 学时) – 阐述按照货物运输公约和由提单证明的典型运输合同或租约,认为船方应负责货物的时间期限		R1

COMPETENCE 2.1	Plan and Ensure Safe Loading, Stowage, Securing, Care During the Voyage and Unloading of Cargoes	IMO Reference

- states that damaged cargo should be rejected or steps taken to ensure that the damage is recorded and endorsed where appropriate on the bill of lading
- explains that bills of lading may sometimes still be drawn up from mate's receipts and the importance of endorsing mate's receipts for the condition of goods and packages
- describes the endorsement of mate's receipts and/or bills of lading for goods in dispute
- describes the endorsement of mate's receipts and/or bills of lading for cargoes where the weight and quality are not known to the ship
- explains the actions to take when a clean mate's receipt or bill of lading is demanded for cargo which is not in apparent good condition
- explains why letters of indemnity offered in return for clean bills of lading should be refused
- describes the documentation which should accompany dangerous goods and is required before loading
- states that containers should have their seals and locks in place when loaded
- states that, if damage to cargo is suspected, protest should be noted before commencing discharging
- explains the procedure for noting protest and extending protest
- states that an independent cargo survey should be arranged when cargo damage is suspected or found on opening hatches
- states that broken or broached packages should be placed in a locker until the contents can be checked and agreed with a representative of the receiver and a receipt obtained for them
- explains how to deal with empty bags or packages, sweepings and other loose goods
- states that cargo spaces should be searched at the completion of discharging to prevent the over carriage of cargo
- describes the procedure for claiming for damage done to the ship during loading or discharging
- explains to whom cargo should be delivered
- explains the potential consequences of delivering cargo to the incorrect party or under a letter of indemnity
- explains the procedure that should be adopted when requested to deliver cargo against a letter of indemnity

4.3 Care of cargo during carriage (4 hours) R1

- plans the loading and stowage of a hold or holds using a cargo list and reference books to take into account the carriage requirements of the various cargoes
- describes the precautions to avoid crushing and chafing damage and states which cargoes are most liable to be affected
- explains how cargo may be damaged by residues of previous cargo, dirty dunnage or leaking fuel oil tanks
- describes how cargo can be damaged by dust and the precautions to take when carrying commodities giving rise to dust

适任 2.1	计划并确保在航行期间货物的安全装载、积载、系固、照管以及货物的卸载	IMO 参考书目
– 描述应拒收损坏的货物或采取措施确保记录货损情况或在相关提单上背书 – 解释有时从大副收据中起草提单以及对货物和包装状况进行背书大副收据的重要性 – 描述有争议货物的大副收据和/或提单的背书 – 描述船舶不清楚重量和质量的货物的大副收据和/或提单的背书 – 解释对货物表面状况不良的货物要求出具清洁大副收据或提单时应采取的行动 – 解释为何应拒绝为换取清洁提单而提供的保函 – 描述在装载危险货物之前应出具相关的材料 – 阐述在装载完毕时集装箱的铅封和锁应是完好的 – 阐述如果怀疑货物受损,开始卸载前应发表声明 – 解释发表声明和延伸声明的程序 – 阐述当怀疑货物受损或开舱时发现受损,应安排单独的货物检验 – 阐述破损或破孔的包装袋应置于小舱室中,直到货物内容能被检测,且与收货方代表达成一致以及从他们那里获得一份收据 – 解释如何处理空袋或包装袋、地脚货以及其他零散的货物 – 阐述在卸完货后应搜查货舱以防额外运载货物 – 描述在装卸期间对船舶受损提出索赔声明的程序 – 解释货物应交给谁 – 解释货物交付错误或接受保函的情况下交付货物的潜在后果 – 解释当被要求接受保函货物交付应采取的程序		
4.3 运载期间货物的照管(4 学时) – 使用货物清单和参考书来计划货舱的装载和积载以考虑各种货物的运载要求 – 描述防止货物压碎和磨损的预防措施并阐述哪种货物最容易受此影响 – 解释货物如何由于先前货物的残渣、不洁衬垫或渗漏的燃油而造成损坏 – 描述货物如何由于灰尘受损,以及装运扬尘货时应采取的预防措施		R1

COMPETENCE 2.1	Plan and Ensure Safe Loading, Stowage, Securing, Care During the Voyage and Unloading of Cargoes	IMO Reference

- states which cargoes are particularly liable to damage by ship or cargo sweat and explains how to minimize the risk of sweat damage
- explains that any goods containing liquids are liable to leak and describes the stowage required to prevent any leakage damaging other goods
- states that many goods can be spoiled by extremes of temperature
- explains that overheating may occur in cargo stowed against engine-room bulkheads, heated double-bottom tanks and deep tanks carrying heated cargoes
- states that high temperatures also occur on the underside of steel decks exposed to tropical sunshine
- describes how to protect cargoes which must be kept from freezing
- describes the measures to take to prevent pilferage of cargo during loading, discharging and carriage
- describes the damage to cargo which can result from the use of fork-lift trucks and similar machinery in cargo spaces and methods of preventing it

4.4 Requirements applicable to cargo handling gear (4 hours)

- outlines the requirements of ILO Convention 152, the Occupational Safety and Health (Dock Work) Convention, 1979, which apply to ships
- defines the terms:
  - competent person
  - responsible person
  - authorized person
  - lifting appliance loose gear
- states that national laws or regulations should prescribe measures to cover, amongst others:
  - safe means of access to ships, holds, staging, equipment and lifting appliances
  - opening and closing of hatches, protection of hatchways and work in holds
  - construction, maintenance and use of lifting and other cargo handling appliances
  - rigging and use of ship's derricks
  - testing, examination, inspection and certification, as appropriate, of lifting appliances, of loose gear (including chains and ropes) and of slings and other lifting devices which form an integral part of the load
  - marking of cargo gear
  - handling different types of cargo
  - dangerous substances and other hazards in the working environment
- describes the requirements for guarding dangerous parts of machinery
- states that machinery includes mechanized hatch covers and lifting appliances
- states the requirements for the marking of beams and portable hatch covers
- states that only an authorized person, preferably a member of the ship's crew, should be permitted to open or close power-operated hatch covers and equipment such as doors in hull, ramps and car decks

适任 2.1	计划并确保在航行期间货物的安全装载、积载、系固、照管以及货物的卸载	IMO 参考书目

– 阐述哪种货物特别容易受船舶或货物出汗的损害,并解释如何最大限度减小货物出汗的危险
– 解释任何含有液体的货物都容易溢漏并描述所要求的防止因溢漏而损坏其他货物的积载
– 阐述许多货物会由于极端温度而受损
– 解释货物积载紧靠机舱壁、热的双层底舱和装有热货物的深舱可能会造成过热
– 阐述暴露在热带阳光下的钢质甲板下面也会产生高温
– 描述如何保护必须防冻的货物
– 描述在装卸和运载期间防止货物被盗而采取的措施
– 描述在货舱里由于使用叉车和类似的机械而可能对货物造成的损坏以及防止的方法
4.4 货物装卸设备的要求(4 学时)
– 概括适用于船舶的 1952 年 ILO 公约、1979 年职业安全和健康(码头工作)公约的要求
– 定义术语:
  – 胜任人员
  – 责任人
  – 授权人员
  – 起重设备
  – 起重设备可卸零部件
– 阐述国家法律或规则应含有以下内容的措施:
  – 进入船舶、货舱、工作平台、设备和起吊装置的安全方式
  – 货舱的打开和关闭、舱口围的保护和在货舱里作业
  – 起重机和其他货物装卸设备的结构、保养和使用
  – 船舶吊杆的索具配备和使用
  – 如果合适的话,形成载荷一部分的起吊设备、可卸零部件(包括链和绳)、网兜和其他起吊设施的测试、检查、检验和认证
  – 货物设备的标记
  – 装卸不同类型的货物
  – 工作环境中的危险物质和其他有害物质
– 描述机械中危险部件的防护要求
– 阐述包括机械舱盖和起吊设备在内的机械
– 阐述横梁标记和可移动式舱盖的要求
– 阐述只有授权人员,最好是一名船员,才允许打开或关闭电动舱盖和诸如船体上的门、活动吊门和汽车甲板之类的设施		

COMPETENCE 2.1	Plan and Ensure Safe Loading, Stowage, Securing, Care During the Voyage and Unloading of Cargoes	IMO Reference
– describes the requirements for fencing of openings – describes the requirements for the testing of lifting appliances and loose gear before they are used for the first time – describes the requirements for periodic thorough examination and inspection of lifting appliances and loose gear – explains what is meant by a thorough examination – describes the records and certificates which should be kept in respect of tests, thorough examinations and inspections of lifting appliances and loose gear – describes the marking of safe working loads required on lifting appliances and loose gear – states that every ship must have a rigging plan and relevant information necessary for the safe rigging of derricks, cranes and accessory gear **4.5 Maintenance of cargo gear (3 hours)** – prepares plans for the inspection of cargo gear – undertakes inspections of cargo gear so that any safety issues associated with machinery, structure, running and standing rigging and associated equipment is identified and addressed before use – maintains the records and plans required for the cargo gear – develops maintenance plans and procedures for the maintenance of machinery, structure, running and standing rigging and associated equipment of cargo gear, including blocks, shackles, wire and fibre ropes – provides instruction to crew and manages the maintenance of cargo gear – states the requirements for the annealing of wrought iron loose gear – describes the precautions to be taken when working aloft for the overhaul of cargo gear **4.6 Maintenance of hatch covers (2 hours)** – states that track ways should be cleaned of loose material before closing hatches – states that the tension of draw chains should be adjusted as required – states that wheels, gears, racks and pinions and other moving parts should be kept lubricated – states that side cleats and cross-joint wedge mechanisms should be kept greased – explains that hydraulic systems should be checked for leakage, especially in tween-decks where leaked fluid may damage cargo – states that drainage channels should be cleaned out and drainage holes checked on weather-deck hatches – describes how to check that compression bars are making complete contact with sealing gaskets – explains that weathertightness may be checked by hose-testing the covers before loading – prepares plans and procedures for the inspection and maintenance of hatch covers		

适任 2.1	计划并确保在航行期间货物的安全装载、积载、系固、照管以及货物的卸载	IMO 参考书目
– 描述舱口围的要求 – 描述在初次使用前,起吊设备和可卸零部件的测试要求 – 描述起吊设备和可卸零部件周期性彻底检查和检验的要求 – 解释彻底检查的意思 – 描述应保存的关于起吊设备和可卸零部件的测试、彻底检查和检验的记录和证书 – 描述起吊设备和可卸零部件上所要求的安全工作重负荷的标记 – 阐述每艘船必须有索具配备图和有关吊杆、克令吊和附属设备的安全配备索具的必要信息 **4.5 货物设备的维护(3 学时)** – 准备货物设备检验计划 – 进行货物设备检验,以便使用前发现机械、结构、吊货钢丝和固定支索以及相关设备的问题并加以解决 – 保存货物设备要求的记录和计划 – 制订机械、结构、吊货钢丝和固定支索以及包括滑车、卸扣、钢丝绳和纤维绳在内的货物相关设备的保养计划和程序 – 给船员提供指导和进行货物设备的维护 – 阐述锻钢可卸零部件的热处理要求 – 描述货物设备检修时高空作业应采取的预防措施 **4.6 舱盖的维护(2 学时)** – 阐述在关闭舱盖之前应扫去滑道里的零散物质 – 阐述应按要求调节牵引链的张力 – 阐述滑轮、齿轮、齿条和小齿轮以及其他活动部件应保持润滑 – 阐述侧夹板和侧面连接楔块机械应保持润滑 – 解释液压系统应进行测漏,特别是在二层舱,溢漏的液体可能损坏货物 – 阐述排水管道应清理干净并应检测露天甲板货舱的排水孔 – 描述如何检查压缩条与密封垫片完全接触 – 解释装载之前可用皮龙冲洗舱盖检查风雨密 – 准备舱盖检查和保养的计划和程序		R1

COMPETENCE 2.1	Plan and Ensure Safe Loading, Stowage, Securing, Care During the Voyage and Unloading of Cargoes	IMO Reference
2.1.5 LOADING AND UNLOADING OPERATIONS, WITH SPECIAL REGARD TO THE TRANSPORT OF CARGOES IDENTIFIED IN THE CODE OF SAFE PRACTICE FOR CARGO STOWAGE AND SECURING **Textbooks/Bibliography:** B21, B71, B72, B73, B74, B75, B76, B77, B78, B80, B81, B82, B83, B88, B89, B90, B91, B92, B93, B94, B95, B97, B98, B101, B102, B104, B106, B109, B110, B113, B117, B128, B129, B130, B146, B152, B153, B156, B158, B159, B161, B162, B167, B182, B189, B190, B191, B192, B193, B196, B197, B198, B215, B216, B217 **Teaching aids:** A1, V53, V57, V58, V59, V69, V70, V71, V72, V74, V75, V76 Required performances: **5.1 Loading, stowage and discharge of heavy weights (3 hours)** – explains how a load should be spread over an area of deck or tank top by the use of dunnage to avoid heavy point loading between beams and floors – states that special supports or cradles will need to be built for awkwardly shaped lifts – explains the use of shoring in a tween-deck to spread the load over a larger part of the ship's structure – states that the ship's stability should be checked to ensure that the resulting list will be acceptable – states that the weight of the lifting gear should be included in the weight of the lift, both for stability calculations and during consideration of safe working loads – explains why double-bottom tanks should be full or empty and the ship upright before starting to load or to discharge – states that additional stays may need setting up to a mast or kingpost – states that only experienced winch drivers should be allowed to handle heavy lifts – states that all movements should be controlled and steady, avoiding rapid stops and starts – describes methods of securing heavy lifts in the hold or on deck		R1
5.2 Care of cargo during carriage (1 hour) – outlines the content of the Code of Safe Practice for Cargo Stowage and Securing – describes how to stow and secure containers on deck on vessels which are not specially designed and fitted for the purpose of carrying containers – describes the stowage and securing of containers and other cargo units in ships other than cellular container ships – describes the contents of the cargo securing manual and its use – lists the elements to be considered by the Master when accepting cargo units or vehicles for shipment – states that cargo spaces should be regularly inspected to ensure that the cargo, cargo units and vehicles remain safely secured throughout the voyage – describes the stowage and securing of road vehicles on ro-ro ships		R1 R66, R69, R60, R61

适任 2.1	计划并确保在航行期间货物的安全装载、积载、系固、照管以及货物的卸载	IMO 参考书目
2.1.5 装卸作业,特别注意货物积载与系固安全操作公约中确认的货物运输内容 **教科书/参考文献**:B21, B71, B72, B73, B74, B75, B76, B77, B78, B80, B81, B82, B83, B88, B89, B90, B91, B92, B93, B94, B95, B97, B98, B101, B102, B104, B106, B109, B110, B113, B117, B128, B129, B130, B146, B152, B153, B156, B158, B159, B161, B162, B167, B182, B189, B190, B191, B192, B193, B196, B197, B198, B215, B216, B217 **教具**:A1, V53, V57, V58, V59, V69, V70, V71, V72, V74, V75, V76 技能要求: **5.1 重型货物的装载、积载和卸载(3 学时)** – 解释如何通过使用衬垫将负荷分散在一个甲板面上或舱顶上,以避免横梁和甲板之间的重点载荷 – 阐述需要为塔形起重机搭建专门的支架或支柱 – 解释为将负荷分散在较大型的船舶结构上,在二层舱里支柱的使用 – 阐述应核实船舶稳性以确保最终的横倾可以接受 – 阐述在进行稳性计算和考虑安全工作负荷时,起重装置的重量应包括在起重机的重量之内 – 解释为何在开始装、卸之前,双层底舱应注满或排空和船舶应正浮 – 阐述可能需要给大桅或将军柱增加稳索 – 阐述只有有经验的绞车操作员才允许装卸重件货 – 阐述所有运动部件必须受控且稳定,避免快速停止和启动 – 描述货舱内或甲板上系固重件货的方法 **5.2 运载期间货物的照管(1 学时)** – 概括《货物积载与系固安全操作规则》的内容 – 描述如何在不是专门设计和配备用来运载集装箱的船舶甲板上积载和系固集装箱 – 描述除了格槽式集装箱船外,船上集装箱和其他货物单元的积载和系固 – 描述《货物系固手册》的内容和应用 – 列出当船长接受运载的货物单元或车辆时应考虑的因素 – 阐述应定时检查货舱以确保整个航次期间货物、货物单元以及车辆保持安全系固 – 描述滚装船上公路车辆的积载和系固		R1 R66, R69, R60, R61

COMPETENCE 2.1	Plan and Ensure Safe Loading, Stowage, Securing, Care During the Voyage and Unloading of Cargoes	IMO Reference
	– describes recommended methods for the safe stowage and securing of: – portable tanks – portable receptacles – wheel-based (rolling) cargoes – coiled sheet steel – heavy metal products – anchor chains – metal scrap in bulk – flexible intermediate bulk containers – unit loads – summarizes the guidelines for the under-deck stowage of logs – describes actions which may be taken in heavy weather to reduce stresses on securing arrangements induced by excessive accelerations – describes actions which may be taken once cargo has shifted	
5.3	**Methods and safeguards when Fumigating Holds (2 hours)** – explains recommendations given in MSC.1/Circ.1264 – Recommendations on the Safe Use of Pesticides in Ships Applicable to the Fumigation of Cargo Holds, contained in the added supplement of the IMSBC Code – explains the reasons for the control of pests – states that the control of rodents is required by the International Health Regulations – describes the methods for the prevention of insect infestation and states the areas to which particular attention should be given – explains how contact insecticides in the form of sprays, smokes or lacquers may be used by the crew for dealing with local infestation – states that all persons not directly involved in the application should be evacuated from the areas being treated for a period not less than that recommended by the manufacturer of the pesticide – states that extensive or hazardous treatments, including fumigation and spraying near human or animal food, should only be undertaken by expert operators – states that a fumigator-in-charge should be designated by the fumigation company or appropriate authority – lists the information about the fumigation which should be supplied to the Master – states that fumigation of empty cargo spaces should always be carried out in port – states that crew should remain ashore until the ship is certified gas-free, in writing, by the fumigator-in-charge – states that a watchman should be posted to prevent unauthorized boarding and warning notices should be displayed – lists the precautions to be taken if essential crew members are permitted to return before aeration (ventilation) of the ship	R1, R56, R19

适任 2.1	计划并确保在航行期间货物的安全装载、积载、系固、照管以及货物的卸载	IMO 参考书目
– 描述以下方面所推荐的安全积载和系固的方法: – 移动式液柜 – 移动式容器 – 底座有轮(滚动)的货物 – 卷片钢 – 沉重的金属产品 – 锚链 – 散装金属片 – 可调式联运散货集装箱 – 单元载荷 – 总结甲板下原木积载指南 – 描述在恶劣天气里,为减小由过大的加速而产生在系固设备上的应力可以采取的措施 – 描述一旦货物移动可以采取的行动		
5.3 熏舱的方法和防护措施(2 学时) – 解释海安会 1264 号通函(MSC.1/Circ.1264)的建议,包含在 IMSBC 规则附录中有关适用于船舶货舱熏舱的杀虫剂的安全使用建议 – 解释控制害虫的原因 – 阐述控制啮齿动物是《国际健康规则》所要求的 – 描述预防昆虫感染的方法并阐述应特别加以注意的方面 – 解释船员如何使用喷雾、烟雾和喷漆式杀虫剂处理局部感染 – 阐述与操作无关的所有人员应撤离该区域至少一段不少于杀虫剂生产商所建议的时间 – 阐述只有专业人员才能进行大范围或危险的操作,包括在人或动物的食物附近熏舱和喷雾 – 阐述熏舱负责人员应由熏舱公司或有关主管机关指定 – 列出应提供给船长的有关熏舱的信息 – 阐述空货舱总应在港内进行熏舱 – 阐述船员应一直待在岸上直到熏舱负责人员书面签发除气证 – 阐述应安排值班人员值守以防止非授权人员上船并张贴警告通知 – 列出如果在船舶换气(通风)之前允许必要的船员回船应采取的预防措施		R1, R56, R19

COMPETENCE 2.1	Plan and Ensure Safe Loading, Stowage, Securing, Care During the Voyage and Unloading of Cargoes	IMO Reference

– states that entry to spaces under fumigation should never take place except in case of extreme urgency and lists the precautions to be taken if entry is imperative
– states that fumigation in transit should only be carried out in ships approved for such process by the flag State Administration and that the application should be with the agreement of the port State Administration
– states that fumigation in transit may be:
  – treatment continued during the voyage in a sealed space in which no aeration has taken place before sailing
  – continuation of in-port fumigation where some aeration has taken place but clearance cannot be issued because of residual gas and the cargo space has been re-sealed before sailing
– states that precautions are the same in both cases
– states that at least two members of the crew, including one officer, who have received appropriate training, should be designated as the trained representative of the Master responsible for ensuring safe conditions after the fumigator-in-charge has handed over that responsibility to the Master
– states that the trained representative should brief the crew before a fumigation
– lists the training which the designated representatives should have
– lists the items which the ship should carry
– describes the procedures for the fumigation and the handing over of responsibility from the fumigator in-charge to the Master
– describes the safety checks on gas concentration that should be made throughout the voyage and states that the readings should be entered in the logbook
– describes the procedures to follow prior to and on arrival at the discharging port
– describes the precautions to be taken during the discharge of cargo until the ship is certified free of fumigants
– describes the procedures for the carriage of fumigated freight containers, barges and transport units that are loaded after fumigation without ventilation
– states that the Master should be informed prior to loading such freight containers, barges and transport units and that they should be identified with suitable warning labels showing the identity of the fumigant and the date and time of fumigation
– describes the methods which may be used for the control of rodents
– describes the use of baits by the ship's crew and the precautions to observe
– explains that the use of pesticides is regulated by Governments, and their use may be limited by the regulations and requirements of:
  – the country where the cargo is loaded or treated
  – the country of destination
  – the country of registration of the ship
– describes the use of pesticides by the ship's crew and the precautions to observe
– describes the measures to be taken if clothing becomes contaminated		

适任 2.1	计划并确保在航行期间货物的安全装载、积载、系固、照管以及货物的卸载	IMO 参考书目

– 阐述除了非常紧急的情况,任何时候都不要进入正在熏蒸的舱室并列出如果必须进入应采取的预防措施
– 阐述只有经船旗国当局批准才能于航行途中在船上进行熏舱并且应征得港口国当局的同意
– 阐述途中熏舱可以是:
  – 在开航前没有换气的密封舱室里,航行期间继续熏舱
  – 在开航之前,发生一些换气但由于残余气体而没能签发干舱证书,且货舱进行了重新密封,是港内熏舱的继续
– 阐述两种情况的预防措施是一样的
– 阐述至少两名船员,其中一名是已接受过正式培训的高级船员,应在熏舱负责人员把责任交还船长之后,被指派作为船长的代表负责安全状况
– 阐述代表在熏舱之前应向船员通报
– 列出指定代表应具有的训练
– 列出船舶应运载的物品
– 描述熏舱程序以及熏舱负责人员向船长移交责任的程序
– 描述在整个航次期间应进行气体浓度的安全检查,阐述检查记录应记入航海日志
– 描述在到达卸货港之前和到达卸货港之后应进行的程序
– 描述在卸货期间直到船舶被颁发无熏蒸剂证书之前应采取的预防措施
– 描述船舶装载在熏蒸之后没有进行通风的货物集装箱、载货驳船和运输单元的程序
– 阐述在装载这样的货物集装箱、驳船和运输单元前,应通知船长,并且它们应使用标有熏蒸剂以及熏蒸的时间和日期的合适警告标签加以识别
– 描述可以用于控制啮齿动物的方法
– 描述船员使用诱饵以及应遵循的预防措施
– 解释杀虫剂的使用受政府的规定,并且可受以下规则和要求限制:
  – 装载或处理货物的国家
  – 目的港国家
  – 船舶登记国
– 描述船员对杀虫剂的使用以及应遵循的预防措施
– 描述如衣服被沾污应采取的措施		

COMPETENCE 2.1	Plan and Ensure Safe Loading, Stowage, Securing, Care During the Voyage and Unloading of Cargoes	IMO Reference

- states that, if contact insecticides are to be applied to grain during loading, the Master should be provided with written instructions on the type and amount of insecticide to be used and on the precautions to be taken
- states the actions to be taken in the event of exposure to insecticides resulting in illness

2.1.6 GENERAL KNOWLEDGE OF TANKERS AND TANKER OPERATIONS — R70

Note that this section is retained in this model course as it relates more to tanker operations than the safety aspects of tankers covered in STCW 2010 chapter V. This may need to be reviewed after the revision of the model courses for basic and advanced tanker operations is completed.

Textbooks/Bibliography: T14, T19, B81, B82, B83, B90, B91, B92, B93, B94, B97, B98, B100, B101, B102, B104, B106, B109, B110, B113, B117, B152, B153, B156, B157, B158, B159, B161, B162, B167, B189, B190, B191, B192, B196, B197, B198, B203, B215, B216, B217

Teaching aids: A1, V50, V51, V52, V54, V55, V56, V61, V62, V63, V64, V65, V66, V68, V73, V78, V83, V84, V129, V137, V138, V174, V175

Required performances:

Note that trainees must be familiar with the content and application of the basic knowledge of tankers and tanker operations from IMO model course 7.03. This knowledge is considered so fundamental for much of the management level content within this course that there is merit in reviewing the operational level content quickly before covering the additional elements required at management level. The learning time has been reduced for many elements on the basis that trainees will be reviewing rather than learning much of this content at this level. It may be necessary for some trainees to refresh their knowledge of such techniques before undertaking this management level content

6.1 Terms and definitions (1 hour)

- defines petroleum as crude oil and liquid hydrocarbon products derived from it
- states that petroleum gases, principally methane, are extracted from crude oils before shipment
- explains that “spiked crude” has additional petroleum gas, usually butane, dissolved in it before shipment
- states that “sour crude” contains appreciable amounts of hydrogen sulphide or organic sulphur compounds
- states that products derived from crude oil include naphtha (gasolines), kerosene, gas oil, diesel oils, lubricating oils, waxes and residual oils such as fuel oil and bitumen
- explains that vapour pressure of any liquid increases with increasing temperature
- defines Reid Vapour Pressure (RVP)
- explains why the pressure in a tank is not necessarily the same as the RVP of the oil it contains, even at the standard temperature
- states that the flashpoint of a liquid is the lowest temperature at which it gives off sufficient gas to form a flammable mixture in a flashpoint apparatus
- explains why flashpoint cannot be used as an absolute measure of safety
- states that “flammable” means “capable of being ignited and of burning”

适任 2.1	计划并确保在航行期间货物的安全装载、积载、系固、照管以及货物的卸载	IMO 参考书目
– 阐述如果在装载期间对谷物使用触杀剂,应向船长提供所使用杀虫剂的类型和数量以及应采取预防措施的书面指导 – 阐述万一暴露于致病杀虫剂中应采取的预防行动 2.1.6 油船和油船作业的常识 **教科书/参考文献**:T14, T19, B81, B82, B83, B90, B91, B92, B93, B94, B97, B98, B100, B101, B102, B104, B106, B109, B110, B113, B117, B152, B153, B156, B157, B158, B159, B161, B162, B167, B189, B190, B191, B192, B196, B197, B198, B203, B215, B216, B217 **教具**:A1, V50, V51, V52, V54, V55, V56, V61, V62, V63, V64, V65, V66, V68, V73, V78, V83, V84, V129, V137, V138, V174, V175 技能要求: 注意:在完成这些要求的内容之前,学员必须熟悉 IMO 示范课程 7.03 中的油船和油船作业内容及其适用。本课程中的知识对多数管理级内容非常重要,以至于在涉及管理级额外要求的知识点之前,在迅速复习操作级内容方面颇具价值。基于学员将复习而不是学习该级别内容,已经减少了许多知识点的学时。对某些学员而言,在学习管理级内容之前,可能有必要更新这些技能的知识 **6.1 术语和定义(1 学时)** – 定义石油为原油及其衍生的液体碳氢化合物产品 – 阐述在运载之前从原油中提炼的石油气体,主要是甲烷 – 解释“强化原油”在运载之前有伴生的溶解石油气体,主要是丁烷 – 阐述“酸性原油”含有大量的硫化氢或有机硫化合物 – 阐述原油衍生产品包括石脑油(汽油)、煤油、轻油、柴油、润滑油、石蜡以及渣油,如燃油和沥青 – 解释任何液体的蒸气压力随着温度的升高而增大 – 定义里德气压(RVP) – 解释为何油舱里的压力甚至在标准温度下,不一定等于油舱内的油的 RVP – 阐述液体的闪点是在闪点装置内液体挥发出足够气体形成可燃混合物的最低温度 – 解释为什么闪点不能作为绝对安全的措施使用 – 阐述“可燃”是指“能被点燃和燃烧”		 R70

COMPETENCE 2.1	Plan and Ensure Safe Loading, Stowage, Securing, Care During the Voyage and Unloading of Cargoes	IMO Reference
	– defines “upper flammable limit”, “lower flammable limit” and “flammable range” and states approximate values for petroleum products – defines the auto-ignition temperature as the temperature at which a flammable material will ignite without initiation by a spark or flame and will continue to burn – describes the viscosity of a fluid as a measure of its resistance to flow – states that viscosity increases as the temperature decreases – defines “pour point” as the lowest temperature at which an oil is observed to flow – appreciates that crude carriers in particular have significant residues in tanks which must be accounted for in order to calculate the cargo loaded – calculates the volume of dry residue as a uniform layer on the tank bottom – calculates the volume of liquid residues as a wedge on the tank bottom – knows the limitation of application of wedge calculation	

6.2	**Contents and application of the International Safety Guide for Oil Tankers and Terminals (ISGOTT) (2 hours)**
	– explains that ISGOTT provides operational advice to directly assist personnel involved in tanker and terminal operations, including guidance on, and examples of, certain aspects of tanker and terminal operations and how they may be managed
	– identifies the contents of ISGOTT
	– states that terminal, local or national regulations may also be applicable and should be known by those concerned
	– outlines the general precautions to be taken on tankers regarding:
	  – smoking, matches and cigarette lighters
	  – naked lights
	  – the galley
	  – electrical equipment
	  – use of tools
	  – entry to enclosed spaces and pump-rooms
	– lists the information which should be exchanged between the ship and the terminal before arrival
	– states that safety procedures are agreed between the tanker and the terminal and include:
	  – means of summoning emergency services
	  – availability and use of firefighting and other emergency equipment
	  – actions to be taken in case of fire or other emergency
	  – emergency evacuation of the berth
	– states that firefighting equipment should be ready for immediate use
	– states that main engines and other equipment essential for manoeuvring should be ready for use at short notice and the written agreement of the terminal and port authority should be obtained for any work or repairs which would immobilize the ship
	– states that detailed loading or discharging plans are agreed between the ship and the terminal
		R1, R28

适任 2.1	计划并确保在航行期间货物的安全装载、积载、系固、照管以及货物的卸载	IMO 参考书目
	– 定义“燃烧上限”、“燃烧下限”和“燃烧范围”并阐述石油产品的近似值 – 定义自燃温度是指可燃物质在没有火星或火焰作用下点燃并将继续燃烧的温度 – 描述液体的黏度是阻止液体流动的度量 – 阐述黏度随温度的降低而增大 – 定义“倾点”是观测到油流动的最低温度 – 认识到特别是原油船,油舱里有大量的残渣,在计算装载的货物时必须加以考虑 – 将干残渣作为舱底的均匀层计算 – 将液体残渣作为舱底的一个楔形物计算 – 了解应用楔形物计算的局限性	
6.2	**国际油船和码头安全指南(ISGOTT)的内容和应用(2 学时)**	R1, R28

	– 解释 ISGOTT 提供操作建议,直接协助油船和码头操作人员,包括油船和码头操作的某些方面的指南、实例以及如何应对
	– 确认 ISGOTT 的内容
	– 阐述可能也适用码头的、地方的和国家的规定,并应让有关人员知晓
	– 概述油船上关于以下方面采取的一般预防措施:
	  – 香烟、火柴和打火机
	  – 裸露灯
	  – 厨房
	  – 电气设备
	  – 工具的使用
	  – 进入封闭处所和泵房
	– 列出到达之前船舶和码头应进行交流的信息
	– 阐述油船和码头之间约定的安全程序并包括:
	  – 呼叫应急服务的手段
	  – 消防和其他应急设备的可用性和使用
	  – 万一发生火灾或其他紧急情况时应采取的行动
	  – 泊位的紧急撤离
	– 阐述消防设备应随时可用
	– 阐述主机和其他重要操纵设备应在短时间内可用,并且任何使船失去动力的作业或修理应获得码头和港口当局的书面同意
	– 阐述装卸计划应由船舶和码头达成一致	

COMPETENCE 2.1	Plan and Ensure Safe Loading, Stowage, Securing, Care During the Voyage and Unloading of Cargoes	IMO Reference

	– explains that safety measures against pollution and actions to take in case of an accident are agreed before transfer of cargo commences
	– states that, before starting cargo transfer, the responsible officer and the terminal representative must formally agree that they are ready to do so safely
	– states that the terminal should be notified of the intention to use crude oil washing (COW) at least 24 hours in advance
	– explains that tanks should be maintained in an inert condition throughout all operations except when entry to tanks for inspection or repair is necessary
	– explains that the inert gas should have an oxygen content not exceeding 5% by volume
	– states that the oxygen content of cargo tanks should not exceed 8% by volume
	– explains that the inert-gas plant will be used to:
	  – inert empty cargo tanks
	  – supply inert gas during cargo discharging, deballasting, crude oil washing and tank cleaning
	  – purge tanks prior to gas-freeing
	  – top-up the pressure when necessary during a voyage
	– explains that, in the event of a failure of the inert gas system, discharge of cargo or ballast or tank cleaning should be stopped, to prevent air being drawn into the tanks, and operations should only be resumed when a supply of inert gas has been restored
	– describes the hold and tank arrangements of combination carriers
	– describes the safety aspects relating to the operation of double hull tankers
	– outlines the change-over from oil to dry bulk cargo and from dry bulk cargo to oil	

6.3	**Oil tanker operations and related pollution prevention regulations (3 hours)** – defines “segregated ballast”, “clean ballast”, “dirty ballast”, “slop tank” – briefly describes an inert gas system (IGS) and sketches the distribution of inert gas to tanks – explains the reasons for ballasting – states that the capacity and arrangement of segregated ballast tanks is intended to provide sufficient weight, to provide a satisfactory trim and to ensure full immersion of the propeller for normal conditions of sea passages – states that on rare occasions weather conditions may be so severe that additional ballast is needed for the safety of the ship – states that in crude oil tankers equipped with COW the additional ballast would be carried in tanks that have been washed with crude oil – states that the additional ballast must be treated as dirty ballast – explains why a ship may have only clean or segregated ballast on board upon arrival at a loading port – states the criteria for the discharge of oil from cargo-tank areas of oil tankers – outlines the procedures for changing ballast at sea – states that, before loading clean ballast, cargo pumps and lines to be used are flushed with clean water into a dirty ballast or slop tank	R1, R28

适任 2.1	计划并确保在航行期间货物的安全装载、积载、系固、照管以及货物的卸载	IMO 参考书目

	– 解释在装卸货物之前应同意防污染的安全措施以及万一发生事故时应采取的行动
	– 阐述在开始装卸货物前,负责的船员和码头代表必须正式确信他们这么做是安全的
	– 阐述使用原油洗舱(COW)的意图应至少提前 24 小时通知码头
	– 解释整个操作过程中舱室应保持惰性状态,除非有必要进入舱室进行检查或修理
	– 解释惰性气体含氧量容积不超过 5%
	– 阐述货舱含氧量容积不超过 8%
	– 解释惰性气体装置应用于:
	  – 惰化空货舱
	  – 在卸货、排压载水、原油洗舱和洗舱期间提供惰性气体
	  – 除气之前货舱驱气
	  – 航行期间必要时加压
	– 解释万一惰性气体系统发生故障,应停止卸货、压载和洗舱,以防空气被吸入液舱,并且只有惰性气体供应恢复时才可继续作业
	– 描述多用途船的货舱和液舱的布置
	– 描述有关双壳油船作业的安全问题
	– 概括从油品到干散货和从干散货到油品的货物转换	

6.3	**油船操作和有关的防污染规则(3 学时)** – 定义“专用压载水”、“清洁压载水”、“不洁压载水”、“污油舱” – 简述惰性气体系统(IGS)并勾画惰性气体到液舱的输送 – 解释压载的原因 – 阐述专用压载舱的容量和布置是旨在提供足够的重量,以得到满意的吃水差和确保在海上正常航行情况下螺旋桨完全浸在水中 – 阐述在极少数天气非常恶劣情况下,为了船舶的安全,需要额外压载 – 阐述在配有 COW 的原油船上,在用原油清洗的舱中应装载额外的压载水 – 阐述额外的压载水应作为不洁压载水加以处理 – 解释为何船舶在抵达装货港时,船上只能有清洁压载水或专用压载水 – 阐述从油船货舱区域卸油的条件 – 概括在海上更换压载水的程序 – 阐述在装清洁压载水之前,所要使用的货泵和管道应用清水冲洗,冲洗过的水排入不洁压载水舱或污油舱	R1, R28

COMPETENCE 2.1	**Plan and Ensure Safe Loading, Stowage, Securing, Care During the Voyage and Unloading of Cargoes**	**IMO Reference**

- describes how to dispose of dirty ballast
- describes how to decant the water contents of the slop tank
- states that a final flushing of cargo pumps and lines to be used for discharge of clean ballast is made to the sea through the oil monitoring and control system
- explains that the operation of discharging dirty ballast, decanting the slop tanks and flushing lines must be done when more than 50 nautical miles from the nearest land and outside a special area
- states that only segregated or clean ballast may be discharged within 50 nautical miles of land or inside a special area
- explains the reasons for tank cleaning
- briefly describes the use of fixed and portable machines for tank cleaning
- describes the use of slop tanks during tank cleaning
- states that an inert atmosphere should be maintained in tanks during tank cleaning in ships fitted with IGS
- briefly describes crude oil washing and the reasons for requiring it in crude oil tankers of 20,000 dwt and above
- states that crude oil washing can only be carried out with fixed washing machines in inerted tanks
- states that the oil residues in the slop tank resulting from tank cleaning and disposal of dirty ballast may be:
  - pumped ashore at the loading terminal
  - retained on board and segregated from the next cargo
  - retained on board and the new cargo loaded on top of them
- states that the process of tank cleaning, changing ballast, decanting the water from slop tanks and loading the next cargo over the retained oil is known as the load-on-top procedure
- states that details of cargo operations, ballasting and deballasting, tank cleaning, discharge of water from slop tanks and disposal of residues are entered in the ship's Oil Record Book
- defines gas-freeing as the replacement of hydrocarbon vapours or inert gas by air
- lists the reasons for gas-freeing
- explains why inert gas is used to purge the tanks of hydrocarbon vapours before introducing air on suitably equipped ships
- states that a mechanical fixed system is used or portable fans are used
- states that checks are made during gas-freeing with combustible-gas indicators, oxygen meters and toxic-gas detectors
- states that the supply of inert gas to the tank is shut off
- explains the need to maintain ventilation and to check the atmosphere frequently when persons are working in a tank
- appreciates that the change of volume with temperature of oils is not linear
- states that cargo calculation is carried out as if the oil were at a standard temperature
- understands that the volume of the oil must be corrected from its actual temperature when measured to the standard temperature

适任 2.1	计划并确保在航行期间货物的安全装载、积载、系固、照管以及货物的卸载	IMO 参考书目

	– 描述如何处理不洁压载水
	– 描述如何排掉污油舱里的水
	– 阐述对用于排放清洁压载水的货泵和管道进行最后清洗的水应通过排油监控系统排入海中
	– 解释排放不洁压载水、排掉污油舱水分和清洗管道必须在距最近海岸 50 海里外和在特殊区域外进行
	– 阐述只有专用压载水或清洁压载水才能在离岸 50 海里内或特殊区域内排放
	– 解释洗舱的原因
	– 简述固定式或可移动式洗舱机的使用
	– 描述在洗舱期间污油舱的使用
	– 阐述在配有 IGS 的船上洗舱期间应保持舱内气体惰化
	– 简述原油洗舱和 20 000 dwt 及以上的原油船上要求原油洗舱的理由
	– 阐述原油洗舱只能在惰化的舱内用固定式机械进行
	– 阐述由于洗舱和处理不洁压载水而在污油水舱内产生的残油可以被：
	  – 在装货码头泵到岸上
	  – 保留在船上并与下一票货物隔离
	  – 保留在船上并在其上面装新货
	– 阐述洗舱、更换压载水、排掉污油舱的水和在残油上装载下一票货物的处理过程被称为顶装法程序
	– 阐述货物作业、装压载水和排压载水、洗舱、排放污油舱水以及残油处理的细节都要记入船舶油类记录簿
	– 以空气代替烃类化合物蒸气或惰性气体定义为除气
	– 列出除气的原因
	– 解释为什么在配备合适的船舶上引入空气之前,用惰性气体驱除舱里的烃类化合物蒸气
	– 阐述可以使用机械固定式系统或可移动式电风扇
	– 阐述在除气期间应用测爆仪、测氧仪和测毒仪进行检测
	– 阐述向舱室充惰性气体以隔绝空气
	– 解释当人员在舱内作业时需要保持通风并频繁检查空气
	– 了解石油体积随温度的变化是非线性的
	– 阐述假设油温为标准温度时进行货物计算
	– 理解油的体积应从实际测量的温度到标准温度进行修正	

COMPETENCE 2.1	Plan and Ensure Safe Loading, Stowage, Securing, Care During the Voyage and Unloading of Cargoes	IMO Reference

- states that the cargo calculation is carried out as if the density of the oil was that at the standard temperature
- explains that the density of oil must be corrected from its actual density to that at the standard temperature
- appreciates that different types of oils have different coefficients of expansion and that there are separate Petroleum Measurement Tables for Crude Oils, Products and Lubricating Oils
- understands the difference between mass and weight in air and that one or the other may be required by different administrations

6.4 Chemical tankers (3 hours)

- states that modern chemical tankers have evolved from oil product tankers to take account of special carriage requirements and associated hazards
- explains that dedicated service usually means that the tanker is designed for the carriage of a particular type of chemical and transports the same type of cargo on each voyage
- explains that a chemical tanker engaged in parcel trade moves a variety of relatively small lots of chemicals between a number of ports
- lists the most important of the rules governing chemical tankers as:
  - international rules and regulations
  - national rules and regulations
  - classification society rules
- states that the sea transport of liquid chemicals in bulk is internationally regulated, as regards safety and pollution aspects, through Conventions adopted by the International Maritime Organization (IMO)
- explains that the Convention requirements are supplemented by recommendations, specifications and Codes adopted by IMO
- states that the IMO Conventions covering the carriage of chemicals in bulk are:
  - the International Convention for the Safety of Life at Sea (SOLAS), 1974, as amended, Chapter VII
  - the International Convention for the Prevention of Pollution from Ships, 1973, as modified by the 1978 Protocol (MARPOL 73/78), as amended, Annex II
- states that the most important Codes and standards covering the transport of liquid chemicals are:
  - the Bulk Chemical Codes
  - Code for the Construction and Equipment of Ships Carrying Dangerous Chemicals in Bulk (BCH Code)
  - International Code for the Construction and Equipment of Ships Carrying Dangerous Chemicals in Bulk (IBC) Code
  - Standards for Procedures and Arrangements for the discharge of Noxious Liquid Substances (P and A Standards)
- defines a chemical tanker as a cargo ship constructed or adapted and used for the carriage in bulk of any liquid product listed in Chapter 17 of the IBC Code
- explains that products are included in the list in Chapter 17 because of their safety hazards or because of their pollution hazards or both

<table>
<tr><td>适任 2.1</td><td>计划并确保在航行期间货物的安全装载、积载、系固、照管以及货物的卸载</td><td>IMO
参考书目</td></tr>
<tr><td colspan="2">
– 阐述假定接标准温度时的油密度进行货物计算
– 阐述油的密度必须从实际测量的温度到标准温度进行修正
– 理解不同类型的油品有不同的膨胀系数以及有独立的原油、成品油和润滑油《石油度量表》
– 懂得在空气中质量和重量的不同以及不同的主管当局对其要求不一
6.4　化学品船(3 学时)
– 阐述现代化学品船是从考虑了许多特殊的运载要求和相关危险的成品油船演变而来
– 解释专门服务通常是指化学品船被设计成运载某一特殊的化学品并且每个航次都运输同样的货物
– 解释散装化学品船在许多港口之间运载各种相对小票的化学品
– 列出有关化学品船的最重要的规则:
　– 国际规章和规则
　– 国内规章和规则
　– 船级社规章
– 阐述散装液体化学品的海上运输有关安全和污染方面受 IMO 所采纳的国际公约制约
– 解释公约要求由被 IMO 所采纳的建议、规范和规则进行补充
– 阐述有关散装化学品运载的 IMO 公约是:
　– 1974 年国际海上人命安全公约(SOLAS)及其修正案第Ⅶ章
　– 由 1978 年议定书修改的 1973 年国际船舶防污染公约(MARPOL 73/78)及其修正案,附件Ⅱ
– 阐述有关液体化学品运输的最重要规则和标准是:
　– 散装化学品运输规则
　– 运输散装危险化学品船结构和设备规则(BCH 规则)
　– 国际散装运输危险化学品船舶结构和设备规则(IBC 规则)
　– 卸载有毒液体物质的程序和设备标准(P 和 A 标准)
– 将建造或改装用于运载 IBC 规则第 17 章列出的任何散装液体产品的船舶定义为化学品船
– 解释第 17 章中列出的产品具有安全危害性或污染危害性或二者皆有
</td><td></td></tr>
</table>

COMPETENCE 2.1	Plan and Ensure Safe Loading, Stowage, Securing, Care During the Voyage and Unloading of Cargoes	IMO Reference

– states that safety hazards may be one or more of the following:
  – fire hazard in excess of that of petroleum products
  – toxicity
  – corrosivity
  – reactivity with water, air or other chemicals or self-reaction (polymerization, decomposition)
– states that, in addition to the survey requirements for any ship, chemical tankers must undergo surveys of the cargo-containment and handling arrangements for the issue of an International Certificate Fitness for the Carriage of Dangerous Chemicals in Bulk
– explains that the Bulk Chemical Codes divide tankers into three ship types, Type 1, Type 2 and Type 3, which reflect the hazard ratings of the cargoes which may be carried
– states that a Type 1 ship is intended for the transportation of products considered to present the greatest overall hazards and Type 2 or Type 3 for products of progressively lesser hazards
– states that the division into ship types is based on the ship's capability to survive specified damage caused by collision or stranding and the location of the cargo tanks in relation to such damage
– illustrates, by means of sketches, the location of tanks for each type of ship
– explains the following descriptions of tanks:
  – independent
  – integral
  – gravity
  – pressure
– states that all materials used for tank construction and associated piping, valves and pumps must be resistant to the cargo carried
– states that some ships have stainless-steel tanks for the carriage of cargoes which cannot be contained in mild steel
– explains that mild-steel tanks are normally coated, to protect cargoes from contamination by steel and to make cleaning, gas-freeing and inspection easier
– states that no single coating is suitable for all cargoes and that the coating manufacturers compatibility data must be used when planning a cargo
– explains that cofferdams and other void spaces may be included in the cargotank area to provide segregation of groups of tanks
– illustrates typical tank arrangements by means of simple sketches
– states that the heating medium may be steam, water or thermal oils
– explains that the heating system may use coils fitted inside the tank or a heat exchanger placed outside the tank
– describes, with the aid of a drawing, a cargo heating system that uses a heat exchanger placed outside the tank
– states that there is suitable protective clothing on board which must be worn by all personnel engaged in loading or discharging operations
– states that, for certain cargoes, there must be respiratory and eye-protection equipment for every person on board for emergency escape		

适任 2.1	计划并确保在航行期间货物的安全装载、积载、系固、照管以及货物的卸载	IMO 参考书目
– 阐述安全危害性可以是以下之一或更多: – 超出石油产品之外的火灾危险性 – 毒性 – 腐蚀性 – 与水、空气或其他化学物质反应或自身反应(聚合、分解) – 阐述除了对任何船舶的检验要求之外,化学品船必须进行货物围护和装卸设备的检验以颁发国际散装运输危险化学品船适装证书 – 解释国际散装化学品运输规则按运载货物的危险性等级将化学品船分为 1 类船、2 类船和 3 类船 – 阐述 1 类船旨在运输整体危害性最大的产品,而 2 类船和 3 类船运输产品的危害性逐渐降低 – 阐述船舶类型的分类是基于船舶应对由碰撞或搁浅所造成的特定损坏的幸存能力以及与这些破损有关的货舱的位置 – 以草图的方式说明每种类型船舶中货舱的位置 – 解释下列液舱的描述: – 独立液舱 – 整体液舱 – 重力液舱 – 压力液舱 – 阐述建造液舱和相关的管道、阀、泵所使用的材料必须能耐受所运载的货物 – 阐述某些船舶具有不锈钢液舱以运载不能装在低碳钢液舱运输的货物 – 解释低碳钢液舱通常应进行涂漆以防止钢污染货物,同时更易于清舱、除气和检查 – 阐述没有一种涂漆适合所有货物以及当计划载货时应使用涂料制造商兼容性数据 – 解释干隔舱和其他空舱可包含在提供隔离不同种类液舱的液货舱区域内 – 以简单草图的方式表示典型货舱的分布 – 阐述传热介质可以是蒸汽、水和热油 – 解释加热介质可以使用舱内的线圈或舱外的热交换器 – 画图说明使用舱外的热交换器的货物加热系统 – 阐述船上有适合所有从事装卸操作的人员必须穿着的防护服 – 阐述针对某些货物,船上必须有供每个人员紧急逃生用的呼吸器和护眼设备		

COMPETENCE 2.1	Plan and Ensure Safe Loading, Stowage, Securing, Care During the Voyage and Unloading of Cargoes	IMO Reference

- states that equipment for evaluation of atmospheres in tanks and other enclosed spaces is provided for
  - detection of flammable gases
  - measurement of oxygen content
  - measurement of concentration of toxic gas
- describes how to use an absorption tube gas detector for measuring the concentration of a gas
- explains what is meant by:
  - the threshold limit value (TLV) of a product
  - the odour threshold
- states that the atmosphere in tanks and enclosed spaces must be considered dangerous unless appropriate checks prove otherwise
- states that information about cargoes to be handled is essential to the safety of the vessel and crew
- states that information for each product may be found on cargo data sheets contained in safety guides or provided by the manufacturer or shipper
- states that, if sufficient information necessary for the safe handling and carriage of a cargo is not available, the cargo must not be loaded
- states that information necessary for the safe carriage of a cargo includes:
  - a full description of the physical and chemical properties, including reactivity
  - necessary for its safe containment
  - action to take in the event of spills or leaks
  - countermeasures against accidental personal contact
  - firefighting procedures and firefighting media
  - procedures for cargo transfer, tank cleaning, gas-freeing and ballasting
  - details of the stabilizer or inhibitor added to those cargoes, that require one (on the manufacturer's certificate, in the absence of which the cargo should be refused)
  - First Aid procedures, including the use of specific antidotes for poisons
- states that tanks are normally subject to thorough inspection and testing for cleanliness before loading
- explains, with the aid of a simple drawing, how cargo is routed from the manifold to tanks on a chemical tanker with separate lines for each tank
- explains, with the aid of a simple drawing, a "closed circuit" loading operation using a vapour-return line
- states that samples are taken from the lines and tanks during loading for purposes of quality control
- states that visual and audible high-level alarms and a tank overflow control system are required for many chemicals
- states that personnel involved in unloading should check the information in the relevant data sheets and take all necessary precautions, including the wearing of appropriate protective clothing
- states that, prior to discharging, samples from tanks and lines are analysed to check if the product has been contaminated on board during the passage		

适任 2.1	计划并确保在航行期间货物的安全装载、积载、系固、照管以及货物的卸载	IMO 参考书目

– 阐述提供检测舱内和其他封闭处所内大气的设备用来：
  – 探测可燃气体
  – 测量氧气含量
  – 测量有毒气体浓度
– 描述如何使用吸收管式气体探测仪来测量气体的浓度
– 解释下列含义：
  – 产品的阈限值(TLV)
  – 气味阈值
– 阐述必须认为舱内和封闭处所内的气氛是危险的,除非相应的检测证明是安全的
– 阐述关于要装卸货物的信息对船舶和船员的安全必不可少
– 阐述每一种货物的信息可以在安全指南里的货物数据表中找到或由厂商、托运人提供
– 阐述如果无法得到安全装卸和运载货物所必需的足够信息,则不得装载货物
– 阐述货物安全运载必需的信息包括：
  – 理化性质的完整描述,包括反应性
  – 安全装载的必要性
  – 溢出或渗漏时应采取的行动
  – 防止人员意外接触的对策
  – 消防程序和消防介质
  – 移货、洗舱、除气和压载的程序
  – 需要向货物添加一种稳定剂或抑制剂的详细情况(厂商证书应载明,如缺少,则应拒装货物)
  – 急救程序,包括毒性物质的专用解毒剂的使用
– 阐述在装载之前,通常要对液舱进行彻底的清洗检查和测试
– 利用画草图解释在各液舱具有各自管路的化学品船上,货物是如何经由歧管输送到舱里的
– 利用画草图解释使用蒸气回路管道的“闭环”装载作业
– 阐述为了控制质量,在装载期间从管道和液舱里取样
– 阐述许多化学品船要求视觉和听觉的高位报警器以及液舱溢流控制系统
– 阐述卸货人员应检查有关数据表里的信息并采取所有必要的预防措施,包括穿着合适的防护服
– 阐述在卸货前,应从液舱和管道里取样,以检查产品是否在船舶航行期间受到污染		

COMPETENCE 2.1	Plan and Ensure Safe Loading, Stowage, Securing, Care During the Voyage and Unloading of Cargoes	IMO Reference

- explains, with the aid of a simple drawing, how cargo is routed from tank to the manifold on a tanker with deepwell pumps and separate lines from each tank
- states that, in tanks containing cargoes that present a major fire hazard, inert gas or nitrogen is used to maintain a small positive pressure during unloading, to prevent air from entering the tanks

6.5 Tank cleaning and control of pollution in chemical tankers (2 hours)

- states that different cargoes require different tank-cleaning procedures
- states that most tank cleaning can be done with hot or cold seawater or fresh water, or by ventilation alone, although a few cargoes require special solvents
- states that fixed or portable tank-washing machines are used
- lists phases in a tank-cleaning operation as:
  - prewash
  - main wash
  - fresh water rinse
  - gas-freeing
  - drying
  - inspection and testing
- explains the use of slop tanks to hold cargo residues and tank washings
- explains, with the aid of a simple drawing, the cycle of a tank-washing system from the seawater inlet to the slop tank
- states that Annex II of the MARPOL 73/78 Convention contains regulations for the control of pollution by noxious liquid cargoes carried in bulk or tank washings from such cargoes
- states that as per the amendments of Annex II of MARPOL, which entered into force on 1 January 2007, a revised annex a new four-category pollution category system for noxious liquid substances; the previous A, B, C and D category system has become X,Y, Z and OS
- states that every chemical tanker is required to have a Certificate of Fitness (CoF) indicating that it is certified to carry certain products. The issuance of a CoF will also require a revised Procedures and Arrangements (P and A) Manual
- states that each ship which is certified for the carriage of noxious liquid substances in bulk must be provided with a Procedures and Arrangements (P and A) Manual that has been approved by the Administration and a Cargo Record Book
- states that the Master must ensure that no discharges into the sea of cargo residues or residue/water mixtures containing substances of Category X, Y, Z or OS take place unless they are made in full compliance with the P and A Manual
- states that carrying out operations in accordance with the ship's P and A Manual ensures that the pollution regulations are complied with

适任 2.1	计划并确保在航行期间货物的安全装载、积载、系固、照管以及货物的卸载	IMO 参考书目

– 利用画草图解释在各液舱具有深井泵和各自管路的化学品船上,货物是如何由舱里输送到歧管的
– 阐述在存在重大火灾危险性的液舱里,在卸货期间使用惰性气体或氮气来保持较小的正压力以防止空气进入液舱
6.5 化学品船的洗舱和污染控制(2 学时)
– 阐述不同货物要求不同的洗舱程序
– 阐述尽管极少数货物需要专用的清洗剂,但大多数货物的洗舱可用热或冷的海水或淡水,或只需通风
– 阐述可以使用固定式或移动式洗舱机
– 列出洗舱操作的短语:
  – 预洗
  – 主洗
  – 淡水清洗
  – 除气
  – 晾干
  – 检查和测试
– 解释使用污油舱储存货物残渣和洗舱水
– 利用画草图解释从海水入口到污油舱的洗舱系统的循环
– 阐述 MARPOL 73/78 公约附件Ⅱ含有控制散装运输有毒液体货物或这些货物的洗舱水的污染的规则
– 阐述根据 2007 年 1 月 1 日生效的 MARPOL 73/78 公约附件Ⅱ修正案,该修订的附录采用新的散装有毒液体物质污染分类系统;以前的 A,B,C 和 D 类系统变为 X,Y,Z 和 OS
– 阐述要求每艘化学品船具有适装证书(COF),证明适合运载某些产品。适装证书的签发需要修订后的程序和布置(P 和 A) 手册
– 阐述持有运输散装有毒液体物质证书的船舶必须提供主管机关批准的“程序和布置(P 和 A)手册”和货物记录簿
– 阐述船长必须确保没有发生含有 X、Y、Z 或 OS 类物质的货物残渣或残渣 / 水的混合物排放入海,除非它们完全符合“P 和 A 手册”
– 阐述根据船舶“P 和 A 手册”进行的操作确保符合污染规则		

COMPETENCE 2.1	Plan and Ensure Safe Loading, Stowage, Securing, Care During the Voyage and Unloading of Cargoes	IMO Reference

- states that pollution prevention procedures during cargo transfer, ballasting and tank cleaning should include keeping a watch on:
  - levels in cargo, slop or ballast tanks
  - hoses or loading arms
  - pumps, valves, gaskets, connections and hatches
  - spill pans and scuppers
  - alarms and instrumentation
  - coordination of operational signals
  - water around vessel
- states that personnel on watch should be present at all times during operations and regularly carry out the inspections mentioned in the above
- states that entries should be made in the Cargo Record Book, on a tank-to-tank basis, of:
  - loading
  - internal transfer of cargo
  - unloading
  - mandatory prewash in accordance with P and A Manual
  - cleaning of cargo tanks
  - discharge into the sea of tank washings
  - ballasting of cargo tanks
  - discharge of ballast water from cargo tanks
  - accidental or other exceptional discharge control by authorized surveyors

6.6 Gas tankers (3 hours)

- states that the transport by sea of liquid gases in bulk is internationally regulated with regard to safety, through standards laid down by IMO
- states that chapter VII of the IMO International Convention for the Safety of Life at Sea (SOLAS), 1974, as amended, makes the provisions of the International Code for the Construction and Equipment of Ships Carrying Liquefied Gases in Bulk (IGC Code) mandatory
- states that a liquefied gas is the liquid form of a substance that at normal atmospheric temperatures and pressures would be a gas
- states that liquefied gas products transported by gas tankers are listed in chapter 19 of the IGC Code
- states that some of those substances are also covered by the IBC Code
- divides gas cargoes into four groups as:
  - liquefied natural gas (LNG)
  - liquefied petroleum gas (LPG)
  - liquefied ethylene gas (LEG)
  - chemical gases
- states that LNG is natural gas from which impurities have been removed, and consists mainly of methane
- states that LPG is the common name for petroleum gases consisting mainly of butane and propane

适任 2.1	计划并确保在航行期间货物的安全装载、积载、系固、照管以及货物的卸载	IMO 参考书目

- 阐述在移货、压载和洗舱期间防污染的程序应包括对以下地方保持关注：
  - 液货舱、污油舱或压载舱的液位
  - 管道或装载臂
  - 泵、阀、垫圈、接头和舱盖
  - 溢油盘和排水孔
  - 报警器和仪器仪表
  - 操作信号的协调
  - 船舶周围水面
- 阐述在作业期间应总是有值班人员并应定时进行以上内容的检查
- 阐述基于舱到舱应记入货物记录簿的内容：
  - 装货
  - 船舶内部货物调拨
  - 卸货
  - 根据“P 和 A 手册”的强制性预洗
  - 货舱的清洗
  - 洗舱水的排放入海
  - 货舱压载水
  - 货舱压载水的排放
  - 经授权的验船师控制的意外或其他异常的排放

6.6 液化气船(3 学时)

- 阐述散装液化气海上运输在安全方面受 IMO 制定的国际标准管控
- 阐述 IMO 1974 年国际海上人命安全公约(SOLAS)及其修正案第 7 章使国际散装运输液化气船舶构造与设备规则(IGC)的规定强制执行
- 阐述液化气是正常气温和压力下是气体的某物质的液体形式
- 阐述液化气船运输的液化气产品列在 IGC 规则第 19 章里
- 阐述 IBC 规则也含有某些液化气物质
- 气体货物分为四类：
  - 液化天然气(LNG)
  - 液化石油气(LPG)
  - 液化乙烯气(LEG)
  - 化学品气体
- 阐述 LNG 是除去杂质的天然气,主要成分是甲烷
- 阐述 LPG 是主要含有丁烷和丙烷的石油气的常用名称

COMPETENCE 2.1	Plan and Ensure Safe Loading, Stowage, Securing, Care During the Voyage and Unloading of Cargoes	IMO Reference

- lists chlorine, ammonia and vinyl chloride monomer as examples of chemical gases
- states that, in addition to the surveys required for all ships, gas tankers must undergo surveys of the cargo containment equipment and cargo handling arrangements for the issue of an International Certificate of Fitness for the Carriage of Liquefied Gases in Bulk
- states that the Certificate of Fitness lists the cargoes which may be carried by the ship and may also stipulate conditions for carriage
- explains the following terms used in the IGC Code:
  - boiling point
  - cargo area
  - cargo containment system
  - gas carrier
  - gas-dangerous space or zone
  - gas-safe space
  - hold space
  - interbarrier space
  - MAR VS
  - primary barrier
  - secondary barrier
  - tank dome
- explains that the IGC divides ships into four types, 1G, 2G, 2PG and 3G
- states that a Type 1G ship is intended for the transportation of products considered to present the greatest overall hazard and Types 2G, 2PG and 3G for products of progressively lesser hazards
- states that the division into ship types is based on the ship's capability to survive specified damage caused by collision or stranding and the location of the cargo tanks in relation to such damage
- describes, in simple terms:
  - integral tank
  - membrane tank
  - semi-membrane tank
  - independent tank
  - internally insulated tank
- explains, in simple terms, the division of independent tanks into:
  - Type A, generally a self-supporting prismatic tank
  - Type B, generally a self-supporting spherical tank
  - Type C, generally a self-supporting cylindrical pressure tank
- states that a cargo tank has shut off valves located as close to the tank as possible for all liquid and vapour connections except for safety relief valves
- states that regulations require remotely operated emergency shutdown (ESD) valves in the cargo piping system
- states that the operation of the ESD system also stops pumps and compressors
- states that all cargo tanks must be provided with a pressure-relief system		

适任 2.1	计划并确保在航行期间货物的安全装载、积载、系固、照管以及货物的卸载	IMO 参考书目

– 列举氯、氨和氯乙烯单体为化学品气体的例子
– 阐述除了对所有船舶的检验要求之外，液化气船必须进行货物围护和装卸设备的检验，以获颁国际散装运输液化气体船舶适装证书
– 阐述适装证书列出了船舶可以运输的货物且也规定了运输的条件
– 解释 IGC 规则所使用的以下术语：
  – 沸点
  – 货物区
  – 货物围护系统
  – 气体运输船
  – 有毒气体的处所或区域
  – 气体安全的处所
  – 货舱
  – 屏壁间处所
  – 安全释放阀最大允许设定值
  – 主屏壁
  – 次屏壁
  – 液货舱气室
– 解释 IGC 把船舶分成 1G、2G、2PG 和 3G 四类
– 阐述 1G 类船是运输存在最大危害性的产品而 2G/2PG 类和 3G 类船所运输产品的危害性逐渐降低
– 阐述船舶类型的分类是基于船舶在由碰撞或搁浅所造成的特定损坏下的生存能力以及与这些损坏有关的货舱的位置
– 用简单的术语描述：
  – 整体液舱
  – 薄膜液舱
  – 半薄膜液舱
  – 独立液舱
  – 内部绝热液舱
– 用简单的术语解释独立液舱分为：
  – A 类，通常是自承式棱形舱
  – B 类，通常是自承式球形舱
  – C 类，通常是自承式圆柱形压力舱
– 阐述除了安全释放阀以外，液货舱的所有切断阀都尽可能靠近该舱，以便所有液体和蒸气连接
– 阐述规则要求在货物管系中有遥控紧急速闭(ESD)阀
– 阐述 ESD 系统的运行也会停泵和压缩机
– 阐述所有液货舱必须具有压力释放系统		

COMPETENCE 2.1	Plan and Ensure Safe Loading, Stowage, Securing, Care During the Voyage and Unloading of Cargoes	IMO Reference

- states that all equipment and piping which can be isolated when full of liquid must be provided with a pressure-relief system
- states that cargo pumps are usually centrifugal, either deepwell pumps or submerged electric pumps, in the tanks with deck-mounted booster pumps, if required
- describes the uses of cargo heaters and vaporizers
- explains the effect of transfer of heat to the cargo on cargo temperature and tank pressure
- states that, except for fully pressurized vessels, means for controlling the pressure must be provided
- states that pressure in cargo tanks may be controlled by:
  - insulation of tanks, to reduce heat transfer
  - leading cargo boil-off to the ship's boilers or main engine as fuel (ONLY with LNG)
  - leading cargo boil-off to the ship's reliquefaction plant, where vapour is liquefied and returned to the tank
  - cooling the liquid in a heat exchanger (indirect system)
- describes the single-stage direct liquefaction cycle
- states that the indirect system is only used for those products which cannot be compressed for safety reasons
- states that inert gas is used to inert hold spaces and inter barrier spaces and to purge tanks
- states that most gas tankers are fined with an inert-gas generator
- states that the liquid level in cargo tanks is commonly measured by means of float gauges
- states that each cargo tank is fitted with a high-level alarm and automatic shutoff valves to prevent overflow
- states that each cargo tank is fitted with means for indicating the temperature and pressure
- explains how cargo leakage through the primary barrier can be detected
- states that gas tankers have a fixed gas-detection system that gives audible and visual alarms of the accumulation of gas in enclosed spaces such as cargo pump-rooms, compressor rooms, hold spaces and interbarrier spaces
- describes briefly the arrangements for firefighting on deck in the cargo area
- describes the water-spray system for ships carrying flammable or toxic products

6.7 Cargo operations in gas tankers (2 hours)

- states that information for each product may be found on cargo data sheets contained in safety guides or obtained from the shipper

适任 2.1	计划并确保在航行期间货物的安全装载、积载、系固、照管以及货物的卸载	IMO 参考书目

– 阐述装满液体时均应能隔离的设备及管路须具有压力释放系统
– 阐述货泵通常是离心式的,或为深井泵,或为电动潜水泵,需要时在甲板上配备增压泵
– 描述货物加热器和蒸发器的使用
– 解释热量转移到货物上对货物温度和货舱压力的影响
– 阐述除了全压式船舶外,应提供控制压力的手段
– 阐述货舱的压力可以由以下方面控制:
  – 货舱的绝热,减少热量转移
  – 将货物蒸发气体导入船舶锅炉或主机作为燃料(仅对 LNG)
  – 将货物蒸发气体导入船舶再液化装置,使蒸气液化后返回货舱
  – 在热交换器里冷却液体(间接系统)
– 描述一级直接液化循环
– 阐述间接系统只用于出于安全原因不能压缩的产品
– 阐述惰性气体用于惰化货舱和屏壁间处所以及净化液货舱
– 阐述大多数液化气船配有惰性气体发生器
– 阐述液货舱的液位通常采用浮标尺测量
– 阐述每一液货舱配有高位报警器和防止溢流的自动关闭阀
– 阐述每一液货舱配有指示温度和压力的设施
– 解释如何能探测货物通过主屏壁的溢漏
– 阐述液化气船有能发出封闭处所如货物泵舱、压缩机舱、货舱和屏蔽间处所气体积聚的听觉和视觉报警的固定式气体检测系统
– 简述货物区内甲板上的消防设备
– 描述运输可燃或有毒产品的船舶水喷淋系统
6.7 液化气船的货物操作(2 学时)
– 阐述每一种货物的信息可在安全指南里的货物数据表中找到或从托运人处得到		

COMPETENCE 2.1	**Plan and Ensure Safe Loading, Stowage, Securing, Care During the Voyage and Unloading of Cargoes**	**IMO Reference**

- states that information needed before loading includes:
  - a full description of the physical and chemical properties that are necessary for the safe containment of the cargo
  - action to be taken in the event of spills or leaks
  - counter-measures against accidental personal contact
  - firefighting procedures and firefighting media
  - procedures for cargo transfer, gas-freeing, ballasting, tank cleaning and changing cargoes
  - special equipment for particular cargoes
  - minimum temperatures of the inner hull steel
  - emergency procedures
- states that products that react when mixed should only be loaded if the complete cargo systems are separated
- states that personnel should be made aware of the hazards and be required to use the appropriate protective equipment provided
- states that the Master should ensure proper liaison between the ship and the terminal before and throughout cargo-transfer operations
- describes briefly the following cargo operations:
  - drying
  - inerting
  - purging
  - cooling down
  - loading
  - cargo conditioning on passage
  - discharging
  - changing cargoes
  - gas-freeing
  - preparing for tank inspection
- states that all operations involving cargo, ballast and bunkers should be carried out in accordance with the applicable international and local pollution regulations
- states that some gas cargoes are subject to the regulations of Annex II of MARPOL 73/78
- explains that a gas tanker requires an International Pollution Prevention Certificate for the Carriage of Noxious Liquid Substances in Bulk (NLS Certificate) to carry such products
- states that such cargoes must be handled in accordance with the Procedures and Arrangements Manual
- understands that the mass of vapour present in the ullage space is included in the calculation of liquefied gases
- calculates the vapour mass

适任 2.1	计划并确保在航行期间货物的安全装载、积载、系固、照管以及货物的卸载	IMO 参考文献
– 阐述装货之前需要的信息包括： – 货物安全围护所必需的理化性质的完整描述 – 发生溢漏或泄漏应采取的行动 – 人员意外接触的对策 – 消防程序和消防介质 – 移货、洗舱、除气、压载和换货的程序 – 特定货物的特殊设备 – 内层船壳钢的最低温度 – 应急程序 – 阐述混合时会发生反应的产品只有货物系统是完全分离的才能被装载 – 阐述人员应意识到危害性并按要求使用所提供的合适保护装置 – 阐述在转驳货物之前和期间船长应确保船与码头之间的适当联系 – 简述以下货物作业： – 晾干 – 惰化 – 净化 – 冷却 – 装货 – 航行中的货物状态控制 – 卸货 – 换货 – 除气 – 准备货舱检查 – 阐述所有有关货物、压载水和燃油的操作应根据适用的国际和当地污染规则进行 – 阐述一些气体货物受 MARPOL 73/78 附件 II 规则管控 – 解释液化气船要运输散装有毒液体物质需要有国际运输散装有毒液体物质防污染证书(NLS 证书) – 阐述这些货物必须根据“程序和布置手册”进行装卸 – 理解空舱里的蒸气质量包括在液化气的计算之中 – 计算蒸气质量		

COMPETENCE 2.1	Plan and Ensure Safe Loading, Stowage, Securing, Care During the Voyage and Unloading of Cargoes	IMO Reference

2.1.7 KNOWLEDGE OF THE OPERATIONAL AND DESIGN LIMITATIONS OF BULK CARRIERS — R56, R64

Textbooks/Bibliography: T35, B71, B72, B73, B74, B76, B77, B78, B88, B89, B95, B104, B106, B109, B110, B113, B117, B128, B129, B130, B146, B182, B193, B198

Teaching aids: A1, V59, V172

Required performances:

7.1 Operational and design limitations of bulk carriers (3 hours)

- explains that the problems that are generally considered to be associated with bulk carriers includes, but is not limited to:
  - high density cargoes, leading to loss of buoyancy or structural failure, if holds are flooded in the loaded condition
  - high loading rate, leading to possible loss of control of load condition, with consequent high stresses
  - vulnerability to internal damage during cargo loading and discharging operations, leading to protective coating damage, accelerated corrosion, and local structural failure
  - low freeboard, leading to high green sea loads on deck structures
  - vulnerability to flooding of forward holds
  - rapid corrosion caused by corrosive cargo
  - minor damage to single sided ship structures or hatch covers can lead to hold flooding
- explains that the nature of bulk cargoes can give rise to a number of problems
- explains that cargoes such as coal produces gas and acidic conditions, high density cargoes produce large void spaces, and other cargoes can produce stability problems due to shifting or liquefaction
- explains that loaded bulk carriers tend to have a low freeboard making forward hatches vulnerable to heavy seas
- explains that a single hold flooding on a bulk carrier, particularly when loaded with high density cargoes, can have a severe adverse effect on stability and hull stresses
- explains that the corrosive effects of some cargoes accelerate the rate of deterioration of internal structures
- describes that ships can be more heavily stressed during ballast passage compared to loaded passage because the use of one or two ballast tanks leads to uneven weight distribution along the hull
- states that hold cleaning, ballasting at sea and ballast exchange carried out at sea are vulnerable aspects of a ballast voyage for a bulk carrier
- describes that improper cleaning during hold cleaning leads to accelerated corrosion and structural faults going unnoticed
- states that additional hull stresses due to redistribution of ballast are imposed on the ship carrying out ballasting at sea and ballast water exchange which is required for operational and environmental reasons
- explains that there is also a possibility of hull damage from “sloshing” when ballasting at sea
- states that this is also one of the reasons why some ships have been fitted with hull stress monitoring systems

适任 2.1	计划并确保在航行期间货物的安全装载、积载、系固、照管以及货物的卸载	IMO 参考书目
2.1.7 散货船作业与设计限制的知识 **教科书/参考文献**:T35, B71, B72, B73, B74, B76, B77, B78, B88, B89, B95, B104, B106, B109, B110, B113, B117, B128, B129, B130, B146, B182, B193, B198 **教具**:A1, V59, V172 技能要求: **7.1 散货船作业与设计限制(3 学时)** – 解释通常与散货船相关的问题,包括但并不限于如下: – 如满载高密度货物的货舱进水将导致浮力损失或结构损坏 – 高速装载带来的高应力导致装载状态的可能失控 – 装卸货期间易遭受内部损坏,导致保护涂料损坏、加速腐蚀和局部结构损坏 – 低干舷导致大浪对甲板结构产生冲击负荷 – 前部货舱易被淹没 – 由腐蚀性货物造成的快速腐蚀 – 对单壳船结构或舱盖的较小损坏可能导致货舱大量进水 – 解释散货的性质可能产生一些问题 – 解释像煤产生气体和酸性环境,高密度货物产生大量留空处所,其他货物可能由于移动或液化产生稳性问题 – 解释装载后的散货船会产生低干舷,使得前部货舱易遭受大浪 – 解释散货船上单一货舱大量进水,尤其是装载高密度货物时,可对稳性和船壳受力带来严重的不利影响 – 解释某些货物的腐蚀作用会加速内部结构的恶化速度 – 描述与装货航行相比,压载航行可能使船遭受更严重的应力,因为一个或两个舱的压载导致沿船体的重量分布不均 – 阐述在海上洗舱、压载和压载航行中更换压载水是散货船压载航行中容易受损的环节 – 描述不当的清洗货舱导致加速腐蚀和不为人注意的结构缺陷 – 阐述由于在海上压载作业产生的压载水的再次分配以及由于操作和环境原因要求更换压载水给船体带来的额外应力 – 解释海上压载还存在“泼溅”损坏船体的可能性 – 阐述这也是为何有些船配备应力监控系统的理由之一		R56, R64

COMPETENCE 2.1	Plan and Ensure Safe Loading, Stowage, Securing, Care During the Voyage and Unloading of Cargoes	IMO Reference
– explains why at shallow drafts ships in ballast are vulnerable to slamming with the consequent risk of bottom damage – explains why loading operation of a bulk carrier has been identified as an area of operations that can have immediate and long term effects on the structural integrity of the ship – describes that loading of bulk carriers requires the careful consideration of the loads imparted to the ship structure – explains that high density cargoes bring high local stresses, particularly in shear, if the vessel is block loaded and can also cause local damage and fatigue when being loaded – explains that loading at excessive speeds can cause high local stresses – describes that high loading rates make it difficult to monitor the amount of cargo being loaded – explains that continued over stressing has a cumulative effect with respect to fatigue – explains that discharging the cargoes causes similar problems to that of loading – describes that in addition to the problems associated with discharging, mechanical grabs, bulldozers, hydraulic hammers, and other machinery produce local damage and loading that can weaken the ship's structure – explains that ballasting operations during discharge can also add to the stresses on the ship if not planned and executed properly – explains as with loading, the need of good coordination at the time of discharge and ballasting of the ship – explains the reason why maintenance and inspection play an important part in the safety of bulk carriers – explains that all ships are designed with limits deliberately imposed on their operations to ensure that structural integrity is maintained – explains that exceeding these limits may over-stress the structure and lead to catastrophic failure – explains that the ship's hull structure is designed to withstand the static loads of the ship's weight and sea water pressure on the hull and the dynamic loads on the hull due to waves and ship's motion – explains that overloading in any one cargo hold space will increase static stress in the hull structure and reduce the capability of the hull structure to withstand dynamic loads when the ship is at sea – explains that many bulk carriers are fitted with very large hatch openings to facilitate cargo loading and unloading and these openings may represent points of weakness in the hull since they reduce the torsional resistance of the hull – explains that when bulk carriers are loaded with dense and heavy cargoes such as iron, dense ores or steel products they rely on large empty spaces in holds, ballast tanks, voids and forward tanks as reserve buoyancy to stay afloat and if seawater enters any of these spaces due to damaged hull, hatches, accesses, ventilators or air pipes, the vessel can lose buoyancy and sink very quickly		

适任 2.1	计划并确保在航行期间货物的安全装载、积载、系固、照管以及货物的卸载	IMO 参考书目
– 解释为何压载状态的浅吃水船舶易受拍底,随之产生船底损坏的危险 – 解释为何散货船的装货作业一直被认为是可能对船舶整体结构具有短期和长期影响的作业范畴 – 描述散货船的装载需要仔细考虑施加到船舶结构上的载荷 – 解释如果船舶集中装载高密度货物,则会产生高局部应力,特别是剪力,且装载中还可能造成局部损坏和疲劳 – 解释过大的装货速度可能造成高局部应力 – 描述高装货速率造成难以监控装货量 – 解释持续的过大应力对于疲劳具有累积作用 – 解释卸货造成与装货类似的问题 – 描述除了卸货相关问题之外,机械抓斗、推土机、液压锤和其他机械产生能削弱船舶结构的局部损坏和负荷 – 解释如计划和执行不当,卸货期间的压载作业也会增加船体应力 – 解释如同装货一样,卸货和压载时同样需要良好合作 – 解释为何维护和检查在散货船安全中起着重要作用 – 解释精心设计所有船舶操作限制以确保整体结构完整性 – 解释超过这些限制可能产生对结构的过大应力和导致灾难性的故障 – 解释船体结构被设计用来承受船舶重量静载荷、海水对船体的压力以及波浪和船舶运动产生的对船体的动态载荷 – 解释任何货舱超载都将增加船体结构的静压力,减小船舶在海上时船体结构承受动态载荷的能力 – 解释许多散货船具有非常大的舱口以便利装卸货,这些舱口可能意味着船体的弱点,因为它们减小了船体的扭转阻力 – 解释当散货船装载像铁、高密度矿石或钢产品等高密度和沉重的货物时,它们依靠货舱中大的空置处所、压载舱、空余处所和前部液舱来提供储备浮力,保持船舶浮于水中,如果船体、舱盖、入口、通风筒或透气管损坏导致海水进入任何这些处所,船舶可能损失浮力而飞快地下沉		

COMPETENCE 2.1	Plan and Ensure Safe Loading, Stowage, Securing, Care During the Voyage and Unloading of Cargoes	IMO Reference

- explains the need for all crew on the ship to be aware that any loss of buoyancy in forward spaces due to flooding will reduce the freeboard forward and dramatically increase the forces of extreme weather on hull structures and hatches
- explains why there is an urgent need for action if a ship takes on an unusual trim or heel, or if her motions become changed
- explains the vulnerability of the bulkhead in bulk carriers between number 1 and 2 holds identified by IACS and IMO and the potential consequences of this failing

7.2 SOLAS, chapter XII Additional safety measures for bulk carriers (1 hour)

- explains the regulations provided as additional safety measures for bulk carriers in chapter XII of the SOLAS Convention which apply to bulk carriers of 150 m in length and upwards, carrying high density dry bulk cargoes, including:
  - damage stability and flotation
  - structure of bulkheads and double bottoms
  - overall longitudinal strength in the flooded state
  - strength and flooding requirements for carrying cargoes with densities of 1,000 kg/m^3 or greater
  - the bulkhead strength requirements for carrying cargoes of 1,780 kg/m^3 or greater
  - hold loading
  - cargo density declarations
  - provision of a loading instrument
  - hold, ballast and dry space water ingress alarms
  - availability of pumping systems
  - restrictions from sailing with any hold empty
  - the imposition of restrictions on loading higher density cargoes and homogenous loading in adjacent holds, including the endorsement of loading information and marking of the ship
- explains that no bulk carrier over ten years old can carry a high density bulk cargo unless she has undergone either a periodical survey or a survey of her cargo holds to an equivalent extent, as required by regulation XII/7

7.3 CSR Bulk (1 hour)

- explains that the IACS Common Structural Rules (CSR) are classification society rules covering structural requirements for bulk carriers and tankers
- states that IACS Common Structural Rules (CSR) Bulk which contains structural requirements are applicable for bulk carriers with L > 90 m signed for construction after 1 April 2006
- explains that vessels built to CSR shall have overall safety of the hull structure equivalent to or better than that currently achieved by present rules

适任 2.1	**计划并确保在航行期间货物的安全装载、积载、系固、照管以及货物的卸载**	**IMO 参考书目**

- 解释需要船员意识到,由于大量进水前部空间浮力损失将减少前部的干舷,大大增加恶劣天气对船体结构和舱盖的作用力
- 解释如果船舶出现异常纵倾或横倾,或其运动发生变化,为什么需要紧急行动
- 解释由 IACS 和 IMO 确认的散货船 1 舱和 2 舱之间舱壁的弱点以及舱壁损坏的潜在后果

7.2　SOLAS 公约第 12 章有关散货船的附加安全措施(1 学时)

- 解释 SOLAS 公约第 12 章里的散货船附加安全措施规定适用于船长在 150 米及以上运载高密度干散货的散货船,包括如下方面的规定:
  - 破损稳性和浮态
  - 舱壁和双层底结构
  - 大量进水情况下的总纵强度
  - 对于运载密度为 1 000 kg/m³ 或以上的货物的强度和进水要求
  - 运载密度为 1 780 kg/m³ 或以上的货物的舱壁强度要求
  - 货舱装载
  - 货物密度声明
  - 装载仪的配备
  - 货舱、压载舱和干的空舱的进水报警
  - 泵系统的可用性
  - 任何空货舱下航行的限制
  - 对装载较高密度货物和邻近货舱同样装载的限制,包括装载信息和船舶标志的附加条款
- 解释超过 10 年的散货船不得运载高密度货物, 除非按照公约Ⅻ/7 规定进行了定期检验或对其货舱进行了同样程度的检验

7.3　CSR 散货船(1 学时)

- 解释 IACS 常见结构规则(CSR)是船级社对散货船和液货船的结构要求的规则
- 阐述 IACS 散货船常见结构规则(CSR)对散货船的结构要求适用于 2006 年 4 月 1 日以后签字建造的船长在 90 米以上的散货船
- 解释按 CSR 规则建造的船舶的整体安全性等于或优于现有规则达到的整体安全性

COMPETENCE 2.1	**Plan and Ensure Safe Loading, Stowage, Securing, Care During the Voyage and Unloading of Cargoes**	**IMO Reference**

- explains that the reasons for implementing these rules are:
  - to eliminate competition between class societies with respect to structural requirements and standards
  - to employ the combined experience and recourses of all IACS societies to develop a single standard, or set of rules
  - to fully embrace the intentions of the anticipated IMO requirements for goal based new construction standards
  - to ensure that a vessel meeting this new standard will be recognized by the industry as being at least as safe and robust as would have been required by any of the existing rules
- explains the general benefits of these rules
- discusses the critical areas of weakness identified in bulk carrier and tanker structure and the requirements for enhanced inspection identified in these rules

2.1.8 LOADING, CARE AND UNLOADING OF BULK CARGOES
Textbooks/Bibliography: B71, B72, B73, B74, B76, B77, B78, B88, B89, B95, B104, B106, B109, B110, B113, B117, B128, B129, B130, B146, B182, B193, B198
Teaching aids: A1, V59, V172
Required performances:

8.1 Application of all available shipboard data related to loading, care and unloading of bulk cargoes (5 hours)

- outlines and describes all relevant information to be appraised prior planning of loading a bulk cargo
- outlines the relevant publications, IMO codes and recommendations that should be referred to prior loading a bulk cargo:
  - SOLAS regulation VI/7 and the related Code of Practice for the Safe Loading and Unloading of Bulk Carriers (BLU Code)
  - International Maritime Solid Bulk Cargoes (IMSBC)
  - International Code for the Safe Carriage of Grain in Bulk
  - Code of Safe Practice for Cargo Stowage and Securing
- explains the procedure for loading a bulk cargo in detail
- prepares cargo stowage plans after carefully considering and assessing information such as seasonal load line zones, port restrictions, shipboard limits, e.g. draft, cargo capacity, stability, stresses and loading rates
- explains that prior to loading bulk cargo, the shipper should declare characteristics and density, stowage factor, angle of repose, amounts and special properties of the cargo
- explains that in preparing the vessel for a safe planning and cargo stowage, the loading and unloading sequences and other operational matters should be informed well in advance by the charterers/terminal
- explains the content of the loading manual

适任 2.1	计划并确保在航行期间货物的安全装载、积载、系固、照管以及货物的卸载	IMO 参考书目
– 解释遵守该规则是为了: – 消除船级社在结构要求和标准方面的竞争 – 利用 IACS 所有船级社共同的经验和资源制定一个单一的标准或一套规则 – 完全接受 IMO 对新建船舶标准将要提出的要求 – 确保满足新标准的船舶被行业认为至少像现行规则所要求的那样安全和坚固 – 解释这些规则的益处 – 讨论所发现的散货船和液货船结构的关键性的弱点和这些规则所确认的进一步检查的要求 2.1.8 散货的装载、照管与卸载 **教科书/参考文献**:B71, B72, B73, B74, B76, B77, B78, B88, B89, B95, B104, B106, B109, B110, B113, B117, B128, B129, B130, B146, B182, B193, B198 **教具**:A1, V59, V172 技能要求: **8.1 与散货的装载、照管和卸载有关的所有船舶数据的运用(5 学时)** – 概述计划装载散货之前需要评估的所有相关信息 – 概述在装载散货前所应参考的下列出版物、IMO 规则和指南: – SOLAS 规则 VI/7 规定和散货船安全装卸操作规则(BLU 规则) – 国际海运固体散货(IMSBC) – 国际散装谷物安全运输规则 – 积载与系固安全操作规则 – 详细解释散货装载程序 – 在仔细考虑和评估季节载重线区带、港口限制、船舶限制(例如吃水、装货能力、稳性、应力和装载速率)之后,准备货物配载图 – 解释在装载散货前,托运人应申报货物的性质和密度、积载因数、静止角、总量和特性 – 解释在准备船舶安全计划和货物积载过程中,承租人或码头方应通知装卸顺序和其他操作事项 – 解释装载手册的内容	

COMPETENCE 2.1	Plan and Ensure Safe Loading, Stowage, Securing, Care During the Voyage and Unloading of Cargoes	IMO Reference

- explains that the consumption of ship's bunkers, consumption/generation of fresh water, during the voyage should be taken into account when carrying out the stress and displacement calculations
- explains that loading and unloading sequences must consider the loading rate, the de-ballasting capacity and the applicable strength and draught limitations
- plans the loading, care and unloading of bulk cargoes using the ship's approved loading manual and the typical information provided
- describes the action that should be taken if the Master does not believe they have been provided with the required or correct information relating to the cargo to be loaded
- describes the requirements for the carriage of loading instruments
- describes the typical information that can be obtained from a loading instrument
- explains the certification, testing and use of a loading instrument
- utilizes a typical loading instrument to plan and monitor bulk carrier loading, ballast exchange and discharge operations

8.2 Code of practice for the safe loading and unloading of bulk carriers (BLU Code) (1 hour)

- outlines the contents of the Code of Practice for the Safe Loading and Unloading of Bulk Carriers (BLU Code) in relation to:
  - planning the sequence of operations
  - communications and coordination between ship and terminal
  - allocation of ships to appropriate terminals
  - condition of ships and terminal equipment
  - training of ship and terminal personnel
  - requirement to be familiar with and comply with local regulations
  - use of safety checklists
  - responsibility of the Master
  - additional considerations in relation to dangerous cargoes
  - the use of the BLU Manual by terminal staff
  - the impact of arrival and departure conditions on manoeuvrability
  - actions to minimize hull and local stress
  - actions to take where acceptable hull and local stress levels may be exceeded

2.1.9 SAFE CARGO HANDLING IN ACCORDANCE WITH THE PROVISIONS OF THE RELEVANT INSTRUMENTS — R56, R64

Textbooks/Bibliography: B21, B71, B72, B73, B74, B75, B76, B77, B78, B79, B80, B81, B82, B83, B88, B89, B90, B91, B92, B93, B94, B95, B97, B98, B011, B101, B102, B104, B106, B109, B110, B113, B117, B128, B129, B130, B146, B152, B153, B156, B157, B158, B159, B161, B162, B167, B182, B189, B190, B191, B192, B193, B196, B197, B198, B203, B215, B216, B217

Teaching aids: A1, V47, V48, V67

适任 2.1	计划并确保在航行期间货物的安全装载、积载、系固、照管以及货物的卸载	IMO 参考书目

– 解释当进行应力和排水量计算时,应考虑航次中的燃料消耗和淡水消耗/制造
– 解释装卸顺序必须考虑装载速率、排压载水能力、所适用的强度和吃水限制
– 利用经批准的船舶装载手册和提供的典型信息,计划散货的装载、照管和卸载
– 描述如果船长不相信已被提供与要装货物相关要求的信息或正确的信息,所应采取的行动
– 描述装载仪的配备要求
– 描述从装载仪可获得的典型信息
– 解释装载仪的认证、测试和使用
– 利用典型装载仪计划和监控散货船装载、换压载水和卸载作业
8.2 散货船安全装卸操作规则(BLU 规则)(1 学时)
– 概述散货船安全装卸操作规则(BLU 规则)的下列相关内容:
  – 计划作业顺序
  – 船舶和码头间的沟通与协调
  – 船舶与码头的适当配置
  – 船舶状况和码头设备
  – 船舶和码头的人员培训
  – 要熟悉和遵守当地规定的要求
  – 安全检查表的使用
  – 船长的责任
  – 有关危险货物的额外考虑
  – 码头员工对 BLU 手册的运用
  – 抵达与离开状况对操作性能的影响
  – 减少船体应力和局部应力的行动
  – 在可能超过可接受应力情况下采取的行动
 	
2.1.9 按照相关文件规定安全装卸货物
教科书/参考文献:B21, B71, B72, B73, B74, B75, B76, B77, B78, B79, B80, B81, B82, B83, B88, B89, B90, B91, B92, B93, B94, B95, B97, B98, B011, B101, B102, B104, B106, B109, B110, B113, B117, B128, B129, B130, B146, B152, B153, B156, B157, B158, B159, B161, B162, B167, B182, B189, B190, B191, B192, B193, B196, B197, B198, B203, B215, B216, B217
教具:A1, V47, V48, V67
		
		R56, R64

COMPETENCE 2.1	**Plan and Ensure Safe Loading, Stowage, Securing, Care During the Voyage and Unloading of Cargoes**	**IMO Reference**

Required performances:

Note that trainees must be familiar with the content and application of the IMDG Code, Intact Stability Code, IMSBC Code and MARPOL in relation to cargo handling from IMO model course 7.03. This knowledge is considered so fundamental for much of the management level content within this course that there is merit in reviewing the operational level content quickly before covering the additional elements required at management level. The learning time has been reduced for many elements on the basis that trainees will be reviewing rather than learning much of this content at this level. It may be necessary for some trainees to refresh their knowledge of such techniques before undertaking this management level content

9.1 Establish procedures for safe cargo handling in accordance with the provisions of the relevant instruments such as:

- **IMDG Code**
- **IMSBC Code**
- **MARPOL 73/78, Annexes III and V (3 hours)**

Note that this section aligns closely with competence 2.3 relating to the carriage of dangerous goods and that the content of competence 2.3 would normally be delivered prior to or in conjunction with this content

- explains the procedures that should be followed for accepting solid bulk cargoes, packaged dangerous goods and marine pollutants for shipment in terms of:
  - the required documentation
  - ensuring that the condition and labelling of the goods are fit for carriage
  - ensuring that the vessel is able to safely stow the cargo in terms of vessel certification, the ability to achieve separation and segregation requirements and the availability of any particular safety equipment that might be required
- develops stowage plans for cargoes that contain multiple packaged dangerous goods and ensure that separation and segregation requirements of IMDG, IMSBC and MARPOL are achieved
- prepares dangerous goods manifests and stowage plans in accordance with IMDG requirements
- discusses the preparations and precautions that should be taken prior to the handling of bulk cargoes, packaged dangerous goods and marine pollutants in terms of:
  - preparation of spaces
  - mooring of the ship
  - information exchange and communication with port and regulatory authorities
  - flag and light signals
  - provision of emergency, fire and protective equipment
- identifies the appropriate action to take in case of general and medical emergencies involving packaged dangerous goods using the EMS and MFAG guidance of the IMDG Code
- discusses the risks that might be created by undeclared dangerous goods or goods that are not packaged or separated/segregated in accordance with the IMDG Code

适任 2.1	计划并确保在航行期间货物的安全装载、积载、系固、照管以及货物的卸载	IMO 参考书目

技能要求:

注意:在完成这些要求的内容之前,学员必须熟悉 IMO 示范课程 7.03 中 IMDG 规则,完整稳性规则,IMSBC 规则和 MARPOL 公约中有关装卸货的内容及其适用。本课程中的知识对多数管理级内容非常重要,以至于在涉及管理级额外要求的知识点之前,在迅速复习操作级内容方面颇具价值。基于学员将复习而不是学习该级别内容,已经减少了许多知识点的学时。对某些学员而言,在学习管理级内容之前,可能有必要更新这些技能的知识

9.1　按照下列文件规定建立安全装卸货物程序:

- **IMDG 规则**
- **IMSBC 规则**
- **MARPOL 73/78, 附件Ⅲ和附件 V(3 学时)**

注意,本节应与危险货物装载有关的适任 2.3 紧密结合,且适任 2.3 的内容通常应在本内容之前或结合本内容进行讲授

- 解释按照下列应遵守的接受固体散货、包装危险品和海洋污染物的程序:
  - 所需文件
  - 确保货物状况和标志适于运载
  - 确保能按照船舶证书、满足隔离和分离要求的能力和可能要求的特殊设备的可用性来安全积载货物
- 制定包括多个包装危险品的货物配载图，确保达到 IMDG、IMSBC 和 MARPOL 的隔离要求
- 按照 IMDG 要求准备危险货物清单和配载图
- 讨论在装卸散货、包装危险品和海洋污染物之前在以下方面要做的准备工作和采取的预防措施:
  - 场所的准备
  - 船舶系泊
  - 与港口和主管当局的信息交换和沟通
  - 旗号和号灯
  - 提供紧急情况、消防和防护的设备
- 确定涉及包装危险品，在发生一般和医疗紧急情况下，利用 IMDG 规则的 EMS 和 MFAG 指南要采取的适当行动
- 讨论未申报的包装危险品、或未按照 IMDG 规则包装或分离 / 隔离货物产生的风险

COMPETENCE 2.1	Plan and Ensure Safe Loading, Stowage, Securing, Care During the Voyage and Unloading of Cargoes	IMO Reference

- explains that the loading and discharge of dangerous goods, bulk cargoes and marine pollutants may be subject to port and national regulations in loading and discharge ports in addition to the requirements of the IMO codes
- explains that there are procedures also given in the safety management system for the reporting of incidents involving the loss, or likely loss of harmful substances
- states that the ship carrying marine pollutants should have a special list or manifest or detailed plan showing the location of these goods as per MARPOL Annex III/4(3)
- states that the Master and chief mate should ensure that marine pollutants are stowed in the location specified in the special list or manifest or detailed plan
- states that the information provided on the special list or manifest should be compliant with section 5.4.3 of the IMDG Code as per MARPOL Annex III/4(3)
- states that the Master and chief mate should ensure that when marine pollutants or any other dangerous goods are loaded on their ship, they must be stowed as required by chapter 7.1, section 7.1.4 of the IMDG Code in order to comply with MARPOL Annex III/5
- states that to avoid accident which may lead to marine pollution, the Master and chief mate should take note that marine pollutants should not be placed on the outer row or out board stow at the side of the ship. In addition, if they are stowed on deck, they should be located in such a way that any leakage will not escape into the sea and containers are not in exposed location where they may be damaged by the action of the sea or weather
- states that as given in MARPOL Annex III/5, the Master and chief officer should ensure that when marine pollutants or any other dangerous goods are carried on their ship, the stowage and securing must be in accordance with the requirements of the Document of Compliance (DOC) and approved Cargo Securing Manual (CSM)
- states that the disposal of dry bulk cargo residues is regulated by the requirements of MARPOL Annex V which governs garbage disposal at sea
- states that as per the guidelines given in MARPOL Annex V, cargo-associated waste means all materials which have become wastes as a result of use on board a ship for cargo stowage and handling and this includes but is not limited to dunnage, shoring, pallets, lining and packing materials, plywood, paper, cardboard, wire, and steel strapping
- states that as per the guidelines given in MARPOL Annex V, operational wastes means all cargo–associated waste and maintenance waste, and cargo residues
- states that as per the guidelines given in MARPOL Annex V, cargo residues, expected to be in small quantities, are defined as the remnants of any cargo material on board that cannot be placed in proper cargo holds (loading excess and spillage) or which remain in cargo holds and elsewhere after unloading procedures are completed (unloading residual and spillage)
- states that this means that under the terms of MARPOL 73/78, discharge of cargo residues, except in limited safety circumstances, is prohibited until the ship is more than twelve nautical miles from the nearest land
- states that minimization of cargo residue wash down and discharge should form part of the ship's Garbage Management Plan and all residue discharges should be recorded as garbage category 4

适任 2.1	计划并确保在航行期间货物的安全装载、积载、系固、照管以及货物的卸载	IMO 参考书目
– 解释在装、卸港口,装卸危险品、散货和海洋污染物可能受除 IMO 规则外的港口和港口国的规定制约 – 解释在安全管理系统中还给出了涉及有害物质灭失或可能灭失的事故报告程序 – 阐述按照 MARPOL 附件Ⅲ/4(3),运输海洋污染物的船舶应当具有一张特别清单或舱单或详细的平面图标明这些货物的位置 – 阐述船长和大副应确保海洋污染物按特别清单或舱单或详细的平面图的位置积载 – 阐述按照 MARPOL 附件Ⅲ/4(3)要求特别清单或舱单上提供的信息应与 IMDG 规则 5.4.3 节相符 – 阐述当船上装载海洋污染物或其他危险品时,船长和大副应确保按 IMDG 第 7.1 章,7.1.4 节的要求积载,以符合 MARPOL 公约附件Ⅲ/5 规定 – 阐述为避免可能导致的海洋污染,船长和大副不应将海洋污染物放在较外一侧或积载在舷侧。此外,如将之积载于甲板上,应放在任何泄漏都不会流入海中的位置,集装箱不应放置在暴露于可能受海浪或风雨损坏处 – 阐述船长和大副应按 MARPOL 附件Ⅲ/5 规定装载海洋污染物或其他危险品,积载与系固应符合接受文件(DOC)的要求和货物系固手册(CSM)的认同 – 阐述干散货残渣应按 MARPOL 附件Ⅴ的规定处理,该附件规定了海上垃圾的处理 – 阐述按照 MARPOL 附件Ⅴ中的指南,与货物相关的废物是指由于用于船舶积载和装卸而成为废物的所有材料,这些包括但不限于衬垫、撑柱、草垫、衬料、包装材料、胶合板、纸张、纸板、钢丝绳和钢带 – 阐述按照 MARPOL 附件Ⅴ中的指南,可利用的废物意味着所有与货物有关的废物和维修产生的废弃物,以及货物的残渣 – 阐述按照 MARPOL 附件Ⅴ中的指南,预计少量的货物残渣被定义为船上货物材料的残留,没有合适的货舱可供装载(装载余数和漏损货)或在卸货程序完成后留在货舱或其他处所(卸货差额和地脚货) – 阐述这意味着按照 MARPOL 73/78 的规定,除了在有限的安全情况下以外,在距最近陆地 12 海里以内禁止卸载货物残渣 – 阐述减少冲洗后的货物残渣和卸载应为船舶垃圾管理计划的组成部分,所有卸载的残渣应作为第 4 类垃圾记载		

COMPETENCE 2.1	Plan and Ensure Safe Loading, Stowage, Securing, Care During the Voyage and Unloading of Cargoes	IMO Reference
– states that discharges of cargo residues also require start and stop positions to be recorded in the Garbage record book – states that cargo materials contained in the cargo hold bilge water is not treated as cargo residues provided that the cargo material is not classified as a marine pollutant in the IMDG Code and the bilge water is discharged from a loaded hold through the vessel's fixed piping bilge drainage system – explains that cargo residues are created through inefficiencies in loading, unloading and on-board handling – states that as cargo residues fall under the scope of these guidelines provided by MARPOL Annex V, it may, in certain cases, be difficult for port reception facilities to handle such residues and is therefore recommended that cargo be unloaded as efficiently as possible in order to avoid or minimize cargo residues – states that spillage of the cargo during transfer operations should be carefully controlled, both on board and from dockside and since this spillage typically occurs in port, it should be completely cleaned up prior to sailing and either delivered into the intended cargo space or into the port reception facility – states that areas on the ship where spillage is most common should be protected such that the residues are easily recovered		

2.1.10 EFFECTIVE COMMUNICATIONS AND IMPROVING WORKING RELATIONSHIPS
Required performances:
10.1 Basic principles for establishing effective communications and improving working relationships between ship and terminal personnel (1 hour)
– explains the necessity for effective communication and working relationships between ship and terminal
– outlines and describes the information that should be exchanged between the ship and terminal:
  – prior to ship's arrival
  – when arriving in a part loaded condition or with residues
  – for combination carriers (OBO or O/O)
  – in relation to the readiness of holds to load cargo
  – in ensuring that the plan and understanding of the operation is up to date and shared by both the ship and terminal
  – ensuring that the cargo declaration as required by chapter VI of SOLAS 1974 is completed
  – provisions for changing loading or unloading plans
– states that the loading plans should be kept by the ship and terminal for a period of six months
		R56, R64

适任 2.1	计划并确保在航行期间货物的安全装载、积载、系固、照管以及货物的卸载	IMO 参考书目
– 阐述在垃圾记录簿中还要求记录货物残渣卸载的开始船位和停止船位 – 阐述货舱污水井中所含货物如果不属于 IMDG 规则中的海洋污染物类别,则可不按货物残渣处理,通过所装货舱的固定污水排放管系排放 – 解释货物残渣由于不充分地装卸或操作而产生 – 阐述货物残渣属于 MARPOL 附件Ⅴ规定范畴，在某些情况下，港口接受设施存在困难,因此建议尽可能充分卸货以避免或减少货物残渣 – 阐述船舶和码头双方应注意在装卸货操作中控制货物溢漏，因为溢漏通常发生在港内,应在开航前清除,既可以送入原本要装的舱内,也可以送入港口接收设施 – 阐述应保护船上最经常发生溢漏的区域,以便回收残渣		

2.1.10 有效的沟通与改善工作关系
技能要求：
10.1 船舶和码头人员间建立有效沟通和改善工作关系的基本原则(1 学时)
– 解释船舶和码头间建立有效沟通和改善工作关系的必要性
– 概述船舶和码头间应交换的信息：
  – 抵达前
  – 到达时未满载或带有残渣
  – 多用途船(OBO 或 O/O)
  – 有关拟装货的准备
  – 确保作业计划和对其的理解都已更新,且为船舶和码头双方分享
  – 确保 SOLAS 1974 第Ⅵ章所要求的货物声明已经完成
– 阐述装载计划应当由船舶和码头双方保存 6 个月
		R56, R64

COMPETENCE 2.2	Assess Reported Defects and Damage to Cargo Spaces, Hatch Covers and Ballast Tanks and take appropriate action	IMO Reference
TRAINING OUTCOMES: Demonstrates a knowledge and understanding of: 2.2.1 LIMITATIONS ON STRENGTH OF THE VITAL CONSTRUCTIONAL PARTS OF A STANDARD BULK CARRIER AND INTERPRET GIVEN FIGURES FOR BENDING MOMENTS AND SHEAR FORCES 2.2.2 METHODS TO AVOID THE DETRIMENTAL EFFECTS ON BULK CARRIERS OF CORROSION, FATIGUE AND INADEQUATE CARGO HANDLING		STCW Code table A-II/2

<table>
<tr><td>适任 2.2</td><td>评估报告中的货舱、舱盖和压载舱的缺陷和损坏以及采取适当的行动</td><td>IMO
参考书目</td></tr>
<tr><td colspan="2">培训效果:

讲授下列内容知识与理解:
2.2.1　对标准散货船重要结构的强度限制和解释给出的弯矩与剪力数据
2.2.2　避免腐蚀、疲劳和不当装卸对散货船造成的不利影响的方法</td><td>STCW 公约
表 A-11/2</td></tr>
</table>

COMPETENCE 2.2	Assess Reported Defects and Damage to Cargo Spaces, Hatch Covers and Ballast Tanks and take appropriate action	IMO Reference
2.2.1 LIMITATIONS ON STRENGTH OF THE VITAL CONSTRUCTIONAL PARTS OF A STANDARD BULK CARRIER AND INTERPRET GIVEN FIGURES FOR BENDING MOMENTS AND SHEAR FORCES **Textbooks/Bibliography:** T35, B71, B72, B73, B74, B76, B77, B78, B88, B89, B95, B104, B106, B109, B110, B113, B117, B128, B129, B130, B146, B182, B193, B198 **Teaching aids:** A1, V60, V120, V121, V122, V155 Required performance: **1.1 Limitations on strength of the vital constructional parts of a standard bulk carrier and interpret given figures for bending moments and shear forces (3 hours)** – states that the longitudinally continuous upper deck of a bulk carrier suffers hull girder stress – explains that the longitudinal bending causes an axial force on the upper deck that may cause cracking of the deck plate at the locations where the stress is concentrated – states that bulk carriers have cargo hatchways for the convenience of cargo handling facilities – explains that these hatchways reduce the ship's torsional strength and invite concentrated stress at the hatchway corners which may be evident by cracking of the deck plates in these areas – states in this regard upper deck plating at hatchway corners is one of the focal points for cracking – explains that cross-deck strips come under stress by transverse bending – explains that the transverse bulkheads provide transverse strength to a bulk carrier and the cross-deck strips provide the strength to withstand the resultant axial forces in a transverse direction – explains that there are various types of cracking in the upper deck – states that those propagating from the cargo hatchways are generally considered serious to the ship's safety – explains that various metal fittings are welded to the upper deck plating and these installations may cause stress concentrations at the welded joints or have defects in the welds – states that deck platings in the vicinity of manholes, hatchside coaming end brackets, bulwark stays, crane post foundations and deck houses, etc. are to be carefully watched for cracking – states that hatch coamings are subjected to hull girder stress – explains that although they are not critical longitudinal strength members, they should be watched carefully to ensure that these cracks do not spread – states that the area around the corners of a main cargo hatch can be subjected to high cyclical stress due to the combined effect of hull girder bending moments, transverse and torsional loading – explains that discontinuous cargo hatch side coamings can be subjected to significant longitudinal bending stress – explains that this introduces additional stresses at the mid-length of hatches and stress concentrations at the termination of the side coaming extensions		R63

适任 2.2	评估报告中的货舱、舱盖和压载舱的缺陷和损坏以及采取适当的行动	IMO 参考书目
2.2.1 对标准散货船重要结构的强度限制和解释给出的弯矩与剪力数据 **教科书/参考文献**:T35, B71, B72, B73, B74, B76, B77, B78, B88, B89, B95, B104, B106, B109, B110, B113, B117, B128, B129, B130, B146, B182, B193, B198 **教具**:A1, V60, V120, V121, V122, V155 技能要求: **1.1 对标准散货船重要结构的强度限制和解释给出的弯矩与剪力数据(3 学时)** – 阐述散货船纵通上甲板所受相当船体梁总应力 – 解释纵向弯曲产生对上甲板的轴向力,可能引起应力集中处的甲板板开裂 – 阐述散货船具有货舱口以便利装卸货设备 – 解释这些货舱口减小船舶扭转强度且在舱口角引发集中应力,这些地方可能常见甲板板开裂 – 阐述就此而言,货舱舱口角上甲板是开裂的焦点之一 – 解释甲板上的横贯带承受横向弯曲应力 – 解释横舱壁提供散货船的横向强度,甲板上的横贯带提供强度承受横向的轴向合力 – 解释上甲板上有各种裂纹 – 解释那些在货舱舱口处产生的裂纹严重危及船舶安全 – 解释各种金属配件焊接到上甲板上,这些装置可能在焊接处造成集中应力或焊缝缺陷 – 阐述要注意仔细检查人孔、舱口围板端肘板、舷樯支柱、克令吊基座和甲板室等附近的甲板板裂纹 – 阐述舱口围遭受相当船体梁总应力 – 解释尽管它们不是纵向强度的关键结构,也应仔细检查以确保裂纹没有扩散 – 阐述由于相当船体梁弯矩、横向和扭转载荷的共同作用,舱口角周围区域可能遭受周期性应力 – 解释不连续的货舱舱口围侧板可能遭受显著的纵向弯曲应力 – 解释这在舱口中部形成额外应力,在边围板延伸部分的端部形成集中应力		R63

COMPETENCE 2.2	Assess Reported Defects and Damage to Cargo Spaces, Hatch Covers and Ballast Tanks and take appropriate action	IMO Reference
– explains that hatch cover operations, in combination with poor maintenance, can result in damage to cleats and gasket, leading to the loss of weathertight integrity of the hold spaces – states that damage to hatch covers can also be sustained by mishandling and overloading of deck cargoes – states that the marine environment, the humid atmosphere due to the water vapour from the cargo in cargo holds, and the high temperature on deck and hatch cover plating due to heating from the sun may result in accelerated corrosion of plating and stiffeners making the structure more vulnerable to the exposures described above – states that when carrying out visual inspection, special attention should be paid to areas where pipes, e.g. fire main pipes, hydraulic pipes and pipes for compressed air, are fitted close to the plating, making proper maintenance of the protective coating difficult to carry out – states that cracking may be initiated at defects in welded joints and metal fittings to the coamings that will invite stress concentration – states that such cracking is considered serious to the ship's safety because it may be the initiation of a fracture on a large scale – states that on typical bulk carriers, the topside and bilge hopper tanks compose a double hull surrounding the cargo space, which together with the double bottom provides hull strength and rigidity – states that if corrosion and waste become excessive, failure of hold frames invites additional loads to the adjacent ones, which may lead to failure throughout the side shell structure – explains that the transverse bulkheads may also be susceptible to accelerated corrosion, particularly at the mid height and at the bottom – states that particular care should be exercised when inspecting hold frames – states that the transverse bulkheads, in that these members may appear in deceptively good condition – states that the tank top and side shell plating generally corrodes from the steel surface facing the cargo hold, and corrosion from inside the double bottom is usually less than that from the cargo hold side – states that cargo hold frames should also be carefully inspected for mechanical damage, corrosion and waste, because many cargoes will damage hold frames through direct contact – states that this damage will invite corrosion from seawater brought on board in loading operations – states that the most important aspects of cargo hold inspections are the condition of side shell structures and their reinforcements – states that special attention should be paid to the condition of hold frames and their connection to the shell plating – outlines and describes the common damage/defects that may occur on watertight transverse bulkheads situated at the ends of dry cargo holds of a bulk carrier – states that cracks may often be found at or near the connection of the stool of the transverse bulkhead and the tanktop in bulk carriers having combination cargo/ballast holds		

适任 2.2	评估报告中的货舱、舱盖和压载舱的缺陷和损坏以及采取适当的行动	IMO 参考书目
– 解释舱盖作业与保养不力可能导致夹板和垫片损坏,进而破坏货舱的风雨密完整性 – 阐述甲板货的错误操作和超载也能造成对舱盖的损坏 – 阐述海洋环境、由货舱货物产生的水蒸气形成的湿气和由于甲板与舱盖板遭受日晒产生的高温都可能导致板材和扶强材的加速腐蚀,使得该结构更易由此受损 – 阐述进行视觉检查时,应特别注意像消防总管、液压管和压缩空气管等管系附近区域的钢板,这些管系使得难以进行正常的防护涂漆保养 – 阐述裂纹可能起始于焊点的缺陷和引起应力集中的舱口围金属配件 – 解释这种裂纹对船舶安全是严重威胁,因其可能是大范围断裂的开始 – 阐述典型的散货船上,顶边舱和底边压载舱在货舱四周形成双层船壳,与双层底一起提供了船舶的强度和刚度 – 阐述如腐蚀和损耗过大,货舱框架损坏对附近结构造成额外负荷,将可能导致船壳板的整体损坏 – 解释横舱壁也可能遭受加速腐蚀,尤其在中部和底部 – 阐述在检查货舱框架时应特别注意 – 阐述横舱壁处的框架可能看似状况良好 – 阐述液舱顶部和舷侧边板一般从面向货舱的钢板表面开始腐蚀,来自双层底内部的腐蚀通常小于来自货舱一侧的腐蚀 – 阐述还应仔细检查货舱框架受机械损坏、腐蚀和损耗情况,因为许多货物通过直接接触会损坏货舱框架 – 阐述装载航行中船舶上浪造成的海水腐蚀会导致该项损坏 – 阐述最重要的检查方面是舷侧板结构及其加强材的状况 – 阐述应特别注意货舱框架及其与船壳板的连接处 – 概述散货船干货舱端部的水密横舱壁可能出现的常见损坏 / 缺陷 – 阐述在散货船上,裂纹可常见于横舱壁底部与货舱顶部连接处或附近起连接货舱 / 压载舱的区域		

COMPETENCE 2.2	Assess Reported Defects and Damage to Cargo Spaces, Hatch Covers and Ballast Tanks and take appropriate action	IMO Reference

– states that wastage/corrosion may affect the integrity of steel hatch covers and the associated moving parts, e.g. cleats, pot-lifts, roller wheels, etc.
– explains that deformation/twisting of exposed structure above deck, such as side-coaming brackets and bulwarks, may result from impact due to improper handling of cargo and cargo handling machinery
– explains that such damages may also be caused by shipping of green sea water on deck in heavy weather
– outlines and describes other fractures that may occur in the deck plating at hatches and in connected coamings
– outlines and describes the damages caused by cargoes in cargo holds, especially to tank top plating and side:
  – at loading and unloading ports for coal or iron ore, large grab buckets, high-capacity cargo
  – loaders, bulldozers and pneumatic hammers may be employed for cargo handling operations
  – large grab buckets may cause considerable damage to tank top plating when being dropped to grab cargo
  – use of bulldozers and pneumatic hammers may also be harmful to cargo hold structures and may result in damage to tank tops, bilge hoppers, hold frames and end brackets
  – lumber cargoes may also cause damage to the cargo hold structures of smaller bulkers that are employed in the carriage of light bulk cargoes and lumbers
– states that side stringers and/or side shells in way of No. 1 cargo hold along the collision bulkhead are often found cracked
– explains that this kind of damage is considered to be caused by insufficient continuity between forepeak construction and cargo hold structure
– explains that on large bulk carriers such as capsize and panamax bulkers, bilge hopper plating around the knuckle line may be cracked along the bilge hopper transverse webs
– states that this is considered to be caused by insufficient local reinforcement
– states that though the water ballast tanks of newer bulk carriers are well protected against corrosion, the upper portion is susceptible to corrosion because the protective coating will easily deteriorate due to heat from the upper deck and the cyclic wet/dry effect of seawater
– states that cracks may be found at the intersections of longitudinal and transverse members
– states that cracks may be found in the side, bottom and/or tank top longitudinal at intersections with solid floors or bilge hopper transverses
– states that cracks also may be found in the floors or transverses occurring at the corners of the slots cut for longitudinal
– states that longitudinal may be cracked at the ends of additional (partial) side girders provided in the double bottom below cargo hold bulkheads or at the side walls of bilge wells for cargo holds, due to additional stress concentration caused by the structural discontinuity at those connections		

适任 2.2	评估报告中的货舱、舱盖和压载舱的缺陷和损坏以及采取适当的行动	IMO 参考书目

– 阐述腐蚀/损耗可影响钢质舱盖及其连接运动部件的完整性,如夹板、罐状千斤顶和滚轮等
– 阐述甲板上露天的结构,如舱口围侧板支架、舷樯可能由于不当的货物操作和装货机械的操作而引起变形/扭转
– 解释这种损坏也可由恶劣天气船舶大量上浪所引起
– 概述其他断裂也可在舱口与舱口围连接处甲板板出现
– 概述货舱内的货物造成的损坏,特别是对货舱顶部钢板和侧板:
  – 在港口装卸煤炭或铁矿、大型抓斗、高容量货物
  – 可能用装载机、推土机和气锤进行装卸货作业
  – 当下落抓货时,大型抓斗可能对货舱顶板造成相当大的损坏
  – 推土机和气锤的使用也可能对货舱结构有害,导致对货舱顶部、边压载舱、货舱框架和端部支架的损坏
  – 木材货物也可能造成对小型散货船货舱结构的损坏,这类船舶被用来运输轻散货和木材
– 阐述 1 号货舱的舷侧纵桁和/舷侧船壳板在沿防撞舱壁方向常发现开裂
– 解释这种损坏被认为是由于艏尖舱结构与货舱结构之间缺乏连续性所致
– 解释在像好望角型和巴拿马型这样的大型散货船上,折角线周围的底边压载舱钢板可能沿着底边压载舱横向框架开裂
– 解释这被认为是由于缺乏局部加强所致
– 阐述尽管新建散货船的压载水舱防腐蚀保护很好,但上部易受腐蚀,因为防护漆由于来自上部甲板的热量和海水周期性的干/湿影响而易于恶化
– 阐述可能在纵向部件和横向部件交接处发现裂纹
– 阐述可能在舷侧、底部和/或液舱顶部与固定底板或底边压载舱横向框架交接处发现裂纹
– 阐述还可能在底板上或为纵向结构所开槽的角部的横断面处发现裂纹
– 阐述纵向部件可能在散货舱端部下面的双层底里的附加(部分)侧梁端部或货舱污水井侧壁开裂,由于这些连接处不连续结构引起额外的集中应力所致		

COMPETENCE 2.2	Assess Reported Defects and Damage to Cargo Spaces, Hatch Covers and Ballast Tanks and take appropriate action	IMO Reference

- states that cracks may be observed in transverse webs in bilge hoppers initiating from the slot openings for longitudinal and at the knuckled corners of the lower ends of the hoppers
- states that corrosion accelerated by heat has been observed in double-bottom water ballast tanks adjacent to fuel oil tanks
- states that in recent years, the grade of bunker oil being used requires the temperature in the tank to be 80°C or more and such a temperature can accelerate corrosion of the steel in the tanks, particularly in the vicinity of the boundaries of the fuel oil tanks
- states that bottom plates are often eroded under the suction bellmouths in tank
- states that a sounding pipe has a pad plate at its bottom end for protection of the tank bottom against the strike of the sounding scale's lead and extent of diminution of the protection plate should be examined during inspections
- states that connection trunks provided between topside and bilge hopper spaces are to be carefully watched for signs of corrosion and waste of the steelworks inside
- explains that on some bulk carriers, bilge hopper tanks and topside tanks form one integral tank connected with trunk spaces
- states that the inside surface of a connection trunk is liable to corrosion and should be examined carefully

INTERPRET GIVEN FIGURES FOR BENDING MOMENTS AND SHEAR FORCES

- states that the bulk carriers are assigned 2 sets of permissible still water shear forces (SWSF) and still water bending moment (SWBM) limit to each ship, namely:
  - seagoing (at sea) SWSF and SWBM limits
  - harbour (in port) SWSF and SWBM limits
- states that the seagoing SWSF and SWBM limits should not be exceeded when the ship is put to sea or during any part of a seagoing voyage
- explains that in harbour, where the ship is in sheltered water and is subjected to reduced dynamic loads, the hull girder is permitted to carry a higher level of stress imposed by the static loads
- states that the harbour SWSF and SWBM limits should not be exceeded during any stage of harbour cargo operations
- explains that when a ship is floating in still water, the ship's lightweight (the weight of the ship's structure and its machinery) and deadweight (all other weights, such as the weight of the bunkers, ballast, provisions and cargo) are supported by the global buoyancy up thrust acting on the exterior of the hull
- explains that along the ship's length there will be local differences in the vertical forces of buoyancy and the ship's weight and these unbalanced net vertical forces acting along the length of the ship causes the hull girder to shear and to bend, inducing a vertical still water shear force (SWSF) and still water bending moment (SWBM) at each section of the hull
- explains that at sea, the ship is subjected to cyclical shearing and bending actions induced by continuously changing wave pressures acting on the hull
- explains that these cyclical shearing and bending actions give rise to an additional component of dynamic, wave induced, shear force and bending moment in the hull girder

适任 2.2	评估报告中的货舱、舱盖和压载舱的缺陷和损坏以及采取适当的行动	IMO 参考书目

- 阐述在底边压载舱起始于为纵向结构的开口槽的横向框架上或在底边压载舱下部的折角处可能发现裂纹
- 解释在邻近燃料舱的双层底压载舱里,可发现由热所致加速腐蚀
- 阐述近年来,所用燃料等级要求液舱内温度达到 80℃或以上,如此高温能加速液舱钢板的腐蚀,特别在燃料舱四周区域
- 阐述在液舱喇叭形吸口下部的底板常被腐蚀
- 阐述测深管的底部有一个保护垫板,保护液舱底部免受测深铅锤的击打,检查期间应检验该保护板的减少程度
- 阐述仔细检查顶边舱和底边压载舱连通管里的钢质构件的腐蚀和损耗程度
- 解释在某些散货船上,底边压载舱和顶边舱通过导管连接形成一个整体液舱
- 阐述连接导管的内表面易受腐蚀,应仔细检查

解释给出的弯矩与剪力数据

- 阐述每艘散货船有两套指定的许用静水剪力(SWSF)和静水弯矩(SWBM)极限,即:
  - 远洋(海上)SWSF 和 SWBM 极限
  - 港口(港内)SWSF 和 SWBM 极限
- 阐述当船舶开航出海或在远航期间,不应超过海上 SWSF 和 SWBM 极限
- 解释在港内,船舶处于遮蔽水域且所受动态载荷减小,允许船体梁承受较大级别的静态应力负荷
- 阐述在任何港口货物作业期间,不应超过港内 SWSF 和 SWBM 极限
- 解释当船在静水中时,船舶空船重量(船舶结构及其机械设备重量)和载重量(所有其他重量,例如燃料、压载水、食品和货物的重量)均由作用于船体外部的总浮力所支撑
- 解释沿船长方向,将存在局部的垂向上的浮力与重力差,这些不平衡的净垂直力沿船长方向的作用造成船体梁剪切和弯曲,导致船体每一部分的垂直静水剪力(SWSF)和静水弯矩(SWBM)
- 解释在海上船舶遭受周期性的剪切和弯曲作用,这是由于连续变化的波浪压力作用在船体所致
- 解释这些周期性的剪切和弯曲作用在船体梁上产生一个附加的动态的、波浪引起的剪力和弯矩分量

COMPETENCE 2.2	Assess Reported Defects and Damage to Cargo Spaces, Hatch Covers and Ballast Tanks and take appropriate action	IMO Reference

- explains that at any one time, the hull girder is subjected to a combination of still water and wave induced shear forces and bending moments
- explains that the stresses in the hull section caused by these shearing forces and bending moments are carried by continuous longitudinal structural members
- explains that these structural members are the strength deck, side shell and bottom shell plating and longitudinals, inner bottom plating and longitudinals, double bottom girders and topside and hopper tank sloping plating and longitudinals, which are generally defined as the hull girder
- states that over-loading will induce greater stresses in the double bottom, transverse bulkheads, hatch coamings, hatch corners, main frames and associated brackets of individual cargo holds, and it can be observed as:
  - increased stress at hatch corners and coamings
  - increased stress in main frames and brackets
  - increased stress in double bottom structure
  - increased stress in transverse bulkhead
  - increased stress in cross deck strip
  - greater distortion of topside tank
- states that exceeding the permissible limits specified in the ship's approved loading manual will lead to over-stressing of the ship's structure and may result in catastrophic failure of the hull structure
- states that when deviating from the cargo load conditions contained in the ship's approved loading manual, it is necessary to ensure that both the global and local structural limits are not exceeded
- explains that all officers should be aware over-stressing of local structural members can occur even when the hull girder still water shear forces (SWSF) and bending moments (SWBM) are within their permissible limits
- analyses and interprets the causes and effects of shearing forces and bending moments on ship's structures
- demonstrates the knowledge gained on the fore mentioned topics by interpreting given figures for bending moments and shear forces
 	
2.2.2 METHODS TO AVOID THE DETRIMENTAL EFFECTS ON BULK CARRIERS OF CORROSION, FATIGUE AND INADEQUATE CARGO HANDLING (3 hours)
- states that deterioration of structure through corrosion, fatigue and damage is identified as a principal factor in the loss of many bulk carriers
- states that failing to identify such deterioration may lead to sudden and unexpected failure
- states that it is critical to inspect the cargo holds, ballast tanks and vital constructional parts of the bulk carriers, after every operation to ensure rapid action can be taken if the inspection reveals any cracks, fracture or other damages
- states that internal degradation through corrosion may be accelerated through chemical action from certain cargoes
- states that certain cargoes, including coal, phosphates and sulphur, transported by bulk carriers can rapidly corrode the hold side frames and promote fractures		

适任 2.2	评估报告中的货舱、舱盖和压载舱的缺陷和损坏以及采取适当的行动	IMO 参考书目
– 解释船体梁在任何时候都经受静水剪力和弯矩与波浪引起的剪力和弯矩的共同作用 – 解释这些剪力和弯矩所致的船舶部分,包括强甲板、侧板、底板、内底板、双层底梁、顶边舱和斜边舱,所受应力由连续纵向部件承受 – 阐述超载会在双层底、横舱壁、舱口围、舱口四周、每个货舱的主框架及其相连肘板产生更大应力,它可被看作是: 　– 在舱口围和舱口四周增加的应力 　– 在主框架和肘板上增加的应力 　– 在双层底结构上增加的应力 　– 在横舱壁上增加的应力 　– 在甲板上的横贯带上增加的应力 　– 顶边舱更大的变形 – 阐述超过批准的船舶装载手册中的许用极限将导致船舶结构应力过大,可能导致船舶结构灾难性的故障 – 阐述对于包含在批准的船舶装载手册中的装货状态,有必要确保不超过整体结构和局部结构的极限 – 解释所有高级船员应意识到,即使船体相当梁静水剪力(SWSF)和静水弯矩(SWBM)处于许用极限内,也可能发生局部结构部件应力过大情况 – 分析并说明船体剪力和弯矩的原因、影响 – 通过给定的弯矩和剪力数据说明来展示获得前述主题的知识 2.2.2 避免腐蚀、疲劳和不当装卸对散货船造成不利影响的方法(3 学时) – 阐述腐蚀、疲劳和损坏造成的结构恶化被认为是许多散货船灭失的一个主要因素 – 阐述未能识别此类恶化可能导致突然和意外的故障 – 阐述关键是散货船每次作业后检查货舱、压载舱和重大结构部件,以确保如检查发现裂纹、断裂或其他损坏,能迅速采取行动 – 阐述与某些货物的化学反应可能加速腐蚀造成的内部老化 – 阐述散货船运输包括煤、磷酸盐和硫在内的某些货物可能会迅速腐蚀货舱舷侧肋骨,加速断裂		

COMPETENCE 2.2	**Assess Reported Defects and Damage to Cargo Spaces, Hatch Covers and Ballast Tanks and take appropriate action**	**IMO Reference**

- states that the scouring effect of abrasive cargoes may cause hold coatings to deteriorate rapidly
- explains that corrosive effects of some cargoes like coal which produces acidic conditions, accelerates the rate of deterioration of internal structures in cargo holds and welds in particular
- explains that since bulk carriers tend to have low freeboard the uppermost continuous deck and other fittings including hatch covers are prone to exposure to green seas, which may again cause accelerated corrosion, and in some cases even structural damages which may again lead to catastrophic result, if not detected early and appropriate action taken
- states that since improper cleaning during hold cleaning leads to accelerated corrosion all crew should be well trained for hold cleaning, and proper checks to be made after the holds have been cleaned, to ensure no remnants of previous cargo is left behind
- states that in ballast holds, sloshing forces due to partially filled spaces during ballast exchange at sea may result in damage to the structure and this damage may go unnoticed if it is in inaccessible positions; this has to be borne in mind while carrying out inspections
- states that coatings are the first barriers to protect metal surfaces against corrosion
- states that ballast exchange, especially for cargo hold, can also cause accelerated corrosion, if the hold has any exposed, unprotected steel surface
- states that intact coatings prevent corrosion of the steel surface, however a local absence of coating (due to coating depletion, deterioration, damage, etc.) can result in corrosion rates similar or greater than those of unprotected steel
- states that periodic inspections at appropriate intervals and repair of coating as required are effective in minimizing corrosion damage
- states that to ensure that such exposures are not neglected, all officers should be well trained in identifying and reporting to the chief officer or the Master
- states that care should be taken to tend any unprotected surfaces in cargo holds caused due to any reasons, after carefully examining the structure for any signs of fatigue or fracture
- states that hold cleaning, ballasting at sea and ballast exchange carried out at sea are vulnerable aspects of a bulk carrier operation, and thus to avoid any kind of undue stress, proper, careful procedures, specified in loading manual, ballast water management plan, among others should be followed
- explains that bulkheads, trunks and ballast tank boundaries in single sideskin bulk carriers can present “hard spots” that concentrate forces where the change in construction occurs (e.g. longitudinal to transverse framing) that may lead to undetected fractures, hence careful examination at periodic intervals is necessary
- states that damage to bow plating is possible through impacts associated with swinging or loosely stowed anchors and may cause an initiating fracture or fatigue in bow shell plating that could lead to failure and subsequent flooding
- states that internal integrity of forward spaces (that are usually used for ballast and/or stores) is therefore of vital importance

适任 2.2	**评估报告中的货舱、舱盖和压载舱的缺陷和损坏以及采取适当的行动**	**IMO 参考书目**
– 阐述磨蚀性货物的侵蚀作用可能使货舱涂料迅速老化 – 解释像煤这样的货物的腐蚀作用产生酸性环境,加速货舱内部结构特别是焊缝的老化速率 – 解释由于散货船往往有低干舷,其最上层连续甲板和包括舱盖的其他配件容易遭受海浪冲刷,这可能会再次导致加速腐蚀,在某些情况下,甚至会导致结构破坏,如果没有尽早发现和采取适当行动,则有可能导致灾难性的结果 – 阐述由于洗舱中的不当清洗导致加速腐蚀,应对所有船员进行良好的洗舱训练,洗后适当检查以确保无先前货物残留 – 阐述在货舱压载情况下,海上换压载水期间,由于未满载空间的泼溅力可能导致对结构的损坏。如该损坏位于不易接近处所,则不易被发现;检查时应牢记此点 – 阐述涂料是保护金属表面免受腐蚀的第一道屏障 – 阐述换压载水,特别是货舱压载水,如果货舱存在暴露而未保护的钢表面,则也可能造成加速腐蚀 – 阐述完整涂层可防止钢材表面腐蚀,然而,局部涂层缺失(由于涂层损耗、变质、损坏等)可能会导致腐蚀速率类似或大于无保护的钢材 – 阐述以适当间隔定期检查,必要时修补涂层在减小腐蚀损坏方面是有效的 – 阐述要确保此类暴露不被忽略,在发现问题和向大副或船长报告方面,应对所有高级船员进行良好训练 – 阐述在仔细检查任何原因造成的结构疲劳或断裂迹象之后,应注意照料货舱里未保护钢材表面 – 阐述在海上洗舱和压载以及换压载水都是散货船易受损的方面,因此为避免任何不当的应力,应遵守装载手册中规定的正当、细致的程序、压载水管理计划以及其他方面的要求 – 解释横舱壁、连通管和单壳散货船的压载舱边界区域,可能出现使力集中于结构变化(例如纵向骨架向横向过渡)处的“硬点”,这可能导致无法探测的断裂,因此有必要进行周期性的定期仔细检查 – 阐述回转或锚收放不牢可能造成船首钢板损坏, 造成船首船壳板初始断裂或疲劳,可能引发故障和随之而来的进水 – 阐述艏部空间(通常用作压载舱和/或物料间)内部完整性至关重要		

COMPETENCE 2.2	Assess Reported Defects and Damage to Cargo Spaces, Hatch Covers and Ballast Tanks and take appropriate action	IMO Reference

- states that to prevent this from happening, the anchor must be fully hauled-in, stowed and retained in position by the lashing arrangement provided, ensuring there is three-point contact of anchor with the ship side at all given times
- states that corrosion degradation will seriously reduce the ability of plating and stiffening to withstand the forces to which it will be subjected
- states that any external forces – horizontal and/or vertical – may cause hatch cover dislodgement
- states that the cargo hatchway, if it loses its protection in this way, is a major access for water ingress and a serious threat to the integrity of the hull
- states that to ensure such thing does not happen, the hatch covers must be stowed, secured, battened down at all given times
- states that metal fatigue is the progressive failure of metal under cyclic loading and as the name "fatigue" implies, it is a mode of degradation in which the steel is worked until it simply gets tired
- states that bulk carriers are susceptible to many modes of cyclic forces that combine with other forces acting upon the vessel's structure and over time these cyclic stresses can seriously weaken the vessel's structural capacity
- states that fatigue failure may result due to loss of cross-sectional area in the plating joints
- states the areas that are prone to fatigue cracks in the cargo holds, which have to be carefully examined during routine, periodic, scheduled inspections, are:
  - corrugated bulkhead
  - shedder plate
  - inner bottom longitudinal (tank top)
  - side frames
  - side longitudinals
  - hopper tank
  - lower stool
  - toes of the hatch coaming termination brackets
- states that carriage of high density cargoes can cause buckling, structural deformities over a period of years, which can result in acceleration of corrosion and fatigue
- states that many terminals have the practice of dislodging cargo from side shell, frames, hoppers using mechanical grabs, bulldozers, hydraulic hammers, and other machineries
- states that these machineries produce local damage and loading that can weaken the ship's structure
- states that precaution must be taken to ensure the terminals are instructed not to use any machinery which may cause damage, clearly, during the formal filling and agreeing as per the ship/shore checklist, contained in the BLU Code, and duty officers to be instructed to stop any such activities that may endanger the ship's structure, also bringing it to the notice of Master
- states that buckling of plating caused due to high density cargoes, found generally on cargo hold tank tops, can lead to fractures or accelerated corrosion, if not inspected thoroughly

适任 2.2	评估报告中的货舱、舱盖和压载舱的缺陷和损坏以及采取适当的行动	IMO 参考书目
– 阐述为防止此类情况发生,必须将锚完全收紧,用配备的绑扎设施将锚安放和保留在固定位置,始终使锚的三点与船壳板保持接触 – 阐述腐蚀老化会减少板材和加强材对力的承受能力 – 阐述任何外力——水平的或纵向的——都可能造成舱盖位移 – 阐述货舱舱口,如果以这种方式失去保护,是主要的进水途径,对整个船体是严重威胁 – 阐述为确保不发生此情况,舱盖必须始终应安放、系固、压牢 – 阐述金属疲劳是一种金属在周期性载荷下的渐进式的失效,正如“疲劳”之名所指的那样,它是一种钢铁在受力下逐渐老化的模式,直至它完全变得疲劳 – 阐述散货船易受到多种周期性的应力与其他力共同作用于其结构,时间一久,这些周期性受力可能严重削弱船舶结构性能 – 阐述疲劳失效可能由于板材横截面上的结合处损坏而发生 – 阐述货舱中易于产生疲劳裂纹,在日常周期性例行检查中必须仔细检验的部位如下: 　– 波形舱壁 　– 挡水板 　– 纵向内底板(液舱顶部) 　– 舷侧肋骨 　– 舷侧纵骨 　– 底边压载舱 　– 下部基座 　– 舱口围端部围座突出部分 – 阐述常年运输高密度货物可能引起弯曲、结构变形,导致加快腐蚀和疲劳 – 阐述许多码头有用机械抓斗、推土机、气锤和其他机械将货物从船壳、肋骨和料斗卸载的习惯做法 – 阐述这些机械产生局部损伤和可能削弱船舶结构的载荷 – 阐述在按照 BLU 规则正式填写船/岸检查表和协议时,必须采取预防措施来保证明确告诫码头方不要使用可能造成损坏的机械,指示值班驾驶员制止任何可能危及船舶结构的此类行动,还应将之告知船长 – 阐述由于装载高密度货物引起的钢板变形通常发生在货舱下的液舱顶部,如不彻底检查,则可能导致断裂或加速腐蚀		

COMPETENCE 2.2	**Assess Reported Defects and Damage to Cargo Spaces, Hatch Covers and Ballast Tanks and take appropriate action**	**IMO Reference**
– states that damage to side shell caused externally through contact with docksides or tugs and internally from impact by cargo dislodging equipment during discharge can result in initiating fractures and/or fatigue of the structure – states that careful examination is of prime importance after any such incidents, to assess the extent of damage and action required.		

适任 2.2	评估报告中的货舱、舱盖和压载舱的缺陷和损坏以及采取适当的行动	IMO 参考书目
– 阐述由于与码头或拖船接触而从外部对船壳板造成的损坏,或卸货期间由于卸货设备撞击产生的内部损坏,都可能导致结构的初始断裂和/或疲劳 – 阐述发生上述事故后,为评估损坏程度和需要采取的行动所做的仔细检查极其重要		

COMPETENCE 2.3	Carriage of Dangerous Goods	IMO Reference
TRAINING OUTCOMES: Demonstrates a knowledge and understanding of 2.3.1 INTERNATIONAL REGULATIONS, STANDARDS, CODES INCLUDING THE INTERNATIONAL MARITIME DANGEROUS GOODS (IMDG) CODE AND THE INTERNATIONAL MARITIME SOLID BULK CARGOES (IMSBC) CODE AND RECOMMENDATIONS ON CARRIAGE OF DANGEROUS CARGOES 2.3.2 CARRIAGE OF DANGEROUS, HAZARDOUS AND HARMFUL CARGOES; PRECAUTIONS DURING LOADING AND UNLOADING AND CARE DURING THE VOYAGE OF DANGEROUS, HAZARDOUS AND HARMFUL CARGOES		STCW Code table A-II/2

适任 2.3	危险货物运输	IMO 参考书目
培训效果: 讲授下列内容知识与理解: 2.3.1 国际规定、标准、规则和建议的内容,包括《国际海运危险货物规则》(IMDG)和《国际海运固体散货规则》(IMSBC 规则) 2.3.2 危险货物、有毒货物和有害货物的运载;装卸期间的预防措施及危险货物、有毒货物和有害货物航行期间的照管		STCW 公约 表 A-Ⅱ/2

COMPETENCE 2.3	Carriage of Dangerous Goods	IMO Reference
2.3.1 INTERNATIONAL REGULATIONS, STANDARDS, CODES INCLUDING THE INTERNATIONAL MARITIME DANGEROUS GOODS (IMDG) CODE AND THE INTERNATIONAL MARITIME SOLID BULK CARGOES (IMSBC) CODE AND RECOMMENDATIONS ON CARRIAGE OF DANGEROUS CARGOES **Textbooks/Bibliography:** B21, B71, B89, B104, B113, B128, B146, B182 **Teaching aids:** A1 Required performance: *Note that trainees must be familiar with the content and application of the basic knowledge of packaged dangerous goods, solid bulk and grain cargoes from IMO model course 7.03. This knowledge is considered so fundamental for much of the management level content within this course that there is merit in reviewing the operational level content quickly before covering the additional elements required at management level. The learning time has been reduced for many elements on the basis that trainees will be reviewing rather than learning much of this content at this level. It may be necessary for some trainees to refresh their knowledge of this content before undertaking this management level content* **1.1 International regulations and codes (3 hours)** – understands and applies the content of international regulations standards, codes and recommendations on the carriage of dangerous cargoes, including the International Maritime Dangerous Goods (IMDG) Code, the International Maritime Solid Bulk Cargoes (IMSBC) Code, International Code for the Construction and Equipment of Ships Carrying Liquefied Gases in Bulk (IGC Code), International Code for the Construction and Equipment of Ships carrying Dangerous Chemicals in Bulk (IBC Code)		R54, R55, R56

2.3.2 CARRIAGE OF DANGEROUS, HAZARDOUS AND HARMFUL CARGOES; PRECAUTIONS DURING LOADING AND UNLOADING AND CARE DURING THE VOYAGE OF DANGEROUS, HAZARDOUS AND HARMFUL CARGOES
Textbooks/Bibliography: T15, B21, B71, B89, B104, B113, B128, B146, B182
Teaching aids: A1, V136, V154, V170, V173
Required performance:
Note that trainees must be familiar with the content and application of the basic knowledge of packaged dangerous goods, solid bulk and grain cargoes from IMO model course 7.03. This knowledge is considered so fundamental for much of the management level content within this course that there is merit in reviewing the operational level content quickly before covering the additional elements required at management level. The learning time has been reduced for many elements on the basis that trainees will be reviewing rather than learning much of this content at this level. It may be necessary for some trainees to refresh their knowledge of this content before undertaking this management level content
2.1 Dangerous goods in packages (10 hours)
– states that the IMDG Code is an evolving document and is updated every two years to take account of:
  – new dangerous goods which have to be included
  – new technology and methods of working with or handling dangerous goods
  – safety concerns which arise as a result of experience
– lists the explosives which may be carried on a passenger ship
– describes the contents of the shipper's declaration of dangerous goods
– identifies the marking and labelling required on packages or cargo units
		R54, R55

适任 2.3	危险货物运输	IMO 参考书目
2.3.1　国际规定、标准、规则和建议的内容,包括《国际海运危险货物规则》(IMDG)和《国际海运固体散货规则》(IMSBC 规则) **教科书/参考文献**:B21, B71, B89, B104, B113, B128, B146, B182 **教具**:A1 技能要求: 注意:在完成这些要求的内容之前,学员必须熟悉 IMO 示范课程 7.03 中的包装危险品、固体散货和谷物的基础知识内容及其适用。本课程中的知识对多数管理级内容非常重要,以至于在涉及管理级额外要求的知识点之前,在迅速复习操作级内容方面颇具价值。基于学员将复习而不是学习该级别内容,已经减少了许多知识点的学时。对某些学员而言,在学习管理级内容之前,可能有必要更新这些技能的知识 **1.1　国际规则和规范(3 学时)** – 理解并应用有关运载危险货物的国际规定、标准、规则和建议的内容,包括《国际海运危险货物规则》(IMDG)、《国际海运固体散货规则》(IMSBC)、《国际散装运输液化气体船舶构造与设备规则》(IGC 规则)和《国际散装运输危险化学品船舶构造与设备规则》(IBC 规则)		R54, R55, R56
2.3.2　危险货物、有毒货物和有害货物的运载;装卸期间的预防措施及危险货物、有毒货物和有害货物航行期间的照管 **教科书/参考文献**:T15, B21, B71, B89, B104, B113, B128, B146, B182 **教具**:A1, V136, V154, V170, V173 技能要求: 注意:在完成这些要求的内容之前,学员必须熟悉 IMO 示范课程 7.03 中的包装危险品、固体散货和谷物的基础知识内容及其适用。本课程中的知识对多数管理级内容非常重要,以至于在涉及管理级额外要求的知识点之前,在迅速复习操作级内容方面颇具价值。基于学员将复习而不是学习该级别内容,已经减少了许多知识点的学时。对某些学员而言,在学习管理级内容之前,可能有必要更新这些技能的知识 **2.1　包装类危险货物(10 学时)** – 阐述 IMDG 规则是一个不断发展的文件,每两年更新一次,主要涉及: 　– 增添了新的危险货物 　– 与危险货物打交道或处理它们的新技术和新方法 　– 实践中产生的安全问题 – 列出可在客船上运输的爆炸品 – 描述托运人声明的内容 – 识别包装或货物单元上要求的标志和标记		R54, R55

COMPETENCE 2.3	Carriage of Dangerous Goods	IMO Reference

– states why additional labelling may be necessary to meet the requirements for through transport
– verifies that the documentation provided to the ship and the packaging and labelling of packaged dangerous cargo complies with the requirements of the IMDG Code
– explains the actions to take when documentation, packaging, labelling or the condition of packages does not meet the requirements of the IMDG Code
– plans the stowage and segregation of a cargo containing dangerous goods when provided with the loading list, the copies of the shipper's declarations and the IMDG Code to plan a stow and segregation and
– prepares the dangerous goods manifest and stowage plan for a cargo containing multiple dangerous goods
– extracts the relevant references to EmS and MFAG
– identifies the appropriate action to take in emergency and medical first aid situations involving dangerous goods
– describes the requirements of SOLAS chapter VII on the carriage of dangerous goods
– explains that the IMDG Code should be followed to ensure compliance with the requirements of SOLAS for the carriage of dangerous goods in packaged form
– explains that the Code ensures safety mainly by stipulating the packaging required and the segregation from other cargoes with which there could be an adverse reaction
– states that the Code comprises 7 parts, which is presented in two books: Volume 1 and Volume 2
– states that it is necessary to use both books to obtain the required information when shipping dangerous goods by sea
– states that the Code also contains a supplement
– lists the contents of Volume 1 (Parts 1-2 & 4-7 of the Code) which comprises:
  – part 1, general provisions, definitions and training
  – part 2, classifications
  – part 4, packing and tank provisions
  – part 5, consignment procedures
  – part 6, construction and testing of packagings, intermediate bulk containers (IBCs), large packagings, portable tanks, multi-element gas containers (MEGCS) and road tank vehicles
  – part 7, requirements concerning transport operations
– lists the contents of Volume 2 (Part 3 and the Appendices of the Code) which comprises:
  – part 3, dangerous goods list (DGL) and limited quantities exceptions
  – appendix a, list of generic and n.o.s. (not otherwise specified) proper shipping names
  – appendix b, glossary of terms
  – alphabetical index
– states that the dangerous goods list (DGL) is the central core of the IMDG Code and presents information on transport requirements in a coded form		

适任 2.3	危险货物运输	IMO 参考书目
– 阐述为什么可能有必要采用附加标记以满足整个运输过程中的要求 – 核实提供给船上的文件和包装危险货物的标志、标记符合 IMDG 规则的要求 – 解释当文件、标志、标记或包装状况不符合 IMDG 规则要求时应采取的行动 – 得到装货清单、托运人声明和 IMDG 规则有关积载与隔离的计划之后,制订危险货物的积载与隔离计划 – 一票货物中有多种危险货物时,准备危险货物清单和积载图 – 从 EmS 和 MFAG 中获取相关内容 – 决定涉及危险货物时紧急和急救情形下采取的适当行动 – 描述 SOLAS 公约第Ⅶ章关于危险货物运输的要求 – 解释应遵守 IMDG 规则,以确保符合 SOLAS 公约关于包装类危险货物运输的要求 – 解释该规则主要通过规定要求的包装和对可能与其他货物产生不良反应的货物进行隔离来确保安全 – 阐述该规则包括 7 个部分,分第 1 卷和第 2 卷两册 – 阐述当通过船舶海运危险货物时,有必要利用两册书来获得所要求的信息 – 阐述该规则还包括 1 个补篇 – 列出第 1 卷(该规则的 1—2 和 4—7 部分)内容,主要包括: 　– 第 1 部分　一般规定、定义和训练 　– 第 2 部分　分类 　– 第 4 部分　包装和液舱准备 　– 第 5 部分　托运程序 　– 第 6 部分　中型散装容器(IBCs)、大型容器、移动液舱、多单元气体容器(MEGCS)和公路液罐车的建造与包装测试 　– 第 7 部分　关于运输作业的要求 – 列出第 2 卷(第 3 部分和规则的附录)包括如下内容: 　– 第 3 部分　危险货物清单 (DGL) 和数量有限的例外 　– 附件 a,类别和 n.o.s. (未另行规定的) 正常运输名称清单 　– 附件 b,术语汇编 　– 字母顺序索引 – 阐述危险货物清单(DGL)是 IMDG 的重中之重,它以编码的形式提供了相关运输要求		

COMPETENCE 2.3	Carriage of Dangerous Goods	IMO Reference
– states that the supplement contains the following texts related to the Code: – emergency response procedures for ships carrying dangerous goods – medical first aid guide – reporting procedures – IMO/ILO/ECE guidelines for packing cargo transport units – safe use of pesticides in ships – international code for the carriage of packaged irradiated nuclear fuel, plutonium and high-level radioactive wastes on board ships – states that the purpose of the IMDG Code's classification system is: – to distinguish between goods which are considered to be dangerous for transport and those which are not – to identify the dangers which are presented by dangerous goods in transport – to ensure that the correct measures are taken to enable these goods to be transported safely without risk to persons or property (both within the port and on the ship) – states that dangerous goods are classified into 9 classes according to properties – states that the way in which different classes of dangerous goods are handled in transport will depend upon these properties and hazards, for example: – the type of packaging that can be used – what classes of dangerous goods can be transported together in freight containers – where the goods can be stored within the port and on the ship – lists the 9 classes of dangerous goods in the IMDG Code, which are: – class 1 explosives – class 2 gases – class 3 flammable liquids – class 4 flammable solids – class 5 oxidizing substances and organic peroxides – class 6 toxic and infectious substances – class 7 radioactive material – class 8 corrosive substances – class 9 miscellaneous dangerous substances and articles – states that the 9 hazard classes have been established internationally by a United Nations (UN) committee to ensure that all modes of transport (road, rail, air and sea) classify dangerous goods in the same way – states that by testing the dangerous goods according to UN test procedures, a shipper is able to classify dangerous goods according to the 9 hazard classes – explains that the hazard presented by each class is identified by an internationally accepted hazard warning label (diamond) – states that this hazard warning label appears on the outer packaging of the dangerous goods when they are being transported as a warning to all those working within the transport chain or coming into contact with them – states that these hazard warning labels are pictured inside the front cover of Volume 1 of the IMDG Code		

适任 2.3	危险货物运输	IMO 参考书目
– 阐述补篇包括有关该规则的下列材料: – 载运危险货物船舶的应急响应程序 – 医疗急救指南 – 报告程序 – IMO/ILO/ECE 包装货物运输单元指南 – 船上安全使用杀虫剂 – 船运包装乏核燃料、钚和高水平放射性废物国际规则 – 阐述 IMDG 规则分类系统的目的为: – 在货物中区分哪些存在运输危险,哪些不存在运输危险 – 识别危险货物运输中的风险 – 确保采取正确措施能安全运输危险货物,而不对人员或财产构成威胁(包括在港口和在船上) – 阐述危险货物按其性质分为 9 类 – 阐述危险货物在运输中的操作方式取决于其性质和危险性,例如: – 可使用的包装种类 – 何种危险货物可用货运集装箱运输 – 在港口和在船上存放于何处 – 列出 IMDG 规则中 9 类危险货物: – 第 1 类　爆炸品 – 第 2 类　气体 – 第 3 类　易燃液体 – 第 4 类　易燃固体 – 第 5 类　氧化物质和有机过氧化物 – 第 6 类　有毒和感染性物质 – 第 7 类　放射性材料 – 第 8 类　腐蚀性物质 – 第 9 类　杂项危险物质和用品 – 阐述由联合国委员会在国际上确立 9 类危险货物,确保所有运输方式(道路、铁路、航空和海洋)以同一方式分类 – 阐述托运人按照联合国的测试程序对危险货物测试,即可按 9 类划分危险货物的类别 – 解释每类危险货物具有的危险性可通过国际普遍接受的危险警示标识(菱形)识别 – 阐述包装危险货物在运输时该危险警示标识应出现在外包装上,警示在整个运输链上工作的人员或与其接触的人员 – 阐述这些危险警示标识被描绘在 IMDG 规则第 1 卷的内封面上		

COMPETENCE 2.3	Carriage of Dangerous Goods	IMO Reference

- states that the dangerous goods, within each of the 9 hazard classes, are uniquely identified by two pieces of information:
  - a four-digit number known as the UN number which is preceded by the letters UN
  - the corresponding proper shipping name (PSN)
  - for example, kerosene is identified in the IMDG Code by its UN number UN 1223 and the PSN Kerosene
- states that together the UN Number and PSN uniquely identifies dangerous goods to:
  - enable rapid and precise identification during transport
  - ensure the correct handling, stowage, segregation etc.
  - in the event of an emergency, ensure that the correct procedures are followed
- explains that the purpose of using a four-digit number to identify dangerous goods is to enhance safety by:
  - overcoming language barriers – the four-digit number is easily understood in all languages
  - avoiding confusing similar names – e.g. TITANIUM POWDER, WETTED UN 1352 which is a flammable solid in class 4.1 and has very different transport requirements to TITANIUM POWDER, DRY UN 2546 which is spontaneously combustible in class 4.2
- states that the PSN must be used for transport purposes on documentation/labelling etc.
- states that no alternatives or variations are permitted unless specifically stated
- states that the PSN is that part of the name which appears in the Dangerous Goods List or the Alphabetical Index in capital letters only
- states that any text in lower case is only descriptive and is not part of the PSN
- states that the Dangerous goods list (DGL) is presented across 2 pages of the IMDG Code and is divided into 18 columns for each individual dangerous good listed
- states that much of the information contained in the DGL is coded to make it easier to present in a table
- states that the DGL is arranged in UN Number order; column 1 and column 18 contains the UN Number
- states that to look up an entry only the UN Number is required
- states that dangerous goods can also be searched using the PSN
- explains that if the UN Number is not given but the dangerous good has the PSN, its associated UN Number can be located by looking at the alphabetical index at the back of Volume 2 of the IMDG Code
- explains that the IMDG Code contains clearly defined recommendations for the training of all staff who handle or process dangerous goods shipments for transportation by sea. The full training requirements can be found in the IMDG Code Volume 1, Chapter 1.3 states that a packing certificate is also required, certifying that a container or vehicle has been properly packed and secured, if loaded with dangerous goods
- describes the information given for individual substances
- states that an index of dangerous goods is included in Volume 1 of the IMDG Code

适任 2.3	危险货物运输	IMO 参考书目
– 阐述 9 类危险货物中的每一类都由 2 条独特信息识别: 　– 一个前缀为 UN 的被称为联合国编号的 4 位数字 　– 相应的正确运输名称(PSN) 　– 例如,煤油在 IMDG 规则中,用联合国编号“UN1233”和“PSN 煤油”加以识别 – 阐述联合国编号和 PSN 作为唯一编号识别危险货物以: 　– 能在运输中快速和准确识别 　– 确保正确装卸、积载和隔离等 　– 出现紧急情况时,确保采用正确的程序 – 解释利用 4 位数字识别危险货物的目的是通过下列方式来提高安全性: 　– 克服语言障碍—4 位数字在所有语言中都易于理解 　– 避免混淆类似名称—例如湿钛粉的联合国编号为 1352,属于 4.1 类易燃固体,与联合国编号为 2546、属于 4.2 类易自燃物质的干钛粉运输要求大不相同 – 阐述 PSN 必须用于运输文件 / 标识等 – 阐述不允许有替代名或他名,除非特别说明 – 阐述 PSN 是出现在危险货物清单的名称部分或以大写字母按字母顺序排列的索引中的唯一名字 – 阐述在大写字母索引下面的任何文本都仅仅是描述,而不是 PSN 部分 – 阐述危险货物清单(DGL)在 IMDG 规则第 2 页,对每一个危险货物分为 18 列 – 阐述 DGL 中的大量信息被进行编码,以使其在表中更易呈现 – 阐述 DGL 以联合国编号顺序排列;第 1 列和第 18 列包含联合国编号 – 阐述要查找一个条目,仅需联合国编号 – 阐述也可利用 PSN 搜索危险货物 – 解释如果没有联合国编号，但有 PSN，则该危险货物 PSN 相关的联合国编号可在 IMDG 规则第 2 卷后面的字母顺序索引中找到 – 解释 IMDG 规则包括对所有在海运危险货物中从事装卸或处理人员进行培训的清晰的建议。全部培训要求可在 IMDG 规则第 1 卷 1.3 章中找到 – 描述单一物质的信息 – 阐述 IMDG 规则第 1 卷中危险货物的索引		

COMPETENCE 2.3	Carriage of Dangerous Goods	IMO Reference

– explains how to obtain the references to the relevant Emergency Schedule (EmS) and the entry in the Medical First Aid Guide for Use in Accidents Involving Dangerous Goods (MFAG)
– describes the information given for individual substances
– states the requirement for a dangerous goods manifest or stowage plan and describes how they should be prepared
– lists, by headings, the information given in an emergency schedule
– defines "dangerous substances", "port authority", "regulatory authority", "designated port office" and "responsible person" as used in the Recommendations on the Safe Transport, Handling and Storage of Dangerous Substances in Port Areas
– explains that a port authority may be empowered to refuse dangerous substances if it is considered that their presence would endanger life or property because of:
  – their condition
  – the condition of their containment
  – the condition of their mode of conveyance
  – conditions in the port area
– states that, if any dangerous substance constitutes an unacceptable hazard, the port authority should be able to order the removal of such substance or any ship, package, container, portable tank or vehicle containing it
– states that a port authority will normally require notification at least 24 hours in advance of the transport or handling of dangerous substances, including those which are not for discharge at that port
– describes the inspections which may be made by a port authority
– states that the designated port officer should be empowered to:
  – direct when and where a ship having any dangerous substances on board may anchor, moor or berth
  – direct a ship to be moved within or to leave the port area
  – attach conditions appropriate to local circumstances and the quantity and nature of the dangerous substances
– states that the regulatory authority may require signals to be shown while transporting or handling dangerous substances
– describes the signals as:
  – by day, flag "B" of the International Code of Signals
  – by night, an all-round fixed red light
– explains how effective communications with the port authority can be maintained
– describes the requirements regarding mooring a ship carrying dangerous substances
– states that at all times there should be sufficient crew on board to maintain a proper watch and operate appliances in the case of an emergency, taking into account the nature and quantity of dangerous substances on board
– states that a responsible person should be designated to supervise the handling of dangerous goods		

适任 2.3	危险货物运输	IMO 参考书目

	– 解释如何获得有关应急医疗措施（EmS）的编号和危险货物事故医疗急救指南(MFAG)的条目
	– 描述单个物质的信息
	– 阐述危险货物舱单或积载图的要求,并描述如何准备它们
	– 以标题形式列出应急医疗措施里的信息
	– 定义关于在港口区域安全运输、装卸和储存危险物质建议书中所用到的“危险物质”、“港口主管机关”、“监管部门”、“指定的港务局”和“负责人员”
	– 解释如果由于下列原因因危险物质的存在危及生命或财产安全,可授权港口主管机关拒绝危险物质：
	  – 它们的状况
	  – 它们盛装的状况
	  – 它们运输方式的状况
	  – 港区的状况
	– 阐述如果危险物质构成不可接受的危害,港口主管机关应能命令移除任何此种物质或移走含有此种物质的任何船舶、包装、集装箱、移动液舱或车辆
	– 阐述港口主管机关通常应提前至少 24 小时告知危险物质的运输或装卸，包括那些不在本港卸载的危险物质
	– 描述港口主管机关可能进行的检查
	– 阐述应赋予港口负责人的权利：
	  – 指导载有危险物质的船舶何时和何处可以锚泊、系泊或停泊
	  – 指导船舶在港内移动或离港
	  – 根据危险物质的数量和性质和当地环境提出附加条件
	– 阐述监管部门可以要求在运输或装卸危险物质时显示信号
	– 描述显示的信号为：
	  – 白天,国际信号规则的 B 旗
	  – 夜间,一盏红色环照定光灯
	– 解释如何保持与主管当局的有效沟通
	– 描述载有危险物质船舶的靠泊要求
	– 阐述考虑到船上危险物质的性质和数量,船上始终都应有足够船员保持正常值班和操作设备以防万一
	– 阐述应指派一名负责人员监督危险品的装卸	

COMPETENCE 2.3	Carriage of Dangerous Goods	IMO Reference
	– lists the measures that should be taken by the responsible person in connection with: – the weather – lighting – protective clothing and equipment – intoxicated persons – fire and other emergency procedures – reporting of incidents and safety precautions – explains that the port authority should be informed of the intention to carry out repair work when dangerous substances are on board – explains the handling precautions which should be observed regarding: – avoidance of damage to packages – access to handling areas – lifting goods over dangerous goods stowed on deck – escape of a dangerous substance from a package entry into enclosed spaces – describes the special precautions for loading or unloading explosives	
2.2	**Solid bulk cargoes (9 hours)**	R56
	– outlines the contents of the International Maritime Solid Bulk Cargoes (IMSBC Code) – states that the main hazards associated with the shipment of bulk solids are: – structural damage due to improper distribution of the cargo – loss or reduction of stability during a voyage – chemical reactions – lists the information which should be supplied by the shipper to the Master before loading – states that a certificate stating the relevant characteristics of the material should be provided to the Master at the loading point – explains that certificates stating transportable moisture limits should be accompanied by a statement that the moisture content is the average moisture content at the time of presenting the certificate – explains how to distribute a high-density cargo between holds when detailed information is not available – states that the loading instrument, loading information and the ship's stability information book should be used to check the suitability of a proposed stow for stresses and stability – describes how to prevent shifting of bulk cargo by reducing an excessively high *GM* – describes precautions to take before, during and after loading of bulk cargo – describes the precautions to take to minimize the effect of dust on deck machinery, navigational aids and living quarters – describes the health hazards which may be associated with bulk materials – states that safety precautions and any appropriate national regulations should be complied with during the handling and carriage of bulk materials – states that a copy of the Medical First Aid Guide for Use in Accidents Involving Dangerous Goods should be on board	

适任 2.3	危险货物运输	IMO 参考书目
– 列出负责人员采取的与下列因素有关的措施: – 天气 – 照明 – 防护服和防护设备 – 醉酒人员 – 消防和其他应急程序 – 事故报告和安全预防措施 – 解释当船上载有危险物质,打算进行修理时应通知主管机关 – 解释应遵守的装卸货预防措施: – 避免损坏包装 – 进入装卸区的通道 – 将货物提升至积载于甲板的危险品上方 – 从包装中溢漏的危险物质进入封闭处所 – 描述装卸爆炸品的特别预防措施		
2.2 固体散货(9 学时) – 概括《国际海运固体散货规则》(IMSBC 规则)的内容 – 阐述与散装固体货物运载有关的主要危险是: – 由于不正确的货物分布而产生的结构破坏 – 在航行中稳性的丢失或减小 – 化学反应 – 列出装货前托运人应提供给船长的信息 – 阐述在装货现场应将载明物质相关特性的证书提供给船长 – 解释载明适运水分限的证书应辅以说明,该水分含量是制作证书当时的平均水分含量 – 解释当得不到详细信息时,如何在货舱间分配高密度货物 – 阐述应使用装载仪、装载信息和船舶稳性计算书来核实为保证应力和稳性所建议的积载的适合性 – 描述如何通过减小过大的 *GM* 来防止散货的移动 – 描述在装载散装货物之前、期间和之后应采取的预防措施 – 描述为使灰尘对甲板机械、助航仪器和生活区的影响达到最小应采取的预防措施 – 描述可能与散装物质有关的健康危害 – 阐述在装卸和运载散装物质期间,应遵循的安全预防措施和任何适用的国内法规 – 阐述船上应有《危险货物事故使用的医疗急救指南》的复印本		R56

COMPETENCE 2.3	Carriage of Dangerous Goods	IMO Reference

– describes how to trim cargoes having an angle of repose:
  – less than or equal to 35 degrees
  – greater than 35 degrees
– describes how to stow material which flows freely like grain
– explains the IMSBC Code method for determining the approximate angle of repose on board ship
– describes the types of cargo which may liquefy during carriage
– states that cargoes which may liquefy should not be carried with a moisture content above that of the transportable moisture limit
– explains that such cargoes may look relatively dry when loaded but liquefy as a result of compaction and vibration during the passage
– states that such cargoes should be trimmed reasonably level, regardless of the angle of repose stated
– explains the precautions to be taken to keep liquids out of holds where such cargoes are carried and the danger of using water to cool a shipment of these materials
– states that specially fined or constructed cargo ships may carry materials with a moisture content above the transportable moisture limit if approved by their Administrations
– describes the test for approximately determining the possibility of flow which may be carried out on board ship
– states that some materials transported in bulk present hazards because of their chemical properties
– explains that some materials are classified as dangerous goods in the IMDG Code while others are Materials Hazardous only in Bulk (MHB)
– states that the IMSBC Code categorizes cargoes into three groups – A, B and C:
  – Group A consists of the cargoes which may liquefy if shipped with moisture content in excess of their transportable moisture limit
  – Group B consists of cargoes which possess a chemical hazard which could give rise to a dangerous situation on a ship
  – Group C consists of cargoes which are not liable to liquefy (Group A) and do not possess chemical hazards (Group B)		

适任 2.3	危险货物运输	IMO 参考书目

– 描述如何调整下列静止角的货物:
  – 小于或等于 35°
  – 大于 35°
– 描述如何积载像谷物之类的自由流动的物质
– 解释 IMSBC 规则中确定船上静止角的方法
– 描述在运载期间可能会液化的货物类型
– 阐述可能会液化的货物不能在水汽含量大于适运水分限情况下运载
– 解释这种货物在装载时可能看上去相对干燥,但在航行期间由于挤压和振动可能会液化
– 阐述这种货物可以平舱到合理的水平,不管其所载明的静止角
– 解释为保持装有这种货物的液体排出舱外应采取的预防措施以及使用水冷却这种货物的危险性
– 阐述如其主管机关批准,特殊配备或建造的货船可以运载水分含量在适运水分限之上的货物
– 描述可以在船上进行的测试以近似确定流动的可能性
– 阐述某些散装运输的物质因其化学性质而具有危险性
– 解释在 IMDG 规则里一些物质被划分为危险货物而其他的是“只在散装时有危险的货物”(MHB)
– 阐述 IMSBC 规则将货物分为 A、B、C 三类
  – A 类由如果装运时含水量超过适运水分限则可能液化的货物组成
  – B 类由具有化学危害性可能在船舶酿成险情的货物组成
  – C 类由既不易液化(A 类)又不具有化学危害性(B 类)的货物组成		

COMPETENCE 2.3	Carriage of Dangerous Goods	IMO Reference
– explains the content and use of the following: that in the added supplement of the IMSBC Code, the IMO documents contained are: – the BLU Code – the BLU Manual – MSC/Circ.908 – Uniform Method of Measurement of the Density of Bulk Cargoes – MSC/Circ.1146 – Lists of Solid Bulk Cargoes for which a Fixed Gas Fire-extinguishing System may be Exempted or for which a Fixed Gas Fire-extinguishing System is Ineffective – Res. A.864(20) – Recommendations for Entering Enclosed Spaces Aboard Ships – MSC.1/Circ.1264 – Recommendations on the Safe Use of Pesticides in Ships Applicable to the Fumigation of Cargo Holds – BC.1/Circ.66 – Contact Names and Addresses of the Offices of Designated National Competent Authorities Responsible for the Safe Carriage of Grain and Solid Bulk Cargoes – explains the list of materials possessing chemical hazards is not exhaustive, that the properties listed are for guidance only and that it is essential to obtain currently valid information about bulk materials before loading – explains the use of the tables for segregation between incompatible bulk materials and between bulk materials and dangerous goods in packaged form – states that the IMDG Code should also be consulted for additional requirements regarding the stowage and segregation of packaged dangerous goods – states that particular care should be taken with the segregation of toxic substances and foodstuffs – uses the IMSBC Code to extract all necessary information for the safe carriage in bulk of a stated cargo, describes how it should be loaded and lists any special precautions or requirements to be observed during loading, carriage and discharge **2.3 International Code for the Safe Carriage of Grain in Bulk (International Grain Code) (7 hours)** – states that the International Grain Code applies to all ships to which the SOLAS regulations apply and to cargo ships of less than 500 gross tons – explains that the International Code for the Safe Carriage of Grain in Bulk (International Grain Code) is based on the recognition that grain-like cargoes have a propensity to shift and that even fully loaded cargo spaces may contain voids that allow dangerous cargo shifts – defines the following terms as used in chapter VI of SOLAS: – grain – filled compartment – partly filled compartment – angle of flooding – explains that the Code requires demonstration, by calculation, that at all times during a voyage the ship will have sufficient intact stability to provide adequate dynamic stability after taking into account an assumed shift of cargo		

适任 2.3	危险货物运输	IMO 参考书目

- 解释下列 IMSBC 规则、IMO 文献包含的附件的内容与使用:
  - BLU 规则
  - BLU 手册
  - MSC/Circ. 908—散货密度的统一测量方法
  - MSC/Circ. 1146—可免除固定气体灭火系统的固体散货或固定气体灭火系统无效的固体散货清单
  - Res. A.864(20)—进入船上封闭场所的建议
  - MSC.1/Circ.1264—关于船舶安全使用适用于货舱的杀虫剂的建议
  - BC.1/Circ.66—指定国家主管部门负责谷物和固体散货安全运输办公室的联系人和地址
- 解释具有化学危险性的物质清单不是详尽的,所列出的性质仅供参考,在装货之前必须获得目前散装货物有效的信息
- 解释不相容散装物质之间以及散装物质和包装形式的危险货物之间的隔离表的使用
- 阐述 IMDG 规则也应考虑有关包装危险货物的积载和隔离额外的要求
- 阐述对于有毒物质和食品的隔离应进行特别的照管
- 为了安全运载所描述的散装货物,使用 IMSBC 规则获得所有必要的信息,描述如何装载货物并列出在装载、运载和卸载期间任何应遵循的特殊预防措施或要求

2.3 《国际散装谷物安全运输规则》(国际谷物规则)(7 学时)

- 阐述国际谷物规则适用于 SOLAS 公约适用的所有船舶和小于 500 总吨的货船
- 解释《国际散装谷物安全运输规则》(国际谷物规则)是基于谷物类货物具有移动倾向,即使货舱满载也可能包含允许货物危险移动空隙的认识
- 定义 SOLAS 公约第 6 章所用术语:
  - 谷物
  - 满载舱
  - 部分装载舱
  - 进水角
- 解释规则要求通过计算表明船舶在航行中的任何时候将具有足够的完整稳性以使船舶在考虑了假定的货物移动之后,能提供足够的动稳性

COMPETENCE 2.3	Carriage of Dangerous Goods	IMO Reference

– states the Code requirements for minimum stability in terms of initial metacentric height, angle of heel due to assumed grain shift and residual dynamic stability
– explains that vessels with appropriate design features may be able to meet the required minimum stability criteria after the assumed movement of cargo without taking further physical precautions to reduce the shift of cargo
– explains the stability and grain loading information that is required to be provided for such vessels if they are to receive a Document of Authorization
– explains the method of verifying that the loading of a vessel supplied with a Document of Authorization meets stability requirements using volumetric heeling moments, cargo details and maximum deadweight heeling moments
– explains that the grain loading stability booklet and associated plans contain all of the information necessary to check that a proposed loading plan complies with the stability requirements of the Regulations at all stages of the voyage
– states that in some countries a certificate of loading, certifying that the cargo has been loaded in compliance with the Regulations, is required before sailing
– explains the importance of trimming to fill all of the spaces under decks and hatch covers to the maximum extent possible
– states that the ability to comply with the stability criteria should be demonstrated before loading
– states that the Master should ensure that the ship is upright before proceeding to sea
– explains the use of physical precautions to reduce cargo movement:
  – describes the use and fitting of longitudinal divisions in both filled and partly filled compartments
  – demonstrates the use of Part C of the Code to determine the scantlings for uprights and shifting boards
  – describes the construction of a saucer as an alternative to a longitudinal division in a hatchway
  – describes the use of bagged grain or other suitable cargo stowed in the wings and ends of a compartment to reduce the heeling effects of a grain shift
  – describes methods of securing the free grain surface in partly filled compartments
– states that the hatch covers of filled compartments which have no cargo stowed over them should be secured as laid down in the document of authorization
– explains the conditions which must be met before a ship without a document of authorization may load grain
– given a ship's data and details of consumption of fuel and of fresh water for an intended voyage, prepares a stowage plan for a cargo of bulk grain and performs the calculations to check that the proposed stowage complies, at all stages of the voyage, with the stability criteria set out in chapter VI of SOLAS 1974		

适任 2.3	危险货物运输	IMO 参考书目

– 阐述由于假设了谷物的移动和剩余动稳性,根据初稳性高度、横倾角,提出了规则对稳性的最低要求
– 解释具有适当设计特征的船舶,在考虑假定的货物移动之后,不用进一步采取物理预防措施来减少货物的移动也可能满足最低稳性标准
– 解释如果这种船舶收到授权书,所要求提供的稳性和谷物装载信息
– 解释使用体积倾侧力矩、货物的细节和最大载重倾侧力矩对提供授权书的船舶装载满足稳性要求进行核实的方法
– 解释《谷物装载稳性手册》和有关的计划含有所有必要的信息以查看预定的装载计划在航行中的任何时候均符合规则的稳性要求
– 阐述在一些国家,在开航之前要求载明船舶已经根据规则装载货物的装载证书
– 解释为最大限度地充满甲板和舱盖下可能的容积而平舱的重要性
– 阐述在装货之前必须表明符合稳性标准的能力
– 阐述船长在船舶开航之前应确保船舶是正浮的
– 解释使用物理预防措施以减少货物移动:
  – 描述在满载舱和部分满载舱内纵隔壁的使用和配置
  – 说明该规则 C 部分的使用,来确定立柱和止移板的尺寸
  – 描述在舱口处放置托盘作为纵隔壁的替代物
  – 描述为减少谷物移动横倾的影响,在货舱的两翼和端部堆放袋装谷物或其他合适货物的使用
  – 描述在部分满载舱里固定自由谷物面的方法
– 阐述应根据授权书里的规定,对舱盖上没有载货的满载舱的舱盖板进行固定
– 解释没有授权书的船舶在装载谷物前必须满足的条件
– 在给定船舶数据和计划航次燃油与淡水消耗细节的情况下,准备散装谷物货物的积载计划并进行计算以核实预计的积载在航行中的任何时候均符合 1974 年 SOLAS 第Ⅵ章里所列出的稳性标准		

Part D2: Instructor Manual

The following notes are intended to highlight the main objectives or training outcomes of each part of the function. The notes also contain some material on topics which are not adequately covered in the quoted references.

On completion of training for this function, officers will be able to use cargo plans and tables or diagrams of stability and trim data to calculate the ship's initial stability, draughts and trim for any given description of cargo and other weights. They will also be able to determine whether stresses on the ship are within permitted limits by the use of stress data or calcula ion equipment, or software.

Officers will be able to plan and supervise the stowage of cargo, taking account of all relevant regulations and safety codes. They will also be able to make the necessary calculations to ensure adequate stability and to check that shear forces and bending moments are within permitted limits.

The safety precautions before entering enclosed or potentially contaminated spaces will be understood and applied.

Officers will be able to supervise the preparation and dunnaging of holds and the operation of ships' cargo gear and will be aware of the importance of adequately securing cargo to prevent damage to the ship of cargo. They will identify dangerous goods and use the IMDG Code (R54 and R55) to ensure such cargoes are stowed and separated correctly. They will know the hazards related to some bulk cargoes and the precautions to take during their loading, carriage and discharge. They will also have a basic knowledge of the piping and pumping arrangements of oil tankers.

Function 2: Cargo Handling and Stowage at the Management Level

2.1 PLAN AND ENSURE SAFE LOADING, STOWAGE, SECURING, CARE DURING THE VOYAGE AND UNLOADING OF CARGOES

2.1.1 APPLICATION OF INTERNATIONAL REGULATIONS, CODES AND STANDARDS CONCERNING THE SAFE HANDLING, STOWAGE, SECURING AND TRANSPORT OF CARGOES (6 hours)

Instructors should refer to the many IMO references concerning this topic and design exercises to let officers practise using information contained in the Code of Safe Practice for Cargo Stowage and Securing and in a typical cargo securing manual.

2.1.2 EFFECT ON TRIM AND STABILITY OF CARGOES AND CARGO OPERATIONS (20 hours)

The time allotted to cargo calculations is based on the assumption that trainees have covered the necessary theoretical work in ship stability and strength to enable them to make calculations based on ship's data.

D2 部分：教员手册

以下注意事项旨在突出主要的教学目标或本职能每部分的培训效果。注意事项也包含了一些所引用的参考文献没有充分涵盖的主题的资料。

完成本功能的培训后，驾驶员将能够在已知货物和其他重物的描述的情况下，利用货物配载图、稳性和吃水差数据表或图计算船舶的初稳性、吃水和吃水差。他们也将能够利用应力数据或计算设备或软件确定船舶的应力是否在允许的范围内。

船员在考虑所有相关的规定和安全规则的情况下，将能够计划并监督货物积载。他们也将能够进行必要的计算以确保足够的稳性和核实剪力、弯矩和扭矩是否在允许的范围内。

在进入封闭的或潜在的受污染的空间之前，应理解并应用安全预防措施。

船员将能够监督备舱和垫舱以及船舶货物装卸设备的操作，并意识到为防止货物对船舶的损坏，充分系固货物的重要性。他们将辨认危险货物并利用IMDG规则(R54和R55)确保正确积载和隔离此货物。他们将知道有关一些散装货物的危险性以及在装载、运载和卸载这些货物期间应采取的预防措施。他们还将具有油船管路和泵设备的基本知识。

功能2:管理级货物装卸与积载

2.1 计划并确保在航行期间货物的安全装载、积载、系固、照管以及货物的卸载

2.1.1 有关货物安全装卸、积载、系固和运输的国际规则、公约和标准的应用 (6学时)

教员应参考许多关于本主题的IMO参考文献，并设计练习题让驾驶员练习应用《货物积载与系固安全操作规则》和典型的货物系固手册里有关的信息。

2.1.2 货物和货物操作对吃水差和稳性的影响 (20学时)

基于认定学员具有基于船舶数据进行船舶稳性和强度计算的理论知识来分配货物计算的时间。

When calculating draughts and trim, solutions are simplified, especially when using calculators or computers, by the consistent use of signs. The convention signs used are:

loading	+	discharging	–
by the head	+	by the stern	–
forward of	+	abaft	–
starboard	+	port	–
hogging	+	sagging	–

If a loading instrument is available, trainees should be given the opportunity to use it to familiarize themselves with the type of input required and the output provided by it. Manufacturers' illustrations and descriptions can be used in addition to or in place of the instrument if trainees do not have access to one.

2.1.3 STABILITY AND TRIM DIAGRAMS AND STRESS-CALCULATING EQUIPMENT (22 hours)

Shear force, bending moments and torsional moments (8 hours)

The load curve is given by the difference between the weight and buoyancy curves. Conventions on the sign of the load and hence on which side of the axis to plot the value vary between authors. The convention chosen is not important, but it is recommended that the chosen one is used consistently to avoid confusing trainees.

During the instruction the following properties of the curves should be pointed out to trainees:

- the total area under the weight curve equals the total area under the buoyancy curve;
- the area under the load curve above the axis equals the area below the axis;
- the maximum values of shear force occur where the load curve crosses the axis;
- the maximum values of bending moment occur where the shear-force curve crosses the axis; and
- the shear force and bending moment are zero at each end.

The classification society requirement for the carriage of a loading instrument for calculating shear forces and bending moments is commonly satisfied by the provision of a personal computer with approved programs on discs. In addition to calculating shear forces and bending moment, programs normally include the calculation of transverse stability, draught and trim. Other facilities to assist with cargo planning are also provided.

The program is arranged to perform a self-check on starting up, with a warning being given to the user if data corruption has occurred. A new copy of the master disc can be made and run to rectify that fault. If a printer is connected, a hard copy of results can be obtained.

当计算吃水和吃水差时,特别是使用计算器或计算机计算时,利用惯用的符号简化求解。常用符号为:

装载	+	卸载	–
艏倾	+	艉倾	–
舯前	+	舯后	–
右舷	+	左舷	–
中拱	+	中垂	–

如果装载仪可用,应给学员使用的机会让他们熟悉所要求的输入和设备提供输出的种类。除了设备外或代替设备,如果学员没有机会操作设备,可以利用生产商的说明书和描述。

2.1.3 稳性和吃水差曲线图以及应力计算设备 (22学时)

剪力、弯矩和扭矩 **(8学时)**

重力和浮力曲线之间的差值给出了载荷曲线。关于载重符号和轴线的哪一边标注数值的惯常做法随作者的不同而异。虽然选择惯常做法并不重要,但是建议应一直使用所选惯常做法,以避免学员混淆。

在教学期间应向学员指出曲线的以下性质:

- 重力曲线下的面积等于浮力曲线下的面积;
- 横轴上载荷曲线下的面积等于横轴下的面积;
- 剪力的最大值在载荷曲线与横轴的交点处;
- 弯矩的最大值在剪力曲线与横轴的交点处;且
- 在各自的端末剪力和弯矩等于零。

硬盘上有经批准程序的个人计算机通常满足船级社关于计算剪力和弯矩的装载仪器的配备要求。除了计算剪力和弯矩外,程序通常包括计算横稳性、吃水和吃水差,还提供辅助货物配载的其他设施。

程序应设计有启动时的自我检测,如果数据发生错误应向用户发出警报。新复制母盘并运行以改正此错误。如果接有打印机,能获得硬拷贝的结果。

Torsion

Torsional stresses tend to produce twisting of the ship's hull about the longitudinal centreline, All ships experience torsional stresses when subject to oblique sea waves. At a particular instant, the sea may be attempting to roll the forward end to starboard while the after end is trying to roll to port. The ship's structure is designed to withstand this wave-induced torsion.

For most ships, normal cargo operations do not induce torsional stresses but in container ships it is possible that an excess of weight to one side at one bay is balanced by an excess to the other side at another bay, thus setting up a torsional stress.

Because of their very large hatch openings, container ships are particularly liable to structural damage, such as cracking at hatch corners, resulting from torsional stress. The classification societies state maximum permissible cargo torsion values. They also recommend that uneven transverse distributions of weights should be avoided and that excess torsion should be monitored for each load condition by means of calculation sheets and graphical representation. If the torsional moments exceed the permissible level, water ballast can be added at appropriate positions to reduce them.

An example of part of a calculation sheet is shown in Figure 1.

The levers for each row are printed on the sheet, the weights are entered and the products are calculated. The resulting moment for each bay is found and recorded, with the correct sign.

An example of loading is shown in Figure 2 (below).

The accumulated moment for each group of bays is plotted on a graph, as Figure 3.

	1	2	3	4
Twin Bays	Torsion moment	Accumulated moments	Torsion moment	Accumulated moments
01/03	+150	+150	+150	+150
05/07	−200	−50	+200	−50
09/11	−1,000	−1,050	−1,000	−1,050
13/15	−100	−1,150	−100	−1,150
17/19	+50	−1,100	+50	−1,100
21/23	−600	−1,700	+850	−250
25/27	−200	−1,900	−200	−450
29/31	−300	−2,200	−300	−750
33/35	+800	−1,400	+800	+50
37/39	−50	−1,450	−50	0

Figure 2: Example of loading

Column 2 shows a total listing moment of 1450 metre-tonnes to starboard and an excessive torsional moment at bays 25 to 31.

Water ballast is added or the anti-heeling tanks are adjusted to reduce the listing moment to zero and at the same time to reduce the excessive torsional moment. In this case, a moment of 1450 metre-tonnes to port has been introduced at bays 21/23.

Columns 1 and 2 are amended to take account of the ballast and are shown as columns 3 and 4. The graph is then re-drawn.

扭力

扭力倾向于使船体绕纵向中心线扭转。当船舶遭遇斜浪时,所有船舶都会受到扭力作用。一个特例是海浪使船首向右横摇而使船尾向左横摇。船舶结构设计成能承受海浪产生的扭转。

对大多数船舶而言通常的货物操作不会产生扭力,但对于集装箱船,在舱的一排有超重货而在另一舱的另一排用超重货加以平衡,会产生扭力。

由于舱口非常大,集装箱特别易因扭力产生结构损坏,例如舱口角的开裂。船级社规定最大允许的货物扭力。他们还建议应避免货物横向分布的不均匀,并用计算表格和图形表示方法监测每一种装载条件下的超额应力。如果扭矩超过允许的范围,应在恰当的位置加载压载水以减小扭矩。

计算表格(部分)的示例如图1所示。

每排的力臂印在表格中,填写重量并进行乘积计算,得出每一列的扭矩并用正确的符号记录。

装载示例如图2所示(如下)。

每两列的累积力矩标注在图上,如图3。

	1	2	3	4
两列	扭矩	累积力矩	扭矩	累积力矩
01/03	+150	+150	+150	+150
05/07	–200	–50	+200	–50
09/11	–1 000	–1 050	–1 000	–1 050
13/15	–100	–1 150	–100	–1 150
17/19	+50	–1 100	+50	–1 100
21/23	–600	–1 700	+850	–250
25/27	–200	–1 900	–200	–450
29/31	–300	–2 200	–300	–750
33/35	+800	–1 400	+800	+50
37/39	–50	–1 450	–50	0

图2　装载示例

第2列显示向右舷的1 450米·吨的总横倾力矩和过大的扭矩在25列到31列。

加载压载水或调节防倾斜舱以减少横倾力矩到零,同时减少过大的扭矩。本例中,在21/23列产生向左舷的1 450米·吨力矩。

考虑压载水后,经修正的第1列和第2列如第3列和第4列所示,接着重新绘制图。

SHIP'S NAME: ______________ VOYAGE: ______ PORT: ______

FOR CARGO LOADED IN THIS PORT – EXPORTS ONLY

TORSION A

BAY	ON DECK ROW	12	10	08	06	04	02	00	01	03	05	07	09	11	EXPORTS: Loaded This Port +P −S	Loaded Prev. Port +P −S	Total on Departure +P −S	ACCUM. +P −S
01	D			9.85 ×	7.39 ×	4.92 ×	2.46 ×		2.46 ×	4.92 ×	7.39 ×	9.85 ×						
	U.D.			9.71 ×	7.04 ×	4.01 ×	1.34 ×		1.34 ×	4.01 ×	7.04 ×	9.71 ×						
02	D			9.85 ×	7.39 ×	4.92 ×	2.46 ×		2.46 ×	4.92 ×	7.39 ×	9.85 ×						
03	D			9.85 ×	7.39 ×	4.92 ×	2.46 ×		2.46 ×	4.92 ×	7.39 ×	9.85 ×						
	U.D.			9.71 ×	7.04 ×	4.01 ×	1.34 ×		1.34 ×	4.01 ×	7.04 ×	9.71 ×						
														SUB TOTAL				
05	D		12.31 ×	9.85 ×	7.39 ×	4.92 ×	2.46 ×		2.46 ×	4.92 ×	7.39 ×	9.85 ×	12.31 ×					
	U.D.		12.38 ×	9.71 ×	7.04 ×	4.01 ×	1.34 ×		1.34 ×	4.01 ×	7.04 ×	9.71 ×	12.38 ×					
06	D		12.31 ×	9.85 ×	7.39 ×	4.92 ×	2.46 ×		2.46 ×	4.92 ×	7.39 ×	9.85 ×	12.31 ×					
07	D	14.77 ×	12.31 ×	9.85 ×	7.39 ×	4.92 ×	2.46 ×		2.46 ×	4.92 ×	7.39 ×	9.85 ×	12.31 ×	14.77 ×				
	U.D.		12.38 ×	9.71 ×	7.04 ×	4.01 ×	1.34 ×		1.34 ×	4.01 ×	7.04 ×	9.71 ×	12.38 ×					
														SUB TOTAL				
09	D	14.77 ×	12.31 ×	9.85 ×	7.39 ×	4.92 ×	2.46 ×		2.46 ×	4.92 ×	7.39 ×	9.85 ×	12.31 ×	14.77 ×				
10	D	14.77 ×	12.31 ×	9.85 ×	7.39 ×	4.92 ×	2.46 ×		2.46 ×	4.92 ×	7.39 ×	9.85 ×	12.31 ×	14.77 ×				
	U.D.		12.38 ×	9.71 ×	7.04 ×	4.01 ×	1.34 ×		1.34 ×	4.01 ×	7.04 ×	9.71 ×	12.38 ×					
11	D	14.77 ×	12.31 ×	9.85 ×	7.39 ×	4.92 ×	2.46 ×		2.46 ×	4.92 ×	7.39 ×	9.85 ×	12.31 ×	14.77 ×				
														SUB TOTAL				
13	D	14.77 ×	12.31 ×	9.85 ×	7.39 ×	4.92 ×	2.46 ×		2.46 ×	4.92 ×	7.39 ×	9.85 ×	12.31 ×	14.77 ×				
	U.D.		12.38 ×	9.71 ×	7.04 ×	4.01 ×	1.34 ×		1.34 ×	4.01 ×	7.04 ×	9.71 ×	12.38 ×					
14	D	14.77 ×	12.31 ×	9.85 ×	7.39 ×	4.92 ×	2.46 ×		2.46 ×	4.92 ×	7.39 ×	9.85 ×	12.31 ×	14.77 ×				
15	D	14.77 ×	12.31 ×	9.85 ×	7.39 ×	4.92 ×	2.46 ×		2.46 ×	4.92 ×	7.39 ×	9.85 ×	12.31 ×	14.77 ×				
	U.D.		12.38 ×	9.71 ×	7.04 ×	4.01 ×	1.34 ×		1.34 ×	4.01 ×	7.04 ×	9.71 ×	12.38 ×					
														SUB TOTAL				
17	D	14.77 ×	12.31 ×	9.85 ×	7.39 ×	4.92 ×	2.46 ×		2.46 ×	4.92 ×	7.39 ×	9.85 ×	12.31 ×	14.77 ×				
	U.D.		12.38 ×	9.71 ×	7.04 ×	4.01 ×	1.34 ×		1.34 ×	4.01 ×	7.04 ×	9.71 ×	12.38 ×					
18	D	14.77 ×	12.31 ×	9.85 ×	7.39 ×	4.92 ×	2.46 ×		2.46 ×	4.92 ×	7.39 ×	9.85 ×	12.31 ×	14.77 ×				
19	D	14.77 ×	12.31 ×	9.85 ×	7.39 ×	4.92 ×	2.46 ×		2.46 ×	4.92 ×	7.39 ×	9.85 ×	12.31 ×	14.77 ×				
	U.D.		12.38 ×	9.71 ×	7.04 ×	4.01 ×	1.34 ×		1.34 ×	4.01 ×	7.04 ×	9.71 ×	12.38 ×					
BAY	U.D. ROW		10	08	06	04	02		01	03	05	07	09	SUB TOTAL				
															TOTAL TO CARRY FWD TORSION			

Figure 1: Example of part of a calculation sheet

船名:__________ 航次:__________ 港口:__________

仅适合本出港所装载的货物

扭 矩 A

跨度 \ 甲板行号		12	10	08	06	04	02	00	01	03	05	07	09	11	本港	上一港	离港	累积
01	D			9.85 ×	7.39 ×	4.92 ×	2.46 ×		2.46 ×	4.92 ×	7.39 ×	9.85 ×						
	U.D.			9.71 ×	7.04 ×	4.01 ×	1.34 ×		1.34 ×	4.01 ×	7.04 ×	9.71 ×						
02	D			9.85 ×	7.39 ×	4.92 ×	2.46 ×		2.46 ×	4.92 ×	7.39 ×	9.85 ×						
03	D			9.85 ×	7.39 ×	4.92 ×	2.46 ×		2.46 ×	4.92 ×	7.39 ×	9.85 ×						
	U.D.			9.71 ×	7.04 ×	4.01 ×	1.34 ×		1.34 ×	4.01 ×	7.04 ×	9.71 ×						
														分累积				
05	D		12.31 ×	9.85 ×	7.39 ×	4.92 ×	2.46 ×		2.46 ×	4.92 ×	7.39 ×	9.85 ×	12.31 ×					
	U.D.		12.38 ×	9.71 ×	7.04 ×	4.01 ×	1.34 ×		1.34 ×	4.01 ×	7.04 ×	9.71 ×	12.38 ×					
06	D		12.31 ×	9.85 ×	7.39 ×	4.92 ×	2.46 ×		2.46 ×	4.92 ×	7.39 ×	9.85 ×	12.31 ×					
07	D	14.77 ×	12.31 ×	9.85 ×	7.39 ×	4.92 ×	2.46 ×		2.46 ×	4.92 ×	7.39 ×	9.85 ×	12.31 ×	14.77 ×				
	U.D.		12.38 ×	9.71 ×	7.04 ×	4.01 ×	1.34 ×		1.34 ×	4.01 ×	7.04 ×	9.71 ×	12.38 ×					
														分累积				
09	D	14.77 ×	12.31 ×	9.85 ×	7.39 ×	4.92 ×	2.46 ×		2.46 ×	4.92 ×	7.39 ×	9.85 ×	12.31 ×	14.77 ×				
10	D	14.77 ×	12.31 ×	9.85 ×	7.39 ×	4.92 ×	2.46 ×		2.46 ×	4.92 ×	7.39 ×	9.85 ×	12.31 ×	14.77 ×				
	U.D.		12.38 ×	9.71 ×	7.04 ×	4.01 ×	1.34 ×		1.34 ×	4.01 ×	7.04 ×	9.71 ×	12.38 ×					
11	D	14.77 ×	12.31 ×	9.85 ×	7.39 ×	4.92 ×	2.46 ×		2.46 ×	4.92 ×	7.39 ×	9.85 ×	12.31 ×	14.77 ×				
														分累积				
13	D	14.77 ×	12.31 ×	9.85 ×	7.39 ×	4.92 ×	2.46 ×		2.46 ×	4.92 ×	7.39 ×	9.85 ×	12.31 ×	14.77 ×				
	U.D.		12.38 ×	9.71 ×	7.04 ×	4.01 ×	1.34 ×		1.34 ×	4.01 ×	7.04 ×	9.71 ×	12.38 ×					
14	D	14.77 ×	12.31 ×	9.85 ×	7.39 ×	4.92 ×	2.46 ×		2.46 ×	4.92 ×	7.39 ×	9.85 ×	12.31 ×	14.77 ×				
15	D	14.77 ×	12.31 ×	9.85 ×	7.39 ×	4.92 ×	2.46 ×		2.46 ×	4.92 ×	7.39 ×	9.85 ×	12.31 ×	14.77 ×				
	U.D.		12.38 ×	9.71 ×	7.04 ×	4.01 ×	1.34 ×		1.34 ×	4.01 ×	7.04 ×	9.71 ×	12.38 ×					
														分累积				
17	D	14.77 ×	12.31 ×	9.85 ×	7.39 ×	4.92 ×	2.46 ×		2.46 ×	4.92 ×	7.39 ×	9.85 ×	12.31 ×	14.77 ×				
	U.D.		12.38 ×	9.71 ×	7.04 ×	4.01 ×	1.34 ×		1.34 ×	4.01 ×	7.04 ×	9.71 ×	12.38 ×					
18	D	14.77 ×	12.31 ×	9.85 ×	7.39 ×	4.92 ×	2.46 ×		2.46 ×	4.92 ×	7.39 ×	9.85 ×	12.31 ×	14.77 ×				
19	D	14.77 ×	12.31 ×	9.85 ×	7.39 ×	4.92 ×	2.46 ×		2.46 ×	4.92 ×	7.39 ×	9.85 ×	12.31 ×	14.77 ×				
	U.D.		12.38 ×	9.71 ×	7.04 ×	4.01 ×	1.34 ×		1.34 ×	4.01 ×	7.04 ×	9.71 ×	12.38 ×					
跨度 \ 甲板行号			10	08	06	04	02		01	03	05	07	09	分累积				
															总和			

图1.计算表格部分的示例

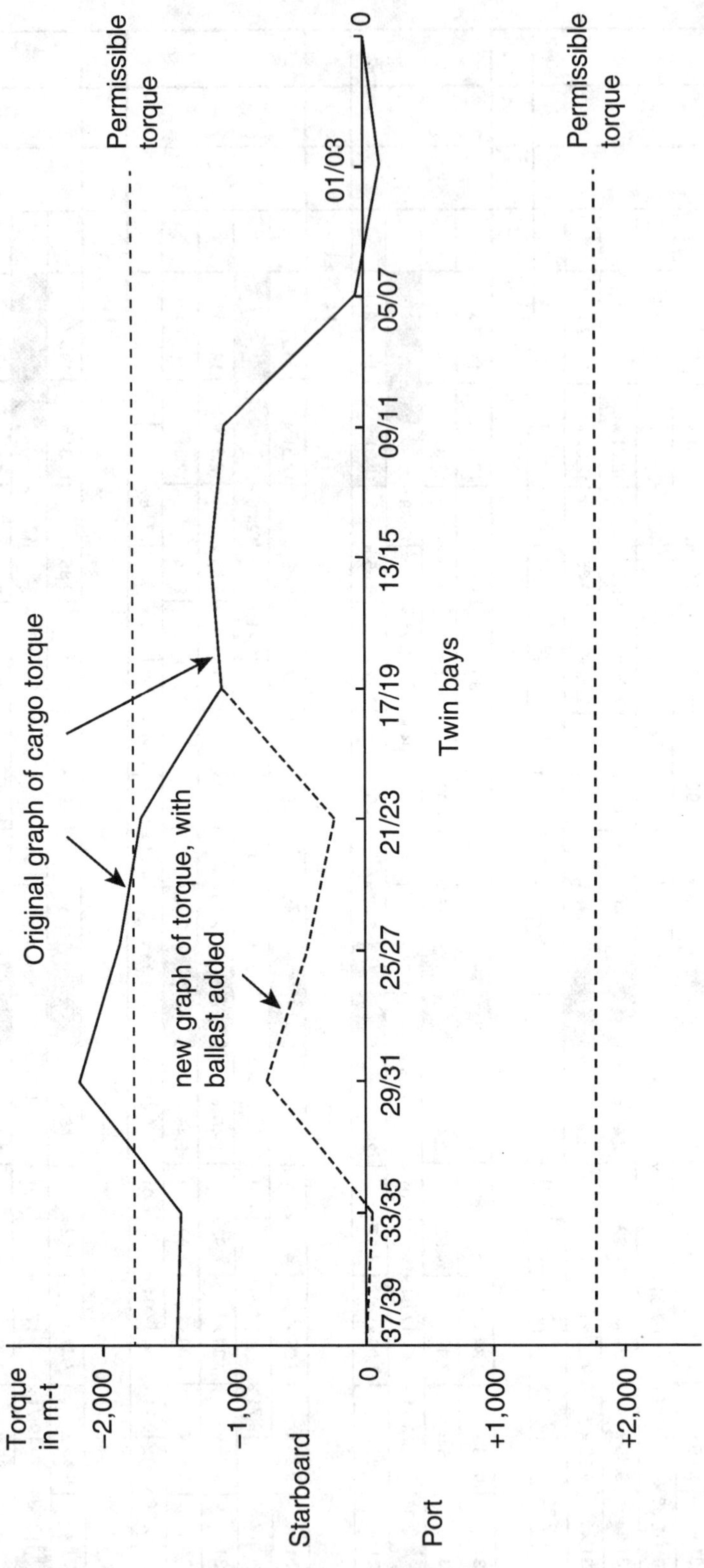

Figure 3: Graph of cargo torque

Knowledge of loading cargoes and ballasting in order to keep hull stress within acceptable limits **(6 hours)**

The importance of devising a cargo stowage plan and loading/unloading plan referring to the loading manual to ascertain an appropriate cargo load distribution, satisfying the imposed limits on structural loading should be pointed out to the trainees. The ship can undergo

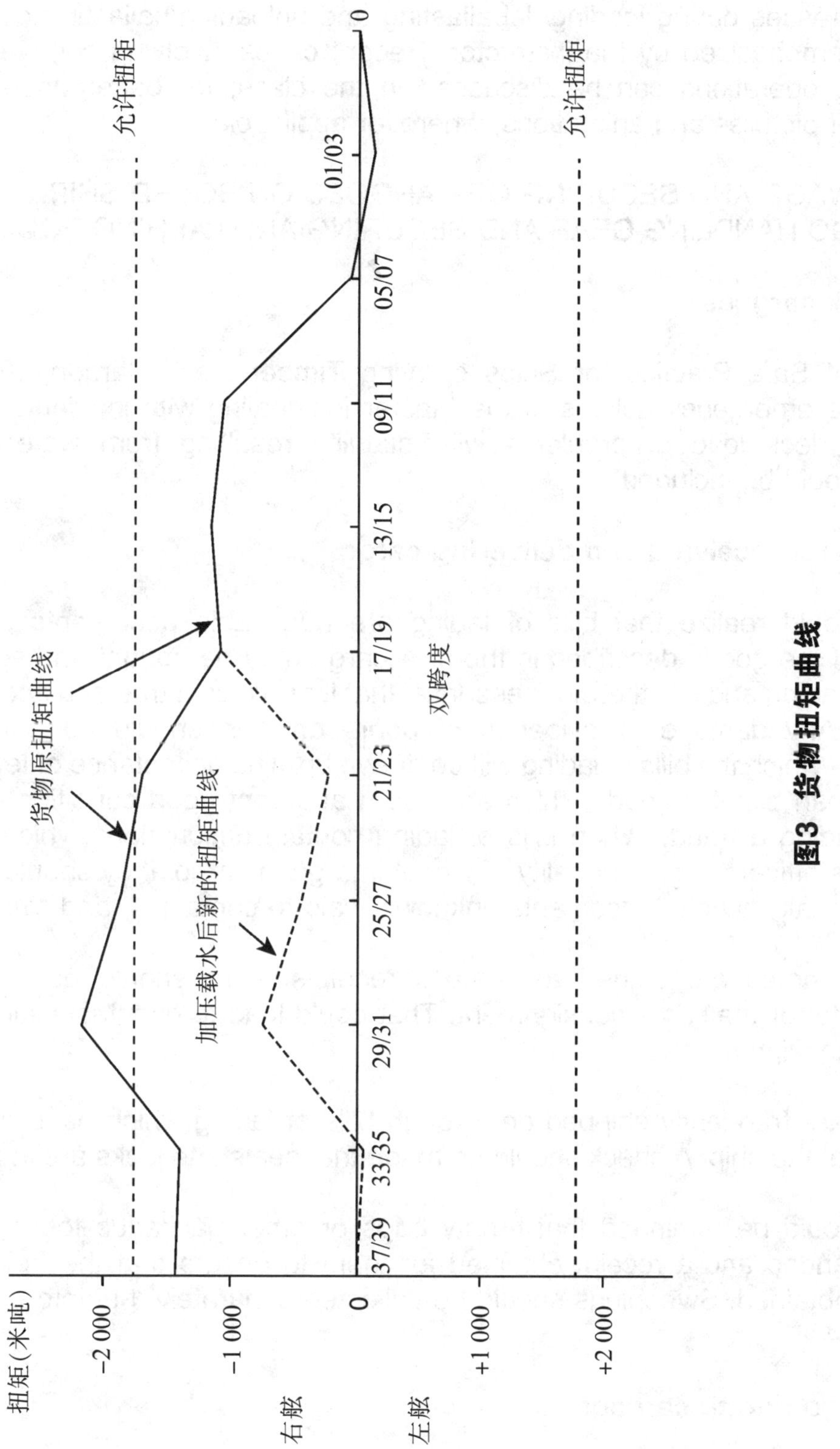

图3 货物扭矩曲线

为保持船体应力在可接受范围内的货物装载和压载知识 **(6学时)**

应向学员指出参照装载手册编制货物积载图和装/卸货计划，确定适当的货物载荷分配,以满足结构载荷限制的重要性。教员有必要强调,在装货/排压载水和卸货/打入压载水作业期间,船

excessive stresses during loading/deballasting and unloading/ballasting operations and these need to be emphasized by the instructor. Recent cases involving complete structural failure during these operations can be discussed in the class, for better understanding, with the assistance of pictures and animations, wherever applicable.

2.1.4 STOWAGE AND SECURING OF CARGOES ON BOARD SHIP, CARGO HANDLING GEAR AND SECURING AND LASHING EQUIPMENT (19 hours)

Timber deck cargoes (3 hours)

The Code of Safe Practice for Ships carrying Timber Deck Cargoes (R9) should be fully covered. The emergency actions of the Master for dealing with incidents such as the partial loss of the deck load or problems with stability resulting from water absorption or ice accretion should be included.

Procedures for receiving and delivering cargo (3 hours)

Trainees should realize that bills of lading are negotiable documents and provide title to ownership of the goods described in them. A cargo may be bought and sold on the evidence of the bill of lading and it is therefore essential that it provides a true and accurate description of the goods. Any damage or evidence of poor condition should be noted on the mate's receipts from which the bills of lading will be drawn up. The acceptance of letters of indemnity in return for clean bills for goods which are not in apparent good condition could be construed as compounding a fraud. When bills of lading contain descriptions which cannot be verified by the ship's officers, e.g. the quality of wheat in a grain cargo, they should be qualified by the inclusion of "said to be...", "contents unknown, said to contain..." and similar expressions.

Where boat notes are signed as mate's receipts, care should be taken not to sign a duplicate note for the same consignment. That could lead to eventual claims for the complete loss of the consignment.

Containers are frequently shipped on through bills of lading which have been issued prior to their arrival at the ship. A check should be made that seals and locks are in place at shipment.

Trainees should be reminded that empty bags or other packages found during discharging should be landed and a receipt obtained for them to ensure that the freight earned on their carriage is obtained. Sweepings should be collected separately, put into bags and discharged as such, V74.

Care of cargo during carriage (4 hours)

The general principles of stowage and care of cargoes should be covered. The requirements for particular commodities can be found in reference books such as T31.

Measures taken for the care of cargo during the voyage, such as the use of ventilation systems or inspections of lashings, should be entered in the logbook. Entries should also be made if ventilation is suspended due to heavy weather or any other circumstances which may have an adverse effect on the cargo. The Master will include such entries in the log extracts to support the noting of protest.

舶可经受过大应力。在课堂上,可讨论近期发生的在这些作业期间整个船体结构受损的案例,如可行,借助于图片和动画,以利于更好地理解。

2.1.4 船上货物积载与系固、货物装卸设备及系固和绑扎设备 (19学时)

木材甲板货 **(3学时)**

应完全涵盖《关于船舶运载木材甲板货安全操作规则》(R9)的内容。应包括船长处理事故,如甲板装载货物的部分损失由于吸水、积冰而产生的稳性问题的应急行动。

接货和交货程序 **(3学时)**

学员应认识到提单是可转让证券,含有货主所有权的条款。在有提单为证的时候货物可以买卖,因此提单中含有真实、确切的对货物的描述是十分必要的。任何货物的损坏或不良状况的证据均要记入大副收据中,据此制定提单。接受作为对表面状况不好的货物出具清洁提单的回报而提供的保函可能被解释为合谋欺诈。当提单中含有不能被船员证实的描述,如谷物货小麦的质量,包含“据说……”,“详情未知,据说是……”以及相似的表述才合适。

对装船单作为大副收据加以签发的货物,应注意不能对同一批货物签发一式两份的收条。那可能导致货物整体损失的最终索赔。

集装箱通常是通过在船舶没有到达之前就签发的提单来运载。在运载期间应检查铅封和锁是否完好。

应提醒学员卸载期间发现的空的袋子或其他包裹应卸到岸上,并获得收据以确保获得其运费。应如V74中所示,应对地脚货进行分别收集,装入袋中并卸载。

运载期间货物的照管 **(4学时)**

应包含货物积载和照管的一般原则。在参考书目如T31中能找到有关特殊商品的要求。

在航行期间采取的照管货物的措施,例如使用通风设备或检查绑扎,应记入航海日志。如果由于恶劣天气或其他可对货物产生不良影响的环境而暂停通风应记入航海日志。船长在提交海事声明时应提供含有这些记录的航海日志摘要。

Requirements applicable to cargo handling gear **(4 hours)**

Where a national register and certificates are applicable, trainees should be made familiar with the requirements of those and the details of tests and examinations which should be entered.

In some ports, the trades union representative of the dock labour force may insist on inspecting the register and rigging plan before work commences. It is important that changes in items such as blocks and shackles attached to a derrick are noted on the rigging plan.

Maintenance of cargo gear **(3 hours)**

This section deals with the practical maintenance and inspection of cargo gear. Attention should be drawn to the requirement that no new item of loose gear should be made of wrought iron. Any existing items of wrought iron are subject to the requirements for periodic heat treatment, unless exempted.

Maintenance of hatch covers **(2 hours)**

The water tightness of hatch covers is vital, both for the safety of the ship and for the protection of cargo from water damage. Before loading a bulk cargo that has a tendency to liquefy or which produces dangerous fumes in contact with water, the hatch covers should be hose-tested for watertightness (V60).

In combination carriers, the proper sealing of hatches is essential to prevent the release of flammable vapour at deck level and for the maintenance of a small positive pressure by the inert gas system.

2.1.5 LOADING AND UNLOADING OPERATIONS, WITH SPECIAL REGARD TO THE TRANSPORT OF CARGOES IDENTIFIED IN THE CODE OF SAFE PRACTICE FOR CARGO STOWAGE AND SECURING (6 hours)

Loading, stowage and discharge of heavy weights **(3 hours)**

Heavy lifts require careful planning before loading. The position in which they are to be stowed must be prepared to accept the lift, possibly requiring the construction of special cradles to support the load. Adequate means of securing must be provided, which often necessitates the welding of additional eye-bolts to the deck. The stability of the ship must be sufficient to limit the list to a reasonable angle both when loading and discharging with the ship's gear. All heavy-lift operations should be supervised by a senior officer (V69).

Methods and safeguards when fumigating holds **(2 hours)**

A thorough knowledge and understanding of the Recommendations on the Safe Use of Pesticides in Ships and its supplement is required.

货物装卸设备的要求 **(4学时)**

在可适用船籍登记和证书的地方,学员应熟悉其要求以及应进行测试和考试的细节。

在有些港口,码头劳工部门工会的代表在开始作业前,可能会坚持检查船籍证书和索具布置图。在索具布置图上标注诸如吊杆附属的滑车和卸扣这些项目的变动是重要的。

货物设备的维护 **(3学时)**

本节涉及货物设备的实际维护和检查。应注意,没有新的可卸零部件应由锻铁制成的要求。任何现存的锻铁部件受制于定期热加工的要求,除非获得豁免。

舱盖的维护 **(2学时)**

为船舶安全和防止货物受海水的损害,舱盖的水密性是十分重要的。在装载与水接触有液化的倾向或产生危险气体的散装货物之前,舱盖应进行水密性的冲水试验(V60)。

在通用货轮中,为防止易燃气体溢漏在甲板以及利用惰性气体系统保持小的货舱正压力,封舱是必要的。

2.1.5 装卸作业,特别注意货物积载与系固安全操作公约中确认的货物运输内容 (6学时)

重型货物的装载、积载和卸载 **(3学时)**

在装载重货之前需要仔细计划。装载的位置必须加以准备以承受该重货,或许要求建造特殊的支架来支撑该载荷。应提供正确的系固方式,该方式通常需要将额外的带环螺栓焊接到甲板上。装卸时,借助索具,船舶必须具有足够的稳性将横倾限制在一个合理的角度内。所有重吊作业应受资深驾驶员的监督(V69)。

熏舱的方法和防护措施 **(2学时)**

要求完全理解和掌握《关于船上安全使用杀虫剂的建议》及其补篇。

2.1.6 GENERAL KNOWLEDGE OF TANKERS AND TANKER OPERATIONS (16 hours)

Terms and definitions **(1 hour)**

Instructors will find much of the material for the basis of lectures in T14.

Contents and application of the International Safety Guide for Oil Tankers and Terminals (ISGOTT) **(2 hours)**

This section is intended to provide a general introduction to tanker operations and the guidance available in the ISGOTT. The instructor should point out the 4 parts of ISGOTT, and brief explanation of each chapter should be discussed with trainees.

Oil tanker operations and related pollution prevention regulations **(3 hours)**

Trainees should be aware of the procedures for ballasting, tank cleaning and gas-freeing and how these are performed within the requirements of MARPOL. A detailed treatment of the operations is not required (V64, V78).

Chemical tankers **(3 hours)**

This section provides a general introduction to the construction and equipment of chemical tankers as set out in the IBC Code. Only a simple treatment of operations is intended since officers who will serve in such ships are required to undertake additional specialized training. Further information on cargoes and operations may be found in reference Textbook Ref. R82 and video V61, V62, V63.

Tank cleaning and control of pollution in chemical tankers **(2 hours)**

The emphasis should be on how tank cleaning and ballasting operations are carried out in compliance with Annex II of the MARPOL Convention and, in particular, on the use of the Procedures and Arrangements Manual to ensure compliance with the regulations.

Gas tankers **(3 hours)**

This section provides a general overview of the different types of gas tanker, their construction and their equipment as set out in the IGC Code. The treatment should take account of the fact that officers who will serve in gas tankers will undertake further specialized training (V56, V129).

Cargo operations in gas tankers **(2 hours)**

The objective of this section is to provide a general insight into the sequence of cargo operations carried out aboard gas tankers without going into detail. Further information will be found in references.

2.1.6　油船和油船作业的常识　(16学时)

术语和定义　**(1学时)**

教员将在T14中发现许多讲课的基本材料。

国际油船和码头安全指南的内容和应用(ISGOTT)　**(2学时)**

本节旨在提供ISGOTT里可供使用的油船作业和指南的一般介绍。教员应指出ISGOTT的4个部分,并与学员讨论各章的简要说明。

油船操作和有关的防污染规则　**(3学时)**

学员应意识到压载、清舱和除气的程序以及如何按MARPOL的要求进行之。不要求详细的操作处理(V64,V78)。

化学品船　**(3学时)**

本节提供了IBC公约中阐述的化学品船的结构和设备的一般介绍。由于在这类船上服务的船员要进行额外的专业培训，所以仅涉及简单的操作处理。在参考教材Ref.T82和录像带V61、V62和V63中可以发现有关货物和操作的进一步信息。

化学品船的洗舱和污染控制　**(2学时)**

强调如何按照MARPOL公约附件Ⅱ，特别是程序和设备手册的使用，来进行洗舱和压载作业,以确保遵循该规则。

液化气船　**(3学时)**

本节提供IGC公约所阐述的液化气船的不同类型、结构和设备的一般概述。操作处理应考虑将在液化气船上任职的船员需要接受进一步的专业培训的事实(V56,V129)。

液化气船的货物操作　**(2学时)**

本节的目的是提供液化气船上货物作业顺序的一般性介绍而不详细讨论。在参考书目中可以发现进一步的信息。

2.1.7 KNOWLEDGE OF THE OPERATIONAL AND DESIGN LIMITATIONS OF BULK CARRIERS (5 hours)

Operational and design limitations of bulk carriers **(3 hours)**

Trainees should be able to identify the problems generally considered to be associated with bulk carriers, such as high density cargoes, leading to loss of buoyancy or structural failure, if holds are flooded in the loaded condition, high loading rate, leading to possible loss of control of load condition; with consequent high stresses, vulnerability to internal damage during cargo loading and discharging operations, leading to protective coating damage, accelerated corrosion, and local structural failure, low freeboard, leading to high green sea loads on deck structures, vulnerability to flooding of forward holds, rapid corrosion caused by corrosive cargo. Many points have been included in the detailed teaching, which the Instructors should point out to trainees.

SOLAS chapter XII Additional safety measures for bulk carriers **(1 hour)**

Instructors should explain chapter XII of the SOLAS Convention which contains regulations of Additional safety measures for bulk carriers with the trainees including, but not limited to, restrictions in carriage of high density dry bulk cargoes, document of compliance, permanent marking on the side shell, damage stability requirements, loading instruments, hold, ballast and dry space water ingress alarms requirements, availability of pumping systems requirements and restrictions from sailing with any hold empty.

CSR Bulk **(1 hour)**

Instructors should point out the reasons, intention and benefit of the Common Structural rules for bulk carriers.

2.1.8 LOADING, CARE AND UNLOADING OF BULK CARGOES (6 hours)

Application of all available shipboard data related to loading, care and unloading of bulk cargoes **(5 hours)**

Procedure for loading a bulk cargo should be explained in detail. The use of ship's approved loading manual, including its content should be discussed thoroughly with the trainees. The trainee's knowledge in respect of planning and loading/unloading should be assessed from a loading computer.

Code of practice for the safe loading and unloading of bulk carriers (BLU Code) **(1 hour)**

The contents of the BLU Code should be discussed in detail with the trainees. Instructors should also point out the consequences of failure to apply BLU Code to the trainees.

2.1.7　散货船作业与设计限制的知识　(5学时)

散货船作业与设计限制　(3学时)

学员应能识别通常被认为与散货船相关的问题,如高密度货物,导致浮力损失或结构损坏,如装货情况下货舱进水,高速装载导致装载状况的可能失控;随之而来的高应力,装卸货期间易受内部损坏,导致保护涂层受损,加速腐蚀和局部结构受损;低干舷导致大量上浪加大了甲板结构的负荷,前部货舱易进水,腐蚀性货物造成的快速腐蚀。教员应向学员指出,许多要点已经包含在具体教学之中。

SOLAS公约第12章有关散货船的附加安全措施　(1学时)

教员应向学员解释SOLAS公约第12章包含散货船附加安全措施，包括但不限于运输高密度干散货的限制、符合证明、船壳永久标志、破损稳性要求、装载仪、货舱、压载和干舱进水报警要求、泵系统可用性要求和任何货舱空载航行限制。

CSR 散货船　(1学时)

教员应指出散货船共同结构规则的原因、意图和益处。

2.1.8　散货的装载、照管与卸载　(6学时)

与散货的装载、照管和卸载有关的所有船舶数据的运用　(5学时)

应详细解释散货装载程序。应与学员全面讨论经批准的船舶装载手册的使用,包括其内容。应用装载计算机评估学员在计划和装/卸方面的知识。

散货船安全装卸操作规则(BLU 规则)　(1学时)

应与学员详细讨论BLU 规则的内容。教员还应向学员指出未能运用BLU 规则的后果。

2.1.9 SAFE CARGO HANDLING IN ACCORDANCE WITH THE PROVISIONS OF THE RELEVANT INSTRUMENTS (3 hours)

Establish procedures for safe cargo handling in accordance with the provisions of the relevant instruments such as:

- IMDG Code
- IMSBC Code
- MARPOL 73/78, Annexes III and V

The safe cargo handling in accordance with these codes and conventions should be discussed with the trainees. The points are covered in the detailed teaching syllabus, which the instructors should find useful.

2.1.10 EFFECTIVE COMMUNICATIONS AND IMPROVING WORKING RELATIONSHIPS

Basic principles for establishing effective communications and improving working relationships between ship and terminal personnel (1 hour)

The information that needs to be exchanged with shore should be discussed in detail with the trainees.

2.2 ASSESS REPORTED DEFECTS AND DAMAGE TO CARGO SPACES, HATCH COVERS AND BALLAST TANKS AND TAKE APPROPRIATE ACTION

2.2.1 LIMITATIONS ON STRENGTH OF THE VITAL CONSTRUCTIONAL PARTS OF A STANDARD BULK CARRIER AND INTERPRET GIVEN FIGURES FOR BENDING MOMENTS AND SHEAR FORCES (3 hours)

Instructors should make use of the points explained in the detailed teaching syllabus, and discuss them in detail with the trainees

2.2.2 METHODS TO AVOID THE DETRIMENTAL EFFECTS ON BULK CARRIERS OF CORROSION, FATIGUE AND INADEQUATE CARGO HANDLING (3 hours)

Instructors should make use of the points explained in the detailed teaching syllabus, and discuss them in detail with the trainees

2.3 CARRIAGE OF DANGEROUS GOODS

2.3.1 INTERNATIONAL REGULATIONS, STANDARDS, CODES INCLUDING THE INTERNATIONAL MARITIME DANGEROUS GOODS (IMDG) CODE AND THE INTERNATIONAL MARITIME SOLID BULK CARGOES (IMSBC) CODE AND RECOMMENDATIONS ON CARRIAGE OF DANGEROUS CARGOES (3 hours)

Instructors should refer to the IMO references concerning this topic and design exercises to let officers practise using information contained in the IMDG Code, the **International Maritime Solid Bulk Cargoes (IMSBC) Code**, which replaces the **Code of Safe Practice for Solid Bulk Cargoes (BC Code)**, which aims primarily to facilitate the safe stowage and

2.1.9 按照相关文件规定安全装卸货物 (3学时)

按照下列文件规定建立安全装卸货物程序:

- IMDG 规则
- IMSBC 规则
- MARPOL 73/78, 附件III和附件V

应与学员讨论按照这些规则和公约安全装卸货物。要点包含在详细的教学大纲细则之中,教员应发现这些是有用的。

2.1.10 有效的沟通与改善工作关系

船舶和码头人员间建立有效沟通与改善工作关系的基本原则 **(1学时)**

应与学员详细讨论需要与岸方交换的信息。

2.2 评估报告中的货舱、舱盖和压载舱的缺陷和损坏以及采取适当的行动

2.2.1 对标准散货船重要结构的强度限制和解释给出的弯矩与剪力数据 (3学时)

教员应利用教学大纲细则中阐述的要点,并与学员详细讨论。

2.2.2 避免腐蚀、疲劳和不当装卸对散货船造成不利影响的方法 (3学时)

教员应利用教学大纲细则中阐述的要点,并与学员详细讨论。

2.3 危险货物运输

2.3.1 有关运载危险货物的国际规定、标准、规则和建议,包括《国际海运危险货物规则》(IMDG)、《国际海运固体散货规则》(IMSBC)和危险货物运输建议 (3学时)

教员应参考IMO有关本课题的文献并设计练习让船员练习使用IMDG规则、《国际海运固体散货规则》(IMSBC) 和IBC规则里所包含的信息。IMSBC取代《固体散货安全操作规则》(BC规则),其主要目的是通过提供与装运某些固体散货相关的危险信息和当考虑装运固体散货时采用的程序相关的指导,以促进固体散货的安全积载和运输。

shipment of solid bulk cargoes by providing information on the dangers associated with the shipment of certain types of solid bulk cargoes and instructions on the procedures to be adopted when the shipment of solid bulk cargoes is contemplated and the IBC Code.

2.3.2 CARRIAGE OF DANGEROUS, HAZARDOUS AND HARMFUL CARGOES; PRECAUTIONS DURING LOADING AND UNLOADING AND CARE DURING THE VOYAGE OF DANGEROUS, HAZARDOUS AND HARMFUL CARGOES

Dangerous goods in packages **(10 hours)**

Trainees should be able to use the IMDG Code to find the information, stowage requirements and precautions to take for a given substance. They should also find the correct emergency schedule and the relevant entry in the MFAG for that substance. Given several substances, they should be able to determine the required segregation between them, including applications to containers and ro-ro units.

It should be pointed out to trainees that safety in the handling and carriage of dangerous goods is primarily ensured by the specification of stringent packaging requirements. Damaged packages should not be accepted for loading. The new requirements as per IMDG Code, for the training of all staff (shore and sea) at both operational and management level, who handle or process dangerous goods shipments for transportation by sea should be pointed out.

Solid bulk cargoes **(9 hours)**

This section deals with the International Maritime Solid Bulk Cargoes (IMSBC Code). A ship may be required to carry a substance not included in the Code. The Master should obtain all relevant information about its properties before loading it. The type of information included in the Code should be used as a guide to what questions should be asked.

Previous loading practices and maintenance activity appear to be important factors in the safety of dry bulk carriers. Instructors should explain the problems suffered by some single skin dry bulkers in the early 1990s. The majority were over 15 years of age and were carrying iron ore at the time of the loss. Masters and chief officers should be able to identify potential weak points and carry out routine inspections to detect unsafe conditions and take appropriate actions. Focus should be on the structural arrangements and hull integrity with emphasis on the critical areas of the structure: hatch corners, coamings; main frames and brackets; topside tanks; transverse bulkheads and any damage caused during cargo handling.

IACS classification societies introduced an enhanced survey programme (ESP) for bulkers and tankers in 1993 covering the preparation and planning of hull surveys, harmonized bottom survey in dry dock with class renewal survey, maintenance of a survey documents file on board and corrosion prevention measures (T35, V59). This was adopted in chapter XI of SOLAS as regulation 2 Enhanced surveys, applicable to oil tankers and bulk carriers from July 1998.

International Code for the Safe Carriage of Grain in Bulk (International Grain Code) **(7 hours)**

An example of a grain loading calculation should be made by trainees.

2.3.2 危险货物、有毒货物和有害货物的运载;装卸期间的预防措施及危险货物、有毒货物和有害货物航行期间的照管

包装类危险货物 **(10学时)**

学员应能够利用IMDG规则找到给定物质的信息、积载要求和应采取的预防措施。他们也应能在MFAG里找到该物质的正确的应急表和相关的记录。在给定几种物质的情况下,他们应能够确定在物质之间所需的隔离,包括在集装箱和滚装单元中的应用。

应向学员指出,安全装卸和运载危险货物主要靠严格的包装要求规范来保证。装载中不应接受包装破损的货物。应指出,按照IMDG规则,对负责装卸或处理海运危险货物的船岸操作级和管理级人员,有新的培训要求。

固体散货 **(9学时)**

本节涉及《国际海运固体散货规则》(IMSBC),可以要求船舶运载该规则里没有包含的物质。船长应在装载之前获得货物的所有相关性质的信息。规则里所包含的信息类型应被用作应考核问题的指南。

先前的装载操作和维护保养活动对干散货船的安全似乎是重要的因素。教员应解释在20世纪90年代初期单壳干散货船所出现的问题。在发生事故的时候,大部分船超过15年船龄,正在运铁矿石。船长和大副应能够识别潜在的薄弱点,并进行例行检查以发现不安全的情况并采取适当的行动。重点应放在结构安排和强调船体完整性结构的关键部分:舱口角、舱盖围,主框架和支架,顶边舱,横舱壁以及装卸货物过程中产生的损坏处。

IACS在1993年提出散货船和油船加强检验程序(ESP),包括船体检验的准备和计划,干船坞船底情况和船籍换证的统一检验,船上检验文件的保管和防止腐蚀的措施(T35,V59)。这已被SOLAS第11章规则2加强检验所采纳,从1998年7月应用于油船和散装船。

《国际散装谷物安全运输规则》(国际谷物规则) **(7学时)**

学员进行谷物装载计算实例。

Master and Chief Mate

Function 3:
Controlling the Operation of the Ship and Care for Persons on Board at the Management Level

船长和大副

功能3：
管理级船舶作业管理和人员管理

Master and Chief Mate

Function 3: Controlling the Operation of the Ship and Care for Persons on Board at the Management Level

INDEX

Page

Part B3: Course Outline **386**
Timetable
Lectures
Course outline

Part C3: Detailed Teaching Syllabus **394**
Introduction
Explanation of information contained in the syllabus tables
3.1 Control trim, stability and stress
3.2 Monitor and control compliance with legislative requirements and measures to ensure safety of life at sea and the protection of the marine environment
3.3 Maintain safety and security of the ship's crew and passengers and the operational condition of life-saving, firefighting and other safety systems
3.4 Develop emergency and damage control plans and handle emergency situations
3.5 Use of leadership and managerial skills
3.6 Organize and manage the provision of medical care on board

Part D3: Instructor Manual **568**

船长和大副

功能3：管理级船舶作业管理和人员管理

索引

页码

B3部分： **课程概要** **387**

时间表

教学

课程概要

C3部分： **教学大纲细则** **395**

介绍

教学大纲细则里的信息说明

3.1 控制吃水差、稳性和应力

3.2 根据立法要求的监督与控制以及确保海上人命安全和海洋环境保护的措施

3.3 维护船员和乘客的安全和治安以及救生、消防和其他安全系统的操作条件

3.4 制定破损控制图并处理紧急状况

3.5 领导力和管理技能的运用

3.6 船上医护的组织和管理

D3部分： **教员手册** **569**

Part B3: Course Outline

■ Timetable

No formal example of a timetable is included in this model course.

Development of a detailed timetable depends on the level of skills of the officers entering the course and the amount of revision work of basic principles that may be required.

Lecturers must develop their own timetable depending on:

- the level of skills of trainees
- the numbers to be trained
- the number of instructors

and normal practices at the training establishment.

Preparation and planning constitute an important factor which makes a major contribution to the effective presentation of any course of instruction.

■ Lectures

As far as possible, lectures should be presented within a familiar context and should make use of practical examples. They should be well illustrated with diagrams, photographs and charts where appropriate, and be related to matter learned during seagoing time.

An effective manner of presentation is to develop a technique of giving information and then reinforcing it. For example, first tell the trainees briefly what you are going to present to them; then cover the topic in detail; and, finally, summarize what you have told them. The use of an overhead projector and the distribution of copies of the transparencies as trainees handouts contribute to the learning process.

■ Course outline

The tables that follow list the competencies and areas of knowledge, understanding and proficiency, together with the estimated total hours required for lectures and practical exercises. Teaching staff should note that timings are suggestions only and should be adapted to suit individual groups of trainees depending on their experience, ability, equipment and staff available for training.

B3部分:课程概要

■ 时间表

本示范课程中没有包含正式的示例课时表。

详细的时间表要根据学员技术等级和对基本原理的复习量来制定。

教员必须根据下面情况制定自己的课程表:

- 学员的技术水平
- 需培训的项目
- 教员数量

以及在培训地的常规实践操作。

教学前的准备及计划是任何课程教学中取得良好教学效果的重要因素。

■ 教学

教员应尽可能在熟悉的背景范围内讲解并结合实际例子。讲课中也应在适当的时候运用示意图、照片、图表等进行图示说明,并联系航海实践中遇到的一些实际问题进行讲解。

一个有效实施方式就是先进行授课,再加强提高。例如:先向学员概述授课内容;然后进行详解;最后进行总结。利用投影仪及向学员分发教学资料幻灯片拷贝等方式有助于其学习进程。

■ 课程概要

以下课程表中列出了对知识、理解与熟练程度及对适任能力的要求,列出了授课、实习的总时数。教员须注意此处的总时数为建议性的,要根据学员的经验、能力、设备及师资力量等不同情况进行调整。

Knowledge, understanding and proficiency	Total hours for each topic	Total hours for each subject area of required performance
Competence:		
3.1 CONTROL TRIM, STABILITY AND STRESS		
3.1.1 FUNDAMENTAL PRINCIPLES OF SHIP CONSTRUCTION, TRIM AND STABILITY		
.1 Shipbuilding materials	3	
.2 Welding	3	
.3 Bulkheads	4	
.4 Watertight and weathertight doors	3	
.5 Corrosion and its prevention	4	
.6 Surveys and dry-docking	2	
.7 Stability	83	102
3.1.2 EFFECT ON TRIM AND STABILITY IN THE EVENT OF DAMAGE AND STABILITY		
.1 Effect on trim and stability of a ship in the event of damage to and consequent flooding of a compartment and countermeasures to be taken	9	
.2 Theories affecting trim and stability	2	11
3.1.3 KNOWLEDGE OF IMO RECOMMENDATIONS CONCERNING SHIP STABILITY		
.1 Responsibilities under the relevant requirements of the international conventions and codes	2	2
3.1.2 EFFECT ON TRIM AND STABILITY IN THE EVENT OF DAMAGE AND STABILITY		
3.2 MONITOR AND CONTROL COMPLIANCE WITH LEGISLATIVE REQUIREMENTS AND MEASURES TO ENSURE SAFETY OF LIFE AT SEA AND THE PROTECTION OF THE MARINE ENVIRONMENT		
3.2.1 INTERNATIONAL MARITIME LAW EMBODIED IN INTERNATIONAL AGREEMENTS AND CONVENTIONS		
.1 Certificates and other documents required to be carried on board ships by international conventions	1	
.2 Responsibilities under the relevant requirements of the International Convention on Load Lines	1	
.3 Responsibilities under the relevant requirements of the International Convention for the Safety of Life at Sea	2	
.4 Responsibilities under the International Convention for the Prevention of Pollution from Ships	3	
.5 Maritime declarations of health and the requirements of the International Health Regulations	3	
.6 Responsibilities under other international maritime law embodied in international agreements and conventions that impact on the role of management level deck officers	35	

知识、理解和熟练	**每一标题的总学时**	**技能要求中每一科目的总学时**
适任:		
3.1 控制吃水差、稳性和应力		
3.1.1 船舶结构、吃水差和稳性的基本原理		
.1 造船材料	3	
.2 焊接	3	
.3 隔舱壁	4	
.4 水密门和风雨密门	3	
.5 腐蚀和防腐蚀	4	
.6 检验和进入干船坞	2	
.7 稳性	83	102
3.1.2 船体损坏并进水对吃水差和稳性的影响		
.1 船体破损并舱室进水对稳性和吃水的影响以及应采取的对策	9	
.2 影响吃水差和稳性的理论	2	11
3.1.3 IMO 关于船舶稳性的建议的理解		
.1 国际公约和规则相关要求下的责任	2	2
3.2 根据立法要求的监督与控制以及确保海上人命安全和海洋环境保护的措施		
3.2.1 在国际协议和国际公约中所体现的国际海事法		
.1 国际公约要求船舶所携带的证书和其他文件	1	
.2 《国际载重线公约》相关要求下的责任	1	
.3 《国际海上人命安全公约》相关要求下的责任	2	
.4 《国际防止船舶污染公约》相关要求下的责任	3	
.5 航海健康声明书和《国际卫生条例》的要求	3	
.6 影响管理级船员作用的国际协议和国际公约所体现的其他国际海事法相关要求的责任	35	

Knowledge, understanding and proficiency	Total hours for each topic	Total hours for each subject area of required performance
.7 Responsibilities under international instruments affecting the safety of the ship, passengers, crew and cargo	4	
.8 Methods and aids to prevent pollution of the marine environment by ships	2	
.9 National legislation for implementing international agreements and conventions	1	52
3.3 MAINTAIN SAFETY AND SECURITY OF THE SHIP'S CREW AND PASSENGERS AND THE OPERATIONAL CONDITION OF LIFE-SAVING, FIREFIGHTING AND OTHER SAFETY SYSTEMS		
3.3.1 KNOWLEDGE OF LIFE–SAVING APPLIANCE REGULATIONS	2	2
3.3.2 ORGANIZATION OF FIRE DRILLS AND ABANDON SHIP DRILLS *See IMO model courses 2.03 and 1.23 and STCW Code, sections A-V1/3 and A-V1/2*	–	–
3.3.3 MAINTENANCE OF OPERATIONAL CONDITION OF LIFE-SAVING,FIREFIGHTING AND OTHER SAFETY SYSTEMS *See IMO model courses 2.03 and 1.23 and STCW Code, sections A-V1/3 and A-V1/2*	–	–
3.3.4 ACTIONS TO BE TAKEN TO PROTECT AND SAFEGUARD ALL PERSONS ON BOARD IN EMERGENCIES	4	4
3.3.5 ACTIONS TO LIMIT DAMAGE AND SALVE THE SHIP FOLLOWING A FIRE, EXPLOSION, COLLISION OR GROUNDING	4	4
3.4 DEVELOP EMERGENCY AND DAMAGE CONTROL PLANS AND HANDLE EMERGENCY SITUATIONS		
3.4.1 PREPARATION OF CONTINGENCY PLANS FOR RESPONSE TO EMERGENCIES	9	9
3.4.2 SHIP CONSTRUCTION INCLUDING DAMAGE CONTROL	4	4
3.4.3 METHODS AND AIDS FOR FIRE PREVENTION, DETECTION AND EXTINCTION *See IMO model course 2.03 and STCW Code, section A-V1/3*	–	–
3.4.4 FUNCTIONS AND USE OF LIFE-SAVING APPLIANCES *See IMO model course 1.23 and STCW Code, section A-V1/2-1*	–	–
3.5 USE OF LEADERSHIP AND MANAGERIAL SKILLS		
3.5.1 SHIPBOARD PERSONNEL MANAGEMENT AND TRAINING		
.1 Shipboard personnel management	10	
.2 Training on board ships	6	16
3.5.2 RELATED INTERNATIONAL MARITIME CONVENTIONS, RECOMMENDATIONS AND NATIONAL LEGISLATION		
.1 Related international maritime conventions, recommendations and national legislation	4	4
3.5.3 APPLICATION OF TASK AND WORKLOAD MANAGEMENT		
.1 Task and workload management	8	8

知识、理解和熟练	每一标题的总学时	技能要求中每一科目的总学时
.7 影响船舶、乘客、船员和货物安全的国际文献相关要求下的责任	4	
.8 防止船舶污染海洋环境的方法和手段	2	
.9 实施国际协议和公约的国内立法	1	52
3.3 维护船员和乘客的安全和治安以及救生、消防和其他安全系统的操作条件		
3.3.1 救生设备规则的理解	2	2
3.3.2 消防演习和弃船演习的组织	–	–
参见 IMO 示范课程 2.03 和 1.23 及 STCW 公约第 A-V1/3 节和第 A-V1/2 节	–	–
3.3.3 救生、消防和其他安全系统运行条件的维护		
参见 IMO 示范课程 2.03 和 1.23 及 STCW 公约第 A-V1/3 节和第 A-V1/2 节	4 4	4 4
3.3.4 紧急情况下保护和安保船上所有人员的行动		
3.3.5 发生火灾、爆炸、碰撞或搁浅后,限制船舶破损和救助船舶的行动	9	9
3.4 制定破损控制图并处理紧急状况	4	4
3.4.1 突发事件应急预案的准备	–	–
3.4.2 包括破损控制的船舶建造		
3.4.3 防火、探火、灭火的方法和手段	–	–
参见 IMO 示范课程 2.03 和 STCW 公约第 A-V1/3 节		
3.4.4 救生设备的功能和使用		
参见 IMO 示范课程 1.23 和 STCW 公约第 A-V1/2-1 节	10	
3.5 领导力和管理技能的运用	6	16
3.5.1 船上人员管理和培训		
.1 船上人员管理		
.2 船上培训	4	4
3.5.2 相关的国际海事公约、建议和国内立法		
.1 相关国际海事公约、建议和国内立法	8	8
3.5.3 任务管理和工作量管理的应用		
.1 任务和工作量管理		

Knowledge, understanding and proficiency	Total hours for each topic	Total hours for each subject area of required performance
3.5.4 EFFECTIVE RESOURCE MANAGEMENT		
.1 Application of effective resource management at a management level	10	10
3.5.5 DECISION-MAKING TECHNIQUES		
.1 Situation and risk assessment	2	
.2 Identify and generate options	2	
.3 Selecting course of action	2	7
.4 Evaluation of outcome effectiveness	1	1
3.5.6 DEVELOPMENT, IMPLEMENTATION AND OVERSIGHT OF STANDARD OPERATING PROCEDURES	1	
3.6 ORGANIZE AND MANAGE THE PROVISION OF MEDICAL CARE ON BOARD		
3.6.1 MEDICAL PUBLICATIONS		
.1 International Medical Guide for Ships	0.5	
.2 International Code of Signals (medical section)	0.5	
.3 Medical First Aid Guide for Use in Accidents Involving Dangerous Goods	3	4
Total for Function 3: Controlling the Operation of the Ship and Care for Persons on Board at the Management Level		**244 hours**

Teaching staff and Administrations should note that the hours for lectures and exercises are suggestions only as regards sequence and length of time allocated to each objective. These factors may be adapted by lecturers to suit individual groups of trainees depending on their experience, ability, equipment and staff available for teaching.

知识、理解和熟练	**每一标题的总学时**	**技能要求中每一科目的总学时**
3.5.4 有效的资源管理		
.1 管理级有效的资源管理的运用	10	10
3.5.5 决策技巧		
.1 情境和风险评估	2	
.2 识别和设计替代方案	2	
.3 选择行动方式	2	
.4 结果的有效性评价	1	7
3.5.6 标准作业程序的制定、实施与监督	1	1
3.6 船上医护的组织和管理		
3.6.1 医学出版物		
.1 国际船舶医疗指南	0.5	
.2 国际信号规则(医疗部分)	0.5	
.3 危险货物事故医疗急救指南	3	4
功能 3 总计学时:管理级船舶作业管理和人员管理		**244 学时**

教员和主管机关应注意到课程概要中各学习任务的先后次序和时间安排仅仅是建议,可根据各班组学员的经验、能力、设备和师资配备等实际情况进行适当的调整。

Part C3: Detailed Teaching Syllabus

COMPETENCE 3.1	Control Trim, Stability and Stress	IMO Reference
TRAINING OUTCOMES: Demonstrates a knowledge and understanding of: 3.1.1 FUNDAMENTAL PRINCIPLES OF SHIP CONSTRUCTION, TRIM AND STABILITY 3.1.2 EFFECT ON TRIM AND STABILITY IN THE EVENT OF DAMAGE AND FLOODING 3.1.3 KNOWLEDGE OF IMO RECOMMENDATIONS CONCERNING SHIP STABILITY		STCW Code table A-II/2

C3部分:教学大纲细则

适任 3.1	控制吃水差、稳性和应力	IMO 参考书目
培训效果: 讲授下列内容知识与理解: 3.1.1 船舶结构、吃水差和稳性的基本原理 3.1.2 船体损坏并进水对船舶吃水差和稳性的影响 3.1.3 IMO 关于船舶稳性的建议的理解		STCW 公约 表 A-11/2

COMPETENCE 3.1	Control Trim, Stability and Stress	IMO Reference
3.1.1 FUNDAMENTAL PRINCIPLES OF SHIP CONSTRUCTION, TRIM AND STABILITY **Textbooks/Bibliography:** T4, T5, T17, T28, T35, T44, B3, B29, B35, B118, B144, B206 **Teaching aids:** A1, A4, V85, V120, V121, V122, V141 Required performance: *Note that trainees must be familiar with the content and application of the basic knowledge of ship construction and stability from IMO model course 7.03. This knowledge is considered so fundamental for much of the management level content within this course that there is merit in reviewing the operational level content quickly before covering the additional elements required at management level. The learning time has been reduced for many elements on the basis that trainees will be reviewing rather than learning much of this content at this level. It may be necessary for some trainees to refresh their knowledge of this content before undertaking this management level content*		

1.1 Shipbuilding materials (3 hours)
(Note that this content is not directly required by the STCW Code but is recommended to be included in training courses)
– states that steels are alloys of iron, with properties dependent upon the type and amounts of alloying materials used
– states that the specifications of shipbuilding steels are laid down by classification societies
– states that shipbuilding steel is tested and graded by classification society surveyors, who stamp it with approval marks
– explains that mild steel, graded A to E, is used for most parts of the ship
– states why higher tensile steel may be used in areas of high stress, such as the sheer strake
– explains that the use of higher tensile steel in place of mild steel results in a saving of weight for the same strength
– explains what is meant by:
  – tensile strength
  – ductility
  – hardness
  – toughness
– defines strain as extension divided by original length
– sketches a stress-strain curve for mild steel
– explains:
  – yield point
  – ultimate tensile stress
  – modulus of elasticity
– explains that toughness is related to the tendency to brittle fracture
– explains that stress fracture may be initiated by a small crack or notch in a plate
– states that cold conditions increase the chances of brittle fracture
– states why mild steel is unsuitable for the very low temperatures involved in the containment of liquefied gases
– lists examples where castings or forgings are used in ship construction
– explains the advantages of the use of aluminium alloys in the construction of superstructures
		R1

适任 3.1	控制吃水差、稳性和应力	IMO 参考书目
3.1.1　船舶结构、吃水差和稳性的基本原理 **教科书/参考文献**:T4, T5, T17, T28, T35, T44, B3, B29, B35, B118, B144, B206 **教具**:A1, A4, V85, V120, V121, V122, V141 技能要求: 注意:在完成这些要求的内容之前,学员必须熟悉 IMO 示范课程 7.03 中船舶建造和稳性的基础知识内容及其适用。本课程中的知识对多数管理级内容非常重要,以至于在涉及管理级额外要求的知识点之前,在迅速复习操作级内容方面颇具价值。基于学员将复习而不是学习该级别内容,已经减少了许多知识点的学时。对某些学员而言,在学习管理级内容之前,可能有必要更新这些技能的知识 **1.1　造船材料(3 学时)** (注意:该部分内容并不是 STCW 公约要求的,而是本培训课程所推荐的) – 阐述钢是铁合金,它的性能取决于所用合金材料的类型和数量 – 阐述造船级社制定造船用钢的规格 – 阐述造船用钢由船级社验船师测试并对其加盖许可标志予以定级 – 解释低碳钢,分为 A、B、C、D、E 五级,用于大部分船体 – 阐述为何高强度钢可用于高应力区,如舷侧列板 – 解释使用高强度船体结构钢代替低碳钢在满足同样强度的情况下减轻了船体结构的重量 – 解释下列名词: 　– 抗拉强度 　– 延展性 　– 硬度 　– 韧性 – 定义张力为延展长度除以初始长度 – 画出低碳钢的应力—张力曲线图 – 解释: 　– 屈服点 　– 极限拉应力 　– 弹性模数 – 解释韧性与脆裂的趋势有关 – 解释应力性断裂可能会由钢板上的一个小裂纹或缺口引起 – 阐述寒冷的情况下增加了脆裂的概率 – 阐述为什么低碳钢不适合作为超低温的液化气容器 – 列出使用浇铸和锻造的船体结构范例 – 解释在船舶上层建筑中使用铝合金的优点		R1

COMPETENCE 3.1	Control Trim, Stability and Stress	IMO Reference
– states that aluminium alloys are tested and graded by classification society surveyors – explains how strength is preserved in aluminium superstructures in the event of fire – describes the special precautions against corrosion that are needed where aluminium alloy is connected to steelwork		

1.2 Welding (3 hours)
(Note that this content is not directly required by STCW 2010 but is recommended to be included in training courses)
– describes the process of manual electric arc welding
– explains the purpose of flux during welding
– describes briefly the automatic welding processes, electro-slag, TIG and MIG
– describes butt, lap and fillet welds
– describes the various preparations of a plate edge for welding
– explains what is meant by a full-penetration fillet weld
– explains what is meant by 'single pass', 'multipass' and 'back' run
– explains how welding can give rise to distortion and describes measures which are taken to minimize it
– describes the use of tack welding
– describes weld faults:
  – lack of fusion
  – no inter-run penetration
  – lack of reinforcement
  – lack of root penetration
  – slag inclusion
  – porosity
  – overlap
  – undercut
– states that classification societies require tests on weld materials and electrodes before approving them
– discusses the electrode type and process of welding high tensile steels
– describes gas cutting of metals
– briefly describes the testing of welds:
  – visual
  – radiographic
  – ultrasonic
  – magnetic particle
  – dye penetrant
		R1

1.3 Bulkheads (4 hours) – states that transverse bulkheads serve to subdivide a ship against flooding and spread of fire, to support decks and superstructures and to resist racking stresses – distinguishes between watertight, non-watertight and oil-tight or tank bulkheads		R1

适任 3.1	控制吃水差、稳性和应力	IMO 参考文献
	– 阐述铝合金是由船级社验船师测试并定级的 – 解释发生火灾时铝合金上层建筑的强度是如何保持的 – 描述必须采取特殊的预防措施来防止铝合金和钢材连接处的腐蚀	

1.2	**焊接(3 学时)**
	(注意:该部分内容并不是 2010 STCW 公约要求的,而是本培训课程所推荐的)
	– 描述手工电焊的程序
	– 解释焊接时使用助熔剂的目的
	– 简述自动焊接程序、电渣、TIG(钨极惰性气体保护焊)和 MIG(熔化极惰性气体保护焊)
	– 描述对接、搭接和角接
	– 描述焊接钢板边缘的各种准备工作
	– 解释全焊透填角焊的意思
	– 解释"一次完成"、"多次完成"和"反面"操作的意思
	– 解释焊接如何引发变形和减小变形的措施
	– 描述点焊的运用
	– 描述焊接缺陷:
	  – 未焊透
	  – 内部没焊透
	  – 未加强
	  – 焊渣
	  – 疏松度
	  – 焊瘤
	  – 下陷
	  – 咬边
	– 阐述船级社在批准之前要求对焊接材料和电焊条进行测试
	– 讨论电焊条的种类和高碳钢的焊接过程
	– 描述金属气割
	– 简述焊接的测试:
	  – 视觉
	  – 射线
	  – 超声波
	  – 磁粉
	  – 染料渗透
		R1

1.3	**隔舱壁(4 学时)** – 阐述横舱壁用来船舶分舱以防止船舶进水和火灾的蔓延、支撑甲板和上层建筑、抵抗挤压应力的作用 – 区分水密、非水密和油密或油舱隔舱壁	R1

COMPETENCE 3.1	Control Trim, Stability and Stress	IMO Reference
– defines: – margin line – bulkhead deck – watertight – weathertight – states that cargo ships must have: – a collision bulkhead, watertight up to the freeboard deck, positioned not less than 5% of the length of the ship (or 10 metres, whichever is the less) and not more than 8% of the length of the ship from the forward perpendicular – an afterpeak bulkhead enclosing the stem tube and rudder trunk in a watertight compartment – a bulkhead at each end of the machinery space – explains that cargo ships require additional bulkheads, as laid down by classification society rules, according to their length or as required by SOLAS – describes the construction of a watertight bulkhead and its attachments to sides, deck and tank top – describes how watertightness is maintained where bulkheads are pierced by longitudinal, beams or pipes – states the rule regarding penetrations of the collision bulkhead – states that watertight floors are fitted directly below main watertight bulkheads – explains that oil-tight bulkheads and bulkheads forming boundaries of tanks are built with heavier scantlings than watertight bulkheads – describes how bulkheads are tested for tightness – gives examples of non-watertight bulkheads – explains the purpose of wash bulkheads in cargo tanks or deep tanks – states longitudinal bulkheads serve to subdivide liquid cargoes, provide additional longitudinal support and reduce free surface effect – distinguishes between Cofferdam, Flat plate and Corrugated bulkhead construction – explains the use of cross ties in tanker construction		
1.4 Watertight and weathertight doors (3 hours) **Explains the general design and construction features of SOLAS compliant vessels in terms of watertight integrity**		R1
– explains the possible effects of sustaining damage when in a less favourable condition		
– states that the number of openings in watertight bulkheads of passenger ships should be reduced to the minimum compatible with the design and working of the ship – categorizes watertight doors as: class 1 – hinged doors class 2 – hand-opened sliding doors class 3 – sliding doors which are power-operated as well as hand-operated – states that all types of watertight doors should be capable of being closed with the ship listed to 15° either way		R2

能力 3.1	控制吃水差、稳性和应力	IMO 参考书目

– 定义:
  – 限界线
  – 舱壁甲板
  – 水密
  – 风雨密
– 阐述货船必须具有:
  – 防撞舱壁,水密至干舷甲板,位于距船首垂线不小于船长 5%(或 10 米,二者之间较小者)和不大于船长 8%的地方
  – 将船尾轴隧和舵柱围在水密舱室内的艉尖舱隔舱壁
  – 机械处所每端的隔舱壁
– 解释按照船级社规则的规定,货船按其船长或 SOLAS 公约要求,需要额外的隔舱壁
– 描述水密隔舱壁的结构和它与船侧板、甲板及船底舱室顶部的连接
– 描述有纵向、横向构件或管道穿过的隔舱壁是如何保持水密的
– 阐述防撞舱壁渗透的相关规则
– 阐述直接安装在主水密隔舱壁下的水密底板
– 解释用比水密隔舱壁更厚重的船材建造油密隔舱壁和组成液舱边界的舱壁
– 描述隔舱壁如何测试密封性
– 给出非水密隔舱壁的例子
– 解释清洗货油舱和深舱隔舱壁的目的
– 阐述纵向隔舱壁用于再分隔液体货物,提供额外的纵向支撑和减少自由液面的影响
– 区分干隔舱舱壁、平面舱壁和槽形舱壁
– 解释油舱结构横向拉杆的使用		

1.4 水密门和风雨密门(3 学时)		R1
解释 SOLAS 标准船在水密完整性方面的一般设计原则和结构特点		
– 解释处在不利条件下时,持续性损坏的可能影响		
– 阐述客船水密舱壁的开口数量应减少到符合船舶设计和建造的最小值		R2
– 水密门分类: 类别 1——铰链门 类别 2——手动滑动门 类别 3——电动兼手动滑动门 – 阐述所有类型的水密门都应在船舶向任何一侧倾斜 15°时能够关闭		

COMPETENCE 3.1	Control Trim, Stability and Stress	IMO Reference
	– describes with sketches the arrangement of a power-operated sliding watertight door – describes with sketches a hinged watertight door, showing the means of securing it – states that hinged watertight doors are only permitted above a deck at least 2.0 metres above the deepest subdivision load line ***Cargo Vessels*** – distinguishes between ships of Type 'A' and Type 'B' for the purposes of computation of freeboard – describes the extent of damage which a Type 'A' ship of over 150 metres length should withstand – explains that a Type 'A' ship of over 150 metres length is described as a 'one-compartment ship' – describes the requirements for survivability of Type 'B' ships with reduced freeboard assigned – summarizes the equilibrium conditions regarded as satisfactory after flooding ***All ships*** – states that openings in watertight bulkheads must be fitted with watertight doors – explains that weathertight doors in superstructure openings are similar to hinged watertight doors – states that drills for the operating of watertight doors, side scuttles, valves and other closing mechanisms must be held weekly – states the requirements for watertight openings to be closed at sea – discusses procedures for ensuring that all watertight openings are closed – states that all watertight doors in main transverse bulkheads, in use at sea, must be operated daily – states that watertight doors and their mechanisms and indicators, all valves the closing of which is necessary to make a compartment watertight and all valves for damage-control cross-connections must be inspected at sea at least once per week – states that records of drills and inspections are to be entered in the log, with a record of any defects found	
	1.5 Corrosion and its prevention (4 hours) – explains what is meant by corrosion – explains what is meant by corrosion of metals and gives examples of where this is likely to occur – describes the formation of a corrosion cell and defines anode, cathode and electrolyte – states that corrosion takes place at the anode while the cathode remains unaffected – describes the galvanic series of metals in seawater – given the galvanic series, states which of two metals will form the anode in a corrosion cell – explains the differences in surface condition or in stress concentration can give rise to corrosion cells between two areas of the same metal	R1

适任 3.1	控制吃水差、稳性和应力	IMO 参考书目
	– 描述电动滑动水密门的布置图 – 描述铰链水密门的布置图,示范系固它的方法 – 阐述铰链水密门只准许安装在货船最大分舱载重线 2 米以上的甲板上 **货船** – 区分 A 类船和 B 类船以便计算干舷 – 描述船长超过 150 米的 A 类船舶应承受的损坏程度 – 解释长度超过 150 米的 A 类船舶被称为"一舱制船舶" – 描述按规定减少干舷的 B 类船的生存能力要求 – 概述所有船舶大量进水后要求满足的平衡条件 **所有船舶** – 阐述水密隔舱壁上的开口必须配备水密门 – 解释位于上层建筑开口处的风雨密门相似于铰链水密门 – 阐述每周必须进行水密门、舷窗、阀门和其他关闭装置的操作演习 – 阐述在海上关闭的水密开口的要求 – 讨论确保在海上关闭所有水密开口的程序 – 阐述在主要横舱壁上所有海上使用的水密门每天必须进行操作 – 阐述水密门与其机械装置及指示器、使舱室水密必须关闭的所有阀门和破损控制横倾调整装置的所有阀门,在海上必须至少每周检查一次 – 阐述演习和检查的记录以及发现的任何缺陷都应记入航海日志	
1.5	**腐蚀和防腐蚀(4 学时)** – 解释什么是腐蚀 – 解释什么是金属腐蚀以及给出可能发生腐蚀的处所的例子 – 描述腐蚀电池的形成,阳极、阴极和电解的定义 – 阐述腐蚀在阳极上发生而阴极不受影响 – 描述海水中的金属电位序列 – 给定金属电解的活泼性序列,阐述两种金属中哪一种可以作为腐蚀电池的阳极 – 解释表面状况或应力集中的差异能够在同一种金属的不同区域产生腐蚀电池	R1

COMPETENCE 3.1	Control Trim, Stability and Stress	IMO Reference

	– states that corrosion can be controlled by:
	  – applying a protective coating to isolate the steel from the air or from seawater electrolyte
	  – using cathodic protection to prevent steel from forming the anode of a corrosion cell
	– explains that cathodic protection can only be used to protect the underwater hull or ballasted tanks
	– states that both of the methods mentioned above are normally used together
	– explains what mill scale is and states that it is cathodic to mild steel
	– describes the treatment of steel in a shipyard and the use of holding primers (shop primers)
	– explains that the required preparation of steelwork depends upon the type of paint to be applied
	– states that many modern paints, such as epoxy and polyurethane, need to be applied to a very clean shot-blasted surface
	– states that paints consist mainly of a vehicle, a pigment and a solvent, and explains the purpose of each
	– explains the suitability of the following paint types for various applications as:
	  – drying oils
	  – oleo-resins
	  – alkyd resins
	  – polymerizing chemicals
	  – bitumen
	– describes the action of anti-fouling paint
	– describes the use of self-polishing anti-fouling paint
	– explains the ban on harmful types of anti-fouling paint
	– describes typical paint schemes for:
	  – underwater areas
	  – boot topping
	  – topsides
	  – weather decks
	  – superstructures
	  – tank interiors
	– states the safety precautions to take when using paints
	– describes the system of cathodic protection using sacrificial anodes
	– lists the metals and alloys which may be used as anodes
	– explains why anodes of magnesium and of magnesium alloy are not permitted in cargo/ballast tanks and in adjacent tanks in tankers
	– states that good electrical contact between the anode and the hull or tank is essential
	– explains why the anodes are insulated from the hull
	– describes the impressed-current system of hull protection
	– explains that the system is adjusted for optimum protection, often automatically, by use of a reference cell	

适任 3.1	控制吃水差、稳性和应力	IMO 参考书目
– 阐述腐蚀可通过以下方法控制: – 在金属表面涂一层保护漆以隔绝钢板和空气或海水电解液 – 利用阴极保护来避免钢铁成为腐蚀电池的阳极 – 解释阴极保护只能用于水下船体和压载水舱部分的保护 – 阐述以上提到的两种方法通常一起使用 – 解释什么是氧化皮,阐述对低碳钢而言,它是阴极 – 描述船厂中钢铁的处理和预处理及底漆的使用(预涂底漆) – 解释所需的钢铁制品的准备工作取决于所上漆的类型 – 阐述许多现代的油漆,如环氧和聚氨基甲酸酯,必须用于非常洁净的喷过砂的表面 – 阐述油漆主要由基料、颜料和溶剂组成,并解释每一部分的用途 – 解释下列油漆种类的适用性: – 干性油 – 精油树脂 – 醇酸树脂 – 聚合剂 – 沥青 – 描述防污漆的作用 – 描述自抛光防污漆的使用 – 解释禁止使用有害的各类防污漆 – 描述下列部位的典型油漆方案: – 水下部分 – 水线带 – 水上舷侧 – 风雨甲板 – 上层建筑 – 液舱内部 – 阐述油漆时的安全预防措施 – 描述牺牲阳极的阴极保护系统 – 列出可作为阳极的金属和合金 – 解释在油船上为什么镁和镁合金不允许用于货 / 压载舱及其相邻液舱 – 阐述必须保持阳极和船体或液舱间有良好的电气连接 – 解释为什么阳极要和船体绝缘 – 描述船体保护的外加电流系统 – 解释该系统通过基准电池通常自动调整到最优的保护状态		

COMPETENCE 3.1	Control Trim, Stability and Stress	IMO Reference
	– states that electrical connection with the hull via slip rings and brushes on the rudder stock and propeller shaft ensures protection of the rudder and propeller – explains that, as the underwater paintwork deteriorates, higher currents are required for protection – states that too high a current can result in damage to paintwork and a chalky deposit on areas of bare metal, which has to be removed before repainting can be carried out – states that a protective shield of epoxy resin is applied for about 1 metre around the anodes to withstand the alkaline conditions there	

1.6	**Surveys and dry-docking (2 hours)**
	– states the frequency of classification society surveys
	– states that intervals between dry-dockings may be extended up to 2.5 years where a ship has high-resistance paint and an approved automatic impressed-current cathodic protection system
	– states that continuous hull survey, in which all compartments are examined over a 5-year period, may replace the special surveys
	– explains all types of survey a ship is subjected to, including but limiting to: Initial Survey, Renewal Survey, Periodical Survey, Intermediate Survey, Annual Survey, Inspection of the outside of the ships bottom, Additional Survey
	– explains the harmonized system of ship survey and certification
	– explains Condition Assessment Scheme (CAS) for oil tankers and Condition Assessment Programme (CAP)
	– lists the items inspected at annual survey as:
	  – protection of openings: hatches, ventilators, cargo doors, side scuttles, overside discharges and any other openings through which water might enter
	  – guardrails
	  – water-clearing arrangements, freeing ports, scuppers
	  – means of access to crews quarters and working areas
	– states that the inspections listed above are also required for the annual inspection under the International Convention on Load Lines
	– lists the items to examine in dry-dock as:
	  – shell plating
	  – cathodic protection fittings
	  – rudder
	  – stem frame
	  – propeller
	  – anchors and chain cable
	– describes the examinations to be made of the items listed above
	– describes the cleaning, preparation and painting of the hull in dry-dock
	– calculates paint quantities, given the formula for wetted surface area as:
	$S = 2.58\sqrt{\Delta L}$
	where S = surface area in m^2
	Δ = displacement in tonnes
	L = length of ship in metres
		R1

适任 3.1	控制吃水差、稳性和应力	IMO 参考书目
– 阐述舵柱和螺旋桨轴通过汇流环和电刷与船体的电子连接以保护舵和螺旋桨 – 解释水下油漆层的状况恶化时,需要较大的电流来保护 – 阐述过大的电流可能导致油漆层的损坏和裸露金属区域的白垩粉沉积，必须在再次油漆之前设法除去 – 阐述环氧树脂保护层应用于阳极周围 1 米左右以抵抗那里的碱性状况		
1.6 检验和进入干船坞(2 学时)		R1
– 阐述船级社检验的频率 – 阐述进入干船坞的间隔在船舶有高阻抗油漆和一个经批准的外加电流阴极保护系统时可以延长到两年半 – 对船体连续性的检验(五年内检查所有的舱室)可代替特别检验 – 列出年度检验应检查的项目 – 解释船舶检验应包括但不限于所有下列检验:初始检验、换证检验、定期检验、中间检验、年度检验、船底的外部检查和附加检验 – 解释船舶检验和发证的协调系统 – 解释油船上的状态评估系统(CAS)和状态评估程序(CAP) – 列出年度检验的检查项目: 　– 开口保护:舱盖、通风筒、货舱门、舷窗、舷外排水口和其他可能进水的开口 　– 固定护舷材 　– 排水系统的布置、排水口、泄水口 　– 船员生活区和工作场所的入口 – 阐述根据国际载重线公约的年度检验对以上所列的检查项目也有要求 – 列出干船坞内检查项目如下: 　– 船壳板 　– 阴极保护装置 　– 舵 　– 船首框架 　– 螺旋桨 　– 锚和锚链 – 描述以上所列项目要做的检查 – 描述干船坞内船体的清洁、准备工作和涂漆 – 计算油漆用量,给出重载水线以下船壳部分的公式如下: $S=2.58\sqrt{\Delta L}$ 式中: S—表面面积(平方米) 　　Δ—排水量(吨) 　　L—船长(米)		

COMPETENCE 3.1	Control Trim, Stability and Stress	IMO Reference

1.7 **Stability (83 hours)**

Approximate calculation of areas and volumes

- states the trapezoidal rule for the area under a curve in terms of the number of ordinates, the interval and the ordinate values
- uses the trapezoidal rule to find the area under a curve defined by given ordinates
- states Simpson's first rule as
  $A = h\ (y_1 + 4y_2 + y_3)/3$
  where: A = area under curve
  h = interval length
  y_1, y_2, y_3 are ordinates
- writes down the repeated first rule for any odd number of ordinates
- uses Simpson's first rule to find the area under a curve defined by an odd number of ordinates
- states that the area is exact for a linear, quadratic or cubic curve but an approximation otherwise
- states Simpson's second rule as
  $A = 3h\ (y_1 + 3y_2 + 3y_3 + y_4)/8$
  where: A = area
  h = interval length
  y_1, y_2, y_3, y_4 are ordinates
- writes down the repeated second rule for 7, 10, 13, etc., ordinates
- uses Simpson's second rule to find the area under a curve defined by a suitable number of given ordinates
- states that the area is exact for linear, quadratic or cubic curves
- states that the first rule has smaller errors than the second and should be used in preference where possible
- states that errors can be reduced by using a smaller interval
- states the 5, 8, −1 rule as $A = h\ (5y_1 + 8y_2 - y_3) / 12$
  where: A = area between first and second ordinates
  h = interval length
  y_1, y_2, y_3, are ordinates
- uses Simpson's rules to find the area under a curve defined by any number of ordinates
- explains that the volume of a body may be calculated by using Simpson's rules with cross-sectional areas as ordinates
- calculates the volume of a ship to a stated draught by applying Simpson's rules to given cross-sectional areas or waterplane areas
- uses Simpson's first, second and 5, 8, −1 rules to approximate areas and volumes of ship structure and *GZ* curves with any number of ordinates and intermediate ordinates

Effects of density

- given the density of the water in the dock, calculates the displacement for a particular draught from the seawater displacement for that draught extracted from hydrostatic data

适任 3.1	控制吃水差、稳性和应力	IMO 参考书目
1.7　稳性(83 学时) **面积和体积的大概计算** – 阐述根据纵坐标数量、间距和纵坐标值计算曲线下面积的梯形法则 – 使用梯形法则求给定纵坐标曲线下的面积 – 阐述辛普森第一法则为 $A = h(y_1 + 4y_2 + y_3)/3$ 式中：A—曲线下的面积 h—长度间隔 y_1、y_2、y_3 是纵坐标 – 写出任何偶数个纵坐标值相应的第一法则 – 用辛普森第一法则求偶数个纵坐标值的曲线下的面积 – 阐述如线性、二次或三次曲线,求得的面积值是准确的,否则是近似值 – 阐述辛普森第二法则为 $A = 3h(y_1 + 3y_2 + 3y_3 + y_4)/8$ 式中：A—曲线下的面积 h—长度间隔 y_1、y_2、y_3、y_4 为纵坐标 – 写出 7、10、13 等个数的纵坐标值相应的第二法则 – 用辛普森第二法则求出给定的纵坐标值的曲线下的面积 – 阐述如线性、二次或三次曲线,求得的面积值是准确的 – 阐述第一法则比第二法则的误差小,如有可能应优先使用 – 阐述误差可以通过使用较小的间隔来减小 – 阐述 5、8、-1 法则为 $A = h(5y_1 + 8y_2 - y_3)/12$ 式中：A—曲线下第一和第二纵坐标值之间的面积 h—长度间隔 y_1、y_2、y_3 是纵坐标 – 用辛普森法则求任何纵坐标的曲线下的面积 – 解释一个物体的体积可以通过将截面面积作为纵坐标,使用辛普森法则计算 – 通过运用辛普森法则求给定的横截面或水线面面积来计算某个吃水下的船舶体积 – 通过对给定的横截面或水线面面积运用辛普森法则,计算船舶指定吃水下的体积 – 利用辛普森第一、第二法则和 5、8、-1 法则,估算任意坐标数和中间坐标数下的船舶结构和 GZ 曲线的面积和体积 **密度的影响** – 根据从船舶静水力参数中取得的排水量，计算在相同吃水情况下给定港内水密度的船舶排水量		

COMPETENCE 3.1	Control Trim, Stability and Stress	IMO Reference

– calculates the TPC for given mean draught and density of the dock water
– discusses the use of the Fresh Water Allowance and how to determine this for a ship
– states that FWA only applies when the ship is floating at or near its summer load line
– explains why the density of the water in the dock should be taken at the same time as the draughts are read
– describes the statical and dynamic effects on stability of the movement of liquids with a free surface
– calculates the virtual reduction in *GM* for liquids with a free surface in spaces with rectangular and triangular waterplanes
– deduces from the above objective that halving the breadth of a tank reduces the free surface effect to one eighth of its original value
– deduces that the subdividing a tank at the centre reduces its free surface effect to one quarter of that of the undivided tank
– states that the quantity 'inertia × density of liquid' is called the 'free surface moment' of the tank, in tonne-metres
– states that information for calculating free surface effect is included in tank capacity tables
– states that the information may be given in one of the following ways:
  – inertia in $metre^4$
  – free surface moments for a stated density of liquid in the tank
  – as a loss of *GM*, in tabulated form for a range of draughts (displacements) for a stated density of liquid in the tank
– corrects free surface moments when a tank contains a liquid of different density from that stated in the capacity table
– given a ship's displacement and the contents of its tanks, uses the information from ship's stability information to calculate the loss of *GM* due to slack tanks
– given a ship's departure conditions and the daily consumption of fuel, water and stores, calculates the *GM* allowing for free surfaces on arrival at destination
Stability at moderate and large angles of heel
– states that the formula $GZ = GM \sin\theta$ does not hold for angles in excess of about 10°
– states that the initial KM is calculated from
$KM = KB + BM$
– uses a metacentric diagram to obtain values of *KM*, *KB* and *BM* for given draughts
– states that the transverse $BM = I/V$
where: I = second moment of area of the waterplane about the centre line;
V = underwater volume of the ship
– states that for a rectangular waterplane $I = LB^3/12$
where: L is the length of the waterplane;
B is the breadth of the waterplane		

适任 3.1	控制吃水差、稳性和应力	IMO 参考书目

– 根据港内的水密度和平均吃水求 TPC(每厘米吃水吨数)
– 讨论淡水宽限的使用和确定船舶的淡水宽限
– 阐述淡水宽限只运用于船舶正浮于夏季载重线或其附近
– 解释为什么读取吃水时应同时读取港内水的密度
– 描述自由液面的移动对静稳性和动稳性的影响
– 计算矩形和三角形舱室中的自由液面引起的 *GM* 减少值
– 从以上结果可以推算出将舱宽减小一半,可将自由液面的影响减少到原来的 1/8
– 可以推算出从舱的中心将液舱二等分,可将自由液面的影响减少到原来的 1/4
– 阐述“惯性矩×密度”的值为该舱的“自由液面力矩”,单位为吨·米
– 阐述计算自由液面影响的信息包含在舱容表中
– 阐述信息可能以下列方式之一给出:
  – 惯性矩(单位:m^4)
  – 舱内已知密度液体的自由液面力矩
  – *GM* 损失值,以舱内已知密度的液体不同吃水(排水量)下的列表形式给出
– 当舱内装不同密度液体时根据舱容表进行自由液面力矩的修正
– 给定船舶排水量和舱内所装液体,利用稳性信息计算未装满液舱的 *GM* 损失值
– 给出船舶离港状态和每天的油、水、储备品的消耗量,计算考虑自由液面后目的港的 *GM* 值
中、大倾角横稳性
– 阐述公式 $GZ = GM \sin\theta$ 中 θ 角不得超过 10°
– 阐述初始 *KM* 是从公式 $KM=KB+BM$ 中计算来的
– 用稳心曲线图得到给定吃水下的 *KM*, *KB* 和 *BM* 的值
– 阐述横向弯矩 $BM = \frac{I}{V}$
式中: *I*—水线面对过漂心的横倾轴的面积惯性矩
V—船舶排水体积
– 阐述矩形水线面的 $I = \frac{LB^3}{12}$
式中: *L*—水线面的长度
B—水线面的宽度		

COMPETENCE 3.1	Control Trim, Stability and Stress	IMO Reference

– shows that, for a box–shaped vessel,
$KM = (B^2/12d) + (d/2)$
where: d = draught
– states that, for moderate and large angles of heel, values of *GZ* found by calculating the position of the centre of buoyancy are provided by the shipbuilder for a range of displacements and angles of heel for an assumed position of the centre of gravity
– uses cross-curves of stability and *KN* curves to construct a curve of statical stability for a given displacement and value of *KG*, making correction for any free surface moments
– explains how to use the initial metacentric height as an aid to drawing the curve
– identifies from the curve the approximate angle at which the deck edge immerses
– describes the effect of increased freeboard on the curve of statical stability for a ship with the same initial *GM*
– states that the righting lever, *GZ*, may be found from the wall-sided formula up to the angle at which the deck edge is immersed
– given the wall–sided formula:
$GZ = (GM + BM/2\tan^2\theta)\sin\theta$
and other relevant data, calculates the value of *GZ* for a stated angle of heel
– shows that, for small angles of heel, the term $BM/2\tan^2\theta$ is negligible, leading to the usual expression for *GZ* at small angles of heel
– uses the wall-sided formula for calculating the angle of loll of an initially unstable ship
– compares the result in the above objective with that obtained by connecting a curve of statical stability
– states that cross-curves and *KN* curves are drawn for the ship with its centre of gravity on the centre line
– demonstrates how to adjust the curve of statical stability for a ship with a list
– describes the effect when heeled to the listed side on:
  – the maximum righting moment
  – the angle of vanishing stability
  – the range of stability
– states that cross-curves and *KN* curves are drawn for the ship at the designed trim when upright
– states that righting levers may differ from those shown if the ship has a large trim when upright
Simplified stability data
– states that stability information may be supplied in a simplified form, consisting of:
  – a diagram or table of maximum deadweight moment
  – a diagram or table of minimum permissible *GM*
  – a diagram or table of maximum permissible *KG* all related to the displacement or draught in salt water		

适任 3.1	控制吃水差、稳性和应力	IMO 参考书目

– 结果表明,对于箱形船舶
$KM=\frac{B^2}{12d}+\frac{d}{2}$
式中:d—吃水
– 阐述对于大倾角稳性,通过计算浮心得到 GZ 的值,造船方应提供不同重心位置时不同排水量和倾角下的 GZ 值
– 利用稳性交叉曲线和 KN 曲线,绘制给定排水量和 KG 值的静稳性曲线,并修正自由液面力矩
– 解释如何借助于初始稳心高度来绘制曲线
– 从曲线中确定近似甲板浸水角
– 描述干舷的增加对于具有相同初始 GM 值船舶静稳性曲线的影响
– 阐述一直到甲板浸水角的横倾情况下的复原力臂 GZ 可以通过垂直船舷公式来求取
– 给出垂直船舷公式:
$GZ=(GM+BM/2\tan^2\theta)\sin\theta$
和其他相关数据,计算给定横倾角下的 GZ 值
– 结果表明,小倾角下的 $BM/2\tan^2\theta$ 项可以忽略不计,得出小倾角时 GZ 的通常表达式
– 使用垂直船舷公式计算初始不稳定船舶的静倾角
– 比较以上计算结果与通过连接静稳性曲线得到的结果
– 阐述稳性交叉曲线和 KN 曲线是根据船舶中心线上的重心绘制出来的
– 表明如何用列表调整船舶的静稳性曲线
– 描述船舶横倾对下列各项的影响:
  – 最大复原力矩
  – 稳性消失角
  – 稳性范围
– 阐述稳性交叉曲线和 KN 曲线是根据船舶正浮状态并处于设定吃水差的情况下绘制的
– 阐述如船舶处于正浮状态且有较大吃水差,则其复原力臂可能与列表的数值不同
简化的稳性数据
– 阐述稳性资料可以通过简化形式提供,包括:
  – 最大载重力矩的图或表
  – 最小许可 GM 的图或表
  – 最大许可 KG 的图或表,所有相关的排水量和吃水都是在海水中的		

COMPETENCE 3.1	Control Trim, Stability and Stress	IMO Reference
	– states that a deadweight moment is mass in tonnes × vertical height of the mass above the keel – states that free surface moments are to be added to the deadweight moments when using the diagram of maximum deadweight moment – states that if, for a stated displacement or draught, the total deadweight moment or *KG* is less than the maximum permissible value, the ship will have adequate stability – reads the maximum permissible deadweight moment from a curve of deadweight moment for a given displacement – given the masses loaded, their heights above the keel and the free surface moments of slack tanks, calculates the deadweight moment and uses the result with the diagram of deadweight moment to determine if the stability is adequate – uses the diagram of deadweight moment to calculate the maximum mass that can be loaded in a given position to ensure adequate stability during a voyage, making allowance for the fuel, water and stores consumed and for any resulting free surface	
	– states that curves of maximum *KG* or minimum *GM* to ensure adequate stability in the event of partial loss of intact buoyancy are provided in passenger ships	R1, R2
	Trim and list	
	– defines longitudinal centre of gravity (*LCG*) and longitudinal centre of buoyancy (*LCB*) – states that a ship trims about the centre of flotation until *LCG* and *LCB* are in the same vertical line – states that the distance of the *LOB* from amidships or from the after perpendicular is given in a ship's hydrostatic data for the ship on an even keel – explains that the *LCG* must be at the same distance from amidships as *LCB* when the ship floats on an even keel – shows on a diagram of a ship constrained to an even keel the couple that is formed by the weight and buoyancy forces when *LCG* is not the same distance from amidships as *LCB* – states that the trimming moment = displacement x the horizontal distance between *LCB* (tabulated) and *LCG* (actual) = $\Delta \times GG_1$ where GG_1 is the horizontal distance between the position of *LCG* for the even-keel condition and the actual *LCG* – states that trim = $(\Delta \times GG_1)$/MCT 1 cm – states that if the actual *LCG* is abaft the tabulated position of *LCB*, then the trim will be by the stern, and vice versa – given the initial displacement, initial position of *LCG*, masses loaded or discharged and their *LCG*s, calculates the final position of *LCG* – using a ship's hydrostatic data and a given disposition of cargo, fuel, water and stores, determines the trim, the mean draught and the draughts at each end – calculates the mass to move between given positions to produce a required trim or draught at one end	R1

适任 3.1	控制吃水差、稳性和应力	IMO 参考书目
	– 阐述载重力矩是质量(单位:吨)与重心距基线高度的乘积 – 阐述自由液面力矩在使用最大载重量力矩曲线时,应加到总的载重量力矩中去 – 阐述在给定排水量或吃水情况下,如果总的载重量力矩或 *KG* 小于最大允许值时,船舶就具有足够的稳性 – 从载重力矩曲线中读取给定排水量下最大许可载重力矩 – 已知装载量及其重心距基线高度和未满载液舱的自由液面力矩,计算载重量力矩,并结合载重力矩曲线图和所得结果来判断稳性是否足够 – 使用载重量力矩曲线图计算可以装在给定位置的最大重量,以确保将燃油、水和储备品的消耗及其形成的自由液面考虑在内,整个航行期间具有足够的稳性 – 阐述最大 *KG* 或最小 *GM* 曲线图以确保万一客船的浮力完整性有部分损失时,提供足够的稳性	R1, R2
	纵倾和横倾	R1
	– 定义纵向重力中心(*LCG*)和纵向浮力中心(*LCB*) – 阐述船舶绕浮心倾斜直到 *LCG* 和 *LCB* 处于同一垂线上 – 阐述船舶静水力参数中,给出平吃水时 *LCB* 到船中或艉垂线的距离 – 解释平吃水时 *LCG* 到船中的距离必等于 *LCB* 到船中的距离 – 显示使船舶回到平吃水状态的力偶曲线图。该力偶是当 *LCG* 和 *LCB* 到船中的距离不同时由重力和浮力所形成的 – 阐述纵倾力矩 = 排水量· *LCB*(列表值)和 *LCG*(实际值)间的水平距离 =$\Delta\times GG_1$,其中 GG_1 是平吃水下 *LCG* 和实际的 *LCG* 间的水平距离 阐述吃水差 = $\frac{\Delta\times GG_1}{\text{MCT}}$ 1 cm – 阐述如果实际的 LCG 在表列的 *LCB* 后面,将艉倾,反之亦然 – 已知初始排水量、初始 *LCG* 位置、所装卸的货物重量及其各自的 *LCG*,计算 *LCG* 的最后位置 – 根据船舶静水力参数和已知货、油、水和储备品的位置分布,计算吃水差、平均吃水和前后吃水 – 为获得要求的吃水差或前后吃水,计算在已知位置间应移动的货物重量	

COMPETENCE 3.1	Control Trim, Stability and Stress	IMO Reference
– calculates where to load a given mass to produce a required trim or draught at one end – calculates how to divide a loaded or discharged mass between two positions to produce a required trim or draught at one end – calculates where to load a mass so as to keep the after draught constant – states that calculated draughts refer to draughts at the perpendiculars – given the distance of draught marks from the perpendiculars and the length between perpendiculars, corrects the draughts indicated by the marks – given draughts forward, aft and amidships, states whether or not the ship is hogged or sagged and the amount – corrects the draught amidships for hog or sag – given the forward and after draughts, the length between perpendiculars and hydrostatic data, calculates the correction for trim to apply to the displacement corresponding to the draught amidships – states that a second correction for trim, using Nemoto's formula, may be applied to the displacement – given Nemoto's formula, calculates the second correction to displacement – calculates the maximum list during loading or discharging a heavy lift, using a ship's derrick, given the relevant stability information and the dimensions of the derrick – calculates the minimum *GM* required to restrict the list to a stated maximum when loading or discharging a heavy lift – calculates the quantities of fuel oil or ballast to move between given locations to simultaneously correct a list and achieve a desired trim – explains how to distinguish between list and loll and describes how to return the ship to the upright in each case – by making use of curves of statical stability, including those for ships with zero or negative initial *GM*, determines the equilibrium angle of heel resulting from a transverse moment of mass **Dynamical stability** – defines dynamical stability at any angle of heel as the work done in inclining the ship to that angle – states that the dynamical stability at any angle is given by the product of displacement and the area under the curve of statical stability up to that angle – given a curve of statical stability, uses Simpson's rules to find the area in metre-radians up to a stated angle – states that dynamical stability is usually expressed in tonne-metres – explains that the dynamical stability at a given angle of heel represents the potential energy of the ship – states that the potential energy is used partly in overcoming resistance to rolling and partly in producing rotational energy as the ship returns to the upright – states that the rotational energy when the ship is upright causes it to continue rolling – states that, in the absence of other disturbing forces, the ship will roll to an angle where the sum of the energy used in overcoming resistance to rolling and the dynamical stability are equal to the rotational energy when upright		

适任 3.1	控制吃水差、稳性和应力	IMO 参考书目
– 为获得要求的吃水差或前后吃水,计算一已知货物的装载位置 – 为获得要求的吃水差或前后吃水,计算在两个位置间如何分配装卸的重量 – 为保持艉吃水不变,计算应在何处装载一负荷 – 阐述计算出来的吃水指的是垂线上的吃水 – 已知吃水标志距垂线距离和垂线间长,修正吃水标志处的吃水 – 已知前、后及船中吃水,说明船舶是否中拱或中垂及其数值 – 对船中吃水进行拱垂修正 – 已知前后吃水、垂线间长和静水力参数,计算吃水差的修正值,以适于船中吃水的相应排水量 – 阐述利用 Nemoto 公式求得的吃水差的第二项修正,可用于排水量的修正 – 已知 Nemoto 公式,计算排水量的第二项修正 – 已知相关的稳性资料和吊杆尺度,计算使用船舶吊杆装卸重大件时的最大横倾角 – 计算装卸重大件时应满足的最小 *GM* 值,以便将横倾限制在规定的最大值以内 – 为同时修正横倾和获得理想的吃水差,计算在已知位置间要移动的燃油或压载水的量 – 解释如何区别横倾和静倾角以及在各种情况下船舶如何恢复到正浮状态 – 运用静稳性曲线,包括具有零或者负的初稳性高度的静稳性曲线 *GM*,确定横向重量力矩产生的横倾平衡角 **动稳性** – 定义动稳性是船舶倾斜任何角度时它所做的功 – 阐述任意角度的动稳性是由排水量和静水力曲线下到此角度的面积之积 – 给定静稳性曲线,运用辛普森法则求某一角度曲线下的面积(单位:米·弧度) – 阐述动稳性通常用吨·米表示 – 解释在给定倾角的动稳性表示船舶的潜在能量 – 阐述潜在能量部分用于克服船体横摇阻力,部分用于产生使船舶复原到正浮的转动 – 阐述当船正浮时,转动能使船舶继续横倾 – 阐述在无其他外力干扰的情况下,船舶将横倾到一个角度,此时所有的用来克服横摇阻力的能量和动摇稳等于船舶正浮时的转动能		

COMPETENCE 3.1	Control Trim, Stability and Stress	IMO Reference
– states that a beam wind exerts a force equal to the wind pressure multiplied by the projected lateral area of the portion of the ship and deck cargo above the waterline – explains that a heeling moment is formed, equal to the force of the wind multiplied by the vertical separation between the centres of the lateral areas of the portions of the ship above and below the waterline – states that the heeling lever equals the heeling moment divided by the ship's displacement – states that a steady wind will cause a ship to heel to an angle at which the righting lever is equal to the heeling over – states that a ship under the action of a steady wind would roll about the resulting angle of heel – on a curve of righting levers, indicates the angle of equilibrium under the action of a steady wind and the areas which represent the dynamical stability at angles of roll to each side of the equilibrium position – by reference to dynamical stability, describes the effect of an increase in wind pressure when a vessel is at its maximum angle of roll to windward – summarizes the recommendation on severe wind and rolling criterion for the intact stability of passenger and cargo ships – by reference to a curve of righting levers and dynamical stability, describes the effect of a listing moment on the rolling of the ship about the equilibrium position		
Approximate GM by means of rolling period tests – states that, for ships up to 70 m in length, the *GM* can be verified in still water by causing the ship to roll and noting the rolling period – defines the rolling period as the time taken for one complete oscillation from the extreme end of a roll to one side, right across to the extreme on the other side and back to the original position – states that for small angles of roll in still water, the initial metacentric height, GM_o is given by: $GM_o = [fB/T_r]^2$ where: f = rolling factor B = breadth of the ship T_r = rolling period in seconds – states that the formula may be given as: $GM_o = F/T_r^2$ where the *F*-value is provided by the Administration – summarizes the procedures for determining a ship's stability by means of the rolling period test – given values of F and T and the equation $GM_o = F/T^2$, calculates GM_o – states the limitations of the method – states that when construction is completed, a ship undergoes an inclining test to determine the displacement and position of the centre of gravity, *KG* and *LCG*, in the light ship condition – states that the displacement and *KM* are calculated from the observed draughts and the ship's lines plans, making allowance for density of water and trim		R1, R96

适任 3.1	控制吃水差、稳性和应力	IMO 参考书目
	– 阐述船舶所受横向风力等于风压乘以水线以上船体和甲板货物的侧面积 – 解释倾侧力矩等于风力乘以船舶水线以上侧面面积中心和水线以下部分侧面面积中心的垂直间距 – 阐述倾侧力臂等于倾侧力矩除以船舶排水量 – 阐述恒定的风会导致船舶倾侧到复原力臂和倾斜力臂相抵消的角度 – 阐述在恒定的风作用下,船舶将围绕风力产生的一个横倾角横摇 – 在复原力矩曲线上，指明恒定的风作用下的平衡角和代表向两舷倾斜到平衡位置时动稳性的面积 – 参考动稳性,描述当船舶处于最大的迎风横摇角时,增加风压的影响 – 概述客船和货船有关完整稳性的强风建议和横摇标准 – 参考复原力臂和动稳性曲线,描述船舶在平衡位置处横摇的横倾力矩的影响	
	通过横摇周期试验估算 *GM* 值	R1, R96
	– 阐述对于长度在 70 米以上的船舶,其 *GM* 值可以通过使船舶在静水中横摇,观察横摇周期来检验 – 定义横摇周期是指从一舷的最大处横摇到另一舷的最大处，然后回到起始点的一个全摇摆 – 阐述在静水中小角度横摇时,初稳性高度 GM_0 由下式给出： $GM_0=[fB/T_r]^2$ 式中： f—横摇因子 B—船宽 T_r—横摇周期(以秒计算) – 阐述该公式也可以表示如下： $GM_0=F/T_r^2$ 此处 F 值由主管机构给出 – 概括通过横摇周期测试确定船舶稳性的程序 – 已知 F 和 T 的值及通过方程 $GM_0=F/T^2$ 计算 GM_0 – 阐述此方法的局限性 – 阐述当船舶建造完成时,要在空载的情况下做一个倾侧试验确定排水量、重心位置、*KG* 和 *LCG* – 阐述排水量和 *KM* 值是通过观测吃水和船舶型线图，同时考虑水的密度和船舶的吃水差计算出来的	

COMPETENCE 3.1	Control Trim, Stability and Stress	IMO Reference
– states that the position of the centre of buoyancy is calculated to enable the *LCG* for the light ship to be determined – describes how an inclining test is carried out – given the mass and the distance through which it was moved, the displacement, length of the plumb line and the deflection, calculates the *KG* – states that the values obtained in a test are corrected for masses to be removed and added to obtain the *KG* and *LCG* for the light ship – states that, at periodical intervals not exceeding five years, a light ship survey must be carried out on all passenger ships to verify any changes in light ship displacement and longitudinal centre of gravity		
– states that the ship must be re-inclined whenever, in comparison with the approved stability information, a deviation from the light ship displacement exceeding 2% or a deviation of the longitudinal centre of gravity exceeding 1% of *L* is found or anticipated		R2

Intact Stability Code
– describes the general precautions to be taken against capsizing
– states the recommended criteria for passenger and cargo ships of all types
– given the initial metacentric height and the *GZ* curve, determines whether the ship meets the recommended criteria
  – states that stability information should comprise:
  – stability characteristics of typical loading conditions
  – information to enable the Master to assess the stability of the ship in all loading conditions differing from the standard ones
  – information on the proper use of anti-rolling devices, if fitted
  – information enabling the Master to determine GM_o by means of a rolling test corrections to be made to GM_o for free surface liquids
  – for ships carrying timber deck cargoes information setting out changes in deck cargo from that shown in the loading conditions, when the permeability of the deck cargo is significantly different from 25%
  – for ships carrying timber deck cargoes, indications of the maximum permissible amount of deck cargo
– states that criteria are laid down for ships carrying timber deck cargoes
– discusses the use of the weather criterion and how to assess whether a vessel complies with this
– states the additional criteria recommended for passenger ships
– states that the information includes a curve or table giving, *as a function* of the draught, the required initial *GM* which ensures compliance with the recommendations on intact stability
		R1, R96

Intact stability requirements for the carriage of grain – states the intact stability requirements for the carriage of grain – states that before loading bulk grain the Master may be required to demonstrate that the ship will comply with the stability criteria at all stages of the voyage – states that the ship must be upright before proceeding to sea		R1

适任 3.1	控制吃水差、稳性和应力	IMO 参考书目
	– 阐述计算浮心的位置以便能确定空船的 *LCG* 值 – 描述倾侧试验是如何进行的 – 根据载荷移动距离、排水量、两柱间长和纵倾角,计算 *KG* 值 – 阐述由试验获得的值要经过加减载荷的修正得到空船的 *KG* 和 *LCG* 值 – 阐述以不超过五年的周期，所有客船必须要做空船检验以核实空船排水量和纵向重心的变化 – 阐述和原来批准的稳性资料相比较,如果发现或预测空船排水量的变化超过 2%或纵向的重心位置变化超过船长 *L* 的 1%,则船舶倾侧试验须重做。	R2

	完整稳性规则
	– 描述防止倾覆的一般预防措施
	– 阐述所有类型客船和货船的推荐标准
	– 已知初稳心高度值和 *GZ* 曲线,确定船舶是否满足推荐的标准
	– 阐述稳性资料应包含：
	  – 常规装载情况下的稳性特性
	  – 使船长能评估不同于标准情况下的各种装载情况的船舶稳性的信息
	  – 如果装有防摇装置,应有关于正确使用它的信息
	  – 使船长能根据横摇试验确定自由液面对 GM_0 修止值的信息
	  – 装运木材甲板货物的船舶,当甲板货物的渗透率明显不同于 25%时,甲板货物发生变化的信息
	  – 装运木材甲板货物的船舶,甲板最大允许载运量的标识
	– 阐述为船舶装载木材甲板货物制定的标准
	– 讨论天气标准的使用以及如何评估船舶是否合乎该标准
	– 阐述推荐给客船的额外标准
	– 阐述这些信息包括以吃水为变量给出要求的初稳性高度的 *GM* 曲线或表格，确保符合完整稳性建议
		R1, R96

	谷物运输的完整稳性要求 – 阐述谷物运输对完整稳性的要求 – 阐述在运输散装谷物之前，可能要求船长证明船舶在运输的各个阶段均能满足稳性标准的要求 – 阐述开航前,船舶必须正浮	R1

COMPETENCE 3.1	Control Trim, Stability and Stress	IMO Reference

– states that grain loading information includes:
  – curves or tables of grain heeling moments for every compartment, whether filled or partly filled
  – tables of maximum permissible heeling moments or other information sufficient to allow the Master to demonstrate compliance with the requirements
  – details of the requirements for temporary fittings and the provisions for the bundling of bulk grain
  – typical loaded service departure and arrival conditions and, where necessary, intermediate worst service conditions
  – a worked example for the guidance of the Master
  – loading instructions in the form of notes summarizing the requirements of SOLAS chapter VI
– explains what are volumetric heeling moments
– states that heeling moment = volumetric heeling moment / stowage factor
– states how the vertical shift of grain surfaces is taken into account in filled compartments and in partly filled compartments
– calculates the heeling arm, λ_0, from:
$\lambda_0 = \frac{\text{Volumetric heeling moment}}{(\text{stowage factor} \times \text{displacement})}$
– draws the heeling-arm curve on the righting-arm curve for a given ship and *KG*, corrected for free surface liquid, and:
  – determines the angle of heel
  – using Simpson's rules, calculates the residual dynamical stability to the angle laid down by regulation 4 of SOLAS chapter VI
– compares the results of the calculations in the above objective with the criteria set out in regulation 4 and states whether the ship complies with the requirements or does not comply		

Rolling of ships – describes the effect on *GM* of rolling – explains how increase of draught and of displacement influence rolling – describes how the distribution of mass within the ship affects the rolling period – explains what synchronization is and the circumstances in which it is most likely to occur – describes the actions to take if synchronization is experienced – describes how bilge keels, anti-rolling tanks and stabilizer fins reduce the amplitude of rolling – states that a ship generally heels when turning – states that, while turning, the ship is subject to an acceleration towards the centre of the turn – states that the force producing the acceleration acts at the underwater centre of lateral resistance, which is situated at about half-draught above the keel		R1

适任 3.1	控制吃水差、稳性和应力	IMO 参考书目

– 阐述谷物装载资料包括:
  – 满载或部分装载的各个舱室所装载的谷物倾侧力矩曲线或表格
  – 最大许用倾侧力矩表格或其他足以使船长证明符合这些要求的资料
  – 临时附件的详细要求和散装谷物绑扎规定的细节
  – 典型的满载运输离港和抵港的状况,必要时,包括中间最恶劣的运输状况
  – 船长指南中的一个工作实例
  – 以注解的形式概括 SOLAS 公约第Ⅵ章要求的装载指南
– 解释何为体积倾侧力矩
– 阐述倾侧力矩 = $\frac{\text{体积货侧力矩}}{\text{积载因素}}$
– 阐述满载舱或半载舱中对散装谷物表面垂直移动的考虑
– 计算倾侧力臂 λ_0:
$\lambda_0 = \frac{\text{体积货侧力矩}}{\text{积载因素} \times \text{排水量}}$
– 对给定的船舶和 *KG*,在复原力臂的曲线上,画出倾侧力臂曲线,对自由液面做出修正,并:
  – 确定倾侧角
  – 运用辛普森法则计算 SOLAS 公约第Ⅵ章第 4 条规定的倾角的剩余动稳性
– 比较以上的计算结果和第 4 条所设定的稳性标准并阐述船舶是否符合稳性要求		

船舶横摇 – 描述横摇时对 *GM* 值的影响 – 解释吃水和排水量的增加是怎样影响横摇的 – 描述船舶的重量分布是如何影响横摇周期的 – 解释谐摇和在何种情况下它最有可能发生 – 描述谐摇发生时应采取的行动 – 描述舭龙骨、减摇舱和减摇鳍是如何降低横摇幅度的 – 阐述船舶转向时通常会发生横倾 – 阐述船舶转向时,会围绕转心产生一个加速度 – 阐述产生加速度的力作用于水下横向阻力中心,约在龙骨以上吃水的二分之一处		R1

COMPETENCE 3.1	Control Trim, Stability and Stress	IMO Reference

- states that the force in the above objective is called the centripetal force, given by $F = Mv^2/r$
  where: M = mass of the ship in tonnes
  v = speed in metres per second
  r = radius of turn in metres
  F = centripetal force in kilonewtons
- explains how the force acting at the centre of lateral resistance can be replaced by an equal force acting through the centre of gravity and a heeling couple equal to the force × vertical separation between the centre of lateral resistance and the centre of gravity,
  $$\frac{Mv^2}{r}\left[KG - \frac{d}{2}\right]^{\cos\theta}$$
- states that the ship will heel until the resulting righting moment equals the heeling couple, i.e.
  $$M \times g \times GM \sin\theta = \frac{Mv^2}{r}\left[KG - \frac{d}{2}\right]^{\cos\theta}$$
  where: g = acceleration due to gravity
  θ = angle of heel
- given the relevant data, calculates the angle of heel from
  $$\tan\theta = \frac{v^2 \times \left[KG - \frac{d}{2}\right]}{g \times GM \times r}$$

Dry-docking and grounding R1

- states that for dry-docking a ship should:
  - have adequate initial metacentric height
  - be upright
  - have a small or moderate trim, normally by the stern
- states that part of the weight is taken by the blocks as soon as the ship touches, reducing the buoyancy force by the same amount
- states that the upthrust at the stern causes a virtual loss of metacentric height
- explains why the *GM* must remain positive until the critical instant at which the ship takes the blocks overall
- derives the formula for the upthrust at the stern
  $$P = \frac{(MCT \times t)}{L}$$
  where: P = upthrust at the stern in tonnes
  t = change of trim in cm
  L = distance of the centre of flotation from aft
- explains that a ship with a large trim will develop a large upthrust, which may damage the stern frame, trip the blocks or lead to an unstable condition before taking the blocks overall

适任 3.1	控制吃水差、稳性和应力	IMO 参考书目
	– 阐述上述的作用力称为向心力,由 $F=\frac{Mv^2}{r}$ 给出 式中: M—船体质量(吨) V—速度(米/秒) r—旋转的半径(米) F—向心力(千牛顿) – 解释作用在横向阻力中心的力如何能被作用在重心的同样大小的力所取代，并且该倾侧力偶等于该力乘以横向阻力中心到重心之间的垂直距离， $\frac{Mv^2}{r}\left[KG-\frac{d}{2}\right]^{\cos\theta}$ – 解释船舶将倾斜直到产生的复原力矩等于倾斜力偶为止,即 $M\times g\times GM\sin\theta=\frac{Mv^2}{r}\left[KG-\frac{d}{2}\right]^{\cos\theta}$ 式中: g—重力加速度 θ—倾斜角 – 已知相关数据,从下列公式计算倾角 $\tan\theta=\frac{v^2\times\left[KG-\frac{d}{2}\right]}{g\times GM\times r}$ **进入干船坞和搁浅** – 阐述进入干船坞时的船舶应: – 有适当的初稳心高度 – 正浮 – 有一个小的或适当的吃水差,通常是艉倾 – 阐述当船舶接触船坞时,部分重量将集中由坞墩支撑,其浮力会减少与其相当的量 – 阐述艉部上冲导致稳心高度的实质损失 – 解释为什么直到船舶整体坐坞之前,GM 值必须保持为正值 – 推导艉部上冲力公式 $P=\frac{(MCT\times t)}{L}$ 式中: P—艉部上冲力(吨) t—吃水差(厘米) L—漂心到艉部的距离(米) – 解释大吃水差船舶会产生巨大的上冲力,可能会在船舶整体坐坞之前损坏艉肋骨、绊倒坞墩或导致不稳定状态	R1

COMPETENCE 3.1	Control Trim, Stability and Stress	IMO Reference
– by taking moments about the centre of buoyancy, shows that, for a small angle of heel, θ, righting moment = $\Delta \times GM \sin\theta - P \times KM \sin\theta$ where GM is the initial metacentric height when afloat – shows that the righting lever is that for the ship with its metacentric height reduced by $\frac{(P \times KM)}{\Delta}$ – by using the equation in the above objective and $KM + KG + GM$, shows that righting moment = $(\Delta - P) \times GM \sin\theta - P \times KG \sin\theta$ – shows that the righting lever is that for a ship of displacement $(\Delta - P)$ and with metacentric height reduced by $\frac{(P \times KM)}{\Delta - P}$ – explains that the righting moment remains positive providing $\Delta \times$ GM is greater than $P \times KM$ or equivalently, $(\Delta - P) \times GM$ is greater than $P \times KG$ – calculates the minimum GM to ensure that the ship remains stable at the point of taking the blocks overall – calculates the maximum trim to ensure that the ship remains stable on taking the blocks overall for a given *GM* – calculates the virtual loss of *GM* and the draughts of the ship after the level has fallen by a stated amount – calculates the draughts on taking the blocks overall – explains that the stability of a ship aground at one point on the centre line is reduced in the same way as in dry-docking – states that when grounding occurs at an off-centre point, the upthrust causes heel as well as trim and reduction of *GM* – explains that the increase in upthrust as the tide falls increases the heeling moment and reduces the stability		
Shear force, bending moments and torsional stress – explains what is meant by shearing stress – states that the shear force at a given point of a simply supported beam is equal to the algebraic sum of the forces to one side of that point – explains that, for a beam in equilibrium, the sum of forces to one side of a point is equal to the sum of the forces on the other side with the sign reversed – explains what is meant by a bending moment – states that the bending moment at a given point of a beam is the algebraic sum of the moment of force acting to one side of that point – states that the bending moment measured to opposite sides of a point are numerically equal but opposite in sense		R1

适任 3.1	控制吃水差、稳性和应力	IMO 参考书目
– 对于倾斜角 θ,通过浮心的力矩可表示为 复原力矩 = $\Delta \times GM \sin\theta - P \times KM \sin\theta$ 此处 GM 是漂浮时的初稳心高度 – 表明复原力臂等于船舶初稳性高度减去 $\frac{P \times KM}{\Delta}$ – 通过运用上述公式和 $KM=KG+GM$ 表明 复原力矩 = $(\Delta - P) \times GM \sin\theta - P \times KG \sin\theta$ – 表明排水量为$(\Delta - P)$时 复原力臂 = 初稳心高度 $- \frac{P \times KM}{\Delta - P}$ – 解释如 $\Delta \times GM$ 大于等于 $P \times KM$, $(\Delta - P) \times GM$ 大于 $P \times KG$,则复原力矩恒为正 – 计算出最小的 GM 值以确保船舶整体坐墩时保持稳定 – 计算给定 GM 值的船舶最大吃水差,以确保船舶整体坐墩时保持稳定 – 计算水位下降至规定水位后的 GM 实际损失值和船舶吃水 – 计算船舶完全坐墩时的吃水 – 解释船舶搁浅在中心线上一点时,稳性的减少同干坞中的情况一样 – 阐述当船舶搁浅在非中心线上一点时,上冲力会产生横倾及纵倾,GM 值也会减小 – 解释落潮时,上冲力的增加,造成倾侧力矩的增加和稳性的减小 **剪力,弯矩,扭力** – 解释什么是剪力 – 阐述简支梁上一个给定点上的切力等于此点一侧的力的代数和 – 解释对平衡梁而言,此点一侧力的和等于另一侧力的和,但符号相反 – 解释什么是弯矩 – 阐述一个梁的给定点的弯矩等于作用在此点一侧力矩的代数和 – 阐述点的另一侧测得的弯矩和此侧在数值上相等但方向相反		R1

COMPETENCE 3.1	Control Trim, Stability and Stress	IMO Reference
– draws a diagram of shear force and bending moment for simply supported beams – states that the bending moment at any given point is equal to the area under the shear-force curve to that point – uses the above objective to show that the bending-moment curve has a turning point where the shear force has zero value – explains that shear forces and bending moments arise from differences between weight and buoyancy per unit length of the ship – states that the differences between buoyancy and weight is called the load – draws a load curve from a given buoyancy curve and weight curve – states that the shear force at any given point is equal to the area under the load curve between the origin and that point – draws a diagram of shear force and bending moment for a given distribution of weight for a box-shaped vessel – explains how wave profile affects the shear-force curve and bending-moment curve – states that each ship above a specified length is required to carry a loading manual, in which are set out acceptable loading patterns to keep shear forces and bending moments within acceptable limits – states that the classification society may also require a ship to carry an approved means of calculating shear forces and bending moment at stipulated stations – demonstrates the use of a loading instrument – states that the loading manual and instrument, where provided, should be used to ensure that shear forces and bending moments do not exceed the permissible limits in still water during cargo and ballast handling – explains what is meant by a torsional stress – describes how torsional stresses in the hull are set up – states that wave-induced torsional stresses are allowed for in the design of the ship – states that cargo-induced torsional stresses are a problem mainly in container ships – states that classification societies specify maximum permissible torsional moments at a number of specified cargo bays – given details of loading, calculates cumulative torsional moments for stated positions – describes the likelihood of overstressing the hull structure when loading certain bulk cargoes		

<table>
<tr><th>适任 3.1</th><th>控制吃水差、稳性和应力</th><th>IMO
参考书目</th></tr>
<tr><td colspan="2">

- 描绘一张简支梁的剪力图和弯矩图
- 阐述任一给定点上的弯矩等于剪力曲线到此点所包含的面积
- 利用上述结果说明弯矩曲线在剪力为零处有一个拐点
- 解释剪力和弯矩是由于船舶每单位长度重力和浮力的不同而产生的
- 阐述浮力和重力之差称为载荷
- 由给定的浮力曲线和重力曲线画出载荷曲线
- 阐述任一给定点的剪力等于从原点到此点之间载荷曲线的面积
- 画出箱形船给定重量分布的剪力图和弯矩曲线
- 解释波浪是如何影响剪力曲线和弯矩曲线的
- 阐述要求船长超过某一长度的每艘船舶备有装载手册，其中列出了可接受的装载模式,以保持剪力和弯矩在可接受的范围内
- 阐述船级社可能也会要求船舶备有认可的计算指定站面剪力和弯矩的设施
- 示范装载仪的使用
- 阐述应用配备的装载手册和装载仪，以确保船舶在静水中装卸货和压载作业中所受剪力和弯矩不超过许用极限值
- 解释什么是扭转应力
- 描述船壳的扭转应力是如何产生的
- 阐述船舶设计中应考虑波浪引起的扭转应力
- 阐述由货物引起的扭转应力是集装箱船上的主要问题
- 阐述船级社规定许多货物排上的最大许用扭转力矩
- 给定装载的详情,计算规定位置的累计扭转力矩
- 描述装载某些散货时船体结构应力超限的可能性

</td><td></td></tr>
</table>

COMPETENCE 3.1	Control Trim, Stability and Stress	IMO Reference

3.1.2 EFFECT ON TRIM AND STABILITY IN THE EVENT OF DAMAGE AND FLOODING
Textbooks: T4
Bibliography: B1, B2, B3, B4, B5, B6, B9, B10, B11, B14, B15, B20, B22, B23, B29, B30, B31, B32, B35, B37, B39, B43, B44, B46, B47, B48, B49, B52, B53, B54, B64, B84, B85, B96, B103, B107, B111, B114, B115, B118, B126, B131, B132, B133, B135, B137, B144, B145, B147, B148, B149, B154, B159, B160, B169, B170, B171, B174, B176, B178, B179, B180, B183, B184, B185, B186, B187, B199, B204, B205, B206, B207, B211, B213
Teaching aids: A1
Required performance:
2.1 Effect of flooding on transverse stability and trim (9 hours)
Passenger vessels
– explains what is meant by 'floodable length'
– defines:
  – margin line
  – bulkhead deck
  – permeability of a space
– explains what is meant by 'permissible length of compartments' in passenger ships
– describes briefly the significance of the Criterion of Service Numeral
– explains the significance of the factor of subdivision
– states the assumed extent of damage used in assessing the stability of passenger ships in damaged condition
– summarizes, with reference to the factor of subdivision, the extent of damage which a passenger ship should withstand
– describes the provisions for dealing with asymmetrical flooding
– states the requirements for the final condition of the ship after assumed damage and, where applicable, equalization of flooding
– states that the Master is supplied with data necessary to maintain sufficient intact stability to withstand the critical damage
– explains the minimum residual stability requirements in the damaged condition with the required number of compartments flooded
– discusses the use of the damaged stability information required to be provided to the Master of a passenger vessel
Cargo ships
– distinguishes between ships of Type A and Type B for the purpose of computation of freeboard
– describes the extent of damage that a Type A ship of over 150 m in length should be able to withstand
– explains that a Type A ship of over 150 m in length is described as a one compartment ship
– describes the requirements for the survivability of Type B ships with reduced assigned freeboard
– summarizes the equilibrium conditions regarded as satisfactory after flooding
		R1

适任 3.1	控制吃水差、稳性和应力	IMO 参考书目
3.1.2　船体损坏并进水对吃水差和稳性的影响 **教科书:**T4 **参考文献:**B1, B2, B3, B4, B5, B6, B9, B10, B11, B14, B15, B20, B22, B23, B29, B30, B31, B32, B35, B37, B39, B43, B44, B46, B47, B48, B49, B52, B53, B54, B64, B84, B85, B96, B103, B107, B111, B114, B115, B118, B126, B131, B132, B133, B135, B137, B144, B145, B147, B148, B149, B154, B159, B160, B169, B170, B171, B174, B176, B178, B179, B180, B183, B184, B185, B186, B187, B199, B204, B205, B206, B207, B211, B213 **教具:**A1 技能要求:		
2.1　进水对横稳性和吃水的影响(9 学时)		R1
客船 – 解释什么是"可浸长度" – 定义: 　– 限界线 　– 舱壁甲板 　– 舱室渗透率 – 解释什么是客船的"可浸舱长" – 简述船舶业务衡准数的重要性 – 解释分舱指数的重要性 – 阐述假定用于评估破损客船稳定的假想损伤程度 – 概述参照分舱指数,客船应能承受的损伤程度 – 描述针对非对称进水的规定 – 阐述对假想损伤后的最终状态的要求,如适用的话,用于船舶均衡进水 – 阐述给船长提供必要的数据,以保持足够的完整稳性来承受临界破损 – 解释在规定数量舱室破损进水状态下的残留稳性要求 – 讨论要求提供给客船船长的破损稳性资料的使用		
货船 – 从计算干舷的目的不同来区分 A 型船和 B 型船 – 描述长度超过 150 米的 A 型船应能承受的损伤程度 – 解释长度超过 150 米的 A 型船被称为一舱制船舶 – 描述减少了指定干舷的 B 型船的生存能力要求 – 概述进水后令人满意的平衡条件		

COMPETENCE 3.1	Control Trim, Stability and Stress	IMO Reference
– states that damage to compartments may cause a ship to sink as a result of: – insufficient reserve buoyancy leading to progressive flooding – progressive flooding due to excessive list or trim – capsizing due to a loss of stability – structural failure **Calculation of vessel condition after flooding** – states that, in the absence of hull damage, the stability is calculated in the usual way using the added mass and making allowance for free surface liquid – states that free surface moments for any rectangular compartment that is flooded by salt water can be approximated by moment = length × (breadth)^3 × 1.025 / 12 – states that virtual loss of $GM = \frac{\text{moment}}{\text{flooded displacement}}$ – states that when a compartment is holed the ship will sink deeper in the water until the intact volume displaces water equivalent to the mass of the ship and its contents – explains that the loss of buoyancy of a holed compartment is equal to the mass of water which enters the compartment up to the original waterline – states that the volume of lost buoyancy for a loaded compartment is equal to the volume of the compartment × the permeability of the compartment – calculates the permeability of cargo, given its density and its stowage factor – states that if the lost buoyancy is greater than the reserve buoyancy the ship will sink – states that the centre of buoyancy moves to the centre of immersed volume of the intact portion of the ship – states that when a compartment is holed the ship's displacement and its centre of gravity are unchanged – explains that a heeling arm is produced, equal to the transverse separation of G and the new position of B for the upright ship – states that the area of intact waterplane is reduced by the area of the flooded spaces at the level of the flooded waterline multiplied by the permeability of the space – states that if the flooded space is entirely below the waterline there is no reduction in intact waterplane – calculates the increase in mean draught of a ship, given the *TPC* and the dimensions of the flooded space, using increase in draught $= \frac{\text{volume of lost buoyancy}}{\text{area of intact waterplane}}$ – states that the height of the centre of buoyancy above the keel increases by about half the increase in draught due to flooding – states that a reduction in waterplane area leads to a reduction in the second moment of area (I) – uses the formula $BM = I/V$ to explain why the *BM* of a ship is generally less when bilged than when intact – states that change in *GM* is the net result of changes in *KB* and *BM*		

适任 3.1	控制吃水差、稳性和应力	IMO 参考书目
	– 阐述货舱的损坏可能由于下述原因造成沉船: 　– 储备浮力不足导致持续进水 　– 由于过度横倾或纵倾造成持续进水 　– 由于稳性减少而倾覆 　– 结构损坏 **进水后的船舶状态计算** – 阐述在船体未受损坏时,稳性通常采用增加载荷并考虑自由液面的方法计算 – 阐述由海水浸入的矩形舱室,其自由液面力矩可由下述公式估算: 力矩 = 长度 × (宽度)^3 × 1.025/12 – 阐述实质损失的 $GM = \frac{力矩}{进水后的排水量}$ – 阐述当舱室出现漏洞时,船体将下沉,直到未沉部分的排水体积等于船体和载荷的重量 – 解释破漏舱室损失的浮力等于原始水线以上进入舱室的水的重量 – 阐述对于一个已经装有货物的舱室,其浮力损失的体积等于该舱室的体积乘以该舱室渗透率 – 已知货物的密度和积载因数,计算货物的渗透率 – 阐述如果浮力的损失大于储备浮力,船体将下沉 – 阐述浮心将转移到船舶未受损部分的浸没体积中心处 – 阐述当舱室出现漏洞时,船舶的排水量和它们的重心不变 – 解释产生的倾侧力臂等于 G 和船舶正浮时 B 的新位置的横向距离 – 阐述完整水线面面积为减少进水后水线处的进水舱室面积乘以舱室渗透率 – 阐述如进水空间完全在水线以下,则完整水线面不会减少 – 给出 *TPC* 和进水舱室的尺度,可计算出增加的平均吃水值 增加的吃水 = $\frac{损失的浮力体积}{受损后的水线面面积}$ – 阐述因进水,龙骨之上的浮力中心高度会增加吃水增加值的一半 – 阐述水线面面积的减少会使二阶面积惯矩(I)减少 – 用公式 $BM = \frac{I}{V}$ 来解释为何通常船舶在有舱底破损进水时的 *BM* 比无舱底破损时的 *BM* 要小 – 阐述 *GM* 的变化是 *KB* 和 *BM* 变化的最终结果	

COMPETENCE 3.1	Control Trim, Stability and Stress	IMO Reference

- explains why the GM usually decreases where:
  - there is a large loss of intact waterplane
  - there is intact buoyancy below the flooded space
  - the flooded surface has a high permeability
- explains why the bilging of empty double-bottom tanks or of deep tanks that are wholly below the waterline leads to an increase in GM
- calculates the reduction in BM resulting from lost area of the waterplane, given the following corrections:
- second moment of lost area about its centroid / displaced volume;

  this is $\frac{Lb^3}{12\ V}$ for a rectangular surface

  where: L is length of the lost area

  b is breadth of the lost area

  V is displaced volume = $\frac{\text{displacement}}{\text{density of water}}$

  original waterplane area / intact waterplane area × lost area × (distance from centreline)^2 / displaced volume

  this is original $\frac{\text{waterplane area}}{\text{intact waterplane area} \times L \times b \times d^2 / V}$

  for a rectangular surface, where d is the distance of the centre of the area from the centreline
- deduces that the second correction applies only in the case of asymmetrical flooding
- calculates the shift (F) of the centre of flotation (CE) from the centreline, using

  $F = \frac{a \times d}{A - a}$

  where: a is the lost area of waterplane

  A is the original waterplane area

  d is the distance of the centre of lost area of waterplane from the centreline
- shows that the heeling arm is given by

  heeling arm = lost buoyancy (tonnes)/displacement x transverse distance from new CF
- constructs a GZ curve for the estimated GM and superimposes the heelingarm curve to determine the approximate angle of heel
- uses wall-sided formula to determine GZ values
- uses wall-sided formula to calculate angle of heel
- states that, for small angles of heel, θ,

  $\tan\theta = \frac{\text{heeling arm}}{GM}$
- explains how lost area of waterplane affects the position of the centre of flotation

Effect of flooding on trim

- calculates the movement of the centre of flotation (CF), given:

  movement of CF = moment of lost area about original CF/intact waterplane area

适任 3.1	控制吃水差、稳性和应力	IMO 参考书目
– 解释为何 *GM* 值在以下的情况下通常会减少: – 完整水线面面积有重大损失 – 进水舱室以下有完整浮力 – 进水舱室具有高渗透率 – 解释完全在水线下的空双层底舱或深舱破损进水导致 *GM* 值增大的原因 – 给定下列修正,计算由于水线面面积的减少而引起 *BM* 值的减少: – 在其质心处的二阶面积惯矩损失 / 排水体积 对矩形面有 $\frac{Lb^3}{12\ V}$ 式中: *L*—受损水线面面积的长度 *b*—受损水线面面积的宽度 *V*—排水体积,等于 $\frac{排水量}{水的密度}$ 原始水线面面积 / 完整水线面面积 × 损失面积 × (距中距离)²/ 排水体积 对矩形面有 × $\frac{原始水线面积}{完整水线面积 \times L \times b \times d^2\ /\ V}$ 其中,*d* 是面积中心至距中心线距离 – 推导第二修正只适用于非对称的进水情况 – 用 *F*= 计算漂心(CE)相对中心线的漂移,即 $F = \frac{a \times d}{A - a}$ 式中: *a*—损失的水线面面积 *A*—原始的水线面面积 *d*—损失水线面面积中心至距中心线距离 – 阐述倾侧力臂由下式给出: 倾侧力臂 = $\frac{损失的浮力(吨)}{排水量}$ × 到新浮力中心(CF)的横向距离 – 构造 *GZ* 曲线确定 *GM* 值,并与倾侧力臂曲线叠加而确定大概的横倾角 – 运用垂直船舷的公式确定 *GZ* 的值 – 运用垂直船舷公式确定横倾角 – 阐述对于小角度的倾斜角 θ $\tan\theta = \frac{倾侧力臂}{GM}$ – 解释水线面面积的损失如何影响浮力中心的位置 **船舶进水对吃水差的影响** – 根据以下的公式计算漂心(CF)移动: CF 的移动 = $\frac{损失的水线面面积相对原漂心(CF)的惯性矩}{完整水线面面积}$		

COMPETENCE 3.1	Control Trim, Stability and Stress	IMO Reference
– explains how the reduction in intact waterplane reduces the MCT 1 cm – calculates the reduction of BML, given the following corrections: second moment of lost area about its centroids / displaced volume; this is $\frac{bL^3}{12\ V}$ for a rectangular surface where: L is length of lost area b is breadth of lost area V is displaced volume = $\frac{\text{displacement}}{\text{density of water}}$ Original waterplane area / intact waterplane area × lost area × (distance from CF)^2/displaced volume This is original waterplane area/intact waterplane area × bLd^2 / v – for a rectangular surface, where d is the distance of the centre of area from the original centre of flotation – calculates the reduction of MCT 1 cm, given, reduction of MCT 1 cm = (displacement × reduction of GM)/100 x ship's length – states that the trimming moment is calculated from: trimming moment = lost buoyancy x distance from new CF where the lost buoyancy is measured in tonnes – given the dimensions of a bilged space and the ship's hydrostatic data, calculates the draughts in the damaged condition – describes measures which may be taken to improve the stability or trim of a damaged ship		
2.2 Theories affecting trim and stability (2 hours) – describes the static and dynamic effects on stability of liquids with a free surface – identifies free surface moments and shows its application to dead-weight moment curves – interprets changes in stability which take place during a voyage – describes effect on stability of ice formation on superstructure – describes the effect of water absorption by deck cargo and retention of water on deck – describes stability requirements for dry-docking – demonstrates understanding of angle of loll – states precautions to be observed in correction of angle of loll – explains the dangers to a vessel at an angle of loll – describes effects of wind and waves on ships stability – lists the main factors which affect the rolling period of a vessel – explains the terms synchronous and parametric rolling and pitching and describes the dangers associated with it – describes the actions that can be taken to stop synchronous and parametric effects		R1

适任 3.1	控制吃水差、稳性和应力	IMO 参考书目
– 解释完整水线面面积的减少如何减小 *MCT* 1cm – 根据以下修正计算 *BML*: 在其质心处的二阶面积惯矩损失/排水体积; 对矩形面有 $\frac{bL^3}{12V}$ 式中: *L*—受损水线面面积的长度 *b*—受损水线面面积的宽度 *V*—排水体积 = $\frac{排水量}{水的密度}$ – 原始水线面积 / 完整水线面积 × 损失面积 × (距 CF 距离)²/ 排水体积 对矩形面有 $\frac{原始的水线面面积}{完整水线面面积} \times bLd^2$ 其中,*d* 是面积中心至原始漂心的距离 – 根据以下公式计算 MCT 1 cm 的减小值: $MCT\ 1\ cm 的减小值 = \frac{排水量 \times 初稳性高度(GM)的减少值}{100 \times 船长}$ – 阐述纵倾力矩由以下公式得来: 纵倾力矩 = 损失的浮力 × 到新 CF 的距离 其中,损失的浮力以吨计 – 已知破损船舱尺度和船舶静水力参数,计算破损状态下的船舶吃水 – 描述为改善破损船舶的稳性或吃水差,可以采取的措施		
2.2 影响吃水差和稳性的理论(2 学时)		R1
– 描述自由液面对静稳性和动稳性的影响 – 确定自由液面力矩并显示它在载重量力矩曲线上的应用 – 解释在航行过程中稳性的变化 – 描述上层建筑表面结冰对稳性的影响 – 描述甲板货吸水以及甲板积水的影响 – 描述进入干船坞对稳性的要求 – 说明对静倾角的理解 – 阐述修正静倾角要求的预防措施 – 解释静倾角对船舶的危险 – 描述风浪对船舶稳性的影响 – 列出影响船舶横摇周期的主要因数 – 解释术语横向谐摇和纵向谐摇及与其相关的危险 – 描述防止谐摇所应采取的行动		

COMPETENCE 3.1	Control Trim, Stability and Stress	IMO Reference
3.1.3 KNOWLEDGE OF IMO RECOMMENDATIONS CONCERNING SHIP STABILITY **Textbooks:** T4 **Bibliography:** B1, B2, B3, B4, B5, B6, B9, B10, B11, B14, B15, B20, B22, B23, B29, B30, B31, B32, B35, B37, B39, B43, B44, B46, B47, B48, B49, B52, B53, B54, B64, B84, B85, B96, B103, B107, B111, B114, B115, B118, B126, B131, B132, B133, 135, B137, B144, B145, B147, B148, B149, B154, B159, B160, B169, B170, B171, B174 **Teaching aids:** A1 Required performance: **3.1 Responsibilities under the international conventions and codes (2 hours)** – states minimum stability requirements required by Load Line Rules 1966 – states the minimum stability requirements and recommendations of the Intact Stability Code – explains the use of the weather criterion – demonstrates correct use of IMO grain regulations – explains how grain heeling moment information is used – describes the requirements for passenger ship stability after damage		R1

适任 3.1	控制吃水差、稳性和应力	IMO 参考书目
3.1.3　IMO 关于船舶稳性的建议的理解 **教科书**:T4 **参考文献**:B1, B2, B3, B4, B5, B6, B9, B10, B11, B14, B15, B20, B22, B23, B29, B30, B31, B32, B35, B37, B39, B43, B44, B46, B47, B48, B49, B52, B53, B54, B64, B84, B85, B96, B103, B107, B111, B114, B115, B118, B126, B131, B132, B133, 135, B137, B144, B145, B147, B148, B149, B154, B159, B160, B169, B170, B171, B174 **教具**:A1 技能要求: **3.1　国际公约和规则下的责任(2 学时)** – 阐述 1966 年国际载重线公约的最低稳性要求 – 阐述完整稳性规则的最低稳性要求和建议 – 解释气象标准的使用 – 说明 IMO 谷物规则的正确使用 – 解释如何使用谷物倾侧力矩资料 – 描述客船破损后的稳性要求		R1

COMPETENCE 3.2	Monitor and Control Compliance with Legislative Requirements	IMO Reference
TRAINING OUTCOMES: Demonstrates a knowledge and understanding of: 3.2.1 INTERNATIONAL MARITIME LAW EMBODIED IN INTERNATIONAL AGREEMENTS AND CONVENTIONS, WITH PARTICULAR REGARD TO CERTIFICATES AND DOCUMENTS TO BE CARRIED ON BOARD BY INTERNATIONAL CONVENTIONS; RESPONSIBILITIES UNDER THE RELEVANT REQUIREMENTS OF THE INTERNATIONAL CONVENTION ON LOAD LINES, SAFETY OF LIFE AT SEA, PREVENTION OF POLLUTION FROM SHIPS, AND METHODS OF AID TO PREVENT POLLUTION OF THE MARINE ENVIRONMENT; REQUIREMENTS OF THE INTERNATIONAL HEALTH REGULATIONS; AND NATIONAL LEGISLATION FOR IMPLEMENTING INTERNATIONAL AGREEMENTS AND CONVENTIONS		STCW Code table A-II/2

适任 3.2	立法要求的监督与控制	IMO 参考书目
培训效果: 讲授下列内容知识与理解: 3.2.1 在国际协议和国际公约中体现的国际海事法,特别是根据国际公约规定的船舶应携带的证件和文件;在国际载重线公约、国际海上人命安全公约、国际防止船舶污染公约、防止污染海洋环境公约和有助于防止污染海洋环境的方法相关要求下的责任;国际卫生条例的要求;为履行国际协定和公约的国内立法		STCW 公约 表 A-II/2

COMPETENCE 3.2	Monitor and Control Compliance with Legislative Requirements	IMO Reference

3.2.1 INTERNATIONAL MARITIME LAW EMBODIED IN INTERNATIONAL AGREEMENTS AND CONVENTIONS

Textbooks/Bibliography: T10, T42, T43, B1, B2, B4, B5, B6, B9, B10, B11, B14, B15, B20, B22, B23, B29, B30, B31, B32, B35, B37, B39, B43, B44, B46, B47, B48, B49, B52, B53, B54, B64, B84, B85, B96, B107, B111, B114, B115, B126, B132, B133, B135, B137, B145, B147, B148, B149, B154, B160, B169, B170, B171, B174, B176, B178, B179, B180, B183, B184, B185, B186, B187, B199, B204, B205, B207, B211, B213

Teaching aids: A1, V2, V77, V79, V80, V81, V82, V86, V87, V89, V90, V91, V92, V94, V95, V97, V99, V100, V101, V102, V105, V109, V110, V111, V112, V115, V117, V118, V119, V126, V127, V131, V156, V157, V158, V169

Required performance:

1.1 Certificates and other documents required to be carried on board ships by international conventions (1 hour) R110

- states that IMO publishes a list of certificates and documents required to be carried on board ship R110
- states how a current version of the IMO list of certificates and documents required to be carried on board ship may be obtained
- identifies the certificates required by MLC (2006) to be carried on board ship
- identifies the certificates and documents that are required to be carried on board a ship of any type using the IMO information
- states the period of validity for each of the above certificates and explains the requirements for renewing or maintaining the validity
- explains how each of the certificates and documents required to be carried on board ships are obtained
- explains the proof of validity that may be required by authorities for the certificates and documents above

1.2 Responsibilities under the relevant requirements of the International Convention on Load Lines (1 hour)

- states that a ship to which the Convention applies must comply with the requirements for that ship
- explains the general requirements of the Conditions of Assignment to be met before any vessel can be assigned a load line
- describes the factors that determine the freeboards assigned to a vessel
- describes the requirements and coverage of initial, renewal and annual surveys
- describes the contents of the record of particulars which should be supplied to the ship
- explains the documentation and records that must be maintained on the ship in terms of:
  - certificates
  - record of particulars
  - record of freeboards
  - information relating to the stability and loading of the ship
- states that after any survey has been completed no change should be made in the structure, equipment or other matters covered by the survey without the sanction of the Administration

<table>
<tr><th>适任 3.2</th><th>立法要求的监督与控制</th><th>IMO
参考书目</th></tr>
<tr><td colspan="2">3.2.1 在国际协议和国际公约中所体现的国际海事法
教科书/参考文献:T10, T42, T43, B1, B2, B4, B5, B6, B9, B10, B11, B14, B15, B20, B22, B23, B29, B30, B31, B32, B35, B37, B39, B43, B44, B46, B47, B48, B49, B52, B53, B54, B64, B84, B85, B96, B107, B111, B114, B115, B126, B132, B133, B135, B137, B145, B147, B148, B149, B154, B160, B169, B170, B171, B174, B176, B178, B179, B180, B183, B184, B185, B186, B187, B199, B204, B205, B207, B211, B213
教具:A1, V2, V77, V79, V80, V81, V82, V86, V87, V89, V90, V91, V92, V94, V95, V97, V99, V100, V101, V102, V105, V109, V110, V111, V112, V115, V117, V118, V119, V126, V127, V131, V156, V157, V158, V169
技能要求:
1.1 国际公约要求船舶所携带的证书和其他文件(1 学时)
– 阐述 IMO 颁发的要求船舶携带的一系列证书和文件的清单
– 阐述如何得到 IMO 颁发的要求船舶携带的证书和文件的清单
– 确定 MLC (2006)要求船舶携带的证书
– 利用 IMO 资料确定任何种类船舶被要求携带的证书和文件清单
– 阐述上述每个证书的有效期并解释证书更新或保持有效的要求
– 解释如何得到要求船舶携带的每个证书和文件
– 解释主管机关要求的上述证书和文件的有效性证明
1.2 《国际载重线公约》相关要求下的责任(1 学时)
– 阐述适用公约的船舶必须符合公约对其的要求
– 解释在勘定任何船舶载重线之前,应满足的勘定条件的一般要求
– 描述决定船舶干舷的因素
– 描述初始检验、换证检验和年度检验的要求和范围
– 描述应提供给船舶的详细物品的记录内容
– 解释船舶必须保存如下文件和记录:
  – 证书
  – 详细物品记录
  – 干舷记录
  – 有关船舶稳性和装载的信息
– 阐述在检验完成后,未经主管机关批准不应在结构、设备或该检验包括的其他事物上做出改变</td><td>

R110
R110</td></tr>
</table>

COMPETENCE 3.2	Monitor and Control Compliance with Legislative Requirements	IMO Reference
	– states that, after repairs or alterations, a ship should comply with at least the requirements previously applicable and that, after major repairs or alterations, ships should comply with the requirements for a new ship in so far as the Administration deems reasonable and practicable – describes the preparation required for renewal and annual load line surveys – states that the appropriate load lines on the sides of the ship corresponding to the season and to the zone or area in which the ship may be must not be submerged at any time when the ship puts to sea, during the voyage or on arrival – states that when a ship is in fresh water of unit density the appropriate load line may be submerged by the amount of the fresh water allowance shown on the International Load Line Certificate (1966) – states that when a ship departs from port situated on a river or inland waters, deeper loading is permitted corresponding to the weight of fuel and all other materials required for consumption between the point of departure and the sea – explains the treatment of a port lying on the boundary between two zones or areas – explains the circumstances in which an International Load Line Certificate (1966) would be cancelled by the Administration	
1.3	**Responsibilities under the relevant requirements of the International Convention for the Safety of Life at Sea (2 hours)** – states the obligations of the Master concerning the sending of danger messages relating to dangerous ice, a dangerous derelict, other dangers to navigation, tropical storms, sub-freezing air temperature with gale force winds causing severe ice accretion or winds of force 10 or above for which no storm warning has been received – lists the information required in danger messages	R2
	– states that when ice is reported near his course, the Master of every ship at night is bound to proceed at a moderate speed or to alter his course so as to go well clear of the danger zone – states that the use of an international distress signal, except for the purpose of indicating that a ship or aircraft is in distress, and the use of any signal which may be confused with an international distress signal are prohibited – states the obligations of the Master of a ship at sea on receiving a signal from any source that a ship or aircraft or a survival craft thereof is in distress – explains the rights of the Master of a ship in distress to requisition one or more ships which have answered his call for assistance – explains when the Master of a ship is released from the obligation to render assistance – describes the requirements for the carriage of navigational equipment – states that all equipment fitted in compliance with reg. V/12 must be of a type approved by the Administration – states that all ships should be sufficiently and efficiently manned – states that manning is subject to Port State Control inspection – lists the contents of the minimum safe manning document referred to in Assembly resolution A481(XII), Principles of safe manning	R2 ch. V reg. 10

适任 3.2	立法要求的监督与控制	IMO 参考书目
	– 阐述在修理或改装之后,船舶应当至少遵守先前适用的要求,并且在大修或大改后,船舶应遵守主管机关认为目前合理和可行的对每艘新船的要求 – 阐述载重线证书换证检验或年度检验要求的准备工作 – 阐述船舶两舷对应于不同季节和区带或地区,当船舶出海时、航行中或抵达时都不得淹没的适当载重线 – 阐述国际载重线公约(1966)表明,在单位密度的淡水中的船舶,载重线可适当地被淡水淹没 – 阐述船舶在内河或内水港口航行出海,允许适当超载。超载部分的重量应对应于船舶在内河航行期间消耗的燃油和其他物资的重量 – 解释位于两个区带或地区之间的边界港口的处理办法 – 解释国际载重线公约(1966)将由主管机关取消的情况	
1.3	**《国际海上人命安全公约》相关要求下的责任(2 学时)**	R2
	– 阐述船长如遇到危险的冰、危险的漂浮物,或其他航行危险,热带风暴,或遇到伴随强风的低于冰点的气温致使上层建筑严重积聚冰块,或者未曾收到风暴警报而遇到蒲福风级 10 级以上的风力时,均有责任将此危险讯息发送出去 – 列出危险讯息要求包含的信息	
	– 阐述据报在其航向附近有冰时,每艘船的船长务必在夜晚以适当的速度航行或改变航向让清该危险区 – 阐述除非船舶或飞行器遇险,否则禁止使用国际遇险信号和会与国际遇险信号相混淆的任何信号 – 阐述海上航行时船长在收到任何有关处于遇险状态下的他船或飞行器或救生艇的信息时的责任 – 解释遇难船的船长有权征调回应其呼叫救援的一船或多船 – 解释何时船长有免除提供救助的责任 – 描述航行设备的配备要求 – 阐述任何满足规则Ⅴ/12 要求配备的设备必须是主管机关认可型号的 – 阐述所有船舶必须配备足够而胜任的人员 – 阐述船上人员配备要接受港口国监督 – 参照 A.481(Ⅻ)大会决议安全配员原则要求,列出最低安全配员文件的内容	R2 ch. V reg. 10

COMPETENCE 3.2	Monitor and Control Compliance with Legislative Requirements	IMO Reference
	– states that in areas where navigation demands special caution, ships should have more than one steering gear power unit in operation when such units are capable of simultaneous operation – describes the procedure for the testing of the ship's steering gear before departure – describes the requirements for the display of operating instructions and change-over procedures for remote steering gear control and steering gear power units – describes the requirements for emergency steering drills – lists the entries which should be made in the logbook regarding the checks and tests of the steering gear and the holding of emergency drills – states that all ships should carry adequate and up-to-date charts, sailing directions, lists of lights, notices to mariners, tide tables and other nautical publications necessary for the voyage – states which ships should carry the International Code of Signals	R2
1.4	**Responsibilities under the International Convention for the Prevention of Pollution from Ships, 1973, and the Protocol of 1978 relating thereto (MARPOL 73/78) (3 hours)** – explains who may cause proceedings to be taken when a violation occurs within the jurisdiction of a Party to the Convention – explains the Parties to the Convention must apply the requirements of the Convention to ships of non-Parties to ensure that no more favourable treatment is given to such ships	R9, R10, R11, R12, R13, R26, R27, R28, R72, R73, R74
	Annex I – Oil – states that, after survey has been completed, no change should be made in the structure, equipment, fittings, arrangements or materials without the sanction of the Administration, except the direct replacement of equipment and fittings – explains the Master's duty to report when an accident occurs or a defect is discovered which substantially affects the integrity of the ship or the efficiency or completeness of its equipment covered by this Annex – states that the dates of intermediate and annual surveys are endorsed on the IOPP Certificate – states that a record of construction and equipment is attached as a supplement to the IOPP Certificate – explains the duration of validity of the IOPP Certificate and the circumstances in which the IOPP Certificate will cease to be valid – states that all new crude oil tankers of 20,000 tonnes deadweight and above must be fitted with a crude oil washing system – states that the competent authority of the Government of a Party to the Convention may inspect the Oil Record Book while the ship is in its port or offshore terminals and may make a copy of any entry and may require the Master to certify that the copy is a true copy of such entry – states that a copy certified by the Master is admissible in any judicial proceedings as evidence of the facts stated in the entry – states that the Master should be provided with information relative to loading and distribution of cargo necessary to ensure compliance with the regulation on subdivision and stability and the ability of the ship to comply with the damage stability criteria	R10

适任 3.2	立法要求的监督与控制	IMO 参考书目
	– 在要求特别谨慎航行区域,船舶应有一台以上并行的舵机电源装置运行 – 阐述在开航前船舶舵机检查程序 – 描述舵机遥控和电源装置的操作指示和转换程序的张贴要求 – 描述应急操舵演习的要求 – 列出有关舵机的检查和试验以及在操舵演习应记入航海日志的内容 – 阐述所有船舶应备有足够的且已更新的海图、航路指南、灯标表、航海通告、潮汐表和其他航行必备的航海出版物 – 阐述船舶应配备《国际信号规则》	
1.4	**1973/1978 年国际防止船舶污染公约及其议定书(MARPOL73/78)的责任(3 学时)** – 解释在公约缔约国的管辖水域发生了违章由谁可以启动要采取的行动 – 解释公约的缔约国必须使非缔约国的船舶遵守公约的要求，以确保没有更多地给予这些船舶优惠待遇	R9, R10, R11, R12, R13, R26, R27, R28, R72, R73, R74
	附则 I —防止油污染规则 – 阐述检验完成后,未经主管机关许可,不应在船舶结构、设备、配件、设施或材料做较大变动,除非直接更换这种设备和配件 – 解释当发生事故或发现实质性影响船舶整体性或本附则包括的设备效率或其完整性的缺陷时,船长的报告责任 – 阐述中间检验和年度检验的日期记录在 IOPP 证书上 – 阐述结构和设备记录作为 IOPP 证书的附录,对其进行补充 – 解释 IOPP 证书的有效期和 IOPP 证书失效的条件 – 阐述所有 20 000 载重吨及以上的新原油船必须配备原油洗舱系统 – 阐述公约缔约国的主管机关可以在该船停泊在其港口或沿岸码头时检查油类记录簿,并对任何记录进行复制,且可以要求船长证明其复印件是该记录的真实复印本 – 阐述经船长证明的复印件在任何司法诉讼中可作为记录中所述事实的证据 – 阐述应提供给船长相关的装载和必要的货物分配信息，以确保船舶符合有关分舱和稳性要求以及船舶符合受损稳性标准的能力	R10

COMPETENCE 3.2	Monitor and Control Compliance with Legislative Requirements	IMO Reference
– states all ships of 400 gt or more must carry an approved shipboard oil pollution emergency plan (SOPEP) Annex II – Noxious Liquid Substances in Bulk – states the duration of validity of the certificate – explains that ships which have been surveyed and certified in accordance with the International Bulk Chemical Code (IBC Code) or the Bulk Chemical Code (BCH Code), as applicable, are deemed to have complied with the regulations regarding survey and certification and do not require to have an International Pollution Prevention Certificate for the Carriage of Noxious Liquid Substances in Bulk Annex III – Harmful Substances Carried by Sea in Packaged Forms, or in Freight Containers, Portable Tanks or Tank Wagons – states that the Master of the ship, or his representative, should notify the appropriate port authority of the intention to load or unload certain harmful substances at least 24 hours in advance Annex IV – Sewage – defines, for the purposes of Annex IV: – holding tank, sewage and nearest land – states the ships to which the provisions apply – states that ships to which the regulations apply are subject to surveys for the issue of an International Sewage Pollution Prevention Certificate (1973) – states the duration of validity of the certificate Annex V – Garbage – explains that when garbage is mixed with other discharges having different disposal requirements, the more stringent requirements apply – describes the provisions for disposal of garbage from off-shore platforms and from ships alongside or within 500 metres from them – lists the special areas for the purposes of this annex – explains the requirements for disposal of garbage within special areas – describes the exceptions to regulations 3, 4 and 5 – describes the form of record keeping required – states records are subject to scrutiny by port State control officers Annex VI – (Regulations for the Prevention of Air Pollution from Ships) of the MARPOL Convention – states that MARPOL 73/78 Annex VI Regulations for the Prevention of Air Pollution from Ships entered into force on 19 May 2005 – states that MARPOL Annex VI sets limits on sulphur oxide and nitrogen oxide emissions from ship exhausts and prohibits deliberate emissions of ozonedepleting substances – explains that Annex VI emission control requirements are in accordance with the 1987 Montreal Protocol (a UN international environmental treaty), as amended in London in 1990		R11

<table>
<tr><th>适任 3.2</th><th>立法要求的监督与控制</th><th>IMO
参考书目</th></tr>
<tr><td colspan="2">
– 阐述所有 400 总吨或以上的船舶必须持有批准的《船上油污应急计划》(SOPEP)
附则Ⅱ—防止散装有毒液体物质污染规则
– 阐述该证书的有效期
– 解释根据《国际散装化学品规则》(IBC Code)或《散装化学品规则》(BCH Code)，如果适用，已被检验和发证的船舶，就被认为已经符合规则关于检验和发证的要求，不要求持有国际防止散装运输有毒液体物质污染证书
附则Ⅲ—防止海运包装或集装箱、可移动液柜或液罐车装有害物质污染规则
– 阐述当计划装卸某些有害物质时，船长或其代表应提前至少 24 小时通知有关港口当局
附则Ⅳ—防止船舶生活污水污染规则
– 有关附则Ⅳ的定义：
  – 集污舱、生活污水、最近陆地
– 阐述规则适用的船舶
– 阐述规则适用的船舶必须通过检验获得国际防止生活污水污染证书(1973)
– 阐述证书的有效期
附则Ⅴ—防止船舶垃圾污染规则
– 解释船舶垃圾与其他有不同倾倒要求的排放物混合时，要满足更严格的倾倒要求
– 描述在海上平台和其靠泊船舶或与其相距 500 m 以内的船舶处置垃圾的规定
– 列出本附则的特殊区域
– 解释在特殊区域处置垃圾的要求
– 描述规则 3、4、5 的例外情况
– 描述记录保存形式的要求
– 阐述上述记录须接受港口国监督官员的仔细审查
附则Ⅵ—防止船舶空气污染规则
– 阐述 MARPOL 73/78 公约 附则Ⅵ防止船舶空气污染规则于 2005 年 5 月 19 日生效
– 阐述 MARPOL 附则Ⅵ限制含硫氧化物和氮氧化物的船舶尾气排放和禁止蓄意排放破坏臭氧层物质
– 解释附则Ⅵ的排放控制要求符合 1990 年在伦敦修正的 1987 蒙特利尔议定书（联合国国际环境条约）
</td><td>
R11</td></tr>
</table>

COMPETENCE 3.2	Monitor and Control Compliance with Legislative Requirements	IMO Reference

– states that MARPOL annex VI applies to all ships, fixed and floating drilling rigs and other platforms, but the certification requirements are depending on size of the vessel and when it is constructed
– explains the requirements for shipboard energy efficiency plans under MARPOL annex VI
– explains that regulation 16 sets out requirements for shipboard incineration and as per 16(4) bans the incineration of:
  – MARPOL Annex I, II and III cargo residues and related contaminated packing materials;
  – polychlorinated biphenyls (PCBs);
  – garbage, as defined in MARPOL Annex V, containing more than traces of heavy metals; and
  – refined petroleum products containing halogen compounds
– explains that under regulation 16(5) incineration of sewage sludge and sludge oil generated during the normal operation of a ship may take place in the main or auxiliary power plant or boilers (as well as in an incinerator), but in those cases, must not take place inside ports, harbours and estuaries
– explains that regulation 16(6) prohibits the shipboard incineration of polyvinyl chlorides (PVCs), except in incinerators for which IMO Type Approval Certificates have been issued
– explains that under regulation 16(7) all ships with incinerators subject to regulation 16 must possess a manufacturer's operating manual which must specify how to operate the incinerator within the limits described in paragraph 2 of appendix IV to Annex VI
– explains that under regulation 16(8) personnel responsible for operation of any incinerator must be trained and capable of implementing the guidance in the manufacturer's operating manual
– explains that regulation 3 provides that the regulations of Annex VI will not apply to any emission necessary for the purpose of securing the safety of a ship or saving life at sea, or any emission resulting from damage to a ship or its equipment, subject to certain conditions
– states that regulation 15 provides that in ports or terminals in Party States any regulation of emissions of Volatile Organic Compounds (VOCs) from tankers must be in accordance with Annex VI
– states that as per regulation 15 a tanker carrying crude oil is required to have a "VOC Management Plan" approved by the Administration on board
– states that ships of 400 gross tons and above engaged in international voyages involving countries that have ratified the conventions, or ships flying the flag of those countries, are required to have an International Air Pollution Prevention Certificate (IAPP Certificate)
– states that the IAPP certificate will be issued following an initial survey carried out by the flag Administration or by a recognized organization on behalf of the flag Administration, confirming compliance with MARPOL Annex VI. For ships with the flag of an Administration that have not yet ratified Annex VI, a Certificate of Compliance with Annex VI may be issued		

适任 3.2	立法要求的监督与控制	IMO 参考书目

– 阐述 MARPOL 附则Ⅵ适用于所有船舶、固定和移动钻井平台及其他平台，但其发证要求取决于船舶大小和建造时间
– 解释 MARPOL 附则Ⅵ的船舶能效计划要求
– 解释规则 16 条规定了船舶焚烧的要求和按照 16(4)项规定,禁止焚烧下列物质:
  – MARPOL 附则Ⅰ、Ⅱ和Ⅲ中的货物残渣和相关的污染的包装材料;
  – 多氯联苯(PCBs);
  – MARPOL 附则Ⅴ中含有超过微量的重金属垃圾;
  – 含卤素化合物的精制石油产品
– 解释按照 16(5)项规定,那些船舶正常作业中产生的污油泥和污油在主要或辅助发电装置或锅炉(也包括焚烧炉)中的焚烧不得在港口附近和河口进行
– 解释按照 16(6)项规定,禁止在船上焚烧聚氯乙烯(PVCs),除非该船持有 IMO 认可类型的焚烧炉证书
– 解释按照 16(7)项规定,所有按 16 条规定配备焚烧炉的船舶须持有制造商操作手册,详细说明在附则Ⅳ到附则Ⅵ第 2 段规定的限制范围内如何操作焚烧炉
– 解释按照 16(8)项规定,负责操作焚烧炉的人员须经培训,并能按制造商手册中的指导操作
– 规则第 3 条规定,附则Ⅵ的规定不适用于为保证船舶或海上救生安全必需的排放,或在某些情况下,船舶或其设备损坏所致的排放
– 阐述规则第 15 条规定,在缔约国港口,油船排放任何挥发性有机化合物(VOCs)的规定须与附则Ⅵ相符
– 阐述按照规则第 15 条规定,要求载有原油的油船上具有经主管机关批准的"VOC 管理计划"
– 阐述要求 400 总吨及以上的国际航行且航行涉及批准该公约国家或悬挂那些国家国旗的船舶,持有国际防止空气污染证书(IAPP 证书)
– 阐述船旗国主管机关或由其认可的代表机构在对船舶进行初次检验之后，证实符合附则Ⅵ,将签发国际防止空气污染证书(IAPP 证书)。对悬挂尚未批准 MARPOL 附则Ⅵ的主管机关国旗的船舶,可签发附则Ⅵ符合证书		

COMPETENCE 3.2	Monitor and Control Compliance with Legislative Requirements	IMO Reference

- states that Annex VI also requires diesel engines with a power output of more than 130 kW which is installed on a ship constructed on or after 1 January 2000 or with a power output of more than 130 kW which undergoes a major conversion on or after 1 January 2000 or with a power output of more than 5000 kW and a per cylinder displacement at or above 90 litres which is installed on a ship constructed on or after 1 January 1990 but prior to 1 January 2000, to carry individual certificates with regard to NOx emissions, named Engine International Air Pollution Prevention (EIAPP) Certificates
- states that Annex VI requires that every ship of 400 gross tonnage or above and every fixed and floating drilling rig and other platforms shall be subject to a schedule of surveys that occur throughout the life of a vessel
- states that the schedule of surveys include:
  - Initial survey: This survey occurs before the ship is put into service or before a vessel certificate is issued for the first time. This survey ensures that the equipment, systems, fitting, arrangements and material used on board fully comply with the requirements of Annex VI. The vessel's International Air Pollution Prevention certificate (IAPP) will be issued to the vessel by an organization authorized to act on behalf of the State, after this survey.
  - Periodic surveys: These surveys occur at least every five years after the initial survey. These surveys confirm that nothing has been done to the ship's equipment that would take it out of compliance. The vessel's IAPP certificate will be re-issued by an organization authorized to act on behalf of the State, after this survey.
  - Intermediate surveys: These surveys occur at least once during the period between issuance of an IAPP and the periodic surveys. They also confirm that all of the ship's equipment remains in compliance.
- states that chapter III of Annex VI (regulations 12 to 19) contains requirements for control of emissions from ships, but the following regulations directly impact vessel operation:
  - regulation 12 – Ozone-depleting Substances
  - regulation 13 – NOx emissions
  - regulation 14 – Sulphur Oxide emissions
  - regulation 15 – VOC emissions
  - regulation 16 – Shipboard Incinerators
  - regulation 18 – Fuel Oil Quality control
- states that regulation 12(1) prohibits deliberate emissions of ozone-depleting substances, except where necessary for the purpose of securing the safety of a ship or saving life, as provided in regulation 3
- states that regulation 12(2) prohibits, on all ships, new installations containing ozone-depleting substances, except that new installations containing hydrochlorofluorocarbons (HCFCs) are permitted until 1 January 2020
- states that all the ships subject to the requirements of Annex VI, are required to maintain a list of equipment containing ozone-depleting substances and, if a ship has rechargeable systems, containing ozone-depleting substances, an Ozone-depleting Substances Record Book is to be maintained on board

适任 3.2	立法要求的监督与控制	IMO 参考书目

	- 阐述附则Ⅵ还要求，2000 年 1 月 1 日及以后建造或于 2000 年 1 月 1 日及以后经重大改装的船舶,安装于其上的输出功率在 130 千瓦以上的柴油发动机,或输出功率超过 5000 千瓦且单缸排量在 90 升以上，安装于 1990 年 1 月 1 日及以后至 2000 年 1 月 1 日之前建造的船舶的柴油发动机,具有单独的 NOx 排放证书,称为发动机国际防止空气污染证书(EIAPP 证书)
	- 阐述附则Ⅵ要求 400 总吨及以上的每艘船舶、固定和移动钻井平台及其他平台,在其寿命期间,应接受各种规定的检验
	- 阐述规定的检验包括:
	  - 初次检验:指发生在投入营运前或首次签发船舶证书前的检验。该检验确保船上设备、系统、配件、设施和材料完全符合附则Ⅵ的要求。检验后,经授权代表国家的组织将向船舶签发国际防止空气污染证书(IAPP 证书)。
	  - 定期检验:初次检验后至少每 5 年进行 2 次的检验。该检验证实船舶设备没有发生不符合规则的改变。检验后,经授权代表国家的组织将再次向船舶签发国际防止空气污染证书(IAPP 证书)。
	  - 中间检验:在签发 IAPP 证书和定期检验之间至少进行一次的检验。该检验也证实所有船舶设备保持合规。
	- 阐述附则Ⅵ第Ⅲ章 (第 12 条至第 19 条规定) 包括控制船舶排放的要求,但下列规定直接影响船舶营运:
	  - 第 12 条—破坏臭氧的物质
	  - 第 13 条—NOx 排放
	  - 第 14 条—硫氧化物的排放
	  - 第 15 条—VOC 的排放
	  - 第 16 条—船舶焚烧炉
	  - 第 18 条—燃油质量控制
	- 阐述第 12(1)项规定禁止蓄意排放破坏臭氧物质,除非像第 3 条规定的那样,是为保证船舶或海上救生安全所必需的排放
	- 阐述第 12(2)项规定禁止所有船舶安装含有破坏臭氧物质的新装置,除了允许新装置在 2020 年 1 月 1 日前含有氢氯氟烃(HCFCs)
	- 阐述要求所有须满足附则Ⅵ船舶保留一份含有破坏臭氧物质的清单，且如船舶具有含破坏臭氧物质的充电系统,则船舶应保留臭氧破坏物质记录簿	

COMPETENCE 3.2	Monitor and Control Compliance with Legislative Requirements	IMO Reference

– states that regulation 13 sets NOx emission limits for diesel engines with a power output of more than 130 kW installed on ships built on or after 1 January 2000, and diesel engines of similar power undergoing a major conversion on or after 1 January 2000
– states that regulation 13 does not apply to emergency diesel engines, engines installed in lifeboats and any device or equipment intended to be used solely in case of emergency, or engines installed on ships solely engaged in voyages within waters subject to the sovereignty or jurisdiction of the flag State, provided that such engines are subject to an alternative NOx control measure established by the Administration
– explains that regulation 13 further contains a 3-Tier approach:
  – Tier I (current limits)
    – For diesel engines installed on ships constructed from 1 January 2000 to 1 January 2011
  – Tier II
    – For diesel engines installed on ships constructed on or after 1 January 2011
  – Tier III
    – Ships constructed on or after 1 January 2016
– states that Engine surveys are described in Chapter 2 of the NOx Technical Code, a supporting document to Annex VI
– states that the four kinds of engine surveys are:
  – Pre-certification survey: This survey occurs before an engine is installed on board a vessel, to ensure the engine meets the NOx limits. The Engine International Air Pollution Prevention certificate (EIAPP) is issued after this survey for each applicable engine, engine family, or engine group
  – Initial certification survey: This survey occurs after the engine is installed on board the ship, but before the ship is placed into service. It ensures that the engine meets the NOx limits as installed. If an engine has an EIAPP, the initial certification survey will primarily ensure that any modifications to the engine's settings are within the allowable adjustment limits specified in the EIAPP
  – Periodic and intermediate surveys: These surveys occur as part of the ship's surveys described above. They ensure that the engine continues to comply fully with the NOx limits
  – Modification survey: This survey occurs when an engine overhaul meets the criteria for a major conversion. It ensures that the modified engine complies with the NOx limits
– states that there are three documents that are essential for completing the engine and vessel surveys. These are the EIAPP or Statement of Compliance, the Technical File, and the Record Book of Engine Parameters
– states that regulation 14 provides for adoption of "SOx Emission Control Areas" – "SECA" where the adoption of special mandatory measures for SOx emissions from ships is required to prevent, reduce and control air pollution from SOx and its attendant adverse impacts on land and sea areas with more stringent control on sulphur emissions		

适任 3.2	立法要求的监督与控制	IMO 参考书目
	– 阐述规则第 13 条对安装于 2000 年 1 月 1 日及以后建造船舶，输出功率在 130 千瓦以上的柴油发动机,和安装于 2000 年 1 月 1 日及以后建造船舶的具有类似输出功率的柴油发动机,规定了 NOx 排放限制 – 阐述规则第 13 条并不适用于应急柴油发动机、救生艇用发动机和计划仅用于紧急情况的装载或设备,或仅航行于船旗国主权水域或管辖水域,假如这种发动机为主管机关建立的 NOx 排放控制替代措施 – 解释规则第 13 条包括 3 层途径: – 第一层 (电流限制) – 针对安装于 2000 年 1 月 1 日至 2011 年 1 月 1 日之间建造船舶的柴油发动机 – 第二层 – 针对安装于 2011 年 1 月 1 日及以后建造船舶的柴油发动机 – 第三层 – 针对 2016 年 1 月 1 日及以后建造的船舶 – 阐述在作为附则Ⅵ支持文件的 NOx 技术规则第 2 章描述了发动机的检验 – 阐述 4 类发动机检验为: – 发证前检验:为发动机安装于船舶前的检验,以确保发动机满足 NOx 排放限制。检验后,对每一适用的发动机、发动机系列或发动机组签发国际防止发动机空气污染证书(EIAPP) – 初次发证检验:发动机安装于船舶后、船舶投入营运前的检验。它确保安装时满足 NOx 排放限制。如发动机具有 EIAPP 证书,则初次发证检验主要确保发动机设置的变更在 EIAPP 证书规定的许可调节限制内。 – 定期和中间检验:这些检验作为上述规定的船舶检验的一部分。它们确保发动机继续符合 NOx 排放限制 – 变更检验:当发动机大修满足大改标准时进行此项检验。它确保变更的发动机符合 NOx 排放限制 – 阐述完成发动机和船舶检验有 3 个重要文件。它们是 EIAPP 或符合声明、技术文件和发动机参数记录簿 – 阐述规则第 14 条提供采纳“SOx 排放控制区”(SECA)。在控制区内要求对船舶 SOx 排放采取特别强制措施,对硫排放采取更严格控制,以防止、减少和控制 SOx 空气污染和随之而来的对陆地和海域的不利影响	

COMPETENCE 3.2	Monitor and Control Compliance with Legislative Requirements	IMO Reference

– states for the purpose of the regulation, Emission Control Areas (ECA) includes:
  – The Baltic Sea area as defined in regulation 1.11.2 of Annex I, the North Sea as defined in regulation 5(1)(f) of Annex V
– states that in these areas the sulphur content of fuel oil used on ships must not exceed 1.5% m/m. Alternatively, ships in these areas must fit an exhaust gas cleaning system or use any other technological method to limit SOx emissions
– states that regulation 15 provides that in ports or terminals in Party States any regulation of emissions of Volatile Organic Compounds (VOCs) from tankers must be in accordance with Annex VI
– explains that regulation 16 sets out requirements for shipboard incineration and as per 16(4) bans the incineration of:
  – MARPOL Annex I, II and III cargo residues and related contaminated packing materials;
  – polychlorinated biphenyls (PCBs);
  – garbage, as defined in MARPOL Annex V, containing more than traces of heavy metals; and
  – refined petroleum products containing halogen compounds
– explains that under regulation 16(5) incineration of sewage sludge and sludge oil generated during the normal operation of a ship may take place in the main or auxiliary power plant or boilers (as well as in an incinerator), but in those cases, must not take place inside ports, harbours and estuaries
– explains that regulation 16(6) prohibits the shipboard incineration of polyvinyl chlorides (PVCs), except in incinerators for which IMO Type Approval Certificates have been issued
– explains that under regulation 16(7) all ships with incinerators subject to regulation 16 must possess a manufacturer's operating manual which must specify how to operate the incinerator within the limits described in paragraph 2 of appendix IV to Annex VI
– explains that under regulation 16(8) personnel responsible for operation of any incinerator must be trained and capable of implementing the guidance in the manufacturer's operating manual
– states that as per regulation 15 a tanker carrying crude oil is required to have a "VOC Management Plan" approved by the Administration on board
– explains that regulation 3 provides that the regulations of Annex VI will not apply to any emission necessary for the purpose of securing the safety of a ship or saving life at sea, or any emission resulting from damage to a ship or its equipment, subject to certain conditions		

适任 3.2	立法要求的监督与控制	IMO 参考书目

– 阐述为符合规则要求,排放控制区域(ECA)包括:
  – 附则Ⅰ1.11.2 中定义的波罗的海地区、附则 V5(1)(f) 中定义的北海
– 阐述在这些地区,船用燃料油的硫含量不得超过 1.5% m/m。或者,在这些地区的船舶必须安装废气净化系统或使用其他技术手段限制 SOx 的排放。
– 阐述规则第 15 条规定在缔约国港口内任何挥发性有机化合物(VOCs)的排放须符合附则Ⅵ
– 解释规则第 16 规定了船上焚烧的要求,按照 16(4) 项规定,禁止焚烧下列物质:
  – MARPOL 附则 Ⅰ、Ⅱ 和 Ⅲ 中的货物残渣和相关的污染了的包装材料;
  – 多氯联苯(PCBs);
  – MARPOL 附则 Ⅴ中含有超过微量的重金属垃圾;和
  – 含卤素化合物精制石油产品
– 解释按照 16(5)项规定,那些船舶正常作业中产生的污油泥和污油在主要或辅助发电装置或锅炉(也包括焚烧炉)中的焚烧不得在港口附近和河口进行
– 解释按照 16(6)项规定,禁止在船上焚烧聚氯乙烯(PVCs),除非该船持有 IMO 认可类型的焚烧炉证书
– 解释按照 16(7)项规定,所有按 16 条规定配备的焚烧炉的船舶须持有制造商操作手册,详细说明在附则Ⅳ 到附则Ⅵ第 2 段规定的限制范围内如何操作焚烧炉
– 解释按照 16(8)项规定,负责操作焚烧炉的人员须经培训,并能按制造商手册中的指导操作
– 阐述规则第 15 条规定,要求载有原油的油船持有主管机关批准的“VOC 管理计划”
– 解释规则第 3 条规定,附则 VI 的规定不适用于为保证船舶或海上救生安全所必需的排放,或在某些条件下,船舶或其设备损坏所致的排放		

COMPETENCE 3.2	Monitor and Control Compliance with Legislative Requirements	IMO Reference

1.5 Maritime declarations of health and the requirements of the International Health Regulations (3 hours)

Arrival documents and procedures R104

International Health Regulations (1969) as amended (IHR)

- defines for the purposes of these regulations:
  - arrival of a ship
  - baggage
  - container or freight container
  - crew
  - diseases subject to the regulations
  - disinsecting
  - epidemic
  - free pratique
  - health administration
  - health authority
  - infected person
  - in quarantine
  - international voyage
  - isolation
  - medical examination
  - ship
  - suspect
  - valid certificate
- states that a health authority should, if requested, issue, free of charge to the carrier, a certificate specifying the measures applied to a ship or container, the parts treated, methods used and the reasons why they have been applied
- states that, except in an emergency constituting a grave danger to public health, a ship which is not infected or suspected of being infected with a disease subject to the regulations should not be refused free pratique on account of any other epidemic disease and should not be prevented from discharging or loading cargo or stores, or taking on fuel or water
- states that a health authority may take all practicable measures to control the discharge from any ship of sewage and refuse which might contaminate the waters of a port, river or canal
- describes the measures which the health authority of a port may take with respect to departing travellers
- states that no health measures should be applied by a State to any ship which passes through waters within its jurisdiction without calling at a port or on the coast
- describes the measures which may be applied to a ship which passes through a canal or waterway in a territory of a State on its way to a port in the territory of another State
- states that, whenever possible, States should authorize granting of free pratique by radio
- explains that the Master should make known to port authorities, as long as possible before arrival, any case of illness on board, in the interests of the patient and the health authorities and to facilitate clearance of the ship

适任 3.2	立法要求的监督与控制	IMO 参考书目

1.5	**航海健康声明书和《国际卫生条例》的要求(3 学时)**
	船舶抵达的文书和程序
	经修订的《国际卫生条例(1969)》(IHR)
	– 有关该条例的定义:
	  – 船舶的抵达
	  – 行李
	  – 集装箱或货运集装箱
	  – 船员
	  – 规则涉及的疾病
	  – 除虫
	  – 传染病
	  – 检疫证
	  – 卫生管理
	  – 卫生当局
	  – 受感染者
	  – 检疫
	  – 国际航行
	  – 隔离
	  – 体检
	  – 船舶
	  – 嫌疑人
	  – 有效证书
	– 阐述如果在船方请求,卫生当局应免费向船方签署此证书,此证书要详细说明适用于船舶或集装箱的措施、要处理的部分、使用方法和实施的原因
	– 阐述除对公共卫生构成严重威胁的紧急事件外,船舶如果没有染疫或染疫嫌疑,港口卫生当局不能以有其他传染性疾病为由而拒绝签发检疫证,不应阻止船舶排放或装载货物和物资补给,或补给燃料或淡水
	– 阐述卫生当局可以采取任何适当的措施控制船舶的生活污水和废物,它们可能污染港口水域、江河或运河
	– 描述港口卫生当局对离港人员可能采取的措施
	– 阐述一国不应对经过其政府管辖的水域而不挂靠其港口或其海岸的船舶施行卫生措施
	– 描述适用于航行中经过一国领土内的运河或水道到另一国领土内港口的船舶的措施
	– 如有可能,当局应通过无线电授权签发检疫证
	– 解释为了病人和港口当局的利益和便利船舶结关,船长在船舶到达之前应尽早向港口当局通报船上的任何病例
		R104

COMPETENCE 3.2	Monitor and Control Compliance with Legislative Requirements	IMO Reference
– states that, on arrival of a ship, an infected person may be removed and isolated and that such removal should be compulsory if required by the Master – states that a ship should not be prevented for health reasons from calling at any port, but if the port is not equipped for applying the health measures which in the opinion of the health authority of the port are required, the ship may be ordered to proceed at its own risk to the nearest suitable port convenient to it – explains the actions open to a ship which is unwilling to submit to the measures required by the health authority of a port – describes the measures concerning cargo and goods – describes the measures concerning baggage **Plague** – states that, for the purposes of the regulations, the incubation period of plague is six days – states that vaccination against plague should not be required as a condition of admission of any person to a territory – states that during the stay of a ship in a port infected by plague, special care should be taken to prevent the introduction of rodents on board – states that ships should be permanently kept free of rodents and the plague vector or be periodically derailed – describes the requirements for the issue of a Ship Sanitation Control Certificate or a Ship Sanitation Control Exemption Certificate and states their periods of validity – states the conditions in which a ship on arrival is to be regarded as infected, suspected or healthy – describes the measures which may be applied by a health authority on the arrival of an infected or suspected ship **Cholera** – describes the measures which may be applied by a health authority on the arrival of a healthy ship from an infected area – states that, for the purposes of the regulations, the incubation period of cholera is five days – describes the measures to be taken by the health authority if a case of cholera is discovered upon arrival or a case has occurred on board **Yellow Fever** – states that, for the purposes of the regulations, the incubation period of yellow fever is six days – states that vaccination against yellow fever may be required of any person leaving an infected area on an international voyage – states that every member of the crew of a ship using a port in an infected area must be in possession of a valid certificate of vaccination against yellow fever – states the conditions in which a ship on arrival is to be regarded as infected, suspected or healthy – describes the measures which may be applied by a health authority on the arrival of an infected or suspected ship		

适任 3.2	立法要求的监督与控制	IMO 参考书目
– 阐述当船舶到港后,受感染的病人可以被转移和隔离,在船长要求下转移应强制执行 – 阐述任何港口不能因健康原因而拒绝船舶挂靠,但是如果港口卫生当局认为,该港口不具备所要求的健康措施,那么该船将被命令自己承担风险航行到最近的一个适当方便的港口挂靠 – 解释拒不服从港口卫生当局要求的措施的船舶所面临的制裁 – 描述和货物有关的措施 – 描述与行李有关的措施 **鼠疫** – 阐述根据本条例,鼠疫的潜伏期为 6 天 – 不得以未打鼠疫疫苗为由拒绝人员下地 – 阐述在船靠泊感染了鼠疫的港口期间,则应特别注意,阻止啮齿动物被带入船舶 – 阐述船舶应始终保持无啮齿动物、鼠疫带菌者或者进行定期除鼠 – 描述船舶卫生控制证书或免予船舶卫生控制证书的签发要求并阐述其有效期 – 阐述到港的船舶被认为受感染、疑似感染或没有感染的条件 – 描述适用于卫生当局对受感染船或疑似感染船到达时所采取的措施 **霍乱** – 描述卫生当局对来自于疫区的健康船可采取的措施 – 阐述根据本条例,霍乱的潜伏期为 5 天 – 描述船舶到达前一旦发现霍乱病例或船上已经出现霍乱病例时,卫生当局所应采取的措施 **黄热病** – 阐述根据本条例,黄热病的潜伏期为 6 天 – 阐述国际航行的船舶,离开疫区可能会要求船上所有人员接种黄热病疫苗 – 阐述挂靠疫区船舶上的每位船员必须有一张有效的接种黄热病疫苗的证明 – 阐述抵达船舶被认为受感染、疑似感染或没有感染的条件 – 描述卫生当局对受感染船或疑似感染船到达时所应采取的措施		

COMPETENCE 3.2	Monitor and Control Compliance with Legislative Requirements	IMO Reference

Documents

- states that bills of health or any other certificates concerning health conditions of a port are not required from any ship
- describes the Master's obligations concerning a Maritime Declaration of Health
- states that the Master and the ship's surgeon, if one is carried, must supply any information required by the health authority as to health conditions on board during the voyage
- states that no health document, other than those provided for in the regulations, should be required in international traffic

1.6 Responsibilities under other international maritime law embodied in international agreements and conventions that impact on the role of management level deck officers (35 hours)

1.6.1 Convention on Facilitation of International Maritime Traffic, 1965, as amended (FAL 1965) (1 hour)

- states that the purpose of the Convention is to facilitate maritime transport by simplifying and reducing to a minimum the formalities, documentary requirements and procedures on the arrival, stay and departure of ships engaged in international voyages
- explains that the Convention lays down 'standards' and 'recommended practices' regarding documentation and procedures for facilitating international maritime traffic
- lists the documents which should be the only ones required by public authorities for their retention on arrival, or departure of ships to which the Convention applies
- explains that the provisions do not preclude the requirement for the presentation for inspection by the appropriate authorities of certificates and other papers concerned with registry, measurement, safety, manning and other related matters
- states that IMO has produced standard forms for:
  - general declaration
  - cargo declaration
  - ship's effects declaration
  - crew's effects declaration
  - crew list
  - passenger list
  - dangerous goods manifest

适任 3.2	立法要求的监督与控制	IMO 参考书目

文件
– 阐述要求船舶具有有关港口健康状况的健康证或其他证书
– 描述船长关于航海健康声明书的责任
– 阐述船长和船医(如果有的话)必须提供港口卫生当局所要求的在航行途中船上有关健康状况的任何信息
– 阐述除规则要求提供的文件外,国际航行的船舶不再需要任何健康文件
1.6 影响管理级船员作用的国际协议和国际公约所体现的其他国际海事法相关要求的责任(35 学时)
1.6.1 经修订的《1965 年国际便利海上运输公约》(FAL 1965) (1 学时)
– 阐述公约的目的是通过将国际航行船舶的进港、停留和出港手续、文件要求和程序简化和减少至最少,便利海上运输
– 解释公约为便利海上运输而制定的有关文件和程序的“标准”和“推荐作法”
– 列出公约适用的船舶进出港时,仅需有政府当局所要求保留的文书
– 解释公约并不妨碍有关当局要求对有关登记、丈量、安全、人员配备和其他相关事物的证书和其他文件进行检查的要求
– 阐述 IMO 已经在以下几个方面制定了标准格式:
  – 总申报单
  – 货物申报单
  – 船舶物品申报单
  – 船员物品申报单
  – 船员名单
  – 乘客名单
  – 危险货物申报单		

COMPETENCE 3.2	Monitor and Control Compliance with Legislative Requirements	IMO Reference

- explains that arrival procedures may be expedited by:
  - providing the public authorities concerned with an advance message giving the best ETA, followed by any information as to change of time, and stating the itinerary of the voyage
  - having ship's documents ready for prompt review
  - rigging a means of boarding while the ship is en route to the berth or anchorage
  - providing for prompt, orderly assembling and presentation of persons on board, with necessary documents for inspection, including arrangements for relieving crew members from essential duties

1.6.2 United Nations Convention on the Law of the Sea (UNCLOS) (2 hours) — R75, R76

- explains that the outcome of UNCLOS III conference convened at Geneva in 1974 was the United Nations Convention on the Law of the Sea commonly known as "UNCLOS"
- explains that UNCLOS attempts to codify the international law of the sea
- states that UNCLOS defines the legal status of the high seas and establishes regulations for the control of marine pollution
- states that UNCLOS is a treaty document of 320 articles and 9 annexes, governing all aspects of ocean space, such as delimitation, environmental control, marine scientific research, economic and commercial activities, transfer of technology and the settlement of disputes relating to ocean matters
- states that UNCLOS came into force internationally on 16 November 1994
- states that UNCLOS sets the width of the territorial sea at 12 nautical miles, with a contiguous zone at 24 nautical miles from the baseline
- states that UNCLOS defines innocent passage through the territorial sea and defines transit passage through international straits
- states that UNCLOS defines archipelagic States and allows for passage through archipelagic waters
- states that UNCLOS establishes exclusive economic zones (EEZs) extending to 200 nautical miles from baselines
- explains that it defines the continental shelf and extends jurisdiction over the resources of the shelf beyond 200 miles where appropriate
- explains that states in dispute about their interpretation of UNCLOS may submit their disagreements to competent courts such as the International Court of Justice (in The Hague), or the Law of the Sea Tribunal (in Hamburg)
- states that the responsibility for enforcement of regulations rests mainly with flag States, but as vessels enter zones closer to the coast the influence of coastal State jurisdiction and, ultimately, port State jurisdiction, gradually increases
- states that Article 94 of the UNCLOS deals with duties of the flag State, while Article 217 deals with enforcement by flag States
- states that Article 218 of the UNCLOS deals with port State jurisdiction
- explains when a vessel is voluntarily within a port or at an offshore terminal, the port State may, where the evidence warrants, begin proceedings in respect of discharges in violation of international rules (i.e. regulations in MARPOL 73/78)
- states that another State in which a discharge violation has occurred, or the flag State, may request the port State to investigate the violation

适任 3.2	立法要求的监督与控制	IMO 参考书目
– 解释到达的程序可以通过下列方法加快: – 提供给政府当局有关进展消息,给出最准确的预计抵达时间,以及有关时间的任何更改,说明本航次的行程。 – 准备好船舶的文书以备快速检查 – 船舶在去泊位或锚地的途中准备好登船的设施 – 以快速、有序地集合和介绍船上人员,提供必要的文件以备检查,包括重要职责船员的更换安排		
1.6.2 《联合国海洋法公约》(UNCLOS) (2 学时) – 解释 1974 年在日内瓦举行的 UNCLOS Ⅲ会议的成果就是被熟知为 “UNCLOS”的《联合国海洋法公约》 – 解释 UNCLOS 意图将国际海洋法编成法典 – 阐述 UNCLOS 定义了公海的法律地位,确立了控制海洋污染的规则 – 阐述 UNCLOS 是一个包含 320 个条款和 9 个附则的公约性文件,调控海洋场所的所有方面,如划界、环境控制、海上科学研究、经济和商业活动、技术转让和有关海洋事务的争端解决 – 阐述 UNCLOS 1994 年 11 月 6 日在国际上生效 – 阐述 UNCLOS 设置了 12 海里领海宽度及从基线开始计算的 24 海里毗连区 – 阐述 UNCLOS 定义了领海的无害通过和国际海峡的过境航行 – 阐述 UNCLOS 定义了群岛国家,并允许通过群岛水域 – 阐述 UNCLOS 设立了专属经济区(EEZs),从基线延伸 200 海里 – 解释 UNCLOS 定义了大陆架和适当时延伸至 200 海里外的资源管辖权 – 解释对 UNCLOS 的解读存在异议的国家向主管法院,如国际法院(海牙)或海洋法法庭(汉堡)提交异议 – 阐述法规执行的责任主要在于船旗国,但随着船舶进入更接近海岸的区域,海岸国家管辖权的影响和最终的港口国管辖权的影响逐渐增加 – 阐述 UNCLOS 第 94 条涉及船旗国责任,第 217 条涉及履行公约 – 阐述 UNCLOS 第 218 条涉及港口国管辖 – 解释当船舶自愿在港或沿岸港口时,在证据确凿情况下,港口国可就违反国际规则(即 MARPOL 73/78 公约规定)的排放提起诉讼 – 阐述在违规排放发生的另一国家或船旗国,可以要求港口国调查违规情况		R75, R76

COMPETENCE 3.2	Monitor and Control Compliance with Legislative Requirements	IMO Reference
– states that Article 200 of the UNCLOS deals with coastal State jurisdiction as applied in relation to pollution provisions – states that where there are clear grounds for believing that a vessel navigating in the territorial sea of a State has violated laws and regulations of the coastal State adopted in accordance with UNCLOS or applicable international pollution regulations, the coastal State may inspect the vessel and, where evidence warrants, institute proceedings including detention of the vessel – states that vessels believed to have violated pollution laws in an EEZ may be required to give identification and voyage information to the coastal State – explains that as per UNCLOS, States must agree international rules and standards to prevent pollution from vessels (Article 211). (This obligation is currently met by MARPOL 73/78) – explains that coastal States may also promulgate and enforce pollution regulations in their own EEZs which may, in some circumstances, include imposition of routeing restrictions – states that in the territorial sea additional navigational restraints (e.g. traffic separation schemes and sea lanes) may be imposed on vessels with dangerous and hazardous cargoes – explains that coastal States and ports may make entry to internal waters and harbours conditional on meeting additional pollution regulations		

1.6.3 Maritime Labour Convention (MLC 2006) (6 hours)
– explains that the Maritime Labour Convention, 2006, is an important new international labour Convention that was adopted by the International Labour Conference of the International Labour Organization (ILO), under article 19 of its Constitution at a maritime session in February 2006 in Geneva, Switzerland
– explains that it sets out seafarers' rights to decent conditions of work and helps to create conditions of fair competition for shipowners
– explains that it is intended to be globally applicable, easily understandable, readily updatable and uniformly enforced
– explains that the MLC 2006, complementing other major international conventions, reflects international agreement on the minimum requirements for working and living conditions for seafarers
– explains that the Maritime Labour Convention, 2006, has two primary purposes:
  – to bring the system of protection contained in existing labour standards closer to the workers concerned, in a form consistent with the rapidly developing, globalized sector (ensuring "decent work");
  – to improve the applicability of the system so that shipowners and governments interested in providing decent conditions of work do not have to bear an unequal burden in ensuring protection ("level playing field" fair competition)
– explains that the Maritime Labour Convention, 2006, has been designed to become a global legal instrument that, once it enters into force, will be the "fourth pillar" of the international regulatory regime for quality shipping, complementing the key Conventions of the International Maritime Organization (IMO) such as the International Convention for the Safety of Life at Sea, 1974, as amended (SOLAS), the International Convention on Standards of Training, Certification and Watchkeeping, 1978, as amended (STCW) and the International Convention for the Prevention of Pollution from Ships, 73/78 (MARPOL)
		R104

适任 3.2	立法要求的监督与控制	IMO 参考书目
– 阐述 UNCLOS 第 200 条涉及沿海国适用有关污染规定的管辖权 – 阐述有明显理由相信,在一国领海航行的船舶违反了沿岸国根据 UNCLOS 制定的法律法规或适用的国际污染法规,沿海国可在证据确凿情况下提起诉讼,包括扣押船舶 – 阐述据信在专属经济区(EEZ)违反了污染法规的船舶,可被要求提供识别信息和航行信息给沿海国 – 解释按照 UNCLOS，各国家必须同意国际防止船舶污染的规则和标准（第 211 条）。(该义务目前由 MARPOL 73/78 公约所要求) – 解释沿海国还可以在自己的专属经济区发布和执行污染法规,在某些情况下,可包括航路实施限制 – 阐述在领海可对危险品或危险货物船实施额外的航行限制（例如分道通航制和分隔航道) – 解释在满足额外污染规则条件下,沿海国和港口可进至内河及其港口		
1.6.3 《海事劳工公约》(MLC 2006) (6 学时)		R104

– 解释 2006 年《海事劳工公约》是一个重要的新的国际劳工公约,2006 年 2 月瑞士的日内瓦海事会议按其章程第 19 条,由国际劳工组织(ILO)国际劳工会议通过
– 解释它规定了海员体面劳动条件的权利和有助于给船东创造公平竞争条件
– 解释其目的是在全球范围内适用、易于理解、随时更新和统一执行
– 解释作为其他主要国际公约的补充,MLC 2006 是反映了海员在工作和生活条件方面的最低要求的国际协议
– 解释 2006 年《海事劳工公约》有两个主要目的：
  – 为了使现行的劳工标准中所载的保护制度以一个与迅速发展相一致的形式更接近相关的、全球化行业的劳动者(确保“体面劳动”)；
  – 为了提高该制度的适应能力,以便提供体面劳动条件的有关船东和政府在确保保护措施方面,并非一定要承受不平等的负担(“公平竞争环境下”的公平竞争)
– 解释 2006 年《海事劳工公约》已被设计成为一个全球性的法律文件,一旦生效,将成为保证运输质量的国际航运质量监管机制的“第四支柱”,对国际海事组织(IMO)的主要公约,如经修订的《1974 年国际海上人命安全公约》(SOLAS),经修订的 1978 年海员培训、发证和值班标准国际公约 (STCW) 和 73/78 国际防止船舶污染公约(MARPOL)进行补充		

COMPETENCE 3.2	Monitor and Control Compliance with Legislative Requirements	IMO Reference

– states that it is sometimes called the consolidated Maritime Labour Convention, 2006, as it contains a comprehensive set of global standards, based on those that are already found in 68 maritime labour instruments (Conventions and Recommendations), adopted by the ILO since 1920
– states that the new Convention brings almost all of the existing maritime labour instruments together in a single new Convention that uses a new format with some updating, where necessary, to reflect modern conditions and language
– explains that the Convention "consolidates" the existing international law on all these matters
– states that the MLC, 2006, applies to all ships engaged in commercial activities (except fishing vessels, ships of traditional build and warships or naval auxiliaries)
– states that ships of 500 GT or over are required to be certified: they must carry a Maritime Labour Certificate as well as a Declaration of Maritime Labour Compliance
– states that ships below 500 GT are subject to inspection at intervals not exceeding three years
– explains that the existing ILO maritime labour Conventions will be gradually phased out as ILO Member States that have ratified those Conventions ratify the new Convention, but there will be a transitional period when some parallel Conventions will be in force
– explains that countries that ratify the Maritime Labour Convention, 2006, will no longer be bound by the existing Conventions when the new Convention comes into force for them
– explains that countries that do not ratify the new Convention will remain bound by the existing Conventions they have ratified, but those Conventions will be closed to further ratification
– describes that the Convention is organized into three main parts: the Articles coming first set out the broad principles and obligations which is followed by the more detailed Regulations and Code (with two parts: Parts A and B) provisions
– states that the Regulations and the Standards (Part A) and Guidelines (Part B) in the Code are integrated and organized into general areas of concern under five Titles:
  – **Title 1: Minimum requirements for seafarers to work on a ship:** minimum age, medical certificates, training and qualification, recruitment and placement.
  – **Title 2: Conditions of employment:** Seafarers Employment Agreements, Wages, Hours of Work and Hours of Rest, Entitlement to Leave, Repatriation, Seafarer compensation for the ship's Loss or Foundering, Manning Levels, Career and Skill Development and Opportunities for Seafarers' Employment
  – **Title 3: Accommodation, recreational facilities, food and catering**
  – **Title 4: Health protection, medical care, welfare and social security** protection: Medical Care on-board ship and Ashore, Shipowners' Liability, Health & Safety Protection and Accident Prevention, Access to Shorebased Welfare Facilities, Social Security		

适任 3.2	立法要求的监督与控制	IMO 参考书目
	– 阐述它有时被称为2006年综合海事劳工公约，因其包含一整套基于1920年以来国际劳工组织(ILO)通过的68个海事劳工文件(公约和建议)的综合性全球标准 – 阐述新公约利用一种新的格式将几乎所有现有的海事劳工文件一并放入在一个新公约中,如有需要进行更新,以反映现代情况和语言 – 解释该公约“合并”了所有这些方面的现有国际法 – 阐述 2006 年《海事劳工公约》(MLC 2006)使用于所有从事商业活动的船舶 (除了渔船,传统方式建造的船舶和军舰或海军辅助船) – 阐述要求 500 总吨或以上船舶持有海事劳工证书及海事劳工符合声明 – 阐述 500 总吨以下船舶应接受间隔不超过 3 年的检查 – 解释现有的 ILO 的海事劳工公约将随着 ILO 批准那些公约的成员国批准新公约而被逐步取消,但将有一个过渡时期,过渡期内一些类似的公约将生效 – 解释批准 2006 年海事劳工公约的国家,当新公约生效后将不再受现行公约的约束 – 解释未批准新公约的国家将继续遵守他们已经批准的现有公约，但那些公约将被终止以待进一步批准 – 描述该公约由 3 个主要部分组成:首先是规定广泛原则和义务的条款,然后是更详细的规定和规则(两个部分: A 部分和 B 部分)条款 – 阐述规则中的规定和标准(A 部分)和指南(B 部分)被整合和组织成下列 5 个标题的共同相关部分: – **标题 1:海员在船上工作的最低要求:**最小年龄、健康证书、培训和资格、招募和安置 – **标题 2:就业条件:**海员就业协议、工资、工作时间和休息时间、休假的权利、遣返、船舶灭失或沉没给海员的补偿、配员水平、海员就业职业技能发展和机遇 – **标题 3:住宿、娱乐设施和餐饮** – **标题 4:健康保护、医疗、福利和社会保障:**船上和岸上医疗、船东责任、健康与安全保护和事故预防、获得岸基福利设施、社会保障	

COMPETENCE 3.2	Monitor and Control Compliance with Legislative Requirements	IMO Reference

- **Title 5: Compliance and enforcement:**
  Flag State Responsibilities: General Principles, Authorization of Organizations, Maritime Labour Certificate and Declaration of Maritime Labour Compliance, Inspection and Enforcement, On-board Complaint Procedures, Marine Casualties
- **Port State Responsibilities:** Inspections in Port, Detailed Inspection, Detentions, On-shore Seafarer Complaint Handling Procedures
- **Labour-supplying Responsibilities:** Recruitment and Placement services, Social security provisions
  These five Titles essentially cover the same subject matter as the existing 68 maritime labour instruments, updating them where necessary

- explains that it occasionally contains new subjects in comparison to the existing ILO maritime labour conventions, particularly in the area of occupational safety and health to meet current health concerns, such as the effects of noise and vibration on workers or other workplace risks
- explains that the standards in the new Convention are not lower than existing maritime labour standards as the aim is to maintain the standards in the current maritime labour Conventions at their present level, while leaving each country greater discretion in the formulation of their national laws establishing that level of protection
- explains that the advantages for ships of ratifying countries that provide decent conditions of work for their seafarers will have protection against unfair competition from substandard ships and will benefit from a system of certification, avoiding or reducing the likelihood of lengthy delays related to inspections in foreign ports
- explains that the Maritime Labour Convention, 2006, aims to establish a continuous "compliance awareness" at every stage, from the national systems of protection up to the international system and it will improve compliance and enforcement:
  - Starting with the individual seafarers, who – under the Convention – have to be properly informed of their rights and of the remedies available in case of alleged non-compliance with the requirements of the Convention and whose right to make complaints, both on board ship and ashore, is recognized in the Convention.
  - It continues with the shipowners. Those that own or operate ships of 500 gross tonnage and above, engaged in international voyages or voyages between foreign ports, are required to develop and carry out plans for ensuring that the applicable national laws, regulations or other measures to implement the Convention are actually being complied with.
  - The Masters of these ships are then responsible for carrying out the shipowners' stated plans, and for keeping proper records to evidence implementation of the requirements of the Convention.
  - As part of its updated responsibilities for the labour inspections for ships above 500 gross tonnage that are engaged in international voyages or voyages between foreign ports, the flag State (or recognized organization on its behalf) will review the shipowners' plans and verify and certify that they are actually in place and being implemented.
  - Ships will then be required to carry a maritime labour certificate and a declaration of maritime labour compliance on board.

适任 3.2	立法要求的监督与控制	IMO 参考书目
– **标题 5:遵守和执行:** **船旗国责任:**一般原则、机构授权、海事劳工证书和海事劳工符合声明、检查和执法、船上投诉程序和海上事故 – **港口国的责任:**在港口的检查、详细检查、扣押、岸上海员投诉处理程序 – **提供岗位职责:**招聘和安置服务、社会保障规定 这五个标题基本上涵盖了现有的、必要时更新了的 68 个海事劳工文书相同主题 – 解释它偶尔包含对现有 ILO 海事劳工公约而言的新主题,特别是在职业安全卫生领域,以满足当前的健康问题,如噪声和振动对工人的影响或其他工作场所的风险 – 解释新公约中的标准不低于现有海事劳工标准,因其目的是为了保持现有海事劳工公约在其现有水平,使每个国家在建立保护水平形成其国内法律方面具有更大自由的裁量权 – 解释批准为海员提供体面工作条件国家的船舶优势将在与低标准船不正当竞争中受到保护,并受益于一个认证系统,避免或减少在外国港口的检查中冗长延误的可能性 – 解释 2006 年海上劳工公约旨在于每一阶段建立一个持续的“合规意识”,从国内保护制度到国际体系,它将在以下方面改进遵守和执行: – 从每位海员开始,按照公约适当告知其权利和一旦声称不遵守公约要求情况下可获得的补救措施,公约承认其在船和岸上索赔的权利 – 它持续涉及那些拥有或运营 500 总吨及以上,从事国际航行或在外国港口间航行的船舶的船东,要求其建立并执行为确保切实遵守该公约制定适用的国内法律、规定或其他措施的计划 – 这些船舶的船长负责执行船东制订的计划,保持适当记录以证实履行该公约的要求 – 作为其对 500 总吨及以上,从事于国际航行或在外国港口间航行的船舶劳工检查更新责任的一部分,船旗国(或经认可的代表组织)将检查船东计划、核实和证明计划切实可行和正在执行 – 将要求船舶携带海事劳工证书和海事劳工符合声明		

COMPETENCE 3.2	Monitor and Control Compliance with Legislative Requirements	IMO Reference

- Flag States will also be expected to ensure that national laws and regulations implementing the Convention's standards are respected on smaller ships that are not covered by the certification system.
- Flag States will carry out periodic quality assessments of the effectiveness of their national systems of compliance, and their reports to the ILO under article 22 of the Constitution will need to provide information on their inspection and certification systems, including on their methods of quality assessment.
- This general inspection system in the flag State (which is founded on ILO Convention No. 178) is complemented by procedures to be followed in countries that are also or even primarily the source of the world's supply of seafarers, which will similarly be reporting under article 22 of the ILO Constitution.
- The system is further reinforced by voluntary measures for inspections in foreign ports (port State control)

- states that the appendices to the Convention contain key model documents: a maritime labour certificate and a declaration of maritime labour compliance
- explains that the Maritime Labour Certificate would be issued by the flag State to a ship that flies its flag, once the State (or a recognized organization that has been authorized to carry out the inspections) has verified that the labour conditions on the ship comply with national laws and regulations implementing the Convention
- states that the certificate would be valid for five years subject to periodic inspections by the flag State
- explains that the declaration of maritime labour compliance is attached to the certificate and summarizes the national laws or regulations implementing an agreed-upon list of 14 areas of the maritime standards and setting out the shipowner's or operator's plan for ensuring that the national requirements implementing the Convention will be maintained on the ship between inspections
- states that the lists of the 14 areas that must be certified by the flag State and that may be inspected, if an inspection occurs, in a foreign port are also set out in the Appendices to the Convention

1.6.4 Collision (1 hour) — R23

International Convention for the Unification of Certain Rules of Law with Respect to Collision Between Vessels (Collision, 1910)

- states that when collision is accidental, is caused by 'force majeure' or if the cause is left in doubt, the damages are borne by those who have suffered them
- states that if collision is caused by the fault of one of the vessels, liability to make good the damage attaches to the one which committed the fault
- explains the apportionment of liability when two or more vessels are in fault
- explains that liability attaches where the collision is caused by the fault of a pilot even when the pilot is carried by compulsion of law
- describes the duties of the Master after a collision
- explains that the Convention extends to the making good of damages which a vessel has caused to another vessel or to goods or persons on board either vessel, either by the execution or non-execution of a manoeuvre or by the non-observance of regulations, even if no collision has actually taken place

适任 3.2	立法要求的监督与控制	IMO 参考书目
	– 也期望船旗国将确保履行该公约的国内法律和规定在发证系统中未涵盖的较小船舶上得到遵守 – 船旗国应对其国内符合系统的有效性进行周期性的质量评估,按章程第 22 条提交给 ILO 的报告需要提供其检查和发证系统信息,包括质量评估方法。 – 船旗国的该一般检测系统(按 ILO 公约第 178 条建立)以程序作为补充,这些程序由抑或甚至是世界主要海员来源国家所遵循,按 ILO 公约第 22 条同样会被报告 – 该系统进一步通过在外国港口(港口国监督)检查的自愿措施而加强 – 阐述该公约附录包括主要范本文件:海事劳工证书和海事劳工符合声明 – 解释一旦核实悬挂其国旗船舶的劳动条件符合其履行该公约的国内法律和规定,船旗国(或经认可授权进行检查的组织)将向该船签发海事劳工证书 – 阐述该证书将为五年有效,须船旗国定期检查 – 解释海事劳工符合声明附于证书上,概述同意实施 14 个方面海事标准的国内法律或规定,制订船东或经营人计划确保船舶在两次检查之间遵循履约的国内要求 – 阐述 14 个方面的内容须由船旗国认证,在检查时可予以检查,在外国港口,还应在公约的附录中载明	
1.6.4	**碰撞 (1 学时)** **关于统一若干有关船舶碰撞规则的国际公约(碰撞,1910)** – 阐述当碰撞意外发生是由"不可抗力"造成的,或如果造成的原因存在疑问,则损失由受害人承担 – 解释如果碰撞是由其中一艘船舶失误造成,那么损失由过失方承担 – 解释两艘或多艘船舶的过失责任分配 – 解释与引航员过失造成碰撞有关的责任,甚至是法律规定强制引航时 – 描述碰撞后船长的职责 – 解释公约延伸到一艘船舶由于进行或未进行操纵, 或未遵守规则造成另一艘船舶或船上货物或人员的损失补偿,即使未发生实际碰撞	R23

COMPETENCE 3.2	Monitor and Control Compliance with Legislative Requirements	IMO Reference
– states that in the event of a collision or any other incident of navigation concerning a sea-going ship and involving the penal or disciplinary responsibility of the Master or any other person in the service of the ship, criminal or disciplinary proceedings may be instituted only before the judicial or administrative authorities of the State of which the ship was flying the flag at the time of the collision or other incident of navigation – states that no arrest or detention of the vessel should be ordered, even as a measure of investigation, by any authorities other than those whose flag the ship is flying – states that nothing in the present Convention is to prevent any State from permitting its own authorities, in case of collision or other incidents of navigation, to take any action in respect of certificates of competence or licences issued by that State or to prosecute its own nationals for offences committed while on board a ship flying the flag of another State – states that the Convention does not apply to collisions or other incidents of navigation occurring within the limits of a port or in inland waters and that the High Contracting Parties are at liberty to reserve to themselves the right to take proceedings in respect of offences committed within their own territorial waters		

1.6.5 Assistance and salvage (3 hours)
International Convention on Salvage, 1989 (The London Salvage Convention)
– defines 'salvage operation', 'vessel' and 'property'
– describes the 'no cure – no pay' principle
– describes the application of the Convention
– describes the duties of the salvor, of the owner and of the Master
– describes the rights of salvors
– states the criteria for assessing a reward as:
  – salved value of property (ship, cargo and bunkers)
  – skill and efforts of salvor
  – measure of success
  – nature and degree of danger
  – expenses of salvor
  – equipment used
  – vessel's equipment used
  – time taken to complete the salvage operation
  – preventing or minimizing the damage to environment
– states the criteria for assessing Special Compensation
– explains that the apportionment of the remuneration amongst the owners, Master and other persons in the service of each salving vessel is to be determined by the law of the vessel's flag
– explains that every agreement as to assistance or salvage entered into at the moment and under the influence of danger may, at the request of either party, be annulled, or modified by the court, if it considers that the conditions agreed upon are not equitable
– describes the reasons for the court to set aside the agreed remuneration in whole or in part (salvor's fault, neglect, fraud or dishonesty)
– states that no remuneration is due from persons whose lives are saved except as provided in national law
		R21

适任 3.2	立法要求的监督与控制	IMO 参考书目
– 阐述如果在公海上船舶发生碰撞或其他航行事故，涉及船长或其他船上服务人员的刑事或纪律责任，刑事诉讼或纪律处罚只能由该船碰撞或航行事故发生时悬挂其国旗的船旗国司法或行政当局做出 – 阐述除了悬挂其国旗的船旗国当局外，任何其他当局都不应发出拘捕或扣押船舶命令 – 阐述在发生碰撞或其他航行事故的情况下，现行公约不妨碍任何国家允许其本国政府,在由该国签发的适任证书或执照方面采取的任何行动,或起诉在悬挂另一国国旗的船舶工作而违法犯罪的本国国民 – 阐述本公约不适用发生在各缔约国港内或内陆水域的碰撞或其他航行事故，各缔约国自由保留在其领海内起诉刑事犯罪的权利		

1.6.5 救助 (3 学时)
1989 年国际救助公约(伦敦救助公约)
– 定义“救助作业”、“船舶”和“财产”
– 描述“无效果—无报酬”原则
– 描述公约的适用范围
– 描述救助人、船东和船长的职责
– 描述救助人的权利
– 阐述评定报酬的标准如下：
  – 获救财产的价值(船舶、货物和燃料)
  – 救助人的技能和努力
  – 成效
  – 危险的性质和程度
  – 救助费用
  – 使用的设备
  – 使用的船舶设备
  – 完成救助作业所花的时间
  – 防止或减少对环境的损害
  – 阐述评定特殊补偿的标准
– 解释由船旗国法律确定在船东、船长和服务于每艘救助船舶人员之间的报酬分配
– 解释在任何一方的请求下,在当时存在危险的影响下签订的有关救助的一切协议,如果法院认为约定的条件不公平,可废除或更改之
– 描述法院撤销全部或部分约定报酬的原因(救助人的过失、疏忽、欺诈或不诚实)
– 阐述除非国内法律另有规定,被救人员支付报酬
		R21

COMPETENCE 3.2	Monitor and Control Compliance with Legislative Requirements	IMO Reference
	– describes the rights of salvors of human life who have taken part in the salvage operations – states that every Master is bound, so far as he can do so without serious danger to his vessel, her crew and her passengers, to render assistance to everybody, even though an enemy, found at sea in danger of being lost – explains that the convention also applies to assistance or salvage services rendered by or to a ship of war or any other ship owned, operated or chartered by a State or Public Authority – explains the provision of security by the owner and the application of the salvor's maritime lien **Lloyd's Standard Form of Salvage Agreement (LOF, 2000) (1 hour)** – states that LOF 2000 should be used where the ship or marine environment are at risk and the Master has insufficient time to request the owner to arrange salvage services on a the basis of a pre-agreed rate or sum – describes the Contractor's agreed endeavours to salve the ship and/or cargo, bunkers and stores and while performing the salvage services to prevent or minimize damage to the environment – explains that the LOF 2000 form does not need to be on board; the Masters of the vessels involved simply need to expressly agree to its terms before the salvage services commence – describes the exception to the 'no cure – no pay' principle – explains that LOF 2000 superseded LOF 95 and where a salvor offers services on LOF 95 or some other terms, the Master of the vessel in difficulties should attempt to get agreement to LOF 2000 terms – explains that LOF 2000 is regarded by the International Salvage Union as a major advance, with clear, user-friendly language and many innovations – states that LOF 2000 is a single sheet (2-page) document (whereas LOF 95 consists of 6 pages) in a simplified format – states that the Contractor's remuneration is to be fixed by arbitration in London and any differences arising out of the Agreement are to be dealt with in the same way – states that the provisions of the Agreement apply to salvage services, or any part of such services, referred to in the Agreement which have been already rendered by the Contractor at the date of the Agreement – states that English Law is the governing law of the Agreement and of arbitration under it – describes the obligation of the owners, their servants and agents to cooperate with the salvors – describes the Contractor's duty immediately after the termination of the services to notify the Council of Lloyd's and where practicable the owners of the amount for which he requires security – explains that the owners of the vessel, their servants and their agents should use their best endeavours to ensure that cargo owners provide their proportion of security before the cargo is released – explains that, pending the completion of the security, the Contractor has a maritime lien on the property salved for his remuneration – briefly describes how claims for arbitration are decided	

适任 3.2	立法要求的监督与控制	IMO 参考书目
– 描述参与救助作业的救助人员救助人命的权利 – 阐述每位船长,只要这么做不会严重危及其船舶、船员和乘客,都有义务对一切处于海上危险中的人员提供援助,即使是敌人 – 解释该公约还适用于由军舰或一国或公共权力机构所拥有、经营或租用的船舶提供的援助或救助服务 – 解释船东的担保规定和救助人海上留置权的适用 **劳氏标准救助合同 (LOF, 2000) (1 学时)** – 阐述在船舶或海洋环境存在风险，船长无足够时间要求船东安排基于预定费率或金额的救助服务的情况下,应使用 LOF 2000 – 描述订约人同意在执行救助服务时,努力抢救船舶和 / 或货物、燃料和物料,防止或减少环境损害 – 解释船上不需要备有 LOF 2000 表格,涉事船长只需要在救助服务开始之前,明确同意其条款 – 描述“无效果—无报酬”原则 – 解释 LOF 2000 取代 LOF 95 和在救助人按 LOF 95 或某些其他条款提供服务的情况下,在危难中的船长应努力按 LOF 2000 条款达成协议 – 解释 LOF 2000 被国际海难救助联合会视作 个重大的进展,具有明确、通俗易懂的语言和诸多创新 – 阐述 LOF 2000 是一个简化了格式的单页(2 个页面)文件(而 LOF 95 共 6 个页面) – 阐述订约人的报酬由伦敦仲裁机构确定，在协议中所产生的任何分歧都以同样的方式处理 – 阐述本协定的规定适用于救助服务或这些服务的任何部分，参见在协议之日由订约人提交的协议 – 阐述英国法律是该协定的管辖法并据此仲裁 – 描述船东、船东雇员和代理人与救助人合作的义务 – 描述订约人在终止服务后立刻通知劳埃德委员会,在可行时,通知其要求的担保金额所有人的职责 – 解释船东、船东雇员和代理人应尽最大努力确保在货物被移交之前,货主提供相应比例的担保金 – 解释在担保完成期间,为获取报酬,订约人对获救财产具有海上留置权 – 简要介绍如何决定申请仲裁		

COMPETENCE 3.2	Monitor and Control Compliance with Legislative Requirements	IMO Reference
– states that the Master or other person signing LOF on behalf of the property to be salved enters into the agreement as agent for the vessel her cargo, freight, bunkers, stores and any other property thereon and the respective owners thereof and binds each to the due performance thereof – states that when there is no longer any reasonable prospect of a useful result leading to a salvage reward in accordance with Convention Article 13 the owners of the vessel shall be entitled to terminate the services of the Contractor by giving notice to the Contractor in writing – describes the provisions for special compensation set out in Convention Article 13 – explains that Personal effects of Master, crew and passengers including any car accompanying a passenger are excluded from reward for salvage as per the LOF 2000 – states that the currency of award as per the LOF 2000 is USA $ – explains that as compared to the old LOF 1995, the duty to cooperate as per the new LOF 2000 is extended to provide information about nature of cargo, plans, stability data etc. – states that as per LOF 2000, the salvors have right to terminate when "no longer any reasonable prospects of useful result" – states that in the LOF 2000, SCOPIC clause is introduced as an alternative to Art 14 set out in the convention – states that as per LOF 2000, the Master is authorized to sign on behalf of cargo interests – explains that LOF 2000 defines the conditions under which a casualty is in a safe condition for redelivery to the owner which can be of crucial importance in the closing stages of a salvage operation **Special Compensation P and I Club (SCOPIC) Clause** – explains that SCOPIC clause is supplementary to any Lloyd's Form Salvage Agreement "No Cure – No Pay" ("Main Agreement") which incorporates the provisions of Article 14 of the International Convention on Salvage 1989 ("Article 14") – explains that the Contractor has the option to invoke by written notice to the owners of the vessel the SCOPIC clause at any time of his choosing regardless of the circumstances and, in particular, regardless of whether or not there is a "threat of damage to the environment" – explains that SCOPIC clause determines the method of assessing special compensation where payable under Article 14(1) to 14(4) of the Convention – explains that special compensation assessed in accordance with the SCOPIC clause is called "SCOPIC remuneration" – explains that the SCOPIC remuneration is payable only by the owners of the vessel (and not by the cargo owners) and is only payable to the extent that it exceeds the total Article 13 award (the salvage award) or, if none, any potential Article 13 award – explains that where the owner of the vessel is a member of a P&I club the club is normally required to pay the special compensation hence interest and involvement of the P&I clubs in drafting the SCOPIC clause		

适任 3.2	立法要求的监督与控制	IMO 参考书目
– 阐述代表待救财产签署 LOF 的船长或其他人员,作为船舶、货物、运费、燃料、物料和任何其他财产以及各自的所有人进入协议,各方均有适当履行协议的义务 – 阐述当按公约第 13 条不再有任何理由期望存在导致救助报酬的有利结果时,船东将有权通过书面通知订约人,终止为其服务 – 描述公约第 13 条中的特殊补偿规定 – 解释按照 LOF 2000,船长、船员和乘客的个人财产,包括载有乘客的车辆不在救助报酬之列 – 阐述按照 LOF 2000,酬劳货币为美元 – 解释相比旧的 LOF 1995,按照新的 LOF 2000,合作职责扩展到提供有关货物的性质、装载计划和稳性数据等信息 – 阐述根据 LOF 2000,救助人在“不再有任何理由期望存在有利结果”时,将有权终止救助 – 阐述在 LOF 2000 中,引入 SCOPIC 条款代替公约第 14 条规定 – 阐述按照 LOF 2000,授权船长代表货物利益方签署协议 – 解释 LOF 2000 阐明了将受害者在安全状态下,交还给在救助作业的最后阶段至关重要的所有人的条件 **船东保赔协会特别补偿(SCOPIC)条款** – 解释 SCOPIC 条款是对包含 1989 年国际救助公约第 14 章条款(“条款 14”)的任何劳氏标准救助协议“无效果—无报酬”(“主要协议”)的一种补充 – 解释不管情况如何,特别是不管是否存在“损害环境的威胁”,订约人任何时候都有权选择向船东发出书面通知,选择 SCOPIC 条款 – 解释根据本公约第 14(1)至 14(4)项下的应付款情况,SCOPIC 条款决定了特殊补偿的评定方法 – 解释按照 SCOPIC 条款评定的特殊补偿称为“SCOPIC 报酬” – 解释 SCOPIC 报酬仅为船东(不由货主支付)应付款项和仅为超出所有第 13 条酬劳(救助报酬)部分或者在无此项情况下,任何潜在的第 13 条酬劳的应付款项 – 解释在船东为船东保赔协会成员情况下,通常要求该俱乐部支付特殊补偿给各利益方和参与起草 SCOPIC 条款各方		

COMPETENCE 3.2	Monitor and Control Compliance with Legislative Requirements	IMO Reference
– explains that the assessment of SCOPIC remuneration commences from the time the written notice is given to the owners of the vessel and services rendered before the said written notice will not be remunerated under this SCOPIC clause at all but in accordance with Convention Article 13 as incorporated into the Main Agreement ("Article 13") – explains that the owners of the vessel have to provide the Contractor within 2 working days (excluding Saturdays and Sundays and holidays usually observed at Lloyd's) after receiving written notice from the contractor invoking the SCOPIC clause, a bank guarantee or P&I Club letter (called "the Initial Security") in a form reasonably satisfactory to the Contractor providing security for his claim for SCOPIC remuneration in the sum of US$3 million, inclusive of interest and costs – explains that the rates are based on time and materials plus an uplift of 25% in all cases – explains that in the absence of agreement, any dispute concerning the proposed Guarantor, the form of the security or the amount of any reduction or increase in the security in place shall be resolved by the Arbitrator – explains that if the owners of the vessel do not provide the Initial Security within the said 2 working days, the Contractor, at his option, and on giving notice to the owners of the vessel, shall be entitled to withdraw from all the provisions of the SCOPIC clause and revert to his rights under the Main Agreement including Article 14 which shall apply as if the SCOPIC clause had not existed – explains that the Owner and Contractor both have option to terminate SCOPIC under certain agreed circumstances – explains that even when the SCOPIC clause is invoked, the duties and liabilities of the Contractor remains the same as under the Main Agreement, namely to use his best endeavours to salve the vessel and property thereon and in so doing to prevent or minimize damage to the environment – explains that the assessment of SCOPIC remuneration includes the prevention of pollution as well as the removal of pollution in the immediate vicinity of the vessel insofar as this is necessary for the proper execution of the salvage – explains that the owner has the right to send on board a casualty Representative (SCR) – explains that Underwriters have the right to send one special hull representative and one special cargo representative (collectively called the "Special Representatives") – explains that the salvage Masters are required to send daily reports to Lloyd's and the owner until SCR arrives and thereafter to SCR – explains that the SCOPIC remuneration is not a General Average expense to the extent that it exceeds the Article 13 Award; any liability to pay such SCOPIC remuneration is that of the shipowner alone and no claim whether direct, indirect, by way of indemnity or recourse or otherwise relating to SCOPIC remuneration in excess of the Article 13 Award is to be made in General Average or under the vessel's Hull and Machinery Policy by the owners of the vessel – explains that any dispute arising out of this SCOPIC clause or the operations is to be referred to Arbitration as provided for under the Main Agreement – explains that a non-binding code of practice has been agreed between the International Salvage Union (ISU) and the International Group of Clubs		

适任 3.2	立法要求的监督与控制	IMO 参考书目
– 解释根据 SCOPIC 条款,SCOPIC 报酬的评定从发给船东书面通知时起算,在书面通知之前提供的服务不计报酬,但纳入公约第 13 条(“条款 13”)主要协议的除外 – 解释船东在收到订约人发出选择 SCOPIC 条款书面通知之后的 2 天内 (按劳氏方法计算通常不含周六、周日和节假日),提供给订约人一份银行保函或 P&I 信用证(称为“初始担保”),对订约人索要包括利息和费用在内的总额为 300 万美元 SCOPIC 报酬,以一种令其合理、满意的方式提供担保 – 解释费率是基于时间和材料,再加上所有情况下上浮 25%计算 – 解释在未达成协议的情况下,任何关于建议的担保人、担保的形式或担保上任何适当减少或增加数额的争端,应由仲裁员解决 – 解释如果船东在上述 2 个工作日内不提供初始担保,给船东发出通知的订约人,将有权选择退出所有的 SCOPIC 条款规定,恢复包括第 14 条在内的主要协议下自己的权利,就像 SCOPIC 条款已不存在 – 解释船东和订约人,在某些商定的情况下都有权选择终止 SCOPIC – 解释即使援用 SCOPIC 条款,订约人的职责仍与主要协议下的相同,即尽最大努力救助船舶和财产,救助时防止或减少对环境的损害 – 解释 SCOPIC 报酬的评定包括防污染, 也包括正常进行救助必要范围内移除船舶附近污染的费用 – 解释船东有权派一位受害人代表(SCR)上船 – 解释保险商有权派一个特别的船体代表和一个特别的货物代表(统称为“特别代表”) – 解释要求救助船长们每天向劳氏保险和船东递交报告,待 SCR 抵达后,改为向 SCR 递交 – 解释 SCOPIC 报酬在超出第 13 条范围时, 不是共同海损费用; 支付这类 SCOPIC 报酬的责任仅在船东方面,船东不得以赔偿或追索或超出第 13 条报酬与 SCOPIC 报酬相关的费用形式, 直接或间接地在共同海损中或在船舶船体与机械设备保单中提出索赔 – 解释 SCOPIC 条款或救助作业引起的任何争议都应按主要协议提交仲裁 – 解释一个不具约束力的例行规则在国际救助联盟(ISU)和国际俱乐部集团之间已达成一致		

COMPETENCE 3.2	Monitor and Control Compliance with Legislative Requirements	IMO Reference

1.6.6 Convention on Limitation of Liability for Maritime Claims, 1976 (LLMC 1976) (1 hour)
– lists the persons entitled to limit liability
– lists the claims subject to limitation of liability
– lists the claims exempted from limitation
– explains the circumstances in which limitation would be barred
– explains that, except for claims in respect of death or injury of passengers, the calculation of limits of liability is based on the ship's gross tonnage
– explains that the limit for claims in respect of death or injury of passengers is based on the number of passengers the ship is authorized to carry, subject to a maximum sum
– describes the constitution of a limitation fund
– states the scope of application of the Convention
1.6.7 Classification societies (1 hour)
– explains the reasons for having a ship classed with a classification society
– states that the majority of ships are built under survey
– explains that the classification society approves plans, examines the manufacture of parts and tests materials during the building of hull, machinery, equipment and, where appropriate, refrigerating machinery
– explains that equipment refers to anchors, chain cables, mooring ropes and wires, mooring arrangements, windlasses and mooring winches
– states that, if requested, the classification societies will also survey and certificate cargo handling equipment
– states that on satisfactory completion of surveys and sea trials the society issues certificates of class, which are kept aboard ship, and enters the particulars of the ship in its register
– states that a classification society will also survey an existing ship and providing it meets the society's rules regarding scantlings, materials, workmanship and condition, assign a class to it
– states that to retain its class a ship must undergo periodical surveys as laid down in the society's rules
– states that periodical surveys are:
  – annual survey
  – docking survey at approximately 2-yearly intervals
  – intermediate survey
  – special survey every 4 years, which may be extended to 5 years
– explains the special survey requirements may be met by a system of continuous survey such that the interval between successive surveys on any given item does not exceed 5 years
– states that an occasional survey, additional to the regular surveys, must be conducted after any damage to the hull, machinery or equipment which may affect the ship's seaworthiness
– states that repairs or alterations must be carried out under survey and to the satisfaction of the society's surveyors
– states that classification societies carry out surveys for the issue of statutory certification on behalf of many governments
		R105

适任 3.2	立法要求的监督与控制	IMO 参考书目

1.6.6 《1976 年海事赔偿责任限制公约》(LLMC 1976)(1 学时)
– 列出享有责任限制的人员
– 列出享有责任限制条件的赔偿
– 列出非责任限制的赔偿
– 解释丧失责任限制的情况
– 解释除海上运输的乘客人身伤亡赔偿外,根据船舶总吨位计算责任限制额
– 解释海上运输乘客人身伤亡的赔偿责任限制额是根据船舶授权承载的最多人数来决定
– 描述赔偿责任限制额的构成
– 阐述公约的适用范围
1.6.7 船级社(1 学时)
– 解释给船舶入级的原因
– 阐述大多数船舶是在检验下建造的
– 解释船级社在船体、轮机、设备和冷藏设备(如可行)的建造过程中批准计划、检查零件的制造和测试材料
– 解释设备系指锚、锚链、系缆和钢丝缆、系泊设施、锚机和绞缆机
– 阐述如果需要,船级社也将对货物装卸设备进行检验和发证
– 阐述在检验和海上测试圆满完成之后,船级社将颁发由船舶携带的入级证书,并记入船舶资料登记簿
– 阐述船级社也将检验现有船舶,如果现有船舶满足船级社有关船材尺度、材料、工艺和条件的规定时,船级社将授予船级
– 阐述入级的船舶为保持其船级,必须按船级社规定的要求进行定期检验
– 阐述定期检验包括:
  – 年度检验
  – 大约每 2 年一次的坞内检验
  – 中间检验
  – 检验间隔为 4 年的特别检验,可延长至 5 年
– 解释特别检验的要求可由连续检验系统满足,对任何给定项目连续检验的间隔不得超过 5 年
– 阐述除定期检验外,任何对船舶适航性有影响的船体、轮机或设备的损坏应进行临时检验
– 阐述船舶修理或改装必须在船级社验船师的检验下,并令验船师满意
– 阐述船级社代表许多政府进行检验并颁发法定证书
		R105

COMPETENCE 3.2	Monitor and Control Compliance with Legislative Requirements	IMO Reference

- states that a classification society may be asked to conduct the loading port survey on its classed refrigerating machinery
- explains that, when convenient, the loading port survey may be combined with a periodical survey for classification

1.6.8 Cargo (5 hours)

International Convention for the Unification of Certain Rules of Law Relating to Bills of Loading, as Amended by the Protocol of 1968 (Hague–Visby Rules)

- defines:
  - carrier
  - contract of carriage
  - goods
  - ship
  - carriage of goods
- lists the duties of the carrier to make the ship seaworthy and fit for the carriage of cargo
- describes the carrier's duty to care for the cargo
- describes the duty of the carrier, Master or agent of the carrier to issue a bill of lading
- lists the information which should be shown in a bill of lading
- explains that a bill of lading is prima facie evidence of the receipt by the carrier of the goods as described in it and proof to the contrary is not admissible when the bill of lading has been transferred to a third party acting in good faith
- explains that the shipper is deemed to have guaranteed the accuracy of marks, number, quantity and weight as furnished by him, and that the shipper is to indemnify the carrier against loss arising from inaccuracies in such particulars
- explains the duty of the carrier, Master or agent to issue a 'shipped' bill of lading after the goods are loaded, provided the shipper surrenders any previously taken up document of title
- explains the mandatory domain of the Hague-Visby rules
- explains the carrier's liability for loss or damage arising or resulting from unseaworthiness
- states that whenever loss or damage has resulted from unseaworthiness, the burden of proving due diligence is on the carrier
- lists the exceptions to the carrier's responsibility for loss or damage
- explains the shipper's responsibility for loss or damage sustained by the carrier or ship
- states the right to deviate for the purpose of saving life or property
- explains the limitation of liability for loss or damage and the circumstances in which benefit of limitation is lost
- describes the provisions regarding goods of an inflammable, explosive or dangerous nature
- explains the liability of the carrier's servants (Himalaya clause)
- explains that this Convention does not apply to charter parties, but, if bills of lading are issued under a charter party, they must comply with the terms of this Convention

适任 3.2	**立法要求的监督与控制**	**IMO 参考书目**

– 阐述船级社在装货港可以对申请入级的冷藏设备进行检验
– 解释如果方便,装货港的检验可以和定期检验相结合
1.6.8 货物(5 学时)
经修订的统一提单若干法律规定国际公约的 1968 年议定书(海牙—维斯比规则)
– 定义:
  – 承运人
  – 运输合同
  – 货物
  – 船舶
  – 货物运输
– 列出承运人使船舶适航和适货的责任
– 描述承运人保管货物的责任
– 描述承运人、船长或承运人代理签发提单的责任
– 列出提单上应显示的信息
– 解释提单是承运人已经按照提单所载状况收到货物的初始证据, 承运人向善意受让提单的第三人的反证不予承认
– 解释托运人被视为要保证所提供货物标志、数量、质量和重量的正确性,由上述资料不正确对承运人所造成的损失,托运人应当负赔偿责任
– 解释承运人、船长或代理在货物装船后签发装船提单的职责,假如托运人放弃先前持有的所有权凭证
– 解释海牙—维斯比规则强制适用范围
– 解释承运人应当对由于船舶不适航所引起的灭失和损失负赔偿责任
– 阐述无论何时由船舶不适航造成的灭失或损失,承运人应承担谨慎处理的举证责任
– 列出承运人对灭失或损失免责事项
– 解释托运人对承运人或船舶所遭受的灭失或损失的责任
– 阐述为救助人命或财产,船舶有绕航的权利
– 解释灭失或损失的赔偿责任限制和丧失赔偿责任限制权利的条件
– 描述易燃、易爆或危险性质货物的条款
– 解释承运人的雇员的责任(喜马拉雅条款)
– 解释本公约不适用租船合同, 但是在租船合同情况下签发的提单必须遵守本公约条款		

COMPETENCE 3.2	Monitor and Control Compliance with Legislative Requirements	IMO Reference

- states that any lawful provisions regarding general average may be inserted in a bill of lading
- explains that, in certain circumstances, goods may be carried under an agreement between the carrier and shipper in any contractual terms not contrary to public policy, provided that no bill or lading is issued and that the terms agreed are embodied in a non-negotiable receipt, marked as such
- explains that the Rules do not prevent a carrier or shipper entering into any agreement regarding loss or damage to goods prior to the loading on, and subsequent to, the discharge from the ship on which the goods are carried by sea
- states that the Convention does not affect the rights and obligations of the carrier under any statute relating to the limitation of the liability of owners of sea-going ships
- describes the scope of application of the provisions of this Convention
- describes briefly the system of documentary credit in the sale of goods during shipment

Casualty Investigation Code

- explains the general procedures for the conduct of casualty investigations under the IMO Casualty Investigation Code

Charter parties

- states that a charter party is a contract between the shipowner and the charterer for the use of a ship or her cargo space
- explains that a voyage charter party is a contract to carry a specified, normally full, cargo between named ports at an agreed freight rate
- explains that the shipowner remains responsible for the operation of the ship and the costs involved, but the charterer sometimes pays the stevedoring charges
- states that contracts are normally drawn up using standard charter party forms amended as required by alterations and additional clauses
- describes the tendering of notice of readiness at the loading port
- explains that if the ship is not ready to receive cargo, whether alongside or not, by the cancellation date the charterer may cancel the charter
- explains what is meant by laytime and the terms ‘running days/hours’, ‘Sundays and holidays excepted’ and ‘weather working days’
- states that the laytime for loading and discharging may be stated separately or as a total
- states that all times relevant to cargo working should be recorded in the logbook and time sheets for the calculations of laytime completed as a check on the charterer’s laytime statement
- explains that if cargo work is not completed within the permitted laytime, the charterer is liable to pay demurrage at the agreed rate per day or hour until it is completed
- explains that time lost due to defects of the ship or its equipment is not counted in the laytime
- explains that in the event of cargo work being completed before the expiration of laytime, dispatch is usually payable by the shipowner to the charterer
- states that bills of lading are normally issued under a voyage charter party and signed by the Master or on his behalf

适任 3.2	立法要求的监督与控制	IMO 参考书目
– 阐述任何有关共同海损的法律规定都应写入提单 – 解释在某些情况下，货物可按承运人与托运人之间在不违反公共政策的前提下订立的协议进行运算,前提是尚未签发提单或,上述协议的条款体现在不得流通且已注有这种字样的收据之中 – 解释本公约不妨碍承运人或托运人就对装载海运货物的船舶在货物的装船前或卸载后所受灭失或损失订立任何协议 – 阐述本公约不影响有关远洋船舶所有人责任限制的任何法令所规定的承运人的权利和义务 – 描述本公约条款所适用的范围 – 简述在装运期内销售货物跟单信用证制度 **事故调查规则** – 解释按照 IMO 事故调查规则进行事故调查的一般程序 **租船合同** – 阐述租船合同是指船舶所有人和承租人就船舶或其舱位的使用签订的合同 – 解释航次租船合同是以约定的运费率在指定的港口间运输指定的通常是满载的货物 – 解释船舶所有人仍然负责船舶营运和相关的费用,但是承租人有时付装卸费用 – 租船合同通常是按要求做更改和附加条款修改后的标准租船合同形式 – 描述在装货港递交装货就绪通知书 – 解释如果船舶没有做好接收货物的准备, 到解约日时无论其是否靠泊，承租人都可解除合同 – 解释装卸时间和“连续工作日/小时”、“星期日和节假日除外”和“晴天工作日”等术语 – 阐述装卸时间可以分开计算也可以作为一个整体来计算 – 阐述与货物工作有关的所有时间都应记录在航海日志和装卸时间表中，以计算完成之后的装卸时间,以此来核对承租人约定的装卸时间 – 解释如果货物装卸未能在所允许的时间内完成，承租人有责任按约定的每天/小时费率支付滞期费直到装卸完 – 解释由于船舶或其设备的缺陷而耗费的时间不计算在装卸时间内 – 解释一旦在装卸时间期满之前完成货物装卸,船舶所有人通常应支付承租人速遣费 – 阐述提单通常在航次租船合同下签发,要由船长或其代表签发		

COMPETENCE 3.2	Monitor and Control Compliance with Legislative Requirements	IMO Reference
– explains that the bills of lading may incorporate the terms of the charter party which, in any case, take precedence over the bills of lading as between shipowner and charterer – explains that when bills of lading have been transferred to a third party they constitute the contract between the shipowner and that party – states that a voyage charter party may be arranged to cover a stated number of successive voyages or an unspecified number of voyages to be performed in a given time – states that in a time charter party the charterer agrees to hire the ship for a specified period of time – explains that the charterer may use the vessel for any voyage he wants within the trading area agreed in the charter party – explains that the charterer pays for bunkers and for cargo loading and discharging, port dues, canal dues and pilotage – states that owners pay crew costs and for provisions, necessary stores, insurance of the ship and the costs of maintaining the ship in class and keeping it in an efficient condition to carry out the charterer's wishes – states that the charter party contains a description of the ship, including its speed and fuel consumption – explains that inability to maintain the warranted speed or consumption as a result of heavy weather or other cause should be substantiated by entries in the logbook – states that crew overtime in connection with the cargo is usually for the account of the charterer, and separate time sheets should be kept – explains that the off-hire clause states the circumstances in which payment of hire ceases during time lost to the charterer – explains that off-hire deductions may be made for time lost due to reduced-speed resulting from defects of ship or machinery, for the cost of additional fuel and for extra expenses – states that the Master is usually required to sign bills of lading as presented to him by the charterer or the charter party may give the charterer the right to sign them on his behalf – states that a time charter party may be used for a single round voyage – describes the Master's actions regarding damage done by stevedores to the ship or cargo – explains that demise or bareboat charter party is a leasing arrangement in which the charterer operates the ship as if it were his own – states that the Master and crew are employed by the charterer, to whom they are responsible as if he were the owner – explains that a tonnage contract or contract of affreightment may be used where a shipper needs to transport large quantities over a long period – explains that the contract does not name particular ships and the shipowner is free to use any suitable ship, his own or chartered, for each shipment – states that the loading dates are specified and that punctual performance is essential – states that each individual shipment is normally subject to the terms of a conventional voyage charter party		

适任 3.2	立法要求的监督与控制	IMO 参考书目
	– 解释提单可合并入租船合同的条款中，但是在任何情况下，船舶所有人和承运人之间的租船合同都优先于提单 – 解释当提单转让给第三方时,提单就构成了船东和第三方的合同 – 阐述航次租船合同可以被安排为包括一个规定数量的连续航次或在给定时间内的不定数航次 – 阐述在一个期租的合同中承租人同意在一个特定时间内租用一艘船舶 – 解释承租人可以在合同允许营运区域内使用船舶完成任何他想要的航次 – 解释承租人付燃油费、货物装卸费、港口使费、运河费和引航费 – 阐述船东应支付船员工资和食品的供应、必要的物料、船舶保险费和保持船级的维修保养费,使船舶保持在承租人期望的状态 – 阐述定期租船合同包含一艘船舶的概况,包括船舶航速和燃油消耗 – 解释由于恶劣天气或其他原因使船舶不能保持在保证的航速或燃油消耗应记入航海日志作为证明 – 阐述与货物有关的加班时间通常记在承租人的账上,且应保存在单独的时间表上 – 解释停租条款规定了在时间损失期间停止支付租金给承租人的条件 – 解释由于船舶或机械的缺陷而造成的减速导致时间的损失可以扣除停租租金，以补偿产生的额外燃油费用和其他的额外费用 – 阐述船长经常在承租人要求下签发提单或租船合同，也可以给予承租人代其签发提单的权利 – 阐述定期租船合同可以用于一个单循环航次 – 描述船长在码头工人对船舶或货物造成损害时所采取的行动 – 解释转让或光船租船合同是一个由承租人好像船舶所有人一样营运船舶的租赁协议 – 阐述承租人雇用船长和船员并对承租人负责,就好像他是船东一样 – 解释托运人需要长期大批量运输货物情况下,可采用吨位合同或租船契约 – 解释合同没有指定具体的船舶且船东为每次运输自由使用自有或租用的任何合适船舶 – 阐述装船日期是特定的并且必须及时履行 – 阐述每个单独的运输通常服从于一个普通的航次租船合同条款	

COMPETENCE 3.2	Monitor and Control Compliance with Legislative Requirements	IMO Reference
"Hamburg Rules" maritime legislation – explains the effect of charges where goods are carried under Hamburg Rules – explains carrier's extended liability for loss or damage to the goods – explains reductions to exception to liability, inward and outward bills of lading, live animals and deck cargo – explains the need to inform P & I Club where goods are carried under Hamburg Rules **1.6.9 General average and marine insurance (3 hours)** **The York-Antwerp Rules, 1974** – states that where the York-Antwerp Rules apply, general average should be adjusted according to the Rules to the exclusion of any law or practice inconsistent with them – defines a general average act – states that general average sacrifices and expenses are to be borne by the different contributing interests on the basis of these Rules – explains that only such losses, damages or expenses which are the direct consequence of the general average act are allowed as general average and that no indirect loss whatsoever will be admitted – explains that rights to contribution in general average when the event which gave rise to the sacrifice was due to the fault of one of the parties to the adventure – states that the onus of proof is upon the party claiming in general average to show that the loss or expense claimed is properly allowable as general average – states that any extra expense incurred in place of another expense which would have been allowable as general average is deemed to be general average, but only up to the amount of the general average expense avoided – explains that general average is to be adjusted, as regards both loss and contribution, on the basis of values at the time and place when and where the adventure ends – states that the general principles contained in Rules A to G are amplified by numbered rules I to XXII, dealing with specific points of practice – states that the Master should make a declaration of general average, as is required by the law and custom of the port, at a port of refuge and at a discharging port when general average damage to the cargo is suspected – explains the duty of the Master to see to it that general average contributions (average bonds) are collected for the benefit of those entitled to them, whether they are cargo owners or shipowners, exercising the shipowner's lien on the cargo, where necessary, until they are paid **1.6.10 Marine insurance and liability (5 hours)** – explains in general terms the purpose of marine insurance – explains what is meant by an insurable interest – describes briefly how insurance is arranged through brokers		

适任 3.2	立法要求的监督与控制	IMO 参考书目

“汉堡规则”的海事立法

- 解释在汉堡规则下货物运输费用的影响
- 解释承运人对货物灭失或损害的责任的延伸
- 解释减少了内、外提单,活的动物和甲板货的免责条款
- 解释在汉堡规则下的货物运输需要通知 P & I 保赔协会

1.6.9 共同海损和海上保险(3 学时)

1974 年约克—安特卫普规则

- 阐述在约克—安特卫普公约适用的情况下,共同海损应按本规则理算,任何与本规则相抵触的法律和惯例就不得予以考虑
- 定义共同海损行为
- 阐述根据这些规则共同海损牺牲和共同海损费用由获益方分摊
- 解释只属于共同海损行为直接后果的灭失、损失或费用才允许作为共同海损,不承认任何间接损失
- 解释引起共同海损牺牲的事故是由航行中一方的过失造成时，该方要求分摊共同海损的权利
- 阐述提出共同海损分摊请求的一方应当负举证责任，证明其损失或费用应当列入共同海损
- 阐述为代替可以列为共同海损的特殊费用而发生的额外费用,可被认为是共同海损,但是总金额不得超过所避免的共同海损费用
- 解释共同海损应根据航行抵达港口而结束时综合考虑损失和获救财产来理算
- 阐述包括规则 A 到规则 G 的总则在实践的特殊情况中，由数字规则 I 扩展到规则 XXII
- 阐述船舶在避难港或卸货港时,如果对货物的共同海损有怀疑,根据港口的法律和惯例,船长应当宣布共同海损
- 解释船长查看船东或货主对于那些有权享有的利益是否提供了共同海损分摊额（分摊保证金),必要时行使船东对货物的置留权直到他们支付为止

1.6.10 海上保险责任(5 学时)

- 以通用术语解释海上保险的目的
- 解释什么是保险利益
- 简述经纪人是如何安排保险的

COMPETENCE 3.2	Monitor and Control Compliance with Legislative Requirements	IMO Reference
	– explains the principle of 'utmost good faith' – explains the effect of misrepresentation or non-disclosure of material circumstances known to the assured – explains 'warranty' and the effect on a marine insurance policy of breach of warranty – describes briefly voyage policies, time policies and floating policies – explains what is meant by deviation and how the insurer is discharged from liability from the moment a ship deviates under a voyage policy – lists permitted deviations – explains that a deviation clause will often permit the assured to extend his cover at a premium to be arranged, provided the insurer is given prompt notice of the deviation ('held covered' clause) – describes briefly the perils usually covered in a marine insurance policy – explains the use of 'Institute Clauses' – explains the 'duty of assured' clause ('Sue and Labour' clause) – distinguishes between partial loss, total loss and constructive total loss – explains what is meant by 'particular average' – explains the doctrine of subrogation – explains the function of Protection and Indemnity Associations (P and I clubs) – lists risks, liabilities and expenses covered by P and I clubs **Noting and extending protests** – explains that a 'note of protest' is a declaration by the Master of circumstances beyond his control which may give, or may have given, rise to loss or damage – states that protests are made before a notary public, magistrate, consular officer or other authority – states that protests should be noted as soon as possible, and in any case, within 24 hours of arrival in port – states that, at the time of noting protest, the Master should reserve the right to extend it – states that protests concerning cargo damage should be made before starting to unload – explains that, although there is no requirement to use a special form, it is usual to do so – explains that statements under oath are taken from the Master and other members of the crew and that such statements must be supported by appropriate entries in the logbook, which must be produced – states that certified copies of the note of protest should be forwarded to the owners and one copy retained on board – explains why protest should be noted at each discharging port and not just at the first port of call	

适任 3.2	立法要求的监督与控制	IMO 参考书目
– 解释“最大诚信原则” – 解释虚假陈述或未能如实告知重要情况对被保险人的影响 – 解释“担保书”和违反担保书对海上保险单的影响 – 简要介绍航次保险单、定期保单和统保单 – 解释什么是绕航以及在航次保单情况下,从船舶绕航那一时刻保险人如何解除责任 – 列出允许的绕航 – 解释绕航条款通常允许被保险人支付一定保险费扩展保险责任范围，前提是立刻通知保险人绕航(“被承保”条款) – 简述海上保险单通常包含的风险 – 解释“公会条款”的使用 – 解释“被保险人的义务”条款(“施救”条款) – 区分部分损失、全损和推定全损之间的区别 – 解释单独海损的含义 – 解释代位求偿原则 – 解释船东保赔协会(P & I)的作用 – 列出保赔协会所覆盖的风险、责任和费用 **提出和延伸声明** – 解释“海事报告”是船长在情况超出其控制,可能或已经出现损失或损坏情况下,发出的声明 – 阐述声明是在公证人、裁判官、领事官员或其他当局面前提出的 – 阐述在任何情况下应该在到港 24 小时内尽快提出声明 – 阐述在提出声明的时候,船长应保留延伸声明的权利 – 阐述应在开始卸货前提出货物损坏声明 – 解释尽管没有要求使用特殊的形式,但通常是这样做的 – 解释宣誓声明来自于船长和其他船员,应有航海日志的适当记录所支持,须予以出示 – 阐述经认证的海事报告副本应送交船东,并在船上保留一份 – 解释为何声明应在每个卸货港而不是只在第一停靠港		

COMPETENCE 3.2	Monitor and Control Compliance with Legislative Requirements	IMO Reference

- states that a note of protest is advisable when:
  - during the voyage the ship has experienced weather conditions which may result in damage to cargo, the ship is in any way damaged, or there is reason to suspect that damage may have occurred
  - normal ventilation of perishable cargo has not been practicable on account of weather
  - cargo is shipped in such a condition that it is likely to deteriorate during the voyage (bills of lading must be appropriately endorsed)
  - the charterer or his agent commits any serious breach of the terms of the charter party
  - consignees fail to discharge cargo, take delivery or pay freight in accordance with the terms of a charter party or bill of lading, any general average act has occurred
- states that, in cases where damage is found to have occurred, it is necessary to extend protest to support claims
- states that the Master should consult his owner's agent about the local requirement and practice for extending a protest
- states that the Master must normally appear in person accompanied by a number, depending upon local custom, of crew members as witnesses

Letter of protest

- explains that a letter of protest, which may also be simply called a "protest", is a written communication intended to convey and record dissatisfaction on the part of the protester (the sender) concerning some matter over which the recipient has control, and holding the recipient responsible for any (legal or financial) consequences of the matter being complained of
- explains that a letter of protest may help to substantiate a claim by the owner, or refute a claim by a charterer, harbour authority, etc., and may prove useful, if properly filed, in the resolution of a dispute long after the related event
- states that a letter of protest should not be confused with a protest noted or lodged before a notary public or consul
- explains that a letter of protest may be sent, in appropriate circumstances, by the Master of any ship, large or small, in any trade, and can be expected to be received by the Master of any ship. They are especially common (in both directions) in the tanker trades, where a variety of reasons give occasion for their sending
- explains that letters of protest are in most cases in connection with cargo operations, although they may be written about almost any matter where there may be legal liability, whether there is a contractual arrangement between the employers of the sender and recipient (as in the case of cargo-related protests) or not (as in the case of a protest sent to the Master of a closely berthed ship that is causing damage to the sender's ship)
- explain that some companies, especially those in the oil, gas or chemical trades, supply their Masters with a stock of printed proforma protest forms phrased in the company's "house" style, while others expect their Masters to compose suitable protest letters when required

适任 3.2	立法要求的监督与控制	IMO 参考书目

– 阐述在下列情况下提出声明是可取的:
  – 航行中船舶经历的天气状况可能导致货损、以任何方式损坏船舶,或有理由怀疑可能已经发生损坏
  – 由于天气原因无法对易坏货物的正常通风
  – 货物的装运条件可能使之在航行中变质(必须相应地背书提单)
  – 承租人或其代理人严重违反租船合同条款
  – 收货人未能卸货、提货或按租船合同或提单条款规定支付运费,发生任何共同海损行为
– 阐述在发现已经发生损坏的情况下,必须延伸声明以支持索赔
– 阐述船长应和船东代理人就延伸声明的当地要求和惯例进行磋商
– 阐述船长通常必须在一些船员陪同下亲自作证
声明书
– 解释声明书简称声明,是旨在传达和记录抗议方(送信人)就收件人控制的某事不满,并责成收件人对此事被投诉的任何(法律或金融)后果负责的书面沟通
– 解释声明书可以帮助证实船东提出的索赔,反驳承租人、港口当局等提出的索赔,如果适当存档,则在解决相关事件以后很久的纠纷中可证实是有用的
– 阐述不应将声明书与提交或呈递给公证人或领事的声明相混淆
– 解释在适当情况下,无论船舶大小或种类,声明书均可由船长送出,并预期能被任何船舶所接受。在油船运输中,有各种理由发出声明书,它们特别常见(双向方式)
– 解释声明书大多数情况下与货物作业有关, 尽管书写的几乎是任何事务有关法律的责任,无论发送者和接受者的雇主之间是存在(像在有关货物的声明一样)还是不存在(像发送给邻近靠泊船舶之船长的声明,该船舶对声明发送者的船舶造成了损坏)契约约定
– 解释一些公司,特别是从事石油、气体或化学品运输的公司,提供给船长具有其公司自身风格的一系列印制好的形式固定的声明表,而其他公司则希望其船长在需要时撰写适当的声明书		

COMPETENCE 3.2	Monitor and Control Compliance with Legislative Requirements	IMO Reference

1.6.11 Stowaways (3 hours)

- explains that as per IMO Guidelines – a "stowaway" is defined as "a person who is secreted on a ship, or in a cargo which is subsequently loaded on the ship, without the consent of the shipowner or the Master or any other responsible person, and who is detected on board after the ship has departed from a port and is reported as a stowaway by the Master to the appropriate authorities"
- explains that an international convention relating to stowaways was adopted in Brussels in 1957, but it has not yet entered into force
- explains that according to the P&I clubs (who deal with many stowaway incidents), certain parts of the world are high-risk areas for stowaways
- explains that since the P&I clubs invariably have the latest intelligence on stowaway risks, Masters should endeavour to obtain their latest club bulletins and information
- explains that at any port in a high-risk area, great care should be taken to ensure that stowaways do not board, and the following safeguards should be observed:
  1. A watch should be kept on the accommodation ladder or gangway
  2. Stevedores should only be allowed to work in restricted areas and a watch should be kept on them
  3. Open spaces should be closed as far as possible
  4. A search of the ship should be carried out before the ship sails
  5. All open-top containers on the quay should be checked. All containers on the quay should be stacked door-to-door, if possible
- explains IMO has introduced various guidelines on stowaway matters, the latest being in Resolution A.871(20), adopted on 27 November 1997, and its Annex, "Guidelines on the Allocation of Responsibilities to seek the successful resolution of stowaway cases"
- explains that the guidelines in the resolution state that the resolution of stowaway cases is difficult because of different national legislation in the various countries involved, nevertheless, some basic principles can be applied generally
- explains that as per the IMO guideline there are nine basic principles which can be applied generally with respect to stowaway cases, the second of these is that stowaway/asylum-seekers should be treated in compliance with international protection principles as set out in international instruments (including the UN Convention relating to the Status of Refugees of 28 July 1951 and the UN Protocol relating to the Status of Refugees of 31 January 1967) and relevant national legislation, the ninth is that stowaway incidents should be dealt with humanely by all parties involved. Due consideration should always be given to the operational safety of the ship and to the well-being of the stowaway

适任 3.2	立法要求的监督与控制	IMO 参考书目

1.6.11 偷渡人员 (3 学时)

- 解释按照 IMO 指南——将“偷渡人员”定义为“未经船东或船长或其他负责人员同意,秘密上船或藏在货物中随后一起装船,待船离港后被发现并由船长作为偷渡者报告给有关当局的人员”
- 解释有关偷渡者的国际公约在 1957 年于布鲁塞尔通过,但尚未生效
- 解释根据船东保赔协会(它处理过许多偷渡人员事故)资料,世界上某些地区为偷渡人员高风险地区
- 解释船东保赔协会总是具有最新的偷渡人员风险资讯，船长应努力获取其最新的公报和信息
- 解释在高危地区的任何港口,要特别注意确保不让偷渡者登船,应遵守以下措施:
  1. 保持人员在舷梯口值班
  2. 只允许装卸工人在限定区域工作,并派值班人员进行监控
  3. 开敞场所尽可能关闭
  4. 开航前搜索全船
  5. 检查所有码头上的敞顶集装箱。如可能,所有码头上的集装箱应门对门堆放
- 解释 IMO 已制订各种有关偷渡事务的指南,最新的 A.871(20)大会决议及其附则已于 1997 年 11 月 27 日通过,为“关于寻求成功解决偷渡事件的责任划分指南”
- 解释决议的指南中阐述，偷渡事件的解决因涉及各种国家的不同国内立法而存在困难,但通常可运用一些基本原则
- 解释按照 IMO 指南,有关偷渡事件通常有九个基本原则可以运用,第二项原则是对待偷渡人员 / 寻求庇护者应符合在国际文件中规定的国际保护原则（包括 1951 年 7 月 28 日通过的有关难民地位的联合国公约及其 1967 年 1 月 31 日通过的联合国议定书)和有关国家的立法,第九项原则是所有有关各方应人道处理偷渡事件。始终应适当考虑船舶的营运安全和对偷渡人员的福利

COMPETENCE 3.2	Monitor and Control Compliance with Legislative Requirements	IMO Reference
– explains that paragraph 5.1 of the IMO Guidelines lists responsibilities of the Master in stowaway cases, which are as follows: 1. to make every effort to determine immediately the port of embarkation of the stowaway; 2. to make every effort to establish the identity, including the nationality/citizenship of the stowaway; 3. to prepare a statement containing all information relevant to the stowaway, in accordance with information specified in the standard document annexed to these Guidelines, for presentation to the appropriate authorities; 4. to notify the existence of a stowaway and any relevant details to his shipowner and appropriate authorities at the port of embarkation, the next port of call and the flag State; 5. not to depart from his planned voyage to seek the disembarkation of a stowaway to any country unless repatriation has been arranged with sufficient documentation and permission for disembarkation, or unless there are extenuating security or compassionate reasons; 6. to ensure that the stowaway is presented to appropriate authorities at the next port of call in accordance with their requirements; 7. to take appropriate measures to ensure the security, general health, welfare and safety of the stowaway until disembarkation. – explains the procedure to be adopted, in general, on the discovery at sea of stowaways, which is: 1. The owner or manager, as appropriate, should be contacted. The owner will normally contact the P&I club's managers to decide on a course of action. The P&I club's correspondent serving the next port of call will normally be contacted by the club managers. The correspondent should be able to advise what information will be required by port State and other officials. 2. An entry should be made in the Official Log Book recording the discovery of the stowaways. 3. The compartment or area in which the stowaways were found should be searched. Any documents or articles of clothing, etc. may give an indication of their place of origin. (Most countries only allow a stowaway to be landed if he has the necessary travel documents to return to his own country. Stowaways rarely have any documentation, however, and some will try to destroy all clues as to their identity.) 4. The clothing of the stowaways should be searched for indications as to their origin. 5. The agent at the next port of call should be contacted and instructed to advise the appropriate authorities of the port State of the presence of stowaways on board.		

适任 3.2	立法要求的监督与控制	IMO 参考书目
	– 解释 IMO 指南第 5.1 段列出了船长在偷渡事件中的责任如下： 1. 尽一切努力立刻确定偷渡人员的登陆港口； 2. 尽一切努力弄清偷渡人员的国籍 / 公民身份； 3. 按照这些指南附则中标准文件列出的信息,准备一份包含所有偷渡者相关信息的声明,并呈报给有关当局； 4. 通知船东和偷渡者登船港口、下一个停靠港的相关当局和船旗国,船上有偷渡者及其相关细节； 5. 不偏离计划航线去寻求使偷渡者在任何国家上岸,除非具有足够文件资料和上岸许可并已做出遣返安排,或具有合理的安全保障或令人同情的理由； 6. 确保按照下一个停靠港有关当局的要求递解偷渡者； 7. 在偷渡者登岸前,采取适当措施确保其安全、身体健康、福利和不受侵害。 – 解释在海上发现偷渡者一般采取的行动如下： 1. 应联系有关船东或经营人。船东通常联系船东保赔协会(P&I)经理,决定如何行动。船东保赔协会经理通常联系其下一停靠港的当地联络人。该联络人应能就港口国和其他机构所要求的信息给出建议。 2. 应在官方航海日志中记录发现了偷渡者。 3. 应搜索发现偷渡者的舱室或区域。任何文件或衣物等均可给出其来源地的标识。(大多数国家在偷渡者有必要的旅行证件时才允许其登陆，以便使其回到自己的国家。然而,很少有偷渡者具有任何文件资料,有些人会试图破坏所有与其身份相关的线索。) 4. 应检查偷渡者的衣物以识别其来源地。 5. 联系下一个港口的代理,指示其通知港口国有关当局船上存在偷渡者。	

COMPETENCE 3.2	Monitor and Control Compliance with Legislative Requirements	IMO Reference

6. Each stowaway found should be individually interviewed in order to establish the following details:
   - name of stowaway;
   - stowaway's date and place of birth;
   - nationality of stowaway;
   - name, date and place of birth of either or both of the stowaway's parents;
   - postal and residential address of the stowaway and either parent;
   - stowaway's passport or seaman's book number, together with date and place of issue; and
   - stowaway's next of kin, if different from above.
7. Stowaway details should be obtained, the completed details should be communicated to the agent and the P&I club correspondent at the next port of call.
8. Photographs of each stowaway should be taken and, where digital camera facilities are available, transmitted to the P&I club correspondent; these may enable travel documents to be obtained more quickly on the ship's arrival.
9. All stowaways should be housed in some part of the crew accommodation which can be locked when necessary.
10. The stowaways should not be locked in their accommodation when the vessel is at sea and well clear of land unless they are considered a threat to the safety of the ship or personnel on board. Consideration should be given, however, to the possibility of unguarded stowaways launching a liferaft or boat in an attempt to reach land.
11. The stowaways should be locked securely in their accommodation when the vessel approaches any port or nears any land. (Consideration should be given to the possibility of the stowaways' escape through open scuttles.)
12. The stowaways should be provided with adequate food, water, sanitary facilities, etc.
13. The stowaways should be treated in a humane manner.
14. The stowaways should not be made to work for their keep.
15. The stowaways should not be signed on the Crew Agreement and should not be entered on any List of Crew. A "Stowaway List" should be made recording any known particulars, ready for production to port officials.
16. Evidence of costs relating to the stowaway case, such as fuel, insurance, wages, stores, provisions and port charges, should be gathered to support the owner's claim on his P&I policy. (The owner's costs associated with the landing of stowaways are usually recoverable from his P&I club.)
17. Full details of all events and particulars relating to the stowaway incident should be recorded in the Official Log Book, if necessary in an annexed document. (This may be used as part of any report required by owners, the club, etc.)

适任 3.2	立法要求的监督与控制	IMO 参考书目
6. 应单独对每名偷渡者提问,以明确以下细节: – 偷渡者姓名; – 偷渡者出生日期和出生地; – 偷渡者国籍; – 偷渡者双亲或父亲 / 母亲姓名、生日和出生地; – 偷渡者及其父亲 / 母亲邮政地址和居住地址; – 偷渡者护照或海员证及其签发日期和地点; – 如不能获悉上述情况,则需偷渡者的亲属资料。 7. 应获得偷渡者详情, 将完整细节传达给下一个 停靠港代理和船东保赔协会联络人。 8. 在有数码相机的情况下,应给每位偷渡者拍照,发给船东保赔协会联络人,这可使其旅行文书在船抵达前就能得到。 9. 应将所有偷渡者安置在船员生活区的某一处所,必要时可以锁上 10. 船在海上和远离陆地时,不应将偷渡者锁在生活区,除非其被认为危及船舶或船上人员安全。然而应考虑无人看守的偷渡者企图释放救生艇筏登陆的可能性 11. 当船舶进港或接近陆地时,应将偷盗者锁牢在生活区。(应考虑偷渡者通过开着的舷窗逃走的可能性。) 12. 应向偷渡者提供充足的食物、淡水和卫生设施等。 13. 应以人道方式对待偷渡者。 14. 在船期间不应强迫偷渡者工作。 15. 不应与偷渡者签署船员协议,他们不应被列入船员名单。应作一个偷渡者清单,记录任何已知细节,准备提供给港口官员。 16. 应收集有关偷渡事件的成本证据,如燃料、保险、工资、物料、食品和港口使费等,以支持船东向其船东保赔机构索赔。(有关偷渡者登陆所花船东成本通常可从其船东保赔协会收回。) 17. 所有事件详情和有关偷渡事故细节均应记入船舶日志,如有必要,以附加文件形式。(这可被用作船东、船东保赔协会等要求的任何报告的一部分。)		

COMPETENCE 3.2	Monitor and Control Compliance with Legislative Requirements	IMO Reference
– explains that arriving with stowaways on board can have complications – explains that the IMO Guidelines on the Allocation of Responsibilities to seek the Successful Resolution of Stowaway Cases state (in paragraph 3) that the resolution of stowaway cases is difficult because of different national legislation in each of the potentially several countries involved: the country of embarkation, the country of disembarkation, the flag State of the vessel, the country of apparent, claimed or actual nationality/citizenship of the stowaway, and countries of transit during repatriation – explains that the IMO Guidelines on the Allocation of Responsibilities to seek the Successful Resolution of Stowaway Cases contain (in paragraph 4) certain basic principles which can be applied generally, the first of these is that there is recognition that stowaways arriving at or entering a country without the required documents are, in general, illegal entrants. Decisions on dealing with such situations are the prerogative of the countries where such arrival or entry occurs, the third is that the shipowner and his representatives on the spot, the Master, as well as the port authorities and national Administrations, should cooperate as far as possible in dealing with stowaway cases – states that in every case the agent should be notified of the presence of stowaways in advance of arrival – explains that under the U.S. Refugee Act 1980 a stowaway who arrives in the USA can request political asylum – explains that the Immigration and Naturalization Service (INS) has taken the position that shipowners are required to provide 24-hour armed guards during the entire asylum process which can take months – explains that there have been cases where the owner has incurred costs in excess of $1m for such detention – explains that many countries impose very heavy penalties (in some cases of over US$200,000) on Masters who fail to ensure that stowaways are kept securely on board in port **1.6.12 Ship's agents and agency (2 hours)** – explains that as per United Nations Conference on Trade and Development, UNCTAD Minimum Standards For Shipping Agents, "Shipping agent" means any person (natural or legal) engaged on behalf of the owner, charterer or operator of a ship, or of the owner of cargo, in providing shipping services including: i. Negotiating and accomplishing the sale or purchase of a ship; ii. Negotiating and supervising the charter of a ship; iii. Collection of freight and/or charter hire where appropriate and all related financial matters; iv. Arrangements for Customs and cargo documentation and forwarding of cargo; v. Arrangements for procuring, processing the documentation and performing all activities required related to dispatch of cargo; vi. Organizing arrival or departure arrangements for the ship; vii. Arranging for the supply of services to a ship while in port – explains the authority of the agency and where it may be actual authority or apparent authority (also called ostensible authority) – explains that actual authority may be express or implied		

<table>
<tr><th>适任 3.2</th><th>立法要求的监督与控制</th><th>IMO
参考书目</th></tr>
<tr><td colspan="2">
– 解释偷渡者随船抵达可能带来混乱
– 解释 IMO 关于寻求成功解决偷渡事件的责任划分指南声明(在第 3 段),偷渡案件难以解决,因为涉及的几个潜在的国家包括:登船国、入境的国家、船舶的船旗国,偷渡者表面的、声称的或实际的国籍 / 公民的国家和遣返国境国,这些国家每一个的立法均不同
– 解释按照 IMO 关于寻求成功解决偷渡事件的责任划分指南(在第 4 段)通常可以运用的基本原则, 第一项原则是偷渡者未携带所需的文书抵达或进入一个国家是非法的。处理这种偷渡事件是偷渡抵达或进入国的特权。第三项原则是船东及其现场代表、船长以及港口当局和国家行政机关应尽可能合作处理偷渡事件
– 阐述在任何情况下,应在抵港前通知代理船上载有偷渡者
– 解释按照美国 1980 年难民法到达美国的偷渡者可寻求政治避难
– 解释移民和入籍处(INS)取代了船东,对整个可能长达数月的政治避难期提供所要求的 24 小时武装保护
– 解释存在船东为此类扣押耗资百万美元的案例
– 解释许多国家对船舶在港期间未能确保偷渡者在船安全的船长征收非常重的罚款(某些情况下超过 20 万美元)
1.6.12 船舶代理人和代理机构(2 学时)
– 解释按照联合国贸易与发展会议,UNCTAD 规定了航运公司代理人最低标准, 航运公司代理人系指代表船东、承租人或船舶经营人或货主从事以下航运服务的任何人员(自然人或法人):
i. 买卖船舶的谈判和实施;
ii. 租船谈判和船舶租赁的监管;
iii. 适当情况下收取运费和 / 或租金,办理所有相关金融事务;
iv. 安排报关和货物文件以及发送货物;
v. 安排获得、办理与分派货物相关的文件和完成所要求的所有行动;
vi. 船舶抵达或离港的安排;
vii. 为在港船舶安排供应服务
– 解释代理人的授权和可能为实际授权或表面授权(亦称为名义授权)的情况
– 解释实际授权可能是明示的或暗示的
</td><td></td></tr>
</table>

COMPETENCE 3.2	Monitor and Control Compliance with Legislative Requirements	IMO Reference

- states that express authority is given by words (spoken or written) such as when an officer is appointed by letter to command of a ship and authority is implied when it is inferred by the conduct of the parties and the circumstances of the case, such as when a ship Master is appointed to command by a shipowner, who thereby implicitly authorizes him to carry out, on the owner's behalf, all the usual things that fall within the scope of a Master's position, e.g. engagement and discharge of crew, signing of bills of lading, and purchasing of provisions
- explains that an exception to this would be where the principal has expressly placed a restriction on the implied authority of the agent, e.g. where the Master is expressly prohibited from signing bills of lading
- describes the different types of agent and agency
- explains that agents are normally either general agents or special agents
- explains that a general agent is an agent who has authority to act for his principal in all matters concerning a particular trade or business, or of a particular nature, many liner agents, for example, act as general agent in a particular city or country for one or more carriers
- explains that a special agent is an agent appointed for the carrying out of particular duties which are not part of his normal business activities
- explains that a special agent's authority is therefore limited by his actual instructions, most port agents are special agents since their authority does not extend beyond their actual instructions
- states that shipmasters are similarly special agents for purposes of engaging and discharging crew, purchasing ships' stores and bunkers, and making salvage agreements in certain cases
- outlines that an agent's duties to his principal are:
  - to perform his duties in person, using ordinary skill and diligence, and if he purports to have special skills, to use his special skills also;
  - to obey lawful instructions of his principal, and when he is not instructed on a particular matter, to act in his principal's best interests;
  - to disclose all information relevant to the agency to the principal, avoiding any conflict of interest;
  - to maintain confidentiality about matters communicated to him as agent, and not to disclose them to prospective third parties;
  - to keep proper accounts of all transactions and render them to his principal on request;
  - not to make extra profits from the agency without disclosing them to his principal
- explains that under the terms of voyage charters port agents are normally appointed, and therefore paid for, by the shipowner. However, many voyage charterers insist on nominating port agents, and are entitled to do so if the charter party is suitably claused to that effect
- explains where a charter party provides that "the vessel shall be consigned to Charterers' agents...", it means that the charterer will nominate agents
- explains that when on a time charter, most of the "voyage costs" associated with earning the freight or other revenue are normally for the time charterer's account, and it can be expected that port agents will be appointed by the charterer in order to look after his commercial interests

适任 3.2	立法要求的监督与控制	IMO 参考书目

– 阐述明示授权通过语言(口头或书面)设定,比如通过信件指定船长指挥船舶;当被从当事人的行为和事例的情节推断出来的时候,授权是暗示的,比如船东指定船长指挥船舶的时候,船东是在含蓄地授权他代表船东,处理船长范围内的一切常规事务,例如聘用和解聘船员、签发提单和购买食物
– 解释该原则不包括对隐含的代理权明确设定了限制,例如明确禁止船长签发提单
– 描述不同类型的代理人和代理机构
– 解释代理通常既不是总代理,也不是特别代理
– 解释总代理在一特定的贸易或业务或特殊性质的所有相关事宜中对其委托人负责,例如,许多班轮代理人作为一特定的城市或国家的一个或多个承运人的总代理
– 解释特别代理是被指定履行不属于其正常经营活动的一部分的一种特殊的职责
– 解释特别代理的授权因为受其委托人实际指示的限制, 大多数港口代理人是特别代理,因其授权并没有超出实际指示
– 船长聘用和解聘船员、购买船舶物料和燃料、在某些情况下签订救助协议,他们就类似特别代理
– 概述代理人对其委托人的职责如下:
  – 使用通常技能和勤奋来亲自履行职责,如果他声称有特殊技能,也用其特殊技能;
  – 服从委托人的合法指示,当他没有收到某一事项指示时,则采取对委托人最有利的行动;
  – 披露所有代理相关信息,避免任何利益冲突;
  – 有关代理事务方面保守秘密,不向潜在的第三方披露;
  – 保留所有交易的适当账目,一经委托人要求,即予提供;
  – 不赚取代理公司的额外利润,不对委托人隐瞒此事
– 解释按航次租船合同,港口代理人通常由船东指定并支付报酬。然而,许多承租人坚持指定港口代理人,并且,如租船合同对此适当签署条款的话,他们有权这么做
– 解释在租船合同规定“本船委托给承租人的代理人……”的情况下,这意味着承租人指定代理人
– 解释在期租合同下,与运费收入或其他收益相关的大多数“航次成本”通常计入承租人账户,可以预见,为照顾其商业利益,承租人指定港口代理人		

COMPETENCE 3.2	Monitor and Control Compliance with Legislative Requirements	IMO Reference

- explains that the charterer's obligation to provide and pay for agents may be in a "Charterers to provide" clause, or a separate Agency Clause or Consignment Clause
- explains that any "protecting" or "husbandry agent" used will be nominated and appointed by the shipowner
- explains that the shipping agents have to adhere to a Code of professional conduct given in United Nations Conference on Trade and Development, UNCTAD Minimum Standards For Shipping Agents, which states that the shipping agent shall:
  i. discharge his duties to his principal(s) with honesty, integrity and impartiality;
  ii. apply a standard of competence in order to perform in a conscientious, diligent and efficient manner all services undertaken as shipping agent;
  iii. observe all national laws and other regulations relevant to the duties he undertakes;
  iv. exercise due diligence to guard against fraudulent practices;
  v. exercise due care when handling monies on behalf of his principal(s)

1.6.13 Port of refuge procedures (2 hours)

- states that a "port of refuge" is a port or place that a vessel diverts to when her Master considers it unsafe to continue the voyage due to a peril that threatens the "common safety", e.g. when there is a dangerous ingress of water into the vessel, a dangerous shift of cargo, the vessel adopts an angle of loll, there is a serious fire on board, etc.
- explains that where such a deviation is for the preservation from peril of property involved in a common maritime adventure, it will usually constitute a general average act and the costs of the deviation to and stay at the port of refuge will be allowed in general average
- explains that where the shipowner or carrier is a party to a contract of carriage, discontinuation of the voyage is a deviation from the contract
- explains that a deviation to a port of refuge will be regarded as a justifiable deviation if the reason can be shown to be a valid one within the terms of the contract. All contractual rights would, in that case, be unaffected
- explains that if the reason for deviating could not be shown to be valid, the deviation would be considered unjustifiable and the consequences could be severe for the shipowner or carrier, in that it would probably constitute a repudiatory breach of the contract, making the owner/carrier liable for all costs of any accident to ship or cargo sustained during the deviation
- outlines that valid reasons for deviating to a port of refuge usually include:
  - weather, collision or grounding damage affecting seaworthiness of the ship;
  - serious fire;
  - dangerous shift of cargo;
  - serious machinery breakdown;
  - any other accident causing some serious threat to the vessel and cargo;
  - shortage of bunkers (if it can be proved that the vessel left port with adequate bunkers for the foreseeable voyage, and ran short as a consequence of weathering exceptionally severe weather, contamination, etc.)

适任 3.2	立法要求的监督与控制	IMO 参考书目

- 解释承租人提供和支付代理费的义务可含在“承租人提供”条款,或单独的代理条款或指定代理人条款中
- 解释任何“保卫代理人”或“船舶管理代理人”应由船东指定
- 解释航运代理人必须遵守联合国贸易与发展会议规定的专业行为准则——UNCTAD 航运代理人最低标准,规定航运代理人应:
  - i. 对其委托人履行诚实、正直、公正的职责;
  - ii. 具有适任能力,作为航运代理人,以认真、勤奋和有效的方式提供所有服务;
  - iii. 遵守与其履行职责相关的所有国家法律和规定;
  - iv. 恪尽职守以防范欺诈行为;
  - v. 代表委托人精心处理钱款

1.6.13 港口避难程序(2 学时)

- 阐述“避难港”是船长认为,由于威胁“共同安全”的危险使得继续航行不安全,而偏航所到达的港口或地点,例如进水危及船舶安全、货物危险性位移、船舶横倾至静止角、船舶严重火灾等
- 解释为避免处于共同海上危险中的财产风险而绕航,它通常构成共同海损行为,去往避难港和在港停留的绕航成本允许计入共同海损
- 解释在船东或承运人为运输合同　方的情况下,按该合同绕航为航次终止
- 解释如按合同条款能证明绕航理由为有效理由,则去往避难港的绕航将被认为是合理绕航。在此情况下,所有合同中的权利将不受影响
- 解释如不能证明绕航理由有效,则绕航将被认为不合理,那它可能将给船东或承运人带来可能构成毁约的严重后果,船东 / 承运人将对绕航期间发生的所有船舶事故或货物损坏费用负责
- 概述去往避难港的绕航的有效理由通常包括:
  - 天气、影响船舶适航性的碰撞或搁浅;
  - 严重火灾;
  - 货物危险性位移;
  - 严重机械故障;
  - 任何对船舶和货物造成严重威胁的其他事故;
  - 燃料短缺(如能证明,船舶携带足够燃料离港进行可预见的航程,由于遭受异常恶劣的天气或污染等,造成该船行驶距离过短。)

COMPETENCE 3.2	Monitor and Control Compliance with Legislative Requirements	IMO Reference

- explains that a "Port of refuge" is a term usually associated with a general average act since, under the York-Antwerp Rules, certain costs and expenses incurred in making for, entering, staying at and leaving a port or place of refuge, even where the ship returns to her port or place of loading, are admitted as general average
- describes the explanation given in Rule X for expenses at port of refuge provided in the York-Antwerp Rules
- explains that a port or place where a vessel seeks temporary shelter from adverse weather is not a port of refuge, since running for shelter is "ordinary" practice and not "extraordinary" in the context of Rule A of the York-Antwerp Rules
- explains that a "common maritime adventure" is said to be terminated on completion of discharge of cargo (or disembarkation of passengers) at the port of destination following a general average act. If the voyage is abandoned at an intermediate port (e.g. a port of refuge), then the adventure terminates at that port
- explains that a declaration of general average should be formally made in compliance with local law and custom before delivery of cargo at the termination of the voyage, in order to initiate an adjustment
- explains that the declaration is usually made by the shipowner or the Master, but in some countries any one of the interested parties may make it. The owners or agent should be able to advise on local requirements
- explains the procedure for any particular port or place of refuge in general, the following basic steps should be followed:
  - as soon as the decision is taken to discontinue the voyage and make for a port or place of refuge (whether under tow or otherwise) inform the owner and charterer (if any), stating the reason for the deviation
  - record the ship's position. Sound tanks for quantity of bunkers on board. From this point until departure from the port or place of refuge, keep accurate records of events and expenditure, etc., for eventual delivery to the owner and average adjuster
  - request the owner to arrange the appointment of an agent at the port of refuge to handle the vessel's visit
  - if the cause of the deviation is an "accident" inform the flag State
  - call the agent as soon as his identity is known. Pass ETA and information necessary for making preparations for the vessel's arrival, including tonnage, length, flag, P & I club, classification society, etc. Request the agent to notify:
    - Port State Administration if vessel is damaged or seaworthiness is affected.
    - harbour master or port authority. Inform port authority of the full facts, as the authority may want to keep vessel outside port until cargo is discharged, etc. Give details of the nature and severity of damage, mentioning any disabled navaids, steering gear, machinery, etc. State any pollution hazard.
    - pilot station, linesmen, boatman, customs, port health, immigration, etc.
    - local correspondent of the owner's P&I club. (See club handbook for name and address, or ask owners.) A representative from the correspondent firm, or a surveyor appointed by the correspondent, should attend on arrival.		

适任 3.2	立法要求的监督与控制	IMO 参考书目

- 解释“避难港”通常是与共同海损相关的术语,因为根据约克—安特卫普规则,船舶前往、进入、驻留和离开避难港口或地点,甚至返回装货港口或地点发生的某些成本和费用都被认定为共同海损
- 描述约克—安特卫普规则中第 X 条所给出的避难港口费用解释
- 解释船舶为躲避不利天气而寻求临时庇护的港口或地点不是避难港,因为按照约克—安特卫普规则中第 A 条,寻求庇护只是“通常”做法而不是“特别的”行为
- 解释据称,按照共同海损条例,在目的港一卸完货(或乘客离船)“共同海上风险”随即终止。如航次在中途港口(例如避难港)终止,则该风险在该港结束
- 解释在航次终止交付货物之前,应按当地法律和习惯做出共同海损声明,以启动理算
- 解释通常由船东或船长做出共同海损声明,但在某些国家可能由任一利益关系方做出。船东或代理应能按当地要求发出通知
- 解释在任何特定的避难港或地点的一般程序,应遵循以下基本步骤:
  - 一旦做出终止航次和(无论是在拖带下还是其他方式)前往避难港口或地点的决定,就通知船东和承租人(如有的话),说明绕航理由
  - 记录船位,液舱测深计算船上燃料数量。从此刻起直到离开避难港口或地点,保持事件和开支等的准确记录,最终交给船东和共同海损理算师
  - 要求船东安排指定避难港的代理以处理船舶来访
  - 如果绕航的原因是一个“事故”,则通知船旗国
  - 获知代理的身份后立刻致电。告知船舶抵港时间(ETA)和船舶抵达准备工作的必要信息,包括吨位、长度、船旗、船东保赔协会(P & I)、船级社等。要求代理通知:
    - 港口国主管机关,如船舶损坏或影响适航性。
    - 港务局长或港务局。告知港务局全部事实,因为港务局可能想要船舶待在港外,直到完成卸货等。详细介绍损坏性质和严重性,并提及任何失效的助航设备、操舵装置、机械等。说明污染危险。
    - 引航站、带缆人员、小艇人员、海关、港口卫生、移民官员等。
    - 船东的船东保赔协会(P & I)的当地联络人(姓名和地址见船东保赔协会手册,或询问船东)。船舶抵达时,联络人公司代表或联络人指定的验船师应在现场。		

COMPETENCE 3.2	Monitor and Control Compliance with Legislative Requirements	IMO Reference

- on arrival at the port or place of refuge, the salvor (if any) will require salvage security, which should be arranged by the owner and cargo owners. Failing this, the salvor may have vessel arrested pending satisfaction of his claim.
- obtain health clearance in accordance with local regulations (as advised by the agent).
- enter vessel in with Customs "under average".
- inform the owner (and charterer, if any) of vessel's safe arrival.
- owners will declare general average. (Any of the parties involved may declare general average, but the owners will normally do this since they are closest to "the action".)
- note protest as soon as possible but in any case within 24 hours, in compliance with local custom (ask the agent about this), reserving the right "to extend at a time and place convenient".
- where there is hull or machinery damage, the agent should be requested to notify local Lloyd's Agent (a requirement of the Notice of Claim and Tenders Clause in Institute Time Clauses – Hulls 1.10.83).
- hull and machinery underwriters normally instruct a surveyor, in major cases from the Salvage Association.
- where there is hull or machinery damage, a class surveyor, if available at the port, will inspect and report on the damage, stipulating repairs necessary for the vessel to maintain class. Temporary repairs may be acceptable.
- if no class surveyor is available, the class society should be contacted, and will advise the appropriate steps to take in order for class to be maintained until a port can be reached for survey, the old practice of requesting two independent Masters or engineers to inspect temporary repairs and issue a Certificate of Seaworthiness should no longer be necessary. Even where a class surveyor cannot reach a damaged ship, the classification society can usually be notified of the damage and asked for instructions.
- if cargo damage is probable, or cargo discharge is necessary before repairs can be made, call a hatch survey before commencing discharge. Employ only registered and unbiased surveyors recommended by the P&I club correspondent. Cargo interests should be notified so that they can appoint their own surveyors. Remember that cargo surveyors are appointed by cargo interests and may criticize the Master's actions or allege that the vessel was unseaworthy. Be guided by the P&I club correspondent as to who to allow on board and about making statements which may adversely affect the owner's legal position.
- if the voyage is being terminated and cargo owners are taking delivery of their consignments, General Average Bond and General Average Guarantee forms will first have to be signed. The owner's lien on cargo should be exercised if necessary; this should be discussed with the owner and agent.

适任 3.2	立法要求的监督与控制	IMO 参考书目
	– 一抵达避难港口或地点,救助方(如有的话)将要求应由船东和货主安排的救助担保。不能提供担保,则救助方可扣押船舶直到满足其索赔。 – 按照当地法规取得卫生许可(根据代理建议)。 – 与海关官员一起进入"受损"船舶。 – 通知船东(和承租人,如果有的话)船舶安全抵达。 – 船东将声明共同海损(虽然任何相关当事方均可声明共同海损,但通常由船东发出声明,因其最接近"该行为"。) – 在任何情况下,遵照当地惯例(有关问题询问代理)在 24 小时内尽快发出声明,保留在方便的时间和地点延伸声明的权利。 – 在船体或机械受损情况下,要求代理通知当地劳氏保险公司代理人(公会定期条款——船体 1.10.83 中的"索赔和报价通知条款"中的要求)。 – 在大多数情况下,船体和机械的保险商通常通知来自于救助协会的验船师。 – 在船体或机械受损时,如港口有船级社的验船师,他将检查损坏情况并报告,明确船舶保持船级所必需的修理。临时修理可以接受。 – 如港口没有船级社的验船师,则联系船级社,建议采取适当步骤保持船级,直到抵达可检验的港口, 原来的习惯做法要求两位独立的船长或工程师检查临时修理情况,签发适航证书,现已不再有必要。即使在船级社验船师不能抵达受损船舶的情况下,通常可通知船级社损坏情况,寻求指示。 – 如可能有货损或修理前必须卸货,则卸货前联系舱盖检验。只雇佣由船东保赔协会联络人推荐的经注册的、公正的验船师。应通知货方,以便其指定自己的检验员。 记住,货物检验员由货方指定,可能批评船长的行为或宣称船舶不适航。关于允许谁上船和谁可能做出不利于船东法律地位的声明, 听从船东保赔协会联络人指导。 – 如果航次终止,货主正交付其货物,将首先必须签署共同海损担保合约和共同海损担保书。如有必要,船东应行使对货物的留置权;船东和代理人应就此进行讨论。	

COMPETENCE 3.2	Monitor and Control Compliance with Legislative Requirements	IMO Reference

  - arrange cargo discharge (under survey) and either trans-shipment or warehousing of cargo during the repairs, if necessary. (This will depend on the length of time in port, nature of cargo, etc.)
  - on receipt of class surveyor's report re hull/machinery damage, the owner will advertise for tenders. (Superintendents and the Salvage Association surveyor will jointly attend to this, bearing in mind the Notice of Claim and Tenders Clause and underwriters' power of veto. Tenders should only be accepted with guidance from Salvage Association surveyor and Lloyd's or IUA Agent.)
  - carry out repairs under class and Salvage Association surveyors' guidance.
  - on completion of repairs, class surveyor will carry out another survey. If, in his opinion, the vessel is seaworthy he will issue an Interim Certificate of Class, and will send his report to the classification society. If acceptable to the society's committee, the vessel will retain class. If the class surveyor is employed by an authorized society, he may also issue provisional statutory certificates on behalf of MCA (or other flag State Administration) to enable the vessel to continue her voyage.
  - reload cargo (under survey) if voyage being continued.
  - extend Protest to include all details of the damage and repairs. Obtain copies for owners.
  - port agent will pay repairers. (If unpaid, repairers will have a maritime lien on the vessel.) Allow general average and Salvage Association surveyors (representing H&M insurers) to see the agent's account before paying.
  - send all relevant documents to the owner for onwards delivery to the average adjuster.
  - enter vessel outwards with Customs (in accordance with local regulations, as advised by the agent). Obtain outwards clearance.
  - continue the voyage.
- explains that in most general average cases the main evidence required for the adjustment comes from the various survey reports, supported by statements by witnesses and ship's records
- outlines the evidence required at port of refuge as listed below:
  - full and accurate records should be kept of the general average incident and the call at the port of refuge, including details of all the various parties involved and their actions
  - photographs and video footage may be useful; the general average statement may take more than a year to produce
  - where salvage services are engaged, a full record should be kept of the salvor's actions and of the equipment used by both parties

适任 3.2	立法要求的监督与控制	IMO 参考文献
	– 安排卸货(在检验情况下),在修船期间必要时或转运或放入仓库。(这取决于停留时间、货物性质等。) – 一收到船级社验船师关于船体 / 机械损坏的报告,船东就将通知报价。(机务主管和救助协会验船师将共同参与,牢记索赔和报价通知条款和保险商的否决权。应仅按照救助协会验船师和劳氏船级社或 IUA 代理人的指示接受报价。) – 按照船级社和救助协会验船师的指示进行修理 – 完成修理后,船级社验船师将进行另一项检验。如他认为船舶适航,将签发临时船级证书,并将报告送至船级社。如船级社认可,该船可保留船级。如船级社验船师由授权的船级社雇佣,他也可以代表英国海事与海岸警卫署(或其他船旗国主管机关)签发临时法定证书使船舶继续其航次。 – 如继续航行,则重新装载(在检验情况下)货物。 – 延伸声明以包含所有损坏和修理细节。从船东处获得副本。 – 港口代理将支付修理费用。(如不支付,则维修人员对船舶享有海上留置权。)允许共同海损和救助协会验船师(代表船体和机械承保人)支付前查看代理人账户。 – 将所有相关文件交给船东,以呈交给海损理算师 。 – 和海关官员一起登上开航船舶(按当地规定,由代理通知)获得出港证。 – 继续该航次。 – 解释在大多数共同海损情况下,理算所需主要证据来源于由证人和船舶记录所支持的各种检验报告 – 概述在避难港所要求的证据如下: – 保留的共同海损事故和停靠避难港的完整、准确的记录,包括涉及的所有各方及其行动的详情 – 照片和录像也许有用;做出共同海损声明可能需要一年以上的时间 – 在进行救助服务的情况下,应保留救助者行动和双方所用设备的完整记录	

COMPETENCE 3.2	Monitor and Control Compliance with Legislative Requirements	IMO Reference

- in order to assess the various contributory values, the average adjuster will require the following documents:
  - all general average security documents including signed average bonds, average guarantees, counterfoils of average deposit receipts and cancelled deposit receipts;
  - casualty reports from the Master;
  - certified extracts from deck and engine room logs;
  - copies of extended protests;
  - survey reports on hull and machinery damage;
  - survey reports on cargo lost or damaged by general average sacrifice;
  - account sales of any cargo sold;
  - copies of any shipping invoices;
  - copies of telexes;
  - accounts for disbursements incurred together with all supporting vouchers;
  - cargo valuation forms;
  - manifest of cargo on board at time of the general average act;
  - copies of bills of lading;
  - portage account for the voyage, and an account of stores consumed;
  - any other evidence relating to the casualty

1.6.14 Master/pilot relationship (2 hours)

- explains that the "maritime pilot" referred to in this section does not include deep-sea pilots or shipmasters or crew who are certificated or licensed to carry out pilotage duties in particular areas
- reviews the applicable contents of IMO Assembly resolution A.960(23), Recommendations on training and certification and operational procedures for maritime pilots other than deep-sea pilots
- explains that the law in most countries makes clear that while a maritime pilot is engaged in pilotage duties aboard a vessel in compulsory pilotage waters the pilot has conduct of the vessel and directs the navigation of the vessel, subject to the Master's overall command of the ship and the ultimate responsibility for its safety. In this respect, the navigation of a ship in compulsory pilotage waters is a shared responsibility between the pilot and the Master/bridge team
- explains that maritime pilots are expected to act in the public interest and to maintain a professional judgement that is independent of any economic pressures to the ship or other desires that do not comport with the needs of maritime safety. Because of these duties, a maritime pilot is not considered a member of the bridge "team", but a maritime pilot is expected to develop and maintain a cooperative, mutually-supportive working relationship with the Master and bridge team in recognition of the respective responsibility of each for the safe navigation of the vessel
- explains the provisions relating to pilotage contained in STCW, section A-VIII, part 4-1, paragraph 49
- explains that the Master has the right, and in fact the duty, to intervene or displace the pilot in circumstances where the pilot is manifestly incompetent or incapacitated or the ship is in immediate danger (*'in extremis'*) due to the pilot's actions or intentions

适任 3.2	立法要求的监督与控制	IMO 参考书目
– 为评估各种分摊费用,共同海损理算师将需要下列文件: – 所有共同海损担保文件,包括签订的共同海损合约、共同海损保证书、共同海损保证金收据和撤销了的保证金收据存根; – 船长的人员伤亡报告; – 经证明的航海日志和机舱日志摘录; – 延伸声明的副本; – 船体和机械损坏检验报告; – 计入共同海损牺牲的货物灭失或损坏检验报告; – 售卖任何货物的销售账目; – 任何货运发票的复印件; – 电传的复印件; – 发生的付款账目及其支持凭证; – 货物估价表; – 发生共同海损行为时的船上货物清单; – 提单副本; – 航次的搬运费账目和消耗的物料账目; – 有关人员伤亡的任何其他证据 **1.6.14 船长/引航员关系 (2 学时)** – 解释本节中提及的"海上引航员"不包括深海引航员或持有在特定地区履行引航职责的证书或执照的船长或船员 – 核查 IMO A.960(23)大会决议、有关除深海引航员之外的海上引航员培训和发证及操作程序建议中适用的内容 – 解释在大多数国家的法律中明确规定,在强制引航水域海上引航员在船从事引航职责时,引航员操船和引领船舶应接受船长总体指挥,船长承担最终的安全责任。在这方面,在强制引航水域船舶航行责任由引航员和船长 / 驾驶台团队共同承担 – 解释要求海上引航员代表公众利益而引航,保持独立于任何船舶经济压力或与海上安全需要不一致的其他欲望的专业判断。由于这些职责,海上引航员不被视作驾驶台团队成员,但在认清船舶航行安全的各自责任情况下,要求海上引航员与船长和驾驶台团队建立和保持一个合作、相互支持的工作关系 – 解释 STCW 公约 A-Ⅷ节,4-1 部分第 49 段中包括的有关引航规定 – 解释在引航员能力明显不适任或丧失能力或由于其行为或意图使船舶处于紧迫危险之中("紧急情况之中")的情况下,船长有权干预或取代引航员,这其实也是其职责		

COMPETENCE 3.2	Monitor and Control Compliance with Legislative Requirements	IMO Reference

- explains that the Master should generally:
  - see that the ship's navigation is monitored (including plotting fixes/positions on charts) as if there were no pilot on board;
  - ensure that officers, helmsmen, etc. attend to the pilot's requests with efficiency and courtesy;
  - instruct the officer-of-the-watch that he has charge of the vessel whilst under pilotage, unless specifically informed otherwise by the Master;
  - clearly state his/her opinion to the pilot on important matters of navigation and manoeuvring
- states that the shipowner is generally liable for the consequences of negligent navigation whilst the ship is under pilotage

1.7 Responsibilities under International Instruments affecting the Safety of the Ship, Passengers, Crew and Cargo (4 hours) R104

Ballast Water Convention 2004 (2 hours) R71

- defines the following:
  - ballast water
  - ballast water management
  - sediments
- describes the application of this convention
- describes the conditions where the application of this convention may be exempted
- describes the management and control requirement based on section B, regulation B1 to B6
- describes the annex – section A, B, C, D and E briefly
- describes the standards that need to be observed in ballast water exchange
- states under regulation B4 Ballast Water Exchange, all ships using ballast water exchange should:
  - whenever possible, conduct ballast water exchange at least 200 nautical miles from the nearest land and in water at least 200 metres in depth, taking into account Guidelines developed by IMO;
  - in cases where the ship is unable to conduct ballast water exchange as above, this should be as far from the nearest land as possible, and in all cases at least 50 nautical miles from the nearest land and in water at least 200 metres in depth
- states as per annex – section B Management and Control Requirements for Ships:
  - ships are required to have on board and implement a Ballast Water Management Plan approved by the Administration (regulation B1). The Ballast Water Management Plan is specific to each ship and includes a detailed description of the actions to be taken to implement the Ballast Water Management requirements and supplemental Ballast Water Management practices
- states that a new paragraph, 4, has been added with effect from July 1, 2010 to SOLAS chapter V, regulation 22 – Navigation bridge visibility. Some changes are operational and others introduce new requirements applicable to navigation records

适任 3.2	立法要求的监督与控制	IMO 参考书目
– 解释船长应通常: – 确保船舶航行处于监控(包括在海图上标绘船位 / 定位)之下,就如引航员不在船一样; – 确保高级船员、舵工等有效而礼貌地回应引航员的需求; – 指示值班驾驶员在引航期间对船舶负责,除非船长另行特别通知; – 有关航行和操纵的重要事务,向引航员清楚地表明其意见; – 船东通常对引航中的船舶航行疏忽负责		
1.7 国际公约中有关船舶、乘客、船员和货物安全的责任(4 学时) **2004 年压载水公约(2 学时)** – 定义下列术语: – 压载水 – 压载水管理 – 沉积物 – 描述该公约的适用范围 – 描述该公约的适用豁免的条件 – 描述基于公约 B 部分 B1 到 B6 条规定的管理和控制要求 – 简述附则——A、B、C、D、E 部分 – 描述在交换压载水中必须遵守的标准 – 阐述根据 B4 条规定压载水交换,交换压载水的所有船舶应: – 考虑到 IMO 制定的指南,可能时,在离最近陆地 200 海里以外,水深至少 200 米的水域进行压载水交换; – 在船舶不能按上述要求进行压载水交换的情况下,应尽可能远离陆地,在离最近陆地至少 50 海里以外,水深至少 200 米的水域交换压载水 – 阐述按照附则的 B 部分船舶管理和控制的要求: – 要求船舶具有主管机关批准的压载水管理计划并加以执行(B1 条规定)。压载水管理计划对每一艘船都是具体的,包括为满足压载水管理要求所采取行动的详细描述,是对压载水管理实践的额外补充 – 阐述 SOLAS 第 5 章 22 条规定——驾驶台能见度,新增加的第 4 段从 2010 年 7 月 1 日生效。有些变化是可操作的,其他的则引入了适用于航行记录的新要求		R104 R71

COMPETENCE 3.2	Monitor and Control Compliance with Legislative Requirements	IMO Reference
– states that as a consequence of this amendment, any increase in blind sectors or reduction in horizontal fields of vision resulting from ballast water exchange operations is to be taken into account by the Master before determining that it is safe to proceed with the exchange – states that as an additional measure, to compensate for possible increased blind sectors or reduced horizontal fields of vision, the Master must ensure that a proper lookout is maintained at all times during the exchange. Ballast water exchange must be conducted in accordance with the ship's ballast water management plan, taking into account the recommendations adopted by the IMO – explains that in accordance with SOLAS chapter V, regulation 28 – Records of navigational activities and daily reporting, the commencement and termination of the operation should be recorded – explains that the navigational records generated during ballast water exchange may be reviewed during ISM Audits and port State control inspections		
Port State control (2 hours) – explains that "port State control" is the inspection of foreign ships present in a nation's ports for the purpose of verifying that the condition of the ships and their equipment comply with the provisions of international conventions and codes, and that the ships are manned and operated in compliance with those provisions – explains that the primary responsibility for maintaining ships' standards rests with their flag States, as well as their owners and Masters. However, many flag States do not, for various reasons, fulfil their obligations under international maritime conventions, and port State control provides a useful "safety net" to catch substandard ships – states that a "port State control regime", where set up under a "memorandum of understanding" ("MOU") or similar accord between neighbouring port States, is a system of harmonized inspection procedures designed to target substandard ships with the main objective being their eventual elimination from the region covered by the MOU's participating States – states that there are eight international PSC agreements currently in force worldwide – identifies how to ascertain which port State agreement a particular port State might be party to and any areas of particular focus that may currently be in place – outlines that the list of certificates and documents which are checked during the inspection are: 1. International Tonnage Certificate (1969); 2. Passenger Ship Safety Certificate; 3. Cargo Ship Safety Construction Certificate; 4. Cargo Ship Safety Equipment Certificate; 5. Cargo Ship Safety Radio Certificate; 6. Exemption Certificate; 7. Cargo Ship Safety Certificate; 8. Document of Compliance (SOLAS 74, regulation II–2/54); 9. Dangerous Goods Special List or Manifest, or Detailed Stowage Plan;		R80

适任 3.2	立法要求的监督与控制	IMO 参考书目
– 阐述由于这项修正案，因压载水交换作业引起的盲区的增加和水平视野的减小都要由船长在决定压载水交换时安全航行之前加以考虑 – 阐述作为一项额外的措施,以补偿盲区的增加和水平视野的减小,船长必须确保在压载水交换期间的任何时候保持正规瞭望。压载水交换必须考虑 IMO 采纳的建议,按照船舶压载水管理计划进行 – 解释按照 SOLAS 第 5 章 28 条规定——航行活动和日常报告记录，应记录压载水交换的开始与结束 – 解释压载水交换期间产生的航行记录在 ISM 审核和港口国监督中可能受到检查		
港口国监督 (2 学时)		R80
– 解释"港口国监督"是港口国对来港外国船舶的检查,目的是核实船舶及其设备的情况符合国际公约和法规的规定以及船舶遵照规定配员与运营 – 解释保持船舶标准的主要责任在于船旗国、船东和船长。然而,由于种种原因,许多船旗国没有履行其在国际海事公约下的义务，而港口国监督提供了一个有用的"安全网"来针对低标准船舶 – 阐述在相邻国家之间签订"谅解备忘录"("MOU")或类似协议的情况下,"港口国监督制度"是一种协调检查程序系统,用来针对低标准船舶,其主要目标是最终消除"谅解备忘录"的参与国所涵盖区域的低标准船舶 – 阐述当前在世界范围内有 8 个生效的国际性 PSC 协议 – 指出如何确定一个特定港口国可能是协议的当事方,当前特别关注的领域 – 概述在港口国监督中检查的证书和文件清单如下: 1. 国际吨位证书(1969); 2. 客船安全证书; 3. 货船安全建造证书; 4. 货船设备安全证书; 5. 货船无线电安全证书; 6. 免除证书; 7. 货船安全证书; 8. 符合证明 (SOLAS 74, II-2/54 规定); 9. 危险货物特别清单或舱单,或详细的配载图;		

COMPETENCE 3.2	Monitor and Control Compliance with Legislative Requirements	IMO Reference
10. International Certificate of Fitness for the Carriage of Liquefied Gases in Bulk, or the Certificate of Fitness for the Carriage of Liquefied Gases in Bulk, whichever is appropriate; 11. International Certificate of Fitness for the Carriage of Dangerous Chemicals in Bulk, or the Certificate of Fitness for the Carriage of Dangerous Chemicals in Bulk, whichever is appropriate; 12. International Oil Pollution Prevention Certificate; 13. International Pollution Prevention Certificate for the Carriage of Noxious Liquid Substances in Bulk; 14. International Load Line Certificate (1966); 15. International Load Line Exemption Certificate; 16. Oil Record Book, parts I and II; 17. Shipboard Oil Pollution Emergency Plan; 18. Cargo Record Book; 19. Minimum Safe Manning Document; 20. Certificates of Competency; 21. Medical certificates (MLC and STCW); 22. Stability information; 23. Safety Management Certificate and copy of Document of Compliance (SOLAS chapter IX); 24. Certificates as to the ship's hull strength and machinery installations issued by the classification society in question (only to be required if the ship maintains its class with a classification society); 25. Survey Report Files (in case of bulk carriers or oil tankers in accordance with resolution A.744(18)); 26. For ro-ro passenger ships, information on the A/A max ratio; 27. Document of authorization for the carriage of grain; 28. Special Purpose Ship Safety Certificate; 29. High-Speed Craft Safety Certificate and Permit to Operate High-Speed Craft; 30. Mobile Offshore Drilling Unit Safety Certificate; 31. For oil tankers, the record of oil discharge monitoring and control system for the last ballast voyage; 32. The muster list, fire control plan and damage control plan; 33. Ship's logbook with respect to the records of tests and drills and the log for records of inspection and maintenance of life-saving appliances and arrangements; 34. Procedures and Arrangements Manual (chemical tankers); 35. Cargo Securing Manual; 36. Certificate of Registry or other document of nationality; 37. Garbage Management Plan; 38. Garbage Record Book; 39. Bulk carrier booklet (SOLAS chapter VI regulation 7); and 40. Reports of previous port State control inspections.		

适任 3.2	立法要求的监督与控制	IMO 参考书目
	10. 国际散装液化气体适装证书或散装液化气体适装证书,二者都适用; 11. 国际散装化学品适装证书或散装化学品适装证书,二者都适用; 12. 国际防止油污证书; 13. 国际防止散装有毒液体物质污染证书; 14. 国际船舶载重线证书 (1966); 15. 国际船舶载重线免除证书; 16. 油类记录簿,第 1 部分和第 2 部分; 17. 船舶油污应急计划; 18. 货物记录簿; 19. 最低安全配员证书; 20. 适任证书; 21. 医疗证书(MLC 和 STCW); 22. 稳性资料; 23. 安全管理证书和符合证明的副本 (SOLAS 公约第 9 章); 24. 相关船级社签发的有关船体强度和机械装置证书(仅在船舶保持船级社的船级时要求); 25. 检验报告档案(按照 A.744(18)大会决议,针对散货船或油船); 26. 对客滚船,关于 A/A 最大比率的资料; 27. 谷物运输授权文件; 28. 特殊用途船舶安全证书; 29. 高速船安全证书和经营许可证; 30. 移动式海上钻井装置安全证书; 31. 对于油船,上一航次的排油监控系统记录; 32. 应变部署表、防火控制图和破损控制图; 33. 有关测试和演习记录的船舶记录簿,救生艇设备设施检查和维护记录簿; 34. 程序和布置手册 (化学品船); 35. 货物系固手册; 36. 登记证书或其他的国籍文件; 37. 垃圾管理计划; 38. 垃圾记录簿; 39. 散货船手册(SOLAS 公约第 6 章第 7 条); 40. 以前港口国监督检查的报告。	

COMPETENCE 3.2	Monitor and Control Compliance with Legislative Requirements	IMO Reference

- outlines that in addition to the general control of above listed certificates and documents, examinations/inspections of the following are generally given priority by Port State Control Officer (PSCO):
  - Nautical publication (SOLAS 74 R V/20)
  - Navigational equipment (SOLAS 74 R V/12 and 19)
  - Emergency starting and running tests (SOLAS 74 R II-2 – 4.3)
  - Lifesaving equipment. Rafts FF (SOLAS 74 R III/20, 23, 26 and 29)
  - Emergency Generator (start/stop only) (SOLAS 74 R II-1/42 & 43)
  - Hull corrosion and damages (Load Lines) (SOLAS 74 R I/11)
  - Main engine & aux. engines (SOLAS 74 R II/26, 27 & 28)
  - Oily water separator 15 ppm alarm (MARPOL Annex I/16(1))
  - Oil discharge monitor (ODM) (MARPOL Annex I/16)
  - Charts corrected and proper scale (SOLAS 74 R V/20)
  - Fire safety Control plan (SOLAS 74 R II-2/20)
  - Ventilation inlets/outlets (SOLAS 74 R II-2/16.9 & 48)
  - Emergency training and drills (Log book rec. SOLAS 74 R III/18)
  - Emergency lighting/batteries (SOLAS 74 R II/42 & 43)
  - Deck and hatches corrosion and damages (LL 1966)
  - Steering gear – incl. auxiliary & emergency (Bridge inspection only – SOLAS 74 R V/19)
  - Cleanliness in engine room (SOLAS 74 R II-1/26 and ILO 134)
  - Cleanliness in accommodation (ILO 92 & 133)
- explains that the port State control inspections may be conducted on the following basis:
  - initiative of the port State Administration;
  - the request of, or on the basis of, information regarding a ship provided by another Administration;
  - information regarding a ship provided by a member of the crew, a professional body, an association, a trade union or any other individual with an interest in the safety of the ship, its crew and passengers, or the protection of the marine environment
- explains that the PSC inspections may be on random, targeted or periodical basis. The following types of PSC inspections are used in PSC:
  1. Initial inspection (random);
  2. More detailed inspection (escalated);
  3. Expanded inspection (targeted/periodical)
- states that the definition of inspection is: “A visit on board a ship to check both the validity of the relevant certificates and other documents, and the overall condition of the ship, its equipment, and its crew”
- explains that the certificates and documents listed above should therefore be readily available and presented to the PSCO at his request during the PSC inspection
- states that the definition of more detailed inspection is: “An inspection conducted when there are clear grounds for believing that the condition of the ship, its equipment, or its crew does not correspond substantially with the particulars of the certificates”

适任 3.2	立法要求的监督与控制	IMO 参考书目

- 概述除了以上所列一般性检查的证书和文件外,港口国监督检察官(PSCO)通常优先核查 / 检查下列事项:
  - 航海出版物 (SOLAS 74 R V/20)
  - 航海仪器 (SOLAS 74 R V/12 和 19)
  - 应急启动和运转试验(SOLAS 74 R II-2—4.3)
  - 救生设备、救生筏 FF (SOLAS 74 R III/20、23、26 和 29)
  - 应急发电机 (仅启动 / 停止) (SOLAS 74 R II-1/42、43)
  - 船体腐蚀和损坏(载重线) (SOLAS 74 R I/11)
  - 主机和辅机(SOLAS 74 R II/26、27、28)
  - 油水分离器 15 ppm 警报 (MARPOL 附则 I/16(1))
  - 排油监控装置 (ODM) (MARPOL 附则 I/16)
  - 海图改正和适当比例尺海图(SOLAS 74 R V/20)
  - 防火控制图(SOLAS 74 R II-2/20)
  - 通风进口 / 出口(SOLAS 74 R II-2/16.9、48)
  - 应急培训和演习(日志记录 SOLAS 74 R III/18)
  - 应急照明 / 蓄电池 (SOLAS 74 R II/42、43)
  - 甲板和舱口的腐蚀与损坏 (LL 1966)
  - 操舵装置——包括辅助和应急(仅在驾驶台检查——SOLAS 74 R V/19)
  - 机舱清洁(SOLAS 74 R II-1/26 和 ILO 134)
  - 生活区清洁 (ILO 92、133)
- 解释港口国监督检查可在以下基础上进行:
  - 港口国主管机关倡议;
  - 另一主管机关请求,或根据其提供的船舶相关信息;
  - 由船员、专业机构、协会、贸易联盟或对船舶、船员、乘客或海洋环境感兴趣的任何其他个人提供的船舶相关信息
- 解释港口国监督检查(PSC)可以是随机的、有针对性的或周期性的。港口国监督检查(PSC)有以下几类:
  1. 初次检查(随机的);
  2. 更详细的检查(扩大了的);
  3. 扩展检查(针对性的 / 周期性的)
- 阐述"检查"的定义为:"到船上进行的一次目的为检查相关证书和其他文件的有效性,以及船舶、设备及其船员总体情况的访问"
- 解释上面列出的证书和文件应该是现成的,在港口国监督检查期间应检查官的要求可随时呈递
- 阐述"更详细地检查"的定义为:"当有明显理由相信船舶、设备或船员与证书记载情况实际上不符时进行的检查"

COMPETENCE 3.2	Monitor and Control Compliance with Legislative Requirements	IMO Reference

- states that the definition of Clear grounds is: "Evidence that the ship, its equipment, or its crew does not correspond substantially with the requirements of the relevant conventions or that the Master or crew members are not familiar with essential shipboard procedures relating to the safety of ships or the prevention of pollution"
- outlines that "Clear grounds" to conduct a more detailed inspection include:
  1) the absence of principal equipment or arrangements required by the conventions;
  2) evidence from a review of the ship's certificates that a certificate or certificates are clearly invalid;
  3) evidence that documentation required by the conventions are not on board, incomplete, are not maintained or are falsely maintained;
  4) evidence from the PSCO's general impressions and observations that serious hull or structural deterioration or deficiencies exist that may place at risk the structural, watertight or weathertight integrity of the ship;
  5) evidence from the PSCO's general impressions or observations that serious deficiencies exist in the safety, pollution prevention or navigational equipment;
  6) information or evidence that the Master or crew is not familiar with essential shipboard operations relating to the safety of ships or the prevention of pollution, or that such operations have not been carried out;
  7) indications that key crew members may not be able to communicate with each other or with other persons on board;
  8) the emission of false distress alerts not followed by proper cancellation procedures;
  9) receipt of a report or complaint containing information that a ship appears to be substandard
- explains that the PSCO during a more detailed inspection generally takes the following into account:
  - structure;
  - machinery spaces;
  - conditions of assignment of load lines;
  - life-saving appliances;
  - fire safety;
  - regulations for preventing collisions at sea;
  - Cargo Ship Safety Construction Certificate;
  - Cargo Ship Safety Radio Certificates;
  - equipment in excess of convention or flag State requirements;
  - guidelines for discharge requirements under Annexes I and III of MARPOL 73/78 which includes:
    - inspection of crude oil washing (COW) operations;
    - inspection of unloading, stripping and prewash operations;
    - guidelines for control of operational requirements – which include:
      - muster list;
      - communication;
      - fire drills;
      - abandon ship drills;

适任 3.2	立法要求的监督与控制	IMO 参考书目
– 阐述“明显理由”的定义为:“船舶、设备或船员与相关公约的要求实际上不符的证据,或船长或船员不熟悉船上有关安全或防污染的基本程序的证据” – 概述需进行更详细检查的“明显理由”包括: 1) 缺乏公约所要求的基本设备或设施; 2) 通过证书检查证实,证书明显失效; 3) 公约所要求的文件不在船上、不完整,没有保持有效或虚假保持有效的证据; 4) 根据港口国监督检查官(PSCO)对船舶的总体印象和观察,可能发生严重的船体或结构恶化,或存在可能使船舶结构、水密或风雨密完整性处于危险之中的缺陷的证据; 5) 根据港口国监督检查官(PSCO)对船舶的总体印象或观察,在安全、防污染或航海仪器方面存在严重缺陷的证据; 6) 船长或船员不熟悉船上有关船舶安全或防污染的基本操作,或没有进行这种操作的信息或证据; 7) 关键船员可能无法互相沟通或与船上其他人员沟通的迹象; 8) 未按适当取消程序撤销发出的虚假遇险警报; 9) 收到船舶似乎是低标准船舶的报告或投诉信息 – 解释在更详细检查期间,港口国监督检查官(PSCO)通常考虑如下方面: – 结构; – 机器处所; – 载重线标志情况; – 救生设备; – 消防安全; – 海上避碰规则; – 货船安全构造证书; – 货船无线电安全证书; – 超出公约或船旗国要求的设备; – MARPOL 73 / 78 附则Ⅰ和Ⅲ排放要求的指南如下: – 原油洗舱作业(COW) 检查; – 卸货、扫线和预洗作业检查; – 作业控制指南包括: – 应变部署表; – 通信; – 消防演习; – 弃船演习;		

COMPETENCE 3.2	Monitor and Control Compliance with Legislative Requirements	IMO Reference

- damage control plan and Shipboard Oil Pollution Emergency Plan;
  - fire control plan;
  - bridge operation;
  - cargo operation;
  - operation of the machinery;
  - manuals, instructions etc.;
  - oil and oily mixtures from machinery spaces;
  - loading, unloading and cleaning procedures for cargo spaces of tankers;
  - dangerous goods and harmful substances in packaged form;
  - garbage;
- minimum manning standards and certification;
- STCW 78;
- ISM; and
- ISPS Code

- states that expanded inspection is an inspection conducted according to non-mandatory guidelines only once during 12 month period for certain types of ships and certain categories of age and size
- explains that oil tankers, bulk carriers, gas and chemical carriers and passenger ships are subject to expanded inspections once during a period of 12 months
- outlines the IMO RESOLUTIONS pertaining to Port State Controls are as follows:
  - A.9/Res.321 Procedures for the control of ships 12/11/1975
  - A.12/Res.466 Procedures of port state control 19/11/1981
  - A.15/Res.597 Amendments to the procedures for the control of ships 19/11/1987
  - A.19/Res.787 Procedures for port state control 23/11/1995
  - A 21/Res.882 Amendments to the procedures for port state control (resolution A.787(19) 25/11/1999
- states that the publication by IMO which gives the General Procedural Guidelines for Port State Control Officers are also of particular relevance to shipmaster
- explains that a record of port State control inspections including safety-related details of many ships is available on the internet from the Equasis database and may be viewed by any member of the public
- explains that Equasis forms part of the Quality Shipping campaign launched by the EU in 1997 which is formally supported by signatories from marine Administrations, classification societies, P&I clubs and the ITF
- explains that more than 40 organizations provide information to Equasis and is used heavily by charterers and insurers as well as marine Administrations with port State control functions

适任 3.2	立法要求的监督与控制	IMO 参考书目
– 破损控制图和船舶油污应急计划； – 火灾控制计划； – 驾驶台作业； – 货物作业； – 机械作业； – 手册、说明等； – 机器处所的污油和油性混合物； – 油船货舱的装、卸和洗舱程序； – 包装危险货物和有害物质； – 垃圾； – 最低配员标准和证书； – STCW 78； – ISM； – ISPS 规则 – 阐述扩大检查是按照非强制指南,对某些种类、某些船龄和大小的船舶在 12 个月内仅进行一次的检查 – 解释油船、散货船、液化气船、化学品船和客船须在 12 个月内接受扩人检查一次 – 概述有关港口国监督的 IMO 决议如下： – 1975 年 11 月 12 日通过的 A.9/321 决议,船舶监督程序 – 1981 年 11 月 19 日通过的 A.12/466 决议,港口国监督程序 – 1987 年 11 月 19 日通过的 A.15/597 决议,船舶监督程序修正案 – 1995 年 11 月 23 日通过的 A.19/787 决议,港口国监督程序 – 1999 年 11 月 25 日通过的 A.21/882 决议,港口国监督程序修正案 (A.787(19)决议) – 阐述 IMO 对港口国监督检查官颁布的一般程序指南,对船长也特别重要 – 解释任何公众也可在互联网上的 Equasis 数据库查看包括许多船舶安全相关细节的港口国检查记录 – 解释 Equasis 成为 1997 年由欧盟发起，并由海事主管机关、船级社、船东保赔协会(P&I)和 ITF 正式签署支持的优质航运活动的组成部分 – 解释 40 多个组织向 Equasis 提供信息，这些信息被承租人和保险公司以及海事主管机关大量运用于港口国监督		

COMPETENCE 3.2	Monitor and Control Compliance with Legislative Requirements	IMO Reference

1.8 Methods and aids to prevent pollution of the marine environment by ships (2 hours)

Convention of the Prevention of Marine Pollution by Dumping of Wastes and Other Matter (London Dumping Convention) (LDC) R106

- explains the aims of the Convention
- defines, for the purpose of the Convention:
  - dumping
  - wastes or other matter
  - special permit
  - general permit
- states that the dumping of wastes or other matter in whatever form or condition, as listed in annex I, is prohibited
- states that the dumping of wastes or other matter listed in annex II requires a prior special permit
- states that the dumping of all other wastes or matter requires a prior general permit
- explains that the provisions of Article IV do not apply when it is necessary to secure the safety of human life or of vessels in cases of 'force majeure' caused by stress of weather, or in any case which constitutes a danger to human life or a real threat to vessels
- states that such dumping should be done so as to minimize the likelihood of damage to human or marine life and must be reported immediately
- states that the Addendum to annex I contains regulations on the incineration of wastes at sea
- explains that the appropriate authority of a Contracting Party should issue prior special or general permits in respect of matter intended for dumping:
  - loaded in its territory
  - loaded by a vessel flying its flag when the loading occurs in the territory of a State not party to the Convention

International Convention Relating to Intervention on the High Seas in Cases of Oil Pollution Casualties, 1969 R107

- describes the rights of Parties to the Convention to intervene on the high seas following a maritime casualty
- defines, for the purposes of the Convention:
  - maritime casualty
  - ship
  - oil
  - related interests
- describes the provisions which a coastal State should apply when exercising the right to take measures in accordance with Article I

适任 3.2	立法要求的监督与控制	IMO 参考书目
1.8	**防止船舶污染海洋环境的方法和手段(2 学时)**	
	防止倾倒废物或其他物质污染海洋公约(伦敦倾倒公约)(LDC)	R106
	– 解释公约的目的	
	– 该公约的定义:	
	– 倾倒	
	– 废物及其他物质	
	– 特殊许可	
	– 一般许可	
	– 阐述无论以任何形式或条件都禁止倾倒附则Ⅰ中所列出的废物或其他物质	
	– 阐述附则Ⅱ中所列出的废物或其他物质事先需要特殊许可方可倾倒	
	– 阐述其他废物或其他物质需要事先获得一般许可方可倾倒	
	– 解释当在由天气影响而引起的“不可抗力”情况下,为保证人命或船舶安全,或者在任何危及人命安全或真正威胁船舶安全的情况下,条款Ⅳ规定不适用	
	– 阐述上述倾倒应把对人类或海洋生物危害的可能性降到最低并应立即报告	
	– 阐述附则Ⅰ的遗补,包括在海上焚烧废物的规定	
	– 解释缔约国有关当局应事先颁布关于倾倒物的特殊许可或一般许可:	
	– 在其领海装载	
	– 悬挂缔约国国旗在非缔约国领海装载	
	1969 年国际干预公海油污事件公约	R107
	– 描述公约缔约国成员干预下列公海油污事件的权利	
	– 该公约的定义:	
	– 海上人员伤亡	
	– 船舶	
	– 油类	
	– 相关利益方	
	– 描述沿海国家根据条款 1 使权利以采取措施时所适用的规定	

COMPETENCE 3.2	Monitor and Control Compliance with Legislative Requirements	IMO Reference
Protocol relating to Intervention on the High Seas in Cases of Pollution by Substances other than Oil, 1973 – describes the rights of Parties to the Protocol to intervene on the high seas following a maritime casualty – defines 'substances other than oil' – explains that the Protocol extends the rights and obligations of coastal States to cases involving imminent threat of pollution by substances other than oil		
International Convention on Civil Liability for Oil Pollution Damage,1969 (CLC 1969) – states that no claim for compensation may be made against the servants or agents of the owner – explains that, with certain exceptions, the owner may limit his liability by constituting a fund for the sum representing the limit of his liability with the Court of a Contracting State where the action is brought – states that claims in respect of expenses reasonably incurred by the owner voluntarily to prevent or minimize pollution damage rank equally with other claims against the fund – explains that where a fund has been constituted and the owner is entitled to limit his liability, no person having a claim for pollution damage resulting from that incident is entitled to exercise any rights over other assets of the owner and that the ship or any other property belonging to the owner should be released – states that the owner of a ship registered in a Contracting State and carrying more than 2,000 tons of oil in bulk as cargo is required to maintain insurance in the sum of his limit of liability – states that the appropriate authority of a Contracting State, after determining that the requirements have been complied with, should issue a certificate attesting that insurance or other financial security is in force – states that the certificate should be carried on board ship and a copy deposited with the relevant authorities – states that a Contracting State must not permit a ship under its flag to which this Article applies to trade without a certificate – states that Contracting States must ensure under their national legislation, that insurance or other security is in force in respect of any ship, whenever registered, entering or leaving their ports of offshore terminals if the ship actually carries more than 2,000 tons of oil in bulk as cargo		R108
1.9 National legislation for implementing international agreements and conventions (1 hour) – explains the process by which international agreements and conventions are ratified and implemented into national legislation		

<table>
<tr><td>适任 3.2</td><td>立法要求的监督与控制</td><td>IMO
参考书目</td></tr>
<tr><td colspan="2">1973 年干预公海非油类物质污染议定书
– 描述参与该议定书国家干预下列事故的权利
– 定义“非油类物质”
– 解释该议定书扩大了沿海国家干预涉及非油类物质污染紧迫威胁时的权利和义务
1969 年国际油污损害民事责任公约(CLC1969)
– 阐述不得对船东的雇员或代理人提出索赔请求
– 解释除某些情况外,船东可以通过事发地法庭,设立与其责任限制额总数相同的基金
– 阐述船东为防止或将污染损害等级降至最低,而主动采取行动产生的合理费用,可与其他索赔一样,向基金会提出索赔
– 解释当基金设立以后,船东有权去限制他的赔偿责任,任何由此事故所引起的污染损失而进行索赔的人不得对船东的其他资产行使权利,并且船舶或者任何属于船东的财产应解除留置
– 阐述要求在缔约国登记注册并载运 2 000 吨以上散装货油的船舶的船东投一份与其责任限制额相同的海上保险
– 阐述当确定要求得以满足后,船旗国的有关当局应颁发证书,证明保险或金融担保具有实效
– 阐述该证书应随船携带,并且有关当局保存副本
– 阐述依据本规定,缔约国严禁悬挂其国旗的船舶无证营运
– 阐述如果船舶载运 2 000 吨以上的散装货油,根据其国内立法,缔约国必须确保船舶保险或其他金融担保具有实效,无论该船何时登记,进入还是离开其沿岸码头
1.9 为履行国际协议和公约的国内立法(1 学时)
– 解释国际协议和公约被批准和填补国内立法的过程</td><td>

R108</td></tr>
</table>

<table>
<tr><td>COMPETENCE 3.3</td><td>Maintain Safety and Security of Crew and Passengers and the Operational Condition of Safety Equipment</td><td>IMO Reference</td></tr>
<tr><td colspan="2">TRAINING OUTCOMES:

Demonstrates a knowledge and understanding of:
3.3.1 LIFE-SAVING APPLIANCE REGULATIONS (SOLAS)
3.3.2 ORGANIZATION OF FIRE AND ABANDON SHIP DRILLS
3.3.3 MAINTENANCE OF OPERATIONAL CONDITION OF LIFE-SAVING, FIREFIGHTING AND OTHER SAFETY SYSTEMS
3.3.4 ACTIONS TO PROTECT AND SAFEGUARD ALL PERSONS ON BOARD IN EMERGENCIES
3.3.5 ACTIONS TO LIMIT DAMAGE AND SAVE THE SHIP FOLLOWING A FIRE, EXPLOSION, COLLISION OR GROUNDING</td><td>STCW Code table A-II/2</td></tr>
</table>

适任 3.3	维护船员和乘客的安全和治安与安全系统的操作条件	IMO 参考书目
培训效果: 讲授下列内容知识与理解: 3.3.1 救生设备规则(SOLAS) 3.3.2 消防和弃船演习的组织 3.3.3 救生、消防和其他安全系统运行条件的维护 3.3.4 紧急情况下保护和安保船上所有人员的行动 3.3.5 在火灾、爆炸、碰撞或搁浅的情况下降低损失和救助船舶的行动		STCW 公约 表 A-Ⅱ/2

COMPETENCE 3.3	Maintain Safety and Security of Crew and Passengers and the Operational Condition of Safety Equipment	IMO Reference
3.3.1 LIFE-SAVING APPLIANCE REGULATIONS (SOLAS) **Textbooks/Bibliography:** T42, T43, B59, B62 **Teaching aids:** A1, V95, V96, V100 Required performance: **1.1 Life-saving appliance regulations (SOLAS) (2 hours)** – demonstrates a thorough knowledge of the regulations concerning life-saving appliances and arrangements (SOLAS), including the LSA Code 3.3.2 ORGANIZATION OF FIRE AND ABANDON SHIP DRILLS Required performance: *Note that trainees must be familiar with the content and application of the requirements for the scheduling and organization of fire and abandon ship drills of IMO model courses 7.03, 1.23 and 2.03. This knowledge is considered so fundamental for much of the management level content within this course that there is merit in reviewing the operational level content quickly before covering the additional elements required at management level. The learning time has been reduced for many elements on the basis that trainees will be reviewing rather than learning much of this content at this level. It may be necessary for some trainees to refresh their knowledge of such techniques before undertaking this management level content* **2.1 Organization of fire and abandon ship drills** – prepares schedules for the conduct of fire and abandon ship drills so that all required drills and equipment are covered within required timeframes – discusses ways in which crew can be motivated to participate fully in drills – prepares plans for effective drills – organizes effective drills including the briefing, conduct and debriefing of the drill – discusses the process for ensuring that required changes are made to the safety management system and on board procedures as a result of the lessons learnt from drills 3.3.3 MAINTENANCE OF OPERATIONAL CONDITION OF LIFE-SAVING, FIREFIGHTING AND OTHER SAFETY SYSTEMS Required performance: **3.1 Maintenance of life-saving, firefighting and other safety systems** – discusses the use and upkeep of the SOLAS training manual in terms of the safety equipment provided and the required maintenance of this equipment – prepares procedures and checklists for the inspection of life-saving, firefighting and other safety systems on board – ensures that regular inspections of life-saving, firefighting and other safety systems on board are undertaken and that any deficiencies are identified and rectified – prepares procedures and schedules for the maintenance of life saving, firefighting and other safety systems on board – prepares schedules for the required survey of life-saving, firefighting and other safety systems on board		R2

适任 3.3	维护船员和乘客的安全和治安与安全系统的操作条件	IMO 参考书目
3.3.1　救生设备规则(SOLAS) **教科书/参考文献:**T42, T43, B59, B62 **教具:**A1, V95, V96, V100 技能要求: **1.1　救生设备规则(SOLAS)(2 学时)** – 表明充分了解有关救生设备和设施(SOLAS)的知识,包括 LSA 规则 3.3.2　消防演习和弃船演习的组织 技能要求: 注意:在完成这些要求的内容之前,学员必须熟悉 IMO 示范课程 7.03、1.23 和 2.03 中的船舶消防演习和弃船演习的计划与组织的内容和适用范围。本课程中的知识对多数管理级内容非常重要,以至于在涉及管理级额外要求的知识点之前,在迅速复习操作级内容方面颇具价值。基于学员将复习而不是学习该级别内容,已经减少了许多知识点的学时。对某些学员而言,在学习管理级内容之前,可能有必要更新这些技能的知识 **2.1　消防和弃船演习的组织** – 准备进行消防演习和弃船演习的时间表,以便在要求的时间段内,涵盖所有要求的演习内容和设备 – 讨论激励船员投入演习的方法 – 准备有效的演习计划 – 组织有效的演习,包括演习情况介绍、进行演习和演习情况汇报 – 讨论由于从演习中汲取了教训,需要对安全管理系统和船上程序做出改变的方法 3.3.3　救生、消防和其他安全系统运行条件的维护 技能要求: **3.1　救生、消防和其他安全系统的维护** – 从提供的安全设备和该设备的保养方面讨论 SOLAS 培训手册的使用与维护 – 准备船舶救生、消防和其他安全系统的检查程序与检查表 – 确保定期检查船舶救生、消防和其他安全系统,并识别和纠正任何缺陷 – 准备船舶救生、消防和其他安全系统的保养程序和时间安排表 – 准备需要检验的船舶救生、消防和其他安全系统时间安排表		R2

COMPETENCE 3.3	Maintain Safety and Security of Crew and Passengers and the Operational Condition of Safety Equipment	IMO Reference

– prepares for and supports the survey of life-saving, firefighting and other safety systems on board
– prepares procedures and checklists for the inspection of watertight doors, side scuttles, cross flooding arrangements, valves and other closing mechanisms
– prepares maintenance plans and procedures for watertight doors, side scuttles, cross flooding arrangements, valves and other closing mechanisms
 	
3.3.4 ACTIONS TO PROTECT AND SAFEGUARD ALL PERSONS ON BOARD IN EMERGENCIES
Textbooks: T3
Teaching aids: A1, V35
Required performance:
4.1 Actions to protect and safeguard all persons on board in emergencies (4 hours)
– states that some crew members will be assigned specific duties for mustering and control of passengers
– lists those duties as:
  – warning the passengers
  – ensuring that all passenger spaces are evacuated
  – guiding passengers to muster stations
  – maintaining discipline in passageways, stairs and doorways
  – checking that passengers are suitably clothed and that life jackets are correctly donned
  – taking a roll-call of passengers
  – instructing passengers on procedure for boarding survival craft or jumping into the sea
  – directing passengers to embarkation stations
  – instructing passengers during drills
  – ensuring that a supply of blankets is taken to the survival craft
	
	R1, R2

Rescue of persons from a vessel in distress or from a wreck This section includes content that is not directly contained within STCW 2010 but which is recommended to be included in training courses for management level officers – states why it is preferable to wait for daylight when no immediate danger exists – states that communications should be established between the ships and the method of rescue agreed upon when time permits – states that rescue boats or motor-lifeboats would be used if conditions permitted – states that unnecessary equipment should be removed from the boats and replaced by lifejackets, life buoys, blankets and a portable VHF radio – states that the rescue vessel should reconnoitre the area to see if there is any wreckage which could be a danger to boats – describes how both ships can spread oil in rough weather – describes the preparations for taking survivors on board from the boats		R1

<table>
<tr><th>适任 3.3</th><th>维护船员和乘客的安全和治安与安全系统的操作条件</th><th>IMO
参考书目</th></tr>
<tr><td colspan="2">– 准备和支持船舶救生、消防和其他安全系统的检验
– 准备水密门、舷窗、横贯进水设施、阀门和其他机械关闭装置的检查程序和检查表
– 准备水密门、舷窗、横贯进水设施、阀门和其他机械关闭装置的保养计划和程序

3.3.4 应急情况下保护和安保所有船上人员的行动
教科书:T3
教具:A1, V35
技能要求:</td><td></td></tr>
<tr><td colspan="2">4.1 应急情况下保护和安保所有船上人员的行动(4 学时)
– 阐述应分派给某些船员特定职责,以集合和控制乘客
– 列出职责如下:
　– 向乘客报警
　– 保证所有乘客撤离舱室
　– 指引乘客到集合地点
　– 维护通道、楼梯和门口的秩序
　– 检查确认乘客着装合适并正确穿上救生衣
　– 乘客点名
　– 指导乘客登艇和跳入海中的程序
　– 指导乘客到登艇位置
　– 指导乘客演习
　– 确保将毛毯带上救生筏</td><td>R1, R2</td></tr>
<tr><td colspan="2">遇难船或沉船人员救助
这部分的内容并不直接包含在 2010 年 STCW 公约之中,但建议列入对管理级人员培训课程中
– 阐述为何在没有紧迫危险时最好等待天亮
– 阐述当时间允许时,应建立船舶间通信和协商救助方式
– 阐述如情况许可,应使用救助艇或机动救生艇
– 阐述去掉艇上不必要的设备,以救生衣、救生圈、毛毯和便携式 VHF 代之
– 阐述救助艇应当侦察此区域,看是否有任何危及救助艇的残骸
– 描述两船如何在恶劣天气下洒油
– 描述把幸存者从救助艇上救上船的准备工作</td><td>R1</td></tr>
</table>

COMPETENCE 3.3	Maintain Safety and Security of Crew and Passengers and the Operational Condition of Safety Equipment	IMO Reference
– describes how to provide a lee and launch boats – describes how boats should approach the wreck and pick up survivors – describes the recovery of boats and survivors – describes the methods of rescue which may be used when sea conditions are too dangerous to use boats **Man-overboard procedure** – describes methods of recovering a person from the sea when heavy weather prevents the use of the normal manoeuvres and boats – describes and explains the actions to take when a person is reported missing at sea 3.3.5 ACTIONS TO LIMIT DAMAGE AND SAVE THE SHIP FOLLOWING A FIRE, EXPLOSION, COLLISION OR GROUNDING **Textbooks:** T10 **Teaching aids:** A1, V24, V25, V28, V29 Required performance: **5.1 Actions to limit damage and save the ship following a fire, explosion, collision or grounding (4 hours)** **Means of limiting damage and salving the ship following a fire or explosion** – describes the use and limitations of standard procedures and prepared contingency plans in emergency situations – describes methods of fighting fires (see IMO model course 2.03, Advanced training in fire fighting) – states that cooling of compartment boundaries where fire has occurred should be continued until ambient temperature is approached – explains the dangers of accumulated water from firefighting and describes how to deal with it – states that watch for re-ignition should be maintained until the area is cold – describes the precautions to take before entry to a compartment where a fire has been extinguished – describes the inspection for damage – describes measures which may be taken to plug holes, shore-up damaged or stressed structure, blank broken piping, make safe damaged electrical cables and limit ingress of water through a damaged deck or superstructure – outlines the measures to be taken when the inert-gas main and gas lines to a mast riser are fractured – states that continuous watch should be kept on the damaged area and temporary repairs – states that course and speed should be adjusted to minimize stresses and the shipping of water		R1 R1

适任 3.3	维护船员和乘客的安全和治安与安全系统的操作条件	IMO 参考书目
– 描述如何做一个下风和施放救生艇 – 描述救生艇如何接近沉船和救起幸存者 – 描述收艇和救上生存者 – 描述当海况太危险而不能使用救生艇时可能使用的救助方法 **人员落水程序** – 描述恶劣天气阻挠船舶不能正常操纵和使用救生艇时,海上救人的方法 – 描述和解释在海上报告人员失踪后所采取的行动		R1
3.3.5 发生火灾、爆炸、碰撞或搁浅后,限制船舶破损和救助船舶的行动 **教科书:**T10 **教具:**A1、V24、V25、V28、V29 技能要求: **5.1 在火灾、爆炸、碰撞或搁浅下降低损失和救助船舶的行动(4 学时)** **发生火灾或爆炸时降低损失和救助船舶的方法** – 描述紧急情况下标准程序和编制应急预案的使用与局限性 – 描述消防方法(参见 IMO 示范课程 2.03 高级消防训练) – 阐述发生火灾的舱室周围的冷却应持续进行,直到接近环境温度为止 – 解释消防积水的危险并描述如何处理 – 阐述应保持防复燃值班,直到该区域冷却 – 描述进入已熄火舱室之前应做的预防工作 – 描述损坏的检查 – 描述采取措施来塞紧洞口,撑起损坏或受力的结构,清空破裂的管路,使损坏的电缆安全可用和限制水从破损的甲板或上层建筑进入 – 概述惰性气体总管和大桅竖管破裂时要采取的措施 – 阐述保持对破损部位连续观察并做临时修理 – 阐述调整航向、航速,将受力和进水降到最低限度		R1

COMPETENCE 3.3	Maintain Safety and Security of Crew and Passengers and the Operational Condition of Safety Equipment	IMO Reference
Procedure for abandoning ship – states that a ship should only be abandoned when imminent danger of sinking, breaking up, fire or explosion exists or other circumstances make remaining on board impossible – states that a distress call should be transmitted by all available means until acknowledged – lists the information to include in the distress message – describes other distress signals which may be used to attract attention – describes the launching of boats and liferafts when the ship is listing heavily – describes the launching of boats and liferafts in heavy weather conditions – describes the use of oil to calm the sea surface and explains why fuel oil is not suitable		

适任 3.3	维护船员和乘客的安全和治安与安全系统的操作条件	IMO 参考书目
弃船程序 – 阐述仅当船舶存在沉没、毁灭、火灾或爆炸的紧迫危险或其他不可能在船停留的情况时方可弃船 – 阐述用所有可用的方法发送遇险呼叫直到收到回答 – 列出遇险信号包含的信息 – 描述其他可使用的招引注意的遇险信号 – 描述船舶横倾严重时施放救生艇筏 – 描述在恶劣天气情况下施放救生艇筏 – 描述海上防浪油的使用,并且解释为何燃油不合适		

COMPETENCE 3.4	Develop Emergency and Control Plans	IMO Reference
TRAINING OUTCOMES: Demonstrates a knowledge and understanding of: 3.4.1 PREPARATION OF CONTINGENCY PLANS FOR RESPONSE TO EMERGENCIES 3.4.2 SHIP CONSTRUCTION, INCLUDING DAMAGE CONTROL 3.4.3 METHODS AND AIDS FOR FIRE PREVENTION, DETECTION AND EXTINCTION 3.4.4 FUNCTIONS AND USE OF LIFE-SAVING APPLIANCES		STCW Code table A-II/2

适任 3.4	制订应急和处置计划	IMO 参考书目
培训效果： 讲授下列内容知识与理解： 3.4.1　突发事件应急预案的准备 3.4.2　包括破损控制的船舶建造 3.4.3　防火、探火、灭火的方法和手段 3.4.4　救生设备的功能和使用		STCW 公约 表 A-Ⅱ/2

COMPETENCE 3.4	Develop Emergency and Control Plans	IMO Reference

3.4.1 PREPARATION OF CONTINGENCY PLANS FOR RESPONSE TO EMERGENCIES
Textbooks/Bibliography: T3, T42, T43
Teaching aids: A1, V24, V25, V29
Required performance:
1.1 Contingency plans for response to emergencies (9 hours)
– draws up a muster list and emergency instructions for a given crew and type of ship
– assigns duties for the operation of remote controls such as:
  – main engine stop
  – ventilation stops
  – lubricating and fuel oil transfer pump stops
  – dump valves
  – CO_2 discharge
  – watertight doors
  – and for the operation of essential services such as:
    – emergency generator and switchboard
    – emergency fire and bilge pumps
– describes options for the division of the crew, e.g., into a command team, an emergency team, a back-up emergency team and an engine-room emergency team
– explains the composition of the emergency teams in the above objective
– states that crew members not assigned to emergency teams would prepare survival craft, render first aid, assemble passengers and generally assist the emergency parties as directed
– designates muster positions for the command team, both at sea and in port
– designates muster positions for the emergency teams
– states that the engine-room emergency team would take control of engine-room emergencies and keep the command team informed
– states that good communications between the command team and the emergency teams are essential
		
		R1, R2

适任 3.4	制订应急和处置计划	IMO 参考书目
3.4.1　突发事件应急预案的准备 **教科书/参考文献**:T3, T42, T43 **教具**:A1, V24, V25, V29 技能要求: **1.1　应对紧急事件的应急计划(9 学时)** – 拟订应变部署表和为给定船员、船型的应急指导 – 分派遥控操作职责,比如: 　– 停止主机 　– 停止通风 　– 停止滑油和燃油输送泵 　– 安全阀 　– 施放二氧化碳 　– 水密门 　– 对于基本服务的操作,比如: 　　– 应急发电机和配电板 　　– 应急消防泵和污水泵 – 描述船员分工的选项,例如分成指挥队、应急队、后备应急队和机舱应急队 – 解释上述目标的应急队的组成 – 阐述设有被分派至应急队的船员准备好救生艇、提供急救、集合乘客和按指示给予应急队成员一般协助 – 指定指挥队在港口和在海上的集合地点 – 指定应急队的集合地点 – 阐述机舱应急队将控制机舱的紧急情况,并向指挥队通报机舱情况 – 阐述指挥队和应急队保持良好通信至关重要	 R1, R2	

COMPETENCE 3.4	Develop Emergency and Control Plans	IMO Reference
– prepares contingency plans to deal with: – fire and/or explosion in specific areas, such as galley, accommodation, container stows on or under deck, engine-room or cargo space, including coordination with shore facilities in port, taking account of the ship's fire-control plan – rescue of victims from an enclosed space – water ingress into the ship – serious shift of cargo – piracy attack – being towed by another ship or tug – heavy-weather damage, with particular reference to hatches, ventilators and the security of deck cargo – rescue of survivors from another ship or from the sea – leakages and spills of dangerous cargo stranding – abandoning ship – explains how drills and practices should be organized – describes the role of a shipboard safety committee in contingency planning		
Actions to be taken when emergencies arise in port – describes actions to take in the event of fire on own ship, with particular reference to cooperation and communication with shore facilities – describes action which should be taken when fire occurs on a nearby ship or an adjacent port facility – describes the circumstances in which a ship should put to sea for reasons of safety – describes the actions to be taken when own ship is dragging anchor towards dangers in port – describes the actions which can be taken to avoid a ship dragging anchor towards own ship in an anchorage – describes the actions and precautions to take when a submarine cable is lifted by the anchor – describes how to buoy and slip an anchor – describes how an anchor may be recovered when no power is available at the windlass		R1, R2
3.4.2 SHIP CONSTRUCTION, INCLUDING DAMAGE CONTROL **Textbooks:** T5 **Teaching aids:** A1 Required performance:		
2.1 Flooding of compartments (4 hours) – defines: – margin line – permeability of a space		R1

适任 3.4	制订应急和处置计划	IMO 参考书目
– 拟订应急计划以处理: – 特殊区域起火和 / 或爆炸,如厨房、生活区、甲板上下堆装的集装箱、机舱或货舱,包括在港口与岸上设备的协调时考虑船舶的防火控制图 – 从封闭场所救援遇难者 – 船舶进水 – 货物严重移位 – 海盗袭击 – 由另一艘船舶或拖船拖带 – 恶劣天气下的损坏,尤其指舱口、通风筒和甲板货的系固 – 从海上或另一艘船上救援幸存者 – 危险货物溢漏 – 弃船 – 解释如何组织演习和实践 – 描述船舶安全委员会在制订应急计划中的作用		
当港口发生紧急情况时所采取的行动 – 描述本船发生火灾所采取的行动,尤指与岸上的协作与通信 – 描述火灾发生在临近船上或与本船附近的港口设施时所采取的行动 – 描述出于安全船舶应离港出海的情况 – 描述本船在港走锚,临近危险时所采取的行动 – 描述在锚地为避免走锚的船靠近本船时所采取的行动 – 描述当锚钩起海底电缆时所采取的行动和预防措施 – 描述如何设锚标和弃锚 – 描述当锚机失去动力时如何收锚		R1, R2
3.4.2 包括破损控制的船舶建造 **教科书:**T5 **教具:**A1 技能要求:		
2.1 舱室进水 (4 学时) – 定义: – 管路边缘 – 舱室渗漏率		R1

COMPETENCE 3.4	Develop Emergency and Control Plans	IMO Reference
– explains what is meant by ‘floodable length’ – explains what is meant by ‘permissible length of compartments’ in passenger ships – describes briefly the significance of the factor of subdivision – states the assumed extent of damage used in assessing the stability of passenger ships in damaged condition – summarizes, with reference to the factor of subdivision, the extent of damage which a passenger ship should withstand – describes the provisions for dealing with asymmetrical flooding – states the final conditions of the ship after assumed damage and, where applicable, equalization of flooding – states that the Master is supplied with data necessary to maintain sufficient intact stability to withstand the critical damage – explains the possible effects of sustaining damage when in a less favourable condition	

– distinguishes between ships of Type ‘A’ and Type ‘B’ for the purposes of computation of freeboard
– describes the extent of damage which a Type ‘A’ ship of over 150 metres length should withstand
– explains that a Type ‘A’ ship of over 150 metres length is described as a ‘one-compartment ship’
– describes the requirements for survivability of Type ‘B’ ships with reduced freeboard assigned
– summarizes the equilibrium conditions regarded as satisfactory after flooding
– states that damage to compartments may cause a ship to sink as a result of:
  – insufficient reserve buoyancy, leading to progressive flooding
  – progressive flooding due to excessive list or trim
  – capsizing due to loss of stability structural failure
		R78

3.4.3 METHODS AND AIDS FOR FIRE PREVENTION, DETECTION AND EXTINCTION **Textbooks:** **Teaching aids:** Required performance: **3.1 Methods and aids for fire-prevention, detection and extinction** – See IMO model course 2.03		
3.4.4 FUNCTIONS AND USE OF LIFE-SAVING APPLIANCES **Textbooks:** **Teaching aids:** Required performance: **4.1 Functions and use of life-saving appliances** – See IMO model course 1.23		

<table>
<tr><th>适任 3.4</th><th>制订应急和处置计划</th><th>IMO
参考书目</th></tr>
<tr><td colspan="2">
– 解释“可浸长度”的含义
– 解释客船“舱室许可长度”的含义
– 简述船舶分舱因素的意义
– 阐述假定损坏程度用以评估客船在受损情况下的稳性
– 概括在考虑分舱因素的情况下,客船能承受的损坏程度
– 描述处理非对称进水的规定
– 阐述假定破损对称进水后船舶的最终状态
– 阐述必须向船长提供必要的数据以保持足够的完整稳性来抵抗严重破损
– 解释当在不利情况下,遭受可能破损的影响性
– 为计算干舷,区分“A”型船和“B”型船
– 描述船长大于 150 米的“A”型船应能承受的破损程度
– 解释船长大于 150 米的“A”型船被描述为“一舱制”船舶
– 解释减少了指定干舷的“B”型船的生存能力要求
– 概括进水后被认为满意的平衡状态
– 阐述由于下列结果引起的舱室破损可导致船舶沉没:
  – 储备浮力不足,导致进一步进水
  – 横倾或纵倾过大引起进一步进水
  – 由于失去稳性而倾覆

3.4.3 防火、探火、灭火的方法和手段
教科书:
教具:
技能要求:
3.1 防火、探火、灭火的方法和手段
  – 参见 IMO 示范课程 2.03

3.4.4 救生设备的功能和使用
教科书:
教具:
技能要求:
4.1 救生设备的功能和使用
  – 参见 IMO 示范课程 1.23
</td><td>

R78</td></tr>
</table>

<table>
<tr><th>COMPETENCE 3.5</th><th>Use of Leadership and Managerial Skills</th><th>IMO Reference</th></tr>
<tr><td colspan="2">TRAINING OUTCOMES:

Demonstrates a knowledge and understanding of:
3.5.1 SHIPBOARD PERSONNEL MANAGEMENT AND TRAINING
3.5.2 RELATED INTERNATIONAL CONVENTIONS RECOMMENDATIONS, AND NATIONAL LEGISLATION
3.5.3 APPLICATION OF TASK AND WORKLOAD MANAGEMENT
3.5.4 EFFECTIVE RESOURCE MANAGEMENT
3.5.5 DECISION–MAKING TECHNIQUES
3.5.6 DEVELOPMENT, IMPLEMENTATION AND OVERSIGHT OF STANDARD OPERATING PROCEDURES</td><td>STCW Code table A-II/2</td></tr>
</table>

<table>
<tr><td>适任 3.5</td><td>领导力和管理技能的运用</td><td>IMO
参考书目</td></tr>
<tr><td colspan="2">培训效果:

讲授下列内容知识与理解:
3.5.1　船上人员管理和培训
3.5.2　相关的国际海事公约、建议和国内立法
3.5.3　任务管理和工作量管理的应用
3.5.4　有效的资源管理
3.5.5　决策技巧
3.5.6　标准作业程序的制定、实施和监督</td><td>STCW 公约
表 A-Ⅱ/2</td></tr>
</table>

COMPETENCE 3.5	Use of Leadership and Managerial Skills	IMO Reference
3.5.1 PERSONNEL MANAGEMENT, ORGANIZATION AND TRAINING ON BOARD SHIP **Textbooks/Bibliography:** T37 **Teaching aids:** A1, B225 – B246, V159, V160, V161, V162, V163, V164, V165, V166 Required performance: *Note that trainees should be familiar with the content and application of the operational level IMO model course 1.39, Leadership and teamwork. This knowledge is considered so fundamental for much of the management level content within this course that there is merit in reviewing the operational level content quickly before covering the additional elements required at management level. The learning time has been reduced for many elements on the basis that trainees will be reviewing rather than learning much of this content at this level. It may be necessary for some trainees to refresh their knowledge of this content before undertaking this management level content* **1.1 Shipboard personnel management (10 hours)** **Principles of controlling subordinates and maintaining good relationships** – identifies sources of authority and power – discusses theories on how effective authority and power may be enhanced or diminished by management level officers on ships – reviews theories in cultural awareness and cross cultural communication – discusses strategies that management level officers could adopt to enhance their effectiveness in managing crews of different cultures – reviews theories in human error, situational awareness, automation awareness, complacency and boredom – discusses strategies that management level officers can adopt to optimize situational awareness and to minimize human error and complacency of individuals and teams – reviews theories in leadership and teamwork – discusses strategies that management level officers can adopt to enhance leadership and teamwork – discusses theories of personnel motivation and relates these to shipboard situations encountered by management level officers – explains that an individual's motivation and well being may be affected by both real and perceived influences on board ship and at home – discusses strategies that management level officers could adopt to optimize the motivation of individuals and teams – discusses theories on coaching individuals and teams to improve performance – discusses approaches to managing and improving the performance of oneself, individuals and teams – prepares for and conducts a simulated formal performance review – identifies the impact of repeated harassment including bullying on individuals – recognizes indications that crew members may be physically or mentally unwell or badly demotivated – describes strategies that can be adopted when a crew member is believed to be physically or mentally unwell or badly demotivated – describes strategies that management level officers can take to ensure that crew remain physically well and are encouraged to remain physically active		R1

适任 3.5	领导力和管理技能的运用	IMO 参考书目
3.5.1 船上人员管理、组织和培训 **教科书/参考文献**:T37 **教具**: A1, B225—B246, V159, V160, V161, V162, V163, V164, V165, V166 技能要求: 注意:在完成这些要求的内容之前,学员必须熟悉操作级 IMO 示范课程 1.39"领导力与团队工作"的内容和适用范围。本课程中的知识对多数管理级内容非常重要,以至于在涉及管理级额外要求的知识点之前,在迅速复习操作级内容方面颇具价值。基于学员是复习而不是学习该级别内容,已经减少了许多知识点的学时。对某些学员而言,在学习管理级内容之前,可能有必要更新这些技能的知识 **1.1 船上人员管理(10 学时)** **管理下属和保持良好关系的原则** – 确定权威和权力的来源 – 讨论船舶管理级船员如何增强或减弱有效的权威和权力的理论 – 文化意识与跨文化交际的理论综述 – 讨论管理级船员在提高不同文化船员效率方面可采取的策略 – 人为失误、情境意识、自动化操作意识、自满和厌倦的应用理论综述 – 讨论管理级船员优化情境意识和尽量减少人为失误和个人及团队自满方面可采取的策略 – 领导力与团队工作的理论综述 – 讨论管理级船员提高领导力和团队工作方面可采取的策略 – 讨论人员激励理论并将其与管理级船员面临的船舶形势联系起来 – 解释个人的动机和良好状态既可能受到现实的影响,也可感受到船上和家庭的影响 – 讨论管理级船员优化个人动机方面可采取的策略 – 讨论指导个人和团队提高绩效的有关理论 – 讨论管理和提高自己、个人和团队绩效的方法 – 准备和模拟进行一个正式的绩效考核 – 辨识重复骚扰包括欺辱行为对个人的影响 – 识别船员可能的生理或心理上不适或严重消极的迹象 – 描述当船员生理或心理上不适或严重消极时可采取的策略 – 描述管理级船员,为确保船员保持身体健康,鼓励保持体力活动可以采取的策略		R1

COMPETENCE 3.5	Use of Leadership and Managerial Skills	IMO Reference
– explains the need for management level officers to be fully familiar with the requirements of national law relating to crew employment and of all crew agreements in place on the ship – discusses the process for signing on and discharging crew under national law – discusses the need to ensure that new crew are appropriately certificated, competent and familiarized with the safety management system, security plan, working procedures and equipment of the ship – explains that procedures for conducting investigations and applying consequences in disciplinary situations are governed by national law, codes of conduct, employment agreements and company procedures – explains the process for investigating and applying consequences in disciplinary situations under relevant national law and procedures – explains the formal process for addressing continuing levels of unacceptable performance by a crew member under national law – explains the process for investigating and responding to incidents of harassment or bullying of crew members under national law – explains requirements for handling crew wages, advances and allotments when this is done by management level officers on board ship		

1.2 Training (6 hours)
Training methods
– reviews training methods that could be adopted on-board ship
– discusses the effectiveness of training methods that can be adopted for training
  – in attitude
  – in skills
  – in knowledge
– describes the preparation needed before the start of a training session
– discusses methods for ensuring that crew are motivated to participate fully in training
– demonstrates how to conduct a training session for a given topic
– lists the areas in which training is required by regulation including the requirements of SOLAS
– identifies other topics where training might be desirable
– delivers a training session to other members of the class
– discusses the resources that may be available on board ship that can be used for training
		R2

适任 3.5	领导力和管理技能的运用	IMO 参考书目
	– 解释需要管理级船员完全熟悉国内法律关于船员雇佣的要求和所有在船协议的要求 – 讨论按国内法律签约船员和解雇船员的流程 – 讨论需要确保新船员持有相应证书、适任并熟悉安全管理系统、保安计划、工作程序和船舶设备 – 解释对违纪情况进行调查和实施结果的程序由国家法律、行为规范、雇佣协议和公司程序所控制 – 解释按国内有关法律和程序对违纪情况进行调查和实施结果的流程 – 解释按国内法律处理一位船员持续的不可接受绩效的正式流程 – 解释按国内有关法律对船员骚扰或欺辱事件的调查和相应流程 – 解释对船上管理级船员管理船员工资、预付款和分配的要求	

1.2	**培训(6 学时)**
	培训方法
	– 审查船上可能采用的培训方法
	– 讨论可用作培训方法的有效性
	  – 态度方面
	  – 技能方面
	  – 知识方面
	– 描述在训练课开始前所需的准备工作
	– 讨论确保船员积极参与全部培训的方法
	– 示范如何就特定主题上培训课
	– 列出规则要求的培训范围，包括 SOLAS 公约所要求的
	– 确认可能希望的其他培训主题
	– 向班上其他成员提供培训课
	– 讨论船上可用作培训的资源
		R2

COMPETENCE 3.5	Use of Leadership and Managerial Skills	IMO Reference
3.5.2 RELATED INTERNATIONAL CONVENTIONS RECOMMENDATIONS, AND NATIONAL LEGISLATION **Textbooks/Bibliography:** **Teaching aids:** A1, V14, V15 Required performance:		STCW Code table A-II/2
2.1 Related international maritime conventions and national legislation (4 hours) **ISM Code** – explains the principles underlying the ISM Code – describes the content and application of the ISM Code **STCW Convention** – explains the principles underlying the STCW Convention – describes the content and application of the STCW Convention – explains how to implement the regulations for ensuring fitness for duty – states that seafarers new to a particular type of vessel require ship specific shipboard familiarization – describes what shipboard familiarization may involve for watchkeeping officers – describes what tasks or duties elementary basic safety familiarization involves for a watchkeeping officer – describes how to organize shipboard training and how to maintain records – states that penalties are prescribed for breaches of STCW Convention,1978, as amended requirements and that these are determined by the flag State – states that national legislation is required to implement the provisions of an international convention – states that for STCW Convention, 1978, as amended, national legislation is subject to scrutiny and checking by IMO appointed persons		R1

– states national legislation may differ from one flag to another
Maritime Labour Convention (MLC)
– demonstrates a working knowledge of the Maritime Labour Convention provisions relating to the management of personnel on board ship, with particular reference to:
  – engagement of crew
  – employment conditions
  – crew entitlements and repatriation
  – medical requirements
		Reg. I/14

适任 3.5	**领导力和管理技能的运用**	**IMO 参考书目**

3.5.2 相关的国际海事公约、建议和国内立法
教科书/参考文献:
教具:A1, V14, V15
技能要求:
2.1 相关的国际海事公约和国内立法(4 学时)
ISM 规则
– 解释 ISM 规则下的原则
– 描述 ISM 规则的内容和适用范围
STCW 公约
– 解释 STCW 公约下的原则
– 解释 STCW 公约的内容和适用范围
– 解释如何执行规则以确保适于职责
– 阐述条约规定特种船上的新到船员对船舶要有具体的熟悉内容
– 描述值班驾驶员应该熟悉船上什么内容
– 描述值班驾驶员应该熟悉的基本安全任务与职责
– 描述如何组织船上培训并保存记录
– 阐述对于违反 1978 年 STCW 公约的,应按修正案要求,由船旗国决定处罚
– 阐述要求国内立法执行国际公约的规定
– 阐述按照经修订的 1978 年 STCW 公约,国内立法要由 IMO 指定人员进行监督和检查
– 阐述各船旗国国内立法有所不同
海事劳工公约 (MLC)
– 说明海事劳工公约条款中有关船上人员管理的工作知识,特别是关于:
  – 船员的雇佣
  – 雇佣条件
  – 船员权利和遣返
  – 医疗需求
		STCW 公约
		表 A-Ⅱ/2
		
		R1
		
		Reg.I/14

COMPETENCE 3.5	Use of Leadership and Managerial Skills	IMO Reference

3.5.3 APPLICATION OF TASK AND WORKLOAD MANAGEMENT
 	
Textbooks/Bibliography: T27
Teaching aids: A1
Required performance:
3.1 Task and workload management (8 hours)
– reviews theories on applying task and workload management from IMO model course 1.39, Leadership and teamwork
– explains that the scope of activity and conflict between activities managed by management level officers is broader than for operational level officers and requires greater task and workload management ability
– plans the task and workload allocation for significant shipboard activities so that the following are considered:
  – human limitations
  – personal abilities
  – time and resource constraints
  – prioritization
  – workload, rest and fatigue
– discusses strategies to monitor the effectiveness of task and workload management during an activity and to adjust the plan as necessary
– discusses strategies to ensure that all personnel understand the activity to be undertaken and their tasks in this
– discusses whether the encouragement of a challenge and response environment is appropriate to the task and workload management of particular shipboard tasks
– discusses the importance of debriefs and reflection after activities have been conducted to identify opportunities for improving task and workload management
		STCW Code table A-II/2

适任 3.5	领导力和管理技能的运用	IMO 参考书目
3.5.3　任务管理和工作量管理的应用 **教科书/参考文献**:T27 **教具**:A1 技能要求: **3.1　任务管理和工作量管理 (8 学时)** – 回顾 IMO 示范课程 1.39——领导力与团队工作中有关应用任务管理和工作量管理的理论 – 解释管理级船员所涉及的活动范围和活动之间的矛盾比操作级船员要求更广泛的任务管理和工作量管理能力 – 计划船上重大活动的任务和工作量分配以便考虑如下因素: 　– 人的局限性 　– 个人能力 　– 时间和资源约束 　– 优先次序 　– 工作量、休息和疲劳 – 讨论监控任务管理和工作量管理的有效性和必要时调整计划的策略 – 讨论确保所有人员理解该活动,参加活动人员知晓其任务的策略 – 讨论鼓励面对相应的工作环境对船上特定任务管理的任务和工作量管理是否合适 – 讨论活动结束后的汇报与反思,以确认改进任务管理和工作量管理机遇的重要性		STCW 公约 表 A-Ⅱ/2

COMPETENCE 3.5	Use of Leadership and Managerial Skills	IMO Reference
3.5.4 EFFECTIVE RESOURCE MANAGEMENT **Textbooks/Bibliography:** T27 **Teaching aids:** A1, V103, V104, V106, V107 Required performance *Note that trainees should be familiar with the content and application of the operational level IMO model course 1.39, Leadership and teamwork in terms of resource management. This knowledge is considered so fundamental for much of the management level content within this course that there is merit in reviewing the operational level content quickly before covering the additional elements required at management level. The learning time has been reduced for many elements on the basis that trainees will be reviewing rather than learning much of this content at this level. It may be necessary for some trainees to refresh their knowledge of this content before undertaking this management level content* **4.1 Application of effective resource management at a management level (10 hours)** – reviews theories on effective communication – demonstrates effective communication in simulated or real situations involving communications on board ship and between ship and shore – discusses how management level officers can encourage other personnel to use effective communications – reviews theories on effective resource allocation, assignment and prioritization – demonstrates the effective allocation, assignment and prioritization of resources when managing simulated or real shipboard activities – reviews theories on decision making that considers team experience – demonstrates the ability to involve team member effectively in decision making when managing simulated or real shipboard activities – reviews theories on assertiveness and leadership – discusses appropriate leadership styles and levels of assertiveness for management level officers in a range of shipboard activities – demonstrates the ability to apply appropriate leadership styles and levels of assertiveness when managing simulated or real shipboard activities – reviews theories on obtaining and maintaining situational awareness – demonstrates the ability to obtain and maintain situational awareness when managing complex simulated or real shipboard activities – reviews theories on the use of short and long term strategies – demonstrates the ability to apply short and long term strategies when managing simulated or real shipboard activities		STCW Code table A-II/2

适任 3.5	领导力和管理技能的运用	IMO 参考书目
3.5.4 有效的资源管理 **教科书/参考文献:** T27 **教具:** A1、V103、V104、V106、V107 技能要求: 注意:在完成这些要求的内容之前,学员必须熟悉操作级 IMO 示范课程 1. 39“领导力与团队工作”的内容和适用范围。本课程中的知识对多数管理级内容是如此重要,以至于在涉及管理级额外要求的知识点之前,在迅速复习操作级内容方面颇具价值。基于学员是复习而不是学习该级别内容,已经减少了许多知识点的学时。对某些学员而言,在学习管理级内容之前,可能有必要更新这些技能的知识 **4.1 管理级有效的资源管理的运用(10 学时)** – 关于有效沟通的理论综述 – 示范在模拟环境或真实在船进行通信的有效沟通,包括船上、船岸间的有效沟通 – 讨论管理级船员可如何鼓励其他人员利用有效沟通 – 回顾关于有效的资源配置、分配和优先次序的理论 – 当进行模拟或真实船上活动时,示范有效的资源配置、分配和优先次序 – 回顾考虑团队经验决策的理论 – 当进行模拟或真实船上活动时,示范在决策中使团队成员有效参与 – 回顾自信和领导力的理论 – 讨论管理级船员在一系列船上活动中适当的领导风格和自信水平 – 当进行模拟或真实船上活动时,示范运用适当的领导风格和自信水平 – 回顾获得和保持情境意识的理论 – 当进行复杂模拟或真实船上活动时,示范获得和保持情境意识的能力 – 回顾利用短期和长期策略的理论 – 当进行模拟或真实船上活动时,示范运用短期和长期策略的能力	STCW 公约 表 A-Ⅱ/2

COMPETENCE 3.5	Use of Leadership and Managerial Skills	IMO Reference
3.5.5 DECISION-MAKING TECHNIQUES **Textbooks/Bibliography:** T27 **Teaching aids:** A1 Required performance: *Note that trainees should be familiar with the content and application of the operational level IMO model course 1.39, Leadership and teamwork in terms of decision-making technique. This knowledge is considered so fundamental for much of the management level content within this course that there is merit in reviewing the operational level content quickly before covering the additional elements required at management level. The learning time has been reduced for many elements on the basis that trainees will be reviewing rather than learning much of this content at this level. It may be necessary for some trainees to refresh their knowledge of this content before undertaking this management level content* **5.1 Situation and risk assessment (2 hours)** – reviews theories of situation and risk assessment – discusses formal and informal approaches to risk assessment – identifies typical risks that management level officers may have to assess – demonstrates the ability to effectively assess risk in the planning and conduct of simulated or real shipboard activities **5.2 Identify and generate options (2 hours)** – reviews theories on identifying and generating options – demonstrates the ability to identify and generate options when making decisions as a management level officer in simulated or real shipboard activity **5.3 Selecting course of action (2 hours)** – reviews theories on selecting the course of action in making decisions – demonstrates the ability to select appropriate courses of action when making decisions as a management level officer in simulated or real shipboard activity **5.4 Evaluation of outcome effectiveness (1 hour)** – explains how to carry out the evaluation of outcome effectiveness and the importance of doing it 3.5.6 DEVELOPMENT, IMPLEMENTATION AND OVERSIGHT OF STANDARD OPERATING PROCEDURES **Textbooks/Bibliography:** **Teaching aids:** A1 Required performance: **6.1 Development, implementation and oversight of standard operating procedures (1 hour)** – discusses approaches to developing standard operating procedures (SOPs) – explains the methods to implement the SOPs – explains why it may be desirable for there to be oversight and approval of many SOPs and explains the dangers associated with it		STCW Code table A-II/2

<table>
<tr><td>适任 3.5</td><td>领导力和管理技能的运用</td><td>IMO
参考书目</td></tr>
<tr><td colspan="2">3.5.5　决策技巧
教科书/参考文献: T27
教具: A1
技能要求:
注意:在完成这些要求的内容之前,学员必须熟悉操作级 IMO 示范课程 1. 39“领导力与团队工作”的内容和适用范围。本课程中的知识对多数管理级内容非常重要,以至于在涉及管理级额外要求的知识点之前,在迅速复习操作级内容方面颇具价值。基于学员是复习而不是学习该级别内容,已经减少了许多知识点的学时。对某些学员而言,在学习管理级内容之前,可能有必要更新这些技能的知识
5.1　情境和风险评估(2 学时)
– 回顾情境和风险评估理论
– 讨论正式和非正式的风险评估方法
– 确定管理级船员可能必须评估的典型风险
– 在计划和进行模拟或真实在船活动过程中,示范有效风险评估的能力
5.2　识别和设计替代方案 (2 学时)
– 回顾关于识别和设计替代方案的理论
– 在模拟或真实在船活动方面,当管理级船员进行决策时,示范确定和设计替代方案的能力
5.3　选择行动方式 (2 学时)
– 回顾关于在决策过程中选择行动方式的理论
– 在模拟或真实在船活动过程中,当管理级船员进行决策时,示范选择适当行动方式的能力
5.4　结果的有效性评价(1 学时)
– 如何进行有效性评估以及有效性评估的重要性

3.5.6　标准作业程序的制定、实施与监督
教科书/参考文献:
教具: A1
技能要求:
6.1　标准作业程序的制定、实施和监督(1 学时)
– 讨论制定标准作业程序(SOPs)的方法
– 履行 SOPs 的方法
– 解释为什么想要进行监督和批准 SOPs,解释与它相关的危险</td><td>STCW 公约
表 A-Ⅱ/2</td></tr>
</table>

<table>
<tr><td>COMPETENCE 3.6</td><td>Organize and Manage the Provision of Medical Care on Board</td><td>IMO Reference</td></tr>
<tr><td colspan="2">TRAINING OUTCOME:

Demonstrates a knowledge and understanding of:
3.6.1 MEDICAL PUBLICATIONS
.1 International Medical Guide for Ships
.2 International Code of Signals (Medical Section)
.3 Medical First Aid Guide for Use in Accidents Involving Dangerous Goods</td><td>STCW Code table A-II/2</td></tr>
</table>

<table>
<tr><td>适任 3.6</td><td>船上医护的组织和管理</td><td>IMO
参考书目</td></tr>
<tr><td colspan="2">培训效果:

讲授下列内容知识与理解:
3.6.1　医学出版物
　.1　国际船舶医疗指南
　.2　国际信号规则(医疗部分)
　.3　危险货物事故医疗急救指南</td><td>STCW 公约
表 A-Ⅱ/2</td></tr>
</table>

<table>
<tr><th>COMPETENCE 3.6</th><th>Organize and Manage the Provision of Medical Care on Board</th><th>IMO Reference</th></tr>
<tr><td colspan="2">3.6.1 USE AND CONTENT OF THE FOLLOWING PUBLICATIONS:
– INTERNATIONAL MEDICAL GUIDE FOR SHIPS
– MEDICAL SECTION OF INTERNATIONAL CODE OF SIGNALS
– MEDICAL FIRST AID GUIDE FOR USE IN ACCIDENTS INVOLVING DANGEROUS GOODS
Textbooks/Bibliography: T13, T26, T33
Teaching aids: A1, A2, V108
Required performance:
1.1 International Medical Guide for Ships (0.5 hour)
– describes the content and application of the above publication
– extracts and applies information for given situations
1.2 International Code of Signals (Medical Section) (0.5 hour)
– describes the content and application of the above publication
– constructs and interprets messages
1.3 Medical First Aid Guide for Use in Accidents Involving Dangerous Goods (3 hours)
– describes the content and application of the above publication
– extracts and applies information for given situations</td><td>

R32</td></tr>
</table>

<table>
<tr><th>适任 3.6</th><th>船上医护的组织和管理</th><th>IMO
参考书目</th></tr>
<tr><td colspan="2">3.6.1 下述出版物的使用和内容：
– 国际船舶医疗指南
– 国际信号规则(医疗部分)
– 危险货物事故医疗急救指南
教科书/参考文献:T13, T26, T33
教具:A1, A2, V108
技能要求：
1.1 国际船舶医疗指南(0.5 学时)
– 描述上述出版物的内容和适用范围
– 特定情况下的信息摘录与使用
1.2 国际信号规则(医疗部分) (0.5 学时)
– 描述上述出版物的内容和适用范围
– 制作和解释信息
1.3 危险货物事故医疗急救指南(3 学时)
– 描述上述出版物的内容和适用范围
– 特定情况下的信息摘录与使用</td><td>

R32</td></tr>
</table>

Part D3: Instructor Manual

The following notes are intended to highlight the main objectives or training outcomes of each part of the function. The notes also contain some material on topics which are not adequately covered in the quoted references.

On completion of training for this function officers will have knowledge of the principal structural members of a ship and methods of construction. They will understand the theory of stability and trim and be able to use tables, diagrams and stress calculators to plan loading and ballasting so as to maintain satisfactory stability and trim (taking account of applicable IMO recommendations concerning intact stability) and to ensure that hull stresses remain within acceptable limits.

The effects of damage to, and the consequent flooding of, a compartment on the trim and stability of a ship and the counter-measures to be taken will be understood.

Officers will also be thoroughly conversant with the certificates required to be on board, their periods of validity and the procedures for their renewal.

The officers will also be aware of their legal obligations and responsibilities concerning international provisions for the safety of the ship, crew, passengers and cargo and for the prevention of pollution from the ship.

They will also be able to follow the correct procedures for all matters concerning the crew: their engagement and discharge, treatment of wages and deductions, discipline and dealing with disciplinary offences, the discharge of a sick seaman abroad, repatriation, deceased seamen and engagement of substitutes.

Officers will have sufficient knowledge of shipping documents related to cargo and the shipowner's liabilities and obligations in respect of charter parties and the carriage of cargo to enable them to protect the ship's interests.

Officers will be capable of organizing and managing the crew for the safe and efficient operation of the ship and be able to draw up an organization for dealing with emergencies. Officers will also know the requirements for training in the operation and maintenance of safety equipment and be able to implement that training on board.

On completion of training for this function officers will be able to use plans and tables or diagrams of stability and trim data to calculate the ship's initial stability, draughts and trim for any given disposition of cargo and other weights. They will also be able to determine whether stresses on the ship are within permitted limits by the use of stress data, calculating equipment or software. The fundamental actions to take in the event of partial loss of intact buoyancy will be understood.

Training concerned with fire prevention and firefighting is covered in IMO model course 2.03.

Training concerned with proficiency in medical care on board ship is covered in IMO model course 1.15.

D3部分:教员手册

以下说明的目的是为了突出各部分职能的主要目标或训练结果。该说明还包含一些在引用的参考文献中没有充分涉及的主题的材料。

完成这项功能培训,驾驶员将具有船舶的主要结构构件和建造方法的知识。他们将懂得稳性和吃水差,能够使用表格、曲线和应力计算器计划装载和压载,以保持令人满意的稳性和吃水差(关于完整稳性考虑适用的IMO建议),确保船体应力保持在可接受的范围内。

将懂得舱室破损和随后的进水对船舶稳性和吃水差的影响并采取对策。

船员还将透彻地熟悉船上需要的证书及其有效期和换证程序。

船员也将注意到有关船舶、船员、乘客和货物的安全及船舶防污染的相关国际规定的法律义务和责任。

他们还将能遵守所有有关船员事务的正确程序:雇佣和解聘船员,工资待遇和扣款,纪律和违纪行为的处理,在国外生病海员、遣返、已故海员的离船和替代者的雇佣。

船员将具有货物装运单据和在租船合同与运输货物方面船东的责任和义务的知识,以使其能保护船方利益。

船员将能组织和管理船员进行安全而有效的船舶作业,并能建立一个组织应对紧急情况。他们还将知道安全设备操作和维护方面的要求,并能在船进行该项培训。

完成本职能的培训,驾驶员将能使用平面图和表格或稳性和吃水差数据曲线,计算任何给定货物和其他重量分布的船舶初稳性、吃水和吃水差。他们还将能通过利用应力数据,包括计算设备或软件确定船舶所受应力是否在许可极限内。将懂得在完整浮力部分损失的情况下,采取的主要行动。

关于防火和消防的培训包括在IMO示范课程2.03中。

关于船上医护培训包括在IMO示范课程1.15中。

Function 3: Controlling the Operation of the Ship and Care for Persons on Board at the Management Level

3.1 CONTROL TRIM, STABILITY AND STRESS

3.1.1 FUNDAMENTAL PRINCIPLES OF SHIP CONSTRUCTION, TRIM AND STABILITY (102 hours)

Shipbuilding materials **(3 hours)**

It is not the intention that officers have knowledge of ship design practice or a detailed knowledge of materials. The focus of teaching should be so that they can explain why various kinds of steel are used in different areas of a ship and understand the advantages and disadvantages of alloys in common use, and how they are maintained.

High Tensile Steel (HTS) has a low corrosion margin and poor resistance to fatigue failures. However, due to a lighter weight of material, compared with mild steel, for the equivalent strength it has been widely used in ship construction.

Brittle fracture occurs when a normally elastic material fractures without any sign of deformation before failure. The structure may not even be highly stressed at the time. The fracture is often initiated at a small notch in a plate edge or at a small fault in a weld. The tendency to brittle fracture is much greater at low temperatures and there is a temperature, depending upon the particular properties of the steel, above which it will not occur. The classification societies specify the use of grade E steel, which has high notch ductility, for those parts of ships above a certain length where thick plates subject to high stresses are found.

Welding **(3 hours)**

If the training institute has an engineering department with welding facilities, the opportunity to use their expertise and equipment should be taken.

Bulkheads **(4 hours)**

The subdivision of passenger ships is dealt with in subject area 3.4.2.1, Ship Construction and Damage Control.

Watertight and Weathertight Doors **(3 hours)**

The provisions of SOLAS for drills and inspections of watertight doors and related damage control devices have been included with the details of construction and operation.

Corrosion and its prevention **(4 hours)**

Trainees should not be required to remember the galvanic series for seawater. It should be used for reference when dealing with corrosion cells and the suitability of metals as anodes for sacrificial anodes.

功能3:管理级船舶作业管理和人员管理

3.1 控制吃水差、稳性和应力

3.1.1 船舶结构、吃水差和稳性的基本原理 (102学时)

造船材料 **(3学时)**

意图并非是要船员具备船舶设计实操或详细的材料知识。教学的重点应该是使他们可以解释为何各种钢材用在船舶不同区域,理解常用合金的优缺点和如何保养合金。

高强度钢(HTS)具有低的腐蚀裕度和较差的抗疲劳能力。然而,由于与低碳钢相比,同等强度下其材料的重量轻,已被广泛用于船舶建造。

普通弹性材料断裂前无任何变形迹象,此时脆性断裂就发生了。该结构甚至可能太注重于时间上。裂缝往往起始于钢板边缘上一个小缺口或焊接上的一个小缺陷。在低温下,脆性断裂的趋势要大得多,钢的特性不同,其发生脆性断裂的温度也不同。船长超过某一长度的船舶的厚钢板承受高应力的部分,船级社指定使用具有高缺口延展性的E级钢。

焊接 **(3学时)**

如果培训机构具有一个焊接设施的工程部门,就应利用机会使用他们的专业知识和设备。

隔舱壁 **(4学时)**

课程章节3.4.2.1——船舶建造和破损控制中涉及客船分舱内容。

水密门和风雨密门 **(3学时)**

SOLAS公约有关水密门及相关破损控制设施的演习和检查规定已包含在建造和作业细节中。

腐蚀和防腐蚀 **(4学时)**

不应要求学员记住海水的电位系列。当处理腐蚀电池和作为牺牲阳极的金属的适用性时将其作为参考。

Many paints contain poisonous substances and release toxic fumes as solvents evaporate. The vapours of most paint solvents will produce flammable or explosive mixtures with air in poorly ventilated spaces.

The risks are greatest when using spray equipment in enclosed spaces. Personnel must wear breathing apparatus, sources of ignition must be excluded and ventilation must be provided while work is in progress. Precautions for entering enclosed spaces should be taken after painting has been completed until the paint has thoroughly dried and no risk of release of vapour remains. Manufacturers' instructions regarding protective clothing and safety precautions should be followed.

Surveys and dry-docking **(2 hours)**

This section deals with the surveys and inspections required by classification societies. The requirements for survey under international conventions are dealt with in subject module 3.2, Maritime Law. The annual inspection required by the International Convention on Load Lines, 1966, is usually carried out by a classification society surveyor, acting on behalf of the flag State Administration. The inspection is similar to that required for the classification society's annual survey.

The hardeners that are used in two-pack (or bi-pack) polyurethane and epoxy paints are toxic and may also cause allergic reactions following contact with skin. Protective clothing and disposable gloves should always be worn when working with these paints.

Stability **(83 hours)**

Calculations on box-shaped vessels have been introduced at a number of places in this syllabus. They are included to illustrate basic principles and to aid trainees' understanding of actual ships' data. The appendix to this instructor manual contains stability data and capacity tables for use in the preparation of exercises. Instructors should make a collection of data for other ships as the opportunity arises. The application of the principles of stability to determining the final draught, trim and initial GM for a given complete distribution of cargo is included in the function, Cargo Handling and Stowage.

Approximate calculation of areas and volumes

This section covers the use of the trapezoidal rule and Simpson's rules for the calculation of areas. The derivation of Simpson's rules and their use for finding moments or second moments of area has not been included. The calculation of volume where the given ordinates are areas is covered.

The use of Simpson's rules is required for finding areas under a *GZ* curve, for checking compliance with recommendations on intact stability. Trainees should also be able to apply them for calculating areas of decks and volumes of compartments aboard ship.

Effects of density

In tidal estuaries the density of the water may vary considerably according to the state of the tide. When checking draughts or freeboard near completion of loading it is essential to check

许多油漆含有有毒物质,当溶剂蒸发时释放出有毒气体。在通风不良的场所,大多数油漆溶剂的蒸气会产生易燃或与空气混合会爆炸的物质。

在封闭的空间中使用喷雾设备的风险是最大的。工作期间人员必须佩戴呼吸器,火源必须排除,并提供通风。喷漆完毕后进入封闭场所应采取预防措施,直到油漆彻底干燥并无释放蒸气的危险存在。应遵守制造商关于防护服和安全预防措施的指示。

检验和进入干船坞 **(2学时)**

本节涉及船级社要求的检验和检查。在课程内容章节3.2——海事法中涉及国际公约对检验的要求。1966年国际载重线公约所规定的年度检验,通常由船级社验船师代表船旗国主管机关执行。该检查类似于船级社年度检验的检查。

用于两重(双重)聚氨酯和环氧树脂油漆中的固化剂是有毒的,与皮肤接触后可引起过敏反应。在使用这些油漆时,应始终穿防护服和戴一次性手套。

稳性 **(83 学时)**

本大纲中的许多地方都引入了对箱形船的计算。列入它们是为了说明基本原理和帮助学员了解实际船舶的数据。本教员手册中的附录包含准备在练习中使用的稳性数据和舱容表。在适当时机,教员应选择数据用于其他船舶。货物装卸和积载职能中包括在给定全部货物分配情况下,应用稳性原理确定最终吃水、吃水差和初稳性高度。

面积和体积的近似计算

本节涵盖了使用梯形法则和辛普森法则计算面积。没有包含辛普森法则的拓展及其用来求面积矩或面积的二阶矩。包括了在给定坐标区域情况下计算体积。

要求使用辛普森法则求*GZ*曲线的面积,以核查符合完整稳性建议情况。学员还应能应用它们计算船上的甲板面积和舱室体积。

密度的影响

有潮汐河口的水密度可能随潮汐的不同会有很大的变化。当装货接近完成检查吃水或干舷的时候,同时必须检查密度:使用当天早些时候得到的密度可能会导致较大的误差。

the density at the same time: using a density obtained earlier in the day could lead to appreciable error.

The term 'inertia' and the abbreviation 'I' are used in keeping with common practice. They may also appear in a ship's hydrostatic data. Strictly, it is the transverse second moment of area of the tank which is involved. Trainees should understand the concept of second moments of area but the method of determining them in general is not required. The formula for a rectangular surface should be known.

Stability at moderate and large angles of heel

The equation $BM = I / V$ has been quoted partly to show that the BM is a function of the ship's dimensions and state of loading and partly to explain the typical behaviour of KM as the draught is increased from light ship conditions. Use is also made of the equation in the treatment of damage stability. The proof of the equation is not required.

GZ curves will normally be constructed from KN curves, but trainees should be able to correct a GZ curve when the value of KG differs from that used in drawing the curve, either by drawing a new curve or by superimposing the curve of GG_1 sin (angle of heel) on the GM should be used as an aid to constructing the curve at small angles should not be expected to deduce the GM from a given curve.

Figure 1 shows a ship with its centre of gravity, G_1, at a distance GG_1 horizontally from the centreline. When inclined to an angle θ, the righting lever is G_1Z_1.

$$G_1Z_1 = GZ = GY$$
$$= GZ - GG_1 \cos \theta$$

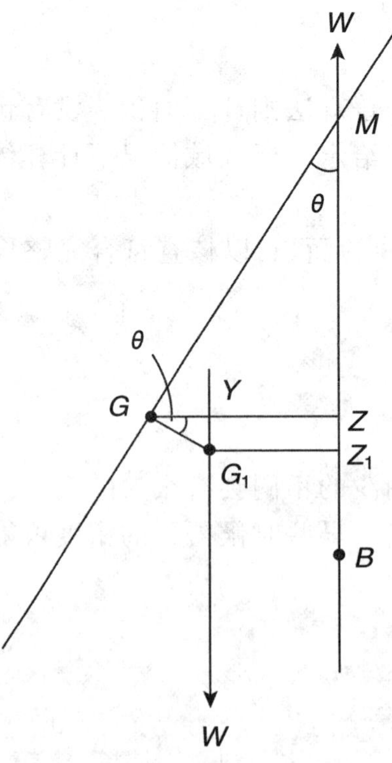

Figure 1

在实践中通常保留"惯性"和缩写"I"的用法。它们还可能出现在船舶静水力参数中。严格地说,它是相关液舱的横向二阶面积矩。学员应理解二阶面积矩的概念,但一般不要求懂得其求取方法。应知晓矩形表面公式。

中等角度和大角度横倾时的稳性

已引用公式$BM = I / V$以部分表明,BM是船舶尺度和装载状态的函数,并部分解释当吃水从空船状态增加时,KM的典型运动。在处理破损稳性中还用到了该公式。不需证明该公式。

通常从KN曲线构建GZ,但当KG不同于在构建曲线所用的值时,学员应能修正GZ,既可画一条新曲线,也可在GM上叠加GG_1×横倾角的正弦曲线,以有助于构建小角度时的曲线,而不应期望学员从给定曲线中推导GM值。

图1表明船舶重心为G_1,至中心线水平距离为GG_1。当倾斜至θ角时,复原力臂为G_1Z_1。

$$
\begin{aligned}
G_1Z_1 &= GZ = GY \\
&= GZ - GG_1 \cos\theta
\end{aligned}
$$

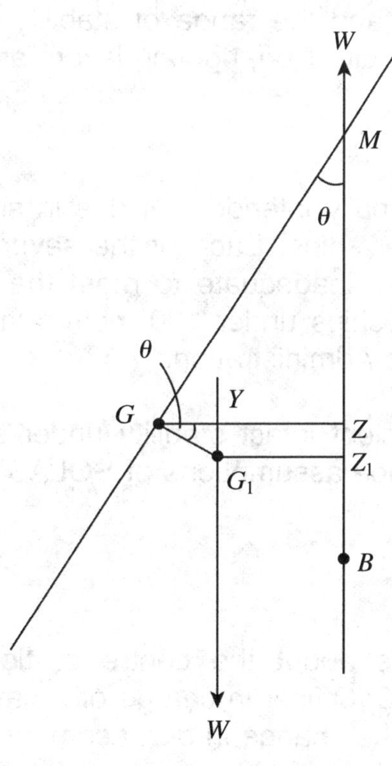

图 1

The values of GZ derived from KN curves can be reduced to $GG_1 \cos\theta$ before plotting or the curve $GG_1 \cos\theta$ can be superimposed on the GZ curve, as shown in Figure 2.

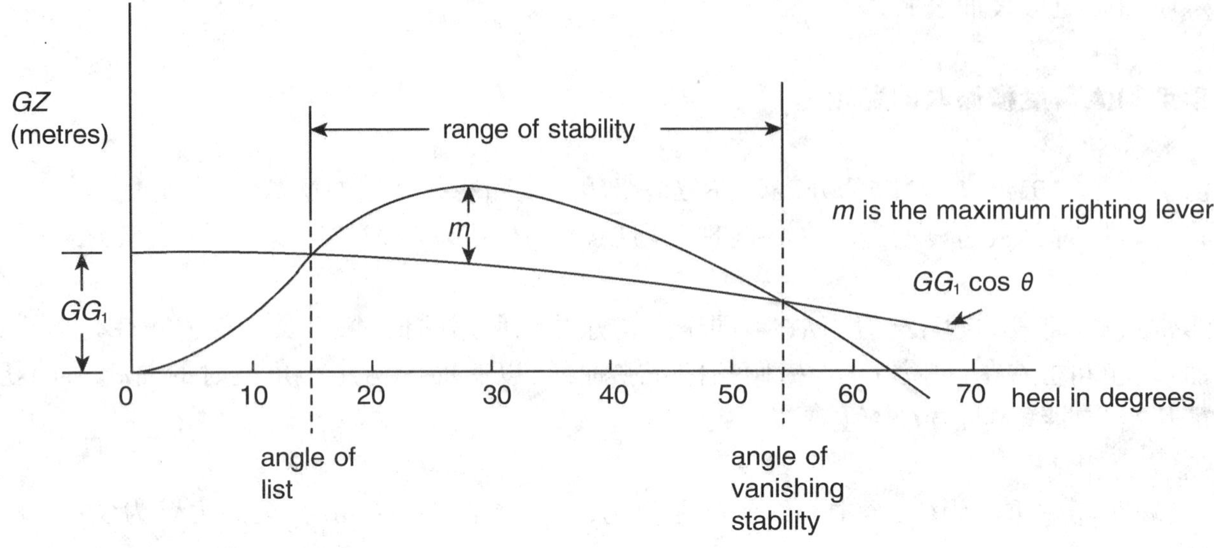

Figure 2

A list reduces the righting levers and the range of stability when heeled towards the listed side. When heeled in the opposite direction, righting levers are increased.

Simplified stability data

Simplified stability data were originally intended for use in small ships, but data in that form may also be found in some larger ships. Each of the several different presentations shows the ship's stability as adequate or inadequate to meet the recommended criteria for intact stability for passenger and cargo ships under 100 metres in length or, in the case of larger ships, the criteria laid down by the Administration.

Data necessary to maintain sufficient intact stability under service conditions to enable the ship to withstand the critical damage assumptions of SOLAS would be provided in passenger ships.

Trim and list

Trim calculations using moments about the centre of flotation or trimming tables were covered in IMO model course 7.03, Officer in charge of a navigational watch. These methods are suitable only in cases where the change in displacement is sufficiently small so that there are no large changes in the position of the centre of flotation or the value of MCT. When large changes in displacement are involved, as, for example, in planning the loading of a ship, the following method should be used.

Figure 3 shows a ship on an even keel with longitudinal centres of buoyancy and gravity indicated. The weight and buoyancy forces form a couple, called the trimming moment, equal to the product of the displacement and the horizontal separation between B and G, in this case acting to trim the ship by the stem. The ship will trim until the centre of buoyancy of the new underwater volume is in the same vertical line as G, which is fixed.

在标绘前,来自于KN曲线的GZ值可被减少至$GG_1\cos\theta$,或$GG_1\cos\theta$曲线可在GZ曲线上被覆盖,如图2所示。

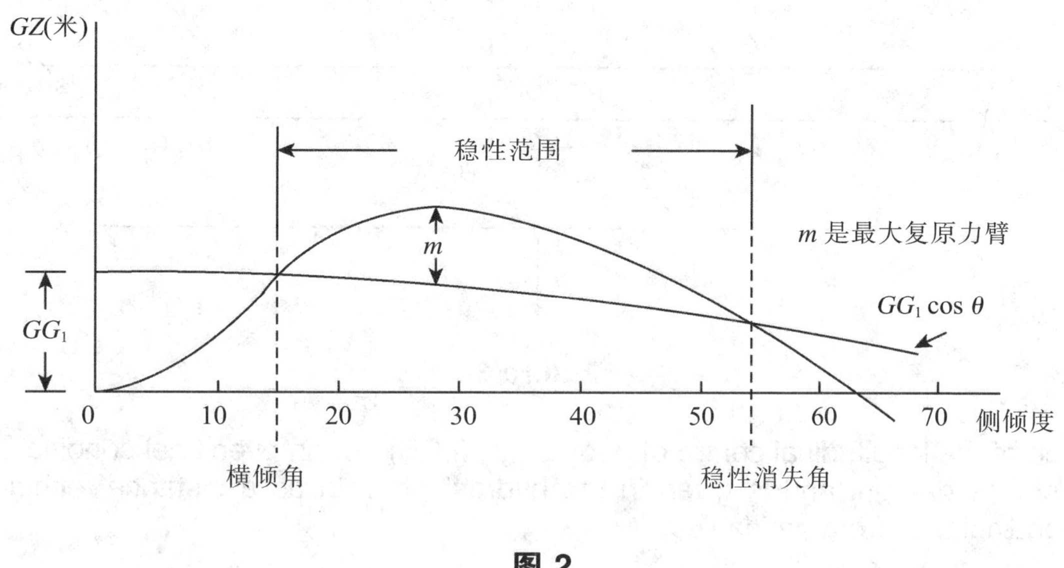

图 2

横倾减少横倾一侧的复原力臂和稳性范围。当反向横倾时,增加复原力臂。

简化的稳性数据

简化的稳性数据最初是打算用于小船的,但该形式的数据也可用于某些大船。每个不同的表现形式表明船舶稳性足以满足或不满足客船完整稳性推荐标准和由主管机关为船长小于100的货船或较大船舶制定的标准。

提供客船必需的数据,保持营运状态下的足够完整稳性,以使船舶能承受SOLAS公约的重大损害假设。

纵倾和横倾

使用有关漂心的力矩或纵倾表计算吃水差包含在IMO示范课程7.03“负责航行值班的驾驶员”中。这些方法仅适用于排水量变化较小的情况,这样漂心位置或MCT 值没有大的变化。当涉及排水量变化较大时,例如船舶计划装货,应使用下列方法。

图3表明平吃水船舶的纵向浮心和重心。重力和浮力形成力偶,称为纵倾力矩,等于排水量和B、G之间水平距离的乘积,这种情况使船舶趋于艉倾。船将纵倾直到新的水下体积的浮心和G处于同一垂线上,才不再移动。

The trim is given by trimming moment/MCT 1 cm where the MCT is taken for the displacement of the ship.

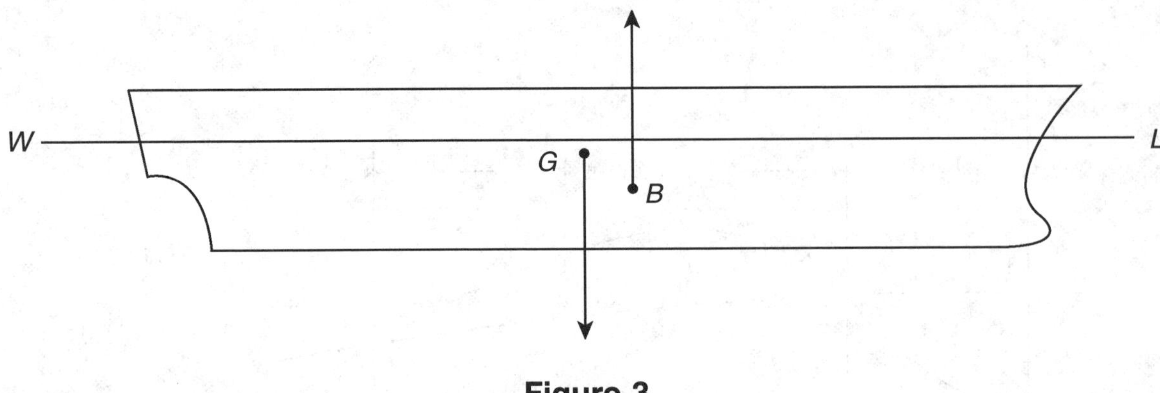

Figure 3

The position of the longitudinal centre of buoyancy (LCB), for an even-keel condition, depends upon the ship's draught and is given in the hydrostatic data as a distance, either from the after perpendicular or from amidships.

The position of the longitudinal centre of gravity is found by taking moments of mass, about the after perpendicular or about amidships, of the light ship and all of its contents. The LCG for the light ship is included in the hydrostatic data, LCGs of tanks and holds are given in the capacity plans or can be measured from the profile plan.

To find the draughts at each end, the trim is divided in the usual way, according to the proportionate distances of the perpendiculars from the centre of flotation, and applied to the ship's true mean draught.

When a ship is hogged or sagged there is a difference between the mean draught calculated from the draughts at the ends and the draught amidships. The difference is the amount of hog or sag. Taking the case of a ship with a sag, the draught amidships is greater than the mean draught. The ship's displacement lies between the values obtained for the two draughts and corresponds to some intermediate draught.

A weighted average of the mean draught and draught amidships is used. The commonly used values are:

corrected draught = 3/4 × draught amidships + 1/4 × mean draught;

or corrected draught = 2/3 × draught amidships + 1/3 × mean draught.

These amount to applying 1/4, in the first case, or 1/3, in the other, of the hog or sag to the amidships draught.

A method known as the mean of mean of means is sometimes used. The mean of the forward and after draughts is found, the mean of that and the draught amidships is found and the mean of that with the draught amidships again gives the required draught. The result is the same as for the first equation above.

吃水差由纵倾力矩除以MCT 1 cm得出,MCT由船舶排水量查得。

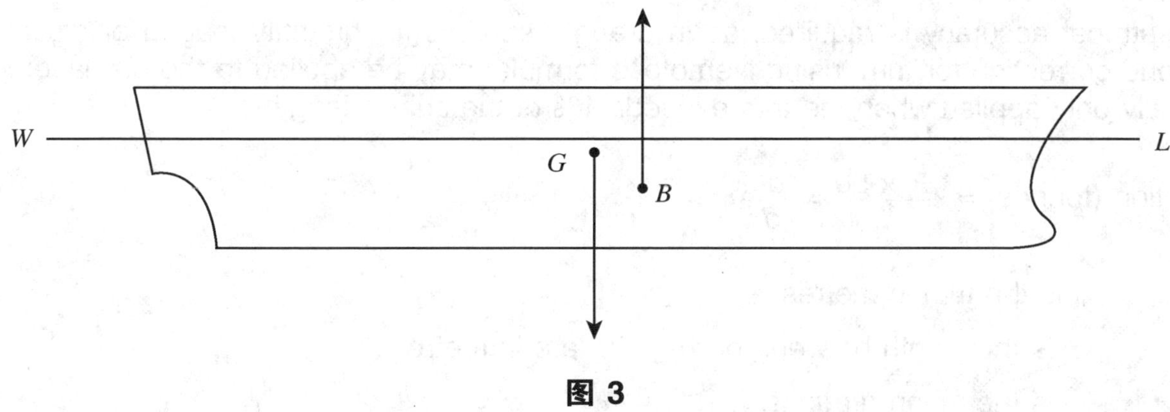

图 3

平吃水状态下的浮心纵向位置(LCB)取决于船舶吃水,在静水力参数中,为距艉垂线或距船中距离。

重心纵向位置通过取空船和所有载荷对艉垂线或船中质量矩求得。空船的LCG包括在静水力参数中,液舱和货舱的LCG在舱容图中给出,或可从剖面图测得。

欲求艏艉端吃水,以通常方式根据艏艉垂线距漂心的距离比例来除吃水差,并应用于船舶真实平均吃水。

当船舶中拱或中垂时,从艏艉吃水计算所得平均吃水与船中吃水之间存在差别。差值即为拱垂值。以船舶中垂为例,船中吃水大于平均吃水。船舶排水量位于从两个吃水得到的值和相应于大约船中吃水得到的值之间。

使用平均吃水和船中吃水的平均值。通常使用的值为:

经修正的吃水= 3/4 × 船中吃水 + 1/4 × 平均吃水;

或　经修正的吃水= 2/3 × 船中吃水 + 1/3 × 平均吃水。

在第一种情况下,将1/4中拱或中垂值(应用于舱中吃水),在其他情况下,将1/3中拱或中垂值应用于船中吃水。

有时候使用平均平均再平均的方法。求艏艉吃水的平均值,再求该值与船中吃水的平均值,再把所得值再一次与船中吃水求平均值,即得需要的吃水。结果和上述第一个公式相同。

Nemoto's Formula

When utmost accuracy is required, as in draught surveys for quantity loaded or discharged, a second correction for trim, using Nemoto's formula, may be applied to the displacement. It is usually only applied when the trim exceeds 1% of the ship's length.

$$\text{correction (tonnes)} = \frac{t^2 \times 50}{L} = \frac{dM}{dZ}$$

where: t is the trim in metres

L is the length between perpendiculars in metres

d is the mean draught

$\frac{dM}{dZ}$ = MCT 1cm at $(d + 0.5)$m – MCT 1cm at $(d - 0.5)$m

The correction is always added to the displacement.

Dynamical stability

In calculating the area under a *GZ* curve to a given angle, using Simpson's rules, the interval between ordinates may be expressed in degrees.

The calculated area would be expressed in metre-degrees, which can be converted to metre-radians, if required, by dividing by 57.3. The dynamical stability is the area under the curve in metre-radians multiplied by the ship's displacement in tonnes. The result is expressed in metre-tonnes, the radians being omitted since they are dimensionless. Usually, it is areas under the *GZ* curve which are required for checking stability criteria which, depending upon the ship's data, may be expressed in metre-degrees or metre-radians.

The area under the *GZ* curve to a given angle represents not only the work done in heeling the ship to that angle but also the potential energy available to return the ship to the upright. By the principle of conservation of energy, the potential energy is converted into rotational energy as the ship moves towards the upright. When upright, all of the energy is in the form of rotational energy, so the ship continues to roll until an angle is reached where the area under the curve is equal to that rotational energy. The energy used in overcoming friction between hull and water and in creating turbulence reduces the angle to which the ship will roll.

The wind exerts a horizontal force on the above-water area of the ship and deck cargo which can be considered to act at the centre of the projected area. That force is resisted by the water acting on the underwater area on the other side, usually considered to act at about half the draught. The two forces form a couple inclining the ship until the righting moment is equal to the inclining couple. In the Recommendation on a Severe Wind and Rolling Criterion for the Intact Stability of Passenger and Cargo Ships of 24 metres in Length and Over, no allowance is made for a reduction in the projected lateral area or the vertical separation between the centres of areas, above and below the waterline, as the ship heels. The wind pressure used in the recommendation corresponds approximately to storm force 10 on the Beaufort scale.

List should always be removed before sailing and cargo should be adequately secured to prevent a shift producing a listed condition while on passage.

Nemoto 公式

当需要最大限度的准确性时,如在水尺检量求装卸数量中,利用Nemoto公式求得的吃水差的二阶修正,可用于排水量的修正。仅当吃水差超过1%船长时使用。

$$\text{改正量(吨)}=\frac{t^2\times 50}{L}=\frac{dM}{dZ}$$

式中: t—吃水差(米);

L—两柱间长(米);

D—平均吃水

$\frac{dM}{dZ}=(d+0.5)$(米)对应的MCT 1 cm $-(d-0.5)$(米)对应的MCT 1 cm

总将改正量加入排水量中。

动稳性

在使用辛普森法则计算GZ曲线下的面积中,坐标之间的间隔可用度表示。

计算出的面积会用米—度表示,如果需要的话,除以57.3可转换为米—弧度。动稳性为该曲线下以米—弧度表示的面积乘以以吨表示的船舶排水量。通常它是GZ曲线下的面积,根据船舶数据核实可能以米—度或米—弧度表示的稳性标准。

GZ曲线下到某一角度的面积不仅表示船舶倾斜到该角度所做的功,而且表示要使船舶恢复到正浮的可用势能。按能量守恒原理,当船舶向正浮运动时,势能转换为转动能。正浮时,所有能量均为转动能,所以船舶继续横倾直到曲线下面积等于转动能的角度为止。用来克服船体和水之间的摩擦,并产生湍流的能量减少了船舶横倾的角度。

作用于船舶水线上的面积和甲板货的水平风力,可被认为是作用于投影面积中心上。该力遭受作用于水下另一侧的水阻力,通常被认为是作用于吃水的一半处。这两个力形成力偶,使船舶倾斜,直到复原力矩等于倾斜力偶。在有关客船和船长为24米及以上货船完整稳性强风中横摇建议中,当船舶横倾时,在侧投影面积或水线上下两个面积中心的垂直间距的换算方面没有留出余地。建议中采用的风压约为蒲福风级表中的10级风暴。

开航前总应消除横倾,货物应适当系固以防止航行中移动产生倾斜情况。

Approximate *GM* by means of rolling period tests

The method is described in The Intact Stability Code.

Inclining test

The purpose of the inclining test is to determine the displacement and position of the ship's centre of gravity in an accurately known condition. It is usually carried out when the ship is as nearly complete as possible, small corrections being made for any components still to be fitted or shipyard stores aboard at the time to obtain values for the light ship condition.

The draughts and water density are carefully measured for use with the ship's lines plan to calculate the displacement, the height of the transverse metacentre above the base (*KM*) and the position of the longitudinal centre of buoyancy.

The test consists of moving weights across the deck under controlled conditions and measuring the resultant angle of list. The angles are deliberately kept small and are measured by long pendulums suspended down holds or engine-room skylights.

The mean value of *GM* calculated from the deflections is subtracted from the *KM* to give the vertical height of the centre of gravity. Since the centre of gravity and centre of buoyancy are in the same vertical line for a ship in equilibrium, the position of the LCG can be calculated from the previously determined LCB.

Recommendations on intact stability for passenger and cargo ships under 100 metres in length

The recommendations are contained in R43. Instructors should refer to the stability requirements of the Administration for ships of 100 metres in length and over.

Intact stability requirements for the carriage of grain

The SOLAS Convention deals with the carriage of grain. The intact stability requirements are laid down, and the loading information required for determining the stability. The method of calculating intact stability is illustrated.

Rolling of ships

A mathematical treatment of rolling is not required. Trainees should know that the natural rolling period is inversely proportional to the square root of the *GM*. Rolling in a seaway is a forced oscillation, the period depending upon the period of encounter of the waves or swell as well as the natural rolling period; when the period of wave encounter equals the natural rolling period, synchronization occurs. Very heavy rolling can be induced by a moderate sea. An alteration of course or speed, or both, changes the encounter period of the sea and breaks the synchronization.

The equation in this objective produces a result in force units (kilonewtons in this case), hence the balancing heeling couple must be expressed in the same units in the equation in the objective relating to the righting moment equaling the heeling couple, by multiplying the usual mass moment by g, the acceleration due to gravity.

通过横摇周期试验求*GM*近似值

完整稳性规则中描述了该方法。

倾斜试验

倾斜试验的目的是在已知准确条件情况下,确定一个船舶排水量和重心位置。它通常在船尽可能完整时候进行,需要对当时仍要配备的任何部件或船厂在船物料进行修正,以获得空船状况下的数值。

仔细测量吃水和水密度以便使用船舶型线图来计算排水量、横稳心距基线(*KM*)高和纵向浮心位置。

试验包括在可控制条件下在甲板上移动重物和测量所得横倾角。刻意保持小角度,通过货舱或机舱天窗悬挂的长钟摆来测量。

从该偏离角计算所得*GM*平均值减去*KM*以求重心高度。因为船舶平衡时的重心和浮心处于同一垂线上,LCG 位置可从前面确定的LCB计算求出。

船长小于100米的客船和货船的完整稳性建议

建议包含在R43中。教员应参考主管机关对船长在100米及以上船舶的稳性要求。

谷物运输完整稳性要求

SOLAS公约涉及谷物运输。公约规定了完整稳性,确定稳性的装载资料。说明了完整稳性的计算方法。

船舶横摇

不需横摇的数学处理。学员应知道自横摇周期和*GM*的平方根成反比。航行中的横摇是受迫摇摆,周期取决于波浪或涌浪的遭遇周期以及自横摇周期;遭遇周期等于自横摇周期时,发生谐摇。中等海浪可引起很大的横摇。改变航向或航速,或改变二者,就改变了海浪遭遇周期,也就消除了谐摇。

该目标方程产生以力为单位的结果(此情况下为千牛),因此在有关等于倾斜力偶的复原力矩目标方程中的平衡倾斜力偶必须以同样单位表示,用g乘以质量矩,这是由于重力加速度的缘故。

In the unusual event of the centre of gravity falling below half draught the heel would be towards the turn.

Dry-docking and grounding

When dealing with stability during dry-docking, it is simplest to consider the righting moment when heeled by taking moments about the centre of buoyancy, which produces the equation:

$$\text{righting moment} = \Delta \times GM \sin \theta - P \times KM \sin \theta$$

directly.

The righting level *GZ*, is given by the equation:

$$GZ = (GM - \frac{P \times KM}{\Delta}) \sin \theta,$$

which is the righting lever for the ship with its *GM* reduced by $\frac{P \times KM}{\Delta}$

By making use of $KM = KG \div GM$, the alternative expression for righting lever can be obtained.

This approach has the advantage of showing that, although different values of *GM* are obtained, the value of the righting moment is the same in each case. The value of *P* for which

$GM - 0$ is also the same for both expressions.

The stability of a ship grounded at a point on the centreline is treated in exactly the same way as the dry-docking problem. A ship grounded forward, say, on a falling tide, would experience a reducing righting lever and the point could be reached at which it became zero. Providing the ship did not touch bottom elsewhere, it would flop over to an angle of loll or possibly capsize.

When grounded at a point off the centreline, a heeling moment is also produced. Considering the case where only heeling moment is involved, at the point of capsize the upthrust from the bottom becomes zero, therefore the ship would not capsize until heeled to its angle of vanishing stability when afloat. In most circumstances, cargo would have shifted, water entered through non-watertight openings or the ship would have slid off before reaching that angle. When the grounding force causes trim as well as heel the angle of vanishing stability may be much smaller.

It should be recalled that buoyancy is provided by the vertical component of water pressure on the ship's hull. When a ship is grounded on firm sand or a bottom of similar nature, water is unable to exert any pressure on the grounded portion and there is a loss of buoyancy compensated by an increased upthrust from the ground. If a ship is grounded over the whole of its bottom there is a large loss of buoyancy for any drop in water level, however small. Stability is not a problem in that circumstance but the fact that nearly all the weight of the ship is supported by the ground must be considered when deciding how to refloat her.

在异常情况下,重心降至吃水的一半以下,倾斜就会趋于转动。

进入干船坞和搁浅

当处理进坞期间的稳性时,最简单的考虑是倾斜时浮心所产生力矩作为复原力矩,直接有下列方程:

$$复原力矩 = P \times GM \sin\theta - P \times KM \sin\theta$$

复原力臂GZ由下列方程:

$$GZ = (GM - \frac{P \times KM}{\Delta}) \sin\theta,$$

即复原力臂等于船舶初稳性高度减去

利用$KM = KG \div GM$,可得复原力臂的另外一种表达式。

这种方法的优点表明,尽管得到的GM值不同,但每种情况下的复原力臂的值相同。两个表达式中对$GM - 0$的P值也相同。

船舶搁浅位置在中心线上时的稳性就像在干船坞中同样处理。前部搁浅, 比如落潮时,复原力臂将不断减小,在搁浅点为零。假如船舶其他地方没有触底,则船舶将会滚翻至静止角或可能倾覆。

当搁浅点偏离中心线时,还会产生横倾力矩。考虑到仅涉及倾覆力矩在倾覆点,底部的上冲力为零,因此船不会倾覆直到漂浮时横倾至稳性消失角。在大多数情况下,货物将产生移动,水通过非水密开口进入船内,或船舶在横倾至该角度前就已倾覆。当搁浅既造成纵倾又造成横倾时,稳性消失角可能会小得多。

应记住,浮力是由作用于船体的水压力的垂直分量所提供的。当船搁浅于坚实的沙滩或类似底质,水压力的垂直分量不能对搁浅部分施加压力,存在损失的浮力由地面增加的上冲力补偿的情况。如果船底部搁浅,对任何水位下降而言,都存在巨大的浮力损失,不过水位下降不大。在此情况下,稳性不是问题,但当决定如何脱浅时,必须考虑到,事实上几乎所有船舶的重量都由地面支撑。

3.1.2 EFFECT ON TRIM AND STABILITY IN THE EVENT OF DAMAGE AND STABILITY (11 hours)

The methods of calculating transverse stability, list and trim in a damaged condition are based upon the principles used in the textbook T4 but the problem has been approached in a way more applicable to the use of a ship's hydrostatic data, although still confined to compartments with roughly rectangular waterplanes.

Flooding of compartments

The requirements for the watertight subdivision of passenger ships are set out in SOLAS. Depending upon the type of service and its size, the ship will be required to withstand the flooding of one, two or three adjacent main compartments.

The International Convention on Load Lines, lays down requirements for the survivability of ships of type 'A', if over 150 metres in length, and for ships of type 'B' which are over 100 metres in length and are assigned freeboards less than the tabular freeboards for type 'B' ships.

Classification society rules stipulate the minimum number of bulkheads to be fitted in dry cargo ships, depending upon length, but do not specify that they should be fitted in such a way that the ship could withstand flooding of a main compartment.

Amendments to the SOLAS Convention provide regulations governing the subdivision and damage stability of cargo ships. They apply to ships over 100 metres in length intended primarily for the carriage of dry cargoes, but exclude those ships already covered by other damage stability regulations in IMO instruments.

The regulations are based on consideration of the probability of the location and extent of damage and the probability of survival after damage. The probabilities of survival conditional upon each possible damage configuration for compartments, singly or in adjacent groups, are summed for the summer draught and for a draught intermediate between light and loaded. The average of the two sums gives a value known as the "attained subdivision index, A" which must not be less than the "required subdivision index, R", which is a function of the length.

Effect of flooding on transverse stability

When a space is flooded without free communication with the sea, the stability can be calculated by taking account of the mass of water and the free surface effect. Examples would be the accumulation of water in tween-decks as a result of firefighting, or flooding through a crack in the hull or through a fractured pipe. The ship's hydrostatic data for the increased displacement are applicable for the calculations.

If a compartment is holed so that water can flow freely in and out of it, that compartment can be considered as part of the sea and no longer part of the ship. The buoyancy of the space up to the water level before damage is lost and the waterplane area of the ship is reduced by the waterplane area of the damaged compartment. These changes give rise to changes in

3.1.2 船体损坏并进水对吃水差和稳性的影响 (11学时)

破损情况下的横稳性、横倾和纵倾的计算方法基于教科书T4中所用原理,但该问题以一种更适用于使用静水力参数的方式加以解决,尽管仍限于对大约为矩形水线面的舱室。

舱室进水

SOLAS公约规定了客船的水密分舱要求。根据航区和船舶大小的不同,分别要求船舶承受一个、两个或三个相邻主要舱室进水。

国际载重线公约规定了长度超过150米的A型船和长度超过100米的B型船的生存能力要求,B型船核定的干舷小于列表计算的干舷。

船级社规范规定干货船隔舱壁的最小数目取决于其长度,但没有明确规定它们以船舶能承受一个主要舱室进水的方式建造。

对SOLAS公约的修订提出了对有关货船分舱和破损稳性的规定。它们适用于船长100米以上主要用于运输干货的船舶,但不包括那些已被IMO其他破损稳性规定所涵盖的船舶。

该规定是基于考虑破损位置和程度的概率及破损后的生存概率。生存概率以每一间舱室可能破损的分布,单个舱或相邻几个舱为先决条件,汇总后即为夏季载重线和空船和满载之间的中间吃水。这两个总和的平均值给出了称之为“达成分舱指数,*A*”,它必须不小于“要求的分舱指数,*R*”,*R*是船长的函数。

进水对横稳性的影响

当进水舱室与外面的海水无连通时,可通过考虑进水质量和自由液面影响来计算稳性。由于消防所致在二层舱积水或通过船体上裂缝或破裂管路进水即为例证。对于增加了排水量的静水力参数适用于该计算。

如舱室破了一个洞,水可自由流入和流出,该舱可被视为是海水的一部分,而不再是船舶的一部分。该舱室在破损前至该水位的浮力丧失,船舶水线面面积减少了破损舱室的水线面面积。这些变化引起计算横稳性和吃水差所需静水力参数的改变。船舶质量及其重心保持不变。这种处理称之为“损失浮力法”,是本课程和教科书T4中所使用的方法。

the hydrostatic data needed to calculate the transverse stability and trim. The mass of the ship and its centre of gravity remain unaltered. Such a treatment is known as the 'lost buoyancy method' and is the one used in this course and in the textbook T4.

The lost buoyancy, expressed in tonnes, is the mass of water which could enter the space up to the original waterplane, i.e. the volume × permeability × density of water in which the ship is floating.

The lost waterplane area is the area of the bilged compartment at the original waterplane. If the compartment is completely contained below the waterline, e.g. a double-bottom tank, there is no loss of waterplane area provided the tank top remains intact. The original waterplane area may be given in the ship's data or it can be calculated from

$$\text{waterplane area} = \frac{100 \times TPC}{1.025}$$

Of the two corrections in this objective, the first is the second moment of lost waterplane area about its own centroid, the second a correction to give the loss about the new centroid of the intact waterplane. In the case of symmetrical flooding, the second correction is zero. For wing compartments, the second correction is very much greater than the first, even for compartments extending half the breadth of the ship.

Generally, the displacement of the ship and the position of the centre of gravity will remain unchanged after bilging. However, if a tank containing a liquid is bilged, the weight of the tank contents is lost, causing a reduction in displacement and a shift in the position of the ship's centre of gravity. The lost buoyancy would be comparable with the lost weight, causing a similar shift in the centre of buoyancy with the result that there would be little change of draught, trim or list. The loss of waterplane area would result in a reduction of GM.

Permeability

The permeability of a space is the percentage or fraction of the space which could be occupied by water. The lost buoyancy equals the permeability × the volume. If a cargo was stowed solidly, with no space for water in infiltrate, it would occupy

$$\frac{1}{density}\ \text{m}^3/\text{t}$$

The space occupied in the hold by one tonne is its stowage factor, so the space available to water = stowage factor $- \frac{1}{density}$ m^3/t

The proportion of the stow which could be occupied by water, i.e. the permeability, equals

$$\frac{\text{stowage factor} - \frac{1}{density}}{\text{stowage factor}}$$

损失的浮力以吨表示,是可进入舱室达到初始水线面的水的质量,即体积 × 渗透率 × 船舶所在处的海水密度。

失去的水线面面积为浸水舱原始水线面面积。如舱室完全在水线下,例如双层底舱,如该舱顶保持完整,则无水线面面积损失。初始水线面面积可在船舶数据中给出或以下式计算

$$\text{水线面面积} = \frac{100 \times \text{TPC}}{1.025}$$

在这方面的两项修正中,第一项为失去水线面在其质心附近的二阶面积贯距,第二项为给出完整水线面的新质心附近的损失。在对称进水的情况下,第二项修正为零。对侧翼舱室,第二项修正远大于第一项修正,即使是对延伸至一半船宽的舱室。

一般而言,船舶舭部进水后其排水量和重心位置保持不变。然而,如含有液体的舱舭部进水,舱内液体重量损失,造成排水量减少和船舶重心位置移动。失去的浮力与所失去的重量相比,引起浮中类似移动,结果是,吃水、吃水差或横倾将很少改变。水线面面积的损失将导致GM减少。

渗透率

舱室的渗透率为水所占据该舱室的百分比或比例。损失浮力 = 渗透率 × 体积。如货物堆码坚实,无水的渗透空间,它将占据

$$\frac{1}{\text{密度}}\ \text{m}^3/\text{t}$$

一吨货物在所占空间为积载因数,所以可进水空间 = 积载因数 $-\ \frac{1}{\text{密度}}\ \text{m}^3/\text{t}$

可由水占据的积载比例,即渗透率等于

$$\frac{\text{积载因数} - \frac{1}{\text{密度}}}{\text{积载因数}}$$

For example, a cargo has a stowage factor of 1.2 m^3/t and a density of 2.5 t/m^3

$$\frac{1}{density} = \frac{1}{2.5} = 0.4\ m^3/t$$

$$permeability = \frac{1.2-0.4}{1.2} = \frac{0.8}{1.2} = 0.67$$

Notice, if a cargo has a permeability of 0.4 but only occupies half of the compartment, the permeability of the whole compartment is 0.4 × 0.5 + 0.5 = 0.7.

The loss of waterplane area is taken to be permeability × waterplane area of the compartment, but if the water level is above the top of the cargo the whole area is lost.

Angle of heel

Buoyancy is lost at the damaged compartment and an equal amount of buoyancy is gained at the position of the new centre of flotation. The transverse shift in the ship's centre of buoyancy is, therefore, lost buoyancy × transverse distance from centre of flotation divided by the displacement. On the assumption that the centre of gravity is still on the centreline, the shift in buoyancy is the heeling arm.

The angle of heel would be given by the intersection of the *GZ* curve for the damaged ship with the heeling-arm curve $BB_1 \cos \theta$. Since *KN* curves for the damaged condition are not available, the *GZ* curve has to be constructed, using values for the intact ship at a displacement corresponding to the damaged draught and a *KG* chosen to give the modified value of *GM*. The angle of heel read from the curve will be approximate. If the angle is small it can be calculated from, $\tan \theta = BB_1 / GM$

Effect of flooding on trim **(9 hours)**

Similar calculations are necessary to find the longitudinal position of the centre of flotation after damage, and the reduction of BML. The change in GML is used to calculate the change in MCT 1 cm.

Buoyancy has been lost at the damaged compartment and replaced at the centre of flotation, hence the trimming moment is the product of lost buoyancy and the distance from the centre of the damaged compartment to the new centre of flotation. The change of trim and the draught at each end are then calculated in the usual way.

Flooding of a compartment near an end of the ship causes a large shift in the centre of flotation away from the damaged end and a large reduction in MCT 1 cm. Combined with the sinkage due to lost buoyancy, this may produce a large increase in draught at the damaged end. The original trim of the ship will influence the chances of the ship surviving the damage.

A ship already trimmed towards the damaged end is more vulnerable than one on an even keel or trimmed the other way.

例如,货物的积载因数为1.2 m^3/t,密度为2.5 t/m^3

$$\frac{1}{密度}=\frac{1}{2.5}=0.4\ m^3/t$$

$$渗透率=\frac{1.2-0.4}{1.2}=\frac{0.8}{1.2}=0.67$$

注意,如货物渗透率为0.4,但仅占据一半舱室,则整个舱室渗透率为$0.4\times0.5+0.5=0.7$。

损失的水线面面积为渗透率 × 舱室的水线面面积,但如水位在货物顶部之上,则整个面积损失。

横倾角

在损坏舱室损失浮力,在新的漂心位置获得等量的浮力。因此,船舶浮心横向移动为损失浮力 × 漂心横向距离/排水量。假定重心仍在中心线上,则浮心的移动距离为横倾力臂。

横倾角由破损船舶的*GZ*曲线与横倾力臂曲线$BB_1\cos\theta$相关求得。因为得不到破损情况下的*KN*曲线,必须相应于破损后的吃水的排水量完整船舶的值构建*GZ*曲线,选定*KG*来求*GM*的修正值。从该曲线读取的横倾角是近似值。如该角较小,则可用公式计算,$\tan\theta=BB_1/GM$。

进水对吃水差的影响 **(9 学时)**

必须用类似计算来求破损后的漂心纵向位置和BML减少值。GML上的变化被用来计算在MCT 1 cm上的变化。

在破损舱室已损失浮力,由漂心处代替,因此,纵倾力矩为损失浮力和破损舱室的中心到新漂心距离的乘积。然后用通常方法计算吃水差和艏艉吃水的变化。

船舶端部舱室进水造成向远离破损端移动和在MCT 1 cm上较大的减少。

结合由于损失浮力的下沉,这将造成破损端的吃水较大增加。船舶的初始吃水将影响船舶幸存机会。

已向破损端纵倾的船舶,比平吃水船或向另一端纵倾的船舶更脆弱。

Measures to improve stability or trim when damaged

The immediate action should be to restrict the flooding and, if possible, to stop it. In the event of collision or stranding damage, it will not be possible to stop the flooding or reduce it significantly by the use of pumps. Even a comparatively small hole below the waterline admits water at a much higher rate than the capacity of bilge or ballast pumps. All watertight doors, valves, dampers in ventilation shafts and access hatches should be closed to prevent flooding progressing to other compartments. Where cross-flooding arrangements are required, they should be put into operation at once to restrict the resulting list.

In passenger ships, the guidance in the damage control booklet should be followed. The same applies to cargo ships where damage control information is provided.

In nearly all cases, damage will result in sinkage, list and trim, loss of stability and loss of longitudinal strength. Corrective action for one condition will affect the others.

Excessive list or trim should be corrected by moving weights, fuel, water or liquid cargoes, when possible. If ballast is added, it increases the sinkage. In some cases it may be possible to pump out ballast to improve list or trim and lighten the ship at the same time. If the ballast is taken from double-bottom tanks, however, the stability will be further reduced.

Stability may be improved by transferring fuel from wing or cross bunker tanks to double bottoms if suitable tanks are empty. Efforts should be made to reduce free surface to a minimum. Water accumulating in upper decks as a result of firefighting should be drained to the lowest level possible if means of pumping it out of the ship cannot be arranged.

After collision or stranding damage, particularly near the middle length of the ship, the longitudinal strength will be impaired and account should be taken of that when deciding on the transfer or addition of weights.

Cases have occurred where a slow leakage of water has been absorbed by a cargo, such as grain, with no water reaching the drain wells. The added weight, high on one side of the hold, has led to a steadily increasing list and eventual capsizing. As the source of the leakage was inaccessible, nothing could be done. Cargo spaces should be thoroughly inspected whenever they are empty for signs of leakage, indicating cracks or damage to overside discharge valve covers.

3.1.3 KNOWLEDGE OF IMO RECOMMENDATIONS CONCERNING SHIP STABILITY (2 hours)

Instructors should refer to the IMO publications referenced in the detailed teaching syllabus.

破损时改善稳性或吃水差的措施

立即采取的行动应为限制进水,如可能则阻止进水。在碰撞或搁浅造成破损情况下,用泵抽水不可能阻止或大量减少进水。即使是水线下的小孔,其漏水速度大大高于污水泵或压载泵的排量。所有水密门、阀、通风井挡火板和货舱入口都应关闭,以防止进水侵入其他舱室。在要求横贯进水设施的情况下,应马上投入运行以限制随后的横倾。

在客船上,应遵守破损手册中的指南。在提供破损控制的信息情况下,这同样适用于货船。

几乎所有情况下,破损将产生下沉、横倾和纵倾、稳性损失和纵向强度损失。对一种情况的纠正行动将对其他情况产生影响。

可能时,应通过移动重物、燃油、水或液体货物纠正过量横倾或纵倾。如泵入压载水,则增加下沉量。在某些情况下,可以抽出压载水以改善横倾或纵倾,同时减轻船舶总量。然而,如从双层底抽出压载水,稳性将进一步减小。

如有合适的舱室空着,可通过从边舱相反方向的燃油舱调拨燃油到双层底舱改善稳性。

努力将自由液面减至最小。如不能将由于消防所致上层甲板积水排出舷外,则应尽可能排至低位。

在碰撞或搁浅后,特别是近船中处,纵向强度受损,当决定转移或增加重量时应考虑此种情况。

在漏水较慢,水已被谷物类货物吸收的情况下,水并没有到污水井。如在货舱上层较高处增加重量,会导致横倾不断增加,最终倾覆。当泄漏源无法接近时,什么都无法做。无论何时,货舱空着的时候,都应彻底检查泄漏痕迹、表面裂缝或舷外排水阀盖的损坏。

3.1.3　IMO关于船舶稳性的建议的理解　(2 学时)

教员应参考教学大纲细则中的IMO出版物。

3.2 MONITOR AND CONTROL COMPLIANCE WITH LEGISLATIVE REQUIREMENTS AND MEASURES TO ENSURE SAFETY OF LIFE AT SEA AND THE PROTECTION OF THE MARINE ENVIRONMENT

3.2.1 INTERNATIONAL MARITIME LAW EMBODIED IN INTERNATIONAL AGREEMENTS AND CONVENTIONS (52 hours)

This area covers those international conventions, regulations and recommendations which directly affect the master in carrying out his obligations and responsibilities.

Those parts of the Geneva Conventions on Law of the Sea of 1958 and the United Nations Convention on the Law of the Sea, 1982, which are relevant to the conduct of a voyage have already been covered at the operational level, however, in order to reinforce previously covered topics, some points have been mentioned in the detailed teaching syllabus, for the instructor. Some brief revision may be necessary with an emphasis placed on the master's legal obligations concerning the requirements for certificates and other documentation, the survey requirements, the provision for inspections by the master or an officer delegated by him, the maintenance of equipment and the records that are required to be kept.

The technical details, where appropriate, are mainly dealt with under other relevant subjects. The International Regulations for Preventing Collisions at Sea are covered entirely in the function Navigation.

We also deal with the necessary basic knowledge of law concerning carriage of cargo and marine insurance. Those subjects, together with a few others, are supplementary to the STCW 2010 requirements and are indicated as such below and in the Detailed Teaching Syllabus in Part C with an asterisk, *.

Instructors should note that the following areas are covered in the training at the operational level. Some areas are covered again with emphasis on the master's responsibilities.

1. An introduction to Maritime Law

2. Law of the Sea
   - 2.1 Conventions on the law of the sea
   - 2.2 Territorial sea and the contiguous zone
   - 2.3 International straits
   - 2.4 Exclusive economic zone and the continental shelf
   - 2.5 High seas
   - 2.6 Protection and preservation of the marine environment

3.2 根据立法要求的监督与控制以及确保海上人命安全和海洋环境保护的措施

3.2.1 在国际协议和国际公约中所体现的国际海事法 (52 学时)

这方面涵盖了这些国际公约、法规和建议,这些公约直接影响到船长履行其义务和责任。然而,1958年日内瓦海洋法公约和1982年联合国海洋法公约中有关航行的部分已包括在操作级内容中,以加强以前涵盖的主题,在给教员的教学大纲细则中已提及某些知识点。某些简要的修订可能是必要的,强调船长有关证书要求和其他文件、检验要求、船长或其指定驾驶员进行的检查设备的维护和需要保持的记录方面的法定义务。

在适当情况下,主要处理其他相关科目的技术细节。国际海上避碰规则全部包括在航行职能中。

我们还涉及货物运输和海上保险的必要基础知识。这些科目与其他几个科目都是对2010年STCW公约要求的补充并在下面指明,在教学大纲细则C部分中用"*"号标明。

教员应注意:下列内容已包括在操作级培训中。某些内容再次强调船长的责任。

1. 海事法介绍

2. 海洋法
   - 2.1 有关海洋法公约
   - 2.2 领海和毗邻区
   - 2.3 国际海峡
   - 2.4 专属经济区和大陆架
   - 2.5 公海
   - 2.6 海洋环境保护和保护区

3. Safety

   3.1 International Convention on Load Lines, 1966, as amended

   3.2 International Convention for the Safety of Life at Sea, 1974, as amended (SOLAS) – General Provisions

   3.3 SOLAS – Subdivision and stability, machinery and electrical installations

   3.4 SOLAS – Fire protection, fire detection and fire extinction

   3.5 SOLAS – Life–saving appliances and arrangements

   3.6 SOLAS – Radiotelegraphy and radiotelephony

   3.7 SOLAS – Radio communications (amended Chapter IV)

   3.8 SOLAS – Safety of navigation

   3.9 SOLAS – Carriage of grain

   3.10 SOLAS – Carriage of dangerous goods

   3.11 International Convention on Standards of Training, Certification and Watchkeeping for Seafarers, 1978, as amended

   3.12 ITU Radio Regulations

4. Passengers

   4.1 Special Trade Passenger Ships Agreement and Rules, 1971

   4.2 Protocol and Rules on Space Requirements for Special Trade Passenger Ships, 1973

   4.3 Athens Convention relating ft the Carriage of Passengers and their Luggage by Sea, 1974

1.1 Certificates and other documents required to be carried on-board ships by international conventions and agreements (1 hour)

The master must be familiar with all the certificates and other documents required by the vessel and by the crew. These will be subject to inspection by both the flag State and by port State control officers. Documents found not to be in order can cause delays on detentions to the voyage.

Relatively new requirements include the Safety Management Certificate denoting that the company and its shipboard management operate in accordance with the approved safety management system. A copy of the Document of compliance shall also be kept on board the ship in order that the master can produce it for verification.

A complete list of certificates and documents, with reference to which convention it is required, is provided in the detailed teaching syllabus.

The requirements for their issue and renewal are dealt with under the appropriate conventions, except for those mentioned below.

3. 安全
   - 3.1 经修订的1966年国际载重线公约
   - 3.2 经修订的1974年国际海上人命安全公约——一般规定
   - 3.3 SOLAS—分舱和稳性、机械和电气设备
   - 3.4 SOLAS—防火、探火和灭火
   - 3.5 SOLAS—救生设备和设施
   - 3.6 SOLAS—无线电报和无线电话
   - 3.7 SOLAS—无线电通信 (经修订的第4章)
   - 3.8 SOLAS—航行安全
   - 3.9 SOLAS—谷物运输
   - 3.10 SOLAS—危险货物运输
   - 3.11 经修订的1978年国际海员培训、发证和值班标准公约
   - 3.12 ITU无线电规则
4. 乘客
   - 4.1 1971年客船特别运输协议和规则
   - 4.2 关于1973年特别业务客船舱室议定书和规则
   - 4.3 1974年关于海上旅客运输及其行李的雅典公约

1.1 国际公约要求船舶所携带的证书和其他文件 (1 学时)

船长必须熟悉船舶和船员要求的所有证书。船旗国和港口国官员将对此进行检查。如发现文件未妥善保存,则可能被滞留造成航次延误。

相对而言的新要求包括“安全管理证书”,系指公司和船上管理符合批准的安全管理体系。船上还应保存一份符合证明的副本,以便船长出示该文件以供审核。

教学大纲细则中提供了证书和文件及其相关公约要求的完整清单。

相关公约涉及了签发证书和换证要求,下列提到的除外。

A certificate of nationality, often called the ship's register, is required by the Geneva Convention on the High Seas, 1958, and by the UNCLOS, 1982. The form of certificate and the conditions for its issue are determined by each national government. In some cases it remains valid until the ship is scrapped or changes ownership or nationality, in others it is subject to regular renewal.

The Panama and Suez Canal Tonnage Certificates are included for completeness; they are not required by international conventions. Any ship wishing to traverse either canal must be measured and obtain the appropriate certificate before doing so. In general, they remain valid until alterations to the ship's structure or in the use of spaces are made.

Tonnage

The International Tonnage Certificate remains valid until alterations in construction or the use of spaces are made, the subdivision load line is changed or the ship is transferred to the flag of another State.

The licence for the ship radio station is required by the radio regulations of the ITU. The form of the licence is determined by the national government which issues it.

There are no international agreements requiring a ship to be classed by a classification society, but practically all ships are. Loss of class would be an indication to a port State control officer that a thorough inspection of the ship should be made. Maintenance of class is a condition for the continuance of insurance in many cases.

The form of the official logbook, the entries made in it and its eventual disposal are decided by each Administration.

The documents listed as the minimum additional documents required at arrival or departure are those mentioned in the Convention on Facilitation of international traffic, the International Health Regulations and the dangerous goods manifest required by SOLAS.

1.2 Responsibilities under the relevant requirements of the International Convention on Load Lines (1 hour)

Instructors should note that the Load Lines Protocol of 1988 entered into force in February 2000. The 1988 Protocol has been modified by the 2003 Amendments which were adopted by MSC.143(77) in June 2003 and entered into force in January 2005.

1.3 Responsibilities under the relevant requirements of the International Convention for the Safety of Life at Sea (2 hours)

Of all the international conventions dealing with maritime safety the most important is the International Convention for the Safety of Life at Sea, better known as SOLAS which covers a wide range of measures designed to improve the safety of shipping.

The convention is also one of the oldest of its kind: the first version was adopted in 1914 following the sinking of the SS Titanic with the loss of more than 1,500 lives. Since then there have been four more versions of SOLAS. The present version was adopted in 1974 and

国籍证书常称为登记证书,为1958年日内瓦公海公约和1982年UNCLOS公约所要求。证书形式和签发条件由各国政府决定。在某些情况下,直到船舶报废或更换船东或国籍它才失效,在其他情况下,须经定期换证。

巴拿马运河和苏伊士运河吨位证书包含在完整性中;国际公约对此并无要求。欲通过运河的任何船舶在通过前须经测量并取得相应证书。在一般情况下,它们保持有效,直到改变船舶结构或使用的空间发生改变。

吨位

吨位证书保持有效,直到船舶结构或使用的空间发生改变、分舱载重线改变或船舶改挂另一国国旗。

无线电台执照为ITU无线电规则所要求。执照形式由签发国政府决定。

没有国际协议要求船舶应由船级社授予船级,但实际上所有船都这么做。失去船级将提示港口国检察官对该船应彻底检查。在许多情况下,保持船级是续保的一个条件。船舶日志的形式、记录内容及其最终处置由各个主管机关决定。

列为要求的到离港最少额外文件在国际便利交通公约、国际卫生条例中提及,SOLAS 要求危险货物舱单。

1.2 《国际载重线公约》相关要求下的责任 (1学时)

教员应注意的是,1988年载重线议定书于2000年2月生效。2003年修正案对1988年议定书进行了修订,MSC.143(77)在2003年6月通过,于2005年1月生效。

1.3 《国际海上人命安全国际公约》相关要求下的责任 (2学时)

在所有涉及海上安全的国际公约中,最重要的是国际海上人命安全公约,称为SOLAS更好,它包含广泛的用于改善航运安全的措施。

该公约是本类公约中年代最久远的一种:随着"泰坦尼克"号带着1 500多条生命沉没,第一个版本的SOLAS公约于1914 年通过。从那以后,已产生4个版本。现行版本于1974年通过,1980年

entered into force in 1980. Some recent additions are covered in the 1996 Amendments in R2.

Reference should be made to the International Safety Management (ISM) Code in Chapter IX, which sets out the master's responsibility with regard to safety and environmental protection.

1.4 Responsibilities under the International Convention for the Prevention of Pollution from Ships, 1973, and the Protocol of 1978 Relating thereto (MARPOL 73/78) (3 hours)

Relatively new additions to maritime law should be noted including MARPOL 73/78 Annex 1, regulation 26 that requires every oil tanker of l50gt and above and every ship other than a tanker of 400 gt and above to have a shipboard oil pollution emergency plan (a SOPEP), and amendments to MARPOL Annex V that require garbage management plans to be in place.

Under Annex IV ships are not permitted to discharge sewage within a specified distance of the nearest land, unless they have in operation an approved treatment plant. Between 4 and 12 miles from land, sewage must be comminuted and disinfected before discharge.

Annex VI entered into force on 19 May 2005. It sets limits on sulphur oxide and nitrogen oxide emissions from ship exhausts and prohibits deliberate emissions of ozone-depleting substances. The instructors should use the topics included in the detailed teaching syllabus, in order to prepare the lesson. The local regulations which may be more stringent than as laid down by Annex VI, pertaining to SECA and ECA, should be pointed out to the trainees.

Pollution

Tanker officers who have had responsibility for loading, discharging and handling cargo will have completed an approved specialized training programme. This includes instruction in pollution prevention relevant to tankers, V2, V79.

Examples of checklists can be found in the references. More extensive checklists are used at many oil installations and include, amongst other things, a list of equipment on board and ashore, whether it is fully operational or not, the communications to be used and emergency procedures. The completed checklists are signed by the responsible persons from the ship and the installation when it is agreed to start the operation.

It is recommended that, whenever possible, disposal of garbage should be made to port facilities. Disposal at sea is strictly regulated by the provisions of the appropriate legislation. Records of waste and garbage disposed of at sea must be kept. These records are subject to inspection and checking by port State control officers.

The annexes to the Convention contain the applicable technical regulations. These are:

Annex I – Oil

Annex II – Noxious liquid substances in bulk

Annex III – Harmful substances carried by sea in packaged forms

Annex IV – Pollution by sewage from ships

生效。一些近期的补充包含在R2中的1996年修正案内。

应参考第Ⅸ章中的国际安全管理规则(ISM),它规定了船长关于安全和环境保护的责任 。

1.4 1973/78年国际防止船舶污染公约及其议定书的责任(MARPOL73/78) (3学时)

应注意的是,对海事法相对较新的补充包含于MARPOL 73/78 附则 1的26条中,要求150总吨及以上油船和400总吨及以上其他船舶具有船舶油污应急计划 (SOPEP),对MARPOL附则V的修正案要求备有垃圾管理计划。

按照附则Ⅳ,不允许船舶在离最近陆地规定的距离内排放污水,除非正在运行认可的处理装置。在离岸4~12海里内,在排放前污水须经粉碎和消毒。

附则Ⅳ于2005年5月19日生效。它对船舶排放硫氧化物和氮氧化物设定了限制,禁止船舶蓄意排放消耗臭氧物质。教员应使用教学大纲细则中的题目来备课。应向学员指出,根据SECA 和ECA,当地规定可能比附则Ⅵ的条款更严格。

污染

负有装卸和管理货物责任的油船驾驶员应完成认可的特殊培训课程。该课程包括油船防污染指导,见V2和V79。

在参考文献中可找到检查表的示例。许多石油设施采用更广泛的检查表, 表上除其他事情外,内容包括船岸设备检查清单(无论设备是否完全运行)、采用的通信方式和应急程序。当准备开始作业时,船岸双方负责人在已完成的检查表上签字。

建议无论何时,只要可能,就应将垃圾送至港口设施处理。相应立法严格规定了海上垃圾处理。必须保持关于海上的废物和垃圾处理的记录。这些检查须经港口国检察官检查和核实。

本公约的附则包含适用的技术法规。它们是:

附则Ⅰ—油类

附则Ⅱ—散装有毒液体物质

附则Ⅲ—海运包装有害物质

附则Ⅳ—船舶生活污水污染

Annex V – Pollution by garbage from ships

Annex VI – Air pollution from ships and NOx technical code

1.5 Maritime declarations of health and the requirements of the International Health Regulations (4 hours)

Arrival Documents and Procedures: these are all very practical requirements that have to be followed.

Officers should be aware that many States will require forms and declarations in addition to those mentioned in the FAL and in the International Health Regulations. The ship's agents should be consulted for the current requirements at any port.

Noting and extending protests: the need to note or extend protests varies from country to country. In many countries it is essential to do so to protect the interests of the ship. For example, failure to do so could debar the master from collecting general average contributions from the cargo. The owner's agent should be able to advise the master regarding the procedure and the number of crew members required as witnesses, if any. Letter of protest is also included in the detailed teaching syllabus, and should be explained to the trainees.

1.6 Responsibilities under other international maritime law embodied in international agreements and conventions that impact on the role of management level deck officers (35 hours)

There are a large number of international agreements and practices that impact on the legal and commercial elements of the role of a master or chief mate. It is important that trainees are familiar with the practical implications of the critical parts of these agreements and that they have the ability to be able to find, extract and understand detail from these agreements. Requirement for trainees to learn detail that in practice would normally be obtained from reference documents should be avoided.

Maritime Labour Convention, 2006

The MLC was adopted on 23 February 2006 at International Labour Organization, Geneva, Switzerland but at the time of writing this book, is still awaiting full ratification. Ratification has now been achieved and the convention is about to come into force. MLC is the result of a joint resolution in 2001 by the international seafarers' and shipowners' organizations, later supported by governments.

The Maritime Labour Convention, 2006 aims to establish a continuous "compliance awareness" at every stage, from the national systems of protection up to the international system starting with individual seafarers.

It sets out their rights to decent conditions of work and helps to create conditions of fair competition for shipowners. It is intended to be globally applicable, easily understandable, readily updatable and uniformly enforced. The MLC will be another pillar of the international regulatory regime for quality shipping, complementing the key Conventions of the IMO.

附则Ⅴ—船舶垃圾污染

附则Ⅵ—船舶空气污染和氮氧化物(NOx)技术规则

1.5 航海健康声明书和《国际卫生条例》的要求 (4学时)

抵港文件和程序:这些都是非常实用、必须遵行的要求。

驾驶员应意识到,许多国家除了要求FAL和国际卫生条例中提到的表格和申报材料外,还要求额外的表格和申报书。现行要求应咨询港口的船舶代理。

提交海事声明和延伸海事声明:提交海事声明和延伸海事声明的需求各国不尽相同。许多国家要求必须这么做以保护船舶利益。例如,如果不这样做,就可能阻止船长从货物收集共同海损分摊。船东代理应能将有关程序和有证人时要求的证人数量通知船长。海事声明书也包括在教学大纲细则中,应向学员解释。

1.6 影响管理级船员作用的国际协议和国际公约所体现的其他国际海事法相关要求的责任 (35学时)

存在大量国际协议和惯例,影响船长或大副作用的法律和商业要素。重要的是,学员熟悉这些协议关键部分的实际含义和有能力去找到、摘录和理解这些协议的细节。应避免要求学员通常从参考文件中获得实际做法细节。

2006年《海事劳工公约》

2006年2月23日在瑞士的日内瓦,国际劳工组织通过了海事劳工公约(MLC),但在写本书的时候,还在等待完全批准。现在已获得批准,该公约即将生效。海事劳工公约(MLC)是2001年由国际海员和船东组织共同决议的结果,后者由政府支持。

2006年《海事劳工公约》旨在从个体海员开始,每个阶段建立从国家保护制度到国际制度的持续"合规意识"。

它规定了海员体面劳动条件的权利,创造有助于船东公平竞争的条件。其目的是在全球范围内适用、易于理解、随时更新和统一执行。海事劳工公约将是国际航运质量监管机制的另一支柱,是对IMO重要公约的补充。

The rather large number of the existing maritime Conventions, many of which are not even ratified by several governments, some totally out of date and not in line with present day situations make it difficult for governments to ratify or enforce them.

MLC is a comprehensive set of global standards, based on 68 existing maritime labour instruments (Conventions and Recommendations), adopted by the ILO since 1920. MLC brings almost all these requirements together incorporating present day conditions and language.

Conventions addressing the seafarers' identity documents which were recently revised in 2003 (Nos. 108 and 185) are not incorporated in the MLC. The Seafarers' Pension Convention, 1946 (No. 71) and one Convention (The Minimum Age [Trimmers and Stokers] Convention), 1921 (No. 15), which is no longer relevant to the sector, are also not included in the MLC.

MLC should help eliminate substandard ships and it would work within the well-established international system for enforcement of the international standards for ship safety, security and environmental protection that have been adopted by the IMO, in other words fall under PSC inspection systems.

Existing ILO Maritime Labour Conventions will be gradually phased out as ILO Member States that had ratified those Conventions ratify the MLC, but there will be a transitional period when some parallel Conventions will remain in force. Countries that ratify the MLC will no longer be bound by the existing Conventions when MLC enters into force since it incorporates the requirements of all these old conventions. Countries that do not ratify MLC will remain bound by the existing Conventions they have ratified, but these will be closed to any further revisions.

Ships flying the flags of countries that do not exercise effective jurisdiction and control will have no choice but to observe the minimum criteria enshrined in the MLC and prevent seafarers from having to work under unacceptable conditions, to the detriment of their wellbeing, health and safety and the safety of the ships on which they work.

MLC is designed on the principle of being "firm on rights and flexible on implementation". This is in line with the Constitution of the ILO and most ILO instruments that seek to take account of national circumstances and provide for some flexibility in their application. The ILO view is to gradually improve protection of workers by taking into account the specific situation in some sectors and the diversity of national circumstances. ILO addresses flexibility on the principles of tripartism, transparency and accountability. When a government exercises flexibility it usually involves consultation with the workers' and employers' organizations concerned, with any determinations that are made reported to the ILO.

Ships of 500 gross tonnage and above, engaged in international voyages or voyages between foreign ports, will be required to carry a 'Maritime Labour Certificate' (MLC) and a 'Declaration of Maritime Labour Compliance' (DMLC) on board. However, most other vessels will also be subject to inspections under MLC; this will get clear on studying the requirements of MLC in detail.

MLC also incorporates the "no more favourable treatment" concept similar to that adopted in the IMO conventions. That is, ships of all countries (irrespective of ratification) will be subject

相当大数量的现有海事公约,其中许多甚至没有几个政府批准,一些则完全过时和不符合当今情况,使得政府难以批准或执行它们。

海事劳工公约(MLC)是一整套基于自1920年以来,国际劳工组织(ILO)通过的68个海事劳工文件(公约和建议)的综合性全球标准。海事劳工公约结合现代情况和语言,几乎把所有这些要求合并在一起。

涉及海员身份证件问题的公约最近在2003年修订(108号和185号)没有包含在海事劳工公约(MLC)中。1946年(71号)海员退休金公约和1921年(15号)公约(最低年龄(扒炭工和司炉工)公约)不再与本方面相关,也都没有列入海事劳工公约(MLC)。

海事劳工公约(MLC)应有助于消除低标准船,将运行于完善的国际系统中,以实施IMO通过的船舶安全、保安和环境保护国际标准,换言之,一切皆在港口国监督检查系统之中。

现有的国际劳工组织(ILO)的海事劳工公约将随着国际劳工组织(ILO)批准那些公约的成员国批准新公约而被逐步取消，但将有一个过渡时期，过渡期内一些类似的公约将有效。批准2006年海事劳工公约(MLC)的国家,当新公约生效时将不再受现行公约的约束,因其合并了所有旧公约的要求。未批准新公约的国家将继续受其批准的现有公约约束,但这些公约将被终止进一步修订。

悬挂不进行有效管辖和控制的国家的国旗的船舶将别无选择，除了遵守海事劳工公约(MLC)中所含的最低标准外,防止海员在不可接受的条件下工作,损害其福利、健康和安全及其工作船舶的安全。

海事劳工公约以“牢固的权利和灵活的实施”为原则设计。这符合国际劳工组织(ILO)和大多数国际劳工组织(ILO)文件寻求考虑本国国情,并在其应用中提供某些灵活性的章程。国际劳工组织(ILO)的观点是要考虑到某些方面的具体情况和国情的多样性,逐渐提高工作人员保护水平。国际劳工组织(ILO)在三方性、透明度和问责制原则上体现出灵活性。当政府行使灵活性时,通常涉及与相关的工人和雇佣组织就向ILO报告的决定进行协商。

要求500总吨或以上,从事国际航行或在外国港口间航行的船舶持有“海事劳工证书” (MLC)及“海事劳工符合声明” (DMLC)。然而,大多数其他船舶还将经受海事劳工公约的检查;这将搞清研究详细的海事劳工公约要求。

海事劳工公约(MLC)还吸收了类似于IMO公约采取的“无更优惠的待遇”概念。即所有国家(不论批准与否)的船舶将受已批准本公约的任何国家检查,如果它们不满足新公约的最低标准,则可能被滞留。

to inspection in any country that has ratified the Convention, and to possible detention if they do not meet the minimum standards of the new Convention.

In covering the Maritime Labour Convention, 2006, and recommendations, the relevant national laws and regulations or collective bargaining agreements, where applicable, should be dealt with. The administrative procedures involved, e.g. the correct procedures for signing off a sick seaman abroad, the disposal of a deserter's wages and effects or the engagement of replacements abroad and similar procedural matters, should be included in detail. Reference should also be made to arrangements to safeguard the shipmaster in the proper discharge of his responsibilities in regard to maritime safety and protection of the marine environment.

The International Medical Guide for Ships, 3rd edition upholds a key principle of the Maritime Labour Convention, 2006: to ensure that seafarers are given health protection and medical care no less favourable than that which is generally available to workers ashore, including prompt access to the necessary medicines, medical equipment and facilities for diagnosis and treatment and to medical information and expertise. By ensuring that this guide is carried on board ships entitled to fly their flags, and following its instructions, countries can fulfil their obligations under the terms of the Maritime Labour Convention, 2006, and ensure the best possible health outcomes for their seafaring population. The Guide was prepared jointly by ILO and WHO.

Collision

The Master's responsibilities under the Convention on the International Regulations for Preventing Collisions at Sea, 1972, are fully covered in the function, Navigation at the Management Level.

Assistance and salvage

At the request of IMO, the CMI drew up a new draft convention on salvage at Montreal in 1981 to update and revise the 1910 convention. The main new features relate to damage to the environment.

Masters and shipowners would have a duty to arrange salvage assistance and to cooperate with the salvors to prevent or minimize damage to the environment.

The draft Convention also made provision for special compensation to a salvor in cases where the salvor has carried out salvage operations in respect of a ship or cargo which threatened the environment but has failed to earn a reward for physical salvage. The International Convention on Salvage, 1989, was adopted by a diplomatic conference in March 1989 and entered into force on 14 July 1996.

Lloyd's Standard Form of Salvage Agreement (LOF) is widely used throughout the world. LOF 2000 superseded LOF 95 and where a salvor offers services on LOF 95 or some other terms, the Master of the vessel in difficulties should attempt to get agreement to LOF 2000. This takes account of the main changes included in the 1989 Salvage Convention and incorporates certain of the Convention Articles, including Article 14, which makes provision for the award of special compensation in cases where the salvor, by his salvage operations, has prevented or minimized damage to the environment. Personal effects of Master, crew and passengers including any car accompanying a passenger are excluded from reward for

在涉及2006年海事劳工公约和建议时，适当情况下应顾及有关国家法律法规或劳资谈判协议。相关的行政程序,例如,在国外解雇生病海员、处理脱逃者工资和影响或雇佣替代者和类似的持续性事务,都应详细包含在里面。还应参考适当免除船长有关海上安全和保护海洋环境责任方面,保护船长所做的安排。

《国际船舶医疗指南》第3版坚持了2006年海事劳工公约的一项重要原则:确保给予海员不逊于岸上个人获得的健康保护和医疗保健,包括及时获得必要的药品、诊断和治疗的医疗设备和设施及医疗信息和专业知识。通过确保本指南在授权悬挂其国家国旗的船上得以实施,并遵守其指示,这些国家可履行2006年海事劳工公约的义务,确保其海员队伍的最佳可能健康结果。该指南由国际劳工组织(ILO)和世界卫生组织(WHO)共同编写。

碰撞

按照1972年国际海上避碰规则,船长的责任完全涵盖在本功能,管理级航行中。

援助和救助

在国际海事组织(IMO)的要求下,CMI于1981年在蒙特利尔起草了一个新救助公约草案,对1910年公约进行更新和修订。主要的新特点与环境破坏有关。

船长和船东有责任安排救援,与救助者合作或使对环境的破坏减至最小。

在救助者对危及环境的船舶或货物进行了救助,但未能获得实质上的救助报酬的情况下,公约草案还对救助者规定了特别补偿。1989年国际海上救助公约在1989年3月外交会议上通过,于1996年7月14日生效。

劳式标准救助合同(LOF)在全世界得到广泛使用。LOF 2000取代LOF 95和在救助人按LOF 95或某些其他条款提供服务的情况下,在危难中的船长应努力按LOF 2000条款达成协议。这考虑了1989年救助公约中的主要变化,结合公约中的某些条款,包括第14款,对通过救助行动防止破坏环境或使对环境的破坏最小化的救助人,做出了给予特别补偿的规定。按照LOF 2000,船长、船员和乘客的个人财产,包括载有乘客的车辆不在救助报酬之列。按照LOF 2000,酬劳货币为美元。教员应向学员指出,相比老的LOF 1995,按新的LOF 2000,合作职责扩展到提供有关货物的性质、计划和稳性数据等信息。根据LOF 2000,救助人在“不再有任何理由期望存在有利结果”时,将有权

salvage as per the LOF 2000. The currency of award as per the LOF 2000 is USA $. The instructor should point out to the trainees that, as compared to the old LOF 1995, the duty to cooperate as per the new LOF 2000 is extended to provide information about nature of cargo, plans, stability data etc. As per LOF 2000, the salvors have right to terminate when "no longer any reasonable prospects of useful result". In the LOF 2000, SCOPIC clause is introduced as an alternative to Art 14 set out in the convention. As per LOF 2000, the Master is authorized to sign on behalf of cargo. LOF 2000 defines the conditions under which a casualty is in a safe condition for redelivery to the owner (which can be of crucial importance in the closing stages of a salvage operation). Since a large proportion of the world's salvage is undertaken under the LOF, the use of LOF 2000 will give effect to the main provisions of the 1989 Salvage Convention, see Appendix.

Special Compensation P and I Club (SCOPIC) Clause, has been added in the detailed teaching syllabus, which is supplementary to any Lloyd's Form Salvage Agreement "No Cure – No Pay" ("Main Agreement") which incorporates the provisions of Article 14 of the International Convention on Salvage 1989 ("Article 14").

The instructors should point out to the trainees that as per SCOPIC the Contractor has the option to invoke by written notice to the owners of the vessel the SCOPIC clause at any time of his choosing regardless of the circumstances and, in particular, regardless of whether or not there is a "threat of damage to the environment". A non-binding code of practice has been agreed between the International Salvage Union (ISU) and the International Group of Clubs.

Proceedings in the event of a collision

Instructors should explain that in the event of a collision or of any other incident of navigation concerning a ship on the high seas involving the penal or disciplinary responsibility of the Master or of any other person in the service of the ship, no penal or disciplinary proceedings may be instituted against such persons except before the judicial or the administrative authorities either of the flag State or of the State of which such a person is a national.

Need to render assistance

Also that every State must require the Master of a ship sailing under its flag, in so far as he can do so without serious danger to the ship, the crew or the passengers, to render assistance to any person found at sea in danger of being lost, to proceed with all possible speed to the rescue of persons in distress if informed of their need of assistance, in so far as such action may be reasonably expected of him, and, after a collision, to render assistance to the other ship, her crew and her passengers and, where possible, to inform the other ship of the name of his own ship, her port of registry and the nearest port at which she will call.

Submarine cables

In the event that a ship breaks or injures a submarine cable so as to interrupt or obstruct telegraphic or telephonic communications, or similarly breaks or injures submarine pipeline or high-voltage power cable it must be understood that this is, except for the purpose of saving lives or ships, a punishable offence.

终止救助。在LOF 2000中,引入SCOPIC条款代替公约第14条规定。按照LOF 2000,授权船长代表货物利益方签署协议。LOF 2000阐明了将受害者在安全状态下,交还给所有人(在救助作业的最后阶段此点可能至关重要)。因为世界上大多数的救助按照LOF进行,LOF 2000的使用将对1989年救助公约的主要条款产生影响,参见附录。

船东保赔协会特别补偿(SCOPIC)条款已被添加在教学大纲细则中,是对包含1989年国际救助公约第14章(14章)的任何劳氏标准救助协议"无效果—无报酬"("主要协议")的一种补充。

教员应向学员指出,不管情况如何,特别是不管是否存在"破坏环境的威胁",订约人任何时候都有权选择向船东发出书面通知,选择SCOPIC条款。一个不具约束力的实践规范已得到国际救助联盟(ISU)和俱乐部国际集团之间的同意。

发生碰撞时的诉讼

教员应解释如果在公海上船舶发生碰撞或其他航行事故,涉及船长或其他船上服务人员的刑事或纪律责任,刑事诉讼或纪律处罚只能由该船碰撞或航行事故发生时悬挂其国旗的船旗国司法或行政当局做出。

提供救助的要求

还应解释,每个国家必须要求悬挂其国旗的船长,只要这么做不会严重危及其船舶、船员和乘客,都应对一切处于海上危险中的人员提供援助,如接到通知需要救援,则以尽可能快的速度航行到遇险人员处,采取当时被预期是合理的行动救援。碰撞后,可能的情况下,对他船、他船船员和乘客提供救援,通知他船本船船名、船籍港和将停靠的最近港口。

海底电缆

必须理解,除了拯救生命或船只的目的之外,一旦船舶损坏或损伤海底电缆,中断或阻碍了电报或电话通信,或类似损坏或损伤海底管道或高压电缆,则属应受惩处的罪行。

However, owners of ships who can prove that they have sacrificed an anchor, a net or any other fishing gear in order to avoid injuring a submarine cable or pipeline should be indemnified by the owner of the cable or pipeline, provided that the owner has taken all reasonable precautionary measures beforehand.

Convention on Limitation of Liability for Maritime Claims, 1976 (LLMC 1976)

The LLMC Convention sets global limits to liability. For example, the limit in respect of death or injury of passengers in Article 7 is the global limit for all claims. Each individual claim is subject to the limitation in the Athens Convention.

Classification societies

Classification societies are independent, normally non-commercial organizations. They were originally established to designate minimum standards on which underwriters could rely before insuring a vessel but have, over the years of their existence, developed into standard-setting institutions for every section of the shipping community. Through their rules for construction and a regime of periodical surveys they are in a position to enhance ship construction and operation. They supervise all stages of the construction or major repairs of a ship, even to the extent of ensuring that the right materials are used. A ship so constructed is assigned a class in accordance with some code.

In order to retain its class, the vessel must be presented for survey at periodical intervals as specified in the rules. Failure to meet these terms or to comply with recommendations issued may result in the suspension or cancellation of its class.

Although it is not a legal requirement to be classed, practically all ships are. It is usually a condition for marine insurance or a maritime mortgage that the ship is classed and is maintained so as to retain her class.

The large classification societies have surveyors stationed at the major ports round the world who, in addition to classification work, carry out statutory surveys required by international conventions under authority delegated to them by national maritime Administrations.

Cargo

A brief description of the use of documentary credit has been included to show how the bill of lading is involved as security for the sale of goods and how important it is that the description of the goods shown in the bill of lading is correct. Trainees should have a working knowledge of carriage of goods conventions so far as these impact on the ship. This content can be found in numerous texts on maritime law or ship's business, only some of which are stated in the resources for this course.

Few management level officers will not at some stage operate under a charter agreement. A working knowledge of the key implications for the ship as a result of charter parties under voyage, time and demise charters is important. Again, this content will be found in any of numerous texts on chartering practice or maritime law in the shipping industry.

然而,假如船东预先已采取所有合理的预防措施,他们能证明,为避免损伤海底电缆或管道已损失一只锚或一张网或任何其他渔具,则电缆或管线的主人应赔偿船东。

1976年海事赔偿责任限制公约(LLMC 1976)

LLMC规定了完全责任限制。例如,第7条中的乘客人身伤亡限制即为所有索赔的限制。每一个体索赔都受雅典公约的限制。

船级社

船级社为独立的,通常是非商业性的组织。当初设立船级社是为保险商在给船舶保险前指定可依赖的最低标准,但经过多年的存在后,它已发展成为给航运界每个部分制定标准的机构。通过他们的建造规则和定期检验体制,他们处在一种提高船舶建造和运营的地位。他们监督船舶建造或大修的所有阶段,甚至到了确保使用正确材料的程度。按照某些规则,授予如此建造的船舶船级。

船舶为保持其船级,必须按规则规定的时间间隔进行定期检验,未能满足这些条款或遵守颁发的建议,则可导致中止或取消其船级。

尽管入级不是法定要求,但所有船舶都入级。船舶入级并维护保养以保持船级通常是一种海上保险或抵押贷款的条件。

大船级社在世界主要港口派驻有验船师,他们除了进行船级相关工作之外,还按照国家海事主管机关的指定授权,进行国际公约要求的法定检验。

货物

使用跟单信用证的简述已包括在内, 以表明提单涉及销售货物安全和其上货物的正确描述是多么的重要。学员应具有到目前为止仍影响船舶的货物运输公约的工作知识。该内容可在许多海事法或船舶业务文本中找到,此处所述仅作为本课程资源。

管理级船员很少在某一阶段不按租船协议操作。航次租船、期租和光租船舶的重要含义的工作知识是重要的。再次重申,该内容可在许多航运业租船实践或海事法文本中找到。

General average and marine insurance

The role of the York-Antwerp Rules in the adjustment of general average is covered in the Marine Claims Handbook, see below. The rules are also included.

Non-disclosure does not include circumstances which the shipowner could not know about. However, it has been held that non-disclosure of circumstances which should have been known but were not, possibly due to the Master's failure to keep the owner informed, would be grounds for the insurer to avoid the insurance contract.

The "duty of assured" clause is intended to encourage the assured to take all reasonable measures to avert or minimize the damage or loss which will form a claim on the policy. Claims under this clause are treated separately from others and are payable in addition to other claims, even in the event of total loss. It is said that the assured should behave as if uninsured.

Stowaways, Ship's Agents and Agency, Port State control, Port of refuge and the Master/ pilot relationship are also included in the detailed teaching syllabus. Instructors should refer to these, which will assist them in preparing their lessons.

1.7 Responsibilities under international instruments affecting the safety of the ship, passengers, crew and cargo (4 hours)

Ballast Water Convention 2004 has been added in the detailed teaching syllabus, all 5 sections should be explained to the trainees. Ballast water exchange must be conducted in accordance with the ship's ballast water management plan, taking into account the recommendations adopted by the IMO.

A new paragraph, 4, has been added with effect from July 1, 2010 to SOLAS chapter V, regulation 22 – Navigation bridge visibility, some changes are operational and others introduce new requirements applicable to navigation records.

The instructors should emphasize that as a consequence of this amendment, any increase in blind sectors or reduction in horizontal fields of vision resulting from ballast water exchange operations is to be taken into account by the Master before determining that it is safe to proceed with the exchange.

The instructor should also point out to the trainees that as an additional measure, to compensate for possible increased blind sectors or reduced horizontal fields of vision, the Master must ensure that a proper lookout is maintained at all times during the exchange.

Trainees should be familiar with the organization and both the effect and coverage of port State control.

The legal and safety implications arising from the use of pilots continues to provide some difficulty. Trainees should have a working knowledge of these topics and be able to discuss how to establish effective relationships and also what action should be taken where the relationship is problematic or the actions of the pilot of concern.

共同海损和海上保险

约克—安特卫普规则在共同海损理算中的作用包含于海上索赔手册中,参见以下叙述。还应包括规则。

不包括船东不了解的非公开的情况。然而,所有人应该知道但可能由于船长未能通知他而不知道的非公开情况已经存在,这将会成为保险商撤销保险合同的理由。

"保证义务"条款旨在鼓励被保险人采取一切合理措施,以避免或将形成保单上索赔的损坏或损失减至最小。本条款的索赔与其他索赔区别对待,可在其他索赔之外支付,即使发生全损。这就是说,被保险人应像没投保一样采取行动。

教学大纲细则还包括偷渡、船舶代理人和代理机构、港口国监督、避难港和船长/引航员关系。教员应参考这些内容,将有助于其备课。

1.7 影响船舶、乘客、船员和货物安全的国际文献相关要求下的责任 (4学时)

2004 年压载水公约已添加到教学大纲细则中,应向学员解释5节的全部内容。压载水交换必须考虑IMO采纳的建议,按照船舶压载水管理计划进行。

2010年7月1日生效的新的第4段已添加到SOLAS公约第5章第22条—— 驾驶台航行能见度,某些变化已在使用,其他的则引入适用于航行记录的新要求。

教员应强调,由于这项修正案,因压载水交换作业引起的盲区的任何增加、水平视野的减小都要由船长在决定压载水交换时安全航行之前加以考虑。

教员还应指出,作为一项额外的措施,以补偿盲区的增加、水平视野的减小,船长必须确保在压载水交换期间的任何时候保持正规瞭望。

学员应熟悉该组织和港口国监督的作用和范围。

由于使用引航员产生的法律和安全含义继续带来某些困难。学员应具有这些主题的工作知识,并能讨论如何建立有效的关系,在关系处于疑难之中或对引航员有关行动存有疑虑情况下,还应采取什么行动 。

1.8 Methods and aids to prevent pollution of the marine environment by ships pollution (2 hours)

This covers the following IMO conventions:

- Convention on the Prevention of Marine Pollution by Dumping of Wastes and Other Matter (London Dumping Convention)
- International Convention Relating to Intervention on the High Seas in Cases of Oil Pollution Casualties, 1969
- International Convention on Civil Liability for Oil Pollution Damage, 1969
- International Convention for the Prevention of Pollution from Ships, 1973, and the Protocol of 1978 relating thereto (MARPOL 73/78) has been covered earlier.

1.9 National legislation for implementing international agreements and conventions (1 hour)

Instructors should develop their own objectives here to ensure that national legislation that is the flag State laws are covered to an extent that meets or exceeds the standards laid down in the international conventions, codes and agreements. Emphasis should be on monitoring compliance, identifying areas where there may be potential for non-compliance or differ ences compared to international standards.

3.3 MAINTAIN SAFETY AND SECURITY OF CREW AND PASSENGERS AND THE OPERATIONAL CONDITION OF SAFETY SYSTEMS

3.3.1 LIFE-SAVING APPLIANCE REGULATIONS (2 hours)

The requirement of the STCW Convention is covered by IMO model course 1.23, Proficiency in survival craft and rescue boats other than fast rescue boats. Trainees who have successfully completed that course and have been issued with a certificate of proficiency in survival craft have demonstrated the ability and knowledge necessary to satisfy the requirements of the regulations concerning life saving.

The obligations and responsibilities of the master under the requirements of the life-saving appliance regulations of the International Convention for the Safety of Life at Sea, 1974, as amended, are dealt with in the subject, Maritime Law, of this course.

SEARCH AND RESCUE

The syllabus for training in search and rescue is contained in IMO model course, maritime search and rescue coordinator surface search. That course provides a thorough knowledge and understanding of the IAMSAR MANUAL and satisfies the requirements of the STCW Convention.

3.3.4 ACTIONS TO BE TAKEN TO PROTECT AND SAFEGUARD ALL PERSONS ON BOARD IN EMERGENCIES (4 hours)

SOLAS Regulations list the duties related to passengers which must be assigned to members of the crew. These duties would usually be so arranged that each member of the catering

1.8 防止船舶污染海洋环境的方法和手段 (2学时)

这包括下列公约:

- 防止倾倒废物和其他物质污染海洋公约(伦敦倾倒公约)
- 1969年国际干预公海油污事件公约
- 1969年国际油污损害民事责任公约
- 1973年国际防止船舶污染公约,其1978年议定书(MARPOL 73/78)已覆盖前者。

1.9 实施国际协议和公约的国内立法 (1学时)

在此,教员应建立其目标以确保船旗国的国家立法水平已达到国际公约、规则和协议所规定的标准。应强调监控适合性,发现潜在的不符合方面或与国际标准相比存在差距的方面。

3.3 维护船员和乘客的安全和治安与安全系统的操作条件

3.3.1 救生设备规则 (2学时)

STCW公约的要求包含于IMO 示范课程1.23"精通救生艇和救助艇"中,除了快速救助艇。成功完成该课程并获得签发的精通救生艇证书的学员,表明已经满足了相关救生规则要求的必要能力与知识。

按照经修订的1974年国际海上人命安全公约要求的船长义务与职责,在本课程的海事法主题中涉及。

搜寻与救助

IMO示范课程——海上搜救协调员海面搜寻,包含了搜救的培训大纲。该课程提供了IAMSAR 手册的全面的知识与理解内容,满足STCW公约要求。

3.3.4 紧急情况下保护和安保船上所有人员的行动 (4 学时)

SOLAS 规则列出了将相关乘客委派给船员的职责。这些职责通常如此安排,每位餐饮人员负责一组房间。一个小组将负责携带额外的供给到救生艇。

staff would be responsible for a group of rooms. A small party would be charged with taking additional supplies to the lifeboats.

Rescue of persons from a vessel in distress or from a wreck

Unless the situation is critical, conditions should be assessed carefully and a plan prepared before initiating rescue action. If the survivors are in no immediate danger and existing conditions make rescue hazardous, consider waiting until conditions have improved or until daylight. Try to establish communications with the survivors to obtain information about their condition and to inform them of the intended method of rescue.

Direct transfer of survivors from a wreck to the ship requires nearly calm conditions and, normally, rescue boats or motor lifeboats will be used.

It is unlikely that the disabled ship or wreck will be drifting at the same rate as the rescue ship so, if time permits, it is a good idea to try to get an estimate of their relative drift rates before launching the boats. At the same time, the rescue ship should reconnoitre the area around the wreck to see if there are any obstructions which might hamper the boats.

During the launching of boats, lifelines, lifebuoys, ladders and nets should be ready in case somebody falls overboard or a boat overturns.

Going alongside a wreck may be difficult. On the lee side the approach may be obstructed by wreckage, and if the wreck is drifting quickly the boat will have difficulty getting away from the side. Sea conditions may make it impossible to approach from the weather side and, since the wreck will probably drift faster than the boat, it will be difficult to remain close enough to transfer survivors. An approach from the weather side is the only possibility when the wreck is on fire or releasing toxic fumes, in which case survivors may have to jump into the water to be picked up by the boats.

If weather conditions make the use of boats too hazardous, and it is not possible to wait for conditions to moderate, a liferaft on a stout line may be towed or floated to the wreck or may be hauled out to the wreck after making connection by line-throwing apparatus. The painter fitted to the liferaft is not heavy enough to be used in this manner.

At the rescue ship, preparations for the transfer of survivors include the provision of a boat rope, nets, ladders, lines and crew standing by to assist. The use of a liferaft alongside as a landing stage releases the boat quickly if it is necessary to make several journeys. Survivors who have been in the sea or survival craft for some time may be suffering from cold, fatigue and sea-sickness and be unable to do much to help themselves.

Man-overboard procedures

The standard man-overboard manoeuvres were dealt with in IMO model course 7.03, Officer in charge of a navigational watch.

The standard full-speed man-overboard manoeuvres, such as the Williamson turn, are not possible in very heavy weather. Turning at speed into a heavy sea and swell could cause serious damage to the ship. The turn should be made in the safest way possible in the conditions and the ship manoeuvred into a position to windward of the person in the water.

遇难船或沉船的人员救助

除非情况危急，否则应在开始救援行动前认真评估情况和准备的计划。如幸存者无紧迫危险,当时情况使得救援变得危险,则考虑等待情况改善或天亮。努力与幸存者建立通信以获得其情况信息,通知他们计划的救援方法。

直接把幸存者从救助艇上转运上船需要几乎平静的天气条件，通常使用救助艇或机动救生艇。

失控船或沉船不可能以与救援船相同速度漂移,所以,如时间允许,好的想法是在施放救生艇前努力获得相对漂移速度的近似值。同时,救援船应侦察沉船周围的水域,看是否存在可能妨碍救生艇的任何障碍。

在施放救生艇期间,救生绳、救生圈、梯子和网应准备好,以防有人落水或救生艇倾覆。

靠泊沉船可能是困难的。从下风接近可能为残骸所妨碍,如沉船迅速漂移,救生艇离开沉船下风舷将有困难。海况使从上风舷接近不可能,因为沉船可能比救生艇漂移更快,保持足够近地转运幸存者将变得困难。当沉船失火或释放有毒烟雾时,从上风舷接近成为唯一可能,在此情况下,幸存者可能不得不跳入水中,以被救生艇救起。

如天气条件使得使用救生艇太危险,不可能等待天气变得温和,可拖动系着一根结实缆绳的救生筏或使其漂浮到沉船,或在通过救生抛绳器建立连接后拖向沉船。救生筏上的艇艏缆强度不足以在此种方式中使用。

在救援船上,转运幸存者的准备包括提供救生艇绳索、网、梯子、缆绳,船员待命协助。 如有必要进行几段航行,使用救生筏作为浮动平台,则迅速放艇。一直在水中或救生艇上待了一段时间的幸存者可能遭受寒冷、疲劳和晕船的折磨,而不能为自己提供太多帮助。

人员落水程序

IMO示范课程 7.03“负责航行值班的驾驶员”,涉及标准的人员落水程序。

在非常恶劣天气下,像威廉姆逊旋回这样的标准全速人员落水操纵是不可能的。高速转向大浪和涌浪可对船舶造成严重损坏。转向应以当时情况下尽可能安全的方式进行,船舶向落水者的上风位置操纵。

The ship will quickly drift down to him. A few fit crew members, wearing immersion suits, lifejackets and lifelines, should be standing by to help the person on board. Use may also be made of the line-throwing apparatus, with a buoyant head, to drift a line to the person in the water. It is essential to keep the person in sight throughout the operation, and this is difficult in a heavy sea and swell, so any crew not otherwise occupied in the rescue should be posted as lookouts.

When a person is reported to the master as missing, it may reasonably be assumed that efforts have already been made to find him. A final call on the public address system should be made and if there is no response the ship should be turned into its wake and a search along the reciprocal course made. At the same time, a thorough search of the ship should be organized and the time at which the missing person was last seen should be established. The track should be searched back to the position where it is known the person was still on board. An urgency call requesting other ships in the vicinity to keep a lookout for the person should be made.

3.3.5 ACTIONS TO LIMIT DAMAGE AND SALVE THE SHIP FOLLOWING A FIRE, EXPLOSION, COLLISION OR GROUNDING (4 hours)

Means of limiting damage and Salving the Ship Following a Fire or Explosion

No definite procedures can be laid down as each occurrence will be unique. Trainees should consider the measures which could be taken in a variety of situations, using materials to be found aboard ship.

It is important to keep observation on damaged areas and temporary repairs, to ensure that there is immediate warning of a worsening situation.

Procedure for abandoning ship

A ship should not be abandoned prematurely. It is generally safer to remain aboard a wreck, to await the arrival of assistance, for as long as possible. This is particularly true in severe weather conditions, when abandoning ship is very hazardous and the condition of the crew will deteriorate rapidly in survival craft. Also, in those conditions, craft are likely to become widely dispersed, making rescue more difficult.

When the condition of the ship is such that sinking or breaking up is inevitable, the ship should be abandoned in time to get clear of her before she sinks or before wreckage makes the launching of survival craft dangerous. In the event of fire or explosion or of the release of toxic fumes it may be essential to get clear of the ship as quickly as possible.

Consideration should be given to the method of passing the ‘abandon ship’ signal. It should be distinctive, so that it is not confused with other signals or instructions which may be given in an emergency. The instruction to abandon ship may have to be given by word of mouth if other communication systems have broken down.

The duties of the emergency party should include provision for the shutting down of any machinery, as required.

船将迅速漂向落水者。几位穿着浸水救生服、救生衣和携带救生绳的健壮船员应在船上待命,以帮助落水者。整个救援期间必须保持落水者在视线之内,这在大浪和大涌浪中是困难的,所有其他参与救援行动的任何船员都应作为瞭望人员。

当船长获得人员失踪的报告时,可合理假定已经做出寻找的努力。最后应在公告广播系统中呼叫,如无反应,则船应掉头,沿相反航向搜索。与此同时,组织全船搜索,应确定失踪人员最后被看见的时间。追踪至据称仍在船的位置。应做出要求附近他船保持瞭望落水者的紧急呼叫。

3.3.5 发生火灾、爆炸、碰撞或搁浅后,限制船舶破损和救助船舶的行动 (4 学时)

发生火灾或爆炸时降低损失和船舶救助的方法

没有明确的程序可以被设定,因为每一个事故的发生都是独一无二的。学员应考虑不同情境下使用船上找到的材料可采取的措施。

重要的是保持对破损和临时修理部位的观察,确保情形恶化时立即报警。

弃船程序

不应过早地弃船。通常尽可能久地待在沉船上等待救援的到达是安全的。在恶劣的天气条件下,这是千真万确的,此时弃船非常危险,救生艇上的船员状况将迅速恶化。还有,在这种情况下,救生艇筏可能变得十分分散,使得救援更为困难。

当船舶当时情况为沉没或断裂不可避免时,应及时弃船,以在船舶沉没前远离船舶或在施放救生艇变得危险前远离沉船。一旦发生火灾或爆炸或释放有毒烟雾, 则可能必须尽快离开该船。

应考虑发出“弃船”信号的方法。它应是独特的,不致与在紧急情况下使用的其他信号或指示相混淆。如其他通信系统发生了故障,则弃船指示可能不得不用口头语言发出。

应急小组的职责应包括按要求关闭任何机械的规定。

3.4 DEVELOP EMERGENCY AND DAMAGE CONTROL PLANS AND HANDLE EMERGENCY SITUATIONS (13 hours)

3.4.1 PREPARATION OF CONTINGENCY PLANS FOR RESPONSE TO EMERGENCIES (9 hours)

Given a brief description of a ship and a crew list, trainees should be able to divide the crew into appropriate emergency teams and draw up the muster list and emergency instructions. Instructions should cover general emergency and fire stations separately.

Plans for dealing with fires in specific areas should be considered. Actual plans would depend upon the construction and arrangement of a particular ship, but principles such as containment of a fire, escape routes, access for fire fighters and the medium to be used can be dealt with. Trainees should be reminded that drills at sea should put these plans into action and that a different location for the fire should be chosen at each practice. It may be found that the plans need revising in the light of practice drills (V29).

Similarly, boat drills should sometimes be organized on the assumption that certain survival craft have been destroyed or are not usable for some reason.

The ship safety committee should be involved in the organization of emergency drills and the evaluation of the plans in the light of those drills. Representatives can bring any difficulties or deficiencies to the attention of the committee and suggest solutions to the problem. The committee can increase awareness of the actions required from crew members through their representatives.

The control centre for the command team in port should normally be at main deck level, at a location suitable for liaison with shore authorities. It should have a shore telephone connection and have emergency equipment and information stored there ready for use.

3.5 USE OF LEADERSHIP AND MANAGERIAL SKILLS

The detailed teaching syllabus for this section builds on the content of IMO model course 1.39, Leadership and teamwork. Many of the concepts introduced in this course are developed further to consider a more senior management perspective to these concepts.

3.5.1 SHIPBOARD PERSONNEL MANAGEMENT AND TRAINING

Officers will have different experiences of personnel management. As officers in charge of a watch they will also have had to exercise their authority. They will therefore recognize and understand many of the learning objectives. It should be possible to build on this and use their prior experience to the maximum to improve their knowledge and ability to cope with seagoing and other personnel such as pilots, ship agents, ship repairers and other shore staff.

There should also be a good opportunity to establish useful facts on the varying conditions of employment experienced by the group of trainees and perhaps to learn something of the advantages and disadvantages of the various systems which the trainees might find to be helpful in the course of their duties.

3.4　制定破损控制图并处理紧急状况　(13 学时)

3.4.1　突发事件应急预案的准备　(9 学时)

给定船舶简单描述和船员名单,学员应能将船员划分为适当的应急队,制作应变部署表和应急指示。指示通常应分别包括一般应急队和消防队。

应考虑涉及特定区域的火灾计划。实际计划取决于船舶构造和布置,但可能涉及诸如封堵火势、逃生路线、灭火方法和使用的介质之类的原则。应提醒学员在海上演习应将这些计划付诸行动,并在每次训练中选择不同的地点。可能会发现,该计划需要国际实际演习修订(V29)。

类似地,有时应组织救生演习,假定某一救生艇已被毁坏或因故不能使用。

在组织应急演习和根据演习评估该计划中应涉及船舶安全委员会。代表们可使委员会关注任何困难或不足,并提出解决问题的建议。委员会可增加通过船员代表提出要求的行动的意识。

港口指挥小组的控制中心通常应在主甲板这一层的一个适合与岸上当局联络的地点。该处应有岸上联系电话,并有应急设备和存有随时备用的信息。

3.5　领导力和管理技能的运用

本部分的教学大纲细则以IMO示范课程1.39“领导力和团队工作”的内容为基础。本课程中介绍的许多概念进一步拓展,以考虑更高级的管理视野来看这些概念。

3.5.1　船上人员管理和培训

驾驶员将具有不同的人员管理经验。作为值班驾驶员,他们还得行使其权力。他们会因此认识和理解许多学习目标。应可能在此基础上建立和最大限度地使用他们以前的经验,改善他们处理航行和其他诸如引航员、船舶代理人、船舶修理人和其他岸上人员关系的知识和能力。

还应有良好机会建立有用关于学员小组经历的不同就业的资料, 学员也许了解在其履行职责的过程中,可能发现有所帮助的各种系统的一些优缺点,如时间允许,应给学员布置小组作业,

If time permits, the trainees should be given group assignments to recreate and learn how to deal with some of the typical arguments and problems which occur on board ship (V111).

Personnel management **(10 hours)**

Management level deck officers have significant responsibility for the management of personnel on board ship. It is important that these officers are aware of national law and the detail of employment agreements that relate to personnel on board. It is equally important, however, that senior officers are able to motivate and manage the performance of personnel as well as dealing with disciplinary situations.

Training **(6 hours)**

Organization and management skills are best learnt through teamwork activities and case studies. As much time as possible should be devoted to this aspect. Role playing exercises may be designed in communications, meetings, organizing drills and training sessions, to name but a few areas (T37). This is an important part of the course as it involves teaching various subjects to the trainees so that they, in due course, have the capability to train staff on board in the same subjects in order to improve safety and operational standards. There is scope in this section to use role playing and group assignments for some aspects of this training.

Nearly all of the training undertaken aboard ship will be on-the-job training, i.e. the trainee uses the normal ship's tools, equipment and materials during the ordinary running of the ship. Off-the-job training will probably be restricted to the use of video cassettes.

For trainee watchkeepers the STCW Convention requires that an approved programme of on board training is supervised and monitored and is adequately documented in a training record book (STCW Code, section A-II/1, paragraph 6). An example of one such book is that produced by the International Shipping Federation. Extensive guidance regarding training is given in the STCW Code, section B-II/1.

Purpose of training

All training is intended to modify attitudes, to increase skills or to provide knowledge which can be applied by the trainee in carrying out his work. The desired outcomes include a reduction in accidents, less need for supervision, greater productivity and improved quality of work. A thorough mastery of a task and knowledge of its relevance to other tasks in the running of the ship also increase the job satisfaction of the crew member concerned.

Preparation

Before starting training, the instructor should prepare what he wishes to teach, decide the order of the instruction and make a note of the important points to be emphasized. Any tools or materials which are needed should be ready to hand and equipment, such as video players, should be tested to ensure that it is working.

以创建和学习如何处理一些发生在船上的典型争论和问题(V111)。

人员管理 **(10 学时)**

管理级甲板驾驶员对船上人员管理具有重大责任。这些驾驶员认识到有关船上人员的国家法律和雇佣协议细节是重要的。然而,同样重要的是,激发和管理人员的表现,以及处理违纪情况。

培训 **(6学时)**

最好通过团队活动和案例研究来学习组织和管理技能。尽可能多的时间应该致力于这方面。可设计通信、会议、组织演习和训练课(T37)这几个方面的角色扮演练习 。这是课程的重要组成部分,它涉及学员的不同科目的教学,以便他们在适当的时候,有能力给船上人员培训相同的科目,以提高安全和操作标准。本节中有一个使用角色扮演和小组作业进行某些方面培训的范围为这部分训练的某些方面。

几乎所有的在船上进行的培训都是在职培训,即在普通船舶的正常运行期间,使用船舶的常用工具、设备和材料进行培训。脱产培训可能会被限制于使用录像带。

对于实习值班人员,STCW公约要求,在接受指导和监控下进行认可的培训计划,并适当记录在培训记录簿中(STCW 规则, A-II/1节, 第 6 段)。国际航运联合会所出版的书就是这样一个范例。在STCW 规则 B-II/1节中给出有关培训的广泛指南。

培训目的

所有培训旨在改进态度、增强技能或提供学员在其工作中运用的知识。理想的结果包括减少事故、不必要的监督、更高的生产效率和改进工作质量。在船舶运营中,完全掌握一项任务和与其他任务相关的知识也增加了有关船员职业满意度。

备课

在开始培训前,教员应准备好他所希望教的内容,决定授课顺序,并注意要强调的重点。需要的任何工具或材料,都应在手头准备好,诸如视频播放器之类的设备应进行测试,以确保其可工作。

Methods of training

For training to be effective, the trainee must be able to see that it is relevant to him and his work or duties on the ship. The instructor should question the trainees before starting to establish what they already know and can do and to explain why the task is necessary.

Nearly all on-board training is of an informal nature, often one-to-one, so trainees should be encouraged to ask questions or have demonstrations repeated, if necessary, during the training. The instructor should also question or test the trainees at suitable intervals to make sure that they have understood, or are able to perform the skill being taught, up to that point. Where appropriate, provide the trainee with a written note to support the tuition.

Changing attitudes

An attitude is an individual's habitual mode of responding to an object or situation. Attitudes are developed by experience within social groups, including those of the work place, and may become firmly implanted. To produce a change of attitude by training is therefore difficult and cannot be done quickly.

A crew member may know the correct safe working practice to adopt for a particular task and yet ignore it when not being directly supervised. The necessary insistence on following safe working practices will not necessarily change a careless attitude to safety. A discussion of the consequences to himself and his family of an accident resulting in permanent disablement might be more effective. Officers should remember that their own attitudes and behaviour help to form those of trainees and new entrants, who will not develop desirable attitudes to required standards if their seniors do not adopt them or if they ignore breaches of them by others.

Training in skills

On-the-job training usually consists of pulling the trainee to watch and work with an experienced person (e.g. a cadet, watchkeeping with a qualified officer). This arrangement fails if the experienced person uses incorrect methods in his work.

In teaching a particular skill, such as a manual task, the instructor should divide the task into self-contained stages, each of which can be taught as a unit. He should identify any critical points at each stage. The job is demonstrated and explained to the trainees in stages, with emphasis on the critical points. The trainee then carries out the job under the supervision of the instructor. Stages are repeated as necessary until the trainees' performances are satisfactory.

Training in knowledge

In the majority of cases aboard ship this will involve an officer or petty officer describing equipment or a particular task to others, for example, instruction in how to launch an inflatable liferaft and board it, and how to survive when in it. Trainees should be encouraged to participate in the instruction by asking questions or making suggestions. Sufficient questions should be directed to trainees to test that the necessary knowledge is being transferred.

培训方法

为进行有效培训,学员应明白培训与其相关,与其船上工作或职责相关。教员应在着手确定学员已了解和能做到的内容和着实解释为什么该任务是必需的之前,进行提问。

几乎所有的船上训练都是非正式的,往往一对一进行,因此,应鼓励学员提问或如有必要,重复培训期间示范的内容。教员还应以适当的间隔对学员提问或测试,以确信学员已经懂得或能完成所教技能,达到该知识点要求。适当情况下,给学员提供书面指示,以利于教学。

转变态度

态度是一种对物体或情景反应的个体习惯模式。态度由社团内的经验所发展,包括工作场所的经验,可被坚定地灌输。因此,要通过培训改变态度是困难的,不能迅速达成。

要进行一项特定的任务,船员可能知道正确的安全工作实践,然而当不被直接监督时就会忽略它。对遵守安全工作实践的必要坚持不一定会将一个粗心的态度改变安全的态度。讨论事故导致永久伤残对他本人和家庭的后果可能会更有效。驾驶员应该记住,自己的态度和行为有助于学员和新人形成其态度和行为,如果他们的长辈不采用要求的标准或他们无视他人违反这些标准,这些学员和新人将不会形成所需标准的理想态度。

培训技巧

在职培训通常包括组织学员观看有经验的人并与其一同工作(如实习生与称职的驾驶员一起值班)。如有经验的人在工作中使用了不正确的方法,这项安排将会失败。

在讲授特殊的技能时,如一个手工任务,教员应将任务分为独立的阶段,其中每一个可作为一个单元讲授。他应识别每一阶段的关键点。在各阶段,给学员示范和解释该项工作,强调关键点。然后学员在教员指导下进行该工作。必要时重复各个阶段,直到学员的表现令人满意。

知识培训

在大多数情况下,船上将涉及驾驶员或普通船员向他人描述设备或一个特定的任务,例如,说明如何施放气胀式救生筏和登筏,以及怎样在里面生存。鼓励学员通过提问或提出建议,参与教学。应针对学员进行足够提问,以测试正在传播必要的知识。

Knowledge which is not often used (how to survive in a liferaft, for example) is forgotten with the passage of time, hence the necessity for repeating such instruction at intervals.

Each trainee should deliver a short training session (about 10 minutes would be sufficient) to the other members of the class. Subjects, drawn from those which would be undertaken aboard ship, should be assigned to the trainees well in advance to allow them ample time for preparation.

3.5.2 RELATED INTERNATIONAL MARITIME CONVENTIONS AND NATIONAL LEGISLATION (4 hours)

It is suggested that where national legislation implementing an international agreement or convention exists, both the national legislation and the international requirements are taught together. For example, a topic could be treated by dealing with the national legislation, including the administrative details necessary for the master to carry out his duties effectively, and making reference to the relevant sections of the international agreement or convention on which the national regulations are based.

In addition to the national laws implementing the international conventions and agreements, the following areas of concern to a ship's master, not touched upon in the syllabus, are mentioned:

- a review of the national system of courts, hearings and appeals
- the procedures for preliminary enquiry and formal investigation of accidents
- contracts of towage
- the carriage of the official logbook, entries and surrender of the logbook at the completion of a voyage
- crew disciplinary procedures, powers and obligations of the master
- the master's disciplinary powers concerning passengers
- calculation of crew wages, rules concerning allotment of wages, deductions of tax and social security contributions, advances, fines, forfeitures, other deductions and payment of the balance
- collective bargaining agreements between seafarers' and shipowners' organizations affecting the employment of crew

3.5.3 APPLICATION OF TASK AND WORKLOAD MANAGEMENT (8 hours)

The importance of identifying fatigue should be emphasized by the instructors. Overload situations can have catastrophic results; the instructors should include case studies involving fatigue, as the major reason for the accident/incident.

Personnel assignment, time and resource constraints and prioritization should be explained to the trainees. Providing opportunities for trainees to apply principles by planning complex typical shipboard activities either individually or in groups will enhance learning and the outcomes for trainees.

不经常使用的知识(例如,怎样在救生筏内生存)会随着时间的流逝而被遗忘,因此必须每隔一段时间重复这样的教学。

每个学员应给班上其他成员提供一个简短的培训课程(约10分钟就足够了)。应事先给学员分派好那些将在船上进行的科目,让他们有充足的时间准备。

3.5.2　相关的国际海事公约、建议和国内立法　(4学时)

在存在国内立法遵守国际协议或公约的情况下，建议将国内立法和国际要求一起讲授。例如,可通过涉及国内立法,包括对船长有效履行其职责的必要行政细节,和参考国内规章依据的国际协议或公约的相关部分来对待一个论题。

除了国内立法履行国际公约和协议外,提到了本教学大纲中没有提及的以下几个方面的问题：

- 国家法院、听证和上诉系统综述
- 事故的初步调查和正式调查程序
- 拖带合同
- 船舶日志的配备、记录和航次结束时的提交日志
- 船员纪律处分程序、船长的权力和义务
- 船长关于乘客的纪律处分权
- 船员工资计算、工资的分配规则、扣除税收和社会保障金、借款、罚款、没收、其他扣减和收支平衡
- 海员和船东之间有关船员雇佣的劳资谈判合同

3.5.3　任务管理和工作量管理的应用　(8学时)

教员应强调识别疲劳的重要性。工作量过大的情形可产生灾难性的后果;教员应把涉及疲劳为事故/事件的主要原因作为案例进行研究。

应向学员解释人员分配、时间和资源限制及优先次序。给学员提供通过以个人或小组进行计划船上的复杂活动来运用原理的机会,将增强学员理解和提高培训效果。

3.5.4 EFFECTIVE RESOURCE MANAGEMENT (10 hours)

This content is intended to build on the learning of trainees through operational level training and experience. The structure follows the concepts from IMO model course 1.39, Leadership and teamwork but develops these to a management level.

Trainees are likely to enhance their learning where they are able to participate in group discussion and practical group activities where the principles of effective resource management can be applied and developed.

3.5.5 DECISION-MAKING TECHNIQUES (7 hours)

Situation and risk assessment, identifying and generating options, selecting course of action and evaluating the outcome effectiveness are covered under this topic.

3.5.6 DEVELOPMENT, IMPLEMENTATION AND OVERSIGHT OF STANDARD OPERATING PROCEDURES (1 hour)

Instructors should explain the methods of developing and implementing standard operating procedures (SOPs) and the reason and dangers of oversighting these procedures. Case studies should be used by the instructors, highlighting these topics.

3.6 ORGANIZE AND MANAGE THE PROVISION OF MEDICAL CARE ON BOARD (4 hours)

The standards of competence required by the STCW Convention are covered by IMO model course 1.15, Medical care, T33, and V91. However, officers need to know where to get appropriate advice and how to apply it correctly. The three main sources of information are the publications mentioned in this section.

3.5.4　有效的资源管理　(10学时)

本内容旨在以学员操作级的培训和经验为基础,继续学习。虽然是按照IMO示范课程1.39“领导力和团队工作”中的概念进行安排,但将这些发展为管理级培训内容。

在学员能够参加小组讨论和小组实操活动,能运用和形成有效的资源管理原则的情况下,有可能提高其学习能力。

3.5.5　决策技巧　(7 学时)

本主题包括情景和风险评估、识别和设计替代方案、选择行动的过程和评估结果的有效性。

3.5.6　标准作业程序的制定、实施与监督　(1 学时)

教员应解释制定和实施标准作业程序(SOP)的方法和忽视这些程序的理由和危险性。教员应使用案例研究,强调这些主题。

3.6　船上医护的组织与管理　(4 学时)

IMO示范课程1.15“医疗”(T33和V91)包括STCW公约要求的适任能力标准。然而,船员需要知道在哪里得到适当的建议和如何正确地加以应用。本节所提到的三个主要资料来源是这些出版物。

Appendix 1

Stability Data

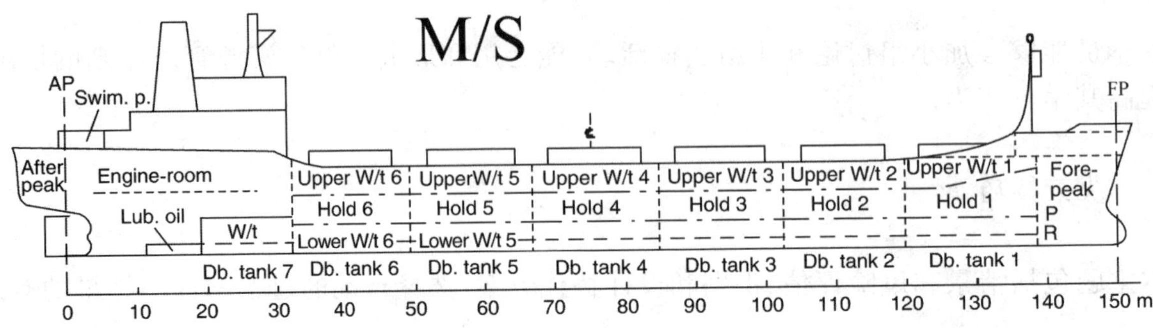

Curves of staflcal stabillty

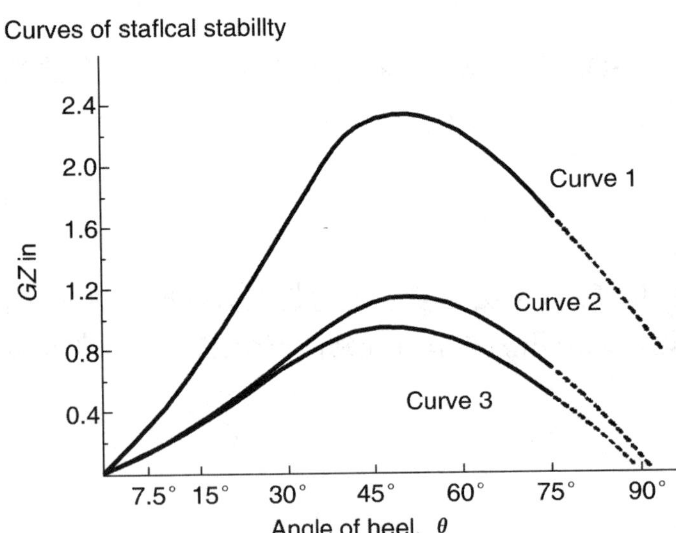

Curve	Condition	Cargo	*H.O.*	*D.O.*	Stores
1	Ballast	–	695.6	155.3	150
2	Load 1	14 894.3	250.0	53.5	150
3	Load 2	16 040.0	200.0	51.2	150

Curve	*F/W*	Ballast	*L/S*	Δ
1	263.3	5070.5	4895	11 229.7
2	104.8	672.4	4895	21 020
3	104.8	–	4895	21 411

Curve	*KG*	GG_1	Corrected *KG*	*GM*
1	6.54	–	6.54	2.56
2	7.113	0.043	7.156	1.484
3	7.320	0.043	7.363	1.307

Capactties in tanks	Volume in m^3	Weights in tonnes					Centre of Gravity		Free surface
		Lub. oil (ρ=0.9)	Diesel oil (ρ=0.9)	Fuel oil (ρ=0.95)	Fresh W. (ρ=1.0)	Bauast W. (ρ=1.02)	*VCG* (metres)	From AP (metres)	$I=\frac{I\times b^3}{12}$ m^4
Forepeak	268.4					275.1	7.28	142.77	67
Db. tank No.1	2×214.0					438.7	1.49	128.44	495
Db. tank No.2	2×296.0					606.8	1.19	110.64	2757
Db. tank No.3	2×328.0					672.4	1.13	93.39	2936
Db. tank No.4	2×328.0					672.4	1.13	75.80	2936
Db. tank No.5	2×191.3			363.5		392.2	0.76	58.22	1094
Db. tank No.6	2×174.8			332.1		358.3	0.76	40.78	785
Db. tank No.7	2×86.3		155.3				1.34	24.69	81
Lower W/t No.5	2×136.1					279.0	1.76	58.46	81
Lower W/t No.6	2×100.8			191.5		206.6	1.89	40.63	55
W/L Eng. Room	2×145			275.5			4.88	26.79	120
Upper W/t No.1	2×149.5					306.1	11.67	127.41	152
Upper W/t No.2	2×204.8					419.8	11.25	110.98	393
Upper W/t No.3	2×204.8					419.8	11.25	93.39	393
Upper W/t No.4	2×204.8					419.8	11.25	75.80	393
Upper W/t No.5	2×204.8					419.8	11.25	58.22	393
Upper W/t No.6	2×204.8					419.8	11.25	40.60	393
After-peak	158.5				158.5		7.98	3.44	206
Swim. pool	32				30	30.8	21.86	2.20	24
Freshw. tank	2×52.4				104.8		11.40	5.27	83
Daily diesel tank	52.2		47.0				10.76	15.00	39
Daily huel oil tank	71.1			67.5			10.82	11.22	102
Diesel oil tank	6.0		5.4				13.99	28.53	1
Lub. oil tank	40.0	36.0					10.76	29.81	4
Lub. oil tank	2×20.8	37.4					0.67	20.50	20
Total:			207.7	1230.1	293.3	6307.1			

附 录 1

稳性数据

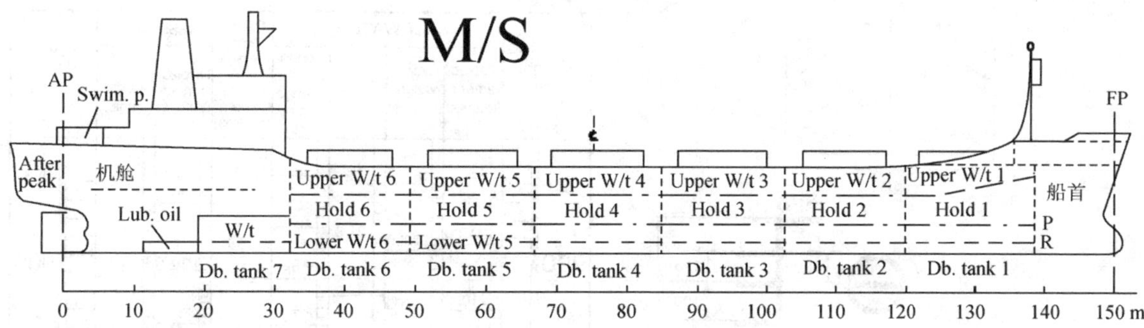

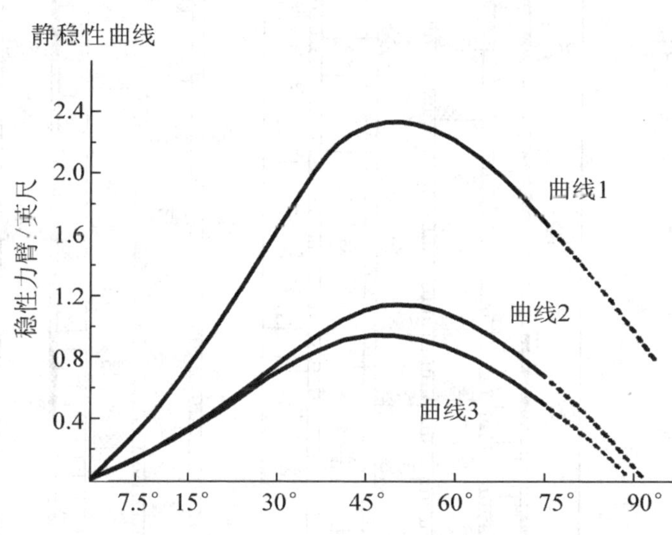

曲线	状态	货物	高位水舱	双层底水舱	备品
1	压载	–	695.6	155.3	150
2	装载1	14 894.3	250.0	53.5	150
3	装载2	16 040.0	200.0	51.2	150

曲线	淡水	压载水	空船重	排水量
1	263.3	5 070.5	4 895	11 229.7
2	104.8	672.4	4 895	21 020
3	104.8	–	4 895	21 411

曲线	KG	GG_1	Corrected KG	GM
1	6.54	–	6.54	2.56
2	7.113	0.043	7.156	1.484
3	7.320	0.043	7.363	1.307

液 体 舱 室	体积/m³	重 量/t					重 心		自由液面惯矩
		滑油 (ρ=0.9)	柴油 (ρ=0.9)	燃油 (ρ=0.9)	淡水 (ρ=1.0)	压载水	重心距基线高	重心距艉垂线距离	$I=\frac{l\times b^3}{12}$/(m⁴)
艏尖舱	268.4					275.1	7.28	142.77	67
双层底舱No.1	2×214.0					438.7	1.49	128.44	495
双层底舱No.2	2×296.0					606.8	1.19	110.64	2 757
双层底舱No.3	2×328.0					672.4	1.13	93.39	2 936
双层底舱No.4	2×328.0					672.4	1.13	75.80	2 936
双层底舱No.5	2×191.3			363.5		392.2	0.76	58.22	1 094
双层底舱No.6	2×174.8			332.1		358.3	0.76	40.78	785
双层底舱No.7	2×86.3		155.3				1.34	24.69	81
低位水舱No.5	2×136.1					279.0	1.76	58.46	81
低位底舱No.6	2×100.8			191.5		206.6	1.89	40.63	55
W/L机舱	2×145			275.5			4.88	26.79	120
高位水舱No.1	2×149.5					306.1	11.67	127.41	152
高位水舱No.2	2×204.8					419.8	11.25	110.98	393
高位水舱No.3	2×204.8					419.8	11.25	93.39	393
高位水舱No.4	2×204.8					419.8	11.25	75.80	393
高位水舱No.5	2×204.8					419.8	11.25	58.22	393
高位水舱No.6	2×204.8					419.8	11.25	40.60	393
艉尖舱	158.5				158.5		7.98	3.44	206
泳 池	32				30	30.8	21.86	2.20	24
淡水舱	2×52.4				104.8		11.40	5.27	83
柴油日用柜	52.2		47.0				10.76	15.00	39
燃油日用柜	71.1			67.5			10.82	11.22	102
轻柴油柜	6.0		5.4				13.99	28.53	1
滑油柜	40.0	36.0					10.76	29.81	4
滑油柜	2×20.8	37.4					0.67	20.50	20
总计：			207.7	1230.1	293.3	6307.1			

Loading Scale

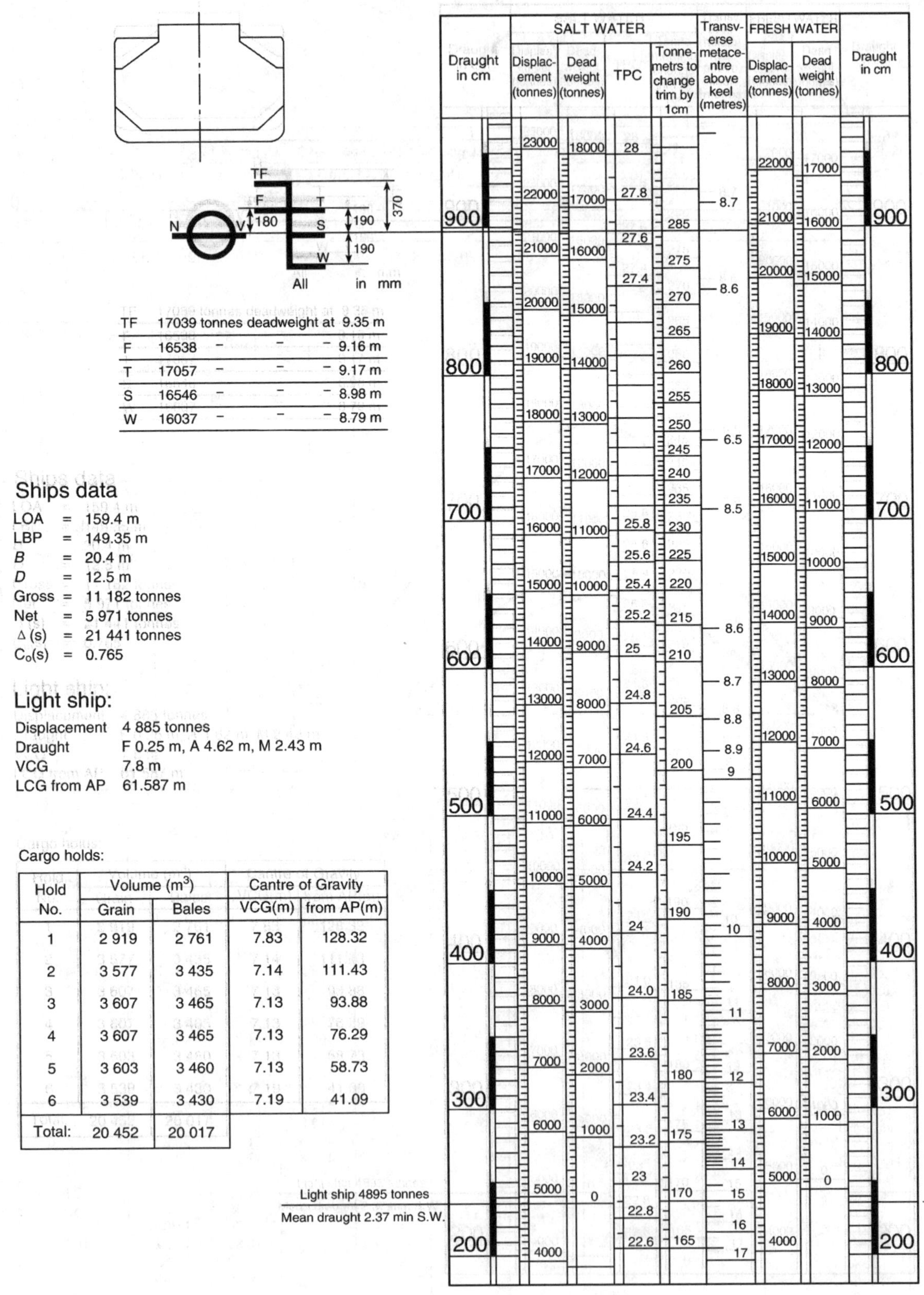

TF	17039 tonnes deadweight at	9.35 m
F	16538 – –	9.16 m
T	17057 – –	9.17 m
S	16546 – –	8.98 m
W	16037 – –	8.79 m

Ships data

LOA = 159.4 m
LBP = 149.35 m
B = 20.4 m
D = 12.5 m
Gross = 11 182 tonnes
Net = 5 971 tonnes
Δ (s) = 21 441 tonnes
C_b(s) = 0.765

Light ship:

Displacement	4 885 tonnes
Draught	F 0.25 m, A 4.62 m, M 2.43 m
VCG	7.8 m
LCG from AP	61.587 m

Cargo holds:

Hold No.	Volume (m^3)		Cantre of Gravity	
	Grain	Bales	VCG(m)	from AP(m)
1	2 919	2 761	7.83	128.32
2	3 577	3 435	7.14	111.43
3	3 607	3 465	7.13	93.88
4	3 607	3 465	7.13	76.29
5	3 603	3 460	7.13	58.73
6	3 539	3 430	7.19	41.09
Total:	20 452	20 017		

载重表尺

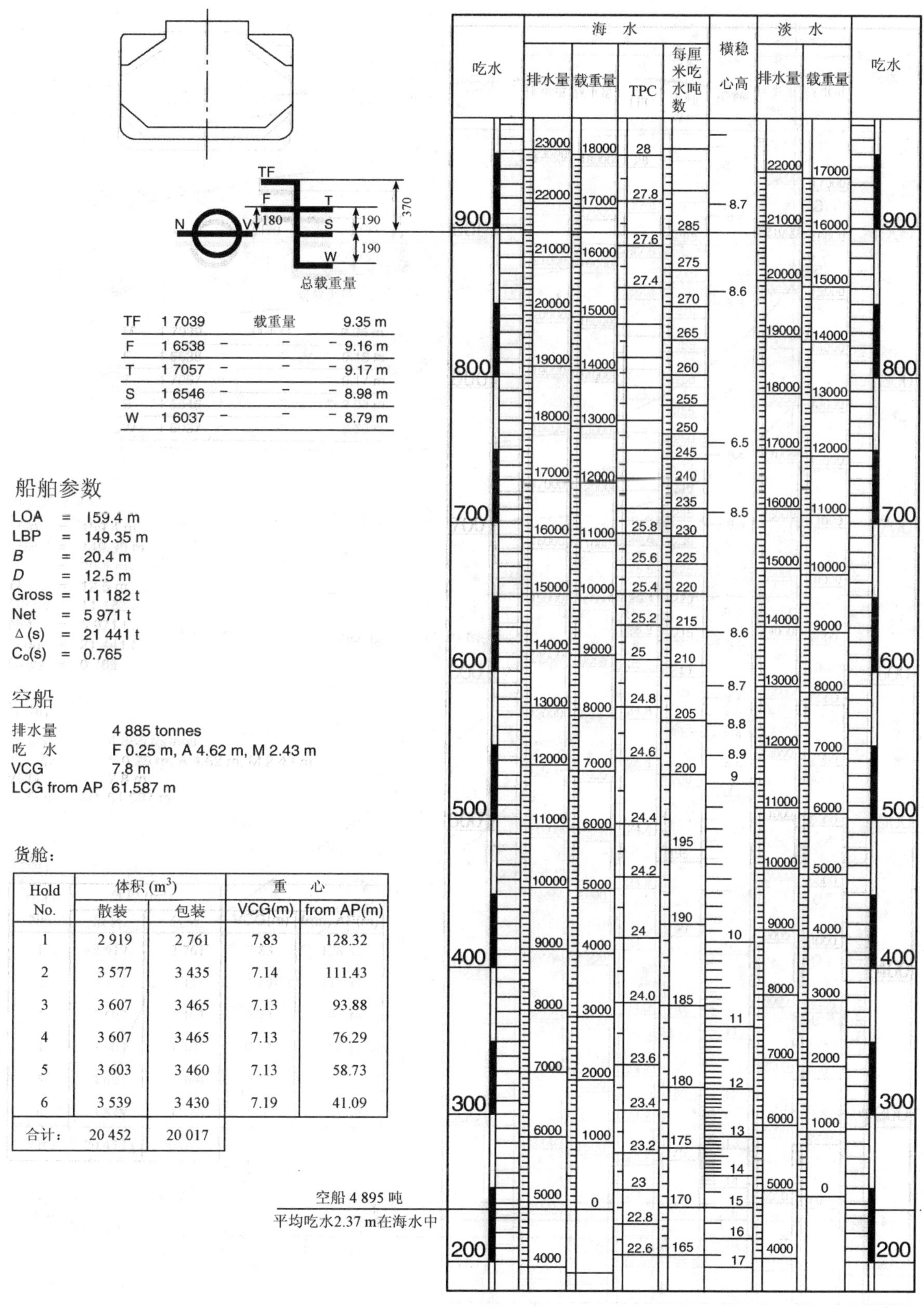

TF	1 7039	载重量	9.35 m
F	1 6538	–	9.16 m
T	1 7057	–	9.17 m
S	1 6546	–	8.98 m
W	1 6037	–	8.79 m

船舶参数

LOA = 159.4 m
LBP = 149.35 m
B = 20.4 m
D = 12.5 m
Gross = 11 182 t
Net = 5 971 t
Δ(s) = 21 441 t
C_0(s) = 0.765

空船

排水量 4 885 tonnes
吃 水 F 0.25 m, A 4.62 m, M 2.43 m
VCG 7.8 m
LCG from AP 61.587 m

货舱：

Hold No.	体积 (m³)		重 心	
	散装	包装	VCG(m)	from AP(m)
1	2 919	2 761	7.83	128.32
2	3 577	3 435	7.14	111.43
3	3 607	3 465	7.13	93.88
4	3 607	3 465	7.13	76.29
5	3 603	3 460	7.13	58.73
6	3 539	3 430	7.19	41.09
合计:	20 452	20 017		

KN Curves

8.0
7.0
6.0
5.0
4.0
3.0
2.0
1.0
KN in metres
75°
60°
45°
30°
15°
7.5°
3 4 5 6 8 10 12 14 16 18 20 22 24
Displacement in thousand tonnes
21441 tonnes

10.0
9.0
8.0
7.0
6.0
5.0
4.0
3.0
2.0
Draught in metres
LCB from AP
LCB from ℄
℄
LCB
LCF
75.0
75.5
76.0
76.5
m 77.0
m
Aft
3 2 1 ℄ 1 2
Ford

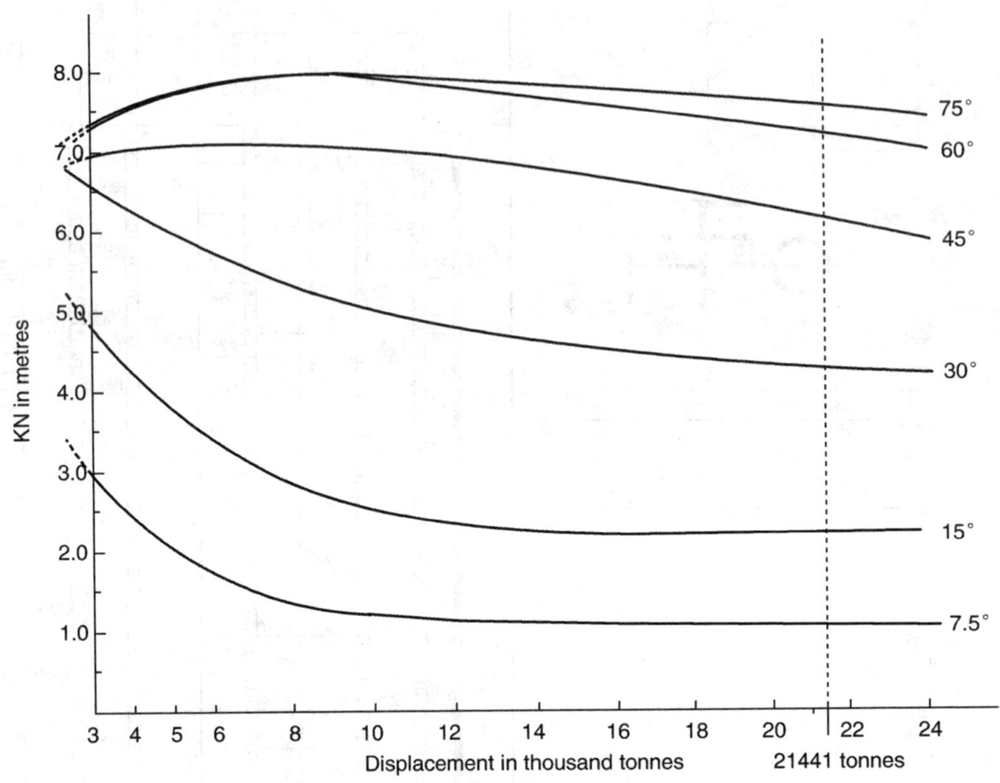

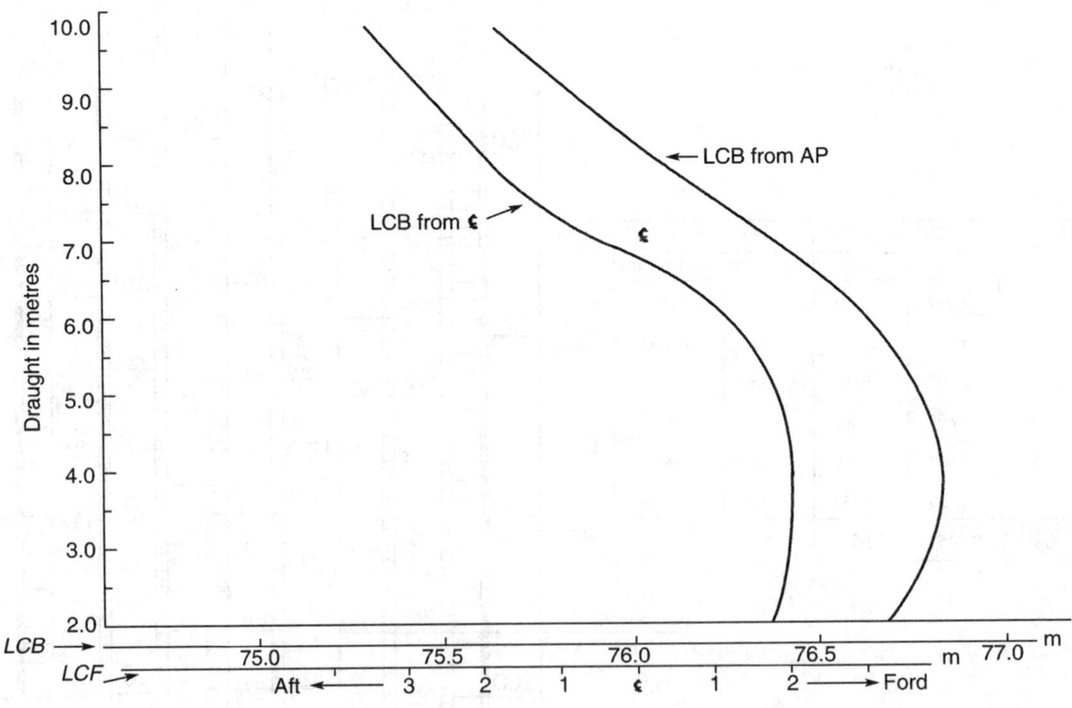

KN曲线

8.0
7.0
6.0
5.0
4.0
3.0
2.0
1.0
型吃水(m)
75°
60°
45°
30°
15°
7.5°
3
4
5
6
8
10
12
14
16
18
20
22
24
排水量×10³(t)
21 441 t

10.0
9.0
8.0
7.0
6.0
5.0
4.0
3.0
2.0
吃水(m)
LCB from AP
LCB from ℄
℄
LCB
LCF
75.0
75.5
76.0
76.5
77.0
(m)
(m)
船尾
3
2
1
℄
1
2
船首

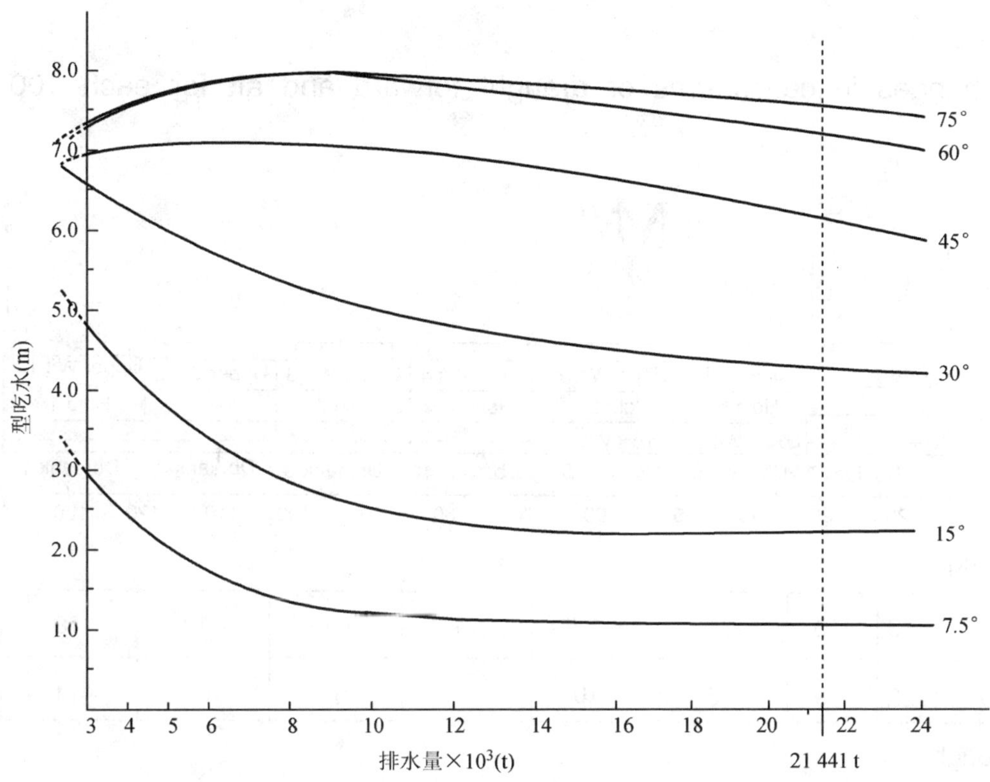

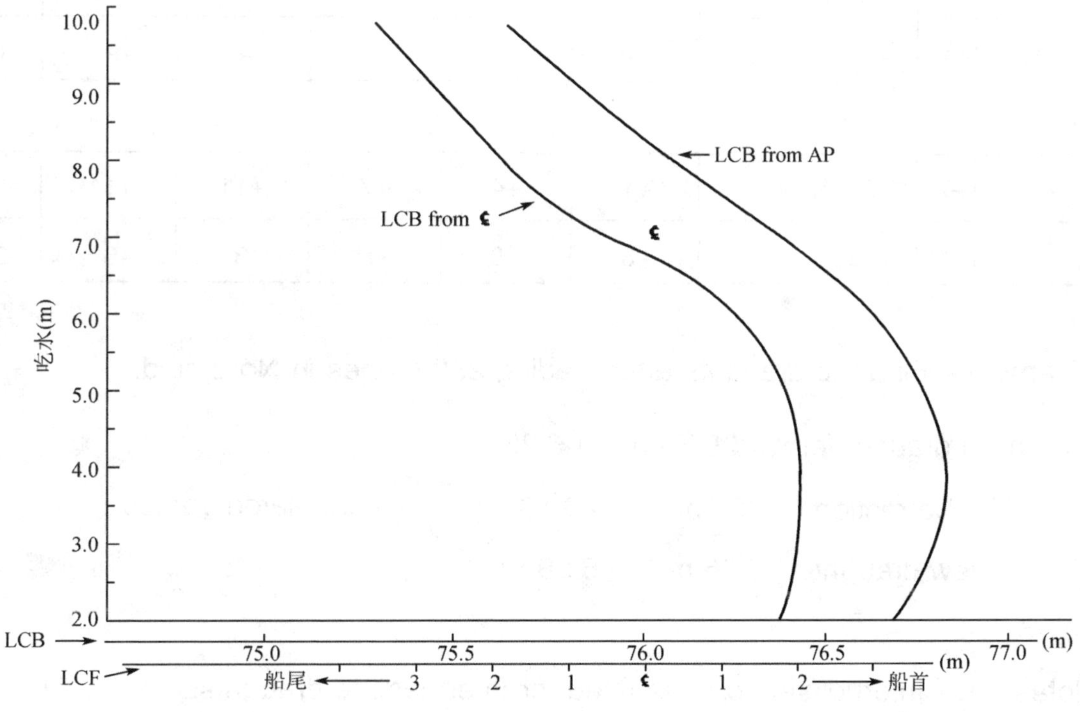

Appendix 2

Trim Table

Tables of changes in centimetres of draught forward and aft for each 100 tonnes loaded.

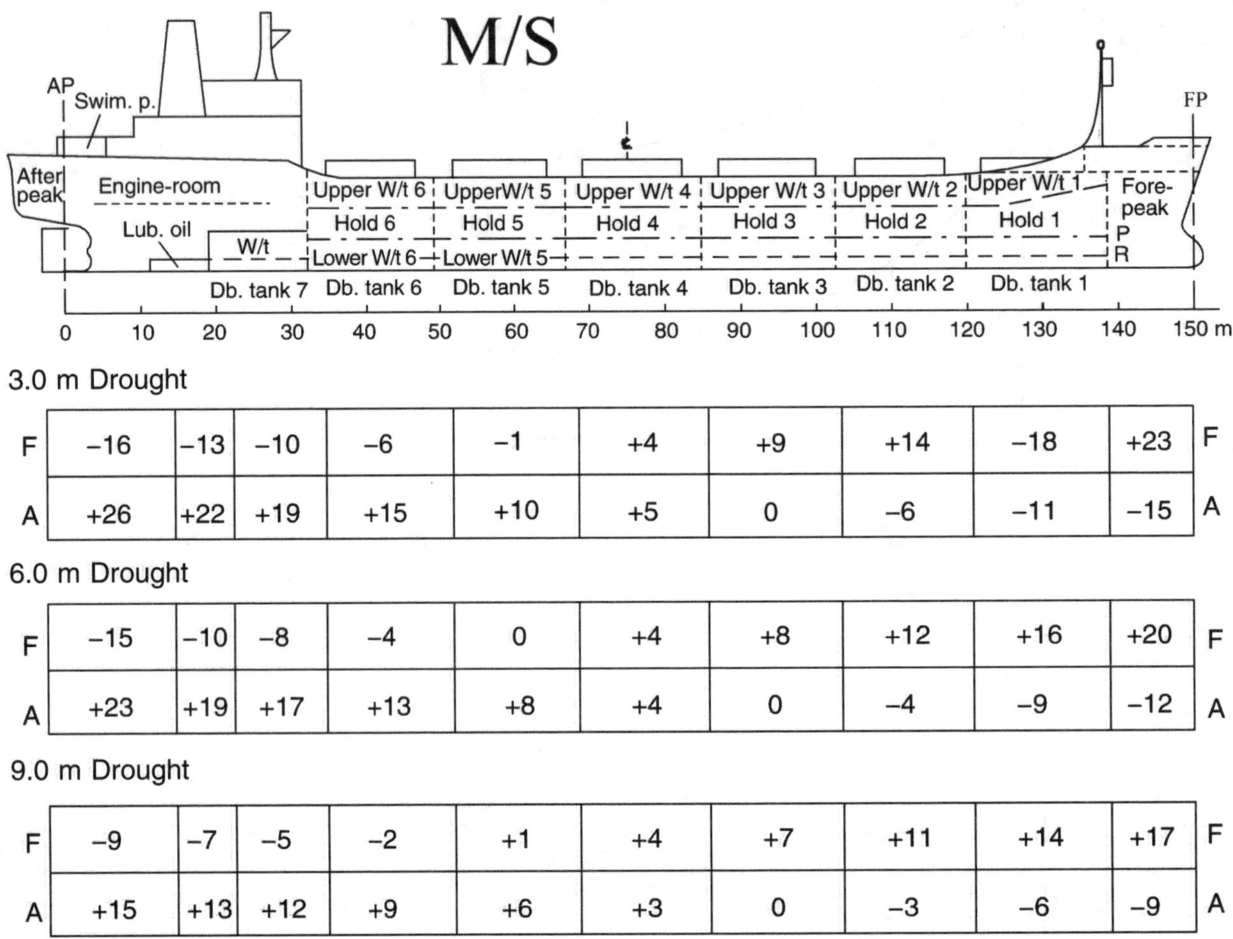

3.0 m Drought

F	−16	−13	−10	−6	−1	+4	+9	+14	−18	+23	F
A	+26	+22	+19	+15	+10	+5	0	−6	−11	−15	A

6.0 m Drought

F	−15	−10	−8	−4	0	+4	+8	+12	+16	+20	F
A	+23	+19	+17	+13	+8	+4	0	−4	−9	−12	A

9.0 m Drought

F	−9	−7	−5	−2	+1	+4	+7	+11	+14	+17	F
A	+15	+13	+12	+9	+6	+3	0	−3	−6	−9	A

Example – Find the draughts after loading 250 tonnes in No.2 hold.

Initial draught forward 5.76 m aft 6.38 m

Correction	+0.30	−0.10	$\left(\frac{250}{100} \times \text{tabulated values}\right)$
New draught	6.06 m	6.28 m	

Notes 1. Interpolation can be used for intermediate draughts.

2. Reverse the signs of the corrections for discharged weights.

附 录 2

吃水差表

每装载100吨在船舶首尾部造成的吃水变化表,以厘米计。

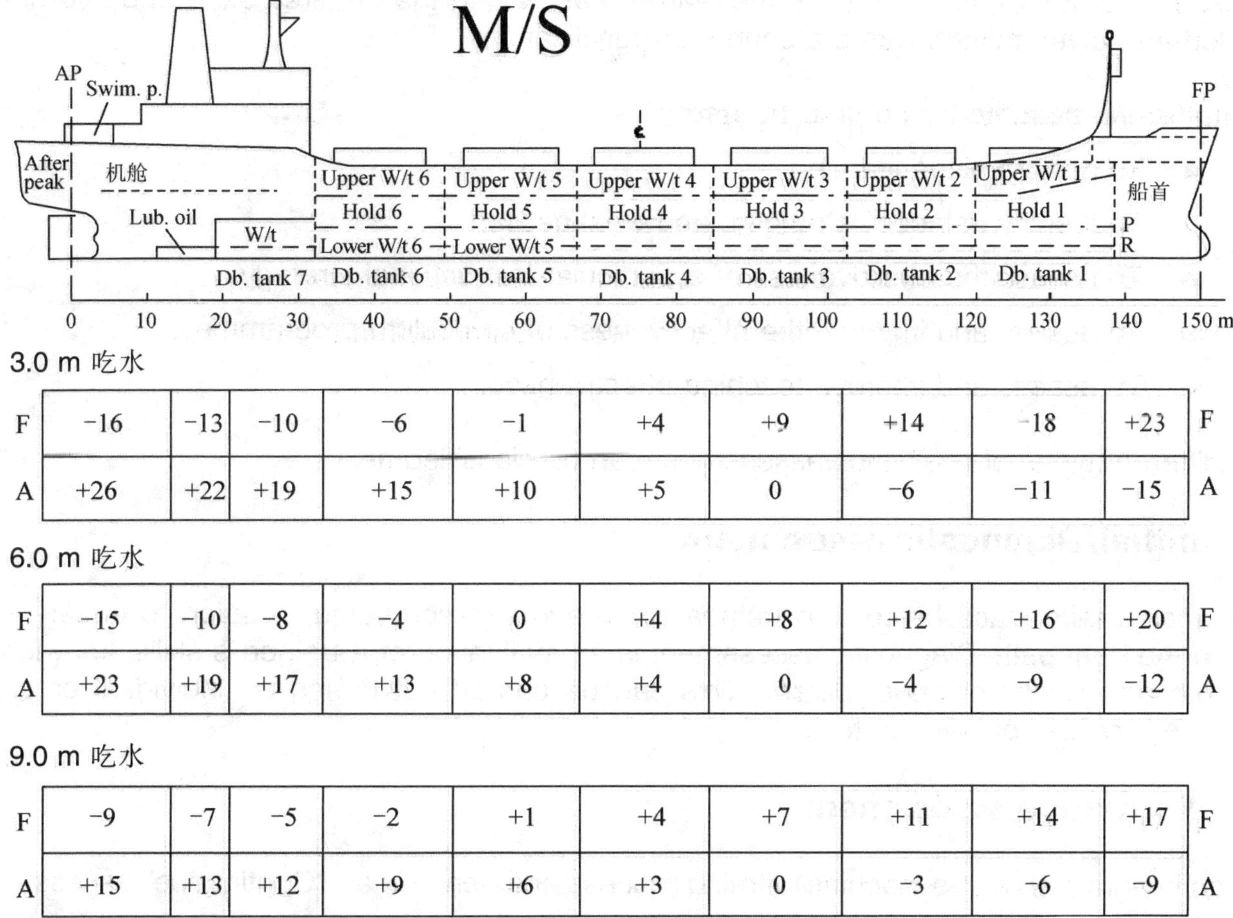

3.0 m 吃水

F	−16	−13	−10	−6	−1	+4	+9	+14	−18	+23	F
A	+26	+22	+19	+15	+10	+5	0	−6	−11	−15	A

6.0 m 吃水

F	−15	−10	−8	−4	0	+4	+8	+12	+16	+20	F
A	+23	+19	+17	+13	+8	+4	0	−4	−9	−12	A

9.0 m 吃水

F	−9	−7	−5	−2	+1	+4	+7	+11	+14	+17	F
A	+15	+13	+12	+9	+6	+3	0	−3	−6	−9	A

举例——找到二号舱装250吨货后的吃水。

初始吃水:前5.76 m,后6.38 m

修正	+0.30	−0.10	$\left(\frac{250}{100} \times \text{表列值}\right)$
新吃水	6.06 m	6.28 m	

注: 1. 插入值可用于中部吃水。

2. 对卸载重量的修正符号应反过来。

Part E: Evaluation

The effectiveness of any evaluation depends to a great extent on the precision of the description of what is to be evaluated. The detailed teaching syllabus is thus designed, to assist the instructors, with descriptive verbs, mostly taken from the widely used Bloom's taxonomy.

Evaluation/Assessment is a way of finding out if learning has taken place. It enables the assessor (instructor), to ascertain if the learner has gained the required skills and knowledge needed at a given point towards a course or qualification.

Evaluation/assessment can also be used:

- To assist trainee learning.
- To identify trainees' strengths and weaknesses.
- To assess the effectiveness of a particular instructional strategy.
- To assess and improve the effectiveness of curriculum programmes.
- To assess and improve teaching effectiveness.

The different types of evaluation/assessment can be classified as:

■ Initial/Diagnostic assessment

This should take place before the trainee commences a course/qualification to ensure they are on the right path. Diagnostic assessment is an evaluation of a trainee's skills, knowledge, strength and areas for development. This can be carried out during an individual or group setting by the use of relevant tests.

■ Formative assessment

It is an integral part of the teaching/learning process and hence is a "Continuous" assessment. It provides information on trainees' progress and may also be used to encourage and motivate them.

Purpose of formative assessment

- To provide feedback to trainees.
- To motivate trainees.
- To diagnose trainees' strengths and weaknesses.
- To help trainees to develop self-awareness.

■ Summative assessment

It is designed to measure trainee's achievement against defined objectives and targets. It may take the form of an exam or an assignment and takes place at the end of a course.

E部分:评估

任何评估的有效性在很大程度上取决于对评估内容的精确描述。教学大纲细则按此方式进行设计以协助教员教学,其采用的描述性动词主要来源于广泛使用的布鲁姆分类中的词类。

评估/评定是查明学员的学习是否有效的一种方式。它使评估者(教师)确定学员是否在给定课程进程点或资格点获得所需的技能与知识。

评估/评定的目的是:

- 帮助学员的学习。
- 发现学员的强项和弱点。
- 评估特定教学方法的有效性。
- 评估和改善课程计划的有效性。
- 评估和提高教学的有效性。

不同类型的评估/评定可分为:

■ 初始性/诊断性评估

这种评估应在学员开始课程或资历学习前进行,以确保他们处于正确的学习方向。诊断性评估评估学员的技能、知识、强项和发展方向。评估期间可采用相关测试对学员进行单人或多人成组评估。

■ 形成性评估

形成性评估是教员教学与学员学习过程中不可分割的一部分,因此,它是一种“连续性”评估。它提供学员的学习过程信息,可用来鼓励和激励学员的学习。

形成性评估的目的

- 向学员提供反馈信息。
- 激励学员。
- 发现学员的强项和弱点。
- 帮助学员发展自我意识。

■ 终结性评估

终结性评估用来衡量学员是否达到确定的学习目的或目标。它可以在一门课程结束之时对学生进行考试或要求其完成规定作业等形式来进行评估。

Purpose of summative assessment

- To pass or fail a trainee
- To grade a trainee

■ Evaluation for quality assurance

Evaluation can also be required for quality assurance purposes.

Purpose of assessment with respect to quality assurance

- To provide feedback to instructors on trainee's learning.
- To evaluate a module's strengths and weaknesses.
- To improve teaching.

■ Assessment planning

Assessment planning should be specific, measurable, achievable, realistic and time-bound (SMART). Some methods of assessment that could be used depending upon the course/ qualification are as follows and should all be adapted to suit individual needs.

- Observation (in Oral examination, Simulation exercises, Practical demonstration).
- Questions (written or oral).
- Tests.
- Assignments, activities, projects, tasks and/or case studies.
- Simulations (also refer to section A-I/12 of the STCW Code 2010).
- CBT.

■ Validity

The evaluation methods must be based on clearly defined objectives, and they must truly represent what is meant to be assessed, for example only the relevant criteria and the syllabus or course guide. There must be a reasonable balance between the subject topics involved and also in the testing of trainees' KNOWLEDGE, UNDERSTANDING AND PROFICIENCY of the concepts.

■ Reliability

Assessment should also be reliable (if the assessment was done again with a similar group/ learner, would you receive similar results). We may have to deliver the same subject to different groups of learners at different times. If other assessors are also assessing the same course/ qualification as us, we need to ensure we are all making the same decisions.

To be reliable an evaluation procedure should produce reasonably consistent results no matter which set of papers or version of the test is used.

总结性评估的目的

- 评估学员课程学习及格或不及格
- 对学员进行分级

■ 质量保证评价

评价也是质量保证的目的。

关于质量保证的评价目的

- 向教员提供有关学员学习情况的反馈信息。
- 评估教学模块的优点和缺点。
- 提高教学质量。

■ 评估计划

评估计划应该是一种具体的、可衡量的、可实现的、实际的与规定时限的计划(英文缩写为SMΛRT)。根据课程情况或学员资历可以采用以下评估方法,评估方法的选择应满足学员个人需要。

- 观察 (在口试、模拟操练、实际演练中进行)。
- 问题(以书面答卷或口试形式)。
- 考试。
- 作业、活动、完成项目、任务和/或案例研究。
- 模拟 (也参考2010年STCW公约A-Ⅰ/12节)。
- 计算机辅助训练。

■ 有效性

评估方法必须基于明确的目标,并且必须真实地表现评估内容,如相关标准、教学大纲或课程指南。在所涉及的课程主题之间及对学员学习的各种概念的知识、理解和熟练程度的测试中必须要有合理有效的评估方法。

■ 可靠性

评估还应具备可靠性 (可靠性指如重复评估类似学习情况的学习小组或学员,评估员应得到类似的结果)。评估员可以在不同的时间给不同组别的学员们设置相同的评估主题,如果其他评估员也进行同样的评估,各评估员间需确保做出类似的评估结果。

可靠的评估过程应该是无论采用哪种测试题或测试方法,都应产生合理一致的结果。

If the instructors are going to assess their own trainees, they need to know what they are to assess and then decide how to do this. The what will come from the standards/learning outcomes of the course/qualification they are delivering. The how may already be decided for them if it is assignments, tests or examinations.

The instructors need to consider the best way to assess the skills, knowledge and attitudes of our learners, whether this will be formative and/or summative and how the assessment will be valid and reliable.

All work assessed should be valid, authentic, current, sufficient and reliable; this is often know as VACSR – "valid assessments create standard results".

- Valid – the work is relevant to the standards/criteria being assessed;
- Authentic – the work has been produced solely by the learner;
- Current – the work is still relevant at the time of assessment;
- Sufficient – the work covers all the standards/criteria.
- Reliable – the work is consistent across all learners, over time and at the required level.

It is important to note that no single method can satisfactorily measure knowledge and skill over the entire spectrum of matters to be tested for the assessment of competence.

Care should therefore be taken to select the method most appropriate to the particular aspect of competence to be tested, bearing in mind the need to frame questions which relate as realistically as possible to the requirements of the officer's job at sea.

■ STCW Code

The training and assessment of seafarers, as required under the Convention, are administered, supervised and monitored in accordance with the provisions of section A-I/6 of the STCW Code.

Column 3 – Methods for demonstrating competence and Column 4 – Criteria for evaluating competence in table A-II/2 (Specification of minimum standard of competence for masters and chief mates) of STCW Code sets out the methods and criteria for evaluation. Instructors should refer to this table when designing the assessment.

It should be noted that this column distinguishes where/how competence can be evaluated by examination, by demonstration and in many cases has requirements for both. The reason for this is that while knowledge and understanding can generally be assessed with some validity, using examination, actual or simulated demonstrations are a far more valid method for evaluating proficiency.

Assessment is also covered in detail in another IMO model course, however to assist and aid the instructors, some extracts from the model course is used to explain in depth.

如果教员要评估自己的学员,首先需明确要评估的内容,然后再决定评估的方法。评估内容来自于其传授给学员的各种标准/课程或资历培训的教学内容。评估方法可以采取布置作业、进行测试或考试等方式。

教师需考虑采取最好的方式来评估学员的技能、知识和学习态度,需考虑评估的类型是否是形成性评估和/或终结性评估,需考虑评估结果的有效性和可靠性。

所有的评估工作和结果都应是有效、真实、现行、足够和可靠的,即所谓的"有效评估创建的标准结果"(英文缩写为VACSR)。

- 有效是指评估工作的相关标准或评估标准的有效性。
- 真实是指评估完全由学员独立完成。
- 现行是指评估工作应与时俱进。
- 足够是指评估内容应涵盖所有公约标准要求。
- 可靠是指评估结果应与学员的学习时间与效果、所处级别水平相对应。

重要的是应注意:没有单一的测试方法可以令人满意地对学员在整个学习期间内所学全部知识与技能以及适任能力进行评估。

因此,教师应仔细选择最合适的测试方法评估学员的特定能力,应注意评估时设计的测试题尽可能与轮机员海上实际的工作要求相关联。

■ STCW 规则

根据《海员培训、发证和值班标准国际公约》的要求,海员的培训和评估应依照STCWA-Ⅰ/6部分的有关规则进行管理、监督和监控。

在STCW公约中,表A-II/2第3列——演示适任能力的方法和第4列——评估适任能力的标准(船长和大副适任能力最低标准)规范,制定了评估方法和标准,当设计评估时,教员应参考该表。

应该注意的是,该列区分在哪里/如何可通过考试、演示,在许多情况下,二者都需要,进行适任能力评估。之所以这样做是因为知识和理解一般可通过考试进行一些有效性评估,而使用检验、实际或模拟演示是一种更有效的评估熟练度的方法。

IMO另一个示范课程也详细介绍了评估,然而使用该示范课程的摘录深度解释评估,以辅佐教员。

When evaluation consists of calculations, the following should be taken into consideration:

■ Calculations

To carry out their duties, Masters and Chief Mates must be able to solve technical problems by performing calculations in various subject areas such as cargo work, ship stability and navigation calculations.

The ability to perform such calculations and to resolve such problems can be tested by having the candidates carry out the calculations in their entirety. Since a large variety of technical calculations is involved and the time necessary for their complete solution is considerable, it is not possible to completely test the abilities of candidates within a reasonable examination time.

Resort must therefore be made to some form of sampling technique, as is the case with the assessment of knowledge, comprehension and application of principles and concepts in other subject fields.

In examinations conducted on a traditional essay-type basis, the sampling technique that is applied in respect of calculation requirements is to attempt to cover as much of the subject area as possible within the examination time available. This is frequently done by using questions involving shorter calculations and testing in depth on one or two topics by requiring the completion of more complex calculations. The employment of this 'gross sampling' technique reduces the reliability of the examination as compared with what can be achieved with a more detailed sampling technique.

A greater breadth of sampling can be achieved by breaking down calculations into the various computational steps involved in their solution. This technique can only be applied to calculations in which the methodology is standardized. Fortunately, most calculations follow a standard format; where alternative methods of solution exist, the examination can be developed so as to allow candidates an appropriate freedom of choice. Such freedom of choice must be a feature of examinations of all types, in any event.

In order to develop a series of 'step test items', covering an entire calculation, it is necessary to identify each intermediate step in each calculation involved by all methods which are accepted as being correct in principle. These questions, after they have been reviewed for clarity and conciseness, form the standard 'step test items' in that calculation topic.

This approach allows questions to be posed which sample the candidate's knowledge and ability to perform parts of various calculations, which process takes up less time than having him perform entire calculations. The assumption is made that if the candidate can or cannot correctly complete a calculation step leading to the solution, then he can or cannot successfully carry out the entire calculation. Such detailed sampling allows a larger number of questions to be answered by the candidate within the time allotted for the examination, thus allowing a broader sampling of the candidate's knowledge and abilities, thereby increasing the reliability of the examination.

当评估包括计算时,应考虑下列部分:

■ 计算

为了履行其职责,船长和大副必须能够通过进行不同学科领域的算术解决技术问题,如货物作业、船舶稳性和导航计算。

执行这样的计算和解决这些技术疑难的能力可以通过测试学员进行完整计算的方法来获得。因为涉及大量技术计算及获得完整的答案需耗费大量的时间,因此在合理的考试时间内它不可能完全测试出学员的能力。

因此,正如对知识、原理的理解和应用、其他学科领域各概念的评估一样,评估方法必须借助于某种形式的抽样技术。

在进行传统的论文式或试卷式考试时,采用抽样技术测试计算能力是为了尝试在有限的考试时间内覆盖尽可能多的主题内容，通常采用的方法是通过设置小型计算题及为测试掌握主题内容深度而设置一个或两个需要更为复杂计算的测试题来进行。与更详细的抽样技术相比,使用这种总抽样技术降低了考试的可靠度。

更大范围或更详细的抽样可以通过分解各种计算于获得答案所涉及的各种计算步骤中,但这种技术只能应用于其计算方法是标准化的计算中。幸运的是大多数计算都遵循标准的格式,由此存在解决问题的可选方法。教员可以制定考试类型以允许学员有适当的选择自由度,但在任何情况下这种选择自由度必须是所有论文式或试卷式考试类型的共同特征。

为开发一系列覆盖完整计算的分步测试项目,有必要分析每个计算的中间步骤,该计算应涉及那些已公认原理正确的所有计算方法。在复核其清晰度和简洁度后,将这些计算作为计算类主题考试的标准分步测试项目。

这种测试方法允许设置问题以抽样测试学员进行各种分步计算的知识和能力，学员花费的时间比其进行完整计算用得少。这种测试方法建立在这样的设想下,即学员是否能或不能正确完成得到答案所需的计算步骤,从而推断其能或不能成功地完成完整计算。采用这样的详细抽样技术可以让学员在规定的考试时间内回答更多的问题,从而允许更大范围或更详细的抽样,以测试学员知识掌握与能力程度,由此提高测试的可靠性。

It must be pointed out that because of the greater number of test items used more time will be spent by candidates in reading the questions and in appreciating the precise step which each question involves.

However, the ability to answer correctly questions that are based on each intermediate step leading to the solution does not necessarily indicate competence in the application of the calculation methodology or in the interpretation of the intermediate or final results. Further questions must therefore be developed which are of a 'procedural' and principle nature.

Such 'step test' and 'procedural' items may be drawn up as 'essay-type' items, supply-type items or multiple-choice items. Marking or scoring is easier if multiple-choice test items are used, but in some cases difficulties may arise in creating plausible distracters.

Detailed sampling can allow immediate identification of errors of principle and those of a clerical nature. It must be emphasized that this holds true, in general, only if the test item is based on a single step in the overall calculation. Multiple-choice items involving more than one step may, in some cases, have to be resorted to in order to allow the creation of a sufficient number of plausible distracters, but care must be exercised to ensure that distracters are not plausible for more than one reason if the nature of the error made (and hence the distracter chosen) is to affect the scoring of the test item.

■ Compiling tests

Whilst each examining authority establishes its own rules, the length of time which can be devoted to assessing the competence of candidates for certificates of competency is limited by practical, economic and sociological restraints. Therefore a prime objective of those responsible for the organization and administration of the examination system is to find the most efficient, effective and economical method of assessing the competency of candidates. An examination system should effectively test the breadth of a candidate's knowledge of the subject areas pertinent to the tasks he is expected to undertake. It is not possible to examine candidates fully in all areas, so in effect the examination samples a candidate's knowledge by covering as wide a scope as is possible within the time constraints and testing his depth of knowledge in selected areas.

The examination as a whole should assess each candidate's comprehension of principles, concepts and methodology; his ability to apply principles, concepts and methodology; his ability to organize facts, ideas and arguments and his abilities and skills in carrying out those tasks he will be called upon to perform in the duties he is to be certificated to undertake.

All evaluation and testing techniques have their advantages and disadvantages. An examining authority should carefully analyse precisely what it should be testing and can test. A careful selection of test and evaluation methods should then be made to ensure that the best of the variety of techniques available today is used. Each test shall be that best suited to the learning outcome or ability to be tested.

■ Quality of test items

No matter which type of test is used, it is essential that all questions or test items used should be as brief as possible, since the time taken to read the questions themselves lengthens the

必须指出,由于测试项目较多,学员将花费更多的时间用于阅读问题和鉴别每个问题所涉及的精确步骤。

然而,在这种测试方法中学员正确回答问题的能力是基于获得答案的每一个中间步骤,而无须显示其对计算方法的应用能力,也不必显示其对中间或最终结果的解释能力。因此,必须进一步开发带有过程性质和原理性质的测试题。

这些“分步测试”和“过程”性考题可以按论文或试卷型、供给型或多项选择题型拟定。如果采用多项选择题型进行测试,改卷或记分更容易,但在某些情况下,创造似是而非的干扰项可能会出现困难。

详细抽样技术的使用允许立即识别原则性错误和书写性错误。必须强调,一般只有在测试项目是基于单步骤的完整计算情况下,以上识别才正确。在某些情况下不得不借助涉及多个步骤的多项选择题型进行测试,采用多项选择题型可以允许创建足够数量的似是而非的干扰项。但如果干扰项错误的性质(干扰选择项)影响测试项目的评分时,须注意确保干扰项具有不合理的多个原因。

■ 测试命题

有关考试时长,虽然每个检查机关都有自己的规定,但用于评估考证学员适任能力的考试时长受制于实操、经济和社会条件。因此负责考试系统的组织和管理机构其主要目的是找到最有效率、最有效果和最经济的方法去评估学员的适任能力。一个考试系统应该能有效地测试学员专业知识的广度,但不可能测试学员各方面的全部能力。所以考试与评估实际上是通过覆盖尽可能广泛的知识内容,在有限的时间范围内抽样评估学员掌握知识的广度与深度。

总的来说,考试与评估应该评估每个学员对原理、概念和方法的理解程度;对原理、概念和方法的应用能力;对事实、想法和观点的组织能力和履行适任证书规定任务的能力和技能。

所有的评估和测试技术都有其优点和缺点。检查机关应认真分析测试内容和测试方法,应仔细选择测试和评估方法以确保使用当下最好的测试和评估技术。每个测试或评估应最好地与学员的学习内容或能力相契合。

■ 试题质量

无论使用哪种类型的测试,至关重要的是使用的所有考题、问题或测试项目应尽可能简短,因为阅读问题本身将拖长考试时间。

examination. Questions must also be clear and complete. To ensure this, it is necessary that they be reviewed by a person other than the originator. No extraneous information should be incorporated into questions; such inclusions can waste the time of the knowledgeable candidates and tend to be regarded as 'trick questions'. In all cases, the questions should be checked to ensure that they measure an objective which is essential to the job concerned.

SCORING TESTS

Scoring subjective tests

The assessment of seafarers is concerned with judging whether they are competent, in terms of meeting sufficient specified learning objectives, to perform the tasks required by the qualification they are seeking. That is, they should be tested against predetermined criteria rather than against the performance of other examinees or the norm for the group as a whole, as is the case in many examinations.

To achieve that end in subjective tests, an analytical scoring scheme should be drawn up in which complete model answers, which would attract full marks, is produced for each question. The model answer is then analysed for the definitions, facts, explanations, formulae, calculations, etc., contained in it and marks are allocated to each item, the aim being to make the scoring as objective as possible. A subjective element will still exist in the original allocation of marks to the various sections and, to some extent, in the scoring of incomplete or partially correct sections.

Either credit scoring or deductive scoring may be used. In credit scoring, marks are awarded, in accordance with the scoring scheme, for each correctly completed part of the answer, no marks being credited for incorrect parts or omissions. With deductive scoring, marks are deducted for errors and omissions from the total mark for the question or part question (where a question has been divided into two or more sections). When applied to essay questions, the two methods should produce virtually the same score. Deductive scoring is usually confined to the marking of calculations.

Deductive scoring can be weighted to take account of the relative seriousness of different types of error. Errors are commonly classed and weighted as follows:

.1 errors of principle; for example, using the formula for righting moment in a calculation of list; deduct 50% of the mark for the question or part question;

.2 major errors; for example, extracting data for the wrong day or time from a publication; deduct 30% of the mark for the question or part question; and

.3 clerical errors; for example, transposition of numbers from tables or question paper, careless arithmetic; deduct 10% of the mark for the question or part question for each error.

In the case of clerical errors, only one deduction for a single error should be made. No deductions are made for incorrect answers which follow through from the original error. If deductions exceed the total mark for a question or part question it is given a zero score; negative scores are not carried over to other parts.

问题必须清晰和完整,为确保这点,由出题者之外的人审查考题十分必要。考题中不应纳入无关信息;这些夹杂的无关信息将浪费有见识学员的时间,并往往被视作“陷阱题”。无论何种情况,应检查考题以确保它们测评的是与工作相关的客观内容。

测试评分

主观测试评分

对海员的评估重点是从满足足够的特定学习目标方面来评判他们是否具有任职资格所要求的适任能力,也就是说,应按预先确定的标准进行测试与评估,而不是像其他考试那样按应试者的表现或整个学习组的表现标准进行测试与评估。

为实现这一目的,应采用主观测试法——一种评分分析方案,其方法是为每一道考题制定完整并可获得满分的标准答案,再分析标准答案中的定义、事实说明、解释、公式、计算等各项,为每个项目分配分数,目的是为评判考卷时能尽可能客观地给出考分。但为各个原始项目配分时,和评卷中对不完整的或部分正确的答案进行评分时在某种程度上都存在着主观因素。

可以使用加分评分或演绎评分的方法进行评分。加分评分是按评分方案,对每个完成正确答案的部分进行计分,不正确的部分或遗漏处不计分。演绎评分是从回答问题的总分中扣除错误回答分和遗漏部分分 (对于分成两个或两个以上部分的考题)。当论文或试卷型考试应用这些计分方法时,这两种计分方法应该产生几乎相同的分数。演绎评分通常限用于计算类的考题计分。

对相对严重的不同类型错误可以考虑采用加权计分的演绎评分法。错误与权重通常归类如下:

.1 原则性错误;如使用复原力矩公式计算横倾时出现原则性错误,从该题或该分题的得分中扣掉50%的分数;

.2 重大错误;例如,从出版物中提取错误的日期或时间数据;对该题目或部分题目扣减30%的分数;和

.3 笔误;如从表或试题中引用数字出错,计算粗心,从该题或该分题的得分中扣掉10%的分数。

对于笔误,只在一个错误处扣分。对由初始错误而获得的错误答案不扣分。如果题或分题的扣分超过了该题或分题的总分,该题或分题计零分,不应出现波及其他部分的负分。

The different types of error can be taken into account in credit scoring schemes by suitably weighting the marks allocated to method, to the extraction of data and to clerical accuracy at each step of the calculation. The steps need to be smaller and more detailed than the division into parts used in deductive marking. As a result, the marks lost for errors of principle tend to be smaller in credit scoring than in deductive scoring.

A small percentage of the total mark, to be credited only for the correct final answer, is sometimes included in a credit scoring scheme. The answer must lie within stated accuracy limits to qualify for that credit. In deductive schemes, an answer that has otherwise been correctly calculated but which falls outside the accuracy limits are treated as a clerical error.

Where tests are to be marked locally at more than one test centre, a well-defined scoring scheme, which will give the same score when applied to the same paper by different markers, is essential for the uniform and fair treatment of candidates. To aid in any subsequent review of marks, possibly resulting from an appeal, the marker should make brief marginal notes on the paper to indicate the reasons for deductions.

Guidance on the treatment of answers produced by pocket calculators is needed. Examination rules usually warn candidates that all working must be shown to gain full marks for a question. The marks to deduct when insufficient working is shown but a correct answer is produced, or when all working is correctly shown but the answer is wrong, need to be known by the marker.

In papers in which all questions are to be answered, the marks may be weighted to reflect the importance or difficulty of individual questions or the length of time which will be needed to answer them. When this is done, it is usual to indicate the mark for each question on the question paper. Optional questions should all be of similar standard and carry equal marks, so that the standard of the complete test is the same regardless of the questions chosen. Use can be made of a compulsory and an optional section in the same paper. Questions on which it is felt that all candidates should be tested can be placed in the compulsory section and suitably weighted, while the remainder of the paper offers a choice of questions each of similar standards.

A problem that arises with optional papers is how to deal with cases where more than the required number of questions is answered. Various solutions are adopted by different examining boards. Many mark all questions and discard the lowest marked question or questions, although that fact is not generally advertised as it may encourage candidates to attempt extra questions. Others take the requisite number of answers in the order in which they are on the question paper and ignore the remainder. A similar problem arises in papers in which candidates are required to answer a given number of questions and including at least some stated number from each of several sections.

The pass mark should be set at the lowest score for which sufficient skills and knowledge are demonstrated for competency in each subject. In practice, that score is difficult to determine exactly for an individual paper and could vary slightly from one examination to another. Such an arrangement would be difficult to administer and would be considered unfair by candidates, so the pass mark is fixed and published in the examination regulations. It is, therefore, essential when preparing papers to maintain as constant a standard as possible, such that the pass mark is an appropriate measure of competency.

对不同类型的错误可以考虑采用加权计分的加分评分法，该方法可对每一步计算中准确的数据及记录予以适当分配分数。加分评分所需评分步骤比演绎评分的评分步骤更细致、更详尽，因此，加分评分法对原则性错误的扣分要小于演绎评分法的扣分。

正确的最终答案在加分评分法中有时只占总分的一小部分，为获得加分评分法的有效计分，答案必须处于规定的精度范围内。而在演绎评分法中，除非进行正确的计算，否则答案无法得分，而且超出精度范围的答案被当作笔误对待。

当评估或测试在当地多个考试中心进行，必须使用明确的评分方案，同一套试卷由不同的评卷者评分时应给出类似的分数，这对统一和公平对待每位学员十分重要。为满足学员对考试分数可能的申诉或复核要求，评分者应在试卷上写明简约旁注以指明扣分原因。

对由袖珍计算器产生的答案有必要给出处理指南。考试规则通常要提醒学员：对每一个问题，如要获得满分，必须标明所有的计算步骤或回答。需要明确说明当答案正确但计算步骤或回答不足时，或所有的计算步骤与回答正确但答案错误时应扣分数量。

在所有问题都需要回答的论文或试卷型考试中，每个考题都需要标明分值或回答问题所需时长以表明该题的重要性和难度。该做法通常会在试卷上显示：试卷上每个问题的分数，可选题计分采用相同的标准，整个试卷无论选择哪一种考题，计分标准都一致。同一套试卷中可以设置必答题和可选题。如觉得有必要测试所有学员的考题可以放在必答部分并给予适当分值，试卷其余部分可设置其他考题作为可选题，但需采取相同的评分标准。

带可选题的试卷中出现的问题是如何处理或评判那些超过要求数量的考题的回答。不同的考试管理局采用各种各样的解决方法。绝大多数采用的方法是对所有的考题都标明分值，舍弃最低分的回答，尽管这一做法并非广为人知，但它可以鼓励学员尽可能尝试回答额外问题。其他的做法是要求学员按顺序回答试卷上的考题，评卷人按顺序给回答评分，舍弃多余的回答。在要求学员回答给定数量的考题并且对每部分的考题回答数量有最少要求的考试中也会出现上述类似问题。

及格分数应设置在对每个课题的适任能力进行充分的技能与知识展示之最低分数水平处。但在实际工作中，很难精确地确定每张试卷的及格分数，而且其可能会因考试地点的不同而略有不同。这给考试管理者带来困难并会被学员认为不公平，所以应明确及格分数标准并在考试规则中予以公布。准备试卷或出考题时尽可能保持恒定的标准十分重要，如此，及格分数才是衡量适任能力的适当措施。

The following instructions are typical of those produced for guidance of examiners on the marking of examinations:

In order to achieve uniformity in marking between the examiners in various centres and to facilitate the review of papers, the following guidelines are to be used at all centres:

.1 When several candidates write the same examination, papers, other than multiple choice, should be marked question by question, that is to say, question 1 of paper 1 should be marked for all applicants before proceeding to question 2, etc. This gives more uniform marking.

.2 All questions should be marked even if it becomes apparent that the candidate cannot achieve the pass mark.

.3 Neatness and Orderly Layout of Work:

Where work is not properly laid out or is not neat, marks should be deducted without regard to correctness of the answer. The number of marks deducted should vary according to the quality of the work up to a maximum of 10% where the correct answer is obtained.

.4 Important Engineering and Technical Terms:

Where, in general calculations or general questions, an incorrect term is used and such a term is incidental to the work, the examiner should exercise his judgement as to whether or not marks should be deducted, but in any case, a deduction should not exceed 10% of the allotted marks. This does not apply to direct answers involving definitions or in answers involving the naming of parts.

.5 Types of Errors:

Errors can be divided into 3 types:

(a) P – error in principle; 50% of marks allotted for the whole or part of the question should be deducted.

(b) C – clerical error; 10% of the marks allotted should be deducted for each such error.

(c) M – major error; 30% of the marks allotted for the question or part of the question should be deducted.

NOTE: Large mark questions should be considered in their main sections and percentages of the sections deducted. Candidates should be given the benefit of any doubt which may exist.

.6 Drawings:

Too much importance should not be attached to elaborate drawings. Often a simple sketch with captions is very explanatory and indicative of a good understanding.

.7 Incomplete Answers:

Where a problem or distinct section of a large problem is only partly worked and a step of principle remains to be made, marks allotted should not exceed 50% of the total marks or the split marks allotted as the case may be.

典型的评估员评分指南说明如下:

为实现各考试中心评估员采用统一的计分标准并便于对试卷复查之目的,所有考试中心应遵循以下评分原则:

.1 除多重选择题外,当诸多学员使用同样的试题、试卷进行考试时,改卷评分对所有应试者的试卷应采用按题逐步打分的方式,即对所有应试者的试卷1试题1评阅打分完毕后,才能评阅试题2,以此类推直至评阅打分完毕,采取这种方式有助于评分标准更为统一。

.2 即使某学员明显不能达到及格分数,仍须对其所有回答进行评阅打分。

.3 卷面的整洁性与有序性:

当考生试卷卷面不整洁、有序性差时,即使答案正确也应扣分。视其卷面质量,扣分量不应超过正确答案得分量的10%。

.4 轮机工程与技术的重要术语:

在一般计算或一般问题类的考试中,术语使用不当或该术语对于考题来说不太重要时,评阅者应行使其判断权决定是否应该扣分,但在任何情况下,扣分量不应超过该题总分的10%。注意这一原则不适用于解释定义、命名部件之类的考题评分。

.5 错误类型:

错误可以分为3种类型:

(a)P——原则性错误:该题或该分题总分的50%应扣掉。

(b)C——笔误:该题或该分题总分的10%应扣掉。

(c)M——主要错误:该题或该分题总分的30%应扣掉。

注意:对大分值问题的回答,应考虑其主要部分内容及所占百分比进行扣分。对有任何疑问的学员回答应尽量给予优惠分。

.6 图纸:

考试或试卷中不必附太多重要的详细图纸。通常带标题的简单草图就能良好地解释和说明题意。

.7 不完整的答案:

学员只完成部分问题或完成一个大问题的不同部分,其他基本步骤有待完善时,给分不应超过该题总分的50%,或视情况分步计分。

MARKING PAPERS:

.8 When marking papers, examiners should enter appropriate marginal notes in brief showing why marks have been deducted, using abbreviations in Paragraph 5. The actual error should be ringed and marked with a brief statement of the reason for the error, e.g., 'wrong answer'. A paper should be so marked that any reviewing examiner can see at a glance just what happened, including a marginal note to indicate award of a 'benefit of doubt'.

.9 In the case of marginal failure, the paper concerned should be carefully reviewed. This review is not to be regarded as having the purpose of passing the candidate; it is to ensure that the foregoing marking standards have been correctly applied and are consistent with those of other responses to the same examination. It may result in either an increase or a decrease in marks assigned. This review having been completed, the examiner should issue a fail result if it is still below the pass mark.

.10 Use of Calculators:

When a pocket, non-programmable calculator is used by a candidate in an examination, all necessary formulae and transpositions must be shown for full marks to be allotted. In the case of a correctly set out answer, or partial answer, which has an incorrect final result, 30% of the whole or part should be deducted on the major error rule.

When the evaluation consists of oral and practical tests, which many topics as per the table A-III/2, column 2, Knowledge, Understanding and Proficiency, require, the following should be taken into consideration:

■ Advantages and disadvantages of oral and practical tests

Some aspects of competency can only be properly judged by having the candidate demonstrate his ability to perform specific tasks in a safe and efficient manner. The safety of the ship and the protection of the marine environment are heavily dependent on the human element. In many cases, STCW actually specifies where practical testing is required. In general, all proficiencies require a practical demonstration which in some cases can be performed within training or in service. It is important that any practical testing used to evaluate competence is valid. This means that where this is to be conducted during a training course, the assessor needs to create an environment that has the key features of the work environment on ship present.

It is generally considered advisable that at least some of the testing of knowledge and understanding of candidates for certificates of competency should be conducted orally. The ability of candidates to react in an organized, systematic and prudent way can be more easily and reliably judged through an oral/practical test incorporating the use of models or simulators than by any other form of test.

One disadvantage of oral/practical tests is that they can be time-consuming and can require expensive equipment and facilities. Each test may take up about 1 to 2 hours if it is to comprehensively cover the topics concerned. Equipment must also be available in accordance with the abilities that are to be tested. Some items of equipment can economically be dedicated solely for use in examinations.

评阅试卷:

.8 当考官或评估员评阅试卷时，应使用第5条中的缩写词在试卷上进行简约旁注以指明扣分原因。试卷上的实际错误处应圈出并简约标明错误原因,如“错误值”。每张试卷都应如此评阅与标注以便任何复审者一眼就可看出错在何方,对有疑问的回答也应旁注说明是“存疑优惠分”。

.9 对于分数接近及格线的未及格试卷,应对其进行仔细复核。复核的目的不是让应试者及格通过考试,而是确保前述评分标准得以正确实施以及实施相同的检查时各结果能一致。复核可能导致增加或减少已评分。复核完成后,如该试卷仍然低于及格分数线,考官应出具评估失败的结果。

.10 使用计算器:

当学员使用便携式非编程计算器进行考试时，为获满分试卷中必须写明所有必要的计算公式与演算步骤。对只写出正确答案,或写出部分正确答案,但最终结果不正确的试题应按主要错误之规则处理,扣除该题或分题得分的30%。

当评估由口试和实操测试组成,对STCW 表A-III/ 2第2栏中诸多课题的知识、理解和熟练程度进行评估时,应考虑以下因素。

■ 口试和实操考试的优缺点

某些方面的能力,只能通过让学员以安全和有效的方式演示执行特定的任务的能力,来适当地判断。船舶的安全和海洋环境的保护都主要依赖于人的因素。在许多情况下,STCW公约实际上明确规定了需要实操考试的情况。一般而言,所有需熟练掌握的内容都要求实操演示,某些情况下,可在培训或在船服务期间进行。重要的是,用于评估能力任何实操考试都是有效的。这意味着,要在培训课程中进行实操,评估人员需要创造一种具有目前船上重要特征的工作环境。

通常认为至少某些适任证书的知识和理解考试应采用学员口试是适当的。学员以一个有组织的、系统的和审慎的方式做出反应的能力,通过结合模型或模拟器进行口试/实操考试可比任何其他形式的考试更容易和可靠地加以判断。

口试/实操考试的一个缺点是,可能需较长时间,并要求昂贵的设备和设施。如果全面涵盖有关主题,每一考试可能需要1至2个小时。设备还必须符合被测试的能力。出于经济上的考虑,一些项目的设备仅用于考试。

Attachment

Guidance on the implementation of IMO model courses

附件

IMO示范课程实施指南

Contents

Part 1 Preparation

Part 2 Notes on Teaching Technique

Part 3 Curriculum Development

Annex A1 Preparation checklist

Annex A2 Example of a Model Course syllabus in a subject area

Annex A3 Example of a lesson plan for annex A2

目 录

第1部分　备课

第2部分　教学技巧注释

第3部分　课程开发

附录A1　备课检查表

附录A2　某一科目示范课程教学大纲的示例

附录A3　附录A2教案的示例

Part 1 Preparation

1 Introduction

1.1 The success of any enterprise depends heavily on sound and effective preparations.

1.2 Although the IMO model course "package" has been made as comprehensive as possible, it is nonetheless vital that sufficient time and resources are devoted to preparation. Preparation not only involves matters concerning administration or organization, but also includes the preparation of any course notes, drawings, sketches, overhead transparencies, etc., which may be necessary.

2 General considerations

2.1 The course "package" should be studied carefully; in particular, the course syllabus and associated material must be attentively and thoroughly studied. This is vital if a clear understanding is to be obtained of what is required, in terms of resources necessary to successfully implement the course.

2.2 A "checklist", such as that set out in annex A1, should be used throughout all stages of preparation to ensure that all necessary actions and activities are being carried out in good time and in an effective manner. The checklist allows the status of the preparation procedures to be monitored, and helps in identifying the remedial actions necessary to meet deadlines. It will be necessary to hold meetings of all those concerned in presenting the course from time to time in order to assess the status of the preparation and "trouble-shoot" any difficulties.

2.3 The course syllabus should be discussed with the teaching staff who are to present the course, and their views received on the particular parts they are to present. A study of the syllabus will determine whether the incoming trainees need preparatory work to meet the entry standard. The detailed teaching syllabus is constructed in "training outcome" format. Each specific outcome states precisely what the trainee must do to show that the outcome has been achieved. An example of a model course syllabus is given in annex A2. Part 3 deals with curriculum development and explains how a syllabus is constructed and used.

2.4 The teaching staff who are to present the course should construct notes or lesson plans to achieve these outcomes. A sample lesson plan for one of the areas of the sample syllabus is provided in annex A3.

2.5 It is important that the staff who present the course convey, to the person in charge of the course, their assessment of the course as it progresses.

3 Specific considerations

3.1 Scope of course

In reviewing the scope of the course, the instructor should determine whether it needs any adjustment in order to meet additional local or national requirements (see Part 3).

第1部分 备课

1 介绍

1.1 任何事业的成功很大程度上都依赖于周全和有效的准备。

1.2 尽管IMO的示范课程的制作已经尽可能全面,但用充分的时间和资料进行备课还是十分重要的。备课不仅涉及管理或组织方面的事务,还包括准备任何可能需要的课程注释、图纸、草图和投影胶片等。

2 总体设想

2.1 应仔细研究整套课程,特别是对教学大纲和相关资料必须专注和透彻地研究。从成功实施本课程所需要的资源这一角度清楚地理解所需要的内容,是十分重要的。

2.2 在备课的所有阶段应当使用如附录A1中所示的那种"检查表",以确保尽早、有效地进行所有必要的行动和活动。检查表能使备课程序的状态受到监控,并且有助于确认满足期限所必需的纠正措施。为评估备课的状况并"诊断"任何困难,有必要经常召集与授课有关的所有人员开会。

2.3 应当与要讲授该课程的教学人员讨论该教学大纲,而且应当接纳他们针对要讲授的特定部分的观点。对大纲进行的研究将决定入学的学员是否需要准备工作以便满足入学标准。教学大纲细则是以"培训效果"的格式制定的。每一个特定的效果准确地阐述了学员必须做什么来表明已经达到了该效果。在附录A2中给出了示范课程大纲的示例。第3部分涉及课程的制定并解释了如何编制和使用大纲。

2.4 将要讲授本课程的教学人员应当编写讲课注释或教案来达到这些效果。在附录A3中提供了大纲示例中某个科目的教案示例。

2.5 讲授本课程的人员随课程的进展向该课程负责人转达他们对课程的评估,这是很重要的。

3 具体设想

3.1 课程范围

在审查课程范围时,教员应当决定是否需要做出任何调整以便满足额外的地方或本国的要求(见第3部分)。

3.2 Course objective

3.2.1 The course objective, as stated in the course material, should be very carefully considered so that its meaning is fully understood. Does the course objective require expansion to encompass any additional task that national or local requirements will impose upon those who successfully complete the course? Conversely, are there elements included which are not validated by national industry requirements?

3.2.2 It is important that any subsequent assessment made of the course should include a review of the course objectives.

3.3 Entry standards

3.3.1 If the entry standard will not be met by your intended trainee intake, those entering the course should first be required to complete an upgrading course to raise them to the stated entry level. Alternatively, those parts of the course affected could be augmented by inserting course material which will cover the knowledge required.

3.3.2 If the entry standard will be exceeded by your planned trainee intake, you may wish to abridge or omit those parts of the course the teaching of which would be unnecessary, or which could be dealt with as revision.

3.3.3 Study the course material with the above questions in mind and with a view to assessing whether or not it will be necessary for the trainees to carry out preparatory work prior to joining the course. Preparatory material for the trainees can range from refresher notes, selected topics from textbooks and reading of selected technical papers, through to formal courses of instruction. It may be necessary to use a combination of preparatory work and the model course material in modified form. It must be emphasized that where the model course material involves an international requirement, such as a regulation of the International Convention on Standards of Training, Certification and Watchkeeping (STCW) 1978, as amended, the standard must not be relaxed; in many instances, the intention of the Convention is to require review, revision or increased depth of knowledge by candidates undergoing training for higher certificates.

3.4 Course certificate, diploma or document

Where a certificate, diploma or document is to be issued to trainees who successfully complete the course, ensure that this is available and properly worded and that the industry and all authorities concerned are fully aware of its purpose and intent.

3.5 Course intake limitations

3.5.1 The course designers have recommended limitations regarding the numbers of trainees who may participate in the course. As far as possible, these limitations should not be exceeded; otherwise, the quality of the course will be diluted.

3.5.2 It may be necessary to make arrangements for accommodating the trainees and providing facilities for food and transportation. These aspects must be considered at an early stage of the preparations.

3.2 课程目标

3.2.1 课程材料中所阐述的课程目标应当非常仔细地予以斟酌，以便完全理解其含义。为涵盖本国或地方性规定对成功完成本课程的学员要求的其他任务，课程目标是否需要做一步扩充？反过来，未经本国行业要求确认的要素是否包括在内？

3.2.2 对课程所做的任何后续评估应当包括对课程目标的审查，这一点很重要。

3.3 入学标准

3.3.1 如果计划入学的学员不能满足入学标准，则应当首先要求入学的学员完成一个提高班，使其提升到规定的入学水平。或者，通过插入会覆盖所需知识的课程材料使受影响的课程部分能够得到扩充。

3.3.2 如果计划入学的学员超出入学标准，你不妨删节或省略不需要教授的或可以用修订的方式来处理的课程部分。

3.3.3 带着上述问题来研究课程材料，并且着眼于评估在参加课程之前学员是否需要进行准备工作。学员准备材料的范围可以是复习笔记、从教科书中选择的题目、技术论文选读，直至讲授的正式课程。将准备工作和修改形式的示范课程材料结合起来使用可能是必要的。必须强调，在示范课程涉及国际要求，例如经修正的《1978年海员培训、发证和值班标准国际公约》(STCW)的条款时，不得降低标准；在很多情况下，该公约的意图就是要求为获得高一级证书而接受培训的申请人对其知识进行复习、更新或深化。

3.4 课程证书、文凭或文件

如果要给顺利完成本课程的学员发放证书、文凭或文件，则要保证能够签发这类证明并且措辞恰当以及本行业和所有相关机关完全知晓其目的和意图。

3.5 课程人数限制

3.5.1 本课程设计人已对可能参加课程的学员人数的限制提出了建议。尽可能地不要突破该限制，否则课程的质量就会降低。

3.5.2 可能需要就学员的住宿、就餐和交通设施做出安排。这些方面必须在早期准备时就予以考虑。

3.6 Staff requirements

3.6.1 It is important that an experienced person, preferably someone with experience in course and curriculum development, is given the responsibility of implementing the course.

3.6.2 Such a person is often termed a "course co-ordinator" or "course director". Other staff, such as lecturers, instructors, laboratory technicians, workshop instructors, etc., will be needed to implement the course effectively. Staff involved in presenting the course will need to be properly briefed about the course work they will be dealing with, and a system must be set up for checking the material they may be required to prepare. To do this, it will be essential to make a thorough study of the syllabus and apportion the parts of the course work according to the abilities of the staff called upon to present the work.

3.6.3 The person responsible for implementing the course should consider monitoring the quality of teaching in such areas as variety and form of approach, relationship with trainees, and communicative and interactive skills; where necessary, this person should also provide appropriate counselling and support.

3.7 Teaching facilities and equipment

Rooms and other services

3.7.1 It is important to make reservations as soon as is practicable for the use of lecture rooms, laboratories, workshops and other spaces.

Equipment

3.7.2 Arrangements must be made at an early stage for the use of equipment needed in the spaces mentioned in 3.7.1 to support and carry through the work of the course. For example:

.1 blackboards and writing materials;

.2 apparatus in laboratories for any associated demonstrations and experiments;

.3 machinery and related equipment in workshops;

.4 equipment and materials in other spaces (e.g. for demonstrating fire fighting, personal survival, etc.).

3.8 Teaching aids

Any training aids specified as being essential to the course should be constructed, or checked for availability and working order.

3.9 Audio-visual aids

Audio-visual aids (AVA) may be recommended in order to reinforce the learning process in some parts of the course. Such recommendations will be identified in Part A of the model course. The following points should be borne in mind:

.1 Overhead projectors

Check through any illustrations provided in the course for producing overhead projector (OHP) transparencies, and arrange them in order of presentation. To produce transparencies, a supply of transparency sheets is required; the illustrations can be transferred to these via photocopying. Alternatively, transparencies can be produced by writing or drawing on the sheet. Coloured pens are useful for emphasizing salient points. Ensure that spare projector lamps (bulbs) are available.

3.6　教员要求

3.6.1　由富有经验的人，最好是有编制教程及整套课程经验的人，负责实施本课程，这一点很重要。

3.6.2　这样一个人经常被称作"课程协调人"或"课程指导人"。为有效实施本课程，还需要其他的人员，例如讲师、教员、实验室技师、车间教员等。需要向从事授课的人员适当地简要说明其将要处理的课程工作，而且必须建立制度来核查可能要求他们准备的材料。为做到这一点，关键是要彻底地研究大纲并且根据被召来授课的人员的能力分配课程工作的内容。

3.6.3　负责实施课程的人应当考虑在下列方面监控教学的质量，如实施的种类和形式、与学员的关系以及交流和互动的技巧；必要时，还应当提供适当的咨询和支持。

3.7　教学设施和设备

场所及其他服务

3.7.1　对使用的教室、实验室、车间和其他场所尽量实际可行地提早预定，这是很重要的。

设备

3.7.2　对在3.7.1中提到的场所中所需设备的使用，必须及早做出安排以便支持和进行课程的工作。例如：

.1　黑板和书写材料；

.2　用于任何相关演示和试验的实验室器材；

.3　车间内的机械和相关设备；

.4　其他场所中的设备和材料（例如用于演示灭火、个人求生等）。

3.8　教具

应当制作被列为对课程至关重要的任何培训教具或检查其可用性以及工作状况。

3.9　视听教具

为加强课程某些部分的学习过程，建议使用视听教具。这类建议将在示范课程第1部分中予以确认。应当牢记以下要点：

.1　投影仪

查看本课程中提供的用于制作投影片的任何插图，并按授课的顺序排好。为制作投影片，需要提供透明胶片。插图可以通过复印转到透明胶片上。或者，可以通过在透明胶片上书写或画图的方式制作投影片。强调重点时，彩色的笔十分有用。应确保有备用的投影仪灯泡。

.2 Slide projectors
If you order slides indicated in the course framework, check through them and arrange them in order of presentation. Slides are usually produced from photographic negatives. If further slides are considered necessary and cannot be produced locally, OHP transparencies should be resorted to.

.3 Cine projector
If films are to be used, check their compatibility with the projector (i.e. 16 mm, 35 mm, sound, etc.). The films must be test-run to ensure there are no breakages.

.4 Video equipment
It is essential to check the type of video tape to be used. The two types commonly used are VHS and Betamax. Although special machines exist which can play either format, the majority of machines play only one or the other type. Note that VHS and Betamax are not compatible; the correct machine type is required to match the tape. Check also that the TV raster format used in the tapes (i.e. number of lines, frames/second, scanning order, etc.) is appropriate to the TV equipment available. (Specialist advice may have to be sought on this aspect.) All video tapes should be test-run prior to their use on the course.

.5 Computer equipment
If computer-based aids are used, check their compatibility with the projector and the available software.

.6 General note
The electricity supply must be checked for voltage and whether it is AC or DC, and every precaution must be taken to ensure that the equipment operates properly and safely. It is important to use a proper screen which is correctly positioned; it may be necessary to exclude daylight in some cases. A check must be made to ensure that appropriate screens or blinds are available. All material to be presented should be test-run to eliminate any possible troubles, arranged in the correct sequence in which it is to be shown, and properly identified and cross-referenced in the course timetable and lesson plans.

3.10 IMO references

The content of the course, and therefore its standard, reflects the requirements of all the relevant IMO international conventions and the provisions of other instruments as indicated in the model course. The relevant publications can be obtained from the Publication Service of IMO, and should be available, at least to those involved in presenting the course, if the indicated extracts are not included in a compendium supplied with the course.

3.11 Textbooks

The detailed syllabus may refer to a particular textbook or textbooks. It is essential that these books are available to each student taking the course. If supplies of textbooks are limited, a copy should be loaned to each student, who will return it at the end of the course. Again, some courses are provided with a compendium which includes all or part of the training material required to support the course.

.2　幻灯机

如果你要排列课程框架中注明的幻灯片，则需对其核对并按授课的顺序排好。幻灯片通常用照片的负片制作。如果需要更多的幻灯片但当地不能制作，则应当使用投影仪。

.3　电影放映机

如果要使用电影片，则检查其与放映机（即16 mm、35 mm、声响等）的兼容性。必须对电影片进行试播以保证没有断点。

.4　视频设备

检查所用录像带的类别是十分重要的。通常使用的两种是VHS和Betamax。尽管存在能够播放任一种磁带的特殊机器，但大多数机器只能放映其中一种。注意，VHS和Betamax不兼容；要求用正确的机型来与磁带相配。另外，检查磁带中使用的电视光栅（即线数、帧/秒、扫描顺序等）是否适合所用的电视设备（这方面可能需要寻求专家的意见）。在课程使用之前应当对所有录像带进行试播。

.5　计算机设备

如果使用基于计算机的教具，则检查其与放映机和可用软件的兼容性。

.6　总体提示

必须检查电源的电压以及是交流电还是直流电，而且必须采取每一项预防措施以保证设备稳定、安全地运行。使用正确设置的适当幕布是重要的；在有些情况下，可能需要遮挡日光。必须进行检查以保证有适当的纱窗或百叶窗。所有要讲授的材料应当予以试用以便清除任何可能的故障并要按播放的正确顺序放好，并且在课程时间表和教案中进行适当的确认和对照。

3.10　IMO参考书目

本课程的内容及其标准反映了所有相关IMO国际公约的要求以及示范课程中注明的其他文件的规定。相关出版物可以从IMO出版服务处获得，如果其注明的摘录没有包含在随课程提供的提纲内，则至少应当向参与讲授本课程的人员提供这些出版物。

3.11　教科书

大纲细则可以引用一本或多本教科书。参加课程的每一名学生能够得到这些教科书是十分重要的。如果教科书的供给有限，则可以将这些教材的复印本借给学生用，在课程结束时再归还。一些课程还配有一个摘要，该摘要包括所有或部分支持本课程所需要的培训材料。

3.12 Bibliography

Any useful supplementary source material is identified by the course designers and listed in the model course. This list should be supplied to the participants so that they are aware where additional information can be obtained, and at least two copies of each book or publication should be available for reference in the training institute library.

3.13 Timetable

If a timetable is provided in a model course, it is for guidance only. It may only take one or two presentations of the course to achieve an optimal timetable. However, even then it must be borne in mind that any timetable is subject to variation, depending on the general needs of the trainees in any one class and the availability of instructors and equipment.

3.12　参考文献

任何有用的补充性原始材料由课程设计人确认并列入示范课程中。应当向学员提供该目录,以便使其知道可以获得额外资料的来源,而且在培训机构图书馆中,每一本书或出版物应当有至少两本供参阅。

3.13　时间表

示范课程中提供的时间表,仅供指导。可能只需一到两次授课就能确定一个最优化的时间表。但是,即使在此时也必须牢记,依据任一班级中学员的一般要求以及教员和设备的可使用情况,任何时间表都有待于变更。

Part 2 Notes on Teaching Technique

1 Preparation

1.1 Identify the section of the syllabus which is to be dealt with.

1.2 Read and study thoroughly all the syllabus elements.

1.3 Obtain the necessary textbooks or reference papers which cover the training area to be presented.

1.4 Identify the equipment which will be needed, together with support staff necessary for its operation.

1.5 It is essential to use a "lesson plan", which can provide a simplified format for co-ordinating lecture notes and supporting activities. The lesson plan breaks the material down into identifiable steps, making use of brief statements, possibly with keywords added, and indicating suitable allocations of time for each step. The use of audio-visual material should be indexed at the correct point in the lecture with an appropriate allowance of time. The audio-visual material should be test-run prior to its being used in the lecture. An example of a lesson plan is shown in annex A3.

1.6 The syllabus is structured in training outcome format and it is thereby relatively straightforward to assess each trainee's grasp of the subject matter presented during the lecture. Such assessment may take the form of further discussion, oral questions, written tests or selection-type tests, such as multiple-choice questions, based on the objectives used in the syllabus. Selection-type tests and short-answer tests can provide an objective assessment independent of any bias on the part of the assessor. For certification purposes, assessors should be appropriately qualified for the particular type of training or assessment.

REMEMBER–POOR PREPARATION IS A SURE WAY TO LOSE THE INTEREST OF A GROUP

1.7 Check the rooms to be used before the lecture is delivered. Make sure that all the equipment and apparatus are ready for use and that any support staff are also prepared and ready. In particular, check that all blackboards are clean and that a supply of writing and cleaning materials is readily available.

2 Delivery

2.1 Always face the people you are talking to; never talk with your back to the group.

2.2 Talk clearly and sufficiently loudly to reach everyone.

2.3 Maintain eye contact with the whole group as a way of securing their interest and maintaining it (i.e. do not look continuously at one particular person, nor at a point in space).

第2部分　教学技巧注释

1　备课

1.1　确认要涉及的那部分大纲。

1.2　充分阅读和研究所有大纲要素。

1.3　获得与要讲授的培训科目相关的必要教科书和参考论文。

1.4　确认所需的设备及其运转所需的辅助人员。

1.5　使用“教案”十分关键,教案能够为协调讲稿和辅助活动提供简化的格式。教案将材料细分成可识别的步骤,使用可能加入关键词的简要陈述并注明为每一步骤分配的适当时间。应当在讲稿中的正确节点做好使用视听材料的索引并留出适当的时间。视听材料应当在授课使用前试运行。在附录A3中给出了一个教案示例。

1.6　大纲由培训效果的格式构成，因此它相对直接地评估了每名学员对授课期间所讲主题的掌握。这类评估可以基于大纲中使用的目标,采用进一步讨论、口答、笔试或诸如多项选择题的选择型测试的形式。选择型测试和简答测试能够提供独立于评估员任何偏见的客观评估。为了发证的目的,评估员应当具有特定培训和评估的相应资格。

记住——准备不足是使一个团体丧失兴趣的必由之路

1.7　在讲课之前检查要使用的房间。确保所有设备和器材备好待用,辅助人员也准备就绪。要特别检查黑板是否清洁,书写和擦拭材料是否立即可用。

2　授课

2.1　要始终面对听课的人;千万不要背对着班级。

2.2　说话声音要清晰、洪亮,让每一个人都能听到。

2.3　与整个班级保持目光接触作为吸引并保持其兴趣的方法(既不要持续地盯着某一个人,也不要盯着场所中的某一点)。

2.4 People are all different, and they behave and react in different ways. An important function of a lecturer is to maintain interest and interaction between members of a group.

2.5 Some points or statements are more important than others and should therefore be emphasized. To ensure that such points or statements are remembered, they must be restated a number of times, preferably in different words.

2.6 If a blackboard is to be used, any writing on it must be clear and large enough for everyone to see. Use colour to emphasize important points, particularly in sketches.

2.7 It is only possible to maintain a high level of interest for a relatively short period of time; therefore, break the lecture up into different periods of activity to keep interest at its highest level. Speaking, writing, sketching, use of audio-visual material, questions, and discussions can all be used to accomplish this. When a group is writing or sketching, walk amongst the group, looking at their work, and provide comment or advice to individual members of the group when necessary.

2.8 When holding a discussion, do not allow individual members of the group to monopolize the activity, but ensure that all members have a chance to express opinions or ideas.

2.9 If addressing questions to a group, do not ask them collectively; otherwise, the same person may reply each time. Instead, address the questions to individuals in turn, so that everyone is invited to participate.

2.10 It is important to be guided by the syllabus content and not to be tempted to introduce material which may be too advanced, or may contribute little to the course objective. There is often competition between instructors to achieve a level which is too advanced. Also, instructors often strongly resist attempts to reduce the level to that required by a syllabus.

2.11 Finally, effective preparation makes a major contribution to the success of a lecture. Things often go wrong; preparedness and good planning will contribute to putting things right. Poor teaching cannot be improved by good accommodation or advanced equipment, but good teaching can overcome any disadvantages that poor accommodation and lack of equipment can present.

2.4　人各不相同，其行为和反应也各不相同。讲师的一个重要作用就是保持学员的兴趣及班级学员之间的互动。

2.5　某些要点或阐述比另一些更重要，因此应当加以强调。为保证能记住这些要点或阐述，必须对其重复说明几次，最好使用不同的措辞。

2.6　如果要使用黑板，其上的任何书写必须清晰并且足够大，让每个人都能看清。使用彩色来强调重点，特别是在草图中。

2.7　在较短时间内保持高水准的兴趣的可能性较低；因此，可将讲课分成不同段的活动，将兴趣保持在最高水准。为达到这一目的，可以使用说、写、画、视听材料、提问和讨论。当班级在写或画时，在他们中间走动、看他们的作业，必要时对个别学员提出评论和建议。

2.8　在主持讨论时，不允许班级的个别学员垄断这一活动，而要保证所有学员都有表达其意见或观点的机会。

2.9　当向班级提问时，不要向全班发问，否则就可能每一次由同一个人回答。相反地，应轮流向每一个人提问，这样每个人都会被邀请参与。

2.10　接受大纲内容的指导而不是受引诱去采用可能太过于深奥或对课程目的作用不大的材料，这一点很重要。教员之间经常存在欲达到太过深奥水平的竞争。另外，教员经常极力抗拒将水准降至大纲要求的水平。

2.11　最后，有效的备课对成功授课起到了主要作用。失误在所难免，但精心的准备和良好的计划将有助于改正错误。拙劣的教学不能用良好的设施和先进设备来改进，但是，优良的教学能够克服不良设施和缺少设备带来的不利影响。

Part 3 Curriculum Development

1 Curriculum

The dictionary defines curriculum as a "regular course of study", while syllabus is defined as " a concise statement of the subjects forming a course of study". Thus, in general terms, a curriculum is simply a course, while a syllabus can be thought of as a list (traditionally, a "list of things to be taught").

2 Course content

The subjects which are needed to form a training course, and the precise skills and depth of knowledge required in the various subjects, can only be determined through an in-depth assessment of the job functions which the course participants are to be trained to perform (job analysis). This analysis determines the training needs, thence the purpose of the course (course objective). After ascertaining this, it is possible to define the scope of the course.

(NOTE: Determination of whether or not the course objective has been achieved may quite possibly entail assessment, over a period of time, of the "on-the-job performance" of those completing the course. However, the detailed learning objectives are quite specific and immediately assessable.)

3 Job analysis

A job analysis can only be properly carried out by a group whose members are representative of the organizations and bodies involved in the area of work to be covered by the course. The validation of results, via review with persons currently employed in the job concerned, is essential if undertraining and overtraining are to be avoided.

4 Course plan

Following definition of the course objective and scope, a course plan or outline can be drawn up. The potential students for the course (the trainee target group) must then be identified, the entry standard to the course decided and the prerequisites defined.

5 Syllabus

The final step in the process is the preparation of the detailed syllabus with associated time scales; the identification of those parts of textbooks and technical papers which cover the training areas to a sufficient degree to meet, but not exceed, each learning objective; and the drawing up of a bibliography of additional material for supplementary reading.

6 Syllabus content

The material contained in a syllabus is not static; technology is continuously undergoing change and there must therefore be a means for reviewing course material in order to eliminate what is redundant and introduce new material reflecting

第3部分 课程开发

1 课程

字典将“课程”定义为一个“常规的学习过程”,同时“大纲”被定义为“对组成学习过程的科目的简明陈述”。因此,通常而言,课程就只是一个教程,而大纲可以被认为是一个目录(传统上,一个“要教授的内容的目录”)。

2 课程内容

组成培训课程所必要的科目及不同科目所要求的精确技能和知识深度,只能通过对课程参加者接受培训并履行的工作职能的深入评估来确定(工作分析)。这一分析确定了培训需求,继而得出课程目的(课程目标)。对此确认之后,才可能界定课程的范围。

(注:确定是否达到课程的目标很可能需要在一段时间内对完成课程人员的“在职表现”进行评估。但是,细化的学习目标很具体而且可以立即评估。)

3 工作分析

工作分析只能通过一个群体来适当实施,这个群体的成员能够代表与本课程所覆盖工作领域有关的组织和团体。如果要避免培训不足和培训过度,通过当时就职相关工作的人员的审查来确认其结果是十分重要的。

4 课程计划

在界定课程目标和范围之后,就可以起草课程计划或概要。然后必须确认本课程的潜在学员(学员目标群),决定本课程的入学标准以及界定先决条件。

5 大纲

这一过程的最后一步就是准备教学大纲细则和相关的时间尺度;确认教科书和技术论文中涉及培训范围的部分,这种涉及要达到足够的程度以便满足但不突破每一项学习目标;以及起草用于补充性阅读的额外材料的参考文献。

6 大纲内容

大纲中所载的材料不是静态的;技术在不断地变化,必须存在审查课程资料的手段以便剔除多余的内容并引入反映当代实践的新材料。如上述所界定的,大纲可以被认为是一个目

current practice. As defined above, a syllabus can be thought of as a list and, traditionally, there have always been an "examination syllabus" and a "teaching syllabus"; these indicate, respectively, the subject matter contained in an examination paper, and the subject matter a teacher is to use in preparing lessons or lectures.

7 Training outcomes

7.1 The prime communication difficulty presented by any syllabus is how to convey the "depth" of knowledge required. A syllabus is usually constructed as a series of "training outcomes" to help resolve this difficulty.

7.2 Thus, curriculum development makes use of training outcomes to ensure that a common minimum level and breadth of attainment is achieved by all the trainees following the same course, irrespective of the training institution (i.e. teaching/lecturing staff).

7.3 Training outcomes are trainee-oriented, in that they describe an end result which is to be achieved by the trainee as a result of a learning process.

7.4 In many cases, the learning process is linked to a skill or work activity and, to demonstrate properly the attainment of the objective, the trainee response may have to be based on practical application or use, or on work experience.

7.5 The training outcome, although aimed principally at the trainee to ensure achievement of a specific learning step, also provides a framework for the teacher or lecturer upon which lessons or lectures can be constructed.

7.6 A training outcome is specific and describes precisely what a trainee must do to demonstrate his knowledge, understanding or skill as an end product of a learning process.

7.7 The learning process is the "knowledge acquisition" or "skill development" that takes place during a course. The outcome of the process is an acquired "knowledge", "understanding", "skill"; but these terms alone are not sufficiently precise for describing a training outcome.

7.8 Verbs, such as "calculates", "defines", "explains", "lists", "solves" and "states", must be used when constructing a specific training outcome, so as to define precisely what the trainee will be enabled to do.

7.9 In the IMO model course project, the aim is to provide a series of model courses to assist instructors in developing countries to enhance or update the maritime training they provide, and to allow a common minimum standard to be achieved throughout the world. The use of training outcomes is a tangible way of achieving this desired aim.

7.10 As an example, a syllabus in training-outcome format for the subject of ship construction appears in annex A2. This is a standard way of structuring this kind of syllabus. Although, in this case, an outcome for each area has been identified–and could be used in an assessment procedure–this stage is often dropped to obtain a more compact syllabus structure.

录，而且，传统上存在着“考试大纲”和“教学大纲”，分别表明试卷中含有的主题以及教师在备课或讲课时要使用的主题。

7 培训效果

7.1 任何大纲中所呈现出的主要交流困难就是如何传达所要求知识的“深度”。大纲通常作为一系列的“培训效果”来编写，以便有助于化解这一困难。

7.2 如此一来，课程的制定利用培训效果来保证学习同一课程的所有学员获得共同的最低水准和广度的成绩，而不论培训机构(即教学/讲课人员)如何。

7.3 培训效果是面向学员的，即这些效果描述了学员要达到的最终结果，并以此作为学习过程的结果。

7.4 在很多情况下，学习过程与技能或工作活动相联系，而且为了适当表明达到了目标，学员的反应可能需要基于实际实施和运用或者基于工作经验。

7.5 培训效果，尽管主要着眼于学员，以保证其达到特定的学习步骤的成果，但也向讲师或教员提供了可以基于编写功课或讲稿的框架。

7.6 培训效果是具体的，并精确描述了学员必须做的事情来表明其作为学习过程最终产品的知识、理解或技能。

7.7 学习过程就是在课程期间发生的“知识获得”或“技能发展”。这一过程的效果就是获得的“知识”、“理解”、“技能”；但仅有这些术语尚不足以精确地描述培训的效果。

7.8 编制具体培训效果时，必须使用诸如“计算”、“界定”、“解释”、“列出”、“解决”和“阐述”等动词，以便精确界定学员有能力做的事情。

7.9 IMO的示范课程计划，目的是提供一系列的示范课程以协助发展中国家的教员提高或更新其提供的海事培训，并使得全世界达到共同的最低标准。培训效果的使用就是达到这一预期目的的可行方法。

7.10 作为一例子，在附录A2中，以培训效果的格式列出了船舶构造科目的大纲。这是编写这类大纲结构的标准方法。尽管在这种情况下，每个科目的效果已经得到了确认——而且可以用于评估程序——但这一阶段往往被降格成要获取一个更加精简的大纲结构。

8 Assessment

Training outcomes describe an outcome which is to be achieved by the trainee. Of equal importance is the fact that such an achievement can be measured OBJECTIVELY through an evaluation which will not be influenced by the personal opinions and judgements of the examiner. Objective testing or evaluation provides a sound base on which to make reliable judgements concerning the levels of understanding and knowledge achieved, thus allowing an effective evaluation to be made of the progress of trainees in a course.

8 评估

培训效果描述了学员要达到的效果。同样重要的事实是,通过不受考官个人意见和判断影响的评价可以客观地衡量这一成绩。客观的测试和评价提供了对学员所达到的理解和知识水准做出可靠判断的牢固基础,这就能对学员的学习过程进行有效的评价。

Annex A1 Preparation checklist

Ref.	Component	Identified	Reserved	Electricity supply	Purchases	Tested	Accepted	Started	Finished	Status OK
1	Course plan									
2	Timetable									
3	Syllabus									
4	Scope									
5	Objective									
6	Entry standard									
7	Preparatory course									
8	Course certificate									
9	Participant numbers									
10	Staffing									
	Co-ordinator									
	Lecturers									
	Instructors									
	Technicians									
	Other									

附录 A1　备课检查表

参考	构成	已确认	预定	电源	购买	已测试	已接受	已启动	已结束	状态OK
1	课程计划									
2	时间表									
3	大纲									
4	范围									
5	目标									
6	入学标准									
7	预备课程									
8	课程证书									
9	参训人数									
10	人员配置									
	协调员									
	讲师									
	教员									
	技师									
	其他									

Annex A1 Preparation checklist *(continued)*

Ref.	Component	Identified	Reserved	Electricity supply	Purchases	Tested	Accepted	Started	Finished	Status OK
11	Facilities									
(a)	Rooms									
	Lab									
	Workshop									
	Other									
	Class									
(b)	Equipment									
	Lab									
	Workshop									
	Other									
12	AVA Equipment and materials									
	OHP									
	Slide									
	Cine									
	Video									
13	IMO reference									
14	Textbooks									
15	Bibliography									

附录 A1 备课检查表(续表)

参考	构成	已确认	预定	电源	购买	已测试	已接受	已启动	已结束	状态 OK
11	设施									
	(a) 教室									
	实验室									
	车间									
	其他									
	班级									
	(b) 设备									
	实验室									
	车间									
	其他									
12	视听教具和材料									
	投影仪									
	幻灯机									
	电影放映机									
	录像机									
13	IMO 参考书目									
14	教科书									
15	参考文献									

Annex A2 Example of a Model Course syllabus in a subject area

Subject area: Ship construction

Prerequisite: Have a broad understanding of shipyard practice

General aims: Have knowledge of materials used in shipbuilding, specification of shipbuilding steel and process of approval

Textbooks: No specific textbook has been used to construct the syllabus, but the instructor would be assisted in preparation of lecture notes by referring to suitable books on ship construction, such as *Ship Construction* by Eyres (T12) and *Merchant Ship Construction* by Taylor (T58)

附录A2 某一科目示范课程教学大纲的示例

科　　目：船舶构造

先决条件：对船厂实践有广泛的理解

总体目的：了解造船所用材料、造船用钢的规格和认可程序

教 科 书：在编制该大纲时没有使用特定的教科书，但参考关于船舶建造的合适书籍会有助于教员准备讲稿，例如Eyres的《船舶构造》(T12)以及Taylor的《商船构造》(T58)

COURSE OUTLINE

Knowledge, understanding and proficiency		Total hours for each topic	Total hours for each subject area of required performance
Competence:			
3.1 CONTROL TRIM, STABILITY and STRESS			
3.1.1 FUNDAMENTAL PRINCIPLES OF SHIP CONSTRUCTION, TRIM AND STABILITY			
.1	Shipbuilding materials	3	
.2	Welding	3	
.3	Bulkheads	4	
.4	Watertight and weathertight doors	3	
.5	Corrosion and its prevention	4	
.6	Surveys and dry-docking	2	
.7	Stability	83	102

课程概要

知识、理解和熟练	每一标题的总学时	技能要求中每一科目的总学时
适任：		
3.1 控制吃水差、稳性和应力		
3.1.1 船舶构造、吃水差和稳性的基本原理		
.1 造船材料	3	
.2 焊接	3	
.3 舱壁	4	
.4 水密和风雨密门	3	
.5 腐蚀及其预防	4	
.6 检验和进坞	2	
.7 稳性	83	102

Part C3: Detailed Teaching Syllabus

Introduction

The detailed teaching syllabus is presented as a series of learning objectives. The objective, therefore, describes what the trainee must do to demonstrate that the specified knowledge or skill has been transferred.

Thus each training outcome is supported by a number of related performance elements in which the trainee is required to be proficient. The teaching syllabus shows the *Required performance* expected of the trainee in the tables that follow.

In order to assist the instructor, references are shown to indicate IMO references and publications, textbooks and teaching aids that instructors may wish to use in preparing and presenting their lessons.

The material listed in the course framework has been used to structure the detailed teaching syllabus; in particular,

Teaching aids (indicated by A)
IMO references (indicated by R) and
Textbooks (indicated by T)

will provide valuable information to instructors.

Explanation of information contained in the syllabus tables

The information on each table is systematically organized in the following way. The line at the head of the table describes the FUNCTION with which the training is concerned. A function means a group of tasks, duties and responsibilities as specified in the STCW Code. It describes related activities which make up a professional discipline or traditional departmental responsibility on board.

The header of the first column denotes the **COMPETENCE** concerned. Each function comprises a number of competences. For example, the Function 3, Controlling the Operation of the Ship and Care for Persons on board at the Management Level, comprises a number of COMPETENCES. Each competence is uniquely and consistently numbered in this model course.

In this function the competence is **Control trim, stability and stress.** It is numbered 3.1, that is the first competence in Function 3. The term "competence" should be understood as the application of knowledge, understanding, proficiency, skills, experience for an individual to perform a task, duty or responsibility on board in a safe, efficient and timely manner.

Shown next is the required TRAINING OUTCOME. The training outcomes are the areas of knowledge, understanding and proficiency in which the trainee must be able to demonstrate knowledge and understanding. Each COMPETENCE comprises a number of training outcomes. For example, the above competence comprises three training

C3部分:教学大纲细则

介绍

教学大纲细则是以一系列学习目标呈现的。因此,该目标描述了学员必须做的事情来表明他已经获得了规定的知识或技能。

因此,每一项培训效果都由一些有关的表现要素来支持,要求学员熟练掌握。教学大纲显示了下述表格中对学员期望的“技能要求”。

为了帮助教员,列出了参考书目来注明教员在备课和授课中可能希望使用的IMO参考书和出版物、教科书和教具。

课程框架中列举的材料已用于拟定教学大纲细则;尤其是,

教具(由A表示)
IMO参考书(由R表示)以及
教科书(由T表示)

将向教员提供有价值的信息。

大纲表格里的信息说明

每个表格里的信息均以下述方式进行了系统的组织。表格抬头一行描述了与培训相关的职能。职能是指STCW规则中规定的一组任务、职责和责任。它描述了组成船上职业素养或传统部门责任的相关活动。

第1栏的标题概述了有关的适任。每一项职能包含了多项适任。例如,职能3“管理级船舶作业管理和船上人员管理”包括了多项适任。在本示范课程中,对每一项适任都做了唯一且一致的编号。

本职能中的适任就是控制吃水差、稳性和应力。其编号为3.1,即职能3中的第1项适任。术语“适任”应当理解为个人运用知识、理解、熟练、技能、经验以安全、有效和及时的方式履行船上的一项任务、职责或责任。

下一项表明的是要求的培训效果。培训效果是学员必须有能力表明了解和理解的知识、理解和熟练的范围。每一项适任包括多项培训效果。例如,上述适任包括了三项培训效果。

outcomes. The first is concerned with the FUNDAMENTAL PRINCIPLES OF SHIP CONSTRUCTION, TRIM AND STABILITY. Each training outcome is uniquely and consistently numbered in this model course. That concerned with fundamental principles of Ship Construction, Trim And Stability is uniquely numbered 3.1.1. For clarity, training outcomes are printed in black type on grey, for example TRAINING OUTCOME.

Finally, each training outcome embodies a variable number of required performances—as evidence of competence. The instruction, training and learning should lead to the trainee meeting the specified required performance. For the training outcome concerned with fundamental principles of ship construction, trim and stability there are three areas of performance. These are:

3.1.1.1 Shipbuilding materials
3.1.1.2 Welding
3.1.1.3 Bulkheads

Following each numbered area of required performance there is a list of activities that the trainee should complete and which collectively specify the standard of competence that the trainee must meet. These are for the guidance of teachers and instructors in designing lessons, lectures, tests and exercises for use in the teaching process. For example, under the topic 3.1.1.1, to meet the required performance, the trainee should be able to:

—state that steels are alloys of iron, with properties dependent upon the type and amounts of alloying materials used
—state that the specifications of shipbuilding steels are laid down by classification societies
—state that shipbuilding steel is tested and graded by classification society surveyors who stamp it with approval marks

and so on.

IMO references (Rx) are listed in the column to the right-hand side. Teaching aids (Ax), videos (Vx) and textbooks (Tx) relevant to the training outcome and required performances are placed immediately following the TRAINING OUTCOME title.

It is not intended that lessons are organized to follow the sequence of required performances listed in the Tables. The Syllabus Tables are organized to match with the competence in the STCW Code Table A-Ⅱ/2. Lessons and teaching should follow college practices. It is not necessary, for example, for ship building materials to be studied before stability. What is necessary is that all of the material is covered and that teaching is effective to allow trainees to meet the standard of the required performance.

第一项是有关船舶构造、吃水差和稳性的基本原理。在本示范课程中,对每一项培训效果都做了唯一且一致的编号。与船舶构造、吃水差和稳性的基本原理有关的培训效果被唯一编为3.1.1。为清楚起见,培训效果被印成灰底黑体,例如培训效果。

最后,每一项培训效果体现了不定数目的技能要求——作为适任的证据。授课、培训和学习应当使学员满足规定的技能要求。对于船舶构造、吃水差和稳性的基本原理,有三个科目技能要求。它们是:

3.1.1.1 造船材料
3.1.1.2 焊接
3.1.1.3 舱壁

在技能要求的每一项编号科目之后,有一个学员应当完成的活动清单,这些活动共同规定了学员必须满足的适任标准。它们用于指导教师和教员设计在教学过程中使用的功课、讲课、测验和练习。例如,在标题3.1.1.1之下,为满足技能要求,学员应当能够:

—阐述钢是铁的合金,其特性依赖于所使用合金材料的种类和数量
—阐述船级社制定了造船用钢的规格
—阐述船级社验船师对造船用钢进行测试和定级并对其加盖认可标志

等等。

IMO参考书目(Rx)列在右侧一栏中。与培训效果和技能要求相关的教具(Ax)、录像(Vx)和教科书(Tx)紧跟在培训效果标题之后。

并不打算按表中所列技能要求的次序来组织功课。大纲表格的组织是与STCW规则表A-Ⅱ/2中的适任相匹配的。课程与教学应遵循大学中的实践情况。例如,没有必要在学习稳性之前先学习建造材料。必要的是,所有这些材料要全部涉及而且教学要有效以便使学员达到技能要求的标准。

FUNCTION 3: CONTROLLING THE OPERATION OF THE SHIP AND CARE FOR PERSONS ON BOARD AT THE MANAGEMENT LEVEL

COMPETENCE 3.1 Control trim, stability and stress **IMO reference**

3.1.1 FUNDAMENTAL PRINCIPLES OF SHIP CONSTRUCTION, TRIM AND STABILITY

Textbooks: T11, T12, T35, T58, T69

Teaching aids: A1, A4, V5, V6, V7

Required performance:

1.1 Shipbuilding materials (3 hours) R1

–states that steels are alloys of iron, with properties dependent upon the type and amounts of alloying materials used
–states that the specifications of shipbuilding steels are laid down by classification societies
–states that shipbuilding steel is tested and graded by classification society surveyors, who stamp it with approval marks
–explains that mild steel, graded A to E, is used for most parts of the ship
–states why higher tensile steel may be used in areas of high stress, such as the sheer strake
–explains that the use of higher tensile steel in place of mild steel results in a saving of weight for the same strength
–explains what is meant by:
- tensile strength
- ductility
- hardness
- toughness

–defines strain as extension divided by original length
–sketches a stress-strain curve for mild steel
–explains:
- yield point
- ultimate tensile stress
- modulus of elasticity

–explains that toughness is related to the tendency to brittle fracture
–explains that stress fracture may be initiated by a small crack or notch in a plate
–states that cold conditions increase the chances of brittle fracture
–states why mild steel is unsuitable for the very low temperatures involved in the containment of liquefied gases
–lists examples where castings or forgings are used in ship construction
–explains the advantages of the use of aluminium alloys in the construction of superstructures
–states that aluminium alloys are tested and graded by classification society surveyors
–explains how strength is preserved in aluminium superstructures in the event of fire
–describes the special precautions against corrosion that are needed where aluminium alloy is connected to steelwork

职能3:管理级船舶作业管理和船上人员管理

适任3.1 控制吃水差、稳性和应力	IMO参考书目

3.1.1 船舶构造、吃水差和稳性的基本原理

教 科 书:T11,T12,T35,T58,T69

教　　具:A1,A4,V5,V6,V7

技能要求:

1.1 造船材料(3小时) R1

—阐述钢是铁的合金,其特性依赖于所使用合金材料的种类和数量

—阐述船级社制定了造船用钢的规格

—阐述船级社验船师对造船用钢进行测试和定级并对其加盖认可标志

—解释A到E级的低碳钢用于船舶的大部分构件

—阐述为什么较高强度的钢可以用于高应力的区域,例如舷顶列板

—解释在相同强度条件下用高强度钢代替低碳钢可减轻重量

—解释下列术语的含义:

- 抗拉强度
- 延展性
- 硬度
- 韧性

—界定应变就是以原长度除以延长

—画出低碳钢应力—应变曲线图

—解释:

- 屈服点
- 极限抗拉应力
- 弹性模数

—解释韧性与脆性断裂的趋势有关

—解释应力破裂可能由钢板上的小裂缝或槽引起

—阐述冰冷条件加大了脆性断裂的机会

—阐述为什么低碳钢不适宜于装运液化气所涉及的超低温

—列出在船舶建造中使用铸件或锻件的实例

—解释上层建筑建造中使用铝合金的优点

—阐述铝合金是由船级社验船师进行测试和定级

—解释在发生火灾时铝制上层建筑是如何保持强度的

—描述在铝合金与钢制件连接处所需要的防腐特别预防措施

Annex A3 Example of a lesson plan for annex A2

Subject area: 3.1 Control trim, stability and stress **Lesson number: 1** **Duration: 3 hours**

Training Area: 3.1.1 Fundamental principles of ship construction, trim and stability

Main element Specific training outcome in teaching sequence, with memory keys	Teaching method	Textbook	IMO reference	A/V aid	Instructor guidelines	Lecture notes	Time (minutes)
1.1 Shipbuilding materials (3 hours)							
States that steels are alloys of iron, with properties dependent upon the type and amounts of alloying materials used	Lecture	T12,T58	STCW II/2, A-II/2	V5 to V7	A1	Compiled by the lecturer	10
States that the specifications of shipbuilding steels are laid down by classification societies	Lecture	T12,T58	STCW II/2, A-II/2	V5 to V7	A1	Compiled by the lecturer	20
Explains that mild steel, graded A to E, is used for most parts of the ship	Lecture	T12,T58	STCW II/2, A-II/2	V5 to V7	A1	Compiled by the lecturer	15
States why higher tensile steel may be used in areas of high stress, such as the sheer strake	Lecture	T12,T58	STCW II/2, A-II/2	V5 to V7	A1	Compiled by the lecturer	10
Explains that use of higher tensile steel in place of mild steel results in a saving of weight for the same strength	Lecture	T12,T58	STCW II/2, A-II/2	V5 to V7	A1	Compiled by the lecturer	15

附录 A3　附录A2教案的示例

科目：3.1 控制吃水差、稳性和应力　　课程编号：1　　学时：3学时

培训范围：3.1.1船舶结构、吃水差和稳性的基本原理

要素 按教学次序列出的具体培训效果，附记忆要点	教学方法	教科书	IMO 参考书目	视听教具	教员指南	讲稿	时间 (分钟)
1.1　造船材料（3小时）							
阐述钢是铁的合金，其特性依赖于所使用合金材料的种类和数量	讲课	T12,T58	STCW Ⅱ/2, A-Ⅱ/2	V5 至 V7	A1	讲师自编	10
阐述船级社制定了造船用钢的规格	讲课	T12,T58	STCW Ⅱ/2, A-Ⅱ/2	V5至V7	A1	讲师自编	20
解释A到E级的低碳钢用于船舶的大部分构件	讲课	T12,T58	STCW Ⅱ/2, A-Ⅱ/2	V5至V7	A1	讲师自编	15
阐述为什么高强度的钢可以用于高应力的区域，例如舷顶列板	讲课	T12,T58	STCW Ⅱ/2, A-Ⅱ/2	V5至V7	A1	讲师自编	10
解释在相同强度条件下用高强度钢代替低碳钢可减轻重量	讲课	T12,T58	STCW Ⅱ/2, A-Ⅱ/2	V5至V7	A1	讲师自编	15